Poured Out Like Water

A Folk Tale of End Times

Poured Out Like Water

A Folk Tale of End Times

Red Egg

—*Kyrie Eleison*

We are not a great people; we are not even a significant people; we are a people who see that life is satisfactory because of our fishing, our goats, and our lemons. Yes, in fishing at dawn, in milking goats, in collecting the lemons from the lemon trees, brushing aside the little green leaves to pluck out the yellow fruit, or by watching an insect sitting at home there, in a little sphere of fragrance that extends so many paces, we see an eminently satisfactory way to live. We are a tiny island with the sea all around us, but we are also an island in the midst of a blaze of sun and a constant stream of wind. The light here holds everything else at bay—all thoughts and emotions. We are undistinguished human animals in a chrysalis of sunlight. There is nothing at all remarkable about us. We have our uninteresting pains and loves. Yet, when one of us dies, that moment of actually seeing the dead face as we all gather around the corpse, seeing a face of little likeness to the living face, seeing in that dead

Poured Out Like Water, pages 1–611.

face always the same thing—listening, somber listening--this is always carved in our memory. Our dead are very alive to us.

When a man dies on this island, earth, that is, this land of sand and dust grains existing one by one, detaches once more from heaven. Few in the world realize how initially earth and heaven are one. The living on our island see it: It is accepted, taken for granted, in the same way that opening the blue and yellow and green painted shutters in our little differently colored houses in the morning will let in sunlight is accepted, taken for granted. Earth is of one mind with Heaven just as those joined by love: Earth says: See, my adored One, I have brought you two dusk-colored doves, an eel moving with its head erect through green serpentine-slow waters, cicadas beginning to saw and buzz with their wings on a midsummer's morning, the frothy pine needles, the grains of sand between your teeth, and Heaven responds—joy, joy, my only one; which are the words in Earth's heart. But when someone dies, Earth turns away from the nuptial embrace to mourn; for Heaven is joyful and doesn't understand tears. Usually, the split between the lover and beloved lasts only a short time. But sometimes it is longer. Earth tears away from Heaven in agony. We are plunged in darkness but repress our cries of anguish for we determine to be patient and wait; someone will bring back the light.

We have started to diminish. Many of our old timers have died—the lingering old folk that we watch withering up like old peaches, withering and withering and still sitting in the sun. One day, their chairs, plastic or cloth, not really their chairs—are vacant. The church bell tolls, and we bury them; sometimes, we go out on the boats and dump the coffin into the sea, there is so little graveyard space; or, depending on the politics of this loosely organized island, we dig up the bones out of favor and dump them into the sea with little honoring ceremony so as to make way for our newly beloved dead. They are gone and the island is quieter. Many of our young people have moved away and do not watch this spectacle of interring and disinterring.

Our children are not born: The shadow of death clings to us and the love making of our newly wedded couples is not fruitful-- has not been fruitful here for fifteen years. The older young people who move away return only once or twice. They usually have on their faces expressions of alternating disdain and apology. Then, they leave abruptly like flocks of startled birds, suddenly, swiftly—and for good. The values of our goods has also changed; our fish, goats' cheese, and lemons fetch less than before on the other bigger island where we sell and buy. Little discrepancies from the old times are visible to the old folk who remain talking of the dead. According to one grandmother, Zoe, there used to be an aura of light around people and things, even foods. God was here—that is, disembodied and everywhere: In the air, sea water, white washed walls of our homes; in the honey that Simon makes himself and has for half a century; in Simon's half crafty, half sweet smile. But God has withdrawn. It is because, my grandmother says, we have become merely eaters and drinkers as Jesus said would happen; as the Son of the Living God said: We are liars now, offended easily. Our homes are as if uninhabited, abandoned even though lived in.

Far away from the world as it is known—the modern world, the world at war, the masses and masses marching in step to a religion or a leader—we still live according to our old ways, but I must admit, a little carelessly now. We have our faith, but we have some who have wandered from this true path. We say it is true because our ancestors have said so. In this way, we hardly have to talk to one another to know what we are all about. There are among the crowd, a few who have taken it into their heads to talk a bit more than others, to pretend there is something we haven't heard yet. Their names include Simon, oldish, but wiry and strong in body, deeply clever, we think—at least, he always puts everything in a crafty way—tricking one out, you see, but about what? Ha, we know it already. Then there is a little circle of friends— they stay up in the night together doing and saying mysterious things—women, of course, who else would be so undercover about their goings on—as if we couldn't guess women's secrets. They are old ladies, dead husbands behind them: They are Cleo, Zoe and Anna and Foti and Agatha; Agatha is the youngest in age, and Foti in understanding.

There is a story about our Agatha, sometimes invited;-- she has gypsy blood and a depressive tendency: She has two sons who are rumored to be great enemies. They are as unlike as can be; perhaps it is just a case of getting on each other's nerves. One of them is a law abider—a man who is molded by the daily turn of the village wheel—fishing, church, fishing, church are his only thought and occupation. The other, ah, the other—a silent, moody, rebellious sort—never in church—piped up one day and said: What need to go to church? Walks in the forest alone, sometimes takes Katrina, another solitary, individual-minded person who smokes. We know Dimitri has always wanted to leave this island. It is too cramped for him, and he wants to fill his mind with something besides fish, lemons and goats' cheese.

The story goes that Agatha, terrified of her older son's unbelief, prayed a terrible prayer. That she would go to hell in place of him—this she asked of God! In some faiths, such a prayer would finish you. But amidst our fish, lemons and goats, we see the faint outlines of Jesus springing up high over our heads laughing and forgiving. Stavros said that but he is half unbeliever. Perhaps he laughs and forgives. In any case, you can tell Agatha from among us—she stands at the back of the church a little scared, praying during the Liturgy never receiving Holy Communion. Several faces and voices appear to her as God: Some are scowling, some are frowning, some are hard, unyielding, unmerciful. One or two is tender. The other women have long since passed under the gaze of the forgiving Son; they eat and drink and talk about anything that comes to mind— unafraid, lazy, chatterboxes, as if Judgment will just be another day. Agatha isn't sure it will be so easy for her. But in any case, what happened just after the old women were sure of Agatha's forgiveness is even more extraordinary: She saw her sons fighting for each other's blood—Jason even with a knife against Dimitri's jugular, and she prayed her terrible prayer again, another time!—for the other one and screamed out—hell! Hell! Hell! until someone came. The boys stopped but it appears she doesn't learn. Offering to go to hell for people twice over! Does she think she has two souls? Besides even for your own children such a sacrifice is unthinkable. What does she know about hell? We know that she can't even stand to sweat come summer.

People murmur that it is for her prayer that we have been cursed; the way old humans are cursed watching their young people grow and go far away and take with them all the love and a lot of the hope; here on this tiny island of a seventy square kilometers where seventy families' dwelling places huddle together in the embrace of a cliff in front of the sea, no children have been born in the ten years since Agatha's prayer. Of course, we are not clowns. We know that she did nothing except go mad twice. We know that it must be an act of a God mysterious and implacable. Why should our rosy-cheeked women and men brought together in holy matrimony—full five of them, bring forth nothing, no fruits? It has perhaps nothing to do with Agatha. And yet people regard her as you might imagine with some antipathy. We understand—so joyless, so strange. To tend that way in mind is a bad sign and we want no bad signs. And so life is not an unending path into the mysterious illuminated forest of infinity, which you can see if you walk around to the back of the houses; it is coming upon the sheer wall of rock that rises up from the sea. A way to a mysterious and ultimate stopping point. An awesome dead end.

Our sea is like a magic carpet. On midsummer days it stretches out in front of us with barely a ripple and the sun makes it glitter gold fire. We've all dreamed of its carrying us away; we half want to go to the great cities, to see the wonders of the world that we hear about in the newspapers and on television. We want to, but we don't; that is, us few don't. Many have made the crossing first by fishing boat and then by ferry, then by airplane, car or rail, but there are still a sacred few who have never gone anywhere but the 'other land'—allied—a neighboring island that is larger and more developed with three towns, four movie houses and five hardware stores, three pharmacies and one hospital with a hundred and fifty beds— because they say they wish to be sure of the ground beneath their feet. We say 'sacred few' about ourselves because we are old believers living and dying on this island—where God lives or used to in the air, or in the fragrances of our food— on the cliff of which stands an old monastery for women, a place, the villagers say of saints and ascetics. Adjacent to the monastery, several paces down the cliff towards the forest, lies the rich foreigner's house; its great white dome like a snowy cloud can be seen from the sea as you approach by boat.

No one knows when it was built—the monastery called the Virgin of the Rocks—because of the two sharp rocks, one little, one big, sticking high up from the sea immediately beneath the cliff on the summit of which it stands (but which one nun said is so named because life there is hard as rocks!)—above the village, which nestles up against the mountain along the beach. The nuns are indeed ascetics, part of an ancient Orthodox tradition; it is said that just a mere century ago there lived in the monastery a great saint and hermit Mother Dora; when she walked a great gust of wind followed and then a fragrance and then a light lighter than the sun because of her great holiness; it was rumored that at night near her people could see in the darkness because of this great aura that followed her; people would shuffle their feet when they came to her but for one unspoken accord never talk, not even whisper. And Mother Dora spoke very rarely and only in a whisper. But no known healing miracles were performed by this holy woman; yet she alone had the true holy feel, they say. For to be truly holy one must radiate the uncreated light. Hard to do. Yet Mother Dora had left all when she was a girl, you could hardly believe she ever was a girl, running and shouting, she had left home and the business of her family for this tiny island and a life of standing on rocks facing the sea at night to pray fiercely, and to put a cool hand on the foreheads of the sick. Can you imagine leaving all for a business of putting your hand tenderly on the foreheads of the sick? Yet they say she was so divinely tender; that her tenderness alone went through their brains into their bodies and healed them or soothed them to their deaths. Miracle cures in the monastery abounded years ago. In fact, there were so many for centuries that the island came to be known as Holy Island and it was known for this beautiful tenderness, tenderness so lovely as to suffice, one priest-monk said, to make it sacred in the rough seas…(anyway, its other name has long been forgotten.) It was said that merely stepping on the sands of our island or swimming in our waters would make whatever illness you were suffering from disappear. It was like, one of the nuns whispered, plunging into the chalice of God. But this was years and years ago, before Mother Dora, the last of the true saints, when the ancient monastery was in full swing. People came, visited, stayed because all our homes welcomed them. We were open and full of bonhomie and any guest was delightful in a sacrosanct way.

The village called, simply Our Saints, because we were each one of us a bit of a saint, housing first this one, feeding then that one, was then and is today a cluster of low houses going up the hillside from the beach and culminating in a tiny church on top, which exists today, all remade new although there are still fragments of very ancient frescos of Christ salvaged from the original structure; the most prominent depicts Christ Pantocrator above and behind the altar on a golden throne in the midst of the 'waters above the firmament,' which swirl around Him without wetting Him as fish leap above the clouds for joy. In the little white washed church the patches of fresco are still as clear as the blue summer.

The artist had a free hand and quite an imagination painting fish above the clouds for one thing as if he took literally the biblical verse 'the waters above the firmament,' setting the throne in the midst of the sky with the sea waves draped around it like diaphanous veils, and the blue he used, a mineral sea blue from rocks that were once found on the island in abundance, is a light ecstatic color, mysterious, joyful and otherworldly. This pigment put the island on the world map for a time. The color, ground into a manageable powder out of the rock, was exported by the monastery for centuries, resulting in wealth for the monastery-- that is, the gold leaf for Christ's throne and the chalices, for the icons and other holy objects. The island flourished with the blue trade. But as other blues easier to obtain were discovered, and the finite stores of the blueschist were used up, the blue pigment trade ended and what remained of the stones, bits and pieces here and there became the sudden rare joy of people who happened to spot some remnant of the beautiful stone walking on the cliffs.

For many years, people around the island said that when the blue trade ceased, so did the holy miracles and the general joy of our little population; people only then began to move away; and babies refused to be born — about seventy years ago. But we know that a number of children were born right up until a decade ago when Agatha brought down curses from hell right here in this place. But the lore of some of us transforms and changes, depending on who is reminiscing.

Take Simon: A carpenter, fisherman, painter, dancer—losing track sometimes because of old age of what's what, yet painting the most beautiful gardens—flowers and trees that seem to be alive, that seem to arrive at the end of a long exhale of the Western wind; he lives, they say, in another world. But we can see, can see that this is reality on Holy Island. It is not that he 'made things up' on his canvas. And yet now and then, the true eye is dimmed and we sense shadows, and a little, banal, stunted place where people see nothing, know nothing, and the waves tumble towards the pebbly shore, aimlessly.

Simon is in love with our blue, the ancient wealth of the island. It takes away burdens for him. Because of his love, he goes around with a little, brilliant light in his old eyes, like a little fleck of gold. Because of this love he also eats with rapture, taste so alive for him. It is an ancient love; as we said, the blue has not been mined for almost seventy years. But he collects the fragments of bluish stone he finds and scatters them around the huge, unwieldy house of his like a litter of beautiful gems, he calls his harem.

He has become a repository, oddly enough, despite the way he has of forgetting what is going on around him, of all the little stories that make up the present day history of the island. He remembers those, well enough, but never chronologically. Things appear to just float in and out of his mind—birth, death, the rebuilding of the church in concrete ten years ago with white plaster covering it. If we ask him about the monastery of the Virgin on the Rocks, the crafty smile returns as does that gold gleam in his eyes.

The sisters are the thoughts of heaven. They aim for one thing: It is not compassion, love or self sacrifice—those are simply the building tools for a deeper more incredible project. They aim to become light. They say it is the secret aim of all of in Christ. Yes, that is it—to transform, to transfigure, to become one with and to become the light that is heaven; he says this laughing a little for joy as if he had hit on an idea that he had been seeking a long time; they aim to dissolve flesh, blood, bone and become the very uncreated light or fire that is God. They aim to become like the saints who shone like the sun. Of course, the steps to believing in such a thing are hard, arduous, torturous, even and many people would be fazed at the undertaking for the strenuous climb to faith alone is just the first step (then to become sinless, and then to live the life of love of God) and many arrive only to tumble down again.

To our uninformed mind, the nuns are just rather hardworking, little talking, genuinely kind types. They do perform terrible fasts and prayer vigils—terrible to us because they are so strict—warm water with a dash of salt, olives and bread for more than half a year, and all night vigils to accompany this. The rare moments when they descend from the mountain in response to someone sending for a spiritual guide to pray beside a sick bed, they seem always exhausted and bony-armed, with dark circles under their eyes. Our nuns are dressed in black, long black skirts and long sleeved tops, shawls and veils; they cover their hair and their necks; one only sees now and then bony forearms when they reach over to embrace the sick person, to lift their head for Holy Communion administered by our priest. They are hard to engage in conversation about their lofty pursuit. Everyone knows they are praying to get to heaven and we seem to see them always standing at the threshold knocking at the final door. We suppose they are right there…but as we indicated, they talk only of mundane things. The amount of lemon curd Agatha made last autumn, the lemon marmalade and pickled fish of Barbara that has been judged the best in our village and was sent for sale to the other island. She got a little stash of money for her sales with which she repainted her house and sent away for rugs and china. The sisters one day, called down for a sick man and stopping by at her house to drink tea, murmured appreciatively about Barbara's rugs and china—how difficult to bring to the island, how exquisite and rare, they murmured all together with shadowy smiles Barbara said, but she didn't know because she never really saw their faces.

The sisters are the mouthpieces of earth to heaven, heaven to earth, Simon says. They are ambassadors and will, when the time comes, announce the Last Judgment. Of course, Simon is Simon—in a world of his own. No one trusts him entirely; for example if he were to say a new shipment of cooking gas tanks had arrived; most people would nod, and amble down to the little port to check—that is, cast an eye. It is so ridiculous to be caught following these words and to find that actually there is nothing there. But gas tanks do arrive, in fact. On the whole, they come all together, twice a month; but now and then people send especially for a couple when they have need. Simon imagines things whenever—in his own time, his own way. That is not to say it won't happen. We all know the Lord is coming, but the idea has entered Simon's brain that the nuns will announce it. So we look at the nuns as if they are, hidden under their bony, bloodless exterior, exquisite gold trumpets. They are the uttermost beauty that cannot always be perceived but that is hidden in all natural things. Only the sisters have understood and refined that hidden inner beauty just as a dancer refines the motions of the body.

When a nun dies, according to Simon, she now casts off the outer clothes of earth and reveals herself a radiant immortal; she stands at the gate of heaven for a full heavenly day collecting supplicants' prayers to take in to God. Her death day is like a birthday celebrated in heaven and on earth. Prayers are shouted from villagers who are sick or in need loud enough so that she might hear them, high up where she stands, and she listens and fills her heart for about a thousand years. Simon probably got this idea from the way, traditionally, at the monastery, it is said that a newly dead nun is living close to, if not already within, the well-spring of uncreated light. If the nun is in her bed, other nuns and villagers encircle her, whispering their prayers into her ears. And she will take these messages on her journey—of possibly a thousand years or until Judgment Day, whichever arrives first.

It is a long way down and a long way up between village and monastery. Steps have been carved into the cliff and if you have the knees of a goat you can climb them easily. One sister once fell off of the edge of the cliff and died, smashed to death on the rocks below. It is rumored that there was another 'accident' of this sort as well. There was of course no question of suicide; in our minds, the half shaded souls of these sisters hung around, peeking in our windows at night, sometimes silently joining a gathering of conversing old women. Prayers were offered and when they had their fill of prayers, they left, climbing up the air to heaven as if it were a ladder.

We all think fondly of our nuns. Some of us think we haven't a care in the world— between the good fishing and the nuns: We eat well on earth and we are sure to get to heaven—owing to their prayers.

Dimitri has been gone six months: For Agatha, a hard day's work begins with getting up in the morning and preparing coffee with brandy for Jason, the almost-murderer son; when he goes out with a flashlight into the darkness of three a.m., Agatha thinks depressively of her other, Dimitri who left a little after the fight with his brother; that's right, she just sits in a chair by the window and thinks, hunched over, we can just see her-- at thirty-six as if already all cramped up with age, looking out into the black sky with large, watery eyes. It's as if, if she concentrates hard enough, brain power will make her son materialize just outside, arriving freshly from the world, flesh, blood and bone on Holy Island.

We know Agatha; for years if you told her she was unhappy, she would give you a peculiar look; if you told her she was happy, she would give you the same look. She has the elusiveness of people gone slightly bad. You think them one thing and in reality, hidden from you—they are quite another. You think she is open, frank and disinterested. In reality, she has her hidden motives, and deep souring vengefulness. She is often a heap of broodiness, with her head bowed, and we rarely see her smile, that is, not the open smile of an honest person. Some of us say it is pain. Her husband died young and left her with the care of two young boys that she raised like a machine for a while; her husband had made her question things that should be taken for granted. He had not been the usual fisherman and believer; he had been a reader of books, a questioner. She said he said to her before he died that what he had discovered was this: There are two paths to truth: One is through the heart, 'spontaneous knowledge,' he called it. The other is through the mind, by tortured argument and counter argument. And then he died, chosen death, Agatha thought, though medically speaking it was meningitis, because he could not stand having to live with these two paths; the thought, she said, of his choosing to die makes her more comfortable; can you imagine?

Agatha didn't commit to one route or the other. And she didn't mourn in the usual fashion. She watched unmoved while they dressed Alex for burial, and the only thing she did, unusual for her, was to drink a little of our strongest brandy after he was lowered into the grave; she usually drinks wine, only wine. And it was then that she smiled. No tears, mind you. A cheerful, easy going smile. We were all shocked.

For Agatha the rest was physical—breathing, eating, nursing, cleaning—except for the brooding that, we think, was intellectual. By the time her boys fought, she had arrived at thirty-five and the surprising thought came that she loved them—so we heard—she said she had just 'turned around;' but Agatha was like that. And there it was suddenly: not of the heart, nor of thinking—an event—then words, among them 'hell'—curses. Now on this comfortable little island, where there has been electricity and gas for thirty years, and the houses lit up like yellow stars in the night, the warm beds, the lemons and recently apricots, the brandy, honey and goats' milk, olives, fried fish and onions, where it seemed so simple to go clean down a straight path, she knows that she takes first one turn on the tortured mind path and then another in the spontaneous heart 'into the wanton wilderness,' we say, for neither provided the answer.

Jason, after the murder that did not result in death, but in his mother's howling, his brother running off by boat to the world, this after ten months of circling one another --he with hard glances, Dimitri with an exquisitely soft smile, has become an exceptionally quiet fisherman and son. Dimitri, the murdered son who is not dead, wrote his mother a postcard from some city in the world, and all things considered, amazingly cheerfully, explained to her how he had gotten a job in the city and enrolled in university for a degree in tourism. It was less cramped than on the island, there were sites to see, longer walks to take. He sent kisses to all, he wrote—meaning, of course, also his brother. We were informed that when Agatha told Jason, he acted as if he had not heard.

Four months passed with Dimitri writing so often that it seemed as if he was beside her and then after that once a month or so, and Jason worrying Agatha as he seemed so stolid, uninterested in anything, going about his fisherman's chores in a slow, steady rhythm that seemed to his mother's heart to be so suddenly mindless and cold; he would go out no matter what the weather, but it wasn't, from Agatha's observations, fortitude that is courage from the heart, rather the ongoing machine numbly, inhumanly continuing.

What is it you do every day? Shouted his mother one day at the end of four years of the same dull routine—she had a propensity to become emotional—fish, fish, fish! But she said to us that she didn't mean that fishing was bad or even that fishing for four years was bad—only that to fish, fish, fish in that mindless way had something unfeeling about it. Of course, it was only an outburst—it didn't necessarily mean anything, but Jason took it ill; he sang a few notes at last—that is how we put it--yelling that she can have her other son and the forest could hear and the mountain could hear and up on the cliff, the sisters all heard. Agatha was both sore and happy about it. A man isn't a man until something like passion comes out of him, she said to Barbara.

For a while there was a lot of shouting going on in that house. We called it a fire in the lungs between mother and son. There was door slamming and Barbara, their next door neighbor, said even horrible cursing. But Agatha proposed to Barbara that it was a better thing—think of that!-- having her and her little son alive and humming and human again with execrations and denunciations rather than dead with saintly politeness and affectations of love. Barbara confided to us that that is just what she expected—this kind of madness made the person think howling and shouting was best! It didn't last. After about three weeks with the whole village with a gleam in its eye expecting a real fight, with broken windows, vases, smashed dishes everywhere, if not murder, there was a sudden lull, and the 'passion' left as it had come—blew away, we said. Jason went back to his cold, mindless routine, with Agatha getting up at three, turning on the single lamp in the kitchen, fixing the hot toddy, and he sitting morose and inhumanly silent for exactly twenty minutes before setting out.

Agatha hasn't gotten a postcard from her older son for six weeks. She obsesses about him, expecting his return, said the priest. It is irrational but even the postcards are not enough for her when they arrive. She wants his homecoming, and not only, but a parade for his homecoming, his haloed presence and something we deem impossible—the loving reconciliation of her Cain and Abel sons. (Of course, we think the Cain son is more the Abel and the Abel more the Cain, but that is another matter.) Now that the postcards have stopped coming she is even more insane. But it is not a madness that is all electric and stunning; rather it is another kind of madness—

deep, and interior, even thoughtful—but with just those little breaks in conversation, a kind of drifting, smiling, frowning as if there is someone else inside her talking in her. How odd! Anna said, when Foti burst out with this. Agatha had murmured to her the day before: There is something and there is nothing. How strange it must be to realize that the something is after all nothing, just as the nothing is something, which is nothing.

Our priest is a thinker but something of a weak one. He reads philosophy, science, history, novels—all available in the monastery where he had come from. He has spent five years following the Orthodox Christian rites, learning his prostrations, the Jesus prayer, the sayings of the saints. Entering the monastery after being ordained, he had cast aside his status as celebrant and bestower of the Holy Mysteries and had become a simple monk for a while. He had looked a little wild, letting his hair and beard grow, walking around in sandals, with only two pieces of clothing in his wardrobe, one for summer and one for winter, and had felt a little like a child. His Elder was particularly kind and Father Isaac had loved him. But he had judged Father Isaac unfit for monastic life. The transfer had been simple with no rancor on either side. One year ago, Father Isaac came to Holy Island with a smile on his lips and a sparkle in his eye. It was fresh, little, beautiful--the perfect place, he had said: beauty is the joy of asceticism.

At first, he conducted our ordinary liturgies and solemn confessions. He seemed harsh—always advising more fasting and prayer. The villagers thought Father Isaac was the picture of propriety, until one day there was news from Michael, the last born on our island, who had spied on him and said that one could see that this new priest was up to something: he had his light on in his room above the church all night; one night, two nights, all week long—the little window in the upper story behind the cross was illuminated. In the dead of night odd things, Michael said—the luxuriant singing of a woman, laughter, shouting; when the villagers had gone watching, there was such goings on that they had wondered if there was a romantic tryst taking place between the priest and a fabulous lady up there in that tiny room. But the turning point came when this new priest told a racy story at a small gathering in the tavern in the center of the town by the large oak tree. At first, there was silence among the men, all large eyed with disbelief. Then laughter, raucous laughter, the men all alive with hilarity and slapping their thighs, roaring so that paunches jiggled and eyes rolled. Around the village they went dropping hints about this 'proper' priest having 'suddenly turned.'

This caused a general stir. When the men who listened were shown with all reasonable argument by Paul and Peter, the twins and our 'managers,' why priests on the whole did not tell such stories they too were dumbfounded. The villagers all desired a good priest, a solid priest who was verifiably holy like old seasoned wood or aromatic chrism oil. They began to suspect that Father Isaac was made of more than one material—a mixture of real and unreal. Why suddenly in the midst of the solemnity—at the tavern, a racy joke? Besides, he had such a strange appearance, they thought now—a look as if he was deceiving people, sallow, sunken cheeks, watery eyes and a discolored beard, he looked unkempt and dirty, underfed and weak; whereas the last priest, Father Raphael, had been robust, and beautiful until the last days—the proper form for a holy man, who has to be strong as a lion, and clean as an angel. Now this laughter and lady singing in the middle of the night and the racy story right there openly from this waif whose stink we carried in our nostrils after sitting near him.

We became uneasy about Father Isaac; and tended to avoid him or to whisper amongst ourselves when he passed, to look at our feet when he smiled. But-- it was one of the days in which Agatha lifted her head-- from her cursed mind, Agatha reasoned that this priest might well have a thing or two to say about himself in self-defense and maybe then some sort of priestly illuminations about the postcard from her son that hadn't arrived. So she toiled up the little hill to the white walled church and up the back stairs to knock at the little rickety green door of his lodgings.

I have come, Agatha, said as a messenger… Yes, yes, said the priest as if expecting her. What is the message?

Agatha thought, and then said: There is no message as yet; but we hope to ask why it is you told that racy story. It is confusing. There, that is the message.

Oh, said the priest, looking at her thoughtfully; It's easy. I thought that a tavern was the place for racy stories and so I told a racy story; the only one I know.

And the woman singing?

A recording.

Of course, said Agatha, looking him in the dimming eye; that is exactly the right answer. She was silent a minute. There is my son, she said at last. As you know he left six years ago.

As for your son, of course he had to leave. Can a man live forever on a cramped little island? Asked the priest, smiling. Now, of course, studying and working at a proper job, he will have less and less time for coming home, for thinking of the old ways; it is only natural. I suspect he'll arrange things so that he can burn the candle at both ends—work, pass his exams, socialize, meet the right people. And then he might drift farther away, said Father Isaac, staring into space.

He was saying all the wrong things in a dreadful harsh nasal tone-- at the same time imagining himself to be sweet and consoling. You mean he'll be one of the ones who go away forever? Cried Agatha, forgetting herself.

Did you think he'd come back? The priest looked all withdrawn as if he lived in a world that made him sad. You see, it is like a fever in the blood, as they used to say—like an erotic urge, this going away with our young people. One finds a new life, like falling in love. There are so many things, of course, wrong with life in general, one could enumerate them for days. But there is a geographical solution—perhaps not lasting or real—and it consists of putting wings on your feet, of getting to the other side where you are free, unmolested; and there perhaps someone will say or do something exactly right; hold out a thread. This urge is strong in young people; I would say that it overtakes even the sex urge. And he had, I think, a reason for taking off suddenly so many weeks ago.

Yes, said Agatha, the tears blurring her eyes. He and Jason fought; I thought there would be blood. It suddenly seemed as if there was somehow a further curse, as if she was not free, nor would ever be free from curses.

Instead, the adventurer took off; the priest looked at her with a kind of remote gentleness.

It was so strange because Dimitri is the stronger. I've always thought that he let Jason taste the feeling of getting his knife against his neck on purpose. Offering himself, laughing, almost. His brother always envied him. I saw that, Father. It was terrible that laughter. Strange that 'offering'.

Boys playing in the end. Sometimes, God knows, it is fatal.

And now he is lost. Out there in the world! He hasn't written…Shall I go to the sisters? I am afraid.…Yet another dismal prediction in a long line of them…

Yes, go to them. Even if your son were a fish among many fish at the bottom of the sea, the sisters with their prayers could find him! Father Isaac said this with a glittering smile that made his face eerie. Agatha thought him almost weird, or perhaps, as the villagers said, deceiving, but she liked him. There is always, she said to herself, a second person that is oneself, not the one generally known.

After Dimitri left, we could almost hear Barbara breathe a sigh of relief. Dimitri was considered the handsomest, and most likely to have beautiful, lively, intelligent children, which drove a knife into her heart. She had read a number of cheap novels—books came in with other supplies on the boats in the morning—in which she sensed deeper- meaning people, more beautiful people, men and women, but it was always the same story with her—how she had looked between her own two sons, about the same age as Agatha's, and lied to herself again and again; there was no question that one boy's head was too small, the other yellowish, and both were fattish and slow. Their lives were the same monotonous, meaningless life. They grunted over their meals at night, talked of fishing, carried on in a sane and normal manner for the village but they were not beautiful. One could not confuse and blindly see ordinary and dull for beautiful and meaningful all of one's life. She often wondered if a fire broke out whether her dull, heavy sons would finally spring to life—running into the middle of a burning house and saving man or woman or child.

Once, in recent memory, a woman had needed rescuing on Holy Island; a tourist from Argentina, coming by big boat and being taken to shore in a dinghy had, for some obscure reason, fallen over board into the sea in her slinky silk dress and hat and glasses. But it was Dimitri who, in a fishing boat nearby, had seen her, dived into the sea and come up with the lady in his arms, swimming gloriously with her to safety. He had also rescued the hat and glasses. For a short time, he was hailed as a hero in the village. He was seventeen, the age of experimentation. One saw him with the lady for a couple of evenings after and a manual of the Spanish language in his hand but then it died down. Subsequent to his heroism, he managed to offend the old villagers in general by saying that he had no loyalties and no faith; people began murmuring—what kind of a son is that? They looked at Katrina—who had been breaking her heart over him for months, although she was as old as his mother—askance, as if to say, and when he abandons you… what then?

Agatha told Katrina that she had seen them in bed. There was this beautiful lady stretched out in among the white cottons, two pillows under her head. And do you know? A horrible disfigurement—something like raw meat splashed across her left breast, which was shriveled and shrunken. Must have been a birthmark, but it was quite violently ugly. It literally looked like something inside the body had been splashed out on the skin. Katrina, she told, to comfort her. (Katrina was just as old as Agatha and everybody said she wouldn't last. She had no hold on him.)

Barbara was glad to see that for all his heroism, Dimitri was not liked or trusted in the end. But still his presence gave her great unease. He was a young, electric, soft-footed, slender-muscled man, his white was brownish and slightly green gold like the sea sometimes when it is churned up after a storm. He was dark eyed and beautiful in a way that you could taste and smiled attractively inward to himself. Barbara sensed that here was all the deeper meaning and beautiful people that the novels talked about. And so, when at nineteen, he faded into the light blue across the sea, becoming another one of those young people who leave, Barbara rejoiced that he was gone forever; for these young people, going was not so much removing to another geographical place but evaporating. He that was once now was not. That was the main thing. Agatha then was less than she, having only one son at home and he hardly more remarkable than her boys. She was to be pitied for there were eruptions, things that showed she didn't bring up her sons properly; that they didn't know how to live. Her own sons dull though they were, were quiet, sane and brotherly.

Before he left, Agatha had talked to her constantly about Dimitri. How he didn't go to the little white washed church with the single priest on Sunday. (Agatha with her perjured soul went faithfully, hoping that God would 'understand' or 'take her even so;' and sometimes she had dreams, strange dreams of the return of Christ, who arrived naked with hair covering his body like a robe—hair down to his knees, more like a phenomenal beast than a man—rampaging through the world furious at the rich, and the complacent, but, when He came to her, a little lenient, growling a little less. She had after all, one guest room with a hand embroidered bed spread on the bed, two embroidered table cloths, a set of blue crystal, a single set of silver-ware, four China coffee cups, four China dishes and the rest of the money went into paying the bills. All this wealth she would lay before the Son of God and say—you see! But she was deformed somehow, not quite right for heaven—her soul bent just beyond the limits of the strait gate; for things, she would say to the Lord, had gone wrong ever since her prayer; she was simply 'off.' This was another sign. She tried to hang on—to rise every morning at four for Jason—Jason didn't seem to like girls or love, showed no interest in getting married, was unpredictable, sometimes cloddish. She prepared the coffee, she had a sip herself, and they spoke a few words. It was all ordinary enough. But if you asked her privately, she would have said that the island seemed to her like a desert and it had become that way, desolate and abandoned, since her son had gone off. Not that the exterior was not in its way beautiful. There was a forest, caves on the other side of the island, and a subterranean lake like a blue crystal. It was something about being there alone in winter—in summer it was a little better—that made it a desert; or perhaps on the interior, as she called it—it was a desert.) Barbara had merely squinted at her, had spoken no words of consolation. So she had mourned, in the end, only mourned—for years madly, mindlessly and now over her absent son, comfortlessly.

The island was is was like a cup brimming over of white sunlight. It was a place where the lizard never seemed to move, lying on the rock with its little slender throat palpitating; and when it moved, it didn't move head or tail; rather suddenly there was a flash and it was gone. Electrical activity for three seconds, then a vanishing. Like the lizard, the island seems utterly static. One doesn't notice changes really; except for the rare pulse of existence, the moving along the main road to the grocery store of a few people, that was really the way of the island of standing still, the things to be expected, motions of motionlessness, lazy smoking in the taverns, the single slap on the rump of the whore Maria serving wine, the old men out early at the fishing boats, the women among the lemons, in the kitchens cooking up lemon curd, pick-ling fish—the beat, beat, beat of a slow, world-forgotten life; as yet the great stir has not happened; nor the vanishing. But one imagines it will; and then earth, creation, emptied, remains as mysterious as ever: When the souls are gone, a zero humanity place, a perch of two, three rocks in the sea in a dazzling diamond sun and the silence of the zero of what made everything tick! The village folk waited for this eventual-ity: the end of the world, when they, the saints, would be summoned to God, be vacuumed up off the earth, sorted out in the accounting, and would take up their new abode after a glorious metamorphosis in the white-gold air of heaven, ultimately muted with still no news about the tick tick or tick tock of human existence. This waiting made them broody often, sometimes cantankerous for they were advised by the priest not to feel worthy of God.

Agatha had brought back a little prayer rope from the monastery and for a while we saw her murmuring the Jesus prayer as she walked in the streets. Trying to be ho-lier than we are! But she in her madness said it was already the end of the world, and 'people' (like us) were getting thrown off course—out, out! Imagine! She had said it of us! It had come quietly, this was the prelude to the mighty appearance in the sky of the hairy, wild Jesus—Agatha's desecrations!— few were going to make it down the path. Agatha also cursed the moodiness, which she called intelligence, which had driven her son away, and the madness that had made her forget herself and say her terrible, cursing prayer. She looked at Barbara on the other side of a white garden wall in that one little window she could see from her kitchen that seemed always to be lit in triumph and imagined her saying the right prayers and watching her sons marry and have children, all proper and correct, setting one foot before another perfectly on the path and arriving in the end, successfully, and happily, at the bosom of an almost hairless Christ sitting in a golden bath of light, eyes like two elegant, unperturbed black swans floating on a lake the color of morning, never having per-jured herself, or having had to watch a son turn away from church and home. Agatha decided she could only hold on to that thread of life that remained to her, hoping that her son would become weary of the outer world and come home at least to rest. For although she couldn't rest but spent the day despite a weak back, cleaning the house, fixing the old furniture, a chair had broken, the table was cracked and she had just figured out a way with a certain glue that she had sent away for to patch up the chair and table, she wanted her home to be a home of rest; she would have Simon whitewash and try to adjust the windows askew. She had become quite the handy-man around the house, and when she wasn't cleaning, fixing, sewing or cooking, she would sit and think over her bad prayer and finger the prayer rope and wonder if there was any way back to the shining path that certain people like Barbara just fell on to, naturally, and if her son would by some miracle transform from a scholar to a fisherman, who maybe read books brilliantly, and return happy to the peaceable island home—if from the wandering in the 'desert' she might not find herself in the end, like Barbara, perfectly fitting on to the bosom of that hairless-chested, golden black-eyed Christ.

But even without the comfort of being on the path like Barbara, she had contin-ued for her second son's sake; large dinners of fish soup and salads of potatoes were his fare, spoonfuls of lemon marmalade at five o' clock, evening coffee and sugar, while she often fasted, tried to fast, sometimes she broke down at five and raven-ously ate whatever she could find in the house; they said of her house that it always smelled delicious, of rice and butter sauce and stewed chicken. As for other women, they became furious in their chests when they saw her—that she could make such a sweet life despite it all as they had put it, and she a widowed gypsy with a disloyal son. Others thought she went around as if she didn't care about the ruination of her household and that she would most certainly be punished in the end. The village folk were never very reliable when it came to standing by one; those who were friends one day easily became enemies—it was enough for an inculpating word to be dropped, as it were, in their ears, while those who were enemies festered in their bad blood towards one. But they were, Agatha thought, like children—little things irked them or brought them pleasure. Nothings changed them from bad to good, from good to bad. But hers—the evil prayer—Agatha thought was something huge; no one else in the daily life of fishing and milking had done something so awful, cataclysmic, though so very, very quiet, and on the inner side, outwardly imperceptible. Agatha with her strange, disordered, cursed mind thought that her soul was irrevocably lost and thus her monologue to God became more insistent as if she had to get a few words in before she had to leave. It was not exactly prayer, nor even confession. It was a rambling, hokey, wild goings-on that spilled from her mouth loudly and softly. What she called her 'talking to'.

When she returned from the visit to the sisters, Agatha was dreamy; she stopped a few people at the market where she was buying oil, saying to them: I know there is a different reality; this is just a side issue. It is the same as if you were writing something and jotted down a note to remember. We are that note not the main piece. Not at all the main piece. When it is done we can be thrown out. Thrown away! Or else, incorporated, as if we, with our distortions, had at the beginning been saying all the conventional things. She had a propensity to dream and to come up with things….

Now it was for certain Agatha was mad. She had let her imagination go—no stopping, checking like holy people do according to the teachings of the Church. We knew already that there was that tendency. Her father was a gypsy singer- poet, and he sang all night long --until he died—until when the birds started up at dawn and he drooped a little, exhausted. He was not cheerful, always, we say, tending towards the melancholy and silent. He told Agatha, a little one then, that he was seeking one meaning in the universe—and proclaimed at the end of his life his revelation—look see an orchid purple and white little blooms on Holy Island—there is one thing one thing to learn! It is known in nature. What it is and why the orchid he never related; he died that evening. Agatha was only ten when his coffin was lowered into the sea and the madness that infected her father's brain showed later in life in her. All so much nonsense and useless expression. It is this kind of thing, the old priest warned her mother, this seeking beyond Scripture to something out there that makes sense— that depletes heart and soul—whether an orchid or an entire universe.

We were not surprised that Agatha married a man who spent hours walking up and down talking to himself as did she. Nor that Dimitri, her first son was mute for a whole six years growing up, becoming an inward, physically restless child, writing brilliant essays in school, yes, but saying nothing not even to his mother—just giving her, as she said, inexhaustible night-sky dark looks. She said he used to tread so softly that she didn't know when he was in the room with her; he would appear by her side sometimes so suddenly that she would scream a little. Her theory of course was that her cursedness had been passed on to him. We know how he came out of that 'fix', as we call it; we call it that for his eyes had a 'fixed look' at times, and we decided he was frozen inside. It was Katrina who brought him 'round—everybody on the island knows it. He must have been sixteen; he was on his way home, carrying goat meat. Whatever she said, the idea is that she lured him away from his path home to the forest; sex has a way of twining its tentacles around a person weaving them in and out with its magic. In any case, when he went in he was a boy, and mute; when he came out he was a man and talking. Agatha didn't ask questions but it seems that while in his non talking stage, Dimitri had acquired a host of opinions that all came tumbling out now. Namely books were all things to be read and criticized rather than read and believed in and that included the Scriptures.

We didn't condemn Dimitri. He was just a person shadowed by the madness in his family. Zoe thought that in the end marrying Katrina would bring him around. Katrina for whatever you might be thinking about her age was a good home-loving girl that had set her mind on marriage. But they didn't marry; they walked in and out of the forest it must have been a thousand times, she smoking with an obstinate, aloof look and he gesturing dramatically—sometimes it was at her bosom, for she was taller than he-- and their loud voices carrying the argument into the square. We thought it would end the usual way with male, female nest building. And we have good reason to believe that Katrina desired it. That she, in fact, waited when Dimitri went away; not that she didn't flirt with the idea of marrying someone else; but that she couldn't let go of Dimitri.

Despite his taunts and scorn, his mockery of our ways, as we said-- we didn't condemn Dimitri. He was feeling his way to manhood, said Anna, our village old woman—it was normal. We just knew that he was much more sensitive than the others; not that there were many others. We had a few children in the village—maybe thirty at that time; we hoped, we have spent a lifetime hoping that they would marry and settle and not travel away never to be seen again. With his intelligence, we hoped for a while that Dimitri would lead the others—that he would be the one, you see, around town, who would make things click. We have no explicitly official mayor or chief. It was an island tradition but always questioned, wrangled about. We have priests and they give us the bread of heaven—that is to say, knowledge on how not to die an eternal death. But we always elect a man to manage things, someone to inform in case something should happen—an accident or a crime. Often we are just swayed to elect a person—we are moved that way—a universal gut feeling, a feeling that the election is necessary. At the time Dimitri left it was Simon, half cracked, seventy year old Simon who painted things that looked wheels and wings but were flowers and pots. He told us it was just sheer accident that he painted. We confess that no one knows how he got elected— except that it must have been by the ladies. It must have been because he alone was so much the islander having never left even to the other island in all his life and our older ladies are prejudiced that way. Perhaps we were swayed a little by guilt—he so old and so useless—made that way by island life, by us; therefore, his madness is our madness. Then Paul and Peter got elected too, or rather 'elevated' by certain of our more aggressive husbands.

Of course, after, we didn't think Simon was the right person for the informal job—just, really a nomination of respect. We thought the twins, Peter and Paul, younger by a generation, like Agatha, but old in their thinking were probably right although their respect was not official because Simon held that place; but the twins had those old expressions in their faces that registered neither young manhood nor age, expressions of our forefathers in our pictures, grim and ghostly. They neither painted nor crafted furniture and houses, as did Simon, but they made children—one son for Paul, little Paul, was his name, and three girls for Peter all of them bland, plump and perfect for marriage and that was worthy in and of itself. For odd reasons, as we said, the motion for we might say patriarch of the island, called manager, passed to old Simon. There was no vote, just several nods among the older folks. All the more apt, because we never could tell what Simon was thinking and we even have imagined that he was not thinking at all just laughing foolishly. But we couldn't say that he was a fool. But when the information was passed on to him about Dimitri, he didn't say anything—smiled his crafty smile, went on carving something out of olive wood. And when he caught wind of the scandalous story of Jason nearly killing his brother, he put down his brush, for he was painting at the time, brushed his hands against his trousers and stared into space until from so much staring and not blinking tears formed in his eyes and ran down his cheeks. Then he asked: He is gone? —meaning Dimitri. They informed him that he was gone. And he began to smile again, that old crafty smile.

We didn't understand. For us it makes more sense to do as Peter suggested—ban Dimitri for a year, watch Jason. Then bring the two men to church when Dimitri came back and see if they kiss as brothers. We know a holy place can work wonders. It used to be that the whole of the island was holy, people were simple, peaceful and pure; we argued but it was all settled with a touch of peace in us not of this earth. The soil was so saintly that the light of heaven was once threaded into it. We think it is right of Peter and Paul to look at this seriously. What madness could creep in to a family here on Holy Island that was always so kind and quiet? Peter and Paul talked of purging the island of mad people and their children as if they had authority. But who could blame them?

Who were we to take care of Agathas, the Agatha-like—should they arise? We could understand someone sick—something not of their own doing, a weak heart, catarrh! But when someone goes and deliberately slams the door on the Almighty there is no question but they will receive punishment in due time!

Father Isaac had acquired a deacon. He was suspected since that incident of the story in the tavern so the only people who gave him whole hearted attention were Anna, the oldest and a little fond of everybody, and Agatha, the cursed--Agatha had 'understood' and had found the answer from the sisters where the priest had advised her to go, and Martha, the imbecilic daughter of the lazy fisherman who despite the destitution of his family, preferred to spend hours lying in bed, drinking brandy, smoking and staring at the ceiling that had gone black with water damage and was rotting. Finally, Max, the son of the village philanderer, anguish-faced and physically contorted, whose hands and feet were too big and thus made him notoriously clumsy: It was Max, of course, who became the deacon;— Max who had run from his father's beating in the middle of a stormy night with a broken nose and blood streaming down his chin! Emerging out of the rain, large frightened gray eyes first into Father Isaac's arms wet with rain water and blood!

They were standing, or rather squatting, as Max crouched down and Father Isaac followed in the doorway of the homey little church; and Father Isaac brushed back Max's rain soaked hair and kissed him on the forehead, said something to him and thus got him to get back on his feet and come into shelter. He took him into his room, laid him on his bed and doctored his nose with homemade ointments and herbal infusions. It is one thing I am good at, the priest murmured—healing broken things. Men, women, cats, birds, lizards, trees, I have made them all come back to life. Then the priest, as Max rested, began to talk loudly.

Your father is now nothing but a broken hearted, dying old man.

Dying? Asked Max incredulously; he can't stop pummeling me—never runs out of breath! How can he possibly be dying?

Now your mother—there!, went on the priest, not listening. A man may have two or three fathers but always only one mother. Years ago she died, giving birth to you—yes, well, then you see Leo went a little mad. Before he was smiling and soft like a little lamb. When she died, he all but killed himself. Then he found out that there was death in him too. He ceased to mourn but took up debauchery. We have a saying that there is a ladder of holiness—usually it starts with a few kind actions and progresses to something genuinely self-sacrificing—well, your father who was up to kindness when your mother was alive, with her gone and his own death looming in his mind, simply lost his grip and slid all the way down. Odd, but a holy brokenness, which should have made him reflect, made him give up virtue.

You know, he paused—there are stories--she was beautiful. Beautiful, unreal.

Who?

Your mother—Magda. One does understand your father's shall I call it—spiritual demise. Girls on this island are just not that beautiful. The islanders themselves say they have simple, goats' herder features—makes one think of cheese and lemons— comfortable but not extraordinary. Your mother was apparently golden in the night like the moon in China, yes, I've been there. Tall, and long-legged with an ever-peaceful face and eyes like little lights, she could run faster than any man. Her skin was smooth and her eyes--blue, green sea-colored eyes were almost invisible for the light in them —she had a look they said like seas upon seas, like she was scanning infinity. She had a moon-like aura, a serene presence. She was more intelligent than the others—knew how to read before the other children her age. But all this you know or have heard?

I have been afraid to. I have always been of the opinion that she made my father what he is.

Your father? Oh, Leo? Puff, who was he—a nonentity, a frightened boy, a heap of dust...? She pulled him out of the dust pile, gave him will power, courage, love. It was as if she injected him with something sweet and vital to the human body, the body of love.

She used to stand around among the adults when she was quite little rather than playing with the other children. When asked why, she answered that she wanted to learn what men and women did together. Of course, the villagers laughed at that—then later regretted their laughter; she stared so solemnly, so long and hard, it made people nervous. Oh, and there was a matter of fortune telling—Magda had been going to the gypsy camps on the other island, eloping with her dreams on the caique that goes out once a month, wandering in amidst the children and women, sitting around the fires, selling her pearls for wisdom; after a few years, it appears they taught her star and palm reading. By the time she was fourteen, she knew how to accurately read the basic shape of a man or woman's life. That is the story, in any case. So she told destinies, little and big—one, two, three—there are rumors that everything she predicted happened; and then when she was about seventeen, she told her own destiny in tea leaves and coffee grains. She looked up at the stars and saw it in inexpugnable writing there. It was as she surmised—dark and painful. Marriage, childbirth, death. Death and birth were to be the same for her.

She threw herself into living and working. She liked repairing roofs of houses more than anything else, she followed Simon around, climbed on to roofs with him, pulled up the old rotted tiles. Eventually she worked on her own. Everything she did had a superior touch. Everything lasted, that is, all the roofs she repaired. Then she ate and drank, feasting enormously like someone trying to forget herself. Then she fasted—smearing her face with dust for the tears she said that she held inside. But the fasts were sincere; she wanted to dissociate herself from her body 'of death', as she called it—find, as she said, another reality. She had her own way with the faith. Her own eating and her own abstaining—nothing to do with the church calendar. Nobody interfered. They saw her as superior, gifted, and the ones that hated her held themselves away, out of fear. In any case, we all waited for her to die.

The story of her marriage has been told time and time again. One day standing on top of a house, she looked down and saw your father mocked and jeered at for being fat and weak. An utterly pitying expression came over her usually impassive face. She made one long jump down from the roof into the midst of the young men, took your father by the arm and kissed him. They went into the forest entwined— the forest was the place for our adolescent lovers! She came out pregnant. She had decided you see—just then—when the baby was conceived; for, as we learned, she had hated bullying and cruelty. She married him in a matter of weeks to a splendid feast but they said there was darkness in her eyes that made even the children pause. Just the expression, I think, of oncoming death. She always said her heart was gay as a wife to your father. And he bowed down to her as if she was not queen but king in their house—a wedding present from his mother who had lived alone with her little Leo after her husband abandoned her and moved to the other land, she praying on prayer beads that he marry well.

And then the newlywed's house was a flurry of fixing, and furnishing; he made the beds in the morning, shaking the sheets, swatting the pillows. He beat the rugs out the window and the dust came out in a cloud—all this midmorning when she was up with her tool kit, in her overalls ready to climb on the roof or fix the plumbing, something Simon had taught her as well, with orders for him to obey. But at dawn, when he awoke, he would spend as he said one 'holy minute'—the first and last of them—watching her breathe. Beauty, more beautiful, more beautiful—and the villagers say he shouted out and whispered—most beautiful thing—a woman who could stand up to anybody and had a face as wonderful as the moon, with naked breasts, breathing.

She had a way of knowing things. It was not that people would come to her to ask what the stars said about them. Rather, she would go to them and tell them things and it would all happen just as she said. With this and her beauty, beauty, Simon told me, like the blue on the island, the sky, the rock, she held the villagers spellbound. There are stories—that her spirit still protects the villagers; they didn't know what to make of her what with the predictions coming true, the ability to look death in the face. The beauty, the divining, made some see in Magda something holy and so, like everything holy, subjected to a cruel fate.

This is your mother. I would say that since her death, a few have become devotees, although the church won't recognize her as a saint, of course: Woman on a roof with her own feasting and fasting. But the fortunes keep coming true. And then there are some who think of her as the devil.

She used to run on the beach in the late afternoon and with her went the light, some of the villagers say. When she got pregnant with you she stopped running. She used to be in the middle of a conversation, your father said, and then drift off. In her third trimester, she suddenly up and left home for awhile. She went up to the monastery laboring with her belly on the cliffs; the nuns welcomed her without a murmur and gave her a little cell to stay ten days. She took with her only a sackful of books—mostly poetry, no change of clothes not even a nightgown and they say she went about nude. And she sat on the cliff each day while the harsh bell rang for prayer staring out at sea and imagining things. What it would have been like if….It seems for all the melancholy, the near despair she went up with she would have come back crying, being nearer and nearer to the fatal day; but in fact she came down smiling.

Death, she said, is finished. They say, when she died, her face though grey, pinched and old looked more beautiful than it ever had in life. The villagers didn't know what it meant to have all this in one of their children. They continue to talk of her; and some, as I said, even pray to her –their homemade 'saint.' Some execrate all this—this beauty—thing of the devil, they say.

And you too, you, the priest shook a playful finger at Max, thought her evil. You listened to your father. After her death your father became a seducer of married women and blamed it on her, a corrupter—as if it was all spite; as if he actually wished to revenge himself on a woman who would go and die on him—who would suddenly transform from flesh and blood, face and breasts, to a hush hush island god some say with the image of the white tailed eagle—a few islanders think that when this bird comes, it is her spirit. Sometimes she is simply 'our saint,' the way the others are not named—not with this kind of leery affection. Seamlessly she passes between myth and religion. The island folk only say to themselves—powerful, perhaps holy— will she do the ultimate magic? As the Jews wondered seeing Jesus.

And, he went on, you like the others thought that I was harboring a woman, in secret, here.

And you are not? Max cried out in a spasm.

Father Isaac picked up a cassette tape—Italian opera, he said. It is wrong to become so ascetic one forgets how to live, how to fill oneself with passion and tenderness up to the gills. How to be ripe flesh and blood. How to make beauty.

In conversations of this kind, the priest planted the seed—the hot blood-seed of love, the beautiful face of a woman—peaceful as the moon, then the sea-like eyes, the soft, queenly walk, the body strong as a storm wind—all this wrapped in a person who went on roofs and fixed them—in the dirt on the roofs of our houses. In the end it was not of course a dead girl that Max fell in love with that happened to be his mother, more a cool breeze in the heat of summer, the fathomless shadowy sea— blue, grey, green, light; but a new thought gave Max a secret ecstasy. He joined in spirit those islanders who thought Magda not Mother Dora the true saint, or rather, island god—a little god, but nonetheless…. And the author of this delight, the priest, talked to him more and convinced him in a half dream to study Scripture with him, as ecstatic song, to stay with him, to drink beautiful tasting herbal infusions, and to listen as he described the Kingdom of God, as a burning coal. And between God and mother—that is, white tailed eagle god and roof-jumping saint, Max lived in a bit of a trance, healing physically, although still not emotionally, so that not a trace was left of his fractured nose. He still twisted when he talked from an instinct of fear. And there were periodically shadows of anguish that passed over his face. But the priest could see that slow step by slow step he was coming away from the old horror of living with Leo.

Of course, the priest knew too that Max was delicate, even dainty. A normal boy his age would have shouted, swung his arm, not twisted himself in a corner, one leg coiled around the other, one elbow in the crook of the other, fatigue stamped all over his mouth, anguish in his green painful eyes. But he was physically filling out a little, moving with less of a jolt, although he still ducked when someone reached out an arm to hold him. The priest grabbed him in big bear hugs, kissed him on the forehead. Amazingly, the boy tolerated him trustingly letting his body meet Father Isaac's skin and bone. So from a few days of staying with the priest until he was better, it became a prolonged stay of a few weeks and then months; finally when Max descended into the village for his things, Leo shouted him out of the house to that priest devil, as he called him, telling him not to come back. Max was fourteen, new to the world as an egg, tremulous as a sparrow.

By then, Father Isaac had made the usual rounds of his parishioners—that is, all seventy households except for Leo, Max's father, who threw an empty bottle at him that crashed into shards under the window at his feet and the priest laughed, like a devil, Leo said, but with a slight grin. But the villagers, those who did the talking in their monthly meetings at Simon's huge house, were still murmuring against Father Isaac. Now that Max was in his tow, and sometimes Martha, whom he called Max's sister—another child saint of the trash heap, meaning the hard, cruel world—Max talking loudly about another world, so unlike him, Martha lagging behind, bending down to stare at insects, they began to think the priest had a secret plan up his sleeve. So they talked about it late into the night, a few heads were seen thrown back in the lamp lit windows, mouths moving, loud talk, a little shouting; one man—was it Paul, got up, hugging himself. Simon himself sat until dawn, frowning and smiling alternately; in the window when the large talkative party had dispersed, some moody, some laughing, the outline of Simon's head could be seen in the window, animated by expression and then frowning or smiling—one didn't know—bent over, brooding or sleeping.

Agatha and Katrina had been at the meeting of course. Agatha had sat silently with a dreamy look. She had been to the monastery and she knew that Dimitri was coming home—knew in her blood, deep in her jeweled mother blood. She had ventured to say about Father Isaac—deceiver or not deceiver he knows us so well… and this gentle addition to the conversation was met with harsh laughter, and anger.

Michael, the fifteen year old, was permitted to attend because he always brought news like a flash in the night of daily existence. At this juncture, he stood up and announced that according to Max who lived with the priest and knew him intimately and more and more each day-- he was busy writing about the villagers, yes, even keeping files on each one of us. Watching us, exclaimed Paul. Spying, said Peter, the twins often talked one after the other. And his plan is this: on earth as it is in heaven.

What? Oh that, oh yes—then I suppose he is alright and all this recording, a kind of fitting us in; —well, but we have been keeping the commandments; different voices chimed in. Bah, keeping the commandments what is that? Don't we all sin?

It is all clear cut, put in Barbara. When we sin, we confess, repent and back we are in heaven.

There used to be heaven here, said Anna, the elder. I remember wild lilies and vines of jasmine, poppies, and anemones, the orchids! There were even vines of wild roses creeping up one fence —there was a real forest of flowers. We hardly had to make our gardens; the flowers just invaded. It was like the beginning of the world—such is a flower, it is a mind, you see and a whole host of flowers—the same mind, tender, considering, shouting the truth; it was magnificent, miraculous! There was no time—delight forever only. But it seems the flowers have stopped growing so profusely. There are larger patches of dust and stones. Perhaps the sun has scorched them. For one thing, there has been too much sun.

This 'forever' ends said Katrina;

In fact, said Peter; what are we to do?

At least we have our ways, said Paul;

And so what is wrong then to say—on earth as it is in heaven? Isn't that what our ancestors came here for?

Well there is nothing wrong, said Stavros a little huffily; only we all know this better than this impossible priest who tells racy stories. We need someone who won't pretend to know more than we do—to say things fancifully and abstractly and to ignore our real problems.

Shall we vote on it—whether to dismiss this Father Isaac, with all his mysterious superiority…asked Barbara, Stavros' wife. The villagers had taken it into their heads that Father Isaac's singing at night, that the opera music which gushed forth from his lit windows and thin walls was an attempt to 'be superior' to the Our Saints villagers.

This is nonsense, said Stavros, loudly, with the sudden change of heart that happened often when he heard his wife's voice. We desired a priest, when Father Raphael died, poisoned by heroin, which he had become addicted to, falling to evil despite his goodness and his sweet manners, we all agreed on it—and look what happened!—we asked for a new priest and we received this one. We are condemned, yet happily, he said laughing strangely as if he had had a new and amusing thought. Suddenly Stavros said: We must accept him. It is our way—the priest is a man of God. He comes from God, doesn't he? He was on the boat that docked in our harbor; besides it will only make us uncomfortable to have to wait for another priest—what if he is worse and we must exchange him too? And then inevitably some will agree and some disagree, he laughed again.

But you said, said Barbara, who was unable to follow the sudden polar changes in the mind of her husband—that he ignores our real problems. I think that is serious.

What we really need is to see able people in positions of authority—not just priests; said Peter.

We have always proposed a mayor and the people would submit if you brought in someone with the old traditions in mind, affirmed Paul.

Like you, laughed Stavros again.

No, bah—what good would a mayor do us? Simon suddenly fixed his intent eyes on Paul. Elections just to subvert our freedom! We are all old folks now; it is shameful that we can't just settle down with an afternoon coffee and some apricot candy, and with the bitter and sweet flavors in our mouths, quietly resolve our differences. You need mayors and things when you have young folks and more and more children being born, many young husbands and wives to be reconciled. With Father Raphael, we had approximately thirty new births—Dimitri, Jason, Little Paul, Katrina—they were born then, and at the end of his tenure, all of Peter's brood, Nico, Elizabeth, Michael, Marta—the last of them and about nineteen more—and even then we thought we were well off with just a priest. But now with the nineteen married and moved off island; there is hardly any movement—we sit and we fish; we don't need a mayor to tell us how to do that, Simon argued. What we need is what we've got— although I don't say I trust him. Still, we old folks need to think a little of heaven.

No but it is on earth as it is in heaven. I like that. I tell you it used to be; this was a holy place—even I can remember. The flowers, the blue stone, the sky that seemed to kiss you like a father…even the dust was holy—it sparkled with a glorious light. Here ancient life mixed in with the newest babes. We had it, it was all here. Somehow we lost it, said Anna.

And you talk, said Barbara—why you hardly believe in God.

Believe, disbelieve, big words in and out of my head like it is for a child growing up, laughed Anna, yawning.

Of course we've lost the holiness here!—what with our refrigerators, radios, gas tanks, TVs—Matrona said in her harsh voice; she was Martha's mother, and essentially jealous because her husband never brought in enough to buy anything new. Her TV had broken long ago and the refrigerator didn't keep anything cold anymore, the radio even with new batteries produced nothing but static. She like any number of people who have given up—said she didn't care—she would buy and eat without storing or even cooking her food often, read old magazines, listen to radios through kitchen windows of other folks' homes. She didn't even have a mop but had to sweep the refuse and grime (and there was always refuse and grime on the floor) with a handmade broom. Then she discovered from Father Raphael that the time was short and she closer to glory for her poverty. So, as she grew increasingly resentful as more and more riches came the way of her neighbors, she also periodically gloated with the sense that they were far behind her on the path to God and that maybe He cast a glance of approval in her direction, offered her admission to the home of light, and looked upon her neighbors with sternness and contempt—for they had it all in this life, wallowed in it—TVs, refrigerators, radios, gas tanks—what was left for the next?

Even this priest had proven to be her ally when she discussed this with him. Except that he said something strange—it is not so much luxury that is the crime—but the hideousness. The curse was they could not make a beautiful refrigerator, beautiful enough to be holy. I myself have only a stove—my gas tanks are my contribution to uglification. I buy them with the pennies they give me each month from the Orthodox Church.

Matrona had tried to see it this way, but the lack of proper kitchen utilities hurt. And a hurtful life was fatiguing and sad. So she beat her only child, Martha, and chased her out of the house often at night. What, she said to her husband and she didn't care if God was listening—do I have to have an imbecile underfoot in the house? She had long since ceased to think of Martha as a daughter; she thought of her, in fact, as a kind of large white rat. And she had a sense that she was understood in any case—that she needn't worry about her lack of maternal instinct. For it was Martha herself, she said to herself, who had ruined it. She played the empty head on purpose.

So despite the fact that people stared at her, she came to the meetings, she held her head high—and she told them—ha, so far behind on the path to the superior place. No one argued with her because they all felt uneasy about Martha. She had fallen down once in Barbara's kitchen and hit her head; perhaps that had contributed to her imbecility; she had hit her head again when a goat kicked her—she had fallen against a stone—that was in Zoe's yard. At Anna's she had stopped breathing for five minutes.

Martha who ambled from house to house, curiously pushing open back doors and eating food that she found, was often found wandering amidst the goats on the hills, without shoes because older children used to steal them. Sometimes, feeling hot or just not liking clothes on her body she would take off her shirt and bare her scrawny breasts. The villagers had willy-nilly inherited Martha, a little after Dimitri was born; she came with the farmyard animals. There was some hostile feeling that her mother wouldn't or couldn't care for her and pushed her out of the house to fend for herself. But that was largely repressed. Martha wandered because it was her nature to wander. Everyone cared for Martha as if it was duty—tossing her scraps of food, but it was Agatha who washed her with sudsy soap, anointed her wet body and hair with fragrant myrrh, set her down to feasts of oregano and tomato baked chicken and peppered goats' cheese, green vegetables dripping with oil, lemon and salt, lemon curd in tarts for dessert and kept her later, reclining on soft cotton scented, new white pillows on her own bed, burping and farting, somnolent with digesting, until, by the nature of her mental disease, Martha got up and went off wandering, sideways like a crab, lurching a little like a drunk person, throwing herself down on the sand and stones against the church in the dead of night to sleep. Martha was a cross, a poor Magdalene, some said. Then came the day, no one exactly knew when, when Father Isaac 'picked her up' like a lost coin and loved her, rejoiced with her—she even smiled that buoyant smile of rejoicing with him. Yet she still wandered about when the rejoicing was done, looking like tragedy, Barbara said. So everyone was silent and swallowed when Martha's mother spoke. Everyone silently accepted her rebukes.

We were not at first concerned about the fact that our young moved away, or simply were not born. We had known dry spells before in the weather and in our women and men. Life continued in the same way. The weather was still what we expected. The summers were a lot hotter and longer, the sun blazing with the ferocity of a white tiger, even prowling into the shaded spaces with its heat; the winters were shorter. But we felt confident that the balance would be restored. As far as the old beauty and holiness—of course, one expects that things like that to be in the past. Some of our grown children—being so uninstructed—whisper among themselves that there is no holiness now on Holy Island. Some of us say that we are waiting for it to come back; it was mysteriously taken from us. Some of our circles of women say that it is hidden and that in one of our people it will shine forth again. Sometimes, a village man, usually one of the old folk, leans his sun-dizzied head against the cool white wall of his little house—as if to say: if only the idea, the thought, the fire of mind would come out in one of us again! And we look heavenward, and we look earthward through the sweat in our eyes in summer; in heaven there is an inscrutable smile at our anguish, not a gloating or triumphant smile, not a smile of satisfaction at our punishment, but a smile that is the smile of all living things—Zoe says so and indeed we have seen it in lizards and just settling on new spring leaves. We have seen it tarrying on the surface of the sun brilliant water enshrouding our land. But there is no help from heaven except that smile if you can call that help.

When we look earthward, we see old age and sorrow. Or, we see helplessness, tenderness. In either case, there is a sense that all that is is mystified about our trouble like little children looking at a great airplane—we see them flying overhead—and wonder how it flies. Heaven asks, earth asks—how can it be? Like little dependent persons.

We know where we came from. We know the stories: how at the time of the Resurrection of Jesus, a man named John, or Simon or Bartholomew or it might have been three men of those names who had witnessed the terrible and cruel Crucifixion, peeped in the door where the disciples were sitting with their raised Master and beheld what they must have thought was a tremendous miracle similar to that of the beginning of all life on earth. They continued to listen in from this cracked open door to the blessed teachings and when the Master left, they ran among a few families that were believers telling the story. Thus it was that the believers, about fifty families, set out for a place to worship and came after many days to this remote island where, because God was with them, they found fresh drinking water, wild lemon trees and wild goats. You can disbelieve it if you like, but there is no question of the radiance of that smile here—smile of life or of the wild lemons and the goats.

There are of course some nay sayers, we know about them—even priests have been among them: they say that the village grew up adjacent to the monastery as a group of helpers—gardeners, goat herders, fishers—a few families who helped the monastery out of their faith in the sisters. And therefore that the village was established during the age of Byzantium alongside the Virgin of the Rocks' monastery; before that there had been only periodic landings by pirates who had buried gold— once it was rumored someone had found a store. The nuns coming from Constantinople had arrived with gold also and possibly, hearing of invasions round about, had buried it. There had been conquering and then liberation. But nothing at all had happened. A few brownish soldiers arrived, counted the population, left. There must have been three hundred souls at the time. Our ancestors gaped at the conquerors-liberators. They gaped back. Nothing came of it but a census and a tax, which died out as the conquerors were conquered.

The buried gold was never found. It is one of those mysterious fantasies that hangs over our heads—the possibility of finding that buried treasure. Several children have been named Gold but that is all that has come of it. There is one single gold icon in the Church and two ancient gold chalices for the Eucharist and a few special gold artifacts that the village stores with Simon, one of which is a beautiful carved crown with a serpent—was an islander appointed king?—which is used today for the best dancer at our dance festivals. The invaders never touched those. Our ancestors knew how to hide them and these things were protected by powers beyond our understanding. Now suddenly, we sense it—those powers are gone.

For years we were protected. Our women bore children and our families stayed, living in little cool multi-colored houses of stone or cement with green or blue shutters and red doors, the men fishing, we women embroidering, and cooking—we are known for our embroidery round about, and there are still a number of women who have a hand for it; there have been, in addition, our 'great' people women and men—healers generally and fixers of things, with minds and souls illuminated a little more than our others. But they ate and drank, slept and died like us in the end. In the end, our eyes are on our children, and our little homes, and we drink sweetened coffee in the afternoon when things get dull. We can't say that anyone was more or less than this and thus….We know them in the end like we know ourselves. We are all the same.

But some have caused misgiving. We began to have uneasy feelings as Magda grew up. Not that she was so different—a girl of the island despite all her beauty—frizzy red brown hair tied back in a white scarf, her honey of a face, her green-blue-dark eyes that always looked concentrated, serious as if she was one living thought. There was something raw about her, we said. Nobody was clear about her. There were those who wanted to call her a witch but in the face of that beauty—who would dare? There were times we couldn't even speak in her presence—we were confused, mute, even stupid; and then we would see as if defying us, one overly large, brown man-hand held up demanding our attention. She had man size hands and feet and they seemed to be part of her beauty. She said things now and then little harsh things—like 'little things keep a man from becoming a beast', told fortunes; seemed to have access to the truth. Of course, it was all coincidence—chance that her fortunes came true. Perhaps it wasn't even that but the subtle fact that in the end we loved her, waddled after her men and women both like fat little toddlers following their mother. Oh yes, we did even though we sometimes wondered if she weren't better off dead. She was too big, you see, for our island. We can take so much not more. There were perhaps always discrepancies in the holiness of our island; but in the past, some strong, able man has handled them. Now, perhaps with the death of Father Raphael, but even before, a priest so sick, so shriveled in musculature from the poison, we have ceased to shoo those elements of unholiness. Agatha has remained. Magda caused confusion, and some of us have weakly yielded ourselves to her spirit.

There were attempts on her life. Well, she had a way of swaying through the throng, with her head held high, with her face exultant and joyous like a conqueror after some ancient war, towering above the other women. And a way of drilling a look through the brains and bodies of men, pinning them down, making them literally shake at times. It was said that she could magically make men impotent. Well, even this sleepy little village woke up at that. Men murmured behind her back. And one day when she was on the roof of one of our larger wooden houses, one of the fishermen climbed up and gave her a push. That is what we have heard. We have heard also and seen with our own eyes how she twisted, writhed and turned in the air in a split second, landing on her feet like a cat; then it was pause and smooth herself a bit, another battle fought and won, you see, and then she walked a cool and easy walk off like a cat does. The would be murderer—oh, he! Didn't stay, we don't think! Melted away. Nothing was heard of him after. She never said a word against him, though undoubtedly she knew who he was. A boy child standing by the house at the time said that he had seen a black cat fall from the clouds and land on its feet and then it transformed into Magda walking that cool and easy walk away. So she transmogrified from the eagle god to the black cat god and there were others to come and oh, yes, of course, the Christian saint—some saint of fates and hearts.

There was more murmuring and then a pause when she married. We saw something in her eyes that was not here and now but there and after and it was final. The men, who would have crowded around the conqueror's marriage bed, stepped back and left her and Leo. Leo we saw smiling sleepily like a sheep. With her, he was always smiling. But she had something big in her look the whole time until she went up to the monastery and came down smiling mysteriously. They smiled and smiled, didn't stop smiling. Then it seemed something about her was faded and frail but on the inside; because before delivering Max, three days before, belly big as a house, she arm wrestled at the tavern—Leo, Simon, Peter and beat them all. But there was still something because she looked as if the outlines were there but the substance faded, as if she had once been one of those rich, full blown paintings by a great artist and now was a sketch by an adolescent with a shaky hand. The day of her delivery was a gusty day, we thought it would storm and the sea would rise over our road. But it all calmed down in a few hours; a baby was heard crying when the winds died in the late afternoon, the sun came out a little before setting and Magda was dead.

Other babies were born at this time—a few, not many. Most of the young parents found work in the big city and took their children away. Max and Leo stayed. Leo had resigned himself to dying further down the line sometime; he had a baby to raise and needs, he told us with a sick grin. Max in Leo's arms: at times he was so tender to that child—we've seen him look like the male version of the All-Holy mother of Jesus; the same very submissive look as if the little body was the incarnate command of God. At other times—we know from the neighbors who were on hand that he left the baby somewhere, anywhere, even on the top of the stove, once in the bathroom sink, and wandered off like a goat after women. Sometimes he would come home drunk, his fly open and penis clearly visible and a sneer on his face. It got to the point where the villagers were agitated like so many chickens hearing a bang next to the chicken coop. Several times crowds of men approached his house and he would appear outrageously drunk and taunting them—what do your wives say? And they would draw back not wishing to make a public spectacle of their own shame. And we know exactly how he went about seducing women. He would appear before them in the market at noon, cool and perfumed with a subtle, engaging man scent imported from the city, the kind that you smell when men flock together like eagles and women wail after them, then he would talk and talk, low, soft, after a while like magic the woman would be laughing. It was the laughter that made her fall into step, walking with him, tossing back her hair—nowhere in particular, then a little spice came into the talk and laughter, spice that could be felt like pepper on the tongue in the arch of the woman's left foot. And so on up her thigh and suddenly up the back of the right leg too. And the love making was absolutely imperative—as if a queen was seated in the love place commanding. Then the slavery—mind, unsuspecting like a child. This would continue for several days. The woman meeting Leo at some designated place, running there as if there was a fire behind her, because often people walking by eyed his house. And then Leo would one day transform into a monster, a petty, vain, lazy boy with a big head and a kind of conceit in his face that would replace the delicacy of sexual engagement; conceit and indifference written all over the body that was once sacred love and the woman would be wooshed out of the house or place of rendezvous ready to cry rape. We know this because women later have gone around in fits of crying unable to stop themselves from confessing. Husbands would get wind of the outrage and there would be maybe uproars in the household; once or twice a wife was shown the door. But we are a placid people about these things and sooner or later the wife was back home and the fisherman husband quiet, sullen—looking at his nets as if they were dear and sweet, the only dear and sweet trustworthy thing in the world. We know their minds: the nets, and thus the marriage. Perhaps we can't explain the logic that connects.

We are so connected to the old beliefs that it is impossible to disconnect us. But there are those who believe that some people today are disparaging them. We know that our lives are like a blink of the eye relative to the ages. Our village took a stand near to the truth—life despite everything, even death. They say our ancestors believed that resurrection, bones and all, was not so strange or unworldly. They believed that the dead came back like rain—gently, sweetly—that some never died. One of their sayings was that in the end, which they thought not as the absolute deadness of things, but simply as the great pause before something greater—there would be born a boy of fire. Of course, this wisdom is like all legend born of ignorance; the old villagers didn't even know how electricity was generated or how the wheel could be used in a million ways other than to move a little cart. What we have now: people stepping out of line, as it were, just a little, perhaps, but it makes them odd and older.

Magda whom some worship, was a sign, we feel of things getting a little odd. She had had a way with her, not that she was cruel, or put herself above the rules; she was after all quiet on the whole, bowing even a little to her elders, to Father Raphael; we imagine that she didn't want to offend. But yet she had provoked—men in particular, but also women—who went murmuring and the like for the men hadn't slept at night because of her. It was odd because of the fortunes that came true, the magic that enshrouded her; and yet there was also anger.

We think that some creatures come out of the half light towards the end. They seem to be a world in themselves—to have in their minds a mystery others can't share. And when they die, although they are as dead as any dead, it seems death has some other meaning in their case as compared with the common one. There was great magic all around Magda like a yellow envelope despite the fact that nothing had happened except a baby. People were expectant—they thought that ah, now her spirit, like a little electric spark or a strange golden furry animal with long, thin limbs coiled around the weather vanes on the house tops where she used to work will make itself heard. Instead all was still! But we could feel the stillness too and then later, after certain events, look back and say—and so her spirit!

The dead in our village have ways of coming back. We see them in people. Not the usual way of ancestors reappearing in the character of somebody; the whole ancestral village has an input in a person. Simon, for example: He has a trace of the character of elder Stavros, his uncle, who left behind no children but saw beauty in everything even in sickness; he died in a rapture about the livingness of the sea. Amazingly gentle, he touched all living things even leaves and flower petals more delicately than you would a newborn child. But, in addition, Simon has the crafty smile of elder Peter, the father of the twins Peter and Paul, the same age as Agatha's mother, a second cousin; elder Peter was agile as a monkey, and used to climb up houses and walk on roofs, leaping from roof to roof with great hilarity when he had a drop too much; he was one of those lively old. And now Simon, with that same vitality and a look as if he has a thing or two up his sleeve that we ought to know about but never will and that way of handling a paint brush so that flowers come forth that seem to be suspended like a spider's thread in midair, or floating like bubbles on a pool of water and beautiful at the same time like bursts of light in the sky. Perhaps the magic is in the blood and by now we all share it, dwindled down as we are to seventy households.

It struck us, around the time that Max was born, to begin to prepare. Anna, who had the sweetness in her of Deborah—an aunt by secret marriage-- who used to bless marriages with such blessing that they would be seamlessly happy—but that was ages ago—we heard it from our grandmothers, Anna said that we had to shift a little back. We thought she meant to our ancestors' way of life and we agreed. But she meant something a little different—just back one single generation at the time of our new refrigerators and the beginning of electricity here.

Anna is not quite one of us—she comes and goes in our circle. Zoe and Cleo belong to us as does Foti although she is younger. Anna moves around a little mysteriously. She thinks she knows deep things—what we sometimes call the 'slight misalignment' of our island now. After Magda died, we began to notice that Anna aroused a strange kind of fear in us sometimes; but she went around with a firm and sweet face always. Some grandmothers are like that;—we are more anxious around them, although our lives are so tranquil and we have nothing in particular to worry about. It is instinct that they arouse in us—readiness. And then there were a few things she said. Anna said we are destined to perish and that this little island that preserved Christ for so many centuries will just die away. Anna made it seem as if a world was already dying—a world of blue and Jesus and a balance so feather fine that the weight of too much wind could tip the scales. Then she says things like—we will change, lose everything, with a look tender and sweet as honey. But we wonder how change? How lose everything? She says life is a dance, and that we should behave more like monkeys, at least take lessons from them and the birds and other wild things. She says this when we tell her of our fears. We could get annoyed but her sweetness is such that we overlook many of those strange, outlandish sayings. She smiles often but it isn't a smile of joy rather one of sadness—a rich, dark smile. She has the sharpest, darkest eyes we have ever seen. She has seen wealth that most of us can only dream of; but despite it all her rich house and her wild sayings, she is a villager, one of us.

She had wanted badly to tell Max of his mother; she had wanted from way back to tell him—so your fool of a father is still carrying on? If she had had the arm muscle, she would have forcibly entered the house and punched Leo. She used to see him sometimes swaggering about with a new pair of sunglasses or expensive trousers on and go up to him and tell him nose to nose what she thought of physical abuse of a child. And she would continue in a long harangue, driving him backwards, step by step. It did our hearts good to see it. We believed Anna would physically muscle the whole village community back into shape, sometimes, even though her faith was such a great question mark. But it didn't change anything. Leo would be carrying on the same as before. And young Max would be walking down the road in that half crouch of someone who is about to be attacked.

When the priest took Max in, Anna rejoiced. But we weren't too sure of the priest, either. Was he the one that could guide us? Could he, in the end, really bring back the holiness of our island? The most important project! We were afraid he was too full of ideas. Did he adopt Max, informally, of course, but still, and tote around Martha here and there—just in order to create followers, a mouth for his ideas, his big head? Max still for a year after he lived and healed in the priest's place went about squinting, cringing, holding up his hands in defense when someone came near him, but also murmuring of heaven—a creation only beautiful and such like. Anna shook her head but smiled. She wanted to tell Max the 'true' things that she knew. She knew though that he was wrapped up in these sayings of the priest. And she didn't want to harm him. She told us some people are best left to heaven. And with that it seemed that she had thrown a mantle of invisible light around him; he became clear and exquisite to us even in his deformity.

We asked her what she believed in because she always had us on her string. In death, she said; in death. But we do not quite understand. We know Anna has always been a prominent member of our charitable groups at Church. (We too have our charities, small and slight though they may be compared to the other island's Church charities!) On second thought, Anna is ever a tough old bird with a twinkle in her eye. We can rest assured that she is jesting, maybe mocking us. She was always one to rejoice at weddings, baptisms, masses. When Father Raphael once mentioned eternal life, she shouted 'Hear! Hear! Eternal living'! Drinking wine, paying the bills! Periodically, one of us breaks out like that.

But here is our deep uncertainty: Isn't this that we are talking about? Isn't this a sign of death after all? The coming of unbelief, the mocking of our traditions? We suspect, we imagine—death after all, and dread like never before the bones of our dead picked clean by the fishes.

We began after this statement by Anna, to think more about the lack of children born. We were afraid and in need of someone to confess us, to give us a neat moral sermon about God and his rewards. Then Anna said something unendurable. She said she didn't believe in God. Not in God God. We became angry—what did she have to say it for? And what did she mean by God God? There was this hullabaloo in our circle where she used to come and go freely—we were afraid of this talk of believing in death, which is as much as to say there was nothing in the end and that the Christ we had cherished so would die! —then she turns around as if nothing can possibly be the matter; as if she can turn and turn like a weather vane in a changing wind. But then she said there was nothing so unchristian in what she had said not even in the carefully preserved Christ dying-- not even in not believing in God, that is, not in God God. She said to our very faces-- here is where spiritual rigor mortis has set in. But her smile was suddenly so sweet—as if to say—everything, even that, is healable. Even that—to us as if we were the ones out of sync, as it were. In this she reminds us somehow of Magda with her own world, or of some of the crazy men, Dimitri, though he was just a boy and sometimes Simon, sometimes Stavros, or even young Nico. They step in and out of their crazy thoughts it seems.

So there was with us periods of intense worry—because she was one of us and whether or not she had intended, Anna, had planted a seed—and periods when we thought that all would somehow be well.

Half way up the mountain towards the monastery, on a promontory of its own, isolated by the stern, stony mountainside on the one side and by the fearsome precipice on the other, looking out to the blue gray sea sits the rich man's villa. The land had been bought and the house built by a Greek ship owner while the villagers who had dozed for years in the tranquility of their ways were, so to speak, too sleepy to notice. In fact, a lot of land had passed into his hands—the forests, the beach; deeds of sale had been easy to sign, and there was of course understanding with the old rich man. He and the Holy Islanders had lived without molesting one another, when the island had still been holy. Indeed, he had made a regular villager, bringing his bread to be baked in the tiny 'oven' in the square that served for the bakery, and now and then made raisin buns and meat buns, drinking at the tavern with the old and young fishermen, dancing at their feasts and dance festivals, it was said he was one of the best dancers, though he had never worn the crown. And the villagers had come to rely on him—to pick up needed supplies from the mainland by way of his high speed yacht, to argue their way into getting electrical cables laid from the other island where they had an electrical factory to this island, to introduce gas cooking stoves and gas in canisters and to be responsible for having them shipped in on supply boats, for coffee, aspirin, paper diapers, rice, flour, sugar and finally for water pipes being installed so that houses had running water. Thirty years ago, Anna, then only just gray at the temples, had taken the rich man's twenty year old daughter, Mini, by the hand and turning into her house had twisted the knob of a new faucet over the kitchen sink, smiling up at her as a thin stream of water poured out. She had been the first to have running water in her house. The village had been like a new born puppy underneath this man, sprawled out helplessly, still unsure how to walk. And he had reached down, picked it up from the scruff of its neck, set it on its feet. Most of the villagers couldn't dream of getting along without him. When he died, there was a month long mourning instituted. Mini had no patience with the village and preserving it. She wanted to make some money and only just barely kept from selling almost all the island to developers. However, the village was saved as it were by the intervention of an American who offered the price and bought the villa, and the land, promising to keep everything as it was, according to the islanders' wishes. The villagers didn't think it was an extraordinary gift of any kind—just the right thing to do as opposed to something that violated every code of respect and honor.

Stavros said that the rich man had paved the way for the Americans. The Americans at first only came during the dead of summer, toiling up the steep path to the promontory in the long days of August. The villa was deserted the rest of the year, empty and white, a place for ghosts. There was hardly any furniture, no curtains around the windows, dead flies and spiders accumulated in the corners. In August, suddenly there was activity on the promontory—moving, house cleaning, and the 'American', as they called the man, dressed always in black --in black shorts with a gray sweatshirt for the wind was seen with his grown daughter in black jeans and a tee shirt holding his hand, descending into the village for rice, tomatoes, olives and goat's cheese. These American people were excruciatingly polite, only using you plural to address people when they talked to them, but they hardly talked to anyone. In fact, though they could speak the dialect of the village rather well, with little stabs at the common accent, they preferred silence as they walked in the village, even amongst themselves. It seems to us that they communicated with short grunts to one another, pointing things out, sometimes to explain things, otherwise by that mystery of familiarity, knowing what each other had in mind. Sometimes three words in English seem to stand for something elaborate --a whole disputation, followed by another two words ending it. Many of the villagers imagined hearing them that English was a language with few words, and grunts to mean things and that far away in places like San Francisco, or New York crowds were stirred up to frenzies by leaders who grunted, and shouted only a few words; they had dreams of people in the streets bumping up against one another, grunting and shouting in monosyllables. Of course, we have whole discourses for our neighbors who collide with us.

The American man has narrow eyes and heavy eyebrow bones and looks like he is constantly frowning; he has grayish cheeks, thin lips and a small chin. He was at first shown our rare respect, and the villagers crowded around to meet him, to invite him to the tavern to drink wine. The wife stays in the villa all day—a remote female and it was rumored she spent her time gazing at the sea and writing in a notebook. The daughter accompanies her father everywhere including to wine drinking parties and dances in the village; she has a strange face, pale and drawn, the look of suffering but there is a glitter in her eyes at times that makes her attractive. A few of the men sitting in the rickety wooden chairs of the tavern, the smell of wine heavy on their breath, make a number of brief, almost sullen overtures. But she would turn down the offers of coffee with brandy in little dirty glasses or walks by the sea from anyone, unaccountably evading those little fragile webs of courtship. Up to the villa, they flitted, black clad father and daughter murmuring their two and three words in their nasal tongue, like flies buzzing, withdrawing to the upper stories.

Our men left were puzzled, one of them angry. The first time it happened, Peter brought his fist down on the flimsy wooden tavern table, shouting for more wine and adding—they drink, drink with us but then all silent and superior!

What would you have them do? Asked another, Nico—he is the youngest drinker of the lot at nineteen—spill out their private lives to you?

You know nothing about Americans, answered Peter; they pretend to become as us—speak the tongue, eat the food, drink the drink—but then, you know, at the slightest inconvenience to themselves—back again they go—to their rich lives, their automobiles, their machines of all descriptions next to their beds! Their machines that open cans, cut weeds—I've seen them in magazines! Why, they don't even have to get up! They are too good for life, it appears. Well, well, added Stavros who was sitting directly opposite, watching Peter, the growler, growing drunker; maybe she doesn't want to be your next wife, what of that? She chose silence when you insisted on saying things. Isn't that actually courteous, relatively speaking?

I looked at them, added Maria, the tavern manager and waitress; she with the dark circles under her eyes and uncannily white face, hair always pushed back under a gray scarf; (she has a bed in a little room she called the office and at night she sometimes offers her company for a fee. She is thin but broadly made and smells comforting.)

And so, growled the fist banger, though a little more moderately.

And so, said Maria, this young woman is sick; it is a burden for her to talk, to make love. Nothing was intended as an insult. They are here because of the sea, the island air. Perhaps medications aren't helping.

I didn't notice anything, said Peter sulkily.

You don't notice said Maria, suddenly affectionately stroking his head, because you only see. Men see things, they don't feel things and you have to feel things to know things.

And so?

Ah, I told you. You can't see the truth. You can only feel it. And so it takes men a long time to understand. What do you see? Odd assortments of color, strange movements, the outsides of things. It's like TV, said Nico, enthusiastically following Maria. It is the feeling part that tells you everything, directly—inside to inside. Seeing does nothing. It's a kind of hypnosis.

Ah, it is the same old thing with Americans; said growling Peter but he had begun to relax as Maria stroked his head. Why are they here? Why are they spread all around the world? Everywhere you hear of Americans. It is a silent invasion and their women—cold, indifferent, unable.

Perhaps she is an intellectual, said Nico, thoughtfully. Waiting for the signs in things you say.

Signs in things I say? Am I not a sign? Man that I am?

I know she is sick, said Maria, making a face. Poor thing!

Idiot, Peter said to her, angrily but Maria was used to his temper tantrums and knew that this one was playing itself out; listen, honey, she said, I am not an idiot but if you keep up your sour grapes over a woman who you don't even remember, I would say you are.

I remember her, replied Peter shrugging.

What does she look like? What color are her eyes?

Black.

No honey, they are grey. What has gotten into you besides wine? You want a woman? Stay a little after. The room's still there. The bed I made today—fresh. Love's like waves coming into shore. You know that—what you always told me. There is high tide and there's low tide—way of nature, you said. Tonight I say it's going to be high tide. Stay a little. Maria pulled off her scarf and shook her head to let her hair down.

The other men finished their wine and headed out.

You're nothing but a whore, said the growler, stroking her naked body in the back room, nothing but an old whore; but you have female dignity. You know how to love.

You hear the priest is going to make earth like heaven. I guess there will be no place for you and me, though adulterers weren't condemned in the end.

But since your feelings are as profound, Peter sneered, as all that and you know the truth…

Almost, said Maria. And I've made a tidy business with the wine shop and conducted myself discreetly in my night time profession. And I have had as a result peace and prosperity and an opportunity to deepen. As good as it gets on earth.

Ha—to deepen? He rolled her over. Will you deepen with me? Kiss me, the way you know.

Maria kissed him starting with his collar bone and going down his body planting kisses in the discreet places of love, ending with the top of his foot. Then she crawled into bed on top of him. She was known for this ritual of kissing;—some men liked it more than others but almost all succumbed to it and it ended abruptly with the soft brush of her lips just below the toes on the right foot.

You leave that American woman alone, she said, crawling into bed and embracing him with her warm thighs—that is what the deep I says.

You're jealous, laughed Peter feeling himself wonderfully inside her.

Not jealous. That woman is sick--needs something holy. You have got to let it happen.

After making love to Maria, Peter slept for about two hours, his mouth hanging open and snoring dreadfully. Then for some reason when a cold draught hit him full on the face through the little window facing the sea, about midnight, he woke up, cursed, kissed Maria, stuffed his gold cross in her hand by way of payment and then stumbled out with his shoes in his hand on the way home to his wife and three bland daughters. We know Peter didn't really wish to be unfaithful to his wife, but he had known Maria for years and she was the best antidote for his temper tantrums. His wife, a wisp of a woman, speaks in a high teeny voice that drives him up the wall. The whole island knows he married her because she agreed to marry him after he had received a load of rejections—women knew about those pissy, cranky tantrums. The marriage contract, the unwritten one said that infidelity and temper tantrums had to be tolerated by Lithia; the other one, written, was the list of possessions—hers and his now all signed over to her. There was never thought of divorce. Lithia was oblivious. Peter free, and, without her oversight and indulgence, penniless.

Peter went through a number of different stages. We remember how he had at first thought of himself capable of anything and his ambition soared and roared in him like a rocket but gradually it became clear that he could not build, or invent machines, or do business, each of which he imagined himself doing, so he fell back disgruntled on what our men do usually—that is, fishing; the last thing he imagined himself to be was a politician along with his brother—sort of rulers of the island. This time, he went about setting himself up in the role very carefully, year by year, continuing to fish but reading, studying and going around as if he was the real follower of the old traditions of the island. His twin brother Paul joined him and after a while they became known, jestingly, as the 'old religion'; of course they had 'ideas' about modernizing—condemning, in general, but as to bringing in the pilgrim trade, in a sensitive way, making a real flow from across the seas—bringing folks to see the very site where…to hear the holy stories, touch a few holy relics, the Byzantine Eucharist chalice cleaned again and again, the carving worn down, the ancient gold crown—what was it for? What did it mean?—discolored on the outside, used for the dancer who won the dancing competition, the moth eaten embroidered vestment of the first priest on Holy Island from the time when they fought miniature wars over the correct interpretation of the Holy Trinity;—they felt they could easily see that and either one of them, Paul or Peter, be mayor, establish Holy Island, as the real holy place, an island in the world's wasteland swirling around like a terrible sea. As far as the absence of children was concerned—his own girls, Peter was sure were fertile and would produce a people. It was enough to get them married off to the young men like Nico, or Jason. The island would probably be small but who knows? Perhaps an American would come and see and marry—an American, yes an American, who would be subdued by the wonder of Holy Island, and leave their unnatural existence where one is mostly machine-bound behind for the Spirit elusive in the world but who could be coaxed back to a properly run Holy island. But still deep down he had a second thought: that one only considered Americans when one was in despair. The island what was it—a heap of stones and sand that God had thrown over his shoulder when he made the world. And they— tiny, shriveled, half way to fools! How could they recapture holiness? Americans were always either salvation or despair—the beginning or the end. An American would see—. Either way you had to go their way. They came very cleverly just as you were thinking and asking what to do? What to do? It was just in this conflicted mind that he had looked at Catherine, the American woman and made certain sullen overtures and had been as he conceived it offensively rebuffed.

It turned out that Maria was right. The American woman was sick. She spent most of her time getting in and out of bed, we heard from the villa's cleaning woman, Kali, whom the American family had inherited from Mini. Kali, comes from the mainland, speaks English, and has seen a lot of the world; she moved first to the other island, where she married, and then managed through contacts to work for the rich man, when her husband died. She is arthritic now but still gets around faster than a cricket. She sings while she works and does her chores without pausing. God knows where she gets the energy all bent and cramped as she is. She says to us that her American girl is called Catherine and that she goes to bed to breathe. She says that the steep cut stairs up the mountainside break her down but she climbs them every day, leaning on her father, or sometimes by herself.

Kali has seen her swim. She practices swimming, swims down off the beach in the afternoon alone, a soft, ethereal breaststroke; Kali has walked down the cliff with her, carrying her towel. She rarely asks questions of the helper, just notices the villagers—stops, looks, continues like someone decided if the person be friend or enemy. Once she asked why so many of our old women are in black. Kali said they're practicing the old faith—when you lose husbands, sometimes sons, you dress like a nun. But not all do it. I did not, said Kali gesturing to her dark green dress. Do they dress so for their whole lives? Unless they marry again. There were also older looking women in jeans and sweaters hanging laundry on the line or seated under a window in little plastic chairs with plastic bowls cleaning green beans and snapping them in two, one by one. There were few men; they had gone out in the boats hours before. Kali said the villagers noticed a thin woman in black jeans walking a little stooped beside her.

In the evening, after the swim, and a change of clothes—Kali holds the towel around her-- she notices the men. At first, as Peter, a few propositioned her—lazy, stupid propositions, now and then whistles, laughs. But after a time, this stopped. Kali said they pulled their heads like turtles when she passed for they were afraid that she had sneered at them—surely being from America, she had seen better men.

Kali says that the American woman thinks that people are saying that she will die behind her back. Not the human destiny—when sick and old you need everlasting rest; no, a latter thing to living, an omnipresent, endless in-coming agony, obliterating all joy;—and a peculiar fate all her own; to Kali she said that she had always looked like death at the edges—like a death-person. Kali said to us—instead of socializing, she has been a loner because of this her death at the edges, which doesn't mix well with people at parties. Kali found out that she had had a love affair but she sometimes didn't remember his name—that he had been an ugly, dilapidated man, the kind sick women find, she said, and she had wandered off home after making love to him leaving him asleep and that that was the end of it.

Looking at her: The feeling of a face in a shadow, frowning, studying us, a look the color of twilight and the cloud of fine dark hair. Long body and flat chest. Of course, she looks entirely out of place on our little island; for a long time, some of the villagers hoped that the family would not stay for that reason. There is something unpalatable even disgusting when such a sick person, looking sick through and through wanders around in the open. But we are not without compassion and some of us want to feed her and make her coffee.

Agatha and Anna made her coffee first. Anna had a way with her—she would burst out with things and we couldn't deny her good humor. She said to us—bah, Agatha has as much right to be a human being as anybody, and by human being, she looked into our eyes—I mean gracious, erect and filled energy, sociable, having fun with a person! What did she expect that we thought —monkeys?—and proceeded to go around with her. So Anna was dilly dallying at Agatha's house, talking of anything that came into her head, when Agatha peeked out of her kitchen window—it was about eight in the morning—and there she was walking all by herself. It was a bit like a gift. A chance to be the first at her, besides Kali. They called her 'she'. She was at that time the 'she' of the island. She's come down off the cliff, whispered Agatha. She'll bring different weather, said Anna, pensively. What do you mean? Asked Agatha, puzzled. I mean between us—that kind of weather. No, said Agatha—she is so quiet and soft and she is strange, not ugly, but too thin. She'll never have much to do or say with us. Anna murmured, sometimes the air here strengthens people, and then! But what do you think? Agatha asked smiling at Anna. Do you think she'd accept? And she gestured, pointing from Catherine who was walking slowly, pausing now and then to breathe, to inside the kitchen. Oh well, why not? answered Anna. So Agatha scuttled out and whistled, caught Catherine's attention and waved for her to come in.

The first thing Agatha did, once the American girl was inside, was to grab her arm as if she was in danger of falling and sit her down in a chair. Then Agatha and Anna began talking both at once to her and to each other. The American woman understood perfectly everything they were saying all disjointedly and all at once; she was very polite and commented on the neatness of the kitchen and the beauty of the embroidered curtains, smoothly working her eulogies of the house into their remarks and questions so that it seemed to everybody after a little while that the beauty of Agatha's house rather than she was the whole point of the conversation. The strange woman's grasp of the proper polite form of the island dialect seemed almost native. Agatha went to work in a thrill to make the coffee, measuring in the grounds and spilling some she was so excited. Am I the cause of all this excitement? She said, as if she were a flea. The American woman was very carefully depreciating herself in the tradition of island etiquette. Oh, Agatha has always been that way, said Anna, showing the well-mannered American by her casual talk that one could be perfectly free around them!

Agatha asked the woman if she was cold and assured her that she had woolen sweaters if she needed one.

The strange woman insisted that she liked the cold, in order, following the island's sense of good manners, not to put her hostess to any extra trouble.

And you sick? Agatha said before she could stop herself.

The woman only smiled. Agatha said she was not even sad. She said briefly that has nothing to do with it. Heat is worse. And she slipped easily, to courteously parallel them, into an entirely inoffensive dialectical familiarity.

How awful, Agatha said with feeling. And now they were talking as old friends.

At one point, the Greek coffee almost boiled over. The American woman told Agatha very softly and mildly to mind the coffee. Agatha rushed to the stove but Anna was there first turning it off, lifting the coffee pot. You could have watched the stove, she said in an angry outburst at Anna. Ah, huff puff, said Anna, waving her aside. She is like that—a little rocket. Get the cups!—the china ones, she said to Agatha. She has been here so often she thinks she owns the place, said Agatha to Catherine. It is my house, my house.

Of course, they were all acting strangely, Agatha was a little uncouth, but it was a little thing to worry about.

The American woman kept saying that the house was beautiful—how beautiful, she said. She loved the furniture, the china, the curtains. Then the women's talk came tumbling out—in brief stories—the fears, even a hint at the loves.

Agatha said that the curtains were Jason's idea—her son, Jason who said that the house needed opaque window curtains because the sun is so strong from May until October—it whitens things; you see this rug, she showed her the rug—faded yellow!—it used to be bright. And here the table cloth, she picked up a corner of the tablecloth—it was cream, now almost white white, speaking, as the island tradition was, depreciatingly about her beautiful decor. The sun on this our own island (there were two words in island dialect for our—one connoting 'our own' more informal—to follow politeness, as they say on this island, with a sweet kiss of familiarity)—it fades fabrics just away like death. Agatha didn't know why she said like death and glanced uneasily at the American woman. And then I have to dye them again, she went on to appear as normal. She set out the blue china cups from her glass cupboard. You see these are special—painted with the pigment that used to be exported from this island. Very little is left. Simon made these for me—he's one of the old ones—proud of me, along with Dimitri or so he says in the postcards! Simon can do a bit of everything—paint, sculpt, craft, even build houses. When you live in a place that is dying out there might be one or two left that keep everyone else going. And when they go….? Anna looked at Agatha at this point as if she had just discovered something about her.

Then she said with her old heartiness, but she doesn't want to hear about these troubles. Staying for the summer? Anna used the informal grammar. Soon Catherine would feel at home.

Actually, my father has a plan to bring us here permanently. I am glad, really, the American woman said.

No, said Agatha, staring, glad to come here? It was one thing to make a visitor at home another to accept a full-time resident. She put down the cups and poured the coffee, a little shakily, offering sugar from the sugar bowl in the middle of the table.

Yes, you don't mind us, do you? Casual talk, informal grammar.

No, no, said Agatha.

Why should we mind you? Anna said, the informal you seemed here slightly impolite, and she was yawning. It is just that this place is so dull, no nightly entertainment except drinking.

This is a kind of threadbare place—the sea, a cliff, the wind, some birds, a little forest. One settles here like a bird because God left one to it. The conversation seemed to take an odd turn. But Catherine's informality was charming.

How true, how true, cried Agatha. Threadbare, socially, Agatha closed her eyes, thinking.

Ha! murmured Anna. She suddenly reared herself up tall and towering; so we are poor and squalid in your mind? But she was smiling.

Holy poor, said this woman, name of Catherine.

Well, there are some here who are, said Anna—Matrona and Martha, the nuns up in the monastery, even Agatha here what has she got to speak of? A cramped little house, goats' cheese and chicken; her husband died penniless. I've never been poor. I had three husbands. Not one was a fisherman. They were each of them in shipping. Built me the best house in town and took me around Europe. I went dancing in Athens and London. Wore furs. We were going to buy an apartment in Paris. It was one of those things talked over and talked over. My second to last husband even apologized for neglecting to buy it on his death bed. With my third husband, this plan was sipped and savored like wine. But in the end—nothing. My house is huge, really; I have no use for its enormity. It feels like death to me sometimes from the inside at night. No doubt you've seen it. The boring one—yellow, not white; the shutters are white. It stands at the end of the village at the beginning of the woods. Too big, really. I have a new TV and new refrigerator, life size refrigerator, not doll size as the others and all sorts of machines. Recently my son bought me a microwave from the other island. He thought it was too dull here—nothing but beach, he said, a few trees and the cliff. An island, he said like an arm bent at the elbow with the hand sticking up vertically over the water ready for arm wrestling but not finding an opponent. It is good if you want to be a nun and spend your life in that everlasting contemplation they call prayer. But for a businessman whose concern is making money....Money is my life, he told me. Quite unashamed. He left but he lives on the other island, the nearest one, two hours by motorboat. Now and then he comes in on his boat; I feed him lunch, Alaskan salmon and butter sauce, (flown in to the mainland and transported to the other island) we talk of the children. The salmon is frozen. He's grown quite fat at sixty five. I can't help laughing about it. Anyway, I've managed quite well without being holy or poor.

The two women ceased to talk much after that. They sipped their coffee and passed into a continued mysterious silence; it is the way with the villagers—that is, to sit, just sit silently. The American woman watched them, her head leaning back against the cool wall. What she saw: Agatha little, cushiony around the hips, her face all knobs; the other was tall and straight as a board, quite aged in the face—severe face, but somehow terribly sweet smile now and then entirely changing her expression. The American woman finally got up to go but it seemed awkward—it was as if she was supposed to sit there all day sipping in a slightly hostile, according to tradition, but also kind circle of island women.

Agatha stopped, got up and looked around then settled her look on Catherine and said in a whisper. I am here you see between the house with the green shutters and the one without the satellite dish on the roof. She bowed and bobbed her head again and again as Catherine passed through the door looking back at Agatha trailing after; Anna came out in the end waved her hand once and then turned in.

Nothing so remarkable—this island, the American woman said later to Kali. A little like a wall. An impenetrable place. But that is what I like about it. It isn't the jewel of the Aegean; it isn't a marvelous oasis in the wastelands somewhere where people are useless. It is the kind of place that by having nothing and being somewhat tedious to get to has come to be remote and almost otherworldly. And the people are the same—ignored, forgotten types. Eating, living—I'm not precisely sure what they live for—following traditions because they help the wheel, the mysterious wheel, go around day by day.

In fact the sameness and unremarkableness of the island makes it seem barren, desert-like. There are of course the little flowers and shrubs, our jasmines pouring over the walls of some of the gardens, and flowers in the forests in the tangled green undergrowth, our butterflies, hordes of them and birds, yellow and red, Zoe knows the names of them, sea birds and in the midst of ever present stones and sand. Every day, the American woman would wake up to sea bird cries and the white sun and the stones and sand. Every day, walking in to the little multi-colored town under a blazing sun with her father after lunch she would say, yet it isn't a desert but a garden —to Kali, who came often now. And her father would look at her and say that is why I've settled on this place; it is like living in the secret heart. After coming for two summers, the American man decided to move in permanently and he was trailed by his wife and daughter. Kali came with them. She said they barely furnished the house because the American man wanted to live simply and cultivate what he called 'old spirituality'.

They arrived one day not in August, their usual month, but in late September—coming in on the boat with several suitcases and some furniture in boxes. They hired our fishermen to give the house a fresh coat of white paint and to sweep and clean the rooms. Simon and Nico helped them install a new toilet and a washing machine. They caught a glimpse of the American wife, mother of the woman. She was not dark; she looked very white and soft, blonde like sleep, Simon said. Blonde like sleep? It didn't make sense to us. The house in the end, he said, looked like a lot of space in which a stove and refrigerator, a toilet and washing machine, a table and six chairs, all folding in wood, three folding divan beds and three tiny plastic desks with plastic and steel stools had all drifted to somewhere more or less in the center.

Kali said that the American man talked like a philosopher, though he called himself 'one who was spiritually informed;' he said that a family did not really consist of persons at all but was an 'invisible river.' Kali found out that he had a lot of money, hidden somewhere or far away in banks. But they lived like poor people. Because of the cold, uncarpeted, cement floors it really was desert-like in the rooms and there was such a lack of furniture and personal possessions, the house sometimes felt abandoned; Kali thought the forced Spartan existence terribly unfair—a crime even against Catherine and her mother that the man was perpetuating in the name of this spirituality. In addition to denuding the house of comforts, this American man insisted that his family eat only one full meal a day, and drink mostly water. However, he was mild-mannered and gentle and he seemed interested in our island saints. He was thinking and thinking now about the Orthodox religion, he told her. The wife, came in and out with a notebook and pen and sometimes she said, you see, Kali we live more on sand, stone, sunlight and wind rather than on soft beds and behind glass. The young woman had neither husband, nor lover, nor employment. Her illness was a heart ailment combined with ongoing sorrow; her room was the only one that wasn't white but blue. Their names were Robert, Ellen, and Catherine and it took Kali a while to pronounce them. They spoke more of the island dialect than the villagers were aware of on first impression. At home they spoke in a mixture of English and our native tongue. Kali had the impression that they didn't speak our tongue for her sake alone. She said they had a horror that they would disrupt the environment, being aware of their alien feel. They sensed that the villagers were all eyes and ears around them, watching, listening for something not right; they had been rebuffed; instantly walls had been erected, doors closed. But it wasn't entirely true either that our villagers were being shut out. Kali said perhaps Robert was sensitive and felt that he was odd and unsightly to our folks. Once you got over the indignation at his ways, once you relaxed and accepted him, he was nothing but a soft man who had the expression of being always at a loss.

Robert said he hoped over time and everybody leaving each other alone, there would come to be just 'living body in the presence of another,' human nearness, again and again that would in the end create a spiritual 'sensation'—he used words that he thought were funny or witty words. He said to his daughter that it was not always talking and talking that does it. Catherine poor thing had nobody to talk to anyway. One sensed that she didn't know much about men, either and that she was well above the age when one finds out. Kali saw that she felt that her father was awkward, slow, blundering, and blunt. That his philosophizing talk was so much smoke puffed out. Kali saw that Catherine, being so home bound and delicate, was good at sensing the subtlest threads of relationships between people; and that the illness, weakening her, had made her patient and discerning. Her mother was withdrawn and remote, and Kali says she thinks of herself as the family victim; she gets up at six, drinks coffee, and goes outside on to the cliffs to sit on a rock and write in her notebook. She is not beloved, says Kali, but the daughter and the father have something in common.

Kali heard that Robert had once burned one of Ellen's notebooks—that Ellen went around with dark circles under her eyes for months after, up at night at one weeping; ferocious with her husband. And Catherine said the loss of that 'treasure' had poisoned her. That notebook had been almost a child to her. And for a while Ellen had sat outside at dawn pen in hand, thinking of the killing of 'the fantastical creature,' as she called it, feeling like when you have a pain and simply can't get comfortable even in a soft bed. Then later, even when she was beginning with a new notebook, the memories! The marriage for this reason slid down to the end like a mud slide. Catherine said Ellen had never hated him before. Now you could see it in her eyes when she looked at him.

But Catherine would deliberate a moment and say, as if at a conference where talking could make things right—I understand you, Robert—she called her parents by their first names—but she is absolutely right. You live in your own world a little like God. And Kali smiled when she heard this. She thought all philosophers lived this way with someone handy to feed and clothe and love them.

Catherine came out of her room in that drifting way of hers and said to him one morning out of the blue—if you don't know, continued Catherine that you have to stay away from her, except to hint at every opportunity that she will write again—another—don't even say 'fantastical creature.'

But she has me, said he, this will help her....

Bother you, said Catherine. You should be invisible. Instead she tolerates your body. Think what a deep, tender, cool thing this forgiveness is in the heat of living together.

But, he went on. She has food, a family, a home—she is where she likes to be.

A fish that floats belly up in the water has the water, said Catherine. You are so limited that it borders on insanity. And on her side, I saw it in her eyes, only love, as she gave the notebook to you—never imagining, and that piteousness in her face when you burnt the beautiful thing in her….

I don't know why they don't have trials in courts of criminal law for people who commit crimes like you. Now your marriage is going to be a place of record keeping—who is accountable for what. And the list of grievances will mount so at your dying day or hers, there may be rancor, things carried to the grave. I call it your fault. Before you burned her notebook, that one precious treasure, all that she had, there were no records, nothing—all your sins were just brushed aside. They didn't even exist. It was a kind of housecleaning to love you for her, she just took a cloth and dusted away the evils. It was all tender and spirited, neat and clean. Now you are filthy and she is not cleaning. She lags; she is listless. She can't help but count all the things you've done wrong. She drags herself around the place. And you, you do all the wrong things—planting yourself in front of her all day long monstrously offering to open the windows and bring in the sun. Cooking delicacies that she used to love. If you gave her a pancake of sunlight, she wouldn't eat it. She doesn't fall for any love play with you now. She doesn't hear your cooing. She only sees you ugly. And this even though she doesn't want it this way.

There must have been a time she saw you different—rough hewn but tender. The blundering was soft like a child's. She was always wondering at the way you had imagination. Catherine mused. There are times we wish for a thousand paths bright as stars to take us to that place we were once with love. That conflagration, the notebook was the end of the years where you had two young lives and one old age. It didn't end until then. You and she, the two young lives, fled away and the last spark of that terrible end-- when something that lived between the pages of that book, or in another immaterial book vanished-- died before your eyes. Your single old age split apart. You after the notebook burned--a strange animal wandering frighteningly near. That notebook kept you husband and wife. Don't you see? Even though you did not write it and did not read it; its existence was the faith. Now you have destroyed the sacred grounds, for this is what it was.

She is being unreasonable, said Robert defensively. To tear apart a marriage…

Poor creature, you never knew you could be hated, at least, not by her, said Catherine. Let her wander around the house, eat whenever she wants to, sleep when she feels the need. Stay away from her. Don't go near. She was your friend. Now a wild beast, herself, with an unpredictable nature. Don't be surprised when you come near if she rears up and hisses that she hates you with wide open jaw like a fiery serpent. I think in my heart of hearts, she is merely being defensive. For her poor mind is back with those sacred grounds; she is keeping you out of the sacred ashes.

But I never knew, said Robert.

You are so plain, said Catherine. Of course, you didn't know. But your hand might have stayed. Does one burn a book one doesn't know? What if it is holy? Made of the most important question....

But to be hated over a book, said Robert, plaintively.

I wouldn't put it past her to come out of her grief and write another, said Catherine. But now, let her go—leave her alone in the house. And Robert obeyed.

Kali, astounded at this exchange, watched as Ellen wandered with dark circles under her eyes for days in her pajamas, forgetting to wash, eating lumps of bread torn out off of the loaf, drinking coffee in the middle of the night, with her new notebook in her hand, writing pages, tearing them up. In the evening, Robert sat hunched in the kitchen doing crossword puzzles from a book under the single light bulb hanging from the ceiling. In the morning, he went to the village. Catherine lay on her blue bed breathing. Kali came in to keep her company and at her request they talked frankly. She said saw her parents as facing two paths—either her mother would start another kind of notebook that would demand division from Robert, or her mother would somehow rebuild and the marriage would recover; perhaps a lack of touching at first, but the old newness would come in the end, but it depended entirely on her mother and the type of notebook. She didn't pity her father, but she loved him—one couldn't help loving him, he never meant any of his evil, and she felt easy about her mother making the choice. It would be in either case magical, the planting of a star. And in a land where stars took root and bloomed, her mother would walk.

Kali thought poor thing, poor thing—mother and father philosophers.

Kali said that the next day, Catherine said that night Ellen had come to Catherine's bed and lain down with her daughter.

All night they had talked and the notebook-writing mother had said: I love him, even now. And if we did separate, I would be always looking for him, in other places, other people. Him burning the notebook was almost as if to say—here I am-- all childlike-- I could not fight, how could I? I even said to him—oh go ahead, burn it. I did not realize how that notebook that I had crafted, bent, toiled to write had an after burn. I kept thinking lift above. Start anew. And the whole project baffles me. And being married only hurts. There are some mysterious things about marriage. But I have forgiven him.

He suddenly acted like a madman.

All the more reason to forgive, wouldn't you say? If I could only adjust, write again, have it be like it was. Restoration is a God-given thing. I knew a woman attacked by a monkey so viciously, so savagely, that they had to remove her eyes. She didn't know about the operation; she had passed out and when she awoke, her eyes were gone. She didn't know and was sure she would see again. It seemed to her that all the pain, the problem was concentrated on her lack of sight. If she could just see again, the world would be fine, what happened wouldn't be much. So little to ask. Of course, the doctors said that is exactly what will never happen. You see, they put it to her frankly, plainly—your eyes are absent. But her brain said—oh well, and now I'll see again. It took her ages to swallow down that she would not see though she knew she had no eyes.

And now? What are you going to do?

Use what strength I have to write a new notebook. Continue in the marriage blind.

And I, Ellen, will murmur in your ear, I believe, I believe, said Catherine. Even if it seems to you impossible.

I wonder about it: The thought of God looking on with all power to restore. Just to make it, as each person would say, a little better. Always that little. The woman with no eyes with magical vision would feel nothing but joy and even that mad savage monkey would be just a dancer that had over stepped, thrown himself out of the music. But lacking that little, that magical God bringing magical vision, (here is where I see God— tiny, light as dust, dancing on closed lids, emanating, enlivening the blank space of forehead, vision transforming the whole face, a seeing face as it were,) the woman has nothing.

Sometimes I don't know if there was malice intended, said Ellen. I realize that although I've been Robert's wife for forty years, there is a part of him that might as well be a monkey, it is so unknowable. And I feel as if I should track him, follow him, make notes of what he does and what he eats, of his habitat so as to have at least a few scientific details on this creature. Then suddenly he may perform again, turn around and look at me with fire in his hand and my new notebook, just coming back to me, the dark vein in it—gone. And this love, this savagery—part of the nature of him, plain, and unknowable. But you, poor sick child, living with almost nothing on this rock and a crazy father hoarding his millions in another country, a mother wandering in the house like a zombie wondering when it will all come back—you remain above all reliable, secure, loving. I know in the sane part of me you always will be. You have nothing of life, health, wealth. But you with all your nothings are devoted to love.

Leave me be, Ellen, said Catherine. I'll get up when the dawn floats in to make you coffee, so that you can grab it and go sit out on the cliff, on the rocks, and write, then--back to bed to think and breathe a bit, then up again in the afternoon, sometimes to slowly wander down with Robert to the village, an hour, no more, and then the fatiguing climb back, I trembling and holding on to him like an elderly woman, back to bed when I get home and then up and cooking dinner, sipping that half sour, half sweet red wine of the island. There are things you learn in weakness—how to reach out to the farthest shore—by tending, by dreaming, by talking. I think my far shores are people. I want to become familiar, thoroughly familiar, memorize the mysterious custom and when I go carry with me in mind whatever bright beauty I may have seen in my travels. You too Ellen are my far shore, perhaps the farthest.

I have been, I know, a little mad as a mother, said Ellen. I never treated you as a child when you were growing up. When you were little I just vanished to another part of the house and wrote. Robert took care of you. We weren't properly introduced until you were sixteen. I think I loved you. You weren't unbeautiful: Serious, and so ready to please. I wondered to Robert how from me and his misshapen body of a man, thin spindly legs, and arms and a sudden paunch could emerge a pretty girl with a brain. Then our confidences, and holding on to you, half needing the care you gave me, half wanting never to let you go, and watching your face as it changed, turned all faded and fatigued when your heart went bad. I know I stayed remote from you when you were sick; I wanted nothing to do with you sick. Robert cares for you. But I thought of you, think of you, wanted to talk to you; when you were well, I loved it—your coming to me, caring for me, getting me coffee, moving in the house. I know if I were judged I'd be a monster as a mother. But you, that is the love of you—you never judge or condemn, really.

This gift was given me, Ellen; I don't call it bad or second rate. I would do it with anyone, rich, poor, bad, good.

You are good, Catherine; most people are not.

I have a little old lamp inside me. I am a rich man's daughter and for some time I thought life would be elegant parties, and idling the afternoons, but....Mine is not the hard life, just what nobody wants.

They lay in bed looking at each other in the moonlight. Ellen has a soft, saggy face, and shadowy eyes that are still blue. Catherine said for all that you think of her when she comes close it is like discovering something in the forest, rare, tender, in its own world—a little animal or bird. But then she has her world of writing and solitude. Although she was in the house, physically, day after day, she was in essence somewhere else. She was in the every day, untouchable; one couldn't get near her. She didn't allow it. Now more than ever. So when she came to be stroked and caressed by her daughter, it was not only an intimate moment but also an intimate moment that would not come again. And yet it was a matter of continuing a conversation they had carried on and would carry on forever or one like it—infinite before and after life. Then the subtle breaks and fading. When those came this time between Catherine and Ellen, they just fell asleep. And sometime in the early hours of the morning, Ellen extricated herself from Catherine's arms without waking her and crept away. In the morning, Catherine was up making the coffee for her and Ellen arrived, untalkative as usual, untouchable, remote, fixed back into her strange solitary orbit, Catherine thought. Never to re emerge! A close body under the silent soft moon for another twenty years, she conjectured, writing her book of holy love, secret and obscure in the world.

We heard from Kali how they were an anguished, mysterious, disjointed family with Ellen wandering in her own world, writing not only language it seemed but magic for they were sure, both Robert and Catherine, that things happened when she wrote—oh, Catherine said to Kali, embroidered fire! Pools of honey. But they had never seen the sparks or tasted the honey. No one ever read those notebooks that she wrote. They all tiptoed around her. Catherine said that the house was too much house for her mother now. It had been a strange, white, naked phantom that breathed and thought, crouched in corners like a cat, hung in the air upside down asleep like a bat. And smelled rarely if ever of cooking, but always of sunlight and salt. Now the house spirit was fat, dusty, sweaty, crept along had no more high mind-edness and there was the maddening machinery of the hours, the hour of coffee, bath, dinner—something with oil and herbs, eaten hastily. And then sometimes time just sat still, bloated, motionless and one minute lasted an age. So Ellen suffered time and the house, day after day.

Catherine and Robert kept company often silent company together. They knew each other enough to know instincts and desires what they meant and how they were manifested in each other. Catherine only had to turn her head, and Robert would appear at her side a ghostly quiet neighbor asking in a low voice—do you want? And Catherine would complete the question—eggs, cheese for tonight? Shall we go down to the village then?

All the men there, some so silent and still like lizards in the sun; drink once with them and then they go, you know the routine. So quick to disappear and then the village and the air over the sea greenish in the evening. Everybody tucked into their unknowable homes. All deserted on the beach and the houses lit like dim yellow stars.

We can, then, Catherine would say. Kali said that meant going places between father and daughter.

Over time Kali made the discovery that not everything was exactly as she had first assumed—there were things underneath about Robert, for example. The family suddenly acknowledged that Robert believed in a spirit --not of the dead --but a spirit from 'another reality'; the fistful of fire he had shown to Ellen, her notebook—was the 'nearness of the spirit' conjured up; one didn't need books or notebooks—that was its message. Kali said the family made out that he was just a p-blunderer—that was Catherine's jest. It was the public version of it and even together or alone they held on to this. Deep down, they knew. Father and daughter went everywhere walking like cripples holding on to one another, talking in hoarse cries sometimes like half dumb people; that is what comes of inventing a god, Kali said, when our true God is just as plain as stones. But Kali said he was very quiet and very soft, that he was kind to her and gave her bonuses regularly. And that in what she called a 'philosophical way' he made sense; who could deny the things he said? Another reality. Spirit near; p-blundering. Kali said he saw everything as spirit—earth and universe and all of life. He once said that life was a process of burning; this was the nearness of Spirit.

According to Catherine, he was always committing unpardonable things.

There is a fourth, a brother to Catherine, Stephen, a Communist for conscience' sake, worked somewhere in a factory, and distributed leaflets. No one took him seriously—he spoke of the new consciousness, the ladder of increasing individual success opposing that of the collective, the love of God, replaced by a saner, more rational love of the superior State and state not to say the present State, or state as opposed to the self. He too like his father and mother shut up in his own world, thinking of the worker, the sufferings of the worker, the injustice around the world. It was a brain thing this Communism—a search for something, like Robert's search for another reality, an everything-immolating Spirit! But now there was a philosophy of I. The mighty I immolating the rest of reality.

The family had woken up in the morning without Stephen for the past twenty years. He didn't even know about the villa on the cliff of our little island, nor of the permanent move there. There had been no way to contact him and Catherine told Kali that if any one of them lived or died he wouldn't know, and vice versa. They were almost strangers now to one another but Catherine said that her parents, seeing him again, would be the same to him. If he came, the house would be open to him, a bed made and they would wait around like little tongue tied children for his plans, and his reasons for things. She knew that they would not argue with him, and if he judged them, they would simply, gently not understand it.

If he never found his way back, not knowing where his family was in the world-- it might be that he was slowly letting the memories fade to four or five, the one like a vision of sitting on Ellen's lap, the TV on, the lamplight in a yellow sphere enclosing them and her singing to them a made up song, the kind mothers sing alone with their babies—when you grow up to be a king, on your little finger a big pearl ring, with all around you little yellow canaries that sing, sing, sing will you remember me when you do your remembering?—they would carry on, a little tired for that deep down never spoken of memory of him, a little old for it. Kali said Catherine wept at times late at night, thinking she would die and never see him again. He, her only older brother, who had once called her his lady wife, and brought her wild strawberries, and leaves, and put spoonfuls of maple syrup into her mouth when she sat with her eyes closed and she all of four, she said; he had sat with her as she painstakingly mouthed out the words in her little books, and who told her once that God was fashioning little wings for her just for her and that one day she would fly. She said he could make a treasure of anything, and anything he gave her was a pearl—a whistle, a train ticket, a dog tag. He had one day incomprehensibly renounced God; —saying all that is meaningless. He had turned away, older, a tighter skin around his mouth, a grimmer look; Catherine said to Kali how is it that certain lovely things children have, like God, have to be put away when you get old? And we reasoned she must be old, as in dying-old, not living-old like us. Then, he had gone just when she began to have her serious illnesses, the ups and downs, fatigues, weaknesses, what she called the loss of self. Catherine fears most never seeing Stephen again, fears it like you might fear dropping down an abyss. With his face in front of hers no matter pain and old age, she would simply lift up from that abyss, all the way like a bubble in champagne, and she could die that way, her old self coming up in her like a bubble in champagne.

This was Catherine's light darkness, Kali called it. We knew of it—a light that is dark, a dark that is light; who can talk of the soul? Only going gloriously, gently free through reclaiming her brother whether he was good or bad.

She was a shy girl. But she was more and more curious about the insides of houses—how we go about living, cooking, tending to our affairs, the slow minutes of afternoon, the steam of the soup, the hot water for the bath—our familiarity. Her determination was to get into it—our circle—in this family or that—to be in the end sipping lemonade on a balcony peering down among the passersby.

She had heard of the priest on the island, and had asked Kali about him. She said that he was always thinking. Catherine had heard of Max, a little of the story, murmured here and there, how the priest helped him find his dead mother, how she was his secret and not so secret bride. Max was disdained of course, but we felt sorry for him too. Kali said the usual thing about Magda—she was beautiful and strong, had eyes like the sea in the evening. Picked for her husband the worst man of the lot, and when her death warrant was signed and the baby was in her, she had gone around singing from dawn until evening that this baby who would never know her face might remember her voice.

And of course he does, said Catherine that is why he is in love with her; dead mothers still speak to their children. (We began to like the girl a little. For this is our kind of cleverness.) Kali went on with the story—Magda had a wild sweet voice, sang her sweet wine song that is what we called it because it got into our veins, warmed us, made us peaceful. That singing down the little streets between the houses left in them a feeling. Catherine wondered what it would have been like to know her. We began to say Magda was the sign of the last of the true islanders. These are little tragedies, perhaps in the big world. Catherine said, yes, little tragedies but she, Magda, should be bowed down to. Of course not, said Kali, rather shocked. Kali asked Catherine about her faith;-- for we believe, she said, and proceeded to tell of the true God. The girl said the sun rising in the morning was the most she could handle of glory, for it burdens her. What she wanted to see at death was Stephen's face and the old, light, wonderful love.

One day, after conferring in Simon's house for three hours, the villagers decided to burn the files of Father Isaac. They moved silently in the evening up the hill in a little black mob with flashlights and matches and kerosene. They were all prepared for a real showdown. The priest was watching them from the window and guessed what they were after. He stood for a few seconds debating in his innermost self whether or not he should try to hide the files. There was a place behind the altar—a cupboard where they kept candles. No one would go into the altar. It was, he said to Max, such a little box; Max was standing beside him; Father Isaac said he was rather fond of his files. They let him see the evil in each one. Eve ill unto Eve ill; he laughed—that is what humanity is all about. What can we do in the end but join forces? Stretch out our hands to one another knowing they are full of contagion!

Have you read the files? He asked Max; Yes, said Max wondering. The priest knew about this. He hadn't minded at all, of course. Max retreated to the back of the little room and held a knife in his trembling hands.

Oh, they will not hurt you, laughed the priest, so gently that Max wept. Father Isaac held him to his bosom. My little Max! They want the files. See they have no weapons. Only matches. Listen, little brother, I will go down and myself deliver to them the files. What does it matter? Ha, we will dance little Max, dance! And he shrugged his shoulder. Then taking Max's hand and picking up the box, the priest led the way down to the door of the church.

What is it you want? The priest called out sternly. Are you not aware that it is late in the day and that I am in my room resting? Do you dare to disturb your priest in his holy contemplations? But there was a slight smile on his lips.

The little throng fell back a step. Then a man came forward, Father Isaac could see in the half light that it was Paul. We want the files, he said, because you have no right to keep written records on us. No priest has done so. It is not part of our holy tradition. Beyond our baptism and marriage certificates, our official, open and public records no written files are kept. What are they but thoughts and imagination? This is not suitable between priest and parishioner. We have come to destroy them. You wrote all about us—fantasies and fabrications—inventions. A good priest hears confessions and remembers things that are real. But writing up notes on our minds and our souls? That is for lazy, dishonest men. And we proclaim that what you wrote about us to be lies. Why? Because they are about us. Who are you to go and tell our stories? We have not authorized such an act. Besides, who knows what you dream up when you write? Is it reality or is it your own imagining, your own desire? We have heard you say you follow a science with theory and experimentation. Good, follow your science. But who is to say that you write what you discover? Who is to say that at that point of writing, you don't fall back into your own hidden secrets as evil as ours? And still the record will go out as us into the world. All about Peter; all about Paul. As truth—these notes, these scribbles! What if we desire to live and die without a record about it for the world to see? For what is told about us cannot be truth for it is written. For what is written cannot be truth for in the writing, in those fancy phrases, scientific or otherwise the truth is lost! There is always your input—exaggeration, imagination! For centuries since the first group of families came here to practice the faith of Christ Resurrected, we have lived in one way; who cares what the world does or does not do? For centuries we have been as we have been—another kind of human….We do not practice the craft of writing fooling the mind. We simply know the truth.

You mean, of course, said the priest, still stern, of people. Another kind of people.

We know what we mean, said Paul, a little peremptorily. The rest of the little crowd shifted feet; some of them looked back over their shoulders as if wanting in reality just to call it a day and go home.

After all that, a woman suddenly called out-- it was Agatha:—we could just burn these few papers. What does it matter in the end? Her voice had a hollow ring. To the priest she was like a person who had suddenly revealed a lost sense of meaning in life. What she said seemed to decide the others. They pressed towards him, reaching for the papers. You are after all a spy, said Barbara in a harsh voice—she was pushing against Stavros in the background; if you were honest you would come forth with it, repent and agree to burn.

It is, as you rightly point out, retorted the priest, not the papers with the writing on it. That is not the point. It is the putting of the heel of the devil, I say the devil, into all the little filaments that work together like embroidery—the heart of the human, yes of the human and the mind—these live filaments, little life-holding filaments, I call them, insignificant, perhaps, in the totality of things, you would crush. But with them crush Man, your pride and joy. And yet there is, you may be aware or not aware, in this universe on which you depend and which you would relegate to a tiny barely breathable place along with crushed Man, a general project being conducted. Something out there or in there, it doesn't really matter where, unnamable, elusive and transient like a wild bird, and impossible to fully comprehend yet close as life—something to love, really—is being studied like math. His space is narrowed down. And the vast arena where he does not walk is being re-examined. These files were part of that ongoing huge cosmic project.

A man laughed in the crowd. It was Stavros, his face was almost joyful. Hush, said Barbara, standing next to him; he is mad can't you see? She said.

It is only these live filaments—so beautifully expressed in such fine detail in our writings that…can capture…

Peter and Paul had raised their fists and had come towards him threateningly.

Good, said the priest, calmly; Max was standing behind him, and, although he was not touching him, Father Isaac could feel his hard heartbeat. Here then are the files; he took a sheaf of paper from under his arm. I suppose you must have your bonfire. What does it matter to you if you succumb to the devil's heel? And in the end, you know, you are all alright, having those moments when you sit and talk in low voices 'round your dinner tables late at night. Perhaps, at times, closer than I to that unnamable, wild, elusive thing.

The priest threw the sheaf of papers on the ground. And Peter bent down and lit a match, setting the pile on fire.

Why? Said Stavros; how foolish this is! It is like being dragged through a very shameful family ritual. We have reached a very low level of human, in fact, resurrection of Jesus or no resurrection. It seems we have on hand here people who are suspicious of the slightest bit of difference in a priest—who burn his writings!

Yet it is the papers with the writing on it, shouted a boy at the back. It was Michael, the bringer of news. You see the paper with writing by a holy man must be holy; the writings must smell of an odor of heaven; we have heard tell of saints who wrote, but always barely—on scraps of things, not as you say, a project—and only when they were very old—just as God told them. But these are things you sat and with your own mind conceived as if God had no part in the priestly life. As if it was all part of some science, all odorless.

There, said Peter, you hear him.

But the priest, watching the fire blaze up and die down, smiled, sadly. Yes, you are right, I was walking along the path lost in thought, thinking, dreaming, planning. I was, after all, a full man, and should have been a shadow of a child, a dreamer, a reciter of verses incapable of writing—in this vocation. What right have I to be a man in it—to think and to conceive cerebrally? To violate heart? And so, he said, dreaming, I thought to have a record—thoughts, impressions—now nothing. Something to refer to in my old age when I was becoming forgetful. But I went about it all wrong. Yet it was, after all, only my own thoughts.

The little throng watched the fire die into ash and then cast uncomfortable glances at the priest. They were all now uneasy; it was hard to gauge exactly whether or not he was angry. Paul and Peter seemed satisfied but Stavros looked angrily down at the ground and Barbara looked in the distance as people sometimes do when covering for embarrassment. The priest looked exceptionally worn in the little light remaining, and stooped as if his back ached like an old man. The crowd started to disappear little by little. Agatha said to him before she left, rather boldly, we have been like thieves. I didn't mean to….In the end, the only one remaining was Michael.

It was just the kind of thing they would think, he said at last, half bitterly, half apologetically. It has all to do with their thinking. I thought that you could keep the files in my heart of hearts. I didn't think you had to destroy them. I thought it didn't matter, you know; determining to do something—by oneself, even as a priest—even, that is, the priesthood. Making up one's own mind about things, shaping one's own way, having one's brilliant thoughts in the confines of one's head, recording them.

There are times things enter our hearts, said the priest putting a hand on his shoulder. It is possible early on to know if they are evil or good even if you don't listen to this inner knowledge. Then again, after the first flash of insight, it becomes more difficult—the knowledge sinks down like a puddle into the earth, deeper, absorbed into your daily mind, almost impossible to touch. Subtly different skeins of worldly thought enter in to distract you or make you question. Soon you are dancing in a web of argument and distraction far from the original knowing. Even about my files, I can only say that they seemed an original, energetic thing to do. I don't remember that first flash of insight.

Write them, said Michael. I will defend you.

I am old and I hurt.

But they are good. I know it. There are certain stoppers and buriers on this island. They are angry at the thought of something going ahead, something new, different. Yet how can it be anything but good?

Yes, I have often thought—how can it be anything but good? Yet we must look also at these creatures—staring at me in the twilight. They thought it was possibly evil—something as it were behind their backs, which it was, of course. One laughs, almost mocks—which I did, of course. And then there was, of course, the desire for a saner conclusion.

Yes, said Michael, nodding earnestly, a saner conclusion. We live in a strange way. Blocking ourselves off, you know. I have often thought what is there for me here? I have seen a great wall in front of me. And they seem to say in my imaginings—here it is better, there is that wall, you see. It doesn't make sense. But there is still something I love about that wall—lizards at the bottom and little weeds grow there. And on the top the brilliant sun and the blue sky. There are times I can't stand this imagining. It is so nothing so much a part of this island. I want to escape, go as far away as possible. Then it seems as if I actually swallow that wall and its whiteness down. I am a child of that wall, now. And even when I feel desperate about the nothingness here, I have a great enthusiasm at the same time—for that wall--the whiteness, the blueness. But all the old folks—they are planted round about and they spy.

Ha, said Father Isaac, spy and sing like crickets?

Yes.

So you spied and sang.

I spied on you, confessed Michael mournfully. And so you see when I delivered the information to the stoppers and buriers....

And now?

Not anymore. It was all so frustrating and confusing before.

Never mind. I have also been a spy—peering into people as best I could. I thought it was for some grand enterprise. I thought it was the grandest fun.

And so you will start again?

Perhaps. But there is business, of a religious sort, to attend to.

Michael incapable of not spilling out the juicy tidbits of information that traveled into his ears, brought news to the village folks gathered in Simon's house that Father Isaac had mocked them in the files. The villagers were doing a lemon curd comparison, tasting Agatha's and then Barbara's curd. Ah, these priests, said Stavros, smiling a little. I am not sure that I don't like him more and more.

I would say that he is a good, spicy man, said Anna, who towered over the others when she stood erect. The mockers and scorners and laughter-mongers are the best in bed. She smiled her stern-sweet smile.

Show me a woman, said Paul in disdain, and I'll show you someone who thinks only of sex.

The point is shall we finally get rid of him? Peter asked, hastily, deflecting Anna's retort.

I say it is too late for such thoughts, said Simon, grinning his mysterious grin in the corner. The moon is up here and the sky is black and the water black. It makes me think that I am only a partial person in our usual days—but something greater in those moon halls up there that just barely touch the earth at times. The night is the time of the light tread. I say, he said, dreamily, that we come clean of this—he waved his hand, vulgarity and anger, otherwise we'll never reach the moon.

Michael, lurking in the background, shouted out—we have reached the moon. Astronauts have—way back when. It's old hat. Now they have a space station. We are up there among the stars, physically. I suppose people like you wouldn't know.

I say, said Simon, with sternness, that we have not reached the moon. We are not clean, nor light hearted, nor magical. Perhaps we might have been under Magda's rule if she had lived and ruled.

It is useless to try to put forth an obvious, necessary plan, said Paul, standing beside Peter. People drift off into this kind of conversation now in our village. And thus we get nothing done.

What is so dirty about us? Asked the irrepressible Michael.

But Simon had lapsed into silence—one of those villager silences that was not to be broken for the rest of the evening. One woman stood up and talked in a honey voice and people listened and didn't listen.

In the end five men and three women voted Agatha's lemon curd best over Barbara's. Barbara thought she saw Agatha walking in front of her swaying her hips in triumph over her and determined that she would never again help her, not if she came begging on bended knee.

The villagers walked out into the night with torches and flashlights. The street lights were dimmed owing to the fact that the electrical company still somehow wasn't supplying the island with much electricity. Perhaps, thought Agatha, they don't believe quite in our existence. If there were a few aging families left, they could simply go to bed at night, they reckon. To sleep like the fairy tales they are in the backwater stories of the modern world.

Agatha in reality was way behind Barbara, had stayed in fact while the others trick-led out, to kiss Simon on the head, Simon who had been once called unkissable by Anna—who had never, as far as anyone knew, had a woman! He had twined his hand around her wrist as she kissed him and pulled her suddenly to him to stare into her eyes: a shocked stare, a coming up out of the darkness to the light stare...but then it vanished. And Agatha more tenderly kissed again, feeling like she had had a deeply intimate moment with someone who touched upon things holily—tantamount to the one secret bifurcated knowledge, love and death. But it seemed, she said later to Anna, who said, and you kissed Simon?—that a little furtive, elusive, poetical creature went off just at that moment. Off, I mean, to get lost in the night. Can't be found again, perhaps, except under certain conditions.

The conditions of the kiss, said Anna.

But it all means nothing. In any case, she said, I went home late just as if we had been lovers. But it isn't so much him, she said, but the way he is, you know.

They were sitting playing checkers and Anna was beating Agatha, game after game. People like Simon, said Anna, I always thought were marvelous—half over the edge, dangling themselves soul and all and pulling up out of their heart something astounding, beautiful, incredibly beautiful. But who am I to know? I always thought one of these days he'd end up crazy. No sex—what can the poor body do?

I am called crazy, said Agatha, and I get along with it.

What do you say of the priest? Asked Anna. The two ancients want to get rid of him. She jestingly called the old religion—twins Peter and Paul, 'the ancients,' mostly because they boasted that they stuck to the old ways of the island, and had, said Anna, a way of waggling their heads that reminded her, she said, of sages.

No, said Agatha, suddenly tender; it was all my fault. He has some real interest in us. Who else would take the time to actually write something down on each one of us? Why I would call that love, you see; that is, from him—modern, but love.

You know something about him.

He told me to go to the sisters—no one would doubt the sisters—and I did and came home, oh, I came home! Agatha, gasping, almost shouted—knowing that Dimitri would come back! Oh, it was a gradual thing like knowing being sure that a man you want loves you. I remember the old days when Alex courted me. He never announced anything, not love, not marriage. But I knew—it grew in me; and like the spring it was suddenly green after all that waiting—one day to the next it happened. And so I went down to his house—it was the worst shack on the island down near the edge of the forest and I said—so when are you and I going to church? Because I knew, you see, that it had happened. In those days it appeared rather dramatic—a little dramatic I should say. We were always a people for these slight discrepancies in the rule. It is the same now. I knew he was coming. And I have written to him. When shall I get your room ready? I was afraid to say things like that before. I didn't know what the answer would be. I didn't want to hear—you know. I didn't want to hear—I can't even say it—that he was gone. Out there.

You are such a hoot, said Anna. Of course, he is gone out there. There, that's your last checker. She jumped a black checker with a red one.

No, said Agatha, barely watching the game, he wasn't entirely gone. I'd have felt it in my heart if he was. Then there was something new with him, turning him away. It wasn't in the last letter. Just in his silence. I was in agony. Then the priest said to go on up—she pointed upward. Then I suddenly knew—not the usual way—prophecies of doom and all, of darkness, end, nothingness—I knew that he was coming. A good thing. I got a letter!

So you pulled a good thing out of the well, said Anna, merrily. Let's have a bite of that famed lemon curd.

Stavros said Michael had nothing else to do on this wretched island except watch people. In any case, about mid-morning the news came via this teenager that the priest had gone up the mountain. He had closed his door, locked it, and taking Max had gone up the steep staircase that led to the summit of the cliff. Further, Michael had seen him go up the staircase of the cliff on his knees. It was a shock to everyone.

It is just a stunt he's pulling to impress us, exploded Barbara.

Well, there was no one around, said Stavros. One imagines he did it because he believes in it. A priest who takes upon himself such a load of penitence—rather impressive, I would say.

Peter arrived at their door, an unusual visit, looking disheveled and goggle eyed as if he had been up all night staring at something in the darkness. What is he trying...? He spluttered as if it was clear from these few vague words exactly what he was trying to say.

Stavros offered him a chair in the middle of the room, dimly lit, despite the five lamps shining, and Barbara brought him a glass of wine. Peter stared into the wine and then drank half of the glass in big gulps. There is something going on that I don't like! He almost shouted the word 'don't'. In his voice, Stavros said later to Barbara, he could hear the assumption that everyone on the island was of one accord with him. He is attempting to sneak his way into the old faith, the old, deep life of our people.

But if we all stand firmly against him, said Barbara, plaintively. It doesn't matter what he takes it into his head to do.

You don't understand, said Peter; it's a matter of argument. This kind of thing you can't argue against. It's delicate. It's metaphysical.

But if he had simply walked up the mountain! Stavros said, fed up with Peter—barging in with this ridiculous upset all on account of some irrational animosity. Not that he didn't feel himself the same strange antipathetic sense towards the priest but at least didn't make such a show of it.

If he had simply walked up the mountain, said Peter, talking as if to a child, of course, he could be a tourist. It wouldn't matter.

You are angry, said Stavros ignoring the condescending tone of voice Peter had used, because he is proving or may prove to you that he is a holy man. And what with the opera late at night and the files, you had wanted to make a list of his unholy acts, proving that he was not fit to be our priest and get him transferred. What is more you are afraid. Afraid because of the sisters like you were of his files. They may be on his side and, as it were, knowing things about us. He might come down a patriarch or saint with a look in his eye that will get to knowledge of the inner most man. And you burned his files. You are afraid because deep down you heartily believe in what he is doing, believe it will prove God or something, writing always proves something!—and in fact wish to do it yourself only fear it because you went against it. And you know, Stavros now couldn't stop himself, if you do that kind of thing only to get it done, to say that you have done it—now there the soul in you can be satisfied before her judge—you will fail, absolutely.

On the other hand, reflected Peter, finishing his wine, I didn't actually see him go up on his knees. I only heard it. I don't have to believe it.

He staggered out of the house not so much drunk as beside himself and still, although somewhat calmer, with his insides all displaced by the whirl of anger and agitation, as Stavros put it to Barbara. In fact, it seemed to Barbara and Stavros that their little house was itself agitated by the visit. Things were lying on the floor—a lamp turned over, a vase unbroken but still lying on its side, newspapers scattered over the rug.

He seems a large man, a whirlwind of a man when he's angry, said Barbara, reflectively. She began to pick things up.

But it is all pointless. A lot of noise for nothing, said Stavros.

If Father Isaac ascended the cliff on his knees then we are all doomed as you know, said his wife.

Why on earth?

Well, for the file burning for one, she was picking up the last of the newspapers and stopped, looking at him, moodily.

It was a foolish thing to do anyway, said Stavros. Of course, we can't seem to keep tabs on this priest. First he is doing one thing, then another. Perhaps we should have let him go. But then he somehow seems right for this island and you can't disagree on his project for us—on earth as it is in heaven.

I wish he'd leave us alone on earth, said Barbara. Heaven is a different matter.

You'd forgive him, then, love him in heaven when you have God in you, said Stavros sarcastically.

Well, what does he expect us to do now? Crawl up the mountain after him?

Ah, ah, afraid for your little honeys of knees, said Stavros laughing. You know he turned on her and whispered with hot breath in her ear, you are supposed to put a little muscle into your holiness.

Soon the village was alive with the news that Father Isaac, old and worn out as he was, had actually climbed the steep cliff steps on his knees in prayer. A new piece of information came in, a witness of sorts: Simon said he thought he had seen him with Max going up the stairs knee by knee, crouching over and heaving himself up with his hands, Max helping. Nico went to the church and confirmed that it was closed until further notice. Martha emerged out of nowhere feebly announcing that the priest had said to her that he was retiring to prepare himself for a 'higher priesthood.'

Paul took her by the arm and pushed her down the road, yelling at her to stay away. Agatha watching, shook her head at this rude treatment of Martha, who shoeless and stinking needed kindness more than anyone else. She went out ignoring the uproar among the villagers over Martha who was wandering crying down the road towards the cliff and took her by the hand. She brought her indoors and prepared the bath with scented oils that she had bought off the supplies' boat.

They are mad, said Agatha to the hunched, crying girl because there are a few things that are going differently in this village. And they are perplexed because they expected the Americans, hated, but welcomed the Americans with their machines and their sex and so they had prepared for something different. No they would not become a tourists' paradise—there was a big fight over that, remember? Agatha talked to herself when she talked to Martha. And now they are faced with something they can't fathom. A holy man in the midst of the ghost of the Spirit? Perhaps. Yet different than they and they want to think that this after all was their identity. The great holy group that parted ways with the world. And yet they knew—no for ages they have not quite been holy—just old, defunct holy as it were. So here is a man so different, perhaps live holy—and they are, of course, enraged. They after all made mistakes about him, censored him. They judged him. And here he is trumping everyone: making a new island, a new island—of holy love—holy, based on penitence that is as Jesus—austere and sweet. Martha was clapping to this soft, enthusiastic little rhythm.

It is because I am big, a too big girl that I couldn't go, Martha said, ceasing to clap. Martha was having a foot bath now with lathery soap and scented oil. As she sat in the bathroom on the side of the bathtub she began to quiet down and then fall asleep listening to Agatha, who was massaging and washing her feet in the hot water.

What a joy you are, Martha, murmured Agatha; hidden in the bathroom, away from people, Agatha could roll out her tenderness like the tide of the sea coming in under the moon. Flood the poor girl with it. With you I don't have to talk about what doesn't matter. With them I feel as you—poor, oversized—a blot on the landscape. A blot on the landscape. Agatha went on talking despite the fact that Martha had fallen asleep. I went wandering too for years. The only difference was that I pretended—pretended that I lived in a nice house with a beautiful family. And yet I did that too, you see. There are my sons—do I love them? There is something about motherhood—you know you are bound at first with a cord. I think the sense of that cord never quite dissolves—since it is your own body. But love? I wonder now and then. Real mother love is something to die for—that was Max's mother. She was grim, fierce. Secretly, I never found her beautiful but alien. But all the men fell right into line. She made houses, lived in a perfect house where the housekeeping was the work of a whirl that quieted down into precise order. Fought, ate, made love like a lioness, or so Leo says. And when it came time to lay down and bear that child, she didn't hesitate—died after. My Dimitri is my pride and joy but could I have done it? Perhaps, if I had known Dimitri. She was impressive. I, like you, something to kick aside—though perhaps, I, unlike you, deserve it.

She dried Martha's feet and helped her to get up. The girl slept on Agatha's shoulder as she walked her to her bed and laid her down for a nap. She could only sleep a couple of hours for then Jason would appear. Last time Agatha had half howled at him—so disgusted was he with everything including poor girls out sweating and stinking with the goats. An animal, he had said and you take her in to this house! A girl trying to live, shouted Agatha—and then she had howled at him—cretin! And the howl had impressed her son and he had shut his mouth for a time. Agatha thought sometimes with his inability to 'reach above,' as she put it—children naturally reach up—for the sun, really; Dimitri had done but Jason—as if under a roof all the time. And that was how it had been since Dimitri had left—under a roof for the both of them in mind and heart. But no, even before that. She was romanticizing Dimitri because he had his own mind and had gone far away as much into the sky as into a different land.

She had seen him break through to the sun. A mysterious, terrible journey! He had always been so. There was that side of him that was so unknowable. The other side that had haunted her house for nineteen years was moody, selfish, so nervous that he bounded around the house at times uncontrollably. He was overly attached to her and for a while she thought him emotionally weak. She thought and he thought he would never survive by himself. And when he had raced off to the mainland with just a wallet full of cash—that skittish boy, she thought to herself —she imagined him in trouble, or sick, or dying. And he had confessed in his letters that he wrote day after day that his mind had been whirling; it was as if that first day in the far away he couldn't find his center of gravity. He hadn't known what to do but had had the presence of mind to buy a newspaper and respond to a wanted ad. It was for dish washer in a hotel and fortunately the manager had a tiny spare room in the back that he could rent by the week at a reduced rate. Dimitri lived on cigarettes, cheap wine and stale bread for a month besides the scrapings from customer's dishes that the waiters of the restaurant left, usually sauce, meat bones and something like a hot pepper garnish.

Agatha missed his beauty. And for days she had been afraid although that had worn off with all the letters coming in. Then there were times when she thought perhaps Dimitri for all that he had been gone fifteen years, knew her more than Jason-- how she wanted above all her loneliness and breathing space not house, kitchen, and food.

She thought how she wanted at times to extricate herself from the old attachments! There was love yes, for a while, with your father, but after he died this love became burden and you and your brother the stones in my sack. What can I say? Is this all taboo on the part of a mother? To confess that children were not what I wanted? And yet it is not dis-love to you and he…

These things she did not write to her son but she wondered if he saw through what she was writing to him to that old script in her heart. Then she began to hope and pray for Dimitri's return. She felt weak with Jason needing her other. When Dimitri ceased to write to her, she pushed all the taboo thoughts out of her head. With him gone missing it felt like a terrible storm had happened and that in the chaos a key, a most precious key, was lost—and that it was lying somewhere unknown in an immensity so huge that simply to think of looking for it boggled the mind. When she climbed up to the monastery, she had said to the nuns—my son is an angel and promptly wept, then became terrified that she had spat out a terrible still unknown truth; that Dimitri was indeed dead and it all had to do with the curse.

Now she knew that he was coming home. Her dark knowing self knew her miserable but blithe upper self barely aware. Usually, this dark knowing self brought negation. No, it couldn't be done. No, it wasn't going to happen. But this time that voice was still and she sensed that certainty like seeing in the dark. It was as if she could but sleep a few nights and he would be there but she must walk lightly, think less 'above' the knowledge—because if you tried to stare a reality in the face in this world, it will vanish.

When Jason came home that evening, the bed was made and the girl was gone. She had a dinner of roast chicken prepared and an infusion to help Jason sleep as he had been missing nights. She had informed him that his brother was coming home for a visit, which is what the nuns had prayed for and Jason and blushed and shouted out—oh for the sake of nuns! She hadn't understood him and had continued serving the food to him. She had wanted to begin the dinner conversation with something to the effect that it was not fair that she had to live under his thumb—that if she wanted to bring in poor hungry girls…but she bit her tongue. She had set out the candles, as always, as the lights were very dim so that it could have, would have been romantic if it had been Dimitri.

She asked him if the chicken was good. Jason had grunted. He was, she decided, an island man more even than Peter or Paul—a nothing person that could sometimes be violent. He was her son and the most of an islander of them all. The lights flickered and she looked at it, holding her breath. She hated it when the electricity went out. But nothing happened and she looked at Jason all tentative and barely breathing and saw that he was exactly like a stone. So this is what the priest had meant by crushing the little filaments…but he had not been there when they had thronged the church and burnt the priest's files. He had not come. Nor crushed, nor burned. To burn something of a priest! Jason had been right—it was shocking and criminal. Not that he had said anything—just stayed at home mending his nets. But Agatha could see that he had meant to say that it was shocking and criminal. He might not be the best but he was there, plain, even good. Dimitri worlds away, so complex. He had never seemed so, but might he not be the one, down under, bad? While Jason, right here under her nose, her pillar—steadfast, reliable. He could never have killed his brother. It must have been all horseplay. And Dimitri could be perhaps slightly dishonest.

Her thoughts had run on but she decided to see if Jason could be engaged in them.

People here don't treat priests as they ought to be treated, she began.

I don't know anything about how people treat priests, said Jason. They do their job and I do mine.

But Agatha desperately wanted to talk to someone about it. She felt guilty suddenly; it dawned on her that they had become a rough, almost wild island and that everyone was going around only seeming to be civilized. She thought over what she had said to the priest—they are just papers. What was she doing? Trying to condone violence to excuse a violent crowd? Would they degenerate with everyone at each other's throats? And had this degeneration penetrated even her? Was that the meaning of this not loving, not wanting of her own children?

They were incidents, here and there—Jason with a knife at his own brother's throat, though it was horseplay, the burning of the files, her own invocation of hell, which people say started it all; they were seemingly small disturbances and yet when you looked at them—they showed—the village, the island itself, the whole of it, was not quite right. It had subtly over the years changed character. It was in fact hugely off course and they were all feeling it good and bad. On earth as it was in heaven—what dreamy words. Visionary—like the early morning on the sea. But impossible! The world was sliding farther and farther from the vision of the priest, of Christ, while earth maintained itself cosmologically on its winged round of the sun. In vision this earthly world was far away and grotesque, and horrible like a face in one of those mirrors which distort the image. Alas it would present itself to God—all the same body, but the vision in his eye so deformed, gross, and absurd.

She suddenly turned to her son; she was about to open her mouth to talk about the urgent thing, the terrible thing, but all she said was—do you want that infusion?

Jason grunted and she went to get it.

It is sweet, she said, pouring it. Best be ready for bed. It does knock you out. Then she thought in despair—best to seem normal, Jason is right; if only one home is an ordinary home, everything according to the clock—time to rise and drink coffee, fish, or clean house, back for lunch—the smell of frying meat, vegetables, potatoes with sauce—at three, and then the dull hours when one thinks a little too much and so takes a little wine, and the men congregate at the tavern, sitting sipping coffee, brandy, talking of women, women whirling in their heads until seven—no other hours in between it seems! Then this above all this will make things return to normal. How can it not?

Jason looked up at his mother and saw that half despair in her eyes, half mesmerism and knew that she was thinking. It was her thinking look. So he pushed his plate and hers together for clean up. Then methodically, he pushed in all the chairs around the table and straightened up the room that was always full of bits and pieces of things it seemed like people's strange minds. After that, without saying a word to his mother, he went off to bed. And what he did there, Agatha thought—she supposed he lay in bed quiet as a stone by a still pool—rigid, frozen in his usual night habits. But what did it have to do with her? And she would let him alone, tacitly concurring that he didn't want to speak. Above all, he didn't want to speak. Not to her nor to anyone. She would wait and see if it was he—the true and steadfast son.

Oddly enough, Dimitri had to have been mute. Oddly, because now one would never dream it of him—so vocal and verbal—bursting at the seams with words, chit chat, expression, noise! He had so much talk in him now—it was part of his flavor! But she remembered him then. It was as if muteness followed him around then, entered into the house, hung around in the corners of the house. And she had asked him, shaken him, beaten him when he was little and all she could elicit was a soundless crying that was so heart wrenching she decided to live with it; besides the ones that waggled their heads like aged patriarchs, Peter and Paul, said it went with the territory of a cursed mother to have a no-good son. Of course, this had been before she actually 'cursed herself' but there were now and then dropped hints and Agatha realized that she was not just a woman who invoked a terrible curse on herself one fatal night; in fact, people had been dropping hints for ages, hints that nobody quite noticed, that is, noticed and not noticed—swallowed it down, she felt she was right, but not remarked on it-- until her terrible prayer, her strange, witch-like scream and then—how everyone had gone around saying—ah Agatha is cursed and with such a one, no wonder…and all the island, she felt, railed against her. She was lame, clawed-handed, when you looked at the picture carefully—not something you'd see right off the bat; but these things—. And Dimitri's silence now; was it that he was in some way mute again—cursed?

Of course; there had been friends through it all. Anna her old standby, for instance. The island loved Anna, forgave her, as money is forgiven, condemned her, or would have, as modern enthusiasm is, in places of ancient piety, or rather felt that she was indispensable; with all her wealth and extravagance—three husbands! Some people could have three husbands modestly, quietly, but with Anna it was all passionate fling in the old style of women with money, hard headedness, but underneath it all kindness—she was the true islander, the woman of their dreams. At least, the men joked about it but strangely no one ran after her, no man lost his head over her. She had married off-island men—one blonde with a look like steel who had spoken their tongue with a strong accent. And she had survived them all but somehow the island assumed she would. They had lived and died beside her and by living whole lives and dying in her bed so to speak they had contributed somehow to her seasoned island character. Three whole man lives melted into one bedded 'she' and vanished like the frost that came to the cliffs winter mornings when the temperature dipped to freezing. That 'she' remained unconverted and with her, their Annina, villagers thought, the island remained—a little nowhere place with its harsh stones and sweet flowers, a place, the villagers liked to think was the end and the beginning, for the good and evil, provided they understood—.

The other friend was, of course, Simon. He had a way of getting to the heart of things—no one doubted that. He could make new light with paint—an island that was itself new light. And it was Simon, dear, strange, perfect— who was part of, partner with, in some abstract fantastic way her secret self, partner to everyone who had a secret self.

Seven years ago, about ten months after her son had plunged into the wide world alone with only his wallet and his cap, Agatha had started to live a secret life. Folks assumed that she was now savoring the bitterness of her curse—her sons having quarreled, and one gone without money or connections to sink or swim as he was able; they murmured that Dimitri was a misfit, Jason a would be murderer. What worse could happen to a woman? What kind of woman would bring up two sons like that? And we expected that she should creep around as one condemned, a weight, as it were on her brain; and that all that would come of her struggling to get it right in the end was further and further drifting off. But Anna said mad, cursed Agatha was looking into her heart of hearts, into her spirit bent as it was with the weight of anathema; and she saw in it a muscular wild woman naked and hairy with a great lion's mane tied in many tiny purple ribbons kicking her toes in the air with her head thrown back and the sound of many bells and it was almost as if as she walked she could hear the tiny ribbons make a soft purple lovely chime. She went to Simon who could diagnose things people saw in their hearts and minds—she assuming that she had, in her cursed mind, seen the whore of Babylon or something and had to repent perhaps go up the cliff on her knees like Father Isaac,— but he told her—dancing! Simon was a little addled at the time just from what we perceived to be his own peculiar body chemistry.

Of course—the villagers dance. Everyone dances in this minute world. They kick, they twirl, they jump to the unending music. Even the octogenarians dance. It is as if they dance at night to keep the white summer sun from getting to them. And they dance to re-illuminate with the energy of their movements the light inside with their own particular lamp that stands against the sun. They sum up enough energy dancing sometimes that it glows white-- almost white like the sun. They have dancing festivals from dusk to dawn and the men in particular, at our time, thought it behooved them to be the best dancers in the village, vying with one another, doing death defying feats to show off to the women, all the women, particularly before their marriages—just to let them all know the kind of man they would be lying awake at night envying one of their woman friends the wiving of. The women all learned the mute little folksy time keeping dances; but on Holy Island it was always the men who practiced tirelessly from the time they were children to dance like fish in the sea swim—as if they had been born to do it and as if therefore they alone were free to spin and leap—to become at last dancers.

Agatha had always been on the fringes of the dancing parties in the village. She had learned our dances, the time-keeping women's steps, body long skirted, feet in the fast, rhythmic, monotonous step and hands lifted gracefully in the hands of partners, one on either side in the long line, the women all equivalent figures to be good, all moving together precisely, while one or another man danced his heart out solo in the spotlight. But Agatha had not been adept with our dances. And there had been a time when, inexplicably, at about seventeen, she had dropped out of dancing altogether. No one noticed much when her little light went out so to speak because there were hosts of other women and although dancing was one of the village rites, it was considered part of sheer exuberance and delight at the life of love, which they as Christians lived; there was no room for one's private bitterness and resentment of man and God; for one cursed, (one assumed as much from her lack of joy, although at the time we didn't quite know), it was no wonder that Agatha couldn't dance—that she couldn't burst out on the days of the great feasts like Christmas and Easter as the others did. She simply drifted, precipitated, out of the thick of the parties and sat still as a stone in the back of the room, trying to wrap herself in darkness like a blanket.

It was there that Alex, her husband found her because of all the men on the island, he alone danced like he had two left feet. And after trying and trying to leap and spin and remain upright and on one toe and never being able, he had finally decided that his best place was congenially applauding the others and acting the good sport, failing with grace and tact. It was there that their courtship began--with failure, and depression but good sportsmanship. But they had managed to make a spark in the end—Alex was singular, affectionate and there was something about Agatha that wouldn't give up neither on marriage, nor on faith; it was a quiet, marriage at first but with, with two depressives, inevitably, ups and downs, twists and turns. But in the end, Agatha had endured, seen a little light behind her prison bars, how could we blame her? And though Alex had died young, he had died, because of Agatha, with his own sense of place in the world. But at the dancing festivals the family of the soon to be cursed one mostly sat—unsmiling, rigid watchers. Jason didn't dance at all. He simply refused; he had never danced and never would, provided he got his way; he was the lone, young non-and-never dancer of the village. Dimitri was a private leaper, dancing on the beach by himself or out on the cliff when nobody was looking but he rarely joined the village dances and when he did, although eyes were on him, he didn't try to distinguish himself. Agatha watched the man dancers keenly at the dances. She said she wanted to be that free—that is, high leaping free and twirling, twirling, twirling free. Ah, we wondered—another mad flight of fancy? Sometimes the cursed see themselves high! She saw Maria the prostitute twirling sometimes suddenly-- her body free there among the wine-drinkers. She said that it was 'unfair' that the women were restricted to line dancing at the festivals, simply beating time with their feet;—that were she mayor, she would have both women and men dancing solo behind the tavern in the light of the candles. She would write a law expressly permitting it.

First dancing, we said to ourselves, now mayor! Ah, she lives in her delusions!

And Paul, our top dancer, said—it just goes to show—the women gone bad want dancing like they want ruling, insatiably. But, for that reason, he said, looking as if filled with hidden enlightenment, it's not part of their business.

Ten years after her husband's death, Simon the Wise had said 'dancing': and it had taken Agatha by surprise. It was as if a great wave of oxygen had filled her lungs. She was dizzy; day after day had been good enough but dark; now the clouds broke, the sun shone through and she suddenly saw in the sun ecstasy that was near her, available to her. This sensation passed in a minute but it left behind a new determination. Then there was the schedule at home, unalterable, an absolute, a kind of prison bar: She had to be up at four thirty to fix the coffee for Jason who swallowed it down in one gulp and went out, his shoulders rounded against the cold. At four, she had the house to herself. She picked up, washed the dishes, changed. At dawn she was dancing.

It seemed to have happened just like that. A decision, steps taken, the end result—whirling and leaping with the winds. In reality, it meant lifting her legs and twirling any way that came to her for days, and then in less than two weeks, sneaking up to Simon's at odd hours to relearn the old steps correctly. At first with Simon, dredging the dance steps out of her memory, stopping every once in a while, unable to go further, her foot placed, but the old rhythm lapsing, it seemed that she had been in error. She had suddenly gotten excited and the whole problem opened itself up again. She could not dance. What was this fuss about? Perhaps Simon had been wrong—the vision diagnosed incorrectly. The wild woman with her hair in purple ribbons—a dream just one of those aberrant fantasies that seem to be signs and that mean nothing! And then Simon had said, bless his holy soul, she thought later, why not? Dance freely like a man. But it was oozing out like liquid pain.

Before she had said to herself—so this is following music, keeping time. And then with Simon teaching her 'man dancing' as he called it, she said to herself so this is dancing, this is freedom, muscle, flying out from the line dancers to dance alone with the sun like the earth itself dances its cruel dance.

There were many wrecks. The little airplane set off and they were dancing high, as Simon said, she not so much following him teaching, as absorbing from him, the sweat, and the song and the rumble that the dance is—like coal miners or production line workers— down she would crash—something weak in her yet, something incapable athletically, of sustaining, landing on a cramped foot, breath that came sore, weeping at midnight. For she would crash too in morale—she would back away, shake her head, stop, give up a hundred times, with Simon at the other end of the dance floor, the living room in his ramshackle house, grinning at her, his head on one side.

You, he said to her, are not a woman only; you are a warrior. Man dance is for warriors only, them who fly despite broken wings, who fly on wings made of tears. Warriors get up after being wounded, vanquished; warriors may lose but make it more brave and glorious to lose than to win! All real defeat stops with the gracefulness of your own resistance, the noble-mindedness of your defense or offense.

For Agatha this stirred old memories. But she didn't want to think—only to lift her head and press on. The dance or battle work was slow. She had to bend and stretch her bent and crooked body into position, first. She had to balance on one toe, closing her eyes, spinning and keeping upright after. Simon taught her how to practice—how to find the energy to balance, how to feel balance rather than see the props. And after her two hours of practice, stretching and leaping, the soft vigor coursed through her limbs and body, whirling in her, raising her up from all sitting, keeping her erect as she moved about the house fixing, washing, preparing lunch, and lifting her heavy feet into little pointed kicks as she walked down the road to buy a few groceries.

All this Jason didn't know. In fact, no one in the village knew. If folks did notice Agatha wandering up to old Simon's house, they thought she was conferring with him on something—perhaps fixing something on her house or building her some furniture. Perhaps she was talking to him about the curse—he was a wise man, perhaps a mystic. Some said he dabbled in magic—white magic, of course, the holy kind. Perhaps he was breaking the curse.

And by lunch time at three in the afternoon, when the fisher boys came home, Agatha was back in her house and the steam from the boiling water and frying oil was carrying beautiful smells out of the window.

When Jason found out that Agatha was often at Simon's house, he simply stared at her for a long time, making her wonder what new twist of his strange, sullen mind was this? But after about forty five minutes, he closed his eyes and said simply—you go to Simon's all the time they say.

Agatha said nothing and Jason never referred to it again. Agatha trusted that whatever his secret thoughts of her, he would continue as before. He had fought with Dimitri, true, held a knife at his throat, and she and he had screamed at one another, but Agatha imagined that whatever he was deep down Jason was not bloody or vindictive. He was like the many island men of what time before?—one that stared sullenly and waited, remote and divorced from the human circle for its humanness and unholiness but not one that actually killed or crushed. But he had an exceptionally stony glance and she had often wondered if a woman would ever get past it.

So Agatha's secret life continued. She was not hugely uplifted as she once considered that she would be—given the beginning twirl, the first step to music. It became more of drudgery than inspiration and dancing had never gone over well with her. But there was just enough elation in the doing of it, the practice at dawn, with her inner eye still steadily on that final beauty, like an inner planet—the Word—that was dance to her, perhaps in reality meant 'yes,' for Agatha to remain dogged and determined about it but it was, remained elusive, a spirit. At the end of four years, she could leap mid-level, they said and drop down into a split. But the perfection of the twirl on the ball of the foot still evaded her.

She came to Simon now after about seven years and said—I think this is a lot of sweat for nothing. I can't do half of what I see the young men doing in the Easter dances. Simon looked at her and smiled. So you want to go back to lolling and lounging, not a drop of sweat in the mornings! Bah, you are not cut out for defeat, creeping away into a hole. The true warrior must press on working; all else is of the devil for the warrior. And as far as the young men go, why care about them? Who are they? Shadows, you'll see. Is all that leg splitting and leaping and standing on one hand dance? It is not a question of achieving something, the highest leap, the amazing physical feat he said to her, gently. It is the doing of dance every day that makes you a dancer. It is sweating and toiling until you finally dance without obstructing your heart. Already, it has become part of your body. You walk like a dancer not like a cripple anymore. Even that is the dance.

But, said Agatha, I never walked like a cripple.

Your back has always been hunched, didn't you know?— you dragged your legs— I thought: Here is someone who is carrying a heavy burden!

Now your shoulders are thrown back, your spine is vertical, your hips move, your chin lifts. Without changing your nose, eyes, bosom, you have gone from being a stumped, cramped, stupid thing to being—ah, there is never quite enough in the word 'beautiful.' You look to me like wedding.

Agatha felt like music with feet and hands had risen up and slapped her in the face by the time she left Simon's. She came home breathless and her mind singing in her so loudly that she didn't hear Jason come in. And she whirled around to meet him when she did hear him on her heel but perfectly, her skirt billowing out, then falling down as she stood in front of him straight as a mast on a sailboat.

He held out a letter. Apparently, you didn't see this, he said and gave it to her, then passed her and sat in his usual seat for lunch, his narrow eyes watching her. She put the letter down. Seven years after she started her secret life of dancing, she made a request of her son. I made a flavored rice with bits of chicken and tomatoes, she said. It's in the kitchen. Do you mind going to get it?

Jason got up slowly. It was of course a strange request in that Agatha had never asked her sons or, for that matter, her husband when he was alive to get anything or do anything in the kitchen. And she had not resented this labor of cooking, serving and cleaning; no, she had embraced it. It had always been relaxing, an occasion for thinking, for talking to --repartee of sorts that she did with one, when no one was around and she the only occupant of her kitchen. But she had begun to change within the private confidence—to reorganize, to unfold as a person. She wanted to change the house; to make it a place of movement instead of stillness, and to make the kitchen, a constant current—the getting up, the going in and out—two bodies were better than one for this.

In fact, Jason said nothing, didn't protest and appeared unmoved by her request. He went lethargically into that kitchen, picked up the platter and serving spoon and brought it to the table, sat down at his place already prepared for him, and began to spoon out the fragrant rice into his dish. In that moment when he was in the kitchen, Agatha glanced at the letter. The address on the envelope was not in her son's hand and a bone chill crept over her. A strange letter perhaps announcing to her that he was dead! Death seemed all over the island, constricting them, making them rigid. Dimitri could not die, she agonized. It was as if she was just stealing life and if death stepped in again to apprehend her the criminal—! Dimitri was slender, strong, movement-oriented with his closed-lipped smile and turn of the head. In the end, it would have to be Dimitri—for all that she had wanted Jason for his plainness, and reliability—his islander soul. Dimitri would understand—even her secret-- without knowing it. She opened herself like wings to fly to him—and thought—yes, he would have said something about going into the kitchen, looked at her, plucked her up in an embrace maybe.

To spend one's life and old age with Jason! Already he was eating as if nothing had happened. He sat like a stone while all around him poised empty air. It was as if he was waiting for something, she thought with a kind of concentration and firm-ness of purpose. For what? She had once murmured to him, innocently, curiously, seeing him sitting in the same way stolid, immovable, just before going to bed with the chamomile that she had served him for his insomnia; just like that she had asked him. She never wanted to talk much or to explain or elaborate to start up the dance of talk with this son. The Kingdom of God, he had said.

No, no, said Agatha to herself, tiptoeing around him. It couldn't have been said in irony or sarcasm—Jason didn't indulge in irony and sarcasm. But there was some-thing dogged in him—a resistance to the usual seductions in young men's lives, a sitting apart that made her slightly sorry. For Agatha prayer meant church, and the trepidation, the sense that hell from all that the priest had said, was richly deserved, a drama of emotions, of the innermost mind, as it strove to be above, clear, and but lucid given the living at hand. Agatha herself felt nervous towards God, on the outs with the Savior—after all, she had prayed and all through her life she had felt that sharp pull to crush herself in the name of humility and to live the rest of her life beseeching the Lord to spare her not for her merit but for his great tenderness of heart. This she thought was thoroughly Jason. But it seemed here was the key—that he sat more righteously than she in the presence of God and ate. It was he who deserved the meal.

She had let these thoughts alone after that minute, spent behind him examining the back of his head, which itself even looked righteous for that minute. No, no, she had said and had gone passed him without collecting his tea things. Shake it off, she had told herself in bed where it seemed to envelope her like a huge sticky web a fly. She had slept that night very fitfully and had dreamed bad dreams.

Jason's Kingdom was nothing like the talking to that she practiced herself without words in which she did not think of sin or evil or righteousness. What came from her came in those moments cooking or sewing and now often in her dancing. It was simple this kind of talking to, and bubbled up and stayed with her sometimes. Sometimes, despite her lost condition, it was very joyful and sweet—a friendship built of gently bubbling up to and popping against God. And it felt, now and then, like touching—only tender and sweet, delicate, it seemed and very fragile and God was not stiff, but soft and extremely delicate. The voice in her was hushed as a person who had undergone much and was sick with pain. But the loveliness bloomed, alive and thriving despite the infirmity. Since words were forcible things and therefore of-ten painful, Agatha talked to without them. This had gone on for ages with Agatha; perhaps she thought, since her tiniest childhood one couldn't know. But she was told in church how God was a hell-bearer and a sin-counter, straight as a ramrod on his golden throne and that salvation, that is, heaven-going was quite impossible. There were exceptions—sly tricks: condemning herself, crippling herself from thousands of prostrations, acknowledging the final righteousness of Paul and the others, who as a male had simply helped himself to a little temptation, that as a female she had wickedly incarnated, and we are all sinners, including she, dancing, winning—murmuring prayers of the fathers ceaselessly—then one creeps to Jesus, half fainting for having given up all joy and all natural sense of justice, sick to death with terror and violently condemned for the ulterior motive of oozing with still the taint of the female under the heavenly door.

But there were times when heaven colluded with her little faint thread of joy. She had found it in her dawn dancing and while Jason was eating the chicken flavored rice he had gotten for himself for the first time in his life. For the letter was from Dimitri announcing to her in a few words that he had succeeded in getting an important job after crawling sweating and hurting up the employment ladder at the hotel where he had begun as a dishwasher. He had had a secretary address the letter. A secretary after only seven years! Agatha thought—her second cousin Lisa had been a secretary to the priest before Father Isaac. In fact they had heard—they had all talked in whispers sitting around her dining table—that he had begun taking pills. Oh well, said Lisa, these priests—they are men, you know. Ah, I heard it from his wife, she said, he found out he was damned. How is it possible? Said Agatha, shaken. Reading Scripture. He said there were levels in Scripture, one couldn't read only for the surface level. That was sheer foolishness. One had to know the signs, the map of signs, he said and the face behind the map of signs—the path each sign represented and how it was going to reveal to us that 'face' after a journey of sorts that was there looking at each one of us. It is all in the way the face looks and it was always from the beginning: an expression.

Then the madness of Father Raphael, as they called it in low voices in her home. That was a sign. Agatha had been depressed over it for weeks until slowly Father Raphael had faded. When they had found him, dead of an overdose, he didn't look like himself. His face looked pinched and rat-like she thought.

But it was at this moment when Jason had said nothing to helping in the kitchen, the lightest, barest kind of help, but nothing, and Dimitri had announced that he was an important man and a thrill of joy passed through her and the thought that she should celebrate that this memory of Father Raphael made her suddenly afraid and sad. He had a long time ago said to her—you are in the right. They will make us say dark is light. And then the back of Jason's head rose in her imagination one more time.

So there was conflict in Agatha's mind again: Before Jason went to bed that night, the night of the serving himself from the kitchen, and the night of Dimitri's letter of such important news, she had asked herself if she was doing the right thing dancing, and 'talking to'. Were these not signs from God—not the events, public and abstract, but the intimate memories dropped into her mind on purpose to remember before it was too late?

For it had gone around the village like wildfire that Father Isaac had repented. Agatha had her share in the common wonderment. In order to sufficiently abase himself before God, the stern, almighty judge who held out to each soul the very last word—eternal pleasure or eternal pain, and the Christians made it worse: endless joy or endless agony—Father Isaac had himself crushed his kneecaps on which he said the prayers to the Holy Spirit, the giver of eternal life. We had not witnessed this: his climb on his knees up the stone steps of the cliffs was done too early in the morning; the goats, maybe Martha, Max definitely for he was with him, knew. And now the little white washed church was closed and the priest was up on the peak of the cliffs in a cell of the nuns up there in their rude little shack of a monastery, drinking broth and confessing his sins.

Strange stories reached us. There were folks who said he was in a cell naked with only a blanket and Max squatting on the floor, howling out the most terrible sins and crimes, bloody, obscene, dreadful things as if he kept hell in his belly all this time and now it had gotten to be too much for him and he was spitting it up. Then there were stories about his agony; his knees healing--there were shooting pains like needles of fire going up his legs. The sisters made him emollients and balms, changed his bed as he lay there unable to walk—he peed freely, apparently, on the sheets and smelled himself with gusto. As he lived on broth for two weeks, he lost so much weight that Max was able to carry him around like a little child. His beard grew whiter and even more tangled and he began to drool on it.

Max didn't leave his side but the poor boy reacted as if bombs were exploding all around when the priest shouted out his confessions. Yes, shouted out! He didn't seem to want to murmur these shocking, shameful deeds that he had done in a whisper but to let them ring out around the mountain top. The nuns go about whispering, of course, and apparently they thought little of this exhibition; nothing changed at the monastery during Father Isaac's visit. The nuns concocted their herbal medicines and gathered their fruit, milked their goats and made their cheese taking turns cleaning and attending to Father Isaac. Fortunately, at that time, there was someone besides the sisters to hear the confessions. A renowned ascetic was residing at the island monastery from Mt. Athos—a priest and an elder and he came and planted himself in Fr. Isaac's cell. And after the initial bout of shouting and screaming, and they said, sometimes cursing dreadfully, the ascetic and Father Isaac struck up quite a conversation that dragged on and on and included God, the devil, heaven and hell, the sun, and moon and earth, humanity, good and evil—everything you can imagine and this conversation wandered in and out of long prayers to the Holy Trinity. And it was rumored that the two believed that the Father, Son and Holy Spirit were attending. And then a story came down from the mountain that the two priests were becoming rather odd and funny and that they said they had seen in a vision the three God-persons and that they were tiny babies black, yellow, and white and clad in diapers and they had spent a lot of time cooing and babbling to them, holding them against their bosoms, and making joy over them as you would over beautiful infants.

So we didn't know how Father Isaac would come home—of another world, no doubt, like so many of these estranged ascetics. Peter paced around quite openly—all nervous and agitated about it. When these stories came, he was in visible agony over them. Were we going to have an idiot saying the liturgy? Paul, his twin brother, was cold, sharp and withdrawn. He murmured that there was obviously need for a mayor in the town for truly religious people…He is a church goer himself of course; believed in appearing in church, shaking hands, nodding to the women, bowing before the altar. The villagers think that of all people Paul is settled in life but Anna commented that he has a rather gray look that is not so much old age, he is forty-eight, but lifelessness. But he kept going, up earliest they say in the village in the morning, leading everyone at the dancing parties, dancing people under the table; we've seen him win the crown at the great Easter dance competition, even. Merciless dancing, Anna calls it. Like a little machine. Just find the battery, pull it out, and it stops. But People say of him that he keeps the island going in some mysterious way.

He is capable of vigorous gymnastics and you have to say that he executes each stunt cleanly and he upholds the old way to all the younger ones. We are astonished and have been for twenty years at his proficiency. We have given him the crown so many times we have lost count. It is strange for Anna to say he is lifeless with those vigorous leaps. Perhaps jealousy. None of her foreign husbands could dance. But there is something about him—distinctly--removed. Perhaps he has least aura as Zoe would put it although we have all lost that. For joy he substitutes triumph. Yes, we can feel that. But that joy has been gone these seventy years. And his certainty of triumph—that comes out in the dance—for he can whirl and flip. Anna said his dancing makes her feel uncomfortable down in her belly but who listens to those kinds of things? Yet we are forced to conclude even in the gaiety of our festivals that there is something terribly off about Paul. A certain lack of heart. Perhaps it wasn't always true. In any case, it is a secret as so many of the most important things in life are partly because they are so hard to put into cold words. And so he continues with the crown Easter after Easter and the respect of so many of the village, but the old dancing that some remember—that miracle of joy when the men became like angels as they used to say—it is gone. For once upon a time we had the dance like no other island and the radiant pilgrims men and women and children used to come to this out of the way place with wooden staffs and knapsacks filled with bread and salt for the Easter dances that were like miracles.…Some said it was a sign of the Holy Spirit! Today the tradition goes on but it is no longer alive. Everybody knows about our tradition, some other islands have it, but no pilgrims come now.

Behind doors, we hear Paul sits at a desk and shuffles papers a lot. He has earned admiration for some rumor that he is in business somehow with the mainland. Peter is just an excitable fisherman, choleric, hopping around, turning over furniture—nothing distinguished. He has a warmer heart. Peter was agitated about Father Isaac's penitence because down deep he felt that he too would have to. He was mad because he felt that he had 'taken away' the old traditional faith that Peter was sure was in his hands, engraved on his heart. Paul wasn't a heart person at all in this sense. In fact, tender things made him impatient. He was curious about Father Isaac from the start although there were times he dismissed him as half-crazed. He would sometimes call him that idiosyncratic monk but we didn't quite know why. When the news came that Father Isaac had toiled up to the monastery on his knees—Paul said: On his way to heaven! But he was not disturbed by it in the same way that Peter was. When he heard of the stories of what the ascetic and the priest were doing, he said, a little disdainfully: He lives in a world of visions now.

In fact, that is how Father Isaac came down off the cliff, riding piggyback on Max's shoulders being too weak and infirm to make it down on his own. He had gone up slender and strong, he was now so emaciated that he looked like a wisp and so enervated he could just barely totter around on his two pencil-legs. He had gone up gray with middle age—he was no more than sixty. But when he next reappeared he was white, pure white—both beard and the thin line of hair around his balding pate; it was as if he had stepped across many years into an old age close to death. But rather than sleep, forgetfulness, feeble-mindedness, he was sharp; his eyes were quick as a bird's. He seemed to have gained an inner life that was vivacious and joyful, full of clear sightings of beautiful unworldly things and a sudden zest for living. Back in his room with Max, it was reported that he exploded with joy singing and even dancing a little, that he ate heartily and drank half a bottle of wine. We have to admit to how bright Father Isaac seemed when we saw him; even his thinness wasn't cadaver-like, but a kind of refinement; his gaunt face appeared translucent now rather than wasted as it had before. And indisputably ugly as he was, there was light in his eyes now, and an ethereality about him that made him to us, when we saw him, the picture of a holy man. He went up to the monastery dark and young and came down light and old, said Simon, smiling his crafty smile. His penitence and his appearance after convinced some of us that Father Isaac was someone in whom we could entrust our holy affairs. Most of us forgave him the files and other minor infractions of our unwritten rules for priests. We forgave him also the watery eyes and unkempt beard. Now he appeared cleaner—perhaps it was just the whiteness of his beard and hair and the serenity in his now clear, lively eyes. After a week getting over the trip down the cliffs, he and Max opened the church again one Sunday and we all huddled in for the liturgy. He was oh, you should have seen—well, even, glorious! It was as if he knew that the Holy Spirit was standing right there beside and he had a wind-blown look as if he had been whirled into that spot from up above. Every little step, he made only little steps, was a dance step; it was as if the dance was set in place—perhaps the singing of the liturgy and our two little chanters—Simon was one, the lesser one, and a man Dino, younger or older, we couldn't tell, who lived as a gardener and helper to the sisters down at the base of the cliffs. And so, though the harsh off tune voice of the priest was the one from before, the one thing that allowed us to say that he was to us the same man, the man we had forgiven, everything else was different. It was as if he knew something and was certain of it. There was only one upset in all the holy ritual. At the elevation of the Body, the priest stumbled and fell heavily against the altar. The pieces of bread fell all over. But Max stepped in bravely, picked up the priest and quickly swept up the crumbs with his hands. Then as the priest lifted the cup of wine, Max wrapped his arms around him protectively.

Apparently he told Max that they were renaming things. The little room above the church was going to be 'Eden'; Max, 'the Beloved,' while he, Father Isaac, was to be 'the near-Traitor, Adam.' Everything was beginning from that room. One day issuing forth, Max would be treated to the vision of new creation. This was of course the treat in the end for following Christ. He said this to his faithful companion in the presence of a few of us, Anna, Stavros—they were there—the priest sometimes gasping a little for a sharp pain in his legs and hips, which had suffered during the terrible climb.

Anna went out of the liturgy when it was over saying bitterly that that penitence had almost killed Father Isaac. And all for the sake of waking up a foolish congregation who had not a shred of holiness left in it. But when Anna said things like that she was quite loud—Barbara swept by with her two heavy set sons undoubtedly thinking the whole time of lunch, as if she hadn't heard Anna, but with a cruel hostile look in her eyes that she always had when someone was a little out of line in the village.

We all expected Father Isaac, so aged and enfeebled, to go under eventually, even to die. But at least to need nursing; but without losing his overnight old age, Father Isaac rallied and grew strong again. He said joking that he had something of the goat in his blood—that he was wiry and tough, could eat practically anything, and easily outlived the domestic dog four, five, six times. He walked more and more now. Max and he preached homilies in the square that were amazing; it was only later that we realized that all the sermonizing had gone by us without registering in our brains. The words seemed very enlightening but now and then when we listened privately after to the memory resounding in us, we concluded that it was unintelligible talk that we only supposed was about the Kingdom of God. And the priest would use funny metaphors to describe heaven—like a pot full of water over boiling, he would say. And 'the intellects of the angels like stars on a cold clear night, seeing all-seeing'. Of course, this went against the grain a little, but we had forgiven Father Isaac; besides the liturgy was now so enlivened, so rhythmic, and white, strong and intelligent, so singing and dancing—what did we care what he had to say? Who were we to argue when he appeared blown in among us as if by the Holy Spirit, moving to his spirit steps? And some of us were so stupefied by this change to our priest and our little church liturgy that we just lost ourselves and stared, drifting around the church like half there people.

We were convinced, all except Stavros, who said alright, alright, he is dancing but he is useless. Maybe he is high on something like the other priest was. We debated this hotly with Stavros—Father Isaac is behaving so differently. Father Raphael just slowly, sadly drifted, mumbled during the liturgies at the end, not at all like.

And in any case, at our Christmas feast, Father Isaac distinguished himself by audibly sending all fasting to hell and eating the most meat of any man. Now Father Raphael who had really been injecting himself, had gone and clean lost his appetite before he died—except for bad wine—so it wasn't those poisons. Some of us thought, drugs—and so?—he was the more holy—bluish, and without appetite, not like this frank salivating for the feast, this craving more and more meat in his gullet of this Father Isaac. Holy! You could taste the flesh on him! We are talking after penitence!

We have an old tradition about God and the soul: Grace is like a balancing act originally set in place by God: a sinner is off balance, having been knocked off by sin; a saint is someone 'knocked back on' by the Holy Spirit. We began to wonder if it was possible that Father Isaac, a mumbling, rambling old fool, intoxicated by singing women had been so knocked back on by the Holy Spirit? But once the soul is knocked back on by God, it has to let go of all else and pray like kingdom come to avoid sin because to get knocked off again would certainly incur the wrath of God, which only the worst kind of penitence could appease. The holy ones knew this and feared it. People had spoken of tearing out of eyes, cutting off of hands. St. Seraphim, who had been thoughtless as a young disciple, knelt on a stone for three years begging for mercy. All joy left these renegade saints and they went around, so it was said, like deflated balloons, haggard, ash colored, repenting day and night.

We wondered therefore if there would be signs around Father Isaac confirming whether he was a saint, or blasphemer. And lo and behold after more dancing liturgies, as the spring set in like a sparkling crystal and winter vanished without a trace as it always does, the fruit trees bloomed like never before, the vegetables yielded a heavy crop, the goats gave more milk than we could ever remember them doing. There was a fragrance around the island of lemon and tomato vine, grapes and flowers of many kinds and warm milk. We smelled this deliciousness night and day. And because we knew that when the Spirit of God is near, the earth bursts into bloom and yields huge amounts of fruit—that even the desert blooms and ripens, we argued amongst ourselves even against our own private misgivings that Father Isaac had indeed brought the Spirit of God and we had to be careful about making fun of him. In any case, he was astonishingly gentle; mocked as he had been, his files taken from him and burned, because of our foolish violence, he acted now as if he were gaiety itself, lighthearted and ever kind. Villagers began trickling back to confession, approaching him at first shamefacedly, and then, when he would shoulder half the blame, saying, but you know—singing opera in my terrible voice in the middle of the night! I should at least have woken you to something sweet sounding. Ah, what to do about this. I should have a lovable voice! What a great and terrible evil in me!—we would gain a little confidence. We would see that what was called evil—our evil, cruelty, violence—was the same in the end as a harsh, dissonant voice to heaven and to others. A tragedy in which we are the most pathetic victims. Villagers said they in fact saw themselves as strange creatures in a dream going to Father Isaac—goblins of sorts with large, bulging white eyes, green, slippery, sagging skin, hands with fingernails grown long into claws; Father Isaac would just nod when they told him this and said that dream is a troubled spirit. And the spirit would be soothed and the dream fade when it was shaping and forming plump little babies out of the green white goblin thighs and bellies.

Agatha and Anna, Agatha because she wanted the curse relieved, and Anna because she loved people, became the prime allies of Father Isaac, cleaning his clothes, sewing up holes in his trousers—this just after he came down from the monastery. When he was up in the monastery, they had tended the church, cleaning it and readying it every day not knowing when the priest would be back. He had left Agatha the key; it was not an act of friendship; just about one week before leaving, when she had come to see him to listen to him with that pathetic dreamy smile on her face, or maybe it had been meeting him in the village and she looked at him with that childlike trust in her eyes that made her in some people's estimation the perfect friend to Martha—in any case, he had suddenly put an extra set of keys in her hands, closed her fingers around them and then left her and also Martha to her care because he found her able. She took Martha, tended her day and night. Agatha and Anna were true allies of Father Isaac; the rest of the village turned and turned like a body on an uncomfortable mattress; but now it was spring, there were signs that he was a saint and so they came back to him. Agatha and Anna acted as if this was the natural thing. For Agatha said to us—of course, the dancing is the first thing when God possesses…or the devil, said Anna, thinking of Paul; but Agatha made it sound as if God possessing Father Isaac were like a lover making love. We expected her to trail after him like a true devotee, and this in fact she did in the end.

Anna was more of a hard nut. She had we want to say a superior mind. But in the end, she simply said—oh, I don't see why not; it was her answer to almost everything it seemed. She had a way of flinging objections to the winds. In fact, she finally bowed to our objections to her atheism—but the reason for God was the same—I don't see why not! And now Father Isaac was a saint for the same ludicrous, preposterous reason—we came to her asking—Anna didn't see why not. When she heard of our goats giving abundant streams of milk and the lemon trees heavier with lemons than they'd ever been, she smiled a little smile and said-- all we need is the old man dancing away ancient Paul, dancing him to smithereens. On the one side a kind of heartlessness, on the other, a saintly lunacy! We went away all cross and frustrated as if we were carrying an unsolved riddle in our minds.

Some of us were shocked thinking she was referring to God, as the old man, others of us thought she was referring to the priest, but he was already dancing, unless she meant dancing with us at our competitions. It was only later that Agatha clarified for us what she had meant.

Five years went by like this with our huge quantities of lemons, our bucket after bucket of milk. The winters were mild, the summers long with cool breezes drying the sweat on our brows. Autumn was a time of change when the cicadas slowly stopped singing, and some of our birds left us. Spring was a time of newness in the air. We had the most glorious springs. There was something magic now in the rain and soil. One could almost see God passing his hand across it. The afternoons were slow. The old folk looked cleaner sipping their red wine. The younger men out in the fishing boats came in sore and tired. The women set out huge dishes of fried octopus and slices of lemon. We all breathed a sigh of relief. We were in our place again—the blue sky like eternity above, the sea infinite at our elbows, the stones and sand ever present, the shrubs little and illuminated with the white sun, our little colored houses cool and the smell of fish frying in the tiny streets between them. The priest now was not making us open our eyes wide. He stopped for dinner with us, spent hours talking to the fishermen. Walking into the square for groceries with Max ever at his side, he became a familiar sight. Who could have asked for more?

Only Agatha counted the days. For five years her son had said that he was coming home. He corresponded now regularly but his letters were brief and she thought rather stern. They lacked some of his former confiding tone. When Agatha went to the priest now, she was welcomed upstairs to his room. Max waited on them, bringing them infusions that the priest made for healing and relaxation. Agatha noticed that Max had gotten taller, that there was something lovely about him physically. It made her feel a little sweetness in her mouth when she looked at him. He had the figure of a runner like his mother had had and the same red brown hair, his face was all his mother's though the skin color was that white white like Leo's, but he had a tendency when she turned to him and came near to ask him something to crouch a little, to raise his hand up slightly as if in fear; it was a very graceful fearful movement. Often, he stopped in his walk on one foot, putting the other down weightlessly the moment after as if afraid someone would hear the footstep.

He is all body, she said to herself, but not touchable body. A different kind of body. Perhaps one ought to be fearful, and a little, light and weak.

But out around the market place addressing the people in a small semi-circle with the priest—the people gathered out of deference now, a little more meekly—now that in all likelihood, this Father was a saint-- he was in his element as the two voices rang out. One clear and precious like a little silver bell urging folks in simple language to believe in the Kingdom of God, saying it was like this or that-- a lover who called his beloved, a woman finding a coin she had missed, the other harsh and nasal sometimes using words they did not understand saying the Jesus prayer and other prayers of the saints. The people were entranced, uplifted and slightly disconcerted because slightly aware that there was underneath it all in that harsh, nasal voice the slightest hint of sweet infantine laughter. But it was evident that Max did not notice; in the market place addressing the crowd—that is, the four, sometimes five people— he came into his own—the beautiful chant-melody as the other held the tone. He reminded Agatha who had seen him there of a snake rising with his little, slow, entranced movements—the way his right hand went up like a cup and turned a little as if it were a perfect arm muscle that he was caressing in wonder when he talked about the Holy Spirit of God and how humanity could come to be filled with it.

Max's father, Leo, was the only one who didn't stop. Seeing his son, he would blush and hurry on; Max would continue his sermon of sorts, entirely oblivious of Leo glancing back as he walked away; and then Leo would smile an indulgent smile for imbeciles. Agatha once met up with him shortly after the sermon had ended, sitting in a little plastic chair in the tavern drinking a glass of wine. She had seen him watching: sweet, isn't he? She said to him. Ah, Leo said; of course. Reminds me of the devil. Agatha looked at him wondering if he was joking. Preaching, said Leo, is the devil's occupation. The old one is simply having a game of it. Sinner down deep. It's the innocent ones whose minds are turned, who are crystal clear; the devil mixes with them like sugar and water. Agatha had in mind that this was a trick—for everyone knew that Leo was the devil incarnate and his son was an angel.

But Agatha thought uneasily of Max, she had long thinking moments, for she had not been quite able to pin down what it was. A stare of fear passing not only in his eyes but over the whole body and then the slight figure emerging, delicately, almost daintily after. She wanted instinctively to like him. Was that a sign of something evil? The devil was sure to make you try to like him. Did one inherit devilry? He was, besides being Leo's son, Father Isaac's protégé and although she might have preferred a robust, shy fisherman such as her husband had been, she had always felt sorry for Max, all things considered with his fear, his clear-voiced faith, his daintiness the islanders' heartiness must have been somewhat repellent to him. Because he had a good, pure-sounding voice, the villagers called Max, Father Isaac's singer. Stavros started it; he put it to them that a saint needed above all a singer. For what was heaven without singing? And he seemed so innocent. Agatha was reminded when she looked at him of cracked glass. A little crack, the kind that made you see the glass. Was this what devils were really like? Father and son, the obvious and, perhaps, the so so subtle.

Leo had been relatively distant with the island women for the last four years or so. He had sent away for hired help even though he was living on a diminishing income from Magda's deceased parents' boat building wealth. Rid of his son he had only himself to feed and clothe and the rest went into the girls—who came and went on the caique in a space of three years—always young, always slender and pretty. Where did he find them? Narrow hips, scant waists, ignorant of our language, some of them must have been all of fifteen. Leo made no secret of the fact that he wanted them for his bed. A devourer, he was. But then, all abruptly, he sent away the blonde one with the narrow eyes rumored pregnant, and stopped having girl-maids altogether. He walked slowly round about the village sighing. His house became cluttered and dirty and he lay around like a pig all day with a bottle of wine.

Agatha, mourning, and celebrating in alternate fits—whether her son would stay away forever, or come home momentarily—that had been the prophecy of the sisters—but still no flesh and blood!—moved closer to Leo at the taverns; he seemed to be 'the real one' to her, perhaps because he too was an outcast, under the disapprobation of the village as she.

One of us said—well, exhausted! Sometimes we crept near to see if we could hear any familiar noises. We heard kitchen pots, smelled food. Man is cooking, we said. We said to the old women if father and son are devils, rather the father whose mind is in food and wine, than in the son who dreams of heaven. In any case, that is women's talk; we are all secretly a little envious of Leo—all that love making, women one after another, each time fresh—we might have dreamed like that when we were young. As for Max, so delicate—something like a child—except for his big hands and feet. Hiding with the priest, we think, because he isn't quite the man.

Max and Leo crept around one another in spirit. Leo seemed to almost never talk of Max; but when someone brought it up—he would smile a little and then roar out—offspring of the devil; he meant, of course Magda. She bewitched me when I begat him, smiling the whole time; Leo talked to us, despite our protestations. We didn't want to hear from him. Our women folk didn't want us listening. Now after a while, he brought out the wine and we finally accepted a cup each. He would smile and say the most outrageous things—women have a certain smell about them. Sometimes they leave that smell all over you. The best thing is bathing with a woman—the smell of the shampoo and the smell of her body. Of course, after a while it sickens you. I would lay on my bed damp, open the windows and long for it to go away, but with the woman in the next room…and coming back, watching her hips, her breasts, it would renew in me the longing for the smell; I would sense the back of my tongue, my lips would have almost no feeling in them. It is the magic of women. But now I am free. I don't indulge myself any longer. Besides, I was never a philanderer; Never seduced women for the wickedness of it. I am a sensualist. I open doors, the doors of the flesh. It is an art, you see, a high art; the goal is a great ideal.

We listened to Leo drinking our wine, laughing a little for shame, but also amusement and a little envy. Some of us remembered when he was a little fat potato-like child, nothing near clever. And then when he married at eighteen still bursting his buttons his devotion to Magda, the most beautiful—too beautiful for him, he confessed to us, his fat face blank of all emotion—used to lie beside her curled up like a fetus. Then silence and after a little while, he would choke with a sob. Those were my clean days, my holy days. And we had to nod—marriage is holy. But there was an exception here, and an exception there: Timos whose wife drank and snored, Nisos whose wife walked around by windows naked. No, but all in all—marriage was holiness and holiness was what we respected.

One of us, George, I think, went back a little drunk to his wife that day and out it came burbling that he had been drinking with Leo. The woman acted as if he had confessed to an affair. She threw things at him. And we heard through the windows his shocked shout—but he doesn't see women anymore. He's a bachelor, a friend.

Leo still ambled solitary through our village. He had done harm, you see; this was acknowledged. He was tainted—he even looked the sinner. Once you begin with that kind of life, it leaves a mark. His flesh was too white—sickness white. But he was one of these people who seemed never to get sick. Besides, he was physically weak and looked it for all his bulk. Next to someone like Paul, the most upright of all of us, clean, athletic and strong, he looked like something that grows out of rot—a fungus, next to a green oak. We drop back when Paul passes, king of dancers, righteous! And they say he has systems for everything, that is what the papers in his office are about; no doubt, we think the island will be holy again owing to his intervention when it takes place. It is all a matter of organization, a moral uplifting such as there never was—because, we hear him say at Simon's house when we all gather—it is in the end why we are here. We drop behind Paul as he walks down the main street. We have heard it is a matter of purging people. A few, he has dropped a hint or two. No doubt Leo. That is an obvious case. But he is busy, Paul is, conceiving who would be best sent away; it is all a matter of discernment—who drags the island down? Who is, Timos says in jest—not a saint in Our Saints? A matter of betrayal-- and Paul is in earnest. A subtle discernment between a violent man who is all instinct and passion and an uncleanliness in someone who purposefully goes against.

Yes Paul, king of dancers, as we've said. There is a long history on our island of dancing to be king of dancers, a position blessed and exalted by our one saint, St. John, little St. John, they called him, who, over a thousand years' ago, wept in this little village, here and there. Yes, wept tears of sorrow and sweetness because he had the name of the Beloved who slept on the bosom of our Lord. You wouldn't think that tears and dancing would go together, but St Little John as he was called would rise up out of one weeping fit or the other and set to work, as he called it, dancing with such energy, jumping, leaping, beating time with his feet so fast that it became an ecstasy. He was the dancing saint of Orthodoxy. And the men strive to follow him, dancing for God. Every time he wept, he danced—bone danced, he called it, for even his bones were rejoicing. He told the little huddled group on Holy Island—if you stop dancing, you'll stop praying. And then he said the enigmatic words: Dance for good or for evil. It is the will of your Lord. He instituted on the day of the Resurrection what used to be called the 'Bone Dancing' competitions for our men and had that crown of gold made to crown the king of dancers. (That is one story. The other is that that gold crown was found on the island when the little band of the elect came and was rumored to be a sign that there would arise a great martyr out of the bones of the villagers—that was the song—and they danced to make it happen. Queer, but Father Raphael explained to us that martyrs and great saints are always born from dead bones, the bones of the prophets and great holy ones—born from the Spirit hiding in their dead bones making them suddenly crackle with sparks of life. Martyrs were a sign themselves of those who, living the eternal life had endured all things even decomposition to bones and dust, and then risen up in a flame of flesh to praise the Lord. Martyrs and great saints were a sign of bones to be re-enfleshed like lightning on the Last Day. Bone Dancing later became 'Holy Dancing,' with the purpose of electric connection, and then, as the island drifted from its original sanctity, just 'Easter dancing' for the villagers tried still, though ambivalent, to follow old rites and rituals.)

In any case, a thousand years' ago this holy dancing was instituted by little St. John and the island has, obedient to the saint, danced ever since. And the dancing crown has gone without prejudice to the one who danced best, good man or bad man. It was St. Little John's command: He crowned the first dance king with these words: this crown to be yielded up without envy or prejudice to the one of the village who dances best. Those were his words, yielded up to—as if he knew we would hold that exquisite piece of carved gold in our possession not wanting to let go. And each time still that we let go and hold the competition, it is a dread and breathless and holy moment for we are afraid, a deep down fear, akin to knowing, that eventually a sign will come this way. What sign? The sign of the Lord. Life or death. Fire or ash. We fear the wearing of that crown even for a night. Yet faithful, joyous that night we crown the King of Bone Dancers. Then the village shifts, the village listens. We believe that certain unnamable powers come with the crowning. The soul rises; it is touched. There is no more possibility of it being altogether different from what we supposed. Paul has won now six times in succession; ever since Ancient Peter retired from dancing, Paul has won. And he is the kind that no one can get to the bottom of. Of course, he is only one of us. Like us he wants the island to regain its holiness. But some of us recoil at having our mirror image in him, bone dancer though he is. We can't quite name it. Peter once said—ah, my brother is cruel but nothing, nothing. Nothing, until….? We wonder. But in the crowning at the Dance, we know him—teeth grinning at us.

But if Leo reforms? Repentance of sorts, not like the priest, that was done on a grand scale; now one or two of us have gone up to Paul, hearing that he wants to revitalize our holiness, and said to him, but you don't expect…and gestured towards the cliffs. Paul said nothing precise about that—just let it loom over our heads. Smashing your kneecaps and praying for each smash. When it comes up, Paul just looks with that far away look out of a window, usually, or towards the other end of the room, or down the road, wherever he happens to be. Once he said answering this kind of question about penitence—the sheep are led back to the fold but there are wolves in sheep's clothing.

We look askance at Leo. Is he in earnest? There Leo is walking alone down the middle of the street; he walks with his head lifted as if listening to something entirely pleasant to hear. And he walks particularly slowly—the amble of someone who will not exert a muscle, lazy, dreaming, savoring the sun. Once he walked in front of Paul and didn't notice that he was holding him up—for Paul walks swiftly and brusquely. It was a little outrage such as we have now and then these days—Paul attempting behind him to get past, and Leo swaying to that side and blocking him, and then Paul moving to the other side and Leo swaying back to that side and blocking him again. Timos and George saw it. Paul got angrier and angrier until he finally gave Leo a violent push and sent him stumbling out of the path. We fell back then and waited. Leo looked astounded and then he squinted his eyes and looked after Paul as if trying to make out what kind of person was this—very strange! In fact, that is what we heard him murmur—as if the world was full of all manner of surprises. He was perhaps too weak to get angry. But Leo is the obstruction; for Paul has won the Bone Dance so often!

The word went around about this 'accident' as things tend to go around in our village, and Anna was the one that smiled. She made no bones about the purging idea getting her goat. Many others were for it, quietly for it—those, that is, who were sure they wouldn't be purged. If a couple of people, or even a family was sent away so that we could be that old group once more—preserving the faith! Anna said indeed it showed we had come a long way since the days of faith. And she wanted to get to the bottom of it and to know, to have it announced loud and clear—who Paul was intending to send away supposing that he could get the village of Our Saints to do it? But except for the idea 'purge' it was all hush hush. Paul had not yet finished conceiving who.

Little Paul was twenty and stuck like a burr to his father. Not only were they seen together more often than not, little Paul also talked with the same voice as his father; they were indistinguishable on the telephone. He had the same face—an alchemist's face, Anna called it—inscrutable, secretive, and cold hearted. Anna would sometimes come up with words or ideas. She had been away in the world, you see, had known wealthy and educated men and women. Anna's idea was that there was something underneath Paul's conceiving of a purge that wasn't about a filthy faith. Trust a woman who has seen the world to come up with hidden meanings to things in order to call us simple minded.

And she, but it was really Agatha, had invited the American woman in. Trust Agatha to do a thing like that. Now that was simple minded. The Americans have of course our welcome. It is said that they are kind and gracious. They do nothing but occupy space here, eat a little, walk among us; they even speak our tongue, now and then we have seen the tall, thin form of the daughter standing in back in church listening. We have no objection. But inside our houses and so soon and so suddenly—in mid-morning! Agatha would not have done it if Jason had been there. There is no question that the Americans are closer to tourists than to us. They come to see, perhaps to take pictures. Not the sort to invite in for coffee in the kitchen for a chat.

Of course, we don't say it was bad of Agatha—just the sort of thing she would do. Barbara would have looked out her window, seen the American girl, and gone on about her morning chores, and Elizabeth's mother, Nitsa, the same. In the end, tourists expose people. They make a place like Hollywood where everyone is carrying on and there is no more faith or truth, such as put our ancestors in heaven. We have limited our tourists. There are no hotels for them. They come for the day, and since they see nothing because we are little, the island like a little child and they are looking for big—as if right over the child's head—so they see nothing, they go away never to come back. Once there was a big noise over a woman from Argentina who fell overboard from a boat; Dimitri saved her. She looked in our faces and cried and smiled. She hugged Dimitri again and again. He smiled and snooped around with her as if he somehow belonged to her and we thought that he would break with Katrina. But she went away after sleeping five days at Agatha's house. It was necessary we suppose for the shock to wear off. But Agatha is a little like that. Her home by her own consent has been a little intruded on. None of our wives would allow it. Something breaks, our folks say, when a tourist comes in to your home. Of course, we welcome them on to our shores, into our tavern where Maria serves red wine. Peter vied with Dimitri for the attentions of the lady from Argentina; kicked his legs a bit, danced on the tavern table in front of her. He has always been dancing, bursting himself kicking and leaping although he is nothing like Paul; isn't capable of making dance and music one slow-fast extraordinary thing. Of course, he didn't stand a chance; Dimitri looks like dancing when he's merely sitting. But he's never come anywhere near beating Paul at our festivals. Paul, when he dances, dances like a king; he owns the dance; athletically, he reigns. Dimitri dances like a poor boy who can't believe anything will ever come of him. His expressive body is dance always, but he never puts any effort into it come the festivals. We, the old men of the island, watch, and jump up sometimes, because we are still able, thank the Lord and our legs—and toss our hearts into the air for the music's sake, and forget ourselves and whirl around a bit. And so we men danced a bit at the tavern those five nights that went by like one evening. The lady laughed a lot and showed us flawless white teeth and then it seemed like in the time it takes for the sea wind to blow out an Easter candle after our vigil until dawn, she was gone.

Anyway, Agatha took her in for those five days. We want to say she is a loose person and sloppy, never caring who sleeps in her house. But Agatha cleans; and she is righteous about who walks through her doors. That lady because she near drowned. And in the end: she sailed through looking like a dream of the big world and we felt she had blessed us. After she left, the island seemed quiet and dull and Timos went and knocked his forehead against a wall in his house until he got a big bump there. Dimitri with the elasticity of the young was seen with his hand curled around Katrina's waist, talking and talking. It didn't matter to him that the world had just paid a call in the body of a knock dead gorgeous woman that we had all exerted and sweated around her; Dimitri had just smiled and poured the wine and talked very politely. Apparently, nothing so tremendous had happened inside Agatha's house and she had stayed in the guest room with the red embroidered bed spread that used to be Alex's studio—he was something of a writer—and Dimitri had mostly gone to his room and slept. They had had family lunches with Dimitri again pouring the wine. Agatha smiling and laughing at the slightly disoriented lady's jokes.

A year or so later when we had all but forgotten the lady, Dimitri suddenly left the island. A few of us then thought he was going to Argentina to find her; we thought that a woman so beautiful would be easy to spot in the middle of even a large country—that she would shine like a light at midnight midst the crowd at lunchtime. But Dimitri went to London to work in a hotel. And so-- he was becoming a rich man, we all calculated. Agatha moped a little, though she was glad because she received a monthly check from him—enough to cover expenses. We dwindled back to our little routines. We have nothing against our little island. When we aren't fishing, we sit and play cards and talk women, and wives. It would be impossible for us to think of any other life. We are bone of the bone of the generations of men who fished, engendered sons and daughters, built slightly crazy cement and wood houses and died here.

Nisos' teeth have mostly rotted; his little belly hangs over thin legs; his back is curved. His mind thinks of nothing but the sea and the sea changes. And when he mends nets you can see his girlish hands getting agile. He's got poetry in him, but he says that he can't put into words. You wouldn't think we'd think much of him, but it's different with us. When he kicked up his heels for the lady, it was really gallant. But in the world they love scientifically—when your teeth aren't in order and your backbone isn't straight—then they judge that dance isn't in you. Dimitri—yes, he is good enough for a young man. But he lacks something. He is almost a tourist here; he's always belonged, we think, to the big world. Now and then the big world comes like resurrection but it doesn't stay like resurrection.

Here on the island we have both salt and fresh water. The salt water is the sea all around us. We are a tiny island just room enough for the village of eighty houses, the monastery on the cliffs, and the forest and the sea is mighty—a huge desert of salt water waves; we don't care that there is in reality somewhere a limit to it. That's the scientific mind of the big world. But no matter what it says, the sea is still infinite— one can see that just standing on the shore down under the cliffs by our two rocks where the waves crash and send up froth during winter storms. There it is spreading out and that spreading out has no end. Our other water is fresh water—a subterranean lake that you can see if you go down into the caves in the forest, on the other side of the mountain. This water is sweet, clean, and utterly delicious. We like to put it that way—not to tourists, not even to that lady from Argentina who looks like a movie—that all around us, up and down and infinitely around—we are salt; even our music and dance is salt; but at heart we are sweet and fresh— the lake like the first mornings of fine weather, brimming sunlight, after winter. When 'the lake' surfaces in the midst of our salty dancing, we have really danced.

Agatha who brings in the tourists can't quite fit in. There are reasons. We sense that in her all is sweat and tears. Not that we mind Agatha. We only wish we could just unfold her, set her right, flush her out, find the heart in her. She was never able to dance. When she was very young and learning, she was all feet. Big feet. Then she began to cry and didn't stop. She would cry on the sly in church even during the years Alex was going out of his way to be kind to her. If she were one of us, she would realize that you have to stop crying. One could cry, cry always cry. Nisos used to cry about his teeth. One by one they fell out of his mouth; now he has only four left. How am I going to eat my chicken when they are all gone? He asks. But now he doesn't cry. Shrugs instead. And dances. And at our festivals, he eats and eats with his four teeth. When he danced for that lady, we've forgotten her name, we thought we almost saw in him that pure, cool sweet water. He danced for something more than the girl; you could almost say he danced for manhood, a forgotten dream.

When Nisos dances, we are reminded too of the way birds dance in the air. That is, just a glimpse because Nisos doesn't really fly; he capers around on the dance floor and we see him all in a rage to kick his legs high and the old, stiff muscles pulling him back. But the intention is written all over him. He has a way of letting his heart come through his body. Humpbacked and thin shanked, one still sees something in his movements, and dreams of him smoothed out leaping in the air. That is because he is a real island man from God knows how many generations. We were made dancing here once upon a time. In some of us, there are these little signs of our original making.

Imagine! Just now—Agatha has found something inside herself belonging to this origin of dance. We noticed it today; we saw her, expecting that old creeping along on the road—a woman stiff, and useless like a broken machine—no doubt thinking bitter thoughts—instead she glided along like a little duck in water; stiffness smoothed out now when she walks, hips perfectly in motion. What, Agatha? We asked ourselves in wonder. After thirty years, we didn't believe she had it in her. We rubbed our eyes. We saw her only for a minute. We old men have dreams—was it our dreaming eyes or was it really she, hunched-in-corners Agatha, walking with a limp ever since she was eighteen? Walking as if one leg didn't quite belong to her.

What to call it if not a miracle? Agatha coming through a door in the blue sky. And her face a different kind of thing. The blue summer sky is planted on her forehead and the sun is something she possesses in a skin like wine and bread, said Thomas, our poet. Women never cease to amaze us. You think they are dead or good as dead and then they pop back, rising high as eagles.

We tend to think no—there are no more miracles. Oh, perhaps a healing, now and then but they say that the great scientists on the mainland would do tests in big laboratories with thousands of machines that tell us all about flesh and blood and come up with a precise reason in this world of shadows for the healing. They say many a miracle they have put to death. We say that miracles rightly belong to the ancient times, but there is no question that both the priest and Agatha have changed. Agatha is a woman. With a woman there is always a turning point, but we expected a grumbling old hag. Yet it is not so unusual for a woman to change shape, magically. There is talk that Magda, a few decades ago, would shape shift from woman to black cat. With Agatha, it is Agatha, of course, nothing different physically; she hasn't grown wings or a tail—and yet it is as if an old skin has fallen away with all that feeble crying. Were we the only ones to think her wrinkled? No, it can't be that she was ever wrinkled. She is after all too young. Smooth as a melon now.

And the priest has changed enormously. Not more enormously than Agatha—and yet what a difference—from one body almost to another. The impression it gives, these two 'miracles', as we call them, having no other way to describe it—is of finding a home—real home in among these little wretched houses of ours. Maybe Agatha, or the dream we had of her passing by, and the priest whom we see white and thin and light as a feather with a smile out of which sunlight flows are two homes that are in reality the same home. Everyone knows that feeling of home. We married wives thinking it was in them and sometimes at the wedding celebrations we could feel in ourselves a certain imaginative straining. There is in any case a feeling—this is how a woman should be—with Agatha—and with the priest, this is how an old man should be. Woman? Old man? No, they are dreams, oddballs, ancient children. In fact, we saw the priest walking by just now with his ever present deacon holding up one side, and his hand on a cane on the other. It is as if he is broken in every place. They say his hair went white for the agony of his penitence.

A few weeks ago our little church was boarded up. Father Isaac was up in the monastery, lying in the little cell with one rough blanket unable to get up for his bowel movements. For five Sundays, we had to make do with our household crosses and icons. Peter and Paul called a meeting one Sunday at Paul's house in which they led prayers. Peter got hold of some incense and marched around with it and Paul stood ramrod straight like a priest and read the blessings even of the holy Eucharist. Afterwards, when we looked at him, talking amongst ourselves about what he was doing—the holy of holies! Without the due process of ordination and consecration—although he didn't actually administer the sacrament, he said in a loud voice that where there was no head to Christ's body on earth…and we knew he was saying something utterly deconsecrating of Father Isaac. That he was, in short, an absent Christ's head as if he had singlehandedly decapitated our priest. That night we gathered at Simon's house as if we were all one reflex. It was the night that Father Isaac was almost expelled from our island.

Katrina saved him that night. We who never listen to Katrina—a woman in the margins now without Dimitri, who had let go of life and love, and settled down to grow plumper and more and more silent as the years passed and to tend her parents who at an early age inclined towards helplessness and senility—we heard a sweet, firm voice that woke us up. She only said a few words but so that all of us could hear clearly and precisely: Father Isaac is at the sisters. We trust the sisters. Won't they turn him around?

We couldn't deny what she had said. Only Leo murmured in response, softly, throwing back his head and lifting his plump face to the ceiling—the sisters! The darling sisters. The sisters whom we fear and adore. But there was a little space around him—as if to say—who would get near such a heap of wickedness?

Agatha lifted her then weary head with her face, made ugly by what we thought were wrinkles, may have been shadows, and said quietly, yes, I trust the sisters.

Both Peter and Paul wouldn't have been caught dead listening to Agatha, and the women all shied away from Katrina as if the lack of a husband and children was something you could catch. But for some reason their words stood out amongst the low murmuring as if they would not be ignored. It was apparent that for all the distaste we had of Katrina and Agatha, today their words have flown like arrows to the target. In fact, that is what had made us all wonder and get flustered: there was no denying it, Father Isaac who had written the files and sang the operas and said the racy joke was now ensconced among our holy people and that our island by virtue of ancient custom belonged first to them.

I think we judged the priest too hastily, said Anna, who had taken Father Isaac under her wing. We judged him simply because he had written down a few things about us. Why consider how many things are written down about people in the world? The governments, the businesses, the schools in the world keep so many records it could fill a million Bibles. And what is more I feel sure, I know for certain, that Father's writings were of the kind sort, possibly examining and explaining away our failings.

And anyway, came Katrina's voice again from the back of the dining room in Simon's house, it may be that he is developing an argument—something beautiful, and original that had as its basis things we told him. It may be that he was merely using our thoughts to come up with something new and insightful about the old traditions. If he was a spy, could he have so easily burned up his files? No, look, he bowed to us—burned up everything solely to please us. Katrina was intelligent, we had to grant her that and had a placid heart and was not so up and down with her temper as some of the others. Was it her fault if, rather than tending children, Katrina had found herself watching over her bedridden mother and her senile father, and this painful difference in Dimitri she had felt down to the marrow of her bones? Yet her evenness of temper did not abandon her. She had a disposition that the mere sight of the sun could make gay. But there were times late at night when out of her bones, she had once miserably confessed to us, would come the anger and the agony. She had related to the priest that she felt that someone was stopping her breath sometimes; she was as capable as anyone of being blithe—did one ever hear a peep out of her as she went about these duties; but it was cruel, she said, the way God had chosen to torment her. And she sent the agony and the ire down to her bones.

Father Isaac had given her some comfort, though no answers. You are impoverished that way, it is true, he said, yet when you look at mothers, they are all lacking. Yes, there are some that toil at it, but many are deficient in understanding the heart of another because they are so ill natured. You would not have been. You would have been the perfect mother, yet you too are cross and bitter. But God sees this deformed, crippled world and us living half lives, lives in which we often feel as if we don't have enough breathing room; and says shout for joy like idiots, get the cantankerousness out of your bones. And Katrina had considered the priest to have real wisdom. For he had told her that life was decrepit, ugly and half real—yet shouting for joy for God was the best thing, although perfect folly. And this seemed to her to be not only literally meant but to introduce her to faith in a philosophical way. As if not faith in the unseen but a purifying shout of love to Jesus is the whole point of it.

The mothers of the island, one and all of the women except Martha and her poor, sore, belabored mother Matrona considered themselves to be superior to Katrina on account of her husbandlessness and childlessness and they patronized her, often switching the conversation when she came in to parties and gatherings among them so that they didn't talk the normal talk of their children and their accomplishments in her presence. Ostensibly, they did not want to make her suffer, but inwardly, they all felt that this was a realm of discourse she was not up to, not having the gift. As a result, all of what Katrina said, except when it came to feeding and caring for the elderly, was more or less discounted. This strange behavior on the part of the mothers happened naturally, in fact, because motherhood was part of a mystery of growing up on the island, and it became therefore a cult once one had progressed into it, with all its rites and its worship of its demigods—grandmothers in families who had single handedly with nothing but a cooking pot and an icon of the Crucifixion raised ten children. Not qualifying for the mystery cult of motherhood on the island, Katrina was condemned to their patronizing, and a lifelong lesser state in the eyes of the other women in all areas open to intimate conversation.

But Katrina had, it was to be seen, far more open mindedness and large heartedness with all the agony and anger, as she told the priest, hidden in her bones. Only once or twice it had surfaced from this skeletal safe as it were. Her bones had, she told the priest, leaked. A horrifying pain and anguish had invaded her brain, making her dizzy. She had seen a knife, a sharp knife, and her mother's thin, loose, old woman's throat. She had thought why it would be like killing a chicken… had gone into the kitchen and put her head under the tap. The anguish and the pain had slowly subsided. And she was able in five minutes to go back to feeding her mother, smiling, encouraging, and talking for the thousandth time about the overly hot weather.

Now the other families couldn't help noticing what Katrina had to say but the fact that she was opening her mouth in support of the priest made them suspect afterwards, yes suspect that perhaps she was not a traditional type, not quite what was wanted…but he was voted in for the moment. And another woman said in a soft voice—but he will be watched, yes, watched. We will not be taken off our guard again. For it is our duty to uphold the priesthood on this island, a duty to God and to our ancestors. If any of us see any suspicious or unusual activity, we must inform each other and call a meeting immediately. Max, they agreed, we must count out. Oh Max, there was a murmur of motherly sympathy—we all of us failed Max. We must buy Max shoes, clothes; Max could still fill out a bit, take a girl, settle down. With Max the priest turned his head, all the more reason…but why the boy chose to run to the priest and refused us always…He thought the priest would comfort him. His father had set him against us. And because this odd bird who talks of nothing but heaven didn't seem to him to talk of the hurtful things of earth….Perhaps he thought the priest would stand between him and his father. In the end it turned out that way. But he stood between Max and us as well and we did nothing but comfort him. No we must entirely discount Max as either for or against us. He must be considered a body, not man or woman on the island, but a poor, shriveled other body—a sign, said someone—of nothing, closing us in. But, we pity him.

When the party broke up, Katrina was out first walking down the dark street alone, not caring, it seemed to even attempt to make that polite small talk that makes women stand by one another; and all of us crowded around the door, supposedly listening to Peter and Paul as they tried to take command at the end—something about the informal liturgy as they called it with the incense and the prayers next Sunday—but really staring after Katrina in the dark.

It's no wonder she hasn't got a husband, Paul said when he came over to our group at the door and poked his head out. She has a way of doing and saying exactly what she wants without thinking of anyone else. She is right about the sisters, proclaimed Elizabeth, one of our younger women, who had still not married and on whom we pinned hopes for a baby—she had a sweet figure with wide unsuspecting hips and long legs but a bit of a mind in the clouds—too thoughtful for the handful of young men. Yes, said Timos with a smile in his eyes—the pure-minded ones are like an umbrella over our souls—they keep out whatever fire God might rain on us from heaven. No one knew whom he meant by the 'pure minded ones'! The men? Katrina? But he had his eyes on Elizabeth's wide unsuspecting hips....

Agatha we found out later had slipped off down the street after Katrina. We didn't see her but then Agatha at least the old weary, limping, slipshod Agatha that we knew wasn't always seeable. Even at the late night meeting where we heard her voice and stopped talking a minute—not because she said anything remarkable but because she said the one thing that we thought we knew just as poetry does—by saying—I trust the sisters, and just like poetry it was all about timing;—even then, we couldn't see her where she was in the back but her voice was like a singing voice— quiet and sweet. She never sang, not like the other women at their washing, but that day it sounded a little like our fresh water lake when you throw a pebble into it. We didn't notice it much then but after, seeing her, she looking like our most fantastic dreams, we remembered that her voice was that way, that it had always been so.

There were certain things happening on the island, little things, nothing terribly remarkable. Agatha was her old self, except she stood straight-backed and looked at us eye to eye with a clear eye. They said she spent some time with the priest—just talking and it turned her head around, cast out shadows. There have been shadows in that girl's mind since she was a child. Depressions, ups and downs—even with her husband. And we know it is worse than that. In fact, it got so bad that her own husband was going to move out, dissolve the marriage. He said it a number of times before he took action. Poor thing! He said that to her first time when she was standing in the middle of the living room with a mop in her hand. She stood listened, then curved her back into an even larger hump—that back so used to being curved at that time—and went on cleaning. Come or go with her husband, she was now comfortable and he couldn't take that away. It was shame of course and such a thing as one's husband abandoning one would have been unendurable for Glendi her cousin, Lisa's sister, who had gotten fat and blasphemous but who still prepared the best goat meat stew with tomatoes for her bloated and sniveling husband—a big complainer, farter, stomper. The two of them as earthy and vulgar as they come had a marriage made in heaven. It just goes to show that some sins are entirely pardonable as Scripture says. It was unthinkable that her husband would leave her really although he was always threatening to sail away to the other island with the little dimpled gray lady Susanna as we called her—lady Susanna because she never went out except in laven- der French skirts, made in boutiques, Anna said, and pearl earrings, stiletto heels and this on our stones and sand. No, some could never part from each other their hearts had grown together, one inside the other, like some blown glass figure with another tinier that you could just see within. Smash the one and the other would smash too. But Agatha and her husband were two separate animals and it is said, for rumors go around this little place, that if he hadn't died, there would have been blow ups and divisions and arguments and divorce even in the way of the world.

Then came the illness, and there were suddenly long periods of holding hands— woman who pulled on one like gravity when one had thought, childishly, that one could fly up weightlessly, leaving all that below. Ah, he learned that there was no de- fying fate—that moment he thought and everyone thought—he redeemed himself in a number of men's eyes at the time of the great escape; how he had conceived of it, planned it—there was to be salt in his nostrils soon as the wind blew at him sail- ing away, a new woman of new womankind vibrating as she walked on the opposite shore. But he was like a bird that just lifts his wings in the wind and doesn't move. Then illness, the wife, as the old men said.

We said that he was lucky and unlucky to their faces. Agatha was there in the room, as familiar as the embroidered bed spread, the one that he loved that had a burn mark in it from a cigarette—embroidered by his mother, and the unruly ciga- rette was his father's. Agatha said to us that it could have worked out that he hated of her, tired of her—a wife isn't perfect. Instead, she seemed to say the right things— present it clearly: death!—but still there is life and those things that one loves that seem to say to one there is and there isn't something more. Best to hold at bay the frustration. But it was clear from what Dimitri said, and Barbara who came around with lemon marmalade and pickled fish, tomatoes, garlic and onions and Anna who brought the sweet pastries that in the end, Agatha was the woman to understand him. Yet what can we say? It was Agatha after all in the end; perhaps he hadn't let go of his chance to marry –and we lifted our hands—so as to mean 'rightly'.

And when he died, Agatha hardly wept, though sickness had slid them back into place with one another. She said she had had her fill of him with a soft smile, a single tear; Zoe thinks she meant something mystical, but Zoe is always looking on the positive side. Alex turned all philosophical and smoky, Agatha said—all grey with cigarette, after cigarette. They became fast friends as he lay in bed, taking his time about dying, looking at death from this angle and then from that; between Agatha and her husband in the end there was nothing sentimental, just really good camaraderie. Even while he was dying, and he died somehow without the usual raw smells and ugly changes in his face but with an amazing finesse, as if some other self in him was finishing off a really good spectacle, savoring it,, pointing to it, he asked for Agatha over the nurse and his last word was directed to her ears only, though the family was gathered around—and it was 'best.'

Agatha at his death, felt she had simultaneously found a new man and lost him. Perhaps the drifting mind of the dying made him turn to her in the end—or perhaps it was some kind of other perspective on this limp and limping girl who never seemed to say the right thing, obscured herself at the back of the room during our dance festivals, cursed herself to hell over her strange and violent sons; some say she had cast a spell on him but what spell would make him simple good company? All that we know is that he took morphine and had some strange, ghastly dreams. Half the island stared as his body was carried out with that suspicious stare; one or two women on Agatha's family's side and even on his—his brother and sister, stood by her. Old suspicions die hard even though family that has gone off island telephoned back from Paris and New York saying above all things—there are no such things as witches. Of course, no! What an idea! Who would dare?

But people looked askance at Agatha, blaming her for the upheaval in the home ten years later, even for her husband's death, even though he had held her hand for fifteen days through his dying—for the moment when she and her sons had stood in a line—Dimitri was eight years old, and Jason only four, a chubby little boy with curly hair, and a soft, soft look that made us all want to mother him—watching as this paterfamilias strode away, perhaps forever; but in reality to go and contemplate the fishing nets laid out on the docks, to walk around the shoreline and stare mournfully at the two jagged rocks under the cliff—to say later at a fish dinner in the tavern to a few morose men drumming a pack of cards with their fingers, waiting for the game to begin—life is a prison of bone, flesh and blood. That is what came of Alex's grand voyage away from a then damp, bent-backed, silent wife who swallowed down words that she was about to say, and the two boys—one mute entirely and the other lisping his baby words. Something passed over them, he said later to Agatha, she repeated this, ten years down the line to Anna—like a net of white fire; they, this quasi mute family with the bent wife were caught in it.

We thought it rude, cruel, cold that Paul said to her face a few months after the funeral at one of our meetings, where we had been all drinking the good red wine of the autumn—Alex died in spring—that it was just so convenient that Alex had died. Now Agatha was free to enjoy all the wealth without having to put up with this up and down type. Anna had given him one of her chill looks, and accompanied Agatha into the corner where she had sat silently staring out the window.

Agatha was much to be pitied but one saw the curse on her from the beginning. She was a strong-minded girl, an angry girl when she was young. Everything seemed to her unjust from the way man and woman are made to life and death to the very hell and heaven of God. That was Agatha just after childhood, a time which had been a little sweet, she had loved life, sung off tune, danced big-footed dances. For a few years she had gone around like a loaded gun; the little things of our women didn't interest her. The women's dances at our festivals aggravated her. Why should she take little steps in a long skirt, when a man can kick his leg up, leap, dance upside down on his hands? Then suddenly, she was out of the dance, in the corners. Just at the time when a woman's face clears into her mating beauty, she stepped aside. And what is more, swallowed down the old anger and the thought of the unjust reality was all ironed out so that there remained only depression. It was as if Anna said later, sorrowfully, that girl has been pinned down, made helpless. She went from being a real firebrand to a weakness and helplessness worse than all the rest. Given the things that she had said, well! It was only natural that hell should come over her. Of course, it was also unfair of the village, Anna proclaimed this unfairness, to call Agatha's sorrow a curse—to believe; but they have their ways, rigid and a little slipped from our once upon a time; they are like old people who have slipped and fallen once and then walk stiffly and fearfully, unnaturally ever after. They had seen this exploding child, with her beautiful arguments, happy big-footedness and expected something amazing, almost revolutionary in the little way of our island--and then had witnessed her sudden inexplicable misery. Years ago so many people would have been sympathetic, secretly rising up, asking questions of the priest! Then how shamefaced they had been seeing her spiritual demise. A curse is a curse. She is no longer really one of ours. And she shouting out in the streets that it is unfair to God, his very hell and heaven, the very divine creation. God is God, they had said, and for the most part, averted their faces, when they passed her—old and hunchback at seventeen, a weeper.

Now twenty four years later, she suddenly sweeps by as if she's royalty. Where did she come from? Yet we know her—her mother and father. Her spine has straightened out, her chest is lifted. You would think it would take God Himself to come down and unroll those vertebrae one by one, setting them back into that delicate poise, like a string of pearls, nothing human could have changed her. Could it be that she has served her time of affliction? In any case, it suddenly looks like she is wafted along, graceful and exquisite too, her feet bearing the same weight but effortlessly, and she swinging her hips playfully, as if she could sway voluptuously or just a little as she might choose, rather than that mindless walk of before where one leg stomped and the other dragged.

The men now ten years after Dimitri left are commenting on her figure. How is it that suddenly she is the envy of our woman folk? What is more she herself walking around hardly seems to notice—as if it is all natural that at forty six she had grown from something ugly, stunted and painful to look at into a real blossom. One would think that a girl child a little ugly and fat would bloom suddenly at sixteen—something commonplace; in fact, Peter's girls went through an ugly childhood and everything smoothed out at sixteen or seventeen. But with Agatha, it has gone beyond. Peter's daughters are heavy steppers, thick-waisted, constipated and jowled women, though young with oval faces and good color. And they do little but eat fruit and candy and listlessly read magazines, although they have their work, and also help cook and sew as they wait for husbands. Agatha whom everybody thought couldn't even straighten her back, is suddenly amazingly brilliant as a flag pole at forty-six and has a way now with her as if she is being blown by a strong wind.

She went to our priest, just arrived at his room one day, a brilliant day, light all around her, stepping almost weightlessly. The priest joked that he was in the presence of an immortal. Ah, he said to Max, the immortals are all women, of course. Those who die in this world but rise up to live in the other reality in which this world is only a tiny piece of the puzzle.

Agatha looked at him and at Max who had anguish written all over his face as she entered and crouched a little, stepping back as she came into the middle of the room like something victorious that ought to be there, standing erect and planted. The priest, smiling and laughing wobbled over to the stove to make her one of his famous infusions.

Why did you do it? Agatha asked in a sharp voice not exactly her former lugubrious one. The village is so unsettled over it.

My knee-walk? Asked Father Isaac with a smile. Oh, fame, he exhaled and then he stopped and bowed his head. But something old had to be put to rest, he countered the jest, softly. It demanded pain.

Oh, for me years and years of it, said Agatha almost unaware that she was speaking. I still think….

But that is not quite true, said Father Isaac his eyes glowing; it was as if they were carrying on a conversation that had not been entirely put into words: We were made naked, erect and looking in the unfathomable eye of God.

And through all this, Father, murmured Agatha, the others saw me pinned down, even Anna!—that pinned -down woman—as if something, the world or God held me like a kidnapper, bound and helpless, continuing that dread night. And through all this I kept talking with Him, in a broken language but not letting go.

God first talks; never acts first. Not the only thing, but the vital part, the libido in him is to raise us up to once more our nakedness, called glory, and to look him in the eye. He wants children, loin persons, love creatures, toilers, sweaters, players, lazy bums, tale tellers, bringers of joy.

I received a letter from Athens; Dimitri lives there now; he was transferred six months ago from London. He is coming home.

Ha, said the priest, thoughtfully. Grew up in England then, said the priest shifting gears. Agatha wanted to say something about the regular checks that arrived from her son—that he is the reason, she had been able to have Simon paint, the reason she didn't have to do everything by herself. Dimitri had, in the end, provided after the pension ebbed—she was a widow with two beautiful, dutiful... but she didn't say it; he was just the man in her mind—a far away creature of hers, and not of hers, more and more secretly beautiful; but Dimitri was coming with a plan to enrich everyone on the little, fading island. For they had, some of them without children, their pensions to consider; the possibility of poverty in old age was looming over many—the childless ones. Of course, no one would permit, no one would allow ...but to be thrown on to the public in that way was so shameful, and pitiful. They say that Nico kept a gun and a bag of clothes with jewels to pawn in case he had to make the great escape!—and he was a young man.

He writes a lot, said Agatha, also shifting gears from these thoughts; I know all about England—how they love roses and fish and chips. And they don't rise with the clock inside them as we do. They have exterior clocks, big clocks tolling the hours with bells. They live by these clocks and they have trains that run by these clocks.

So I have heard about England, said the priest. And we just half know time to do things. We see it in the sun, here. And the hours of wind shifts. The summer/winter differences in light, we have memorized and account for them as we work. It is one of those studies that you might make—stranded in the middle of the sea as we are, he jested. And the birds and animals know the light differences. At Easter the vigil runs from midnight to dawn. It has never been the case where I have ended a vigil after the appointed hour—that is, not of the 'exterior clock,' as you so eloquently put it, but of exactly when the birds begin to sing, in that long pause of darkness, before the pre-dawn light comes into the sky. Somehow the vigil ending has always been precise though not clocked to the first singing of the birds. And there have been different Easters some more towards summer, some still chilly. Of course, we have watches and clocks. One of them set by the radio to perfect time at Simon's house. I can always set my watch by his. They say that the American family up on the cliffs have the kind of clock that keeps exact time according to the electromagnetic band of atoms. These clocks I admit are beautiful, to be much admired—one can after all hardly fathom the complexity of these machines. But our rhythm—who knows it except us?—a slow, steady, swaying measure like our music and it comes out of singing and chanting and out of dancing. Sometimes before dawn, I open the church and our two chanters go and practice and they know to sing twice at the right speed the whole of St. Basil's liturgy just as the smells of frying garlic start emanating from the windows of their houses. I have seen and heard in the slow afternoons, the men gathering behind the tavern and twirling to the musicians—Mimo and Pipo; they are carrying the few bars of the Trisagion and six or seven repetitions of the soft stomp and kick in our guts, we get through a mini practice—what would it be—about an hour and forty seven minutes by the clock, once I timed it by my old watch that I carry now and then in my pocket-- give or take, with a slow walk home—it makes it about two hours.

Then there are poor souls—Katrina's parents who sit and suffer time—the second, breath by breath, drop of sweat by drop of sweat in the summer although she tries, God bless her, to keep them cool in the shade, under the leaves, by the window with the shades drawn in that white white house so quiet you could hear a pin drop. For them the minutes are breaths and pains, breath by breath, pain by pain, soft groan, loud groan; sometimes, the gross hours—feeding--swallowing and swallowing.

But anyway, said Agatha, pulling at his arm, he was seated in his broken straw armchair by the window and was drifting off into thought, the sun on his face. As Agatha saw it, the sun was always on his face and the flesh of his face was ringed all around with white like a cloud. He didn't bathe often enough and smelled a little of soiled flesh, although also of fragrance, men would have said he needed a woman, an efficient woman, not Martha, the lambkin, as he called her, to run behind him, but it was part of monastic vows not to have one and Father Isaac looked as if he hadn't renounced all that—the needy flesh—happily, but was bereft like a perennial widow. His various smells didn't offend him but the villagers for the sake of the smell of soil, which came through the fragrance refrained from downright idolizing him also the miracle of the goats brimming with the sweetest milk still smelled goat and the earth bursting suddenly with massive amounts of fruit had some still rotten after his huge penance. For he had never actually, the women said—you know, to their friends—put his hand out, glorified God, and commanded the goats to bear more milk and more fragrantly!

Yes, anyway—said Father Isaac, smiling at her, then remembering—yes, so Dimitri is coming. I predict that this little island will gather around—every last man and woman and stare, withdraw, poke their heads out, glance out of windows…Is he still one of us? Of course, he will have that slight look of otherness, and what is worse, also that slight disdain for them.

Disdain? How can he?

No but—now his head is stuffed full of ideas. As you say he lives by the clock of the world, is known as all good employees are known for punctuality to it—that is, the long clock hand on the twelve usually when they march in to their offices, not the feelings in their digestive tract, the brain throbbing above their eyes. When he comes in to this little world that he left not much bigger than a child, and sees how people wake up like little birds in the dark, intone a word or two in their homes, cross themselves, and then step softly away to their little boats, unable to see the water well until they are out in it—all without looking at the face of the clock—I think he will give it half a thought of sorrow and love and half a thought of disdain. That is what I think. And the shores, the village, the boats will all be littler and more fragile than what they had been on his going away.

Agatha sat down on the floor in one soft drop, her knees catching her, bearing the weight so that she landed lightly and to one side. Max stood to one side watching, until the priest gestured to him to come and sit opposite in the other straw chair.

There is something I wanted to tell you before my son comes, she said, but—she looked at Max.

There are things one reads in the bodies of people, said Father Isaac, softly. They may not be an explicit, word by word description of fact, history, event as the world sees fact, history and event. But there are subtle engravings of human agony of one kind or another; joy, on the other hand does not leave traces, obliterations, fictions and lies. It is almost a nothingness on the skin in the bone—except perhaps for a quiver there. In the great myth of Icarus and Daedalus it is commonly held that Icarus was proud, ambitious, vainglorious and therefore wanted to fly right up against the sun, whereas Daedalus knew his place and was wise, lowly, and prudent. But I see it completely reversed: it was Icarus who truly knew joy and knowing it like a child let go of all restraint. Similarly, it was Eve who utterly gave herself to joy—reached out for the fruit, for surely, as the serpent beguiled her—she would be as the gods and would not die! How perfect and pure and true to God, the God-shadow in her. And do you know the saints at the monastery that is, those of the holy mind—strive for such true holiness, immortality, as theosis, deification, for without this ambition—to experience utter joy, to become as God, that is, to achieve God-spiritedness, one is neither going to heaven nor saved. Utterly unashamed, the sense of joy still on her, wonderingly, she told God—the serpent beguiled me, in other words, not that she disobeyed, that she regretted her growing desire but that the tempting, subtle, rebel snake had told her an untruth passed off as truth—that he had spoken with the mouth of God, out of line. But God saw Mary in her, herself a rebel but un-beguiled and for God and faster than Lucifer could jump to forestall, sent Jesus, Eve's true desire to be God eternally, to free the beguiled human soul on that thousands' of years trip—for that wonderful joy—at the right hand of power—does not mean death. And Jesus, another Serpent but this time the Word of all authority, and in line, said let be to the Serpent-death: I am— and to His followers suffer the liar, even die under him if he kills you, for love, for love, slip on your belly underneath the Serpent. And the apostles saw their Master do it, preferring God even as curse, as abandonment... There are many who believe this joy to be a lie. One can't deny the death bringers' death. But, in love, dying and suffering is the glory of God, love is not just a tender light but a terrible, anti-human, cruel toil and travail that breaks down the barrier of limited imagination, which confines the small-minded. This is the article of belief to abide by, the only one. In this dread toil and travail that is love is the eternal quality of God—tender, crushing metamorphosis to soul. Sometimes I think it consists of just one extra day like this, with this blue that seems to be made up of millions of age old afternoons and afternoons to come—and one more meal of rice, tomatoes and goats' cheese—the strenuousness of living through the lift and lift again of that weight of beauty and fulfillment. Surely, we'll not die indeed, we who commit ourselves to the dread toil, for we are only dying to a Life—what we've lived for— that is larger than our death and our blood will give it more life.

The priest went on, looking at Agatha but not seeing her—narrowing his eyes and seeing something far away: At the cross, there was a change in Jesus Christ, subtle, slight but distinct. He was no longer angry, not the least; now he was passionately loving—(here is the true Christ in the Christian facing suffering)--loving and wanting to say it—the uttermost speech of love—My God, My God! Why hast thou forsaken me? with the broken bone in his throat-- it was as if immanent death unleashed a huge cosmos of love in Jesus; he loved the faces in front of him—John, Mary, but also the torturers with the same torrent of hot fire of passion, a mother tiger with her cubs—and God who was withdrawn! For that moment, because of the hugeness of his love far above and beyond the torture-- they were his children—he provided for them and pleaded with God for them. Before, because of his trust, everything was in order. Now he saw the chaos and he was part of it. He saw at last, long last, the pathetic face of humanity—the unknowing face, the lied to face, the obscened face of man and woman seeking the secret, holy joy in other than truth, sometimes the mad face, the viciously torn face, the worn face but fading into mere innocence and fear before a great cruel absurdity. There is a crossing at the cross: some say that Jesus saw the truth, shouted my God, my God why have you forsaken me? And died into nothingness. But the love-strength of the Master does not diminish --he and God were one—for before death, even if soul forsakes soul, the living recoil from the dread dead but love remains riveted love to love. What more manifest in this whole story than this final despair? We've seen bones. They are nothing. It is the putting out of the well-spring of light, light that is not of the sun, but that clothes the self, the world;--that is, terrifying nakedness. And God is none other than this nakedness, lost nakedness, beautiful, innocent and joyous, love making nakedness— but terrifying and cruel and dread. Yet our priest says that Jesus laughed when He said this terrible truth. For He was naked, so he was alive. He was God Himself and a mere child, dying; it was a terrible and a God-playful thing for the Messiah, Son of the Living God to die. As it is a terrible and playful thing for the Big Bang to begin time and space, birth, death and suffering.

And what strange renewal after! The confessions of St. Paul of the Christ alive: from the tone, not the ghost of Christ, not despair and fanaticism—but flesh and blood body as if quivering within him—flesh and blood whole- joy! Naked and unashamed joy burning in the depths of the heart. For Jesus, the Christ lived on whichever way you look at it. The victory of contempt over that ignominious figure horribly tortured, contempt which now in its final mockery stretches its arms wide to embrace us all is still not yet; there is real love still. And if we look for the God who is gone, we see only risen life dancing for joy—Jesus whirling through the walls enclosing the disciples who stand petrified within barriers of material limitation un-believing; His dance is now truly limitless—even bastions of walls, secure protective barriers cannot shut it out. It is clear to the disciples that only the life of love is resurrected life—the end-beyond-God-life or Christ's nakedness—and so give away the safe holdings, possessions, strip off the robes of pride, dignity, passionately compassionating the poor, for life begins—begins! on the other side of this final poverty—the loss of self! Death, no, what a life! Not the half a cup of earthly living but the (eternally) overflowing cup—the giving back which some beggar of beauty did for you: a raped woman who lifts her leg straight and high to the stars and points her toe, leaping like Jesus returned, her genitals open. And it becomes clear that Scripture is all about this—resurrected Life—resumed from some origin when Love was engraved on our heart, and we were eternal! Love was engraved in us then—but not as the sentiment— sexual, or moral: as a mad awe, rather. Points to it, St. Paul does, from the tone—St. Paul with his arms outstretched as if crucified in the bowels of a Roman prison—rejoicing, unafraid—a new movement, skipping joyously with only love in his head to death as if skip hard enough and you leap past it—and his severed head bounced thrice leaving fountains for each bounce. All there is to go by—a tone. Did not our hearts burn like torches within us—soft as water, lovely as wine? A trace. And the unlikely, incomprehensible, unshakable holy dance of joy in the few who laugh off the sneer of contempt, the shadowy, bodiless, specter of mind—intelligent, technological, with even the leisure to be relatively kind, the other joy of God.

It was this contempt that I recognized as a universal force in humankind against the risen Body when I was up on the cliff. Contempt not only for the man carrying the cross, for suffering, for human nakedness, but also and above all for the only joy. And so I said, ah, to hell with it, I will go down feasting, skipping as St. Paul on the way to his execution for if we accept resurrection there is nothing other than risen joy, body given back, self a piece of music that is it. There is pain in these legs and yet I skip, laugh, dance. For if the depth of evil and suffering is profound, this cup of joy is so far profounder. While the death bringers are darker-faced than atom bombs, true Christ, Jesus, that is, resurrected Life is the re-beginning Dancer, the gift of Body and Blood as if stepping on water, the delicacy of the poets and lovers, delicacy of nakedness—the inner core of a person naked. Joy for that as the lover beholding. For Mary Magdalene the weeping was unfathomable that night and the joy such a shock as to make her delirious and fragrant with jasmine. Her backbone base that had disappeared, restored and she immortal-touched. Smiling ever after celestially.

Yes, your son will return, Father Isaac concluded suddenly. And I predict his will be the way of atheism but not antagonism, not antagonism—a non-seer, impatient, but kind, genuine.

Like Anna, said Agatha. .

Godlessness, a different kind of life, said the priest, not answering, shifting his gaze at last and looking out of the window. There is scientific evidence of course that we are marooned in a sea of almost nothingness—what is death but the decay to worm's meat?— and that we are in ourselves fantasticating creatures of time, powerful as God. And we who cling to God seem to hold on to the fantasy, a fairy tale, some sort of wishfulness. But is it less real, I wonder? These fairy tales, I must say, have a living reality beyond the reach of the anthropologists and mythologists. How they live in rose blooms, in leaves, in forests endowing with mystical life the very green leaf—a life as tangible as a snow flake that is our only hope for beauty, truth or love. Of course, when they bring in the tools of science they die immediately, obediently like little, frail creatures, butterflies being pinned and analyzed. Victorian child women offered up to the marriage bed and a husband not the most understanding. The cold hard heavy tread of the inexorable law or fact of nature discovered like the ingredients of a cake, it's why and how of rising. But the cake is more than all that. It has a perfection that cannot be found in its ingredients or its rising. Love is not in the pinning. Sometimes it comes to me that the hydrogen becoming helium in a star is a dream. And this dream is the star, not the hydrogen and helium; for who can prevent my dream? Indeed stars just blow up sometimes like children laughing. There, I said it: this is the life of a star, the life of life. Yes, of course there is the law that says hydrogen will become helium in a star factory. But I wonder if the blowing up is in fact the sign of the way also—the way of Christ—the flinging down of the temple, the blowing up of holy spite. The Hydrogen becoming Helium of human agony on the cross. Woe becoming blessing, the passionately compassionate defense of the rage-distorted school children who have less so much less than the gentle and mighty heroism of the Spirit of Justice and Love intrinsic to but not of and beyond, ever beyond us.

But he is coming home? Said Agatha, rising up and standing on her toes, and wanting a scientific yes. He said so; he assured me so. But there is something that makes me doubt.

I haven't read the letter. But it is my sense of things from what you told me.

Max suddenly sprang up and moved to the stove, bending a little over it when he arrived.

Oh, said the priest, I have been talking all this time and forgetting the infusion. It will be a little strong.

Shall I pour it out, Father? Max had a high clear trembling voice. Agatha saw him as a person who lived as she, perhaps, a secret life.

Yes, said Father Isaac. He is somebody, he said to Agatha in a whisper, gesturing to Max, whom I hover near and have everything to do with but pretend most often not to see. I have a superstition that if I don't look at him very much, great, unexpected and almost magical things will come out of him. You know we have a shortage of true followers of the cross; and of course it seems rather hideous. I would say shockingly hideous. I don't say deny yourself and pick up your cross to him. He is so innocent. And we have just come to holding, trusting, and chanting the eight tones. The hallowed halls for him are my arms, you see. Men are too harsh and women, if you forgive me, untrustworthy. I was once hideously angry at those who made him so delicate and breakable. But now I am rather thankful for it.

Max came back with the infusions in two cups and offered Agatha one, bowing a little, holding the rim of the china tea cup and pointing the handle towards her hand. Once he was sure she held it, he took away his hand shaking it a little.

Is it hot? Said the priest, smiling, shaking his head when Max offered the other cup to him. It's fine, said Max, sipping the cup refused for his sake and closing his eyes.

So beautifully, beautifully sweet, said Agatha, sipping, still on her feet.

Making infusions are something I learned to do after much trial and error. It is all rational deduction and a little guesswork, extrapolation from old recipes but with the goal of making them the most delicious ever, whereas in some of these ingredients there are old prejudices, for in one root there is medicinal value, in another an undeniable fragrance. These prejudices have held sway for a long time. I concocted for taste alone taking into account changes between hot, warm and cold, reheating too, and prolonged as opposed to short steeping. There are two or three that I make now that are quite addicting they are so delightful. And all except one provide a little stimulus.

We live for these teas, suddenly exclaimed Max. Whatever the reason for drinking one—headache, grumpiness, lack of loving feeling—he is over there by the stove brewing. You'd think watching him every other hour that there'd be no time for work even, for reading the Scriptures, contemplating the liturgy! Amazingly, he gets his golden hour in, as he calls it --the study sometimes all night for Sunday morning—and yes, he is prepared. But the labor of the day goes into making infusions. He says that herbs alter chemical reactions in the body. And almost each time he makes an infusion—maybe ten a day sometimes, he is right there with his notebook. He believes in solving, chemically solving, the problem of sin: One sip for inner calm, a rich sweetness for humility, full- bodied flavor for love. He believes that such things talk to the brain cells and changing, converting, through means of a tea. This, he raised his cup, gesturing, is his main preaching. Max stopped talking as abruptly as he began and looked down.

Agatha looked at him and imagined his face asleep—the high bridged nose, the pale eyelids, barely pink lips all his mother's physiognomy except for the pallor—something deathly looking, at the same time an outline—warm. She thought there should be in his life something to wake him up. Then he would talk with a firmer voice.

The priest didn't respond to this outburst of Max, except to smile slightly. It was clear to Agatha that he loved him in a frank, fond way almost like a grandfather. So whatever his faults, whatever his comments, he saw him as a child, as a bright light so that it was as if, when he himself faded and became decrepit, Max would be the brighter light having learned a few lessons; Agatha knew that these lessons that the priest undoubtedly wished to impart to Max were such that it took time, many months of application to for them to eventually take root. And she knew also that the world of young people was a fast one, and though she had never been to the great cities, never seen the highways and the quick movements of the people going about their business, she could imagine the young people in crowds surging like seas at high tide. A young person in New York grows up in the blink of an eye; getting jobs, going to France and India, writing books, wrote Dimitri. It made Agatha wonder—Peter's girls were twenty six, twenty eight and thirty and still at home with their father and mother, huffing and puffing when they had to move very far, downing their fried fish, stewed chicken, and popping into their mouths after the long siesta, fat ripe apricots. Of course, they worked—one of them at the grocery store, another apprenticed at the monastery to embroider priestly vestments; the last milked goats and fed chickens and was up early, rubbing the sleep out of her face with the plump upper part of her arm. But still the days wore by very slowly; and the burden of three semi somnolent daughters grown but not yet married was felt keenly by Peter who had been slow moving away from home himself.

In the city, Agatha heard from Dimitri, people expect changes fast—like turning on an electric switch and getting light. The development of a new medicine that will entirely eliminate a dire disease, a machine that will connect one country to another in a few heartbeats is perceived as suddenly there, no one thinks of it as other than right—created, functioning, beside one's right hand. There they don't know the meaning of the waiting for. Here there is only waiting; boats bringing things are slow and as far as disease is concerned, people sit and endure in the hot sun and flies and sometimes scream a little for death. Her father, she remembered, came home one night suddenly by the light of the moon; next night, bathed in sweat, one arm bone like a knife waving a little, crying, and screaming loudly enough for the neighbors to hear; her mother or she waving a newspaper to fan him on hot days wishing he'd die for he lasted a long, laborious summer of stink and pain and heat. He was eaten away, day and night no relief from the pain. One begins to live differently, to walk cautiously, because even a heavy footstep made him scream. Here was a kind of holiness, in fact—the stepping lightly. So much so she hesitated to bring all of herself to her wedding two years later because she would walk normally down the aisle then. She looked at Max now—that fresh, unaware look was still on him. Undoubtedly the priest would try to get there so that one day when he saw pain like that or felt it—real pain, the kind that couldn't be borne…but you couldn't hurry the lessons that were slow, light and left only the faintest imprint. And the priest loved him, real, physical, all out love—and that made the impress slower, the impression fainter as Max saw himself already perfect in the Father's eyes needing no alteration or reform.

Agatha put down the little cup on the little glass table under the window and bowed to the priest. You have perfected a science in these infusions, Father, she said to him.

It is my hobby, said Father Isaac. It gives me great relief to dedicate myself in one aspect entirely to pleasure. How could I not in Eden, he gestured around the room that was piled with old books mostly on God and herbal medicines, and where

clothing—a sweater, a shirt hung drying, and there was a fragrance coming of tomatoes like red suns sitting in a pile on the counter by the stove. I believe that the taste
is just right; now how to create a paradisiacal fragrance, a perfume without spoiling
it? This occupation gets my mind off the pains in my body. I live for taste and smell.
A science that I believe will bring love to the world.

Father, she said suddenly; I have doubted you and Max, wondered about you.
Now I think you are all about frankness and honesty. I think I know what you want.
It has to do with our humanization, our materialization into the human material.

Go away now, said Father Isaac waving at her. Your son is coming home. Make
merry; eat something sweet. Don't think ill of Max. He's just beginning. He may be
twenty six or so but he's a little fuzzy chick for all that.

I have just thought that when pain comes....

Well, we have faith, hope and love.

Yet it can defeat all of them.

Never mind let it come and defeat then. Then it's no use talking is it? Now you
will go.

Agatha bowed a little awkwardly; she looked into the priest's face to see if it was
all harsh and stern; but she could only see that he was looking down and to one side
as if thinking and suffering being looked at.

What an impossibility, she said to herself as she went out. To find a guide on this
earth. Better to look at nature—the flowers, the weeds, the stones, the sea—they all
seem to know entirely what they are about and to love it. And when the pain comes,
well, there must be a move, or a moment that lessens it for maybe a breath. Of
course, she didn't even confess to herself before that she wanted a guide; it suddenly
seemed obvious that that was what she was seeking.

And when the pain comes, she thought, again, it spreads out over life like a terrible storm. And the little body goes still or tilts. I remember my father clear as day
now; it wasn't in the end the pain of the cancer that really got to him, as one day, in
the middle of the afternoon with a fly on his cheek, he suddenly felt toothache and
it came on stronger and stronger until the pain was splitting his head. This pain on
top of the other pain made his screw up his face until he looked like a crying infant.
He died with the screwed up face still on him, and when at last, he relaxed, I saw
something so blue grey and sorrowful as if he was looking back, I thought from the
kingdom, at that dark pain cloud spreading over poor bodies on earth. Agatha didn't
remember death in so graphic a form on the island, although of course she had seen
many of the people who had died.

Every time Agatha went to the priest and she went oftener than the others because she thought he was a full blooded saint, although so quaint—it was hard. Hard
because she thought things, remembered things—like her father dying and pain and

more pain. It was hard, very hard, to start up again at dawn. Easier to just walk incessantly around the dark house when Jason left; easier to just turn over in bed, push herself down in the soft warm nest of covers. Every time she encountered the priest in his eyrie, as she called it, on the top of the hill, she couldn't help thinking that there was no answer and no way out. That even her son coming home lovely though it was, was coming as a stranger to move around as if house and village were not part of him nor he of them as he'd begun to do years ago. And the rest of her life would be taken up with creeping after him, as she used to do and that irritated him terribly—wanting just to see into his mind; this obsession was a little like the madness of an illicit passion for she wished a little to be his wife; he seemed to sense it and move away become more withdrawn, which made it worse. She was always at his side saying take me there with you, or watching him, not properly with affection, but envying him, idolizing him. And, he had wished to exclude her. Never once brought Katrina home.

There were voices in the night just outside the windows, and she would hear him and her and think—of course, he is sixteen, seventeen, eighteen and handsome. Sometimes, in the morning, he was all arms around her, picking her up, kissing her on the lips. But she had reconciled herself to the fact that a boy growing into a man goes into a place in himself and his mother must lose the map to get there.

He had written all his letters in his old affectionate tone reassuring her. It was only these last few addressed by a different hand that had put her off a little. How was it that he could have a stranger address his letters to her? It put a kind of barrier up between them—and the barrier was cold and pitiless. She had written this to him: Why couldn't he address the letter himself? It was to her, his mother; didn't he know how she longed to first thing see his handwriting when she got the mail? He had entirely ignored her plea, acted as if he had not heard it, strangely, incomprehensibly, and the next letter came addressed by that same stranger.

Nor could she complain. Of all people, she would have complained to Anna or the priest or Simon. But they would have chided her—you got the letter; he is coming home; what more can you ask? Her grief was such a little thing. It was utter foolishness to talk of this as pain. Pain she had seen in the human body; agony, even. How dare she say it, breathe it--? And then there was old pain, and that too, wasn't pain like other people have. Agatha was used to this in her life, little things, big things, maybe, but she could never complain. She couldn't even find the words; people wouldn't see the importance. Or, when she finally found the words, and wrote them, as she had to her son—they were proven to be so much of nothing; they were tossed into the blank wind--and swallowed up there. It was as if she had never written them. He wrote affectionately as always but she thought in a fit of irritability that it could have been a blank sheet sent to her for all he answered her.

And so she continued with her secret life that she plucked like a full blown rose and held out to us in corners, under cover of night. There we saw no anger or pain for the injustice of it all, no. No creeping back into the old hole as she had often enough with her husband, with her sons. No, perhaps because the dawn has something other in it—brilliant, tender and joyous. It must be that she wants the dawn in her. We see her whirl around on one toe, light as a summer cloud when she was forty three and the old men said old women can never be young again but a woman becoming a woman is never old…but it was impossible to say exactly what she was doing. Becoming a ballerina at her age? But she danced, forced herself, even after she saw the priest; for if she didn't wind up her body and stretch it out, she said she would 'lose it.' Ah, what did that mean? For years, she felt she was 'going nowhere' building and building and what was there? But the red light of the rising sun made her feel as if there was another country lovelier than anything on earth; and only a bare margin of time between it and her-- but then she felt she danced.

When the old men saw her walk by, no longer a lady, now a lord, as if lords have always had cleavage, a kind of trance came over them. They expected her going by to fold over as she had for so many years into her permanent bow; they had seen her fade all those years and had expected nothing more; lady-style, she had had children, the old curse bearer in the end—that was what a woman was for, they muttered amongst themselves. But what good can come out of her? Of course, she would be the one almost abandoned. Alex at last got fed up. But where could he go? Went mad in the end—brain affected; and so he held hands with her whom he would have gladly hurled down an abyss and talked nonstop with her until he died. She could have been a stranger; it would have been the same. The onset of death makes one reach out. Strangers become close as lovers. Old hated wives become strangers who are suddenly close as lovers. But here she was saying to them, whispering to them—soul to a group of dried up, whoring old men—that a woman…and going past looking like majesty. As if the curse were on them!

But we saw her at the market buying onions. She looked her little self. Her back was straighter, yes, that's true. Alex used to slap her up over hunching after they were married. He didn't always insinuate himself into her intimate places with kindness and a light touch; we thought he was a hero of sorts to go into that web of misery, and sullenness that was Agatha at seventeen, eighteen, nineteen—the cursed one. She behaved herself; during her marriage, she held herself at bay. Her husband was her husband, she told us. Husband seemed to her to have a special meaning. But then he began to get fed up—slapped her on the back and told her to straighten up, for the thousandth time. The old black moods got to him at last. Ah, he wanted a woman, we thought, not a thin, shriveled crab with nothing to say for herself. Those were the hard years for Agatha with her back smarting. Then, the near abandonment. Finally, illness, the collapse, the madness, philosophizing, death. Ah, how he had wanted someone to talk to.

Maria, our whore, says there is a conspiracy against us living. A blackness, no not blackness like night or like rocks—for that was deep-hearted as God; no but there was a blackness even so that was so grim; it was a place of no living—not of death, for death has living in it. She had heard of black holes, black prisons, places in cold outer space that you could just glimpse but were farther even than night—places where stars can't live but fall upside down into. Maria imagines that this blackness actually surrounds us, exists inside, and, in some cases, outside; for although the universe is way beyond us, it is also, she says, in us. And so there is a certain desire—ah who, what is she talking about?—just desire, she says, loose here that we not live. It took a while to get to Holy Island.

We said to her—is it possible? What madness has entered your head? There is only God and the devil—but if it is the devil you mean…it sounds like the devil. She said she thought she had seen it in operation—this blackness. Years ago. She was coming out of the night, passing a window full of light on her way home, the electricity was full blast then. Perhaps she had taken a different route. She doesn't remember ever passing that way—whatever the reason, she was there under that window that turned out to be Paul's bedroom window. He must have been seventeen and Maria herself was nineteen, both parents dead and she in a fix because they had been poor. Aunt Dema who owned the tavern at that time had hired her for a pittance and given her goat cheese and watered wine for dinner but Maria had made her way herself with her shapely hips and soft, slender legs that seemed to blow in the wind like pine branches. She had charged a lot for the old men, a little for the young men and not a few tried to court her in the end, because she knew how to navigate a man's mind. Maria in any case there under the window would arouse no suspicions—she knew all the young men naked. But she had seen—Agatha there, breasts bare, her arms holding herself. It was not so strange for a boy to have a girl even for a while in secret. But what Maria had seen, what she had known after looking into Agatha's face was that the girl didn't want to be there. Behind she saw Paul with his shirt unbuttoned to the belly and a pink smile, as she called it on his cold face. She wished with all her heart that she could have substituted herself for Agatha, she said.

Of course we knew that there was something up between Agatha and Paul way back when. But that had been one of those little experiments between female and male. We knew, we were not children, that a woman and man didn't often marry as virgins. What happened, happened. We say no more about it. Certainly Paul was slightly miffed after. Can you imagine? He said, smoking cigarette after cigarette with a group of boys, Peter and I think Basil was among them—Katrina's father—she laughed at me, he had said. But in the end I made her scream and plead for mercy. In fact, the story went around that Paul did Agatha a 'favor.' She was 'a gypsy'—and I think he talked of doing favors because some of the villagers are disgusted with gypsies—a people discontented with everything, the women folk with wild hair, fierce eyes, maniacs that no man can love, but she changed after.

But I saw, said Maria, that he did not want her to live. That blackness came, the kind the stars fall into, and took over one of us. What was it now—more than a quarter of a century later that made Maria herself bring forward that impossible piece of news. Paul was a family man; married Ella two years later and danced so spectacularly at his wedding the villagers, all of us, felt it augured so well. A wedding in church with the bridegroom leaping and snapping his fingers—higher than the others, longer than the others; he had legs of steel in those days and one felt he could do anything. There was no denying it. The men murmured that he could take on the world. Paul's father boasted that his son had a brain like a great scientist.

He developed impeccable manners with his wife and her family. She was neat, sweet smelling, and smiling. Her hair always shone in the sun. We sensed that of all the families round about Paul's was a cut above our others. Agatha, the cursed, married earlier on, almost right after Maria's vision of her with Paul; right after the cigarette smoking, laughing, cursing of her; the ceremony itself took place on the other island before the Justice of the Peace; there were festivities, of course, but we simply swallowed a little brandy, ate apricots stewed in a syrup like honey and watched them toil away, Agatha both dull and bright like a face full of tears colored to us in a tight faded yellow dress—she had refused a new white one and had used her mother's who had similarly married not in white but in faint candlelight yellow—had taken little steps holding on to the arm of her new husband who had perhaps married, we thought, a little by accident. He had known her, of course, but to propose right after the whispers about her and Paul—on the heels of that night of experimentation. But then our villagers are not so fastidious. Alex didn't seem troubled in the least by the whispers. In fact, at the time, it had seemed that he had felt for her and wanted to marry to smooth things over, make things right—the way Joseph had thought about the All-Holy One after the visitation of the Spirit. And Agatha's parents had put by a little; we thought gypsy men were idle but Agatha's father was clever and hard working, fishing and leading the musicians at our festivals. Left her mother with something stored up for her. Dimitri was born exactly nine months after Agatha's marriage. With this Alex was no longer, if he ever was, put out. He wasn't present at the birth; men usually aren't in Our Saints' village. Paul had received a tongue lashing from his father because he had been so indiscreet as to arouse the neighbors' curiosity in what should be private matters. Paul smiled sneeringly a little when he passed them, but on the whole avoided Agatha and her husband.

When Paul married it was an elaborate affair; Paul's family was rich not like Anna but they had stores and abundance—a large house, orchards, goats that went half way up the mountain—they owned the supplies' boat and conducted the major buying and selling of goods in the village. Paul and his wife were the focus for years of our little village. There were rumors that Paul was working on something big. He had a studio made by his house--in a little tower overlooking village and sea. There, his wife said, he does his great and weighty cogitations that are so delicate. If he loses a thought the whole thing is ruined and he gets angry, smashes a dish, and storms back and forth from his tower, swearing that if he sees anybody come near, he'll leave for good. A few hours later maybe, Ella lays out dinner, not daring to call him, but he comes in always on time for the food, and asks in a voice like a lamb why he wasn't informed that the meal was ready?

Thus these remarkable cogitations that appeared in Paul some five years after their marriage, three years after little Paul was born, left Ella shaken and thin. Paul was still foremost in prostrations and offerings in church, in fishing, and in dancing. We believe that of all of us on the island, he looks most professional and smart. Calm and cool even on hot days—killer-cool, says Michael. One of these days, we know, he will make a great discovery, end up with a prize, an invitation to lecture before a crowd of university students on the other island. He did after all attend high school on the other island. One day when Ella hand in hand with little Paul leaned against the table in the tavern where she had come for him, her face white, Maria informed us that something had to be done. The village's old men came by stiff as rods and stood around him as the Paulines sat at the dinner table, little Paul staring, and said—this smashing of things can be heard by the neighbors.

Paul lowered his head. Ella shrunk closer to the child. But then he looked up and smiled his somewhat cold but still affable smile and said—if we disturb the neighbors, we must cease to do so.

Alex and Agatha meanwhile were living, we must confess, a blameless life. Agatha learned to do everything—cook, clean, wash, sew, embroider, fix broken furniture, redo lampshades; the house in the beginning, her grandfather's house, more or less a shack, had to be entirely renovated and Simon had fixed rotten beams and whitewashed while Magda had gone out on the roof, torn up the old where it was broken and put in the new. Paul used to say vulgar things of Magda but he was quiet to her face. He said he'd never hire a woman roofer. But in the end, there she was on his roof too, quietly replacing some tiles.

Agatha admired Magda; we know that they rarely spoke but it was as if when they did they said a few memorable things to one another and were great friends. Agatha told Magda: men think we want only love. Magda told Agatha: you'll never be given what you want. Somehow, you have to wrest it from God.

Then they would pass; go their separate ways—Agatha to raise Dimitri and now the little one, Jason, to breast feed and mend clothes, and fix chairs; to clean windows, to mop floors, to embroider covers and rugs, to clean the stove, and adjust the shower head that was always slipping to one side, to knit blankets for the winter, to repair various items that had been broken in ingenious ways—Magda to Leo to tear out of him the man she wanted, as the villagers said; but they were not sneering anymore, rather waiting to see if all her predictions would come true.

When Magda died, there was a hush. Paul said later that bad luck follows women who put themselves in the man's place. And Paul came out after, looking more and more perfect, dancing better than everyone at the festivals. Agatha and Anna were found together. Agatha now was nothing more than a low voiced talker in our gatherings, a sitter in dark corners. We heard that Alex and she were now always at odds. She said to Anna something like I think there is love still left in us. Anna said Agatha is the strong one and we all laughed at that.

Alex died and Dimitri grew into a man before we could breathe in and breathe out. His expression reminded the casual observer of Paul's cold, unapproachable face, but on closer look, it wasn't anything like. For one thing, Dimitri looked like a poet, not like a scientist; he was warm and gentle like a glass of red wine. The breadth of his forehead was greater than Paul's, his skin was darker, and his eyes dark and electric. He was white skinned but not white as Paul who was blue eyed and thin lipped. For another thing, in Dimitri we saw gypsy blood and Alex's philosopher-mind; there was no likeness to Paul—that was just an emotional mirage, the mixing up of opposites in mind—water and desert that happens when one stands too long in the blazing island sun. Dimitri had an inner life so intense that he brimmed over with it, while Paul was political, and hard, and had nothing so deep in his self. For another thing, Agatha informed us that she had ordered book after book for her son and he had devoured them like olives one after the other. Paul considered that you could have thoughts on your own without books—that it was almost unnecessary to read.

Simon had said to her: Send Dimitri to university. It was only friendly advice, but there were so and so feelings about Agatha and her family. She had a way with her, so depressed, and brooding, lonely and turned away—it wasn't quite what suited us. She must have gotten a lot of cold shoulders; she seemed so unable to let go of the past. And Dimitri too, spectacular though he was had a certain superior way of looking at us, after reading all those books, as if everything was packed into his head—all the truth of earth and heaven. There were times at the tavern when Maria heard the men—Peter, especially and Paul, but others as well, saying, just letting it out, that they wished that family were not with us. Then Peter would ask Paul—and so what about you?

Ah, they are not right for us.

But what about that time

And he would get angry. What time? You are dreaming. Nothing happened.

She has never been quite right up there—said Peter, pointing to his head.

Now it is late in the story. Agatha is behaving just a little bit differently. The men think it is something great—the old ones. We all think that she has somehow pulled herself together but deep down some of us think that it is unfair.

Agatha, the cursed one. We were ready to overlook the petty displays of temper and sullenness, the withdrawal, the tears in public—she was our littlest child in a way, not in physical stature but in importance in the village. Even Martha sometimes had more of a place—with the animals—and her mother was a strong, tearless kind of woman who would have been foremost in the village if her husband wasn't lazy and good for nothing and kept them poor. Agatha in a sense had her trial and there were ups and downs—and the worst kind of indignity looking all of her gypsy side standing outside with her children while Alex got ready to abandon her. She just didn't know; didn't sense which way is up in the village.

But even the priest heard of her cursing herself to hell—bargaining with God— myself for my son and then again as if she had two souls to perjure. And he took it back to the books and discovered, putting things together in his old grey head, though of course he was slightly addled at the time with so much poison in his brain that this might well be the unforgivable sin, the sin of all things against the Holy Spirit. And then wonder of wonders the babies stopped coming. Of course, said Zoe—'giver of life'! We are born by the Holy Spirit. It is he who sees to it that we come out alive not dead. But she didn't seem perturbed.

So for twenty years the old men gathered at the tavern and Maria served them wine and brandy, and one or two of them leant on their sticks and said well I am a sinner, I make no bones about it, but I haven't gone there...!—as if to say they hadn't quite step foot in hell, a place of no return, whereas Agatha had landed there with both feet. Anna said they are all self-righteous, pompous nobodies, and laughed at them. And do you think our god, she said, even though she had turned away, who is a kind god, will have half an ear for their say so? Our priest is nothing but an addle-minded fool. Of course, Agatha didn't sin against the Holy Spirit—what does she know about it? Wasn't it the spirit of utter self-sacrifice that was in her to offer herself for damnation in place of her faithless son? Ah, if only this village had half a grain of intelligence, let alone a mustard seed of faith! As I see it, she should be rewarded the highest paradise! But Anna was an unbeliever and so often away dancing at the nightclubs of Paris and London that these words weren't often heard.

And then, you see, the priest told the assembly of faces, for they had gathered together about this very point once when Agatha had just lost Dimitri to the big world, it is a matter of secret pride or presumption. Because how does she know she is going to heaven? That is a lifetime of struggle, a hair of difference distinguishes the saint from the demon. And it is those who assume that they have a place in paradise, although assuming gently, with the protection of the Theotokos is alright, but it becomes presumption when you make it into a bargaining chip—to save one soul from hell, I will take their place, their rightful punishment—so long as this wicked soul can have my place in heaven?

Several of the men and women, including Paul and Ella nodded with a large eyed, solemn look. Persons like that, said Paul, bring bad luck.

Yes, but, said Barbara, finding her voice, not liking the idea that her neighbor should be so black marked as it were—you see, the condemned soul was her own son. What if it had been Jesus?

What on earth do you mean? Are you suggesting…as if Jesus was a gypsy!

What if it had been Jesus, shouted Barbara, now really carried away, who had committed a terrible faithless act and Mary had stood or tried to stand in the way of God's wrath asking that it fall on her instead of him?

Some women show themselves to be really feeble minded, said our former priest, primly.

But Stavros was looking at his wife as if he was warmly, tenderly amused. We two are lovers, he said to her, shamelessly in the middle of the solemn meeting, and laughed. Lovers start with the mind, of course, he told the assembly. Why, did you think that love making began with the things between our legs? He asked Paul.

The meeting broke up. The priest looked himself more weary and afraid than bitter and self-righteous, according to Zoe. It was Anna exclaimed later, why a little thing, a laughable thing, but the village was all solemn about it and this infected even Barbara and we must admit even us, although we tend to think a little person, an insignificant person what use could God have with him in hell?

Agatha had been at the meeting. She had stared quietly ahead and had not spoken in her own defense. After, the rumor circulated that the island had lost its holiness because of her. At first, we tried to counter that—surely, the island had not lost its holiness because of one poor little mistake. It was after all no more than a dream, a nightmare—the kind where words all mean something entirely different… and perhaps, we thought, that was it—when these things happen it can only have one meaning: that the island had lost its holiness because of bad blood mixed with ours. For Paul had told us time and time again that seeing as her mother married a gypsy—making Agatha only half gypsy but still—and you couldn't marry a gypsy without something in the creation of the children going wrong, not to mention their souls and thus in all of us evil by its very nature…!—and that that explained Agatha. Besides most gypsies were Muslims, and therefore traitors to Christ. And he, oh, he, her father!—had been in church alright but one knows, through a whisper that flows, that he had a Muslim Bible. But I must admit for years we had been so out of step, as it were, with our old traditions—with Magda on the rooftops—there's another one! And she too wandered among the gypsies. Agatha didn't but what difference did it make? The gypsy family, half gypsy if you like still did their thieving and fortune telling, played their wild music. Agatha was a branch off the old root. And look the women wore scarves—and Agatha, but so did Barbara. But actually going among them, eating with them as a fourteen year old girl! No wonder Magda's destiny turned evil—though what a girl she was, beauty like magic! But Agatha's father, a poisonous presence on the island undoubtedly and the fact that he came back! No wonder the priest himself as we found out later—injecting himself, poisoning his blood, dissolving his very brain, killing his spirit. As Cleo said at one point and the old men later echoed—bah! If we are wild and rotted by blood and spirit--then let the tourists come. But Paul said—the answer is a thorough purgation, and whisked by with eyes set forward in determination. We knew it was Agatha, even though Agatha's cursing of herself came after Fr. Raphael's poison.

It appeared to us that Agatha at that meeting was her old raggedy, sullen self, hobbling out, bent backed as any witch and there had been several glances of aspersion cast in her direction; but the priest died and we were taken up with that—found dead a few weeks down the line with that poison by his side. And then the new priest, Father Isaac came in and we waited, wondering.

Father Isaac's penitence so inflamed us that we didn't know what to do-- having in our minds the image of him climbing up the hard stone steps of the mountain on his skinny knees for days and days, and all of us in an uproar, half wanting to expel him for first the 'scientific spirit', then the madness and the holiness—we were boggled— how could they mix? Science and holiness—from flesh to God—we suspect some lying tale of the world;—we, missing the syrupy voice of the old priest who had come from the old monastery in spirit, although the new priest had also physically walked those halls—he our old priest so properly preoccupied with hell, we, half wanted to see what the new might say and if he had found a way if not sanctified by the ancients, at least, a reasonable way to live with our goats and tomatoes and our purple, crabbed little vines and assure us of a victorious death;—we, the same we, half cracked up for wanting our holiness back, simply don't know when Agatha started walking erect and like there was life in her legs and something we can only call liquid grace in her hips. We watched her and didn't watch her for the beauty in her, the danger in her. The watching must have stopped a minute and then in a flash, she was there, glorious like a young tree in full spring leaf.

We must have felt a little like birds on their way South—the call had come, we had seen it; where were we going? We had in our mind an idea of blessed and free—and Agatha looked like the incarnation of all that. Brought smiles to our lips despite ourselves and yet, and yet: there were those who thought beyond the loveliness of the rolling buttocks on the woman, the holding herself erect like distinction with that inward curve in the small of her back, to the fact that that glory was hidden evil; they couldn't get beyond a woman who had damned herself and not repented for it! For ourselves, we were headed only back to the old traditions, in the end, but with now in a woman, evil and all, a sense of going beyond to a magical land, we were driven blessed to the early land of the island, when the group that had witnessed the resurrection, crossed the sea singing, landed dancing. It couldn't be that Agatha's evil made us better in soul! Some like Nico said that our beatific dancing place was non-existent; he was following in the footsteps of the absent Dimitri who had read a thousand books and could whip anyone verbally around the village with questions,

questions that shook us, that told us in the end that faith was not faith, Jesus not Jesus, even that God could crumble like a house in an earthquake and fall with pieces of Him here and there—a nose, or a finger sticking ominously out of the dust. But we still held fast to that magical land—there were stories of so many cures, of a dust that held the light captive in it, and the blue that reminded one of angels in chariots racing across the sky. Where had it gone? There were still fragments of it here and there, a crystal in among the stones, bits of blueschist in the rubble. There was holy land of course but there were also holy lands, offspring of this one place on earth. Our island was one, we thought the one—translocated by God, planted in this sea –for Jerusalem had fallen and was now a tourist trap-! Our holy land burst white with sunlight, like a blossom—ah it was rare that heaven was anything but blue above it, a temple of blue perfect without a crack. And then like white linen soiled, always a shame to see, it had been ruined. Not physically; but then, again, even there. There were fewer flowers, more dust. So many blamed Agatha. It was natural, we think; she had had her head down always in those days, she with her moody, intelligent son— hadn't the Lord warned us about intelligence?-- her eyes that had been bleared with misery for so long, her back bent horribly like a witch's—bad luck for any place, we thought. And after the old priest, Father Raphael, of course, drugged to the gills, but still-- revealed to us that no one could do as she had done without sure damnation!

And what was she doing, it seemed like days after, but in reality it was seven years—swaying into the little throng with a bright blue scarf on her head with gold spangles sewn into it holding her head up as if she was wearing a crown, a face like the crust of new baked bread—golden brown from the sun and gypsy blood, erect as a baby sitting up? Walking with the kind of highness… as if she lived in a realm of fragrances.

Maybe she found her way out of hell, said Simon, but he pulled wisecracks, mon- keying around in his mind even about serious things.

Hey said Peter, turning to him—we were all at the tavern; it was one of those slow Sundays—we've seen her trudging over to your place quite a lot at all hours. Is it your magic hand by any chance that has pulled her out of the dumps?

Simon's smile never falters. His eyes glitter a bit like the sea with the sun on it. Oh, she comes and goes as she pleases, said Simon; so does everybody. I've never even locked my door. Who would think of it? I've no secrets.

It's been a long time since you've been with a woman, growled Peter. And then they all turned on him—what has it been, cough up the truth: twenty, thirty years? An impossibility, muttered Stavros.

Yes, so, said Simon, leaning forward and adjusting his backseat in the chair. An impossibility. But I've done it. I've gone without a woman for thirty years.

What did it dry up and fall off? Is that why Agatha comes to you less and less—now that she's found out? Or are you lying? Said Timos. Better to have found yourself in your old age, said Stavros.

Thus, they all went away thinking that Agatha essentially brought her ass to Simon, despite all his protestations—anyway he made them all with that strange crafty smile of his so that you knew he was lying—and that that is what changed her.

No, said Anna, later; Simon's a monk in disguise—a true monk; he has a cunt in the seat of his soul that's sealed up like the seventh seal reserved for the marriage in heaven.

Agatha said, I've kissed him on the brow. More about him I don't know. I never thought once about him as a man for all that he's made me sweat dancing. And he looks at me like he would look at a pot or a painting of his, tenderly, craftily with warmth in his old yellowish and sparkling black eyes.

Some of the village men might have said it—so that is why, Agatha like any woman rears herself up like a serpent, wiggling and waggling, once she's got it from a man. Witch dancing! But there was something so lofty about Agatha now; she saw them as if at a distance whispering about her. There was a stone or two thrown; in the end, our village didn't take to the idea of Agatha coming out of her hole so independently, as it were, very kindly. And the assumption that she was of all things—Simon's slut—opened the door for them to say wicked things and throw the stone or two. And Agatha wept but she continued erect and strong and the village had to admit that something other than love had gotten into her, maybe derision!—since love is so easy to break.

Was it a dream? Or were those men and women surrounding her house one night just after midnight with fire in their hands at the ends of long sticks—phantom like creatures with shadows for faces? Did she go up on to the roof and stand there and see—a sort of grotesque cartoon—as the worst sorts of things in life are— suddenly among them Robert and Catherine horrified, absurdly, calling out at the people to stop? And Barbara stood by screaming, Stavros waving his hands and Nico standing in front shouting to the people would you really burn flesh and blood, your own flesh and blood, as if there was meeting point between philosophy and human feeling? One of those who came with the others Body of Christ to this island in the bodies of our ancestor? And then the priest arriving late in his slippers with Max shuddering behind him, holding the Eucharistic cup on high in his hand, saying—I will refuse communion for an act of human slaughter....moreover this soil, which has been pure and holy would be stained with murdered blood and may that never be forgiven you. I know your faces and the names! You have been baptized every last one of you. For shame!

But she has been a curse on us, one man, or was it phantom, hissed. Gypsy-blooded, our babies not born....

Idiots to believe that Agatha is the reason. More likely evil like this....

We believe that an anathema has brought about God's curse on us, Father; what do you believe? I believe, bellowed the old man— that Father, Son and Holy Spirit have blessed her, the words were shot out hot and furious and the man, or spirit, writhed and twisted.

But some man with a towel thrown over his head cried out—come away, come away—Paul, judging by the voice. And by two in the morning, all was eerily still. Lights were on, she and Jason were sitting at the dinner table drinking warm brandy. Agatha and Jason were both trembling—both mad as hell;—Agatha that they would dare; Jason at the transformation in his mother that had started the rage.

In any case, dream or no dream, the next day was Sunday and at the liturgy the priest substituted the regular Gospel reading with the reading of the woman taken in adultery. And his voice rang out, stern and beautiful, some of us thought like Christ's: Neither do I condemn you. He looked at Agatha and Agatha for the first time in a number of weeks bowed her head. Almost everyone in the church except for the few of us old women, thought it was an admission of guilt and shame.

Anna went out with Agatha later, walking erect and proudly, saying it is all such utter foolishness. We have no dignity in this village—people spying, making comments, coming up with fictions and fantasies about one another. Of course, Simon is still a virgin. That is Simon. It is the way he is now. Oh once, he was a little different; but you know how it is; in old age, you are granted a second nature. And at the next meeting, that evening, in the tavern, Anna went, stood up and said to the crowd gathered there murmuring; I know you are all fools just as Jesus knew those old horny bastards who had spied on that poor woman in love were fools. Agatha goes to Simon for some important guidelines. That man will never touch a woman. He thinks women are disgusting in bed. At this the others all fell silent. Well then, said Peter, solemnly, we've judged when we shouldn't have judged. Ah, said Paul, it was a mistake. But it shows you we still have that good, old, traditional righteousness in us. Doesn't Christ say that the angels will divide the just from the wicked?

I wouldn't be surprised if angels really do come for those who are despised, retorted Anna, in the same way Christ did.

Several of the men opened their mouths and inhaled and then gently exhaled and looked at the ground. Yet it seemed to them the very reason that she had brought that instant of holiness to them, that startling vision of female glory, constituted the very pressing reason why Agatha should be punished, something that they had grasped earlier, even before she had been seeing going in that flagrant way to Simon, the virgin's house in the morning, regularly, seen by Martha and by Paul and others; ah, one can understand a person, that is the point, here; it clicks in the mind—the reason for her curse; and no one can say they didn't put up with her for a long time for she had married, had sons and one was solid—Jason. It seemed to them clear that she should be punished—oh abundantly clear; what with the sign from God—the babies that weren't coming. Not of one couple who could go to the other island and get fertility treatments, but of five couples! Now that defied science! That was an act of God. But now it was hazy; they were losing their grasp on it. It suddenly seemed as if she was just Woman walking down the road. There was nothing in the least extraordinary, although women were always devious. But one had to say in the end-- that she had rediscovered her beauty, and every woman had a right to. Ah, but they say that that is exactly how the devil comes—not of course the way they used to think in the poor, the sick, the ugly, no, but in those who suddenly stood upright, beautiful as the day—walking erect, as if she had in her head a country to rule and this one day, yes, simple as that. One day the old men had seen her; she who had been bent and aged prematurely was suddenly straight and ageless. They knew no miracle would come to a woman cursed, who had, after all sinned against the Holy Spirit. No, now the devil was deceiving them.

And when they cease condemning you to hellfire, said Anna, kissing Agatha, one noontime in her kitchen, you'll be courted.

Agatha supposed the village really had almost burned her to death on Tuesday midnight because in came Catherine and Robert, a little breathlessly, Wednesday morning to check on her—that is, to take her by the wrists and look into her eyes.

I swear, she said to them, softly, that it seemed like a dream, a nightmare. I don't know what gets into me; sometimes, things that happen—I can't remember after whether or not they were dreams or reality. And once in a while during an event, it seems to me that it may be a dream. I can tell you, I don't even know how I got to the top of my house. And then I heard an uncanny noise like I have never heard—of Jason crying and pleading. I felt sad after—my poor son, I wanted to say to him; but already things had changed. We sat all mad in that kitchen, glaring and hating—Jason, me and I, everybody.

Eventually she had to say to them—things get a little like that in this village. A little bit passionate and out of hand and dreamy, the everyone is mad as hell. Of course, when it comes to flesh and blood....There have been a few near murders—nothing real, though. Nothing happened, nothing, she assured them. Could we be called Holy Island, could we be Saints' Village if there was cold-blooded murder? No, of course not. And you know these islands, sunny, everyone walking slowly in the sun, eating their onions, cheese, fish, wine; everyone dying so old and placid. In the end, Agatha had to soothe Catherine and Robert as if they were children, she told Anna. But they went away, offering their services—their villa as a place of refuge. Robert had a gun, they told her; a little antiquated, said Catherine, but sure. A gun? Said Agatha, and smiled as if she had had an idea. What a thought! But of course we have the services of the police on the other island—which is so big compared to ours. All I have to do is dial on the telephone and they come on one of those fast motorboats; they come with their dogs. At least they did when the other priest died.

One of us found out the drugs that he was unfortunately injecting himself with, dialed the police and they came over—but the dogs ran into the church—it was awful to think of—ran upstairs to the priest's quarters and smelled all around his dead body. The police searched the entire room with gloves on, and the dogs, big, gold black hairy beasts, German Shepherds, they call them, sniffed around and they found, among various old theological books, packets of white powder. The police kept asking the kinds of questions only the priest could answer. And of course he was dead and the dead tend to say nothing, nothing at all, which was quite irksome to the police. Anyway, they had guns. And they kept firing questions into the quiet throng of lookers on as if they were shooting them with their mouths. I think it was a little to intimidate us. Perhaps they thought we would become a sort of hot spot for people who took that white powder, seeking release, from some sweat and pain. I thought it really rather sad that they would take away the one refuge from pain— would have taken away—for he was dead…of course our dead priest said things about me too and there was a time I thought him an old bastard but then I thought how crazy to live this short life so twisted with fear. And I've read that those powders and the other potions he injected himself with have almost a magical power on the brain that casts out all fear but substitutes a kind of wild evil.

Of course like all witchery, said Catherine, drugs can turn quite evil on you.

But there are hints of it here and there. Father Raphael himself tried to cast a spell on me I think, telling me I had committed the sin of sins and could not obtain forgiveness. Wasn't that a kind of spell, all things considered? A psychological spell.

My son Dimitri smiled when I said this and then, his face frowned, terribly; I think he said something like this priest is obsessed, Mother; everyone seeks release from this life and everyone fears death but to say that a good, kind soul like you because you belted out a strange kind of bargain plea with the Almighty-- and for that reason, only— was definitely going to be tortured eternally! What kind of rational mind is left in that old man?

Between the fairy magic and the reading of Scriptures he had brought himself into these unreal obsessions, I think, said Agatha. For there are certain books, you see, and the Bible is one, that will cast a spell on you—so you see, along with the drugs…they say he was seeing demons, miserable, fat, grinning monsters—before he died.

Odd, said Catherine; I've never quite read the Bible. I suppose I shall give it a shot. But you are alright? She asked, putting her hand on Agatha's shoulder. Oh, said Agatha, you know it all in the end flows away like water. My own mother told me that. What if it is all you know, all this sorrow and pain, tragedy and torture, in the end just resolved in an utterly beautiful experience? Not this life, but death, death itself. I am resolved to die so that it is a perfect experience—a kind of stepping out on to rain.

I often think of dying, said Catherine. Not such a popular way of conceiving of living, but more common than not.

Then they were gone. Agatha didn't quite know how it happened. They had neither sat down and eaten the lemon curd, which she offered, which stood in a jar on her white clothed table, nor taken the little cups filled with coffee. They had come and had had this strange fearful, fearless conversation, which went in all directions, as Agatha later put it to Anna, and then they had gone off, dissolved out of the circle of seeing and hearing. The only real thing left between that yesterday and today was a little can of kerosene that she discovered three days later around the corner on the windy side of her house in among the weeds.

We are a weak and helpless people. When we have our passionate moments, our furies, driven by god knows what force, we calm down after; we come out of it like children out of a nightmare—crying for a while, maybe, but then all rinsed and cleansed with water-like sleep and sweet forgetfulness. It gets put in perspective, the fury and the ghastly, flaring anger. People like Paul and some of the old men—say yes, well, it was not right but then again—what were we to do? We thought...

In other words, the island went to sleep and woke up after, went to sleep and woke up, and went to sleep and woke up and after-- the episode with the burning sticks around Agatha's house where a group of men, known on the island, were going to burn to death Agatha and her family was put to rest. The tortured shock washed away with the slow time of the island, the lunch meals, the brandies at five in the afternoon, the talking and re-talking, the scorn of Maria for them—hooligans, she shouted and hooligans, again, and the priest with that strange convulsed Max at his side, sternly rebuking us; but in all this there was the effect of water on a hole in the sand—the memory, reality, began to wash away; the grisly attempt— a scar, on the landscape of the usually serene island was filled up with the talk, the lunches, the brandies, until gradually, inexplicably, it turned into a mere white scratch on our consciousness like a sun blanched bone.

The men, guilty and innocent but fantasizing guilt, and truly guilty in their minds, were reshuffled; none of those that were at Agatha's house that night with torches of fire were seen on the streets—except out of the corners of eyes, creeping away on the side to their homes, which appeared now to be not in the forefront, on the beach, except for Paul's but in the center to the back, towards the forest. Agatha was amazed at how quickly the 'story' was forgotten, the hooligans became the one or two quiet fishermen, sitting in their close circles expounding their various little faiths—apricot 'wedding' brandy, the unending fish, the steady white-white moon; when she walked pass them so sober and quiet, yet somehow vibrating wrath, she began to feel eerily as if she was perhaps cursed and they had only acted naturally in wishing to expunge her, to burn her up, to leave of her body, her cursed body vivid with inexplicable desire, nothing but ashes. It was as expected as leaves turning. I guess, she thought, I am their natural enemy—Woman who didn't quite fit in—who was supposed by their order of nature to be bent, but who had instead walked by erect. How she had predicted something in her heart when Father Raphael, poor soul, had in a way allied with her—calling her damned without hope, yes, and the village had reacted, but hadn't he thought in his heart of hearts that he too for some strange magical, mad reason was damned without hope? He had wished to carry her to the pinnacle of spiritual experience, which is always inverted. No that was an excuse, it went back further.

Woman alone crying each afternoon in the pale sunlight, wearing black skirts as if for mourning and one brown headscarf just to indicate that she was not a widow yet; how they had woven a web of widowhood around her like cruel spiders! No she was not a widow, had a man, a girl and a boy. The boy had gone off island—roved on the other island, a little wild, playing the violin, with long hair and dirty feet in old worn down sandals; then sickened, died. And the girl had grown—oh joining in, she too—the grandmothers caressing her along with the others, although some shaking their heads—had eaten the soft apricot candy, coated with confectioner's sugar and delectable and thought when I grow up I will dance like the sun. But they had not stayed—and they had been, just smilers, turning away from her; and then she had thought and I will dance to the song of the sun and she had gone with the burning resolve of youth to the one who could dance, the head dancer, the acrobat and prancer. Had come back understanding, not in words, but in stabs of pain—the mother widow in black who blocked the afternoon sun. Holding in her mind the boy, dead and gone.

Man kind, worshipping a different God. A little bit bent before his time. Played the violin and all sorts of instruments—ever sweet, the girl would remember. She lingered at his knee in the festivals, long dark hair, a look in her face as if she could hold the world in one hand. That is what fathers are there for to put the globe into their hands like an enormous apple. Ah, they played dirty tricks—paid him less than the others at the festivals; the charity, which was supposed to help pay to renovate the little house—like the others, colored with brightly painted shutters, actually meant in the end that he had to pay a large amount and work and work and never get a break. Called an oversight. Of course, there were the stories going around that he and his daughter…Stories that he had other wives—all this because he worshipped a different God or God by another book. As for his having gypsy blood—blood is all one thing—but there were those who thought he was trash for his blood and for his book.

And still, said Anna to Agatha sternly, there is no reason except for foolish superstition. Superstition is the degrading of faith—when one or two elements fall into the hands of crude, vulgar men. It is entirely dependent on you now, which it usually is—the victim of the people carries the entire hope of the world in the end; it is you who must rise up…and Anna proceeded to portray a woman of dignity getting up from a table, just that and Agatha saw dancing again as she had with the purple ribbon—a vision, the hairy female body like a new silver wedding, like the soft rain that falls when the west wind blows. In a way, Anna said, the Father was right—there are demons all around us with sleek porcine flesh. And it is all a matter of cutting the pig-fat.

Cutting the pig-fat? Said Agatha

They want to destroy —see here, the woman at a table, with china, delicate tea cups with their lovely handles, the fingers of her children resting there. They want to smash all this even the fingers of the children for they have surrendered to the scar, the untruth, or partial truth, therefore an untruth— an actor's world losing connection to the whole in favor of the delusional self's world—a world in which the self, the prerogative of the stronger is in control cutting tenderness, and love—Not only that, they revel in the bits of china flying in the air, blood on the white table cloth, children crying and pleading. You must rise up dancing with your vivid alien body and with you the scene like magic will be restored. I believe that.

Anna and Agatha were sitting at the dining table talking over coffee. Anna had come dressed in gray, more formally than usual; she was on her way to the other island that afternoon to see her son. Agatha was thinking, drifting off, coming back— in and out of the conversation.

Thinking back on it, what Father Raphael had once announced—that is, that she was damned like himself— a strange kind of love actually, she realized, out of his poor poison filled head—before his death and Dimitri's departure and her seven years of toil when the men hadn't noticed— to now the sudden all-eyes-on-her, and then after the admiration yanked out of them like an unwanted orgasm, the ruffians that had only then crept out of the woodwork, or come in from somewhere on the hillsides, sought to kill her and then dissolved again—she conceived that all of this was not so blameworthy as that night of police and dogs in the church. She could never forget their muddy tracks all over the nave and by the altar as they came around it to pass through the narrow door and go up the stairs to find Father Raphael's body. That was a horror. An obliteration of the holy. And it was all as if not one of them, these law enforcement officials thought for one moment that their great wet boots and their grisly golden and black dogs would leave heavy marks of mud on their dainty, antique, white plastered church with the slender Jesus in pain and dancing. She thought it the worst crime committed even today, years later. Paul had been on their side—babbling in a low voice of all that he had known about Father Raphael whose cause against her he had so ardently espoused. And the village had trusted: Paul was there. Paul and the village hardly noticed the mud marks. And Agatha had cleaned them alone. Yet, I suppose, she said to herself, that such is sin in God's eyes. Thoughtless, cold, grisly sin: that I or he, for instance, would trample in to a delicate place even without my absurd bargaining, thinking heaven was in the end all a matter of a desperate trick that made one overlook! I can see why Father Raphael with his distorted brain, dying so long, would rant and rave. And I as if to rub in the horror, upcoming horror doing it all over again after he was gone—shouting out, wishing hell on myself to rescue one son and the other. The fire I was in, inside, I think hell wouldn't have hurt.

The years of Agatha grey, bent and crushed, were years when she was, according to the men, like Paul, at least that is what we heard, rumors flying—that sort of thing—at least in her place. Then there was the year of her cursing, and her wickedness began to affect the land. How can one curse oneself, said Paul; it must be a sign not of the great sinner souls, but of one soul fallen into such corruption…She is an old woman at thirty six, ten years ago, husband almost left her for her black moods, came back only to die, and that in itself…—and her children sucked at that breast!— Jason is man enough thanks to the grace of God, but Dimitri with his ideas! She is the sign and substance of our lost holiness. Babies aren't born; Paul said that we had gone and lost our holiness for some reason—but we know he meant Agatha and her cursed body, sign and cause.

Anna said, well, well, and he has something on his mind, doesn't he? This man with his political ambitions. He would never say—a curse is on us—he is far too modern. But he will use some people's foolish superstitions to make them act.

It is all your uprising, though, said Anna, softly, caressing Agatha's face—your straight back, the luminosity of your face these days—that is what they—he!—can't stand, really. Grace rising up out of corruption! Well, well. But you seem so determined to let all antagonisms go.

I believe I am to live and die here, said Agatha, simply. And I have a race to run—I can't be burdened, weighed down.

Yes, said Anna; I am all ears.

To rise like the sun, know it with my brain, the pit of my stomach. I read in the Bible, once opening to a page at random and letting my eyes fall: Rise up my love, my fair one, and come away! That I think is the whole of living, and living, real living, eternal living. To come away from bitterness, envy, and wrath—the taste of ash. I had a dream like a ladder—a hairy monster of a woman with purple ribbons, so purple they chimed in my eye-tongue going up and up.

You lack one thing, said Anna.

What is that?

A bridegroom. For that passage is a love song.

Agatha turned away. I measured out my compliance—marriage, children—day after day. I received, it is true, a certain amount of protection. The village, she groaned slightly, left me alone. Now I feel that I'd almost rather be-- would you believe it? An astronaut! There is a space station and I can't help but feel they, those live and intelligent men and women out there, know something more than we about being on an island, lost somewhere to the world.

No, said Anna, an expression of sensing the pain of another suddenly taking the place of her severe, set face and making it wonderfully fine, and Agatha looking up thought suddenly that even a hair makes a difference in the universe—imagine the pain of a pin prick magnified; you know the truth, she said, softly, of what it is like to be on a remote island with all the outdated implements of civilized life, the old washing machines and refrigerators, the thirty watt bulbs—out in the desert places of the ocean.

I know and there is something still about this place; I have my house, my son, my other one coming home. I am not sure it is even love, oh, sometimes, yes, but there is forever a certain attraction....

To what?

To Dimitri. He reminds me of the island—all that is beautiful here, all the secret knowledge that is the sun. I think somehow that he belongs here—in this lost place or where it's as if home is narrower and narrower-- a hall going up, Agatha had gotten a little dreamy and was speaking as if Anna was and wasn't there, a listener, only, and she telling this ear and wide eye and brain finally those heart-felt words she'd held inside for so long, but which, when she spoke them, came all differently—the word 'lost' when she might have meant 'forgotten' the week before, the image of the narrowing hall—when she wanted to say that she had a long journey still to go, not a hall to toil on into a larger structure, home and trap, but a precise path bearing infinite expanse to infinite expanse.

You have an attraction to your son, smiled Anna; ha! Few mothers would say these sorts of things.

Of course, I have an attraction to Dimitri—he is life to me, the way no one else is; his bitter olive eyes would see the small minded prejudice and stink of hatred— the whole island would have if they allowed themselves. Jason was jealous and Dimitri didn't help the situation—riled him up somehow. Of course, I can see Jason wielding a knife, the blade against someone's throat; his arm that it seems he hardly uses, except to fish with, suddenly rearing up with the knife, and the days and days, months and months, years and years, of just being in this place—still as a stone, heavy with the presence in him, suddenly all collected, and all projected with that knife so that it isn't even enmity so much as attachment via knife blade to something beyond this tragedy of small sameness. Strange, you might say, but Jason must strike because he doesn't talk. I am not sure that he ever learned many words. Oh, words, yes to get by—from one place to another in a crowd; but not words to make things come alive in heart and soul. Whereas Dimitri the mute one, who for six years never used a word, knew words, many words, words close and laden as blood. He could fish you out of the darkness, mind and soul, with words, I always thought. And then the sight of him, as if all those words come together in a ball of electricity—it gets to me, sparks up in my body.

What did you feel about Katrina?

Oh, Agatha shrugged, a woman not of his choosing. Young man, hormones—that sort of thing. He began talking and coming out of his shell. But he didn't want to marry her. She was more useful than intriguing to him. Katrina sat and longed for him for quite some time on those bluish nights when the men and women got together at their house—her father and mother, quite a love match between them, they used to invite all sorts to their house and it was lively with the clatter of dishes, the clink of glasses and chatter. But there was news in a letter early on from Dimitri that he had found a woman over there, Agatha tossed her head. Over there, meant the world and since it was all around, she simply indicated a point beyond her little physical sphere to mean where her son lived, loved, lay.

Are you jealous?

Not really. I think that woman just touches on the shell of him—beautiful, I'm sure, but the little truly naked piece not skin but soul—the innocent, the wonderer—I almost believe is meant for no woman, or at least, not in the sense you mean. What must capture him there, at the true piece, is a fellow. Fellow day laborer, fellow thinker, the other mouthpiece. I almost think it could be a man. Love, deep love even—and if it went there…you understand my drift—it would be largesse, generosity of spirit, nothing lurid. And perhaps one wouldn't be enough. There would be a circle of beloveds and then I among them, no difference really from all the rest—love making with our glances, our deference to one another's bodies in the way.

You're dreaming. But I don't think badly of you or of him.

What condemns love is wrong faith. The one questions the soul, but the other the truth, so my husband used to say.

One thinks to believe in God is easy, he said—one must merely hate the devil. After all, the devil's existence is almost unmistakable. One can point—a turning point, a cutting off: there he is, there! And so they haul in a poor wretch caught committing adultery or homosexual love and throw stones—thinking to crush the life out of him, the one true light, is to crush the devil. But the devil is far subtler than they—in every hating eye, every murderous thought of the stone-throwers —he lives powerfully still, lives far more robustly than in the victim of their hate. And so, while the crowd is busy stoning the glass eye of the mirrored deceiver, away he walks singing, their small minds, and souls, in his bag like so many potatoes. Singing, I tell you, having gathered a large harvest of the blindest and most foolish—those deluded by piety itself.

I have been told I was 'an accomplice' to evil for my one moment of laughter at the crime. I haven't repented for that laughter, I can tell you. It saved my soul. For I thought, on the cross there in that squalid teenager's room for three hours-- and the cross is a vile, vicious thing, cruel and hateful—what an absurd little half man is my crucifier. But the wounds were real; they were fatal wounds. I gained the knowledge that I was of the dead margin of the village—must truly be a cursed person. No one was for me. I myself even thought I was a beast. You might imagine a naked, hairy creature picking lice off her head. And so I would have been had not my husband, who had his little nobility, you know, come along and hauled me away! Next thing you know, I was pregnant. But it was not my choice, no, not to have those children, not to be a mother. I wanted to kill the criminal who had deceived me, my body wanted it; this was my holy temple—this desire to kill and I let myself feel and I danced from the feeling later.

I worked like a machine raising my children, until one day, not long ago, I looked at them—fell in love with him, not the young one who hardly seems to move during the day, who lives alone despite the people around him for sheer pity; but the older one, whom I first imagined with horror!—for sudden attraction, attraction of the mind. He fed me and nursed me imaginatively –loved me like one would the sun—almost with awe and joy—it was as if his heart knew how I had wanted to kill him and he was drawn to me like water down a drain. He taught me that this was not the only world, but that there were worlds under the sea, among the stars, inside people and he had words to go along with them—galaxy, consciousness—but he used those rarely. It was not my husband, who married me because I was little and would not dance—who had the romance in him, but my older son whose birth was agony who is my beloved. It is said that my husband at the tavern swallowed a lot of insults over me; ultimately, it agitated us. But my son was smart as a whip; he swept through the village cracking insults back, once he began talking; then he appeared with Katrina, the good family's daughter, in the village tavern—she recoiling, turning green before the hairy, hoary old men—and he with his arm around her, forcing her down into a white plastic chair and the men, seeing him, sitting beside as gracefully as an angel and beautiful as a horse whip, the most beautiful of all the young men, couldn't help but smile slightly; and there was no insolence. Yes, I was glad of my one time laughter --one isn't desperate, and groveling, a beast, but a creature of God...so why submit? One prefers justice and tenderness. That is what my son taught me and yet I taught it him first, a long time ago without knowing it.

You must know more than any of us about real living said Anna, thoughtfully, and yet you have spent your life here raising children, washing curtains.

Anna left leaving behind as she always did a little wake of perfume that Agatha was content to inhale. She was like one of those heirlooms kept in tissue paper that always smell sweet and delicious of antiquity like the oils of embalmment. Anna must be, thought Agatha, well over ninety; she has gotten to the point where she can look on life with a smile of amusement coiling on her lips—past the long lugubrious middle age when one regrets one's evil and the endless list of youthful things lost. It was almost as if she saw a theater before her, rather poorly acted, and it was as if she knew or they knew that reality was far better, more imaginative, beautiful, stunning. She had emptied herself of all her desires in the end by indulging in them: three husbands, one after the other, one doesn't know how many lovers, friends in Paris, London, Athens and Rome, dancing from dusk 'til dawn, reading periodicals during the day, one after the other, which she was so fond of and having guests to talk about them at night—intellectuals, artists, journalists flocked to their house for there had always been lobster and oysters, champagne, pasta with truffle sauce and other delicacies varying from night to night. Anna had told her that she had even started an amateur theatrical company in the hills of Delphi, and that she had once engaged a martial arts' master to teach her Karate. Her life is replete, thought Agatha, my life is poor. And yet nothing tangible had come out of Anna's richness of life except this smile of amusement and the friendship that she, Agatha, treasured. Of course, Anna's wealth, which stunned the village in the end—little Anna, whom no one remembered now, but who was said to have been an ordinary girl with a yellow dress that she wore day to day to help her mother in the kitchen—is what kept the village from daring to ostracize her along with Agatha for spending so much time in her company—for being seen, as it were with that old gypsy. Anna who turned around one summer and married a shipowner who sent cruises to Norway and Alaska, the Caribbean, Morocco and then went off for a honeymoon lasting two years to Florence, and traveled on after that, came back to the island only in her mid-sixties and spent her time unpacking extraordinary things—paintings, pottery, and reading wonderful magazines, hiring village folk to install the latest plumbing—they had just built the sewer lines—and then got to know this strange girl with darker skin, and fierce eyes. Got to know—well, her eye was on Agatha before she was even conscious that she was wronged. Anna heard of stories by letters when she was in distant lands, Agatha along with the other one—the beautiful one, Magda, how they were both wild-- Agatha a Rom by origin, Magda sojourning on the other island in the Rom encampment, to learn from them. And the way the two of them, something she gathered from the letters, Magda, the beautiful big one, towering above Agatha, the little one with the look of raw, passionate anger, used to linger together a little as children—that Anna used to love.

Anna had told her all this, and Agatha had said—yes, Magda. I cried when she died. There was a time, when we were just little chicks that we were like sisters. But she wanted a man; I didn't. I wanted a sovereign self. We went our separate ways— she 'to prepare,' she said—she was nine. I was seven and I, I said, 'to climb mountains alone.' Anna looked at her, and did you climb mountains? No, not even this cliff to the sisters as she did, not then. Do you know I had never been up—all those years until I went running after Dimitri lost in the cloud-colored horizon across the sea...? But Magda prepared, climbing the mountain to receive holiness, eating magical herbs, reading the stars. She ended up for a few years becoming the village magic woman; no harm could touch her. The villagers went from running after her to trying to kill her, because she was the devil, to cozying up to her because it seemed she had a life like a charm. But she didn't care because she knew exactly when and how she would die.

It didn't seem so shocking to me that a man on a rooftop would try to kill her. I almost felt that I lifted my head, you know how my head I used to hold bowed way down—and said oh, yes, of course, even the beautiful ones, so beautiful that another thus might never be—get the same treatment from these people. These people—meaning our neighbors—are blockheads, lumps of humanity that may do all sorts of evil if the faithless spirit takes them. But in the end, she had them all bowing down to her as if she was holy! I saw in my own case—how it was not impossible… Not that I want to be worshipped as a saint—but for one glorious moment to take back the old free sweet body covered with my lacy soul that they tore and took from me in one evil evening and then hour after hour.…

Anna and Agatha had had this conversation when Agatha was still bringing up children. Anna was in her seventies and she and Agatha subsequently had clung together becoming friends. They were friends because Anna scoffed at the superstitions and prejudices of the island folk, and because Agatha loved her for her very tender and very imperious scoffing with the soft sweetness of a child who must by nature love. They were free with one another, free to come and go with each other—although Anna was exceptionally private in reality-- to become moody and argumentative, family-style, with one another, to press faces together in the moonlight. Agatha didn't quite believe as Anna believed that life consisted of increasing one's pleasure as far as one was able. She thought that life was about getting closer and closer to the truth. For to Anna, Agatha thought, it was a matter of self at the center of the circle and then, of course, throwing away the whole thing with oneself, death—with a laugh. But Agatha was not sure that self was the center of the circle. But the delicious, irreplaceable thing about Anna was that she was just unimaginably sweet to Agatha and that it was indescribably pleasurable to love her.

As it turned out, Dimitri didn't come home that summer. Nor the next. It was not until three summers had passed from when his second suggestion that he would be returning that he wrote and said that he had packed his bags. Agatha was living all this time as closed up as a clam. Except for Anna and Katrina and sometimes Catherine, the American, she didn't see anybody. She seemed to barely even open the windows, summer evenings. But there was no question that she was flourishing; she often wore jeans and a tight clinging shirt, instead of her old black skirt, and her thighs, from dancing and leaping, filled the pants' legs like the flesh of Eve in the hollow of the hand of God; you could see the beauteous curves of her hips and the arch in the small of her back. In addition to everything else she was doing, she procured a small oil press and collected the olives on her property that would have gone to waste and started to make olive oil. In the fall of the year before Dimitri came home, after supplying Anna and Katrina and Catherine with jars' full, she decided to take some oil to Leo—out of simple good will.

He had been living alone in his house that stood separately on the hill for a number of years as a recluse. People said he had completely forgotten how to take care of himself. He lived like a pig with garbage strewn around the house—bottles and orange rinds, paper bags, rotting fish carcasses. In fact, Agatha noticed a foul smell as she approached the house and half expected that Leo would rise up like a swimmer suddenly out of all the trash she saw lying round about. She had an instinct of love for him—just out of sorrow –for it seemed to her that here was life lived as a tragedy, and she knew of his addictive inclination. She called out to him several times and heard in the end a faint voice recognizing her, the sound of febrile pleasure, and the sound of old age. Leo emerged after she had waited another ten minutes, in his underwear, his hair tousled, his mouth slathered over with saliva. He had been sleeping, he said. What at eleven in the morning? Asked Agatha. You're limping, he said. No, said Agatha, her voice quavered a little. No, said Leo, looking at her from the side of his face like a child whose said something naughty. No, he repeated, exhaling, looking down. No. Well, come in, if you want to. Nobody has wanted to for the past four years. I have chairs and a table. Some meat with bread and onions. It has been a little hot. Yesterday I discovered a lady's fan on a dresser in a room I never use. It must have been from way back when, when I used to spruce myself up and entertain, you know, the ladies. I'd be gratified if you used it now.

I brought you some olive oil and wine, said Agatha; I didn't intend to stay. But it seems you could use a helping hand cleaning this place up.

Has it become untidy? Said Leo absentmindedly. Oh, there are a few things strewn around but that is what makes it home, you know. People's messes are always what makes their homes.

It's more than a mess, retorted Agatha; it's a pig sty.

Well, if you wouldn't mind cleaning—but it seems such a rotten thing to do to a visitor. First to invite you to eat bread and meat and fan yourself—I also made some lemonade with heaps of sugar—but anyway, then to have you cleaning. I was of course much neater a few months ago.

Agatha handed Leo the little container of olive oil, and unwrapped her shawl.

Leo looked at her. You look, if I may say so, sculpted; he spoke reflectively. Ah yes, a woman's body—the best of creation. Don't mind me, though; I have turned inward. I seek spiritual beauty and perfection, he spoke in a slightly artificial voice.

You look and behave like a slob, said Agatha, shortly.

That too, he sighed.

Agatha went into the house; it looked inside like a hurricane had ripped it apart. Pans and empty bottles were on the floor, a coffee maker that had the cord ripped out, paper bags with crusts of bread, sauce bottles one of them lying sideways and oozing an unidentifiable red sauce, along with the food and cooking ware and containers, there were newspapers, a jacket or two, papers, shoes, a beret, a yellow shaded lamp lying on its side, two pillows, a child's chair with a leg broken off, and a mattress with a sheet on it.

This is my sitting room, said Leo, walking in behind her. I thought I might use it. The bedroom is cluttered with books and clothes. The guest room has suitcases in it and odd bits of furniture that I don't ever use. Here, I live. This garbage dump gives me inspiration.

You can't live here, said Agatha; you must clean.

I realize that to you it must look like an impossible mess. But you must understand that a mess, a real authentic mess, unlike some of those farcical half way messes such as you find on old lady's desks, has for one thing a specific genesis. It is just that, for instance, when I am lying on this mattress in this room, which gets the most cool air, I might reach to the side for some bread, and then, of course the crumbs in the bag are left there—at my elbow. The pans here, once contained chicken—I am good at frying chicken parts in a pan, but then after, you see, when I have eaten directly from the pan so as not to hazard making a mess of a dish, I simply forget, for a while, the pan there on the floor, and then when I remember, a delicious full-fed sleep is already upon me. How can I possibly get up to clean the pan?

Agatha stepped over the objects on the floor into the kitchen where there were more pans and pots some broken on the floor, and a few whole on the table, bread, bits of meat, chicken bones and water jugs, more wine bottles, beer bottles and brandy bottles strewn around on the floor and on the table. Foraging in amongst the shelves, she came up with a largish plastic bag and began to fill it with the trash.

She worked for two hours, picking things up, deciding which things were broken beyond repair and which could be mended with some ingenuity. At the end of two hours, there was some space to walk between kitchen and living room where Leo slept. Now, she asked looking at Leo who was watching her the whole time—making little murmuring sounds—quite right! Absolutely! That too, I hadn't seen it.—now! How was I meant to sit?

I have rarely had the pleasure…began Leo; I forgot how you were meant to sit. I was for a moment, just overcome….

Agatha wondered if he was slightly ironic, or really just sentimental—for they had been children together.

Well, I finally thought of Magda, she said, gently; you see I, like all the others, went around judging you and then, remembering Magda, I thought what if in the grand scheme of things, a man or woman has the right to make others a little angry—to step on a few toes? Heavens, our villagers, the men and women down there—Agatha pointed out the window down the hill—they'll shift on you and get angry or love you for the most absurd of reasons. Perhaps you haven't heard how—years ago, the old priest considered me damned without any possibility of mercy. And you, you know—were a devil! And yes, I can see it in their sense, but then I wonder—what on earth for?

Then it does make sense, said Leo, pensively, for the damned and the devil do go together.

At first it disturbed me, continued Agatha not listening, but I had my sons to consider. Dimitri was moody and complex. He was a reader, a constant thinker. He wanted to solve enormous questions—God, if God exists—what is his nature? Reality—what is it? He was wayward in school, refusing to talk, but always scoring highest of all his classmates. Jason, poor dear, I always call him my poor dear, and well he knows that I am most in love with Dimitri, Jason is strange in a solid, dull way. He seems sometimes almost inarticulate whereas Dimitri always had words even when he refused to talk. I think Dimitri was most the island man but Dimitri left, had to, wanted to—both I think. And so I have thought of him, you see. And then it seemed to me as if here I was existing and that I might as well be dancing…And why on earth not?

I don't know why I am telling you all this. It is just a long way of saying that I judged you once and now I am sorry for it and I feel like I am breathing great breaths of relief for being sorry for it.

You are trash-dancing, said Leo, smiling sweetly. You, muscular and light, picking up trash!

But one thing is strange, said Agatha: You have a son, and you loved her mother and yet you are content to let him go and to wallow in this misery—because I think it is misery that makes you so slothful. Me, on the other hand, I've been working like a horse for my one son who lives with me it's true, but also thinking of Dimitri. I could never let my sons go like you have. I don't mean of course physically so much. But mentally, emotionally. It is not so much love—though I have found I love them. But curiosity, following as if they lead somewhere. Don't you feel it ever? You don't even talk to Max. Aren't you at all curious about what is going on inside his head? Don't you want to, just for a kind of intrigue, follow him around?

Hmm, hmm—there are breakages. Ruptures. Besides I have my theory about him—fatherly of course.

What is that?

Hmm, hmm.

Well, I will be going.

Leo closed one eye and looked at her out of the other. Far?

I'll come back with a bottle of dish washer detergent soon.

Of course, few things in the village world are really private; a window may be two or three meters from another across the way, but somehow the noses in the one invade the little hollow reflected in the other and in the village it was not uncommon to see an anonymous nose, but irrefutably a villager's nose in the intimate space of friend with friend, and it was impossible not to know that a villager's ear was set a little distance away. Thus it was, not so surprising, that although Agatha had gone up the hill to where Leo lay neglected by everybody—that it was suddenly everybody's business that she had done so. The piece of factual information that she had been in his house was suddenly all around in all the houses. Of course, we took it lightly—delivering what was it? Olive oil and wine—mere piece of thoughtfulness. Since when had we even thought to inquire, that is, to ascertain whether Leo was alive or dead? For all we knew, he might have been a feast for flies, worms, rats by the time she got there. For months, years even, we'd have rather pass over in silence the terrible metamorphosis of the man after the strange, power-filled wife died. Some still worshipped her—slipped in a prayer or two to her they had been so in awe—the stories were so beyond belief. Surely, she had not quite died. But he—why had he turned to evil? Such fluffed and ornamented adulteries! He was not only a connoisseur of women such as we'd had in the past, but a real, snorting glutton for female flesh. We are used to the crude ways of men—but here was our poor little sot, fattened, as a child, coddled, married, now wallowing. Of course the men laughed, and some of our women shivered with a kind of half delight, half disgust—but we all stood a little in awe of his excesses. And then nothing, a moaning and groaning came faintly from the lone house on the hill. Penitence? We asked ourselves. But every morning he descended to the grocery store to pick out a chicken and some vegetables and bread, the rings under his eyes, still smelling of cigarettes and alcohol, unshaven, bloated looking from face to face with a faint smile—making commentary on the chicken flesh. Then, off to the bakery to have a platter made up of roasted chicken and potatoes and vegetables. So he was hardly fasting. Month after month went by and not a peep was heard from that house. It seemed as if the house itself was comatose.

When Agatha went up to find him, Leo emerged quite obviously from sleep. And we felt like questioning her—so has he really been just sleeping and eating for four years? But we noticed that she had in her face a look like business and the kind of happiness that comes from accomplishment.

It flowed in and out of the eighty homes of the village that she had gone and cleaned up Leo's place a bit and we turned our heads, we old women as we embroidered and made lace, and asked ourselves—what is to happen next?

Agatha, the gypsy-blooded woman with the curse on her, and now the miraculously 'lifted' head, was never one to ignore someone down. Perhaps for all those mechanical years—cleaning, washing, cooking—her body worked without relief for all the men around in her home, nothing womanly—sensing herself so cut off, and cut out—she needed now more than ever—what we will half in jest call heart. Of course, she was past the years when one falls in love, makes plans for a grand escape and ends up with oh so much abandon, physically, in a house of one's own, perhaps the house of one's grandparents that hover around as kind souls embracing, scolding, praising. There are always one or two things in marriages—the naked night swim in our village is one and sometimes candles are brought down to the dark water and the villagers surround the couple softly laughing; but then one finds that a new pace is called for and one must at last conform; the dreams vanish; sometimes the soul remains going a little crazy in a corner somewhere. In any case, it just wasn't to be with Agatha. Her marriage was dull; we thought pathetic, although Alex had brains. There was, at times, blessed conversation. It seemed he wanted something very quiet—in a hole, hidden, almost. He was that kind. Agatha was already down deep, faded and weak morally but she too with brains. For years, she had followed the old traditions. For years no one had bothered to think that Agatha would once more lift her head. And now we remember that even then she had gone with meat and jam to Matrona's house day after day.

Matrona is not the kind to be effusive with her affection. She is too numb with years and years of poverty. But we have seen her go to Agatha in a pinch. And it is known that Agatha has more than once offered to pay the bills with the little she had. To turn on the electricity again when it was shut off because they hadn't paid. Leo, whose father had bought shares in the electrical factory on the next island, could still pay his bills off the interest of this inheritance. He was a kind of prince, they said on the island—but Matrona was a poor woman, a faithful woman, a sad woman and the villagers said they were all one thing. Agatha sensed that and forgave her her bitterness. But we never felt that Matrona fought back except to cruelly foist her daughter on the village and that she almost couldn't help doing, the pain in her was so fatiguing; she had no energy to care for an imbecile.

We all thought Agatha would be the one sick, desperate with rags on her body. But somehow for all that the village was against her, she had taken a few of our wellworn steps—marriage with a reliable fisherman, and had borne sons, one of whom sent her a check each month from the wide world. She had done well for herself and now she was in middle age. And she had never been above helping others. As with Matrona, Martha, now with Leo, we thought; we kept our mouths closed about her going to see him. But some people have to talk; they talked, we say, her down into a more deeply bent posture when her husband was going to leave her. And now that the men had come to burn-- because her backbone was straight and her eye clear-- and left unfulfilled, they were talking again. The mere fact that she had been seen at Leo's house, abandoned of the villager's one accord, as punishment, payment for the wives plucked out of their little domestic garden pots—got their tongues wagging. We knew it would not be seen as a matter of the heart. Sympathy? Compassion? The man is a pig! One ought not to cast pearls.... The villagers considered dignity of primary importance. One's maleness was the issue when one's wife was rooted up out of her conjugal soil where the man's seed had given her everything—formed her, even made her bloom like heaven does.

Let Leo rot in his filth and gluttony! Many of the village men scorched by their shame for stranger cock pre-empting cock of the roost wished for it. And the more Agatha went to him with detergent, washed clothing, a basket of green peppers, or figs or grapes, a loaf of bread, a jar of lemon curd, a napkin filled with raisins, the more the tide once again turned against Agatha.

We had almost believed that Agatha could become a nonentity—that is, totally inconsequential. That nobody would have distinguished her as the one who…and thus she could have traveled the road of simple homemaking like the other village wives and like Ella, striven to be oh so little in the man's eye so as not to rouse his damning ire as if the merest rustle of a skirt, like the rustle of a wild thing in the leaves near a lion that sets him on his feet, roaring. We thought she had been there, almost there—that the curse had been wearing off. But no, never did she quite do it—even when Alex deserted her there was that almost showing off about it—what did she do but step out of her house where she should have been closeted up for shame and exhibit herself and her two children under the naked eye of the village sun. There she stood in the road and we blinking our eyes for the white sunlight in which she stood, and it started there, we think. The curse in her, the spirit which brought about that curse, the gypsy blood rising up like the mercury in a thermometer on this hot day—all conspired against Agatha's peace with us. And now years later, after one thing after another, after nearly being burned to death in her home, heaven forbid—she toils up the hill, erect- back, lifted face to Leo, the sinner, the devil. What does she want to run the village her own way? Paul shouted. We heard. We thought well, after all—he is hungry in his anger against her. But there are some who don't care for our unspoken accords.

Catherine had a desire to see Father Isaac. Kali said that she asked night and day for an interview so that the maid finally had to run down the cliff—her legs had gotten quite agile going up and down running errands and taking the sick American girl to the beach—and up the hill to the little whitewashed church. Kali presented her request very simply to the priest.

It is a kind of tourist thing, said Father Isaac from his armchair. But I will hazard a guess that more tourists will come soon. There is hardly anything here compared to the world and it has always almost amused me that the villagers cling so close. But the tourists will come and change everything. There is sea, wind, forest, quiet, distance, a certain community of birds. A man with a little money could make it into a retreat— the monasteries of the world: little whitewashed hotels, with air conditioning in the rooms, desks, TV, and downstairs tables, and, for dinner, fish dishes with lemons, the lemons of the island and goat cheese, from the very goats of the island.

Max sat in the chair opposite to Father Isaac's wicker armchair reading Scripture. Father Isaac continued: It will be comfortable. No sweat or headache or hunger. And you talk about believing! No, all that will have died out. And this little church will remain as an artifact from a past age that they will have to excavate and write books about to get at; and then, as more people come, the church will change from artifact to souvenir—a little of the blue sky or a fragment that reflects our glorious sun somehow. Max looked up. The days of the elect will be shortened, he murmured.

Yes, for it is not only a physical war that we are fighting but an internal one. It is present in everything—even in the way we move, look around us and talk. But come let's see this woman—Catherine? Kali nodded, smiling her polite smile. A good name, continued the priest. And you tell me she is sick. But I am afraid if it is healing that she wants…I am not good on demand like that, you see; I find things in obscure places, creatures who are helpless and they put themselves in my hands. It is a different thing. Logical, I would say. The healing comes. Love, like an elixir of life flows between my hand and the hurt creature. I have healed even flowers and insects, not only men. But what a different story. They do not come loudly asking, planting themselves before my face. I happen on them. God wills it. It has to do with fitting something together in spirit. Not with fractured knees, labored breath—that happens millions of years after the fact—though it is all in a flash, of course. Vast speed one realizes in the tiny space. Something for the whizz in an imperfect world goes off course, even something like a butterfly—ah it affects generations and generations—first weather, then diseases of water and air, then sin—eventually. But surely, thought Eve, we shall not die. For the devil it was sheer lie, but not for God! Truth in Christ means the devil thinks to have won. Alas, poor devil, content to eat and drink and save the soft or virile body—his mistake is assuming that God will keep his lie holy and not realizing that God is the more cunning.

Yes, tell her—and let our shortened days be full of sweetness and kindness.

She can come whenever she likes except on Sundays.

Catherine said then—let's go immediately, to the panting Kali who had almost run back up the cliff to her. And they set out with Kali explaining what the priest had said to her.

Of course, healing is a priority with me, said Catherine, but I think I understand. Still if I stay in this place, day after day, I think I won't be so like—what he imagines I am.

When they arrived at the whitewashed church, Kali went away to do some grocery shopping and to sit and gossip with Agatha and Anna who was just back from seeing her son and full of tidbits of news.

Catherine found the priest to be, as she described it, like a large white summer butterfly. He spoke English but Max didn't so Catherine used each a bit of English and the island dialect so as not to cut out anybody, as she put it later to Robert. The priest said to her in English—I can see that you are sick. You are thin, and malformed-- your chest appears to be most of your body. It is the chain that has brought me here, said Catherine. But I use my time well.

What do you do? The priest asked, gently.

Well, I tend people, she said in the island tongue—just now my mother and father. I fight to keep my health and that takes many hours during the day. I fix old machines for a hobby. And I am making a study.

Which study is that?

A study of love, said Catherine simply. One has the sense that it is not only in people.

No, agreed Father Isaac. I wouldn't wonder if we were really a marginal concern where love is.

Is it ridiculous to say that I see it in the leaves, the dust, in the air my poor lungs fill with, sometimes painfully.

Not so, said the priest, shaking his head, quickly—not ridiculous. It is just strange that you come upon me, like a little animal coming out of the water and tell me this; I have suddenly beheld, you see; I didn't expect it. I thought you were a tourist and would ask me things about the history of this place, or religion, or if it is true that one could get a faith cure. Even the villagers, you know, are not so, how shall I say it? Honest, I guess. First they talk of one thing, then another—their baptisms, marriages, funerals; they murmur behind my back that I am odd, unfit to be their priest; then they come to me again with pots of lemon curd and bottles of wine. Never will they say—what is this, Father, am I made of lust or envy? How to love?

You have told me something direct. I have indeed never known you before now. I have only imagined you—as I watched you toiling up the steep cliff stairs. I did think when I heard the story, because stories get around in the village—what are you doing here? Isn't it true that in America you can get all sorts of doctors' attention, and medicines and lifesaving technology? But now I see some faint reason for you and for you here. There should be a reason for our existence. God asks for that. If I don't give you one, He says, in His booming barely audible voice, make one for yourselves. One reason even if it is washing floors in hospitals. And that is a good one. Hygienic! Here you have told me what you do—study love. And you have found it to study it in our hard-hearted men's camp, in us believers' hard-heartedness—what we call that God's will.

I think even trampling on a flower or a branch of leaves is a terrible thing, said Catherine, her voice trembling. There is love running like a fingertip along the honeysuckle petals and leaves. Or perhaps they too sin and look away in disdain. I have often thought that the flowers were like pretty disdainful adolescents.

Yes, eventually this vain finger of burdened nature moving, said the priest construing Catherine's discourse differently, leads to sins of the worst nature, hubris and narcissism, said Father Isaac. For in our story, that of Jesus, the continuing story of the Gospels, it wasn't the actual breaking of the taboo that Jesus saves us from but evil itself, that can be more present in the smooth moving of the disdainful eye of the classically virtuous Pharisee than in the many transgressions of God's Com-

mandments of the publican who lives them for a culminating moment with the
sweetness and tenderness of a child.

I was never baptized a Christian, said Catherine, but when I was little, I was quite
sure that the greater I am existed. Yet God was more of a place than a person. I can't
explain it—a between place closer to my love and me. And God was fragile, and
fragrant and only kind. My love went off—it was my older brother—an unbeliever
in the end—and the realm that was between us became chaotic and dark. Although
God continued like some sweet grandmother—fragile, fragrant and kind. Nothing
can restore now that old beautiful realm of love, I don't think; but broken off, as it
were, I study love and it does make me lesser even near a leaf—a consolation.

The priest spoke to her suddenly in a low tone in English. You see my assistant
there, he said; so assiduously studying the Bible. The god he really worships is his
dead mother. I say dead advisedly because she died for all we know in childbirth. But
she is alive, you know. Some of the villagers pray to her. They saw her with great
powers during life, you see, and even the power to consent to death. It is a great,
heroic power. Of course, we all die, but sometimes it is given us to consent to a death
as did Christ. That death was to marry and have a child knowing that she would die
in childbirth. Of course, you can wonder if she really knew? Perhaps not. Perhaps
her divining was just the sort of thing that catches foolish fatuous people in a net. I
don't know. But she lives enough after death to make him into a secret adorer. Oh, he
believes in Christ, alright; goes to him with his prayers. But He is a stiff and formal
Christ. The thee and thou of great pomp and wealth. His Jesus is full of the wrath
and pity of rich and powerful men. When something is not quite right—mother,
mother, his soft painful heart calls. That is love for our true God.

It does not matter to me. It would have mattered to my predecessor. Now he was
a man of rule. What is written is written. But I think that all Jesus the Christ, Son
of the Living God left in the Gospels, in the Scripture, itself, was a trace. Love God,
love one another. Neighbor, enemy, believer, unbeliever. To be able to love—the
test is the poor, ugly, fly-covered corpse-like man, the test is the despised one—to
love him or her. Put yourself down in front of the worldly. How often have you too
gone about on giant human legs crushing the little and tender? And it means, as Max
knows, to kiss her or him with your soft painful heart right on your lips, sleep with
your tender, weak body pressed against your Sweet as did John. Love is love not rules,
rods, forced confessions, artificial lives, inquisitional condemnations. What would a
child say? Love is your soft painful heart against a breast, which loves forever driven
in like crazy mad nails.

It used to be that way for me, said Catherine.

Put leaves on your breast, said the priest—ones that you find. Don't try to pray
right now or believe with your mind.

As far as tending goes do it naturally. Not forced. Not as if the rod is held up.
Foolish fathers behave that way—not God. My tending will come—he indicated

Max, and, as far as I am concerned, if it does not—good riddance to it. But Max now cooks, you know. I am very proud of him. He can do everything with eggs. He is so clever cooking; one senses sensitivity, tenderness towards the swelling breast-omelet. It is sure that he will give me my medications when I grow old, holding up my shaking head.

I haven't thought of growing old, said Catherine, reflectively. But it seems to me that the old people here, and there are so many, are like little Oriental charms, pieces of carved jade, black, white, green. That they sit around inscrutable and ageless in their ancientness—looking at us from the perspective of having seen so much.

Nonsense! What have they seen? A few men and women, a child or two. They grow old here because of the sun, fish, goats' cheese, the olive oil and wine; their healthy digestive tracts make their lifelines longer as they process the fresh uncontaminated food each day. And then they rear their heads and look around in the sun! You know they are no more than worms. Healthy worms, ageless worms. And yet, said the priest pensively; one can go from worm to man in a single instant.

I prefer to see them as all men and women, said Catherine. If one could approach them with that one difference—what is it tone of voice, freedom from all grudges and ask them—what was it that made you thus? Not in one question, but in many. I think they'd be like encyclopedias—but as you might wish them to be, Father, not of events on a large scale, or knowledge that would impress at the university—but of small reflections, ramifications on the general theme of living this crude physical life of eating and sleeping. I think they would know things about tomato and eggs, about cross old husbands or wives, about the man dancing, the sole, solitary figure midst the crowd keeping time with their feet that would lift your mind over the profound like an abyss and carry it high into endless meditation like the sun in the blue summer. I believe that is love.

Yes, love can moisten and make live again a dried out old plant, like myself. I was reading recently that even certain dead organisms, what were they fungi? Bacteria?—fossils found in the sand somewhere in the world can, if placed in water, come to life. And so, and so—water in the physical world is like love in the mind and soul, absolutely yielding, essential, all-powerful. So few people, in this I am correct, know of love. So few. They have affection, eros, and for a while it is beautiful enough; one is caught up with so many things. But then there comes a time—when one asks: What was it there that I missed?—As if one could not think of a word and yet knows the word, or thinks one does—but at the right time to use it, it just eludes one's memory. And so love, the lone figure dancing trying to tenderly take the thorn out of the foot of the crowd. Up it has come, here, there—perhaps perfect but elusive—missing the mark when called for. And so some a kind of horror becomes apparent—am I really one who has lived all my life without love?

I would have thought, said Catherine, I would have minded....I am not sure that family love was the core thing in our house. But recently I began to see love, or some such beautiful mystery that is all frankness, tenderness and utter relief as of solitude—just, as I said—in the leaves. And I believe that we have the power—to settle into peacefulness, that is tenderness, that makes us littler than leaves—partakers thus.

Ah, ah, said the priest for pleasure listening to her, leaning back in his armchair. You need no catechism, no baptism, he said.

Isn't that anathema in your faith? Asked Catherine, a little startled.

No—did the little children of whom Christ told the disciples a little ironically to 'suffer' to come unto him—imagine the stiffness and scowling of Peter, John and James!—did the little ones need baptism? How would it have been possible for Christ to take a little child and put him in the midst of the crowd, saying, the kingdom of heaven is of such as these if that child still needed baptism? You have shown to me a little child-spirit. With all that you have not, yet you have. And to those that have, more will be given. Oh, that it were given to me to be, and not only to understand.

Catherine and the priest talked until evening filled the room with its green and grey, and she emerged only when stars began to appear low down in the sky. Kali had been waiting for about an hour in the church, sitting, her eyes on the altar, murmuring prayers. Catherine took her hand and as they went out asked her about her afternoon. Anna has news about her boy, said Kali—he is old but he has two wives now. He divorced the old one for his desire for something fresh, you see; but then the old one came to live with them at his request because she mends his socks and cooks what he likes without any complaints like the young one. All goes on as usual in a home with husband and wife. Sometimes he comes to the old one even at night—for the young one is overly vigorous, and an all-night talker. He has grown children with the old one—three sons, and with the new young one, one daughter, a child of three. On the other island, they have all sorts of things going on, said Anna, and no one seems to care. Besides he inherited the ship owning business from his father and wealth excuses any number of sins. He even goes to church! He reasons that since he still makes love to his divorced wife, it's as if he isn't really divorced and adulterous only half adulterous, given that there are two women, and the Lord forgave one after another, adulterous women, even prostitutes, not to mention the men who went to them—then the chances are he is quite alright with his soul. Anna thinks this blasphemy is outrageously funny. And I have to admit I joined in with her laughter, and laughed myself ten years' younger. But one thing I can't get out of my head is that Anna is an unbeliever, she confessed that she didn't believe in God, and one knows that the devil comes unawares—to the laughing, to the sleeping. I wondered a little at myself then.

They say the devil is subtle, said Catherine.

And you think you are what you are—but in reality—poof, gone, insubstantial. Not the salt with savor. To me evil is what you think is there—and you point to it there, and then, it dissolves away, it becomes irretrievable, and it has decamped, gone to another place in the blink of an eye.

That is because everybody likes to point like little children—the ugly, the sick!

And the devil won't have this pointing, said Kali. They walked down the hill towards the cliff, Kali pulling Catherine along pressing her hand against her bosom and hurrying along so as to make it up the cliff before darkness.

It happens sometimes that the bowels of one's heart gets scooped out like butter; a friend becomes ill and prepares to die—and one goes around town, following the usual steps in the same old road, but with a feeling like this great, dreadful change that makes me into a ghost, or almost, why it can't happen. And it isn't happening. Look I am not dying; I am living as much as you or he! And so, and so, she too cannot be dying. And this seems in love to have all the logic in the world. Look a dragon fly crosses my path; the sun this autumn is like a million slender dancers, leaping and landing lightly, soundlessly—as if they had not landed on earth: there is no one dying, least of all my heart and soul.

At her son's house, Anna coughed a lot. They put a warm woolen shawl around her shoulders. Nothing was said or done. She is an old woman, said her son wisely and periodically, she will cough or have constipation. But the cough lasted for a month after Anna returned home until finally Agatha and Anna took the same trip across the water to the other island and met her son who was expecting her, having sounded the cough last time she was there, and all three went to the hospital for x-rays. When they came out with the news, Anna smiled slightly; Agatha looked at her and said cancer—she'll out live it; her son smiled that closed in kind of smile, as if pleasing all the crowd waiting in the dark belly regions of the soul. Inwardly, though Agatha immediately thought death.

When they returned back to Holy Island, Agatha looked at her, her eyes filled with alarm, and Anna said to her quietly—don't be silly. You can get along without me. What are you going to do? Asked Agatha. Watch for it. Wait for it. Life is about life, despite death. Ah, I am a great believer.

You said you didn't believe in God.

Well, not in the great enthroned, golden crusted—man-head. I've had three husbands and what I know of men is that they are pathetic, and often spineless, highly egotistical, and absurd. Why if one of those clowns were in heaven! No, I believe more in the power of one little sparrow. Remember: even they are counted.

Jesus, said Agatha, sighing, and tensing.

We are to love—wasn't that the commandment of commandments? God and neighbor. It is good I have had all this love.

Agatha stayed that night and put her to bed, tenderly; you know, she said, just as her friend was about to leave: as a matter of fact, I have not had love. Could that be the truth?

Of course, it is not the truth, said Agatha: you have had husband, son, friends.

Ah yes, said Anna—husbands, son, friends, she echoed like a little child. Then she sat up in bed and looked at Agatha with an ominous look. Agatha looked back, hardly breathing—sometimes they say the dying know things. What is it? She asked her, fearfully.

Why, I have NOT loved. Now this is something to outlast the devil for. I must love before I die, she said. Why, it doesn't matter who or even what: I must love the gypsy that visits sometimes peddling, stealing, or I can love Martha, even a lizard, a moth. Whatever comes, she said to Agatha in her old sprightly way. Go home, as you see; I am not dying. No, you know as well as I that they say death can be held off until the dying person is ready. Don't you remember, or perhaps you were too young, elder Stavros wanted to see his long lost daughter who reconciled with him when he was breathing his last on his bed, and came over on the slow boat ride from the other island. Ah yes, you should have seen him fight, refuse to go. And then the tenderness when they were at last together and how he died so peacefully.

Bah, I don't have longings like that for anyone I know. No—I have been exceptionally hard hearted. I need the courage to be indignant, the delicacy to break my heart, the inward luxury to lay my blood from the heavens at the feet of whomever—even the enemy.

But that is not true, said Agatha, shocked. The whole island knows you—you with good humor, taking people as they come, not holding grudges, not judging, condemning…what do you call that?

Why, amusement, said Anna, smiling at her. Warm hearted, yes, but--. No, love must be something different. I have heard of that Catholic saint—St. Francis, who went mad for Christ and then tried to pick up love—all over the universe he traveled for it. Sister Moon, Brother Sun, Brother Wolf and so on. And the sun and moon and wolf looked at him and questioned: Who are you? And went smiling away. And so have they questioned me—not the wolf, nor the butterfly. I have danced and made love. But oh, I long for something more. Rousing up the old life like an electrical cord plugged in. Not just a greeting! Energy! Ecstasy! Leaping over boundaries. I used to think the best thing in the world was to be warm-hearted. Generally warm hearted. Now I am beginning to think it is to have that moment of hot headed, brilliant, brave ecstasy even from the worst—the rapist, the murderer. Look even the body wants it. How can we be surprised at our wanton males and females? Searching all over for that release into physical fireworks. I was desired myself—what did my first husband want but to bury his hot gummy seed, deep in my body? What did I want but hot quivers down my thighs, up into my belly? Again and again I desired, drooled, ached for the sweetness—my legs stretched wide to encompass summer. I have to admit that this mad pleasure I thought was all there was to love. So I heaped my plate full. I lived to have three luscious man-fruits in my lap.

I suppose one day I woke up with one husband or another and said—in fact, you have become a bore. There was a time I pitied one And one, not the one I made my son with; he, I later despised; no, the third one who had come to me when I was a sixty year old woman and flirted my eyeballs out—now he had a smile that was not a fool's smile. I wondered audibly to him if I had any faith. He said to me if Jesus Christ danced, he'd dance our breath away. I believe that, said Anna. And since I found that I could believe him, if not the priest, we grew together comfortably. I got close to loving, then, because I was close to a warm faith—but what was it after all—agreement, affection, consolation, slight beautification.

If Jesus Christ danced, said Agatha, musing, the cross dance.

Yes, if Jesus Christ danced— our dance, the dance of stuffed eggplant.

Agatha and Anna sat together for a few more hours in the old village silence. Anna had her eyelids lowered, reflecting but for a long time she did not sleep. She was scheduled for a follow up visit at the hospital on the other island. They were going to take measures to prevent her from dying soon. She was thinking—oh operations and chemicals to keep this old carcass of mine alive? Isn't it better to leave in a less complicated way with all good humor, a blessing on the young ones. What can death be after all? I have a cough but no pain, or not much to speak of. And if it gets bad, why slip me a pill and I will go out. But first, to have that one experience—to love with all one's strength.

Agatha had a dream—while she was sitting watching Anna drop off—of light, white light, brilliant, scintillating and rolling downwards into a dark space and flooding it like water. And beneath, at the bottom of the abyss, in the lightened night, a single little lit candle that seemed, she couldn't have put it any other way, to have lumbered along in the darkness for ages-- that still shone and was still visible to her below this tissue of light. And then the flood of light covering it receded, the lit candle remained but how different it appeared; before it had been a little joyful rustic thing. After, when all had been illuminated, and then become dark again, it appeared so minutely solitary and helpless, forlorn yes, but holy—a memory of light but of light of light of light and so on until this memory was the reborn physically real and not cocked up in the mind like theater.

She wanted to linger but there was house, dinner, Jason; Anna and dreams would keep. When she left the sun had gone down—she thought back, Anna's house had been flooded with light; perhaps the dream had been real—but there had been no candle, and no special holiness. What on earth did Anna mean when she said she had not loved? A human being was as secretive and inward as a star. When they've loved, she thought, there is some great 'thereness,' a knowing that one has hit the mark—a difference in the human flesh and blood. Here was Anna, whom she thought, but then again—righteously speaking—one could see; one didn't want to say that she was selfish—she was so affectionate. She was the kind that could gather up friends like farmers gather up the rich grain in an abundant harvest. And she was kind, there was no question. All this time when the others had abandoned her, not quite abandoned, but acting as if she could just drop off the branch and wither away for all they cared—Anna came, now it seemed she could hear her voice, for amusement, Agatha—for amusement! Yet there was her undeniable bonhomie; she never seemed sad; had always given her a shoulder to lean on. She had at times imagined that Anna brought with her great light—but there was that severity in her face, beautiful still but severe; she was all shadow. How was it possible? Affection, bonhomie—and severity. Ah did she mean that she did not love the others? Was the severity that was always in her face, despite the sweet smile—was that the telltale sign of it, this unlovingness?

Agatha had always thought to herself—oh Anna can do or say anything—she is so kind and so affectionate at bottom.

But Anna had said to her today—I stuff myself with treats—marinated fish, pickled onions, lemon curd and strawberries that are imported, imported in their leaves, paid for by the berry it seems they are so expensive, and I, alone, have the money for them; I didn't bring you any; I ate them all myself. Delicious—the fruits of this earth are still sweet and good. And she had kissed her and for a moment Agatha had wondered if she had relished the kiss like the strawberry she had refused to share. It was a kiss on the side of the mouth, just brushing Agatha's full-blown lips. And she had once said to her—oh to be as Sappho and to fall in love with women; only a woman really knows what is delight for another woman! And Agatha had seen this as the height of beauty and truth. But now stuffed with unshared strawberries and these sorts of reflections on beauty and truth—that is, utter delight—she suddenly with tumor in lung, reported that she had not loved.

Blow the golden trumpet with the snake sculpted on top: Bring them in! she had said to Agatha as she was leaving her. The men and women, lovers, wives, kings and queens of the earth who did not love, in the end, despite their amours, and their delights, their luxuries. What luxuries!: red velvet curtains, peacock feathers, dried figs and raisins, dates and coconuts, and, locked with golden locks to be opened only with golden keys, the aromatic chests of carved wood containing pearls and rubies and diamonds! Hanging from the domed ceilings of white, white marble—chandeliers of gold leaf, fragrant candles and sticks of incense, diaphanous silk dresses, rustling and fragrant as the haunches of a woman passed clad in them—I had them all in my glad paw or nearly all. I could afford in my idling here on Holy Island to strike up a conversation with this brow beaten girl with her abandonment, and her sullen, silent fishing son. Ah what conversation! It gladdened me. Were we Sappho's children what immortal delight would have been between us!

Agatha was glad that the old spark in Anna was untouched by the cancer. I suppose in the end, she said, in the throes of her talking with, going home to the cold house and Jason who sat still for the Kingdom of Heaven, it all has to do with those who rush and those who take their time. Anna is a rusher, she wants the loveliness now. Where is the honest person who isn't the same, at bottom? But you are slow—oh you! See the millions of years it took to make Anna—and then, even then, with all her elegance, severity and affection—what depth, what glory—you—oh you!—drew back, disgruntled. There is one, maybe two, three—you—oh you-- consider finished. When we are slow, slow as Simon who crouches over his paintings — which he lays down on the floor— like some kind of insect, crouching, with folded wings—crouches there making his hips sore until he reaches out like a flash, hand flying—and another stroke is added—when we are slow, we are closer to you—oh you! When we feel every pain as we come slow, not skidding swifter than a thought over the ground as if it were ice and we supreme skaters—when we lumber along, heel toe, heel toe, graceful despite ourselves, but blundering, awkward, clumsy too—going lurching and slipping along like drunks, like sleepwalkers to the X across your bosom…something in the slowness—oh you—changes us. For the metamorphosis is painful—happens only when we feel, yes feel.

And when they had gotten over the tip toeing around Anna, and the getting of glasses of water, the bringing of sweet lemon jam, oil, bread and cheese, Agatha shared these reflections. Perhaps, she said to Anna, you are a rusher. And back and forth she had gone, trying to figure it out: why Anna had not loved?

In the end, Anna said to her: Well, it is simple. There are many out there, crowds and crowds that I saw in Paris and London, well wishers, kind hearted—some Christian, some of other faiths—and they too are waiting to love. Not love as in family matters, or affection with friends, but love—passionate, in-dwelling love, sometime painful. The closest people come is compassionating, vaguely, almost coldly.

That first night that Agatha left Anna, she went home and found Jason moving around in his slow way—he had brought a fish. Here, he had said to her and presented it to her still flipping a little, quivering, in her hands.

It was the first time he had brought her home a fish. Other fishermen had brought home fishes to their wives and children, to their mothers—but Jason had tallied up his catch exactly for the sale and had come home to sit silently and empty handed of gifts in his mother's house.

What did you do this for? Asked Agatha with the fish—she could still feel the life in its body. Why should we be murderers? She spoke unreasonably—they always ate fish like all of us, but suddenly, well, there it was reasonable even so. That happens on our island—the most unreasonable thought one day after a million years sets the world in place and becomes our reason.

We eat chicken and fish, said Jason, shrugging his shoulders. He didn't see it. Our islanders sometimes fail to see reason. Sometimes lamb. What do you think happens—the animal is killed. I will kill it if you like. And he took the fish into the kitchen and cut off its head.

Agatha watched her face turned away half in disgust, half in pity. How beautiful the life in its body—she said. You cook it, said Jason, abruptly, depositing the headless fish in her hands. There are things that have to be done, he said. The killing of this soul is one such thing. Agatha wondered less about the word he used than about the whole bit of drama from him, the never never actor.

Agatha went obediently into the kitchen and filled a pan with oil. She turned on the cold water faucet and slit the belly of the fish and began to clean out the guts, depositing the heart and liver on an old newspaper.

We found out later that Agatha had now and then the most profound of thoughts. She said to us that cleaning the freshly killed fish, she discovered that it was not that dead body that she had loved, although she still loved it—and yes, why not love a fish?—it was after all the quivering, helpless creature that she had loved. And that that quivering, helpless creature could be a woman, for instance. Quivering and help-less in the hands of death, in the hands of men, or of God. And the way we turned away—as if, go along now, just do it—aren't there things that have to be done? There was obedience, willed submission. That was the cruelest. And we had to because we wanted to rush things—there was no time to question, that takes reflection, and someone was taking charge. We could eat potatoes—not crush this live, quivering, silvery thing—this other body of love.

Agatha was like that—always getting upset over little things—exploding now and then. We said to her wasn't it a miracle that your son who never participates in the home, finally gave you a fish? You should be grateful; didn't our Lord do miracles with fish? And this seemed just to irk her, although it should have shown her the way. But we stepped back from condemning Agatha, now. She was with Anna day and night. We also visited. We brought our home made infusions for pain and digestion, our magazines for reading pleasure, our wine for savoring. Some of us brought can-dies, lemon and apricot candies the kind that we serve at weddings. But Anna wanted Agatha. Why on earth—we wondered. Oh they had been friends, but she was friends with everybody and anybody. She had that way with her—excessive good humor, we called it; perhaps Agatha because now Agatha walked more like a woman and looked like she was somebody and because Anna was angry that ruffians-- now that we have lost our holiness we have them even here on Holy Island—had wanted to kill her.

Perhaps Anna had taken up the Agatha cause on her deathbed.

As for us, we were worried. We talked to Anna and Anna said—the world, the world! It has come here, you see, more and more. One imagined…but that was all a myth such as many people have about old times, places where things are unchanged for centuries. The altar —is it not filled with golden antiquities, shining ancient things? We told her about Agatha's fish and she laughed. You thought you could go free from death, that you were treasured, eternal. Secretly you thought you were the eternal treasures in the midst of the crowd of the dead—and how do you prove it—by bowing towards the altar of Christ. And we walked away saying to ourselves, she has a mighty foul temper towards us, her friends.

And those two—Agatha and Anna—are now like two grapes hanging together on a vine. Rubbing elbow to elbow as they walk around together, bobbing a little at people passing. Anna walks with a stick now. She has pain medicine and cough syrup she didn't want anything else.

Paul murmurs, sitting nights in the tavern, that a woman without God and a God-cursed woman together—both will die, have died. What we see are just ghosts, not living treasures—he actually said that. But the old men—Nisos, and Timos piped up and said that considering the shape of Agatha's thighs there was no mistaking her for a ghost. And we have to admit that Cleo and Zoe and all of us laughed 'til we cried. But Paul got angry and said again and again that he had heard things of grave consequence…that he wouldn't be surprised if Agatha slipped from her high perch….

We must admit we thought him almost mad. What high perch? It was just the way she tilted her head back as if she was out on the beach in a bathing suit letting the sun come down inside. People did that when they were sick sometimes—even when their minds were dark and sorrowful. But to Paul it looked rebellious when Agatha did it, stood and looked a little up with her graceful chin and closed her eyes at the sun so often.

For a while, Paul stood back. It was clear to us that he was waiting for Anna to die. For one thing, his great purpose to purge the island—we were not clear what that meant—to regain anyway our holiness—would have been interfered with by Anna. Even his attempt to run for mayor, though we never had a mayor and never needed one, would have been blocked by Anna first and foremost. She thought, she confided to us, that he was mean and petty. That his notion of holiness smelled to her like dead fish. He had gotten after Max for example, since now no one dared approach the priest—what with his penitence and the brimming fruit trees, nets of fish after—and had told him on his own authority to clean and clean the altar. There is nothing cleaning won't do. Detergent on the paving stones, polishing the icon cases with glass cleaner. And Paul made sure that numbers of people heard him ordering the deacon around. He even wanted to collect donations to embellish and renovate the little church of ours—call in architects and restorers. Perhaps, he said aloud in the tavern surrounded by men eating olives and bread, a new fresco! The artist who created this last was as loopy as Simon. Whoever heard of fishes leaping and quivering for joy a hair's breadth from the hand of the Lord in the heavens? No, not fish, but tiers of angels in a row and the Lord above—that is how the fresco should be.

But I've always loved that one peculiar fresco of ours, said Maria, breaking into the conversation. And the little old icon off to the corner—with Jesus walking on water. You can see he is happy, though contorted with the agony of surprise and wonder.

I've never seen it, murmured Paul and a few voices.

That is because, said Maria, you go in just to repeat your prayers, not to offer a bellyful of love and joy to Him.

Which I suppose you do when you stretch your legs wide open for a man, said Paul sarcastically.

At least I know who I am regarding Him, said Maria demurely. There are some here who are puffed up like cocks crowing and they really have not much more to say to Him, the Creator and Cross-bearer.

Saluting the sun—murmured Timos. He was not part of the argument.

So we all have our place, said Maria. His is letting everyone know the sun is coming up, mine is kissing the laughing foot of our Savior in the icon.

The place of a whore, said Paul, with disgust is—

But Maria is right, said Timos, suddenly. The place of the whore is on the ground kissing Jesus' foot; we have it on authority.

Peter turned and looked at her. Is that why you kiss…he was going to say but checked himself.

In fact, said Maria in a musical tone, I do; I kiss the feet of my men. They think of course, but I don't care what they think. For me it's just in case the Son of God were to come back in the guise of one of them.

Ha, said Paul, foul thoughts of a whore—what blasphemy.

Every mother's son likes to be held naked. We know he was unashamed of being naked. He went naked to the cross.

I've always seen him in little pants, said Zoe. We were in consternation. Was the Lord ever naked?

He had a brilliant body, said Cleo, dreamily.

I've seen him thin, fat, stooped, bald, ugly, and sound with a whopper of a behind and naked, said Maria. That one I most doubt was he. But I may be wrong.

This is a disgusting conversation, said Paul righteously. Peter was going to wallop Maria's backside but thought better of it and sat very still, eating.

She raises a point, said Zoe; we can't condemn her. I say the Lord was naked on the cross but that he never slept with a woman.

He often came to us whores, Maria persisted. We fed him, we bathed him. We saw ourselves in him, you know. Ill-used and sick. And he held us and told us we weren't beneath him. That's why I know he was naked. The way I've cried over some men— dying ones. They could have been him.

I don't want to hear anymore of a whore's fixations, thundered Paul. Maria wilted a little and moved herself into the corner bar.

In fact, said Paul, I propose a tax on her prostitution ring to discourage clients.

Where would the money go? Asked Zoe

For the town hall.

We haven't got one, said Nisos, laughing with hilarity.

It is in the making, retorted Paul.

No one wants to make you rich, snapped Zoe, angrily.

That is the reason nothing can happen in this village. Did you hear her talk? Talk is free of course, of course, and it is only Maria talking—but do you realize how many ears her talk falls into?

You're joking of course, said Peter with a ghost of a voice.

Well, we'd have to vote on it. I think any number of wives might agree—true wives, he murmured, thoughtfully. Isn't the whole objective to make our island, Holy Island, holy again? What are we a farce? That whore makes us into a farce! She and others. Yes, there are others. A true wife brings holiness to her husband, sanctified by her obedience according to the wedding sacrament performed and joining them together before God! She needn't support his waywardness, his carnal nature.

You're joking, said Peter; the other day you said yourself—

I've made a little study of it, interposed Paul. It seems to me decent and upright. A wife should be clean to her husband, a light in the home, while he may, according to nature, have his more masculine side.

But all that taxing Maria will do, commented Cleo, will be to punish the poor masculine natures heavily, while the rich ones will carry on as before, hardly caring.

No, the opposite is true, retorted Zoe, misinterpreting, for someone poor in carnal nature will not be tempted by a prostitute at all and therefore refrain, while the richly endowed will find themselves severely punished and who knows whether or not it isn't after all a question of nature.

The priest says that true carnal nature is not a man's longing for women at all—that is simply poetry; the carnal nature of St. Paul is composed of vice, and viciousness—that sin is not the burning you carry between your legs at all but deep, cold, calculating cruelty of a heart divided from God.

It will punish me, said Maria in a hollow voice. God knows I've lived here as long as you have, Paul, and if it weren't for the death of my two parents and me with nowhere to go…while you have always been fed and comfortable.

A whore's place is not to concern herself with an honest man, Paul replied with a slight frown. Besides, if you had shown a different interest, if you had taken another path—you might have yourself been a married woman.

I went wrong, I don't deny it; but I stepped off the high path of virtue lightly with love in me. There are folks who never make a wrong move but who don't have love in them.

Enough, said Peter, uneasy at the crossfire between his brother and Maria. Let's talk of other things. This island has its shortcomings but surely as you say—a whore cannot be the real cause—it isn't even her place. She manages everything discreetly, and we men come here to drink and ease our minds. That she is here is common knowledge and there has been a common accord about it for years!

You know, if we were with other girls, our wives would divorce us, piped up Nisos—but Maria, she hardly counts as another girl. She is part of our home-- in our house—the tavern is just visible from our back windows!

I say things have to change. We have lost the key element—what makes us ourselves—our meaning, our truth and our hope. And all because we have let ourselves go—one is a whore, another is a Muslim, Paul continued in a stentorian voice. What are we going to do just go naked with our love?

Impossible, laughed Peter—impossible.

Agatha is a Muslim.

No, not she. She comes to church.

Who? What? What are you talking about? Suddenly half shouted Zoe who had closed her eyes. Cleo looked away as if she was not going to permit herself to comment.

You have been against Agatha, murmured Peter in a low voice; and she may have been all that you say—well, a bit of a troublemaker for her way and manner, but she is no Muslim.

Gypsies are, said Paul. Her father was. He had a prayer mat and bowed to Mecca on it.

Didn't you know? Asked Zoe softly.

What do they worship? Asked Timos, curiously.

God in the shape of a sea urchin, laughed Nisos.

No, said Peter, sternly; the prophet Mohammed.

What did he do? Timos continued with his inquiry. Die on the cross?

No, said Peter, conquered with the sword and married three wives.

Now that sounds reasonable, interrupted Nisos. What is life but fighting and marrying? The sword and love making. One sword of steel for the enemy, a sword of flesh for women. Now the cross, ah—it hurts. And there is an end to all joy.

But Christ was humble, murmured Zoe.

In any case, said Cleo, on this island we have Christ. That is what makes us…

Yes, said Paul, suddenly turning to her—that is what makes us. And we are losing that for sheer foolishness; a little correction would bring us round. And since we are left now with only ourselves, creatures who will only get old and die—we can now gather in, turn to our ancient ways, and once more be at peace and be holy. But to gather in, as I am an honest man, we must throw out anything that is degenerate, anything that is wicked.

We must return to our holy households, we must resume our fishing, we must go back to our businesses. There are certain elements on our island—not only Agatha, but Anna too—the two of them conspiring—it is as if men don't even exist between them, Paul added, incongruously.

I saw Agatha—she looked like she was sent from heaven, said Nisos.

Like a vision of gold, said Zoe;

This kind of thing is why the devil deceives, said Paul.

Nisos piped up: I wish that Agatha would befriend Maria and set up shop with her. Then we'd see business resume and peace come to our island.

Everybody except Paul laughed. This is what is happening, he muttered angrily. Instead of our return to holiness—these distractions. It is clear that we will never progress. But it is within our power...we could become a holy place, a shrine! Were not our ancestors the very Greeks who witnessed our Lord's resurrection, saw Him raised flesh and blood from the dead—who decided to search the world over for a secluded place to dedicate themselves to worship; who were directed here to this island through Providence, found enough to eat, and fresh water to drink through Providence and took root here? We have it within ourselves—our blood, our heritage. We are a living shrine ourselves—our very flesh and blood. But to do this we must painstakingly and with great effort come away from our lax and unholy ways and remake ourselves as the Lord taught us. It was the same at Nineveh. Doesn't the Lord say that he will send only the sign of Jonah to us?

But as you say, said Peter, quickly lest his brother should really get angry—we are just flesh and blood and there are not many of us left. You wouldn't want us to wither away before our time.

From among the great sinners, piped up Zoe, Christ selected his greatest saints.

In the end, Paul strode out, annoyed at the others. Peter tipped Maria lavishly and groped under her dress. I'll come soon, he whispered to her. Nisos and Timos went out holding hands, slightly drunk.

Zoe and Cleo who held their liquor well, sailed out serene as cream.

It was two in the morning on Monday, and Maria leaned on her broom. Poor Agatha, she murmured; just as she is getting out of so much broken heart, the old, cold hoary monster has to come back preying on her, getting her down again. I don't much mind for myself; I can close up shop and go away and open up again somewhere else; a whore is always in business. But she—she isn't right with herself yet. Somehow I think if she ran away she would die. Maybe that is the holiness here—

what still lingers in the air to make her stay. A judgment has to be given; a fair judgment! Then she will take her place here, first among us because we have so cruelly abused her, and Maria started sweeping under the chairs and tables.

Zoe had whispered the message into Anna's ear about Paul one day as the woman's circle came visiting the newly diagnosed patient. Anna smiled—oh, he wants my death, does he? Cold little man—quite switches one off. And so they say prostitution is to be taxed and that you are a Muslim, my dear, she said to Agatha, who stood by her pillow.

My father was, said Agatha; my mother didn't want to have us baptized on his account. I always retained something of my father. Privately, I consider myself both Muslim and Christian. I don't find there to be any discrepancy.

Only for men, said Anna, laughing. Fornication and religion are their main themes. For them, such distinctions as whore and wife. For us, pleasure, pain! For them, the great dream of the spirit. For us, the real body.

We thought you should know, said Zoe; she had brought some white roses and was arranging them in a glass vase on Anna's table.

You brought white? Said Anna suddenly focusing on the flowers. I like red. Wine red. Blood red. Since I am shortly to become the vine and the wheat field, wine and bread in the very tangible worm. My dying passion nobody will know however—except you, perhaps, she said to Agatha.

I? said Agatha, she was brooding. You are right, she said to Anna—what do they know about me—that I keep a Qu'ran, and a Bible I read a little here and there in each one. It seems to me that there is only a trace of God—in one a vision, in the other, a voice, and yet they would call me Muslim or Christian and then begin to argue it one way or another! I don't really deserve to be called either one.

You see, said Anna to Zoe, how faithful she is. She keeps God—a closet full and does not let go.

Anna, listening to you I would say you are hardly sick. You'll outlive all of us in the end.

Ha, I am ready! My foot is hovering, pointed like a dancer's down to the open grave.

With other pleasantries like this—where it seemed that Anna thought nothing of the shadow hanging over her—the little meeting was brought to a close and Zoe went away.

Agatha stayed behind to wash tea cups—for they had drunk a lot of excellent tea, very green and fragrant; tell me said Anna, as she watched her bringing the china cups out from her bed—how is it you can have two Gods? I thought one was enough; I certainly could not handle even that many.

For me God is like saying the great sky, the huge pit. There is something about it that either wipes out everything else or else is itself a kind of non-existence. No you are right—a closet full! But there must be one—how can I say it—precise truth. And consolation for the passing of the day, the week, the year…

I would call it the scar, said Anna.

But it does not exist if we are just flesh and blood, bread and wine. Then it is just a woman with her legs spread open on a hospital bed waiting for the doctor to rip out of her another bag of flesh with legs --a desecration, a violation, Agatha's voice surged up. But yet it exists. This I call holiness—the birth; yes, what you call the scar. Oh, you could call it that scar of birth, but the more you look at it, the more it has a life of its own separate from that wound of birthing.

And it becomes a beautiful calligraphy, divine, godly—the writing in the end of love…said Anna, because of that life of its own.

I can hardly bear it.

Old scar-bearer, said Anna to her affectionately. Of course, that is its nature. Do you expect me to believe these pitiful Christians with their white roses for the sick, their little houses, marriages, children…their money under the mattresses, their supplications when they are sick, their copulations under all sorts of secret covers, their bowings to the icons, their kissings of the gold-leaf covered crosses? No, but you with that endless pain—and then something more to it--Christ, the Crucified One: it seems sometimes like we are passing up the one truth—as we pass on the right by the believers, on the left, the unbelievers.

I can hardly complain, murmured Agatha, talking now more to herself than to her friend. I could wish that the work in the morning was easier. I thought that dancing was just a matter of getting up and kicking one's legs higher and higher as the practice went on; but it isn't really. It's the frost on the grass, the light on the water. It's that barely touching quality of nudity. And toiling behind, coming up the hill to it. Not somersaulting in the air.

That's Paul, laughed Anna, deliciously—Paul who's captured the dancer's crown, the last little distinctive piece of culture on our island; he captured it by kicking and kicking, flipping, splitting, stretching the ligaments. He was determined you know—drove himself, split himself. I personally don't think he ever danced at all. But you were saying—

It is harder, a matter of unfolding—getting down into the secret places where the wings are really kept, listening with your body for the rhythm of the slightest rain; it's coming naked to the air, parting the curtains of the day. I can't explain any other way. I too have driven myself. And there are so many mornings when after an hour or so, back I go defeated into my little hole, my bedroom, in which you can still see the picture of my husband smiling stupidly—he hated being photographed—and I look into his eyes and think—well, he was as good as any other. I managed. Why not marry again if I can and settle down? Give up this anger and pain in me that survived even the relatively happy marriage; let go of it, drown it in the sea…but in the dance…

Ha, said Anna, frowning, you want your vengeance.

For what? Didn't I consent?

Never, said Anna; the door was shut and locked, the windows also. You were trapped. But you went naked to it.

It has to do with the body not being just the body…

Well, those are places in the mind I have never been. But above all don't give up.

Hold on to yourself. I don't see why we shouldn't be Muslim and Christian, Hindu and Buddhist here—they are just meaningless categories, God never calls us anything but children-- and those that follow hollow rituals and rites are as empty headed as the others –with one idolizing one fanciful idea another another. Any man secretly knows whether he is truthful or not. And a woman, well a woman I don't think can ever quite tell a lie.

They ranted on and on as Anna called it later to Zoe. Our group was astonished to find that she was in such great good humor. The prospect of death just seemed to buoy her up—this unbeliever, godless as they come. Paul said that when the pain of the cancer hit, she would bow her head in agony and despair; we could see him willing it on this old lady with his very loins. Walking past her, thrusting his pelvis forward a little in fury. But she would always greet him with a serene smile and often together with Agatha, once—how used we were to seeing it—bowed down as if under a great weight, her head downwards, eyes on the ground, and one leg dragging—now quietly erect, not so much defiantly, although now and then perhaps; but often it was just that she couldn't help herself. Her spine had straightened; she no longer dragged her leg and our sense was that she was feeling, what could we call it but a kind of glory?

We saw her and thought—impossible that she should be brought low again. And many of us thought that God had healed her, raised her from her affliction. When we heard it was dancing that she was up to, our breath came short. And then laughter—well, yes of course. She never used to dance. It is the other time with her on this island. Not only the fishing time, the lunch time, the tavern time, the whoring time—that was all one thing. This was a different time, something else entirely. There was no night or day when we danced, no God or man. Timos said that we were eagles and Nisos that we were flying fish. But those are old men's dreams. We were just the male and female naked in naked air long ago—first creatures in our day on the rim of a bright new earth like a young moon with a lapis lazuli shadow.

When we had young people, many a romance started at our dance festivals. A man would pick out a woman if he had danced well enough for her satisfaction and even if he had not and all sweaty and panting he'd be, and she with glistening eyes. We thought that Agatha perhaps was going to put herself in the line of women on purpose now so that there would be a crown of orange flowers in her hair soon, and a white bridal dress. As if one couldn't sense the difference—Agatha, the anathema—creeping back, at last, to our ways and traditions. Paul said it is this sort of thing—those who cannot partake, creeping back in, eating and drinking with us—that ruins holiness.

But objected Cleo, she would be a believer like anyone of us. She couldn't dream of anyone not baptized joining in in the Easter dance, or of even being capable of dancing.

She can't be a believer. She would have never brought that terrible curse upon us. Why she would have known that murder itself is preferable.

As if there isn't a personal history behind your hate, snapped Anna at Paul losing all patience.

What personal history? Who isn't guilty of a little dalliance? Wasn't it that that Jesus forgave us—when all the rest, he looked around at the little throng—they were gathered by the grocery store to buy last minute items before it closed for the night--- were so prepared to stone the sinner? But didn't he also say that we were not to be forgiven the sin against the Holy Spirit and hasn't the priest said…

Of course not, said Anna. He was crazed by poisons. Agatha is doing the one thing needed.

Now prayer… started Paul, intending to object--.

Rising up, said Anna, interrupting, her tone flat and final.

In rebellion, said Paul, not obedience.

To you and your notions of curses and to all of you. Why you are nothing but contemptible. Unkind, foolish, and cruel—if you were honest you would confess to your own sins with shame instead of denouncing others'.

But you, squeaked Timos are an unbeliever and as such…

Precisely, said Paul sighing. It is obvious that we have on hand good, kind people, dear people who would like to see this island what it always was—holy, and pure. And then others….

Anna had to be quiet. There was in her a clear and profound degree of memory that saw things differently—the island had been beautiful and holy; holy because it was so beautiful, perhaps; and there was no question that things had changed. People had changed. She knew that Paul was a liar. At the same time, he spoke truth. The very people that she had shouted at half convinced of Agatha's cursedness as they called it, frightened that she had committed the absolute sin, were also inexpressibly dear to her. It was all affection, of course, nothing deep; but although she didn't believe as they believed in God, she wanted the little island to succeed, to raise up itself a nice little boast—that they maintained a simple, beautiful life in the midst of what she knew to be a chaotic, complex world on the way to losing everything good, rare and absolutely true, above all to utterly devaluing the beloved old people of belief. Agatha was a bit of a disturbance. What was this wanting of her own world as it were plop in the midst of this slightly disturbed but still humming and vibrating perfect refuge? This seeking of holiness in moody broodiness—in her hell—as it were? What was this 'thing of her own'—this dancing in her closet?

Our dances were all together at the dance festivals; Agatha was not with us, and was therefore against us in some inscrutable way. We knew Anna would raise her voice and rail at us but wouldn't blame us forever. Besides Agatha had always gone about her business—she and Jason, although one could see at a glance that Jason was with us while she was not.

We never disturbed Agatha, in any case. She was perfectly free even to join our little circle. Sometimes she came, sat apart—made a big thing of pouring the tea, as if where on that pot that she put her tea-colored hands, browner than the rest of her, was of some concern to us. She sat quietly; never spoke a word; to look at her, said Cleo, made one think of a bee buzzing. Summer and its intense clarity. Perhaps we wanted a bee to buzz—to startle a girl who looked like she could never be startled— from just behind her head. That she might give a little cry, flail her arms in quite a profane or undancer-like way.

We guess what bothered us, if you call it bother—was that she had crawled into a pit on her own and on her own was crawling out. She had no need of anybody. It was as if she had worked out life completely on her own. She was, how can we say it—so content to be just as she was. She was not needy, little, chit chatting; she didn't need our group, nor did she need to gather at the tavern. She was suddenly by her own and on her own —one glorious woman. Well, of course, God bless women who can by their own industry—after years of being as it were so deeply disturbed—rise up in the world. But then let her go and face the world—she seems to want to take it on like a wrestler.

But there is dissent in our group. Some say she is like a wrestler, some say like the Virgin mother; how the two go together, I can't say. Only someone like Agatha would have us so confused. Of course, that is nonsense. Of course the Virgin mother… but here we are tongue tied. Who is to say that the Virgin mother gathered with the cronies in a group and chatted? Who is to say that she did not rise up and walk—that is to say walk like the queen she was? But with Agatha—it is as if: Behold the truth, she says, haughtily. Although, we must admit it isn't so much haughtiness. A kind of sorrow, separateness—alas who can blame her? But well, if that sorrow leads to this—this we can't help saying it, exquisite walking in our sight—it would have us all jealous almost. But this is not the end yet.

Anna said to us a strange thing concerning Agatha: She said I think it was just like a drug for a long time-- her sorrow. She held it in her heart and feasted off it; same as an addict chewing cannabis!-- same as Father Raphael who saw his sister in her; remember how he took powders and chewed leaves? And in him, hallucinations, a broken mind; in her sorrow upon sorrow—the whirling down the abyss in her mind—the keeping apart, the not quite fitting in. That she has broken this sorrow fixation, this eating of tears inside like an addict eating hash is in itself admirable. The change is little but immense. She walks erect; she carries herself well. She has worked seven years to simply lift her head!

But the beauty? There was undeniable beauty.

Did anyone ever see her face when she walked hunched over? Did anyone ever see her womanliness when her breasts were caved in, when her hips couldn't move properly?

And they wanted to kill her.

Are you so surprised? With the way our little island has lost its soul—that hooligans should creep out of our forest, the end zone of our village… Of course, they could have targeted you or me….

Were they ever found?

The same men that we see every day, you know that. They are there, one or two fish among the throng. Who could really know them by their faces? They weren't seen in the darkness by the sparks of their matches. We from our windows only saw shadow noses, jaws, eyes so contorted as to be not human at all but phantoms that whirl on the edge. Perhaps the priest knows them to be flesh and blood faces within our circle and keeps it to himself. He was there. We were at home. We know them only by their hearts. Resentful, angry. It suited them-- and they danced at the dance festivals kicking their heels up high—when one of us was a prisoner, like Agatha, a real prisoner at last. The old war flared up again—they wanted that woman to keep her back bent, bent as it was—ah they could see and hear the battle—for a man's sake: a cold, cruel man who said he brought justice, from God, of course. And he would even sit as one or two or three in amongst others of a more modern frame of mind.

Ah, more modern. You mean the ones who admire her behind? They are fickle. Blow on with Paul's trumpet. Holiness, he proclaims through his horn—and his music plays the song of the bent backed women while the men stand straight like strength –the words. I know the scoundrels who admire Agatha, said Zoe, scornfully.

When Anna was with us and putting it so clearly, we saw that Agatha was really a good friend. It was just when she sat in our circle, so quiet, so distant—as if a thousand thoughts separated her heart from us—it was then that we knew that she was a different fruit, of a different root; there was nothing that could be done about it. Before, we gathered that she was mourning—her husband, and before that, the parents that had died. But this mourning was never for the death of anybody, ultimately. It kept her apart; and it seemed that she preferred that shadow of sorrow to us. Now, something else—a new wisdom, it seems. She has that look in her eyes, how terribly annoying, says Cleo, as if she could write a book. We try to be with her. We realize, oh, of course, we realize, that the men have unjustly…but there is the fact, the undeniable fact, that she although beautiful, and although we come smiling up to receive her, with her straightened spine, when she comes in like a gift or something—we can't quite help feeling that well she got there by herself, perhaps her solitude is best for her.

She is aiming for something, said Anna to us smiling.

A new man, we said it as with one voice. There is no question that one wants at this point in time, a man to bring in the light. Different to the sun, no question. But then again there is something of the sun in it—the hollow of a man's hand on your thigh—something of the sun in his thigh against your thigh, something of the sun when he fills your place, penetrates to the deep inside, something of the sun when you feel his hot seed in you. But it is different from the sun. A different kind of light. Leaves you knowing something. With all those shining eyes of our last young wives coming away from the altar—who had in the usual way, met, tested—it appears to be something almost ineffable. But we would call it love.

Even gypsies, says Foti. And we have visions of a woman doing it in the dust with a man. We are embarrassing ourselves needlessly; when has Agatha ever lived in the dust? She's had a roof over her head even when—now we remember—someone did set fire, a pathetic attempt and it was a long time ago—a brief memory: a burned doorway. Ah yes, she has had a roof over her head, and we thank God for it. It appears her mother told her the fable of the phoenix rising from the ashes. Ashes family, someone called them once; but it was all patched up and healed over quickly. We were all shocked. These things simply do not happen on Holy Island. There was a rumor that the gypsy father had himself…but no, he had tears in his eyes, that day sitting in the sun. A quiet man and suddenly his house door on fire! Well, it was quenched and there was nothing more. Ashes to ashes, Paul's father had said. We know he meant that the episode was over, the terror was dead, the cruelty was dead. But now we suddenly realize: Could he have meant—the ashes were the gypsies, dead to us?

He had been the one to say: gypsies are the enemies of civilization. Why doesn't he return to his camp in the other land? And he called Agatha herself jestingly—that ashes girl. For a while, she had been taunted—ashes girl, ashes girl, but the voices grew fainter; mothers and fathers had hushed them; but then her mother did an unusual thing. She said to her –perhaps you will find in yourself some spark still glowing. You have fire in you and perhaps one day it will blaze high. A different light from the others, and closer to the sun.

But in sum, it had all been nearly wiped away. Agatha's father, died young from smoking pack after pack—smoked nervously and that makes all the difference—he was a little ever-wrinkled man in a dusty old jacket, ate little, and played all kinds of instruments—the violin, the cello, guitar, flute, oboe, clarinet; he became head of the musicians that play for our festivals. We remember his wrinkled face, his bent head over the strings, the reed and the nonstop music; it was as if better to play music than to live, he said, although he didn't quite say it. He wasn't quite, as a gypsy, you understand, well meaning. He left his family—although he died in bed at home with his wife and daughter. But he left Agatha, a girl of ten, twined around her mother—because she was both a little spitfire and a soft, melancholy clinger to her mother—persons are never one thing like they say in the novels—but he took the boy. And so woman and man separated. There was a break like the other world coming between, and the woman looked out on the sea and saw nothing but an abyss into which husband had fallen, abyss of nothingness and the day after day that followed him there; and she was knitting him a scarf in case he should come back and find it cold at night; and it never came right—she would knit a little and unravel it; one day the woolen scarf knit with blue yarn was entirely unraveled. And then she would try and try to remake it but she said the pain in her made her put it down.

What pain, what foolishness—we tried to comfort her. You are young—she was just forty; find another. But then the light went on in the house at night, and whenever we passed, we saw her with that ball of yarn attempting to do it up again—like Zoe does or Cleo, but at that time it was our mothers. And they had men, you see, click in place—like the knitting needles click click; everything was click click. You can't have it if it isn't; that is quite clear. He came home alone and died on their marriage bed with Agatha's mother fetching tea and cold compresses uselessly, futilely against the pain of cancer; her eyes saw a shape on the bed, but her heart didn't recognize him. And then after they buried him, it was as if he had never returned. Agatha's mother died about ten years later trying—sitting up for the return of him—of who? Of course, she was a little addled -- click click, knitting him a scarf over and over—without a man or with a man just hidden, wrapped up in absolute air. Perhaps unfolded somewhere—man born of air—and walking next to a woman in that other land, or going back to his ancestors—the men and women who do it in the dust and live in camps with their dirty, dusty children. In any case, we all in the end saw him as the one who had left not the cracked pot who had returned, whining and in pain, and we remembered—a small figure with his violin and jacket, nothing else, on board a caique and his wife alone at home near a window now and then, seeing the backs of several men down by the dock, not him. The boy had got sick and died.

Unnatural, said Paul's father; undoubtedly, he said, springing with his genius to another thought—she wanted with all the lust in her—that man—he came with a violin, and in those days a guitar too—pretty things that make women pant; undoubtedly—a gypsy makes women think wild—what was it? Music and stolen Mercedes Benz', not that he ever produced one for her and they heat up like bitches...But then he was silenced. Paul's mother did not like that word, nor the idea that a woman would want in that way, when she had children by him.

Perhaps, said Paul's father, she couldn't bear seeing him off. The house was her only refuge.

She had had enough of him. When lust dies down in a woman, she will become cold, heartless and bitter.

And love? Asked Paul at the time he was about eight, active as a little rabbit.

Love puts them on your string forever.

And it was Paul, a little child then, white, brown and blue-eyed, bounding around, jumping and cartwheeling—the kind of child a mother would ache and pray to have—who said to Agatha, older by two years—I am going to make you love me.

How some memories come we will never know. Perhaps it is just talking of Agatha—how the whole village secretly thinks it is unfair that she is walking tall and as secretly thinks—how could we not be delighted? Hasn't she been down in the dumps long enough in her affliction—an inherited thing, a depression that has no end because of the blood. Gypsies may be wild and beautiful, but they have no ability to love as we do. Look at them committing crime after crime—robbery, and murder, incest even. And we have heard, although we never saw it, how they market their own children—sell them for money. It was, of course, not Agatha's fault. She went to school with our daughters and sons. Not quite one of them. In those days, she was a stout girl and used her fists. The priest, Father Raphael, new at the time, coaxed and reprimanded; she was not unintelligent. She listened in class, read her books; she even had a friend or two. But she spent most of her time lurking in the forest and she was like a little outlaw then—didn't care if the thorns scratched her, if she was penetrating into that forest alone with no protection.

We say that we didn't discriminate. How could we? Agatha grew up with our children. When her father left, she was more thoughtful. Our mothers came with the lemon curd, the gift of a bottle of brandy, the blankets, the embroidered curtains; the woman sat silently at the dinner table not responding to our questions. We say she would have gotten over it, but something stuck in her head—one or two of his songs, the love that flew out of her and down the path of the little figure with the finely wrinkled face, meek like a little tame dove. We say it was love. A woman and man don't quite marry in their usual bodies. One might be a badger, the other a dove. But alas, man or woman can metamorphose yet again.

In any case, it appears to us that it was the lapsed island woman that didn't want to join us. And that Agatha took right after her. But that is not so rare with gypsies. They prefer to be outcasts, wild folk. Then Agatha couldn't quite come up to our way of doing—how she made much of a little slip on Paul's part. We saw her at seventeen parade into Paul's place one evening. Now come, what would a woman expect—tea and apricot candy? She said she was going to learn dancing. Well, she took it too much amiss. After all, he never came to her house.

We are glad that Agatha is over all that. At least, she doesn't display that foul mood that gypsies often have. Though the gypsy man was meekness and mildness itself on the exterior, he had a will of iron in the family. The woman picked up a foul mouth like a disease and cussed at us often. We must say that for love, we know of course that it was love—but it took on quite a character way back then. Agatha didn't inherit that ugly tongue. She was a well-spoken child, then silent. And some of the men whisper that Paul was the reason. Of course not, though, we say, though misery made her silent. We thought: what right has she to be miserable? A man married her in the end—a husband who died at home. And then also we thought –how can we express it—what right to rise up now—with husband dead and son gone? And we were not quite allowed, none of us was quite allowed except Anna, Katrina, now that American girl—to come with the proper solace ever. When her husband died—no one. What was going on inside the home would have been unknown as the Creator except for Barbara who has a kitchen window next to Agatha's living room. With her screaming at the top of her lungs—of course, the village heard the news. Cursing herself. It was such a spectacle, but in a sense only one more pathetic little incident of Agatha. And then Dimitri gone—only a few remained who really heard and saw: Barbara, who saw really nothing but a dim light, candles lit and then heard the hoarse cracked scream almost like the shouts at the dance festivals only horrifying, Simon, who holds himself aloof from all judgment, who with Anna who loves and laughs at everybody was passing on the narrow stone street outside.

Now, ah now—we have known Agatha since she was born! Now she is a stranger. She has always been a stranger. Anna said she is aiming to bring a flood of fire to us.

At last the news came, every ear in the village heard it: Dimitri was coming home. He was bringing a man with him, a rich man; we had had Anna's rich men-husbands and we knew what they were like. They came in shorts, and sunglasses, walked on the beach, threw an arm around a man's shoulders, rested a hand on an old woman's hip, ate one or two of our lumps of goats' cheese, talked over a platter of chicken with potatoes and tomatoes, looked up and back from the table at a poor musician and held out to him a fistful of change to take home and buy something on this little island, a fistful of sand and stones, where we sit and wait, one day like any other—for the return of our holiness. For God has his ways…. But in any case, the rich men don't wait for them. If they can't abide the caique, off they sail in a small yacht—the extra one.

We gathered in Simon's house. Agatha was bringing the news. For once, she would face us and explain this thing. There were plastic and wooden chairs all around the house. People dropped into them, lit cigarettes. There were little glasses on Simon's long dining table—shining and dark wood that could seat at least twenty; here we were about three hundred and it still looked long, imposing, stately in his big, cavernous dining room. Some of us were seated on cushions—red and white and yellow, about fifty of them scattered around the carpeted floor. Some were seated directly on the floor—men sitting cross-legged with their pants hitched up exposing their long ankles. The rest had found chairs.

There were the mumblers—what does it matter to us! Drag us out of our homes in the middle of our evening smelling dinner cooking or digesting it still warm in our bellies—all for what? A rich man—pah! What do we care for a rich man? Let them have their tours of the world, their women, their play—we have our old ways; the old times are coming back to us soon because we are taking steps; a different earth it was—right here on our shores, in our forest, on our cliffs! Our monastery knows. Born, made of discipline; people really applied themselves to what we call the little life: fishing, embroidery, prayer. We had, they say, the light. The sun still shines same as ever but in those days—we were of the light. Sun people and more than sun people—of the light, the light—what is here, in this world, in the sun, only a crude sign. Babies were born on this island under the sun, and more than under the sun. We had children with the light shining on their foreheads. Is this rich man going to bring us children?

When Agatha came in, everyone was still. She was wearing her old black mourning skirt and a white blouse. She stood light and taut like a tree in the forest. Just before she spoke, one cleared his throat and spat, about three others lit cigarettes inhaled deeply, tilted back their heads and blew smoke in her direction.

Dimitri is coming bringing with him a man who wears high fashion jeans and a white Panama hat who owns luxury hotels and might build one right here, she said.

We were all buzzing at once. Luxury hotel—you mean here? What would we want with a luxury hotel? I don't know but there are beautiful women that come along with money….And where will he build? We must sell him the land or the church—I doubt whether the church….Of course, the church—everything goes for money.

It is only a testing ground, said Agatha. She walked to the rear of the room.

How like a gypsy, said one man in a raincoat evilly—in the end to sell us and get rich.

But some others of us would get rich as well.

There is the good and the bad, said Simon, who always spoke as if he was half imbecile, but, made you think twice—as if he was a sage. They live together in the same nut, bitter and sweet; it is, you see, one flavor.

This island, said Stavros, wisely, like everywhere else in the world, has to face development. What are we going to remain the innocents of long ago because modern civilization has turned on its heel and walked out on us?

You scoff, said Peter but they are players, players! They play with God himself. Here we have everything we need.

And, of course, said Paul, coldly, it was not part of the design.

But the murmuring had picked up—a luxury hotel on our island! Will we have our faces on postcards? Asked Nisos. That is what I want to know.

Yes, then, said Anna, mocking and smiling all together, people will have collections—the Eiffel tower, the Coliseum, the Acropolis, and Nisos' face—Americans no doubt, or Japanese, with his face, right in their bedrooms.

That is because here we have people, the people, said Michael. What the world is looking for.

Awkward, contorted, pleasure-seeking, wizened, said Stavros laughing heartily. The men with teeth rotted from years of apricot brandy and apricot candy, the women with soft, heavy flesh from growing up on goat's cheese and lemon curd. Men with brains dried into nuts from long hours on the sea—thinking of brandy. Women half mad from embroidering, cleaning house. Think of it! The people! Whereas in America women travel to the moon.

And what do they learn there? Barbara asked harshly, that they can't learn making lemon curd at home?

Why as a matter of fact, said Stavros, smiling, unimportant things—all about galaxies, planets, the possibility of life –in a far away world.

That is exactly what we have here, said Timos, dreamily—.

Yes, said Stavros nodding, his round face, serious for once—in fact! The possibility for life in a far away world.

It is what excites the developers, said Paul, drily.

We knew that Agatha was sensing the uneven reception to her news; she had of course known that it would be like this. Even something mundane from the outer world, like a new refrigerator, or heavens! Computers—for the possibility of wiring the island had still not been explored, but this was something that would take our island shake it dead as a dog does a squirrel and then resurrect it into a different life—a life of yachts and business men who owned hotels and golf courses, lived with swimming pools in their back yards and all sorts of gadgets; we would become a sort of super island despite our tininess—a getaway prized for the fact that there are no cars, the sea is clean and cool, the forests brilliant with white and yellow butterflies in summer, for our wealth of birds, that there is a cliff, and a really old monastery where a dissonant bell still tolls faintly in the early morning and every so often for prayer—and even that would be in the end—a comma, a pause in the luxury people's day—a little memory. While on the side, peering in, would be our faces, our fisher faces—like little unidentified birds collecting on the seashore that seem to situate themselves there for some biological reason so far unrecorded. And there would be picture after picture of our different colored houses, the white washed church, and the patches of fresco of God in the waters above the firmament with the joyful fish who live somewhere in the sky. And in this new resurrection, we, some of us, fewer and fewer, would go on living as the trinket, beloved natural trinket, of a million, million tourists. We would have to live for the sake of the world that has turned on its heel and moved on but still wants to see, sometimes to turn back and know—those people are still there. The natural trinket people with their white washed church, their celestial fish, their monastery bell that tolls faintly! Ah, we know all this: we see it in the future. Magda taught us how. And she was of another world, ah she! Beautiful and unsuspecting, she died. There might be a little surreptitious resistance in saying her name—prayers to, simple devotions. And maybe she too would be 'raised'—a story for the amusement of people with white Panama hats to down with apricot brandy at the tavern.

And Paul seeing what we were afraid of, would one day, when the furor died down come round to—perhaps too late, begin to creep around warning us—no good can come of this sort of thing. Development perhaps but not on our terms.

And we listened. Paul was the rationalist, the reasonable one. How could we let all go to the winds…But many of us had just enough curiosity. We wanted to see this rich man in a white Panama hat and exquisite jeans who would come, we presumed in a yacht sail into our waters, with us vying with each other—who should present him with a gift of apricot brandy or lemon curd first. In any case, he hadn't come. What is the use of a story among us—whispers and murmurs, Agatha wouldn't respond to questions—when the real thing is going to turn up any moment? But we were in full force. Prepared: we would put it to him plainly—development but only on our terms.

Then come up with the money, growled Stavros. Don't you see that when you have sold a piece of this land, most of this land because how can a hotel like that stand in a narrow lane, off of an alley?—you lose the land, the island forever? Gone it is for so much gold. You can't then come around and dictate something to the builders, the architects, the contractors. They will say: What have you to do with it? Are you mad? Useless for you to say—but I know this land, my blood is in it, my ancestors sleep just off the shores in a ring 'round about; some underneath—so many that the coffins knock against one another in the ground. I know all the stories; I have eaten the food for years and years….

So Stavros talked on the fishing boats at dawn. The fishermen couldn't understand his drift. Of course, the development was to be on their terms. It was always would be—their island. That can't change. What a Christian you are! They even said to Stavros—hooligans that they are. Was Jesus the property of the Pharisees who paid good money for him? The fishermen even had the gall to ask.

Stavros was always a talker. Out they went when it was quiet and he would be murmuring, saying things—as if his noise didn't count as far as the fish were concerned. But for years and years, the other fishermen were convinced that he scared away fish. He would start to talk and they would try to persuade him to be quiet. For these were the finest fishing waters in the Aegean. Pity for it all to go to waste because of one big mouth. And Stavros had to comply.

Barbara in his home took the side of everybody else. Seeing as Dimitri didn't come right away with the rich man with the white Panama hat and the light colored jeans who would ask us right away—so this land or that land? You, pointing to Nisos, maybe, what do you think? There we would be assembled...And then Stavros shouting at her no! Wake up!—there was time in any case to prepare. Each house was given the task of polishing up, so to speak; Barbara spent back breaking hours in the garden weeding, and then painted her shutters that bright other worldly blue the island was once famous for. Other women sewed again, embroidering with all their talent as if this time they might win a kind of competition. Maria cleaned up the tavern with Simon's help so that it looked immaculate—little white-cloth draped tables with empty wine bottles and flowers coming out of their necks.

Everyone did something, changed a little. Jason ate more and put on weight quickly. Agatha said something to the effect that she was sure the two boys would fight again and Jason— now with his mass of flesh that always appeared hard to her, like a shield against all tenderness, against Dimitri who was slim and quick as she remembered like a tender thing struggling for survival—would have an unfair advantage. She actually took it into her head, she told Anna one day—Agatha was wearing skirts now and wrapping her head in a brown scarf—to visualize a fight with knives as that which had one time occurred...but that had been hushed, dropped, all but forgotten, left as it were in the silence of the stones of the streets. Agatha told Anna that now that she was celebrating and cooking dish after dish, dancing in a way that she couldn't imagine herself dancing, there had come into her deep heart new/old fear that grabbed her like a fist. There is nothing I can do—even if all the world is joyful—if they decide to go at one another with knives!

But of course, they will not. They parted boys; they return together as men. Together they will see this island raised up. Of course, of course—how can they not embrace one another—the one who came from far away with this new call for us; the other who stayed and kept the place alive—just barely. Can't you see that one and the other are on two ends of a balance—without either one we would be destroyed.

Agatha went around town with a crease in her forehead though. She had that look of whatever happens she would keep going—almost despair, but not quite. She too had to absorb that the island was creeping towards her. There was of course suspicion, there was anger—Paul was coldly wrathful at times—he said we'll see, we'll see—but in general the village was coming in like the tide towards Agatha who held out, it seems, infinite multiples of rich men to them with white Panama hats.

If she could put real money where her mouth is, said one, a shadowy face on him. But think, said another—a million in a real bank! Wiry, with gleaming eyes. What are we good for anyway, said a third; I'm fifty and I've dreamed of many things. All came to nothing because of this island. I'm cooped up here with a sterile wife—all I see is sand and stones and death. You're young yet, said the wiry one. With a million in the bank you could have an apartment on the mainland.

Michael ran up to the group. Agatha received a phone call from the mainland at the tavern where there is one pay phone. It appeared Dimitri had flown in. In three days, he'll be here. Arriving on a private yacht. He and the rich man.

With Dimitri?

Perhaps not, said Michael. Dimitri you see is just a greeter and a guide. They have some sort of arrangement, but he does not work directly for the hotel owner. It is his place to be here, in a certain way, and for the hotel owner to ask him questions. Dimitri speaks English and can translate.

Do you mean we cannot even speak to this developer? This rich man who wants our island?

Everything will be translated by Dimitri.

At the tavern that evening, playing checkers, Peter and Stavros tried for a time to pretend that everything was as usual. But at a certain point, Maria broke in with—if the rich man buys our island were will be live? In the waves? This tavern can't float.

Ah, listen to her, said Peter in frustration, stamping with his foot. But it is odd now, isn't it? I am fifty years old—fished for a living. Dreamed many things. Used to turn over in bed and dream again. And now they tell me that this one and that one –a gypsy's son are coming in to buy my house! Ha, you know, I don't believe it.

We can say no, said Stavros.

How like a gypsy in the end—everything is money for them.

For years Agatha has lived on practically nothing. And I would say, she has given much, very quietly. I myself don't know how much of her goods and money she has actually given away to Matrona, but it has been something substantial. We just stood idly by, content to let her just somehow exist. And she treats Martha like she is one of us—gathering her up half naked, so to speak, bringing her in like it's a natural thing to do.

Trying to show us Christians up. But now—what is going to happen to us? Alright, we'll have money in our pocket—but where am I to go? I never liked Agatha. For me, underneath that face which says nothing and never did say anything there is nothing but savagery.

She was miserable for years but always subdued and gentle.

Misery comes from going against heaven. Didn't she cry out a terrible curse from hell? Ah, she is a very subtle one. Subdued and gentle! For years she had something to say against my brother. Ah, she is the violent one within down deep and very slyly, the way women are violent. What could my brother possibly have done? It is hard and wearing to have a heap of misery and slyness pointing the finger at you for no earthly reason. It was right that she should pay for it. I think they once engaged in a sort of horse play! But everybody does that when they are seventeen.

Dimitri...

What about him, snapped Peter, angrily.

He has made a world for himself.

A deserter who thinks that with money he can come back and set everything to rights. Ah, it takes much more than that. It takes an act of God.

Yes, because something is lacking here; we will be dead soon, said Maria suddenly appearing at the side of the table and joining in.

Too much screwing has gone to your brains, said Peter, disgustedly.

No, I know—I too hear from God.

And what does he say? Stavros, smiled a little.

He doesn't speak in words, Maria looked over the men's heads as if she was seeing something in the air. Perhaps he doesn't speak at all. But something clutches at my deep inside. There are to be a few more moments—that is what that means.

A few more minutes and a few more minutes; Peter misquoted. We will live a lifetime in a few more minutes. It has always been the same here. For some reason, years ago or a few years ago, it doesn't matter, we went off. A little out of line. Now see what it takes to come back, practically a miracle. Now how is it that a gypsy could make so much money? Peter grumbled.

So you think, really, now, that we'll come back, as you put it, with this luxury hotel? Stavros was still smiling.

I never said that nor ever would say that, said Peter, hastily.

But there are things that reveal themselves when you speak, softly continued Stavros, and—

Nothing reveals itself, shouted Peter. Nothing.

Yes, honey, Maria sidled over to Peter. We still have that few minutes. My gut instinct tells me that you'd rather be somewhere comfortable, warm and tender...

In a minute, no, go away, Peter pushed her hand off his hair. He looked at Stavros in an embarrassed sulky way. I don't spend much time with her, of course, he muttered. You see the kind of girl she is—half crazy. I come out of pity. Besides these days—so many important things...

It is not said that anything will ever be built here, Stavros said reflectively. There is much agitation. It makes me think that the island was asleep for my entire lifetime and only now has half woken up. He looked around him—look at this tavern; what a job Maria has done.

I polished everything—the glasses, the dishes. I washed the awning; I threw out the old wine bottles with candles and put new ones. I spent from my savings and bought new white linen for the tables. Why didn't you notice?

Well, grumbled Peter—all this for a man you don't even know! I guess you expect that he'll pay more for your services.

Why—he's a guest, honey. Coming across the water.

And so?

Why—it means weddings! The last thing we can do in the few minutes left us.

Ha, laughed Peter, shortly—you, a whore planning to marry a rich man.

Rich or poor, of course I am planning to marry. Someone will take me—of course they will. I still have all my teeth and hair. I know how to wash and clean and keep company.

Well, Maria, said Stavros getting up after finishing the fifth game with Peter, fish well. Peter stayed behind to keep Maria company and Stavros plunged into the night.

We think that the electrical company has done us wrong, depriving us of a full ration of electricity. We have not always paid, it is true, but some of us have been very faithful and paid in full. During these days when we were expecting, as Maria said, our guest, who was to bring along if not weddings, similar feasts—because for a rich man like that we would have to go all out—the electrical company could have been more understanding. We sent Nico, a talker like Dimitri, and an arguer of some ability. But they didn't listen.

And he said: But we aim to have a feast like a wedding! An awesome feast!

Use candles, one insignificant worker replied. Nico never got to talk to anybody important over there on the other island. But he came back full of the same stories: They have huge houses, some of them, with gold domes and porches; they have roads and cars and trucks and buses. Simon laughed and whirled around Nico dancing a little kick step—and the whole world glitters and glows, he shouted. Imagine, us having voted him in for chief on our island. Then again, half maniac that he is, he still has a streak of the sage.

It is like that for us. It is for us to listen and for us to learn of Simon, and the one or two that remain who still tap into the old mind. The world never would.

Yes, we have, Simon knows—the sign of light, the flesh and blood-- the sign that would come—flesh and blood that would live or die in the light—one mind; that is the difference. There is talk that Agatha's father was the ruination of our island, that the one mind split or dissolved because of him. But what was he? A person who stayed home Sundays when we went to church—who had another Bible. Yes, perhaps, that is serious. A great division. But see who he was—a quiet man, a man who thought in music; a soft man with his girl, Agatha. Took his boy with him everywhere. A gentle man with the poor. Turned his back on his wife when she blasphemed. Sent his money to his brethren in the gypsy camp on the other island where they lived like beggars, filthy children, building fires in the fields to cook.

If it wasn't him, who was it? Where can we point the finger and say—there, there, everything changed, there! We think it wasn't Agatha's father, but Agatha's mother: A woman who would willingly, knowingly change the face of the island. A woman who would go out to the other island and bring back one of the 'different elements' as we might put it that live in clusters there. Oh, there it is ok. They have long since given up their old traditions. People from all over the world live there in their own little groups. But we are different—we have clung to each other. Without speaking about it, undercover, as it were, we have told each other—in hints, gestures—take the man or woman that sews the island together, not the one that frays our customs. No matter who it is. No matter if it is the child of that mother or this father.

At the same time, we must say that we did feel that Agatha had, shall we say, almost settled. We had forgotten and forgiven. She was almost one of us. It was an embarrassment when Father Raphael, muddled in the mind as he was, proclaimed that he was damned and she was damned. We think he rather liked her. It may have been an odd sort of love. Of course, there were some that took it seriously. And Paul went around saying that curses hold on earth when they do in heaven. Supposing, I guess that because of her father, Agatha, who had never been baptized—her mother having never in the end had the courage to—was cursed in heaven. We did feel that she had tried, though Paul was never content. It was when we found her walking like a woman does who is coming from the wedding or going to it—how shall we say— taller than usual, with a beautiful face, almost brighter than sunlight—that motions against her started. For she was not supposed to, we reasoned—be at that 'wedding'. And now the news—that gold for her was on its way. And her hand was held out to us with gold from the 'wedding' in it!

So the village crept to her, a little warily. But it didn't learn anything of her other than what she had said at the meeting: Gold, that is, Dimitri was coming. A rich man with a white Panama hat for the 'wedding.' Some of us said—this is God forgiving us. Imagining a real wedding, somehow!

The village crept to her, that is not to say it loved her. We are certain many would have rathered, yes, many would have rathered someone else bring us gold. And we sat around at times, eating apricots stewed in syrup, the kind that practically dissolve in your mouth, saying and what earthly good is the gold going to do us anyway? There are only a few youth left, the airy few—like plums sitting out all newly washed and sprinkles of water on them—smooth faces and flesh full of juice—while we dissolve away like dust, webs of sunlight. We are going to disappear, though not without a fight. Old, drying, crinkling at the edges—readying ourselves for the second life! And she is bringing us gold! He will come along this rich man, wretched as they all are, secretly, for don't you think we've seen them—they've come before—to bargain with us for permission to build low roofed, 'native' like hotels—brightly painted one color or another or whitewashed, unforgettable in the blue of summer, that is what they will build and people will come and learn our dances, drink our apricot brandy and pay and pay. But we'll be the ones losing, said our chiefs—we have in mind something else—meaning the offer wasn't good enough. Our villagers have all calculated well: present to make them look dignified to the family on the other island, and something immense in the bank—something that means living, as they say. For one or two of these rich hotel owners offered to buy the entire village! But no, to lose our holiness for a piddly sum! It is, after all, otherworldly; can one calculate heaven's worth in money? A little more, therefore, until the immensity of the sum makes it look and feel like fairy poetry. Who can blame us then if we get a little lost to the magic? Ah, we've lost our holiness, some argue back, and how can we find it again? It's a thing for children. And then Paul came of age—fifty years old or so, on this island, late for us, now that we have no young folks, and declared: This island will be what it once was. And some of us were new enough with our one time life to think ah—the island that we did, after all, love: And grandmother Zoe, who is a grandmother to nobody and consequently to everybody said: The light come back— meaning the light in things and people. And we said the taste come back, the sweet taste! And someone said yes, the light—I can remember when my life was spun light! Anna said—if you ask me, there is too much light; the sun is hotter than ever before. In any case, people are weak in faith. For all that they want the holiness, the flavor again, they do creep towards Agatha and her announcement of gold, smacking their lips; they like money.

Simon said, wise Simon, with his monkeying around, that these kinds of transactions never bring love. And yet when you think of it, said Katrina, who is at present tending two people who bend their heads and drool and the flies settle on them, on their stained shirts, one who looks as if his head is an empty house, staring, sleeping, staring; the other who is cracked and rattles on senselessly—what does love matter? I'm a nonentity—a virgin, in the Scriptural sense, who's waited and waited for the perfect and beautiful marriage with the crown of orange flowers, to be steeped in love like wine, to feast on love like aromatic meat—and I have instead two aged parents who are like children, yes, goblin children and I do not will not love them. So, in any case, I live without.

A virgin, ha ha, the old men laughed months after; we know she's lying. They don't know what virginity is, said Katrina with disdain; I don't mean some accident of the body between my legs. Why, there's a kind of virginity, what would you call it—spiritual, answered one, winking wisely. And so she was called 'the virgin' for a while and even 'the perpetual virgin'—in other words no matter how much she fornicates—because of that virgin love for Dimitri-- until our old men got tired of it.

And they have a strange tenacity when they are mocking someone; they don't tire of the game for a long time.

Katrina is still waiting for Dimitri, said Zoe to our assembly. I am sure of that without doubt. Some of us will never give up, said Cleo, yawning; it was the day she put on a little make up and made her rounds—visiting and gossiping. She's as old as his mother… That is what makes it all the more spicy—an unsung tragedy, an embarrassed tragedy, said Anna. Katrina never behaved like one of us. She had the best family in town—everything was perfect in her home—everything the old island style. I felt visiting once that here at last there was breath—we lived. You have to understand, they didn't just decorate like we used to, they lived like we used to—smiling, hospitable; in those days poor folk from the other land used to arrive on our shores; and Katrina's parents were the first to open their doors. To one man who was sick in mind and soul somehow, couldn't work, her father said: Take my seat—be king of the table! You because you are poor are king in our home. Ask for anything. And they put him in the best bed, served him the best food. I don't know what happened to the poor man—he drifted on. They were beyond all fear and reproach, Katrina's parents were. They did everything old style. Those were the days that Zoe says people, stones were full of light. Now there is sun and sun and we don't have it.

Everyone is shut in their houses. If someone visits our island, especially if they are poor in old clothes, we squint out at them once from our windows, someone may bring them a good sandwich, Agatha or Foti, sometimes Katrina—we don't let them starve, but then we leave them alone. Everybody's got to fight for life. It would be unfair any other way; that is what we say. And then there are those who go out on the fine days, when our island seems suspended in a great cave of blue light, and they look around them, and they whistle, or laugh for no reason and they say to themselves—see we have solved everything—the problem of living, money, food! Here there are no poor. No one complaining. Old happy monkeys, Anna would say, carefree, swinging from one place to another place in this little oblong of sand and stones—catch them when a tooth is rotten!—and then everyone is astonished at their howling—simply can't relate. When one of their monkey friends is dead—how it seems unreal—ah, the other world, world of rotting, dusts, cold, endless black.

Katrina's parents were open: be king at our table, they said to a poor man, and put him at the head of the table, waited on him, brought him all that he desired. What wind blew their souls on to the old true path?

Katrina's parents—now they were gold, in the real soul sense. They had a pearl of a marriage, and to Katrina said always: you have our blessings. You have our blessings. Katrina was a shy, ugly girl. Thin wispy black hair, although it filled out later, a beak nose, and tendency to overweight. The parents for one thing did nothing to breed her up properly. They just offered their hands to her head, their fragrant hands and said—you have our blessings. After a few years, when Katrina was fifteen, Agatha was busy staring down men, leaping in the streets, it was discovered that

Katrina had a whale of a sexual appetite. An old man had discovered it, she was you see, so ugly that only old men came around. But when she saw Dimitri, years later, she was, so to speak, born again. She was determined to melt his flesh into her flesh. And sometimes determination of this sort leads to an energy that accomplishes the intent. Then, she became 'the virgin.' Yes, simple joy over a man's body put it back, the old men said; it was kind mockery, hiding cruel mockery. Spiritually, of course, but almost physically too. There was even something about her, despite the cigarette-smells in her hands and hair that led us to say—ah, a new bride. But we looked at this matron with her seduction born of despair, and the hot loins generated by the dark, electric glance, the broad forehead of a thinker despite it all, and thought, poor soul, driven to swallow up the youth. People tried to tell her parents, to let them just think about it. Katrina as old as Agatha, Dimitri's mother, and Dimitri—what of him? But they simply nodded seriously, sighed, served tea. It was as if our mothers and fathers were talking about a severe pestilence in Africa. A terrible thing, no doubt, but how and what should one do? Besides, they were getting ill. Five years after Dimitri left they were in wheelchairs. Helpless, we said, as they had always been. And Katrina with an expression like a tree on which great branches have been torn off in a hurricane, stunted, broken and irreparable, tended them; and they all lived off the state pension that her father, Angelo, made fishing.

It was a miserable life, sure enough, but that didn't make Katrina holy. No, we don't think so—not after a life like hers! Now she was clamoring that Dimitri was coming, Dimitri! Like she had lost her mind. She would stand at the dock and weep and stretch out her hands. Such demonstrations! She had been quiet enough for these ten years, tending and washing her parents. Perhaps she thinks this kind of madness will make her young again. Bride-young! And she was going around saying with that old ring of despair in her voice that we can remember years ago when she used to call him and he would come to her as if he had something in mind—as if he was fixing something in himself—anyway she was going around—'listening' to him! imploring us!

Even Agatha wasn't cracked like that over her son's coming home. We expected a flood of joy, and instead beheld a quiet, reserved little smile. We investigated further—Cleo went to tea and found Anna there—Anna now bent a little with the red sweet cough syrup at her elbow, but smiling, although the smile was not as fine and gracious—the lower lip protruded a bit after. How she was holding on!

Agatha had clearly cleaned her kitchen. Even the stove sparkled—not only the enamel but the burners had been cleaned and below them where the stains accumulate. The floor had been cleaned and the table polished. It was winter now, but sunny and that restrained sunlight of winter penetrated and warmed us sitting there around the little wooden table.

What is all this about, Agatha? Was the question on our minds. But no one dared ask. We knew she wouldn't answer. There would just be silence, perhaps an invitation to go. So we chose another track: You have been very kind to Leo just now, Cleo said, looking at her. We would have all forgotten him, thinking this abandonment was well deserved; she looked meaningfully into Agatha's face. In any case, you have Jason, still unmarried. What makes you go up there and tend that pariah?

Oh well, said Agatha, turning her face to one side—I am good at cleaning, when I set my mind to it. He made me clean my own home better in the end. Who can say that that is wrong? Then—she meant after she had cleaned-- he cooked for me. Astonishingly, he is quite a good cook. Chicken mostly, but also vegetables and all with the expert use of herbs. We had everything—chicken stew, chicken soup, baked chicken and so between cleaning and cooking, cooking and cleaning… We did in the end sit down and sort of congratulate one another and we got to talking.

But he wouldn't with you…

No, he's past all that.

Genuinely?

Yes. He is something of a joker, you know, but the joke is on him. He's benign, woolly headed—I mean not only that he has his tight grey curls, but that there is a quality about him—fuzzy, absent-minded. He's sorting something out, he says; something concerning his son in his own mind. He goes on in this fashion: A creature that I wholly don't understand. Holy, not holy—that is no concern of mine. But the artifice! I want to go to the priest and belt it out—none of this is honest! And yet I have to admit, and here he rubs his hands in that old greasy way, Max is very pretty! Already he looks like a saint in an icon—clean, silvery, goldy.

And you—what do you do when he goes on this way? Asked all of us there.

Oh, I responded: but the question is are you comfortable with it?

What does it matter?

It matters to me, said Agatha.

You would judge me?

Judge whether or not you can remain sane about it.

Then again, he went on, disregarding me: there is an honesty about being dishonest. The priest has such a jolly time. Just bursting with enthusiasm. I hear he kisses my poor Max on the lips. The boy just submits tamely and the fellow is a wild smacker. Leo puts his finger to his lips. I am not implying anything, of course. It is just a slight insanity on his part. My boy is being accommodated with kisses and hearty hugs. I, in my saner moments, beat him. And now he is holding golden covered bibles at the altar, the golden cup that holds the sacrament. Ah bosh, I say. I too took him in infancy, when I doted, and drooled over him with his slightly auburn hair and the face carved like his mother's with a delicate chin and thin nose, and held him for the bit of wine-soaked bread. And then I began to think—yes you know the story—what if I sin? The Lord loves sinners. And round I went, round the globe in my heart sinning. And then I saw them all hypocrites, fools! Thinking to get to heaven by repeating their proper prayers with hearts full of violence and scheming and lust. But I felt sorry for them too. I gave them something to concern their pious heads about, something to ejaculate over. But the time for that has passed.

So you attacked the human machine. We are weak in the face of sickness and carnality. Why prove it?

Just to see how humanity goes when it runs off course-- wobbles, you know, and tilts, first, smiling, then, enraged, crying.

That is vanity and conquest.

Yes, he said meekly. I had my moment in the sun.

I guess our nature tends towards falsification, vanity.

It is after all a little thing in the end, a disease, he was reflective, murmuring; and the sun shone gold behind his head. And then he said to me: Would you like some onions? They are good onions. I was thinking you'd want to make a soup for Dimitri.

And I came away with the bag of onions. I haven't stopped thinking about our conversation. It was getting late. The afternoon was grey but I enjoyed it, walking home. Seemed more than ever that we were snug in the bosom of the sea.

But that is just like you, said Cleo, perturbed—you tend to such thoughts. Despite what you call falsification, vanity--we are seekers of the true light, you can't forget that. When all the world has gone to ruin—the lapses of old traditions, the violence, and here and there the sudden glimpse of the truth but like an orphan, cut off—with us it was always different. And with you, those inconsequential thoughts.

How different? Agatha said, ignoring Cleo's last pronouncement.

You can't forget that our ancestors...we were all one then.

If they beheld God then why...

Well there is why and why, when people are stubborn.

Agatha looked down. One can be a Christ follower without all that bile.

Perhaps, but the truth is that no good will come of not being baptized. You will see everything in a more comfortable light when.... The argument that arose over your family you cannot deny. We were stuck in our ways, as you know-- a little boring, a little sleepy, perhaps, but still.

All that is a lie, Agatha almost shouted. The village was just as unholy before my father came.

Well, well perhaps—we don't deny that we were imperfect. And yet, and yet. See the holiness of Katrina's family and how they fell off. The babies unborn. There is no question that with that outcast bible in your house....

If holiness were just a formula with one institution or another presiding then Leo would be right; it would not be part of us, retorted Agatha.

Well, well, Dimitri is coming, said Cleo soothingly; I imagine that you will be happy and a happy mother is after all a holy thing.

I am happy enough, said Agatha said loudly. I have the onions for the soup.

A fly entered in through the open window and began to buzz and fly in zig-zags.

I hate flies, Agatha murmured, flushing. They are filthy.

Oh no, smiled Anna; she had gotten up and joined them, feeling better in the past few hours, and sat listening quietly cracking and eating almonds that Agatha had set out in a little china dish permanently on her table. I don't mind flies. Remind me of something. Onions, Leo—you have to admit he has that bloated white white face a fly could settle on—forms part of the picture! They remind me of my grandmother who used to sit in a bonnet of sorts, partly made of lace and say things like—this fly is here to tell me that I am not far from decay and rot; heaven has no need of this bread filled stomach, this muscle pump. Ye who think you are so great—are nothing but food for worms and flies—for I am a thing of decay and rot, and you, love, you too.

Death, said Cleo with a face. She rose to leave clasping her little satiny white purse. She leaned down after a thought, and kissed Anna. We are here of course if you need anything, she said.

No, said Agatha to Anna, anxiously looking into her eyes, after Cleo had left. Not death—just old, seasoned flesh.

It is mighty fine, said Anna, caressing her face.

It is beautiful, said Agatha kissing her.

And when they resurrect me, ha—sometimes I imagine things—I will say, well then—it is mighty fine; I was right. It was just a lover's hypothesis before.

My mother wanted to wrap my father in a blue shawl, blue like heaven, like God. She knit and knit and unraveled and unraveled. The more she found herself alone, not alone so much physically, that was bearable, even desirable, but alone in the way that people desert you by just lapsing off when they should be saying that one word of love—the more that was, the more she knit and then unraveled. I think she wanted to say to him—the old flesh is mighty fine. Only you said it. She never got a chance to say it to her other half. And there were times I would have said it to her. But you said it. I think things get passed around—things that make up one truth. Not stars, galaxies, historical moments —when the heart or lung is created; but that night we wanted so much to wrap the blue shawl around a person because we loved them and their old flesh was mighty fine.

You are exquisite, said Anna. You make me dream.

Anna followed as Agatha led her out of the house, putting on her grey coat for Anna and taking a sweater for herself. Anna got cold easily; and suddenly, in the last two days, the beginning it seemed of the cold winds on the island, she had looked excruciatingly infirm, as if she was crumbling. A woolen shawl, a beautiful one, to be worn with great dignity and majesty even, would have been suitable. But even leaning on the stick, frail, and white, draped in grey, Anna gave her one, two, three times that invincible smile that dressed her again, Agatha thought, like royalty.

A few paces before they reached Anna's house, it began to rain. Anna couldn't hurry and Agatha hadn't thought to bring an umbrella. The rain came down cold and relentless. Agatha thought only of the clump clump of the stick on the pavement and how it couldn't be hurried. These winter days, she said to Anna, you don't know when the heavens will unleash. Anna looked up at her with still the smile, but a kind of fadedness in her eyes. By the time they finally reached the door of Anna's house, they were both drenched, the clothes clinging to their bodies.

Anna opened the door and invited Agatha in. It was a big old house with rose-colored wallpaper with embossed a strange design of naked women bearing fruit in their hair; there were chandeliers and heavy polished wooden chairs, paintings, glass bowls of potpourri, polished dark chestnut tables, and red Turkish carpets on the marble floors. Agatha had been all of once before to this mansion. For reasons of her own, Anna rarely invited anybody to her home. Anna and Agatha had been friends for years, but of the kind that meets outside house and home, though, more recently, Anna had visited Agatha. Perhaps, thought Agatha, without meaning to be unkind or resentful, it is just convenience.

Tell me where your dry clothes are, said Agatha, after stopping a minute before the splendor.

No need, said Anna breathlessly. Just a bathrobe. It is upstairs. There is a linen closet—a yellow linen closet. You will find it if you go up, turn immediately to your left, by the bathroom.

Wait, then, Agatha ran upstairs, soon found the linen closet and the bathrobe, soft terrycloth white folded among the linens.

She ran down again; Anna was standing, swaying a bit with closed eyes. Agatha began to undo buttons, feeling her arms and breast, saying in consternation—you're soaked, soaked. She pulled off Anna's black linen dress and then began to tear off her underclothes…

Right here, murmured Anna with the same invincible smile on her lips and faded looking eyes.

Why not? said Agatha. And then she looked and saw Anna's naked body. It was still slender and she thought for a minute that it should be framed in an oval portrait, the title elderly woman, naked. There were differences between youth and age undeniably, but there was also something seamless that connects in some people. There is beauty on you, said Agatha to Anna. I told you, said Anna, stretching out her arms for the bathrobe. Before handing her the bathrobe, Agatha stooped down and kissed her breast wonderfully warm from the blood heating in woolens against the cold. Anna took the bathrobe, put it on, and folded her arms, smiling at her. So you think because I am an old lady, she began... Agatha put her hand to her mouth. It was just, it was just... Nonsense, said Anna; it was charming. But you and I are standing in this doorway. I, a new person, born of the rain and a soft kiss on my breast, you seduce with your innocence and truth, an old person, the reverse of everything people would say is real—for that is the business of true life...and she laughed.

Forgive me, cried Agatha, as if it was torn out of her.

Nonsense, Anna repeated, I said it was charming. Now take me, please, to bed. Upstairs to the right is my room.

Yes, said Agatha and they went up the stairs, Agatha leading the way, and when she had settled Anna in her yellow bed, she stepped back and said to her—I didn't know that you were so lovely an old lady.

Anna coughed. I always thought that beauty of one's person was an important thing. Pagan conception, no doubt; I determined long ago to preserve myself. I face death with certain equanimity now, you see, she said picking up a bottle of cough syrup on her dresser. You see, or you don't see? A sculptor who makes a statue—who knows how long it will last—not forever but there is in it still beauty, the sign of the immortals; he has hit the target. He has made beauty that spurts out like juice when you bite into an overripe plum. Now that is the important thing. Here, as I open my bathrobe, scent me with this fragrance. It smells clean and lemony.

Agatha complied. Anna looked still slender, lovely, wrinkled, translucent. Bones on her visible—the knees down, the chest—like carvings. She was a carved gem— old age, magnificent. Agatha touched her here and there hesitantly as she rubbed in the fragrance in the yellow light.

There are some things, said Anna with stateliness, that people forget. Women can and do find beauty in the bodies of other women; and there are times when we discover that old age in a woman has its body too. A beautiful body, even.

I don't want to leave you, said Agatha, after she was finished.

I am fine, said Anna. Clothe me.

Agatha softly wound the bathrobe around her delicate body like spun honey. I'll leave then, said Agatha, softly, something aching in her like a wound.

Goodnight, said Anna and thank you. Don't turn out the lights.

Agatha crept down the stairs and found her sweater and handbag. She opened the front door of Anna's home and then stopped, looked around at the chandeliers and the paintings, breathed, smiled reflexively, a little smile.

A real person, a real person—that is what it is all about. Being a real person—naked. No, I won't tell my Dimitri—he would of course be understanding, but deep down—no, it would violate. It is about being a real person, she said again. Hurrying away through the rain and darkness.

I kissed her, she said, at last, when she got home and turned her back to her closed door, facing the little hall that went to the kitchen. She was sopping wet, her hair was plastered to her head, her sweater was heavy with water; everything on her was dripping—her skirt, her underwear. But she was smiling, saying, yes, yes! And in her nostrils was the fragrance that she had rubbed on Anna's body—clean, lemony—a beautiful fragrance that never grew tiresome.

When the news of Dimitri's impending arrival with the rich man had shot through the village, everybody became softer, lighter. Even Barbara was all smiles these days, bowing at the priest. When her husband asked her about this radical change, considering how she had once hated Father Isaac for his 'unholy ways' ways that he had dared bring to the island, masquerading under true concern, a project for the village folks' spiritual welfare, she looked only a little thoughtful. Ah well, she said to him enigmatically, a peacock is not an eagle.

A few months ago she and the islanders would have been more disposed to judge and condemn the wayward Dimitri. But his new 'gesture of reconciliation,' although some people thought of it as buying their forgiveness, and the little memories that cropped up of their handsomest, made them reinterpret his abandonment of them. He was, Nico thought, a hero type, a little larger than life: one is commanded to go far afield by the gods, then. There was nothing he could do. He jestingly made this remark to Nisos and Timos, who were arguing on weighty issues. Oh that kind can lead battles, fight monsters, but woe to their wives, said Nisos. They never settle down, added Timos.

What monsters will he fight here? Asked Nico, uneasily.

I am sure there will be monsters, said Timos. And the girls will gather around him like flies for the honey, said Nisos, solemnly. Ah, they don't know, said the fishermen together, shaking their heads.

So with a hero, a sea monster…and women.

Certainly said the fishermen and their voices had a childlike tone. At first, we wanted him gone. There was agitation on the island over him. He said things. Not to our girls, of course, but to the lads. So we thought it best. Over the sea and no return. But it was somehow not the best plan, said Nisos. We want him here; he was born here. He is an island man; sometimes we feel we even love him, continued the fisherman, you know love for a son of ours. We are even ready to make him governor of the island, he nodded, his eyes wide, though of course the real head of our village is Simon, but he is so wise and batty all at the same time. Dimitri's election would just be something to calm us all down. And he wouldn't have any power really. Just to organize a more frequent supplies' boat, that sort of thing. And that way he would have some release for his pent up tensions, and we other folk would be able to live as we always have—like the sea today, and both men looked out over the water-- barely a ripple.

Of course, said Nico, heroes are a bit like the weather. You never know what the winds will bring. He took leave of the arguing two. They had stood in the background of the inquisitorial crowd that had gone to condemn Father Isaac's files to the fire with a look of incredulity, an almost blank gaze, on their sun burned faces. They had stood in the background on voting night at Simon's. They reminded Nico of fleshed out paper dolls with just the slightest indication of expression. Their wives had them on edge always; both of them were like hot pepper to the tongue.

Nico was standing by the grocery store in the piazza at the end of the road along the beach, when Simon walked by, wheezing a little, because his lungs were no good. Who is a hero? He asked Nico, smiling. We were hypothesizing that Dimitri is, said Nico. Oh, we all know that. But what made him that? I think evil, not good. Although I must say I am looking forward to seeing him—that night his mother tore him out of hell at the cost of her own soul.

Nico said but you know that heroes are beyond good and evil.

No, really? Asked Simon, surprised. I thought the contrary. I thought that the only truly good or evil creatures were the heroes, the mythological ones.

It depends on whether or not you think them men or gods. As men they are beyond good and evil, of course. As gods…they are at the heart of good or evil, mysteriously so. For their good and evil is not our good and evil. They condescend to us out of duty, or for the same reason abandon us. But when they are gods, they mysteriously love and bring goodness or utter destruction, if they are evil.

But how can we, Simon, frowning, said, almost to himself, separate the man from the god in this case?

What god? asked Nico

Simon coughed. Oh nothing. Perhaps, we are secretly all gods.

Oh no, said Nico, smiling gently. I can assure you. I haven't the slightest ambition in that way. I just get through the day. Day weaves into night. I live alone came down from the other island so I eat well, cook splendidly for myself, with a bit of wine each night. That is as far as I go. Down the path of the human animal. I live a little, cook, drink, read; my brain cells are stimulated, my lungs expand. In time, my bones ache, my gums shrivel, my skin turns slack. At last, I die. When I die, my flesh is eaten away, by bones are bared—such is my final commentary. There is nothing else for me.

They say the immortals exist. The ancients say it.

What—you are not a Christian?

That is separate. That is the true faith; an inheritance. But there is also the main thing-- dying and living, dying and living—the spirit of the poet. I read a little po-etry—only that written by the intelligent poets; the ancients wrote of immortal-ity—whether it was in a flower or fruit, but wait-- perhaps that was forgetfulness and death; in any case, there were some who achieved it. It was a long and arduous pro-cess; one reads the hero performed impossible tasks. The problem for us to resolve is whether the hero was in fact a kind of god? If not, of course, the stories would be nothing but fantasy. I would wonder at intelligent men wasting their time with it. But this is where I hesitate; is there a grain of truth? And then you see it would be fair to talk of good and evil. When the human approaches god.

Even our faith, our precious faith—hell and heaven, do you think these are fair? When a shriveled up monster, a crappy human, one of our saints-- goes to heaven? An illustrious one, illustrious in the richness of mind-- goes to hell for not spitting out dogma? Even were it the other way around, it would not be fair, for in richness of mind, one is pompous, vain, absurd too. What the little twisted, pathetic mind of man, the bleached little virtues, one, two, barely three—awarded heaven, that is the pleasure of the Divine? The vice, even if it is rampant, ugly, and lifelong, awarded hell, a place of never redemption, never pause in torment, and despair. How can it be fair? The only answer is that we are in some mysterious way not only persons facing God, but gods facing God. That somewhere in our petty, insipid lives we are immortally good or evil: the disgustingly simpleton reality of the inconsequential deformed bug beautiful compared to the rampant lithe sick half fever-wish of the classically configured ballerina.

You know, he went on smiling slyly at Nico, the women think we have only good on this island. Bah, what do we have? Fish, olives, goats, vegetables. The south wind. For the most part wives go to their husbands beds, husbands come home at night. The priest is in his church. There is nothing that we don't have that is worth anything and nothing that we do have that is worth anything. You see what I mean? That is not good as in hard won flesh and blood good! But I know of something that might give us a little more, a little spirit, if spirit can stir us unworldly folk. Maybe it is too late; we are already to set in our ways.

What are you talking about?

The rich man coming here with Dimitri. I say let them build and build: A luxury hotel, a helicopter pad. Then the drama of the spirit will begin.

Yet, I've been thinking myself --a luxury hotel on this island? However could it be? Nico murmured.

A palace of gold with a blue swimming pool, waiters in brocade, footmen, maids…and us toads and sea urchins smiling in the sun.

But there is nothing here, said Nico. And who would come? How strange. What a dream—the island suddenly in the focus of the world!

There is nothing a tourist wants to find so much as a place where no tourists go. Besides, this is a beautiful island we have forest, cliff, sea. And we have the caves, the mountain and the holy monastery. It is paradise, he said stretching his hands up in the air and laughing. A while ago, when you were too young to know about it, other men came proposing to build a hotel. We voted it down. You see we had the millionaire on the mountain, he brought us things, economy. We wanted our own ways; we desired that nothing should change. But we have changed since then. We have pondered in our hearts like the Virgin. (You know even here sometimes wives get restless and rove. Some of us think of work, work that tourists bring, cooking and trinket making, embroidering for the women, curtains, shirts, dresses, the old selves would wake up out of their laziness and day dreaming and become industrious, hard working. Besides, they would get money for their efforts, they would be happy.) We would be building and expanding our reality.

There would be other tragedies, said Nico, a young man like a god, day dreaming about the world out there. I have seen movies when I lived on our neighbor island. There is always some tragedy attached to these sorts of things.

These are not tragedies, said Simon. The ancients had tragedies—the killing of a king! The killing of his child—the great wars and blood purges. The sacrifice of immortality of the god to live among us dead.

That would be Jesus.

Christ is the great God, not one of those gods like us. In any case, you see what I am saying. Tragedy overturns the mind. Brings it down into dumbfoundedness, up into new thinking. The beautiful young goddess raped by death forced to be mortal, dead, cold, but for only a few months!—Persephone though dead, resurrected; she was too beautiful to stay dead. Joy comes from the real tragedies. Human joy—dead sons back alive with their mothers but it is a great secret as to where and when. Look at Agatha—her 'dead' son returns with gold, gold enough to make paradise! But our villagers who would kill for paradise will continue with our usual sort of nonsensical thing—girls entranced by the handsome man-- that is not tragedy, only lesson. We need lesson.

So nodding at Nico, Simon walked on past him down the street towards the beach. Nico went into the store, looking after him wondering if the old geezer had become a bit foolish after all. This old home so shaken up and rebuilt! There was a part of him that protested—no, I could never endure it. Another part of him that said wait—perhaps one can offer opinions, advice; the thing need not be a disaster.

Nico had once at age fifteen offended the village folk in the way people usually offend by disturbing certain things taken for granted. Women in the village married their lovers, on the whole, or else they quickly found other lovers and the original affair faded in memory not being talked about out of respect for dead hopes and expectations. A few women, perhaps one or two in fifteen years went up the mountain to the monastery and stayed. These women were different from the ordinary. They stayed clear of men from the beginning. One noticed in them a tendency to sit alone, to frequent the church with their eyes down, apparently pondering something. They spoke little, ate less. There was something 'going on' in them from which it was impossible to distract them. Some of them had a piercing gaze, which however was directed to something other than the object that their eyes rested upon—something in their minds. When these changes occurred in a young girl, the family gathered together before the household icon, the father whispered a blessing to the girl; it was settled that she would, at age sixteen, separate from them and become one of the strange, numb, alien nuns responsible for the salvation of the island, maybe of the world.

Nico had met such a girl, four years after Dimitri had left the island. She was a little younger than he, maybe nineteen. He was twenty, a virgin, reclusive, and a doubter. It seemed he wanted neither woman nor God. The girl was one of those with that other type of gaze. People had earmarked her for a journey up the mountain soon. When she looked at folks, it seemed she saw the heights of the mountain, heaven, or whatever the nuns see suspended in the void before God. Then, one day, she looked at Nico and focused; she saw not the uncreated light, but a man, slightly smallish compared to her, examining her with hostile eyes.

This appeared to her like all the injustice in the world. Yes, she said to him—it starts here: when one person, for no reason, looks at another in this way. No, in fact, when you, Nico, look at me, Elizabeth, though you don't even know what I am like. They had an argument. And so the relationship suddenly began. He couldn't put it down, so to speak. That was the ball she had tossed him; he was angry, ticked off to the core. He left her exploding with anger. And sought her out the next day to tell her what he thought of her and her ideas. She answered in a high handed way. It has to do with religion, she said, something you wouldn't understand from what I hear.

In fact! Religion has never righted any wrongs. Which mouths has it fed? Religion has meant war and more war.

Of course, when there is desecration, men desecrating it…

There is nothing sacred. There can be no desecration.

Everything true is holy. There are desecrations all the time.

I only looked at you. What possible harm can there be?

But the affair had gone well past the look. Already Nico and Elizabeth were boiling in their bellies. When she kissed him, Elizabeth said, hotly, you started this, remember! Nico grabbed her by the hair, the blood in him stinging, his lips hot as pepper and kissed her hard. Their embrace was more like the grappling of two wrestlers. Slowly Nico got the upper hand propelling Elizabeth behind the church—they had been in front, alone, taking the air at dusk—he and she, one of those chance meetings that are never chance. Behind the church, Nico swept Elizabeth from behind with his foot, she fell as she tried to step back, fell hard on the sand.

I've broken something, she gasped, her eyes wide.

Good, said Nico cruelly. He tore off her clothes and his own. Then he stopped and looked at her.

Elizabeth pushed herself up on her hand, encircled Nico's head and pressed her lips to his mouth pushing her tongue into his mouth.

Scoundrel, she said when she had done.

It was you, he said hoarsely—you all the time; I hope I split you open, drench you with blood.

But it was Nico who was the virgin, not Elizabeth. She lifted up her legs in the air and arched her back. Nico plunged down on top of her in a fever. They made love madly until the next morning.

When at last they slept at dawn, Nico felt a great terror had been lifted from him. It is all so easy, after all, he said; her flesh was fragrant and tasted sweet. They slept together naked, shamelessly, under the altar window. Father Isaac saw them from his bathroom window. It is like a sounding of the depths of the sea, he said to himself; and I have only self obliteration and contempt for not, for not engaging myself ever.

The mad affair between Nico and Elizabeth under the altar window continued for months. They spoke cruelly to each other of one another; yet they learned nothing but more postures and hotter, spicier ways of making love. In the end, thoroughly seeded by fire for one another, they realized they could not abide reality without one another.

For once Nico took her hand and held it as they walked silently together. What has happened? He asked her. I would have done anything to hurt you only just yesterday. It is strange to say this, and all the fear comes back. I am just a little child.

You love me, said Elizabeth, but she didn't have a triumphant or scornful voice.

Yes, whispered Nico and the tears welled up from his heart.

I, too, said Elizabeth in a strong, firm tone.

I can't marry, said Nico, in anguish; it would ruin it. Or do you think differently?

No, we can't marry.

What are you thinking, my love, what is it? I shall die if I don't know.

Elizabeth turned to him and kissed him tenderly. How much I would like to have a child with you and to live somewhere far away where the old fools of this place can't come to haunt us.

She turned to go; she had her own laws it seemed to him, suddenly. Wild, internal laws; it was not that she was so arrogantly in control as it had seemed to him at first. He had, he knew and secretly delighted in, wanted to subdue her. This was the fight at first. It was exciting, sexually, morally, imaginatively. But then suddenly all that had seemed second rate, cheap, and trivial. Besides, she didn't 'have her own mind' exactly; this he began to understand after being internal with her for days and days, hours and hours of frantic, frenzied sex. She responded to a will, which was not precisely her own. And he became afraid and little. He knew that he was up against something gigantic, invincible, and unrelenting. It was like the call to migrate for a wild bird; when it came, it would fly irrevocably.

When it came, she did fly. Beautifully, swiftly—she was suddenly out of his life, up and away. She climbed the mountain to the monastery. She closed herself in. Apparently, she prayed. Incomprehensibly, she cut off all ties—even this profound love tie that he was sure he had died for—died, as it were, in a different dimension, where he was immortal and she—and yet died nonetheless, died absolutely, immortally. He walked, when she climbed that mountain, the walk of the utterly dead. He had felt, yes, he remembered, he thought to himself that day, morbidly, that he had known it was coming. There had been that night-- after she had left him with the thought of running away to live somewhere even with an old ramshackle hut in the midst of the overgrown forest living on whatever wild berries they found, letting their hair grown long-- a sense of some other body—the baby, he had at first thought—she is pregnant—'turning within him' around the place of the diaphragm; this new creature had squirmed and then left—flew. This was his experience. His first and last spiritual metaphor. He thought, a little 'out of it' that he had given birth to a bird. But it was not a good dream; it was a nightmare and this he felt—sensation of panic: abandonment! Eternal, absolute. It was Nico's descent into hell.

He learned then that one can die many deaths before even being born. The one thing that kept him humanly the same was the thought, and he clung to it, that it was infinitely unfair. Were not these laws, were not these supposedly just laws that she responded to in her mind? What business did they have of existing if they were not?

Nico lived and worked for five years after in a dream, clinging to this sense of injustice that was so profoundly rooted in her that it was beyond all conceiving. He even knew, knew, did not guess or hypothesize, that the Christian injunction to endure injustice because who among us is without sin?—fell short in this case. This was not about his own shortcomings, lack of faith, whatever. This was about necessity, the law that overrode all other laws; his hand went out in the night still to encircle and claim the beautiful body, which had been both his downfall and crown. He had discovered himself to be immortal, then became mortal for her sake and then immortal once again, but as a wish-defunct thing rather than as glorious being, the fulfillment of all wishes. Now he, a citizen of this realm of glory was among the dead shades. He was periodically in a fever, then in such a depression that he could not speak. He grew thin, then, in a few weeks, fat. His body did not seem substance to him but ethereal spirit but shadow, nerveless and dumb. His flesh seemed perhaps ceaselessly cold and yet he did not know. He didn't know touch or sensation; muscles, nerves and skin were abstract, imponderable things. He ate and defecated, mechanically, responding to instinct as if it were a command button being pushed. Sexuality was a thing of horror, a kind of grotesque cadaver rising in a grave yard with both eyes missing from their sockets and black dead blood streaming down from where its throat had been cut.

After a time, in which shock and panic, as well as a sort of dazed, horrified acceptance, similar to someone living through a terrible crime or natural disaster, dominated him, he began to develop another 'person' intellectually, a character that could handle things just to survive. This was so real to him that he wondered if he should take a new name. But there was some advantage to retaining what remained of his other self, and particularly his name. The island folk knew him from birth, but they did not know of the affair with Elizabeth. He and she had been fire, hot blood, flesh, sexual parts and yet they had known how to walk around serene as summer clouds by their inconceivable cleverness; only the old priest knew, and they knew he knew. But it was one of those situations where they trusted like children --in the air, the wind, the rain and in Father Isaac. Without any communication, any agreed upon course of action, they reasoned he would keep their secret—it was obviously a secret. This trust was seamless with their very existence with their trust the sun would rise tomorrow; it was as if their lovers' faith was gene in the coil of DNA. And they sensed the same flame of love in the aged, luminous old man—he had a taste that strengthened the old faith in them; he had once said in a sermon that one is not to judge another but to see the different acts of people as one would see, if one could, all the details of how flowers bloomed. Father Isaac had no need to tell anyone their secret. In a sense, it was, after all, not a secret, there was no need that it should be, but just something that one doesn't need to talk about like a personal letter disclosing news that no one would understand.

For five years, people in the village thought Nico was rather odd. The old matrons wisely thought he needed to marry. He was getting old and the urge they imagined, must be strong. Strangely, Nico did not mind being among these women. When they smiled at him and insinuated he needed a woman, he would consider it like a mathematical problem; he had always liked such equations, worked at them, solved them at last, but he wasn't a genius and couldn't conceive of another woman. Slowly, that part of his brain had gone into disuse. Now, how to activate it again? This was his question to the aged ladies who took such an interest. And it was true, as they saw, that he went among the young women with looks of polite indifference, a look of inactivity. Many a good match in the old matrons' opinion was passed over this way and they puzzled about this, wanting to ask Nico intimate questions and not being able to.

For there was something entirely congenial about Nico to the old ladies. He was tender, not too talkative, rather a good listener. They reasoned that they needed a man, an intelligent man to work something out and oddly, they thought that Nico was the perfect choice. Nico had developed with this new 'person' in his mind, no particular likes or dislikes, enthusiasm or objection to people in his home town. He began to feel empty but with it came lightness and a certain blessed forgetfulness. He could move around with a kind of innocence he had not known before since one part of his life that he imagined somehow free, almost criminally, brilliantly free was now closed and buried since he and Elizabeth were in their death-life. Thus he absent-mindedly even courted the young women, the old ones picked out for him, listened politely to their talk, chatted, mechanically, but in a low, soft tone so that no one would notice the lack of all interest. But oddly to these women, who unanimously would vote him a spectacular catch, describing him in such words as gentle, devoted, so considerate, deep hearted, he postponed passion time after time. And his kisses were fatherly and on the brow.

A compilation of opposites, thought the matrons, until a light dawned in one aged, clouding eye: he is perhaps not normal, the old lady began, hesitantly; what are your thoughts—snappishly, defensively asked another. They were sitting on plastic chairs on a little patio in the courtyard of a house by the garden, washing greens in buckets of cold water. Well, it is said that some men prefer men to women. What you are saying is shocking, the other responded. Besides, piped up one of the younger ones, it is impossible; love can only be performed one way. You are a fool, said an exceptionally aged crone, picking the snails out of the chard to the young one. Nonetheless, what you— to the other— are suggesting is a crime against human nature. But it would explain things, said the first, heavily and suggestively. I have heard the men here vow to rout out these deviations to our traditions with violence if necessary. They have suggested that such men deserve execution.

I say we keep it to ourselves. After all, he has done nothing to excite suspicion. And perhaps, it is just a matter of feeling a bit superior.

Why superior?

All skeptics feel that way to true believers.

And so Nico's kiss that one girl had described as a pat on the head from God, abstract and careful, excited many a long disputation in the hearts of the old ones. Not only unusual in a young man, but positively unheard of in one long chaste and celibate. So the whispering began. And when the old men heard of it, a degree of pent up rage. Because daughters were being disdained, lithe-bodied, beautiful girls that needed to be opened and swallowed up like wet little oysters for their balletic beauty, which, if you squinted enough you could see.

They would have even pardoned Nico his atheism, as they had pardoned Anna; she, for her wealth, he, for his youth and eligibility.... Perhaps atheism was only obtuseness, a kind of bluntness, plainness without any sweetness; it was a man thing that he would in time learn to put to the use it was intended for not against God but to block the woman factor. Here too the usual kind of lady would help. These were always pious and suffered the males to come. But this aversion to the female—not even aversion that might be a secret hot masculine eros, but a tender coldness-- one could sense it, the men said, in the scrotum. And so the old men and some of the old ladies, who sensed vicariously, burned at Nico inwardly. This enmity was all they actually experienced as soul.

But the old women of the village never gave up hope. They spun the tale that a girl would come along who would pull Nico off his pillar of tedious chastity. The fall would be delightful, breaking several things, sore, sweet in the bone and muscle. At the end of a year, however, Nico had pretty much established an identity. He was hot in argument, burning with intelligence, but with women sealed up, mysterious and cold. It was at this time that Father Isaac climbed his penitential climb on his knees —in short there was a dramatic change to village life and the matrons forgot Nico and his concerns. The men too forgot their suspicions. Nico was a loner, a fisherman by choice, and a good reader; although the village folk felt that you could never be friends with him, like a different species he could be tolerated, even enjoyed. There was room enough on the island for him. The islanders would return to the 'burning question' about him later.

But when Nico went back into the village square, he was met by Agatha, Katrina and Barbara. They had been talking about him, their own differences patched over by their collaboration on this mission to Nico. It was apparent that they had once again opened up the island's 'Nico question.'

We need to change the atmosphere on the island, began Katrina, shyly.

It is marriages that we need, said Agatha; our men and women are drying up. We are not courting, loving, mating, having children.

It is not right under God, said Barbara, stoutly.

Why do you come to me? Asked Nico, a little testily.

In our circle, you are the most eligible, said Agatha. You have refrained for years. Yet you have been seen passionate.

That is my business, he said curtly, and passed on, almost pushing them away.

There, said Barbara to Katrina, as they stood looking after him—what did I tell you? He is immovable.

It is true isn't it, said Agatha, softly, that no woman has conceived on this island for the past ten years?

What is more, husbands and wives don't engage in the act of holy matrimony, said Barbara.

Something is askew, said Katrina. But Nico has a right, you know, not to breed. It seems foul of us to push people into that.

Oh but you know, said Barbara turning red—it is natural and good.

She was 'pushed,' Agatha murmured.

It's as if, however, Nico is pointing to a new path, said Katrina. It is from the top—from the mind, spirit.

It is all wrong and deceitful, said Barbara, hurriedly. I am almost sure now that he is not normal.

That is a hasty conclusion, said Agatha, thinking with apprehension of Dimitri, who had his own mind also and who would certainly be subject to a little pushing when he returned.

Barbara spat. There are three blooming girls almost next door to Nico. Two are a little young it is true, but the other would make a good wife.

Nico knew the little knot of women stationed in the middle of the road was looking after him with amazement and anger. He had heard too of the stories going around that he was not normal. But the young man ruled himself with a fist of steel. He had had love, and although he couldn't imagine that God existed, he had created his own holiness that he would not, come hell or high water, jeopardize. Love was holy. Breeding shattered the shrine whether it was done in a moment of thoughtlessness for pleasure, or because one felt constrained to have a family. But there were moments when alone with his breath and the great sea and sky, he would become uncertain. It was so long ago…Was it really love or just a kind of dream for us? Some say that love, this definition, doesn't exist. Was it only the sex impulse made particularly sweet? And he had through an intellect they did not share, enshrined and mythologized it until it was like a mysterious cloud and through it the girl even a little faint now so that whoever he was holding out for he did not really know. And this 'really' first spun him like a spinning table away into weakness and then cracked his mind like a hammer into fragments that sensed infinite possibilities.

About this time, Nico began to develop vertigo and faintness. Simon who since their discussion enjoyed a little more of Nico's confidence, went to the neighboring island by fishing boat to fetch the doctor. The doctor could find nothing wrong with him but sensing that Nico was under some kind of stress, left advising him to take it easy. A shock like this could end up affecting your heart. Nico had said nothing about shock but he listened in silence. Nico himself knew, as people sometimes know about themselves hearing, as it were, the ghost of an oracular voice in their minds that this vertigo and the fainting fits had to do with thinking with wonder about Elizabeth, and beginning to doubt. His organism was so eager for her, her taste, feel, smell, that when he thought that it was not love, it threw him off center. This was the shock. For although he had developed strong defenses against outer attack, he was ill prepared for subtle, inner warfare.

Where, he wondered often, did these thoughts come from? I lived once in absolute certainty. It is as if one day, looking at the broad blue sea, a voice crept in, a haunting deep voice, a godly voice: do you know that it was love, is love? And there is nothing in the sea, nothing that answers. The question is one of infinitely many. All of which are dissolved and held in the great waters. Suddenly it seems as if there is nothing in the human question that answers at all. One could live and die a million miles away the same as here and the question would not be answered. One could bend tragically under the weight of the sorrow. Still the blue waves and the question, the golden question, the question of salt-- unanswered. Then suddenly the vertigo, the fainting. He tried to hide it as much as he could, considering that the old men and even he at times would think with old peasant logic that this sudden effeminacy of his body came from his refraining.

As yet he didn't despair. For these deep attractions weave fine gossamer threads of hope around us, catch our bodies like cobwebs catch flies. There is no thinking that the web is other than benign at first. And the caress of love that is perceived by all the senses, though sometimes imaginary, is deeply delightful. And Nico was the kind of person that needed above all a secret; the secret was the center of his existence. He could not think, in fact, he knew it was not, the same with every man and woman in love. He thought, rather, that his love affair with Elizabeth had been distinctly other. He felt that with her he stood at the origin of things. He knew her and did not know her. But he knew that she was woman in his invention, an invention that came from his soul. And that equally, he was man in hers. And rapidly, without analyzing it, he had known that this was love. And yet, now an inner voice, a godly voice, caused him to doubt. This secret, his one true delight, the new core of his existence, unique and rare in the universe, could in a moment, simply because of a 'voice' that arose, apparently from the deep, broad sea, vanish forever.

Now it was hard to keep himself from running to them—Agatha, Barbara, Simon or whomever, and flinging himself down on the ground at their feet, and crying out—yes, I am normal. I will marry. Only marry. The circle that enclosed him, that Elizabeth had drawn around him, unwittingly, unconsciously, but surely was terrible. He was lonely, uncertain, and his one beautiful secret hung in the balance; he suddenly felt his soul might not for sin, so defined, but for the possible non existence of this secret, be lost. This was too much.

He had always doubted God—that is, since he was tiny. So the idea of a spirit, a relentless spirit, an intelligence unattached to him but taking up a kind of residence within him came to him out of the blue. That he could be told things by this other intelligence seemed to him extraordinary. But the godly voice that told him all that had passed between him and Elizabeth might not be love --certainly was not his. He struggled like a weak child against a far stronger force. I love her, he repeated in his thoughts constantly, and yet, over days, weeks, it grew hollow sounding in his mind. Fantastically, he wished he were climbing a mountain, crossing a burning desert, rather than on a minute island where God, if God there was, was conspiring to keep them richly fed with fresh eggs and goats' milk and in a tiny sphere where everything great swirled around them far away.

Nico had at first not noticed the islanders' miracles. Then he laughed when they had mentioned the priest in connection with the fruit growing abundantly on the trees and the goats giving milk, saying the weather had come, the combination of rain and sun, no saint had ever had anything to do with it; it couldn't be that that awkward priest with his disease of the imagination magically made crops grow or goats give milk. He fasted; good, there were people with mental illnesses who starved themselves; he danced with joy; well, he had learned an old island tradition. He was radiant, light-filled like an angel; well, he was thin, diaphanous and if people saw him in the light...

And so Nico had remained for two reasons on the margins of the circle of island folks. He was an uninvolved bachelor; and he didn't follow the faith of the little church though he gathered there on Sunday with the villagers. His skepticism was common knowledge. But now his own system, as he called it to himself, was shattered. There were times he looked on the folks' simple belief and wondered. It may at least have been better to be one of those pious folk praying senseless words but full of conviction in front of the icon of the Virgin and Child with its little light in the corner of the church. And he, where had he to go, to whom could he pray?

It had been wild, fire, treasure, tender live chick—all these things-- and he had brought it with him, this love, wherever he went. Ah, if they only had known, how illuminated he had been on the inside—not brains and stomach and liver at all, but an elaborate, vivid, glittering letter was he like those illuminators craft on manuscripts; it was so ornate and bright one could hardly recognize it—first for all the detail of the embellishment, then for the shining ink—but it was the letter E. And it just needed her body to complete the letter, suddenly swirling with meaning more than any other on earth.

Because Nico did not believe, he did not see the compulsion in the faith and thought that because of this love, brilliant letter, wondrous name, tender chick, the girl would come out of her morbid seclusion on monastery mountain, which is what he called it, and return to him. And he thought this for a good five years without hesitating or growing tired.

His new disease of vertigo and faintness made him feel ashamed—as if he was a feeble woman! At first, resisting, Nico finally recognized that 'inner earth-shaking' changes were occurring-- all of a sudden for no reason like the creation of the world. At length feeling a strange assurance that Elizabeth was his anyway, because they had recognized each other—the one male, the one female, mysteriously, the way monogamous wild animals do—he let go of all resistance. When the godly voice came, sounding in the hollow caverns of his mind and imagination, saying—what if it is not love? He simply answered, perhaps not. But the music of the letter and the letters following, finally sounded, sung, spelled-spilled his whole being.

But owing to the voice, he would go to the base of the mountain and look up at the monastery, a collection of crazily built wooden shacks, perched on the summit of the cliff above the Isolet's villa over the rocks and sea, and he would wonder if Elizabeth too heard a voice. He asked himself these moments if it was this madness that had driven her, poor tender chick, blazing letter, as he called her then, to vanish up the mountain into that ramshackle dwelling to give her life to God, as a slave; or to give her life to God as a slave. And everything seemed solemn, mournful and still. He would think that there is something—another nature to it, but he didn't believe there was anything but death there—a long slow lament for it. For five years he had avoided the cliff; the sight of that monastery chilled him to the core. Now he frequented it. He thought about her; he masturbated fantasizing her naked and making love to him. Now and then he wanted to bite her with a passion and to hear her cry out in pain.

God is behind a mask in any case, if there is a God, he told himself one day rambling over by the rocks under the monastery. They worship in all the disguises, names, books to promote marriages and feasting. But this was for the changes, the helplessness he felt in himself. He kept firing up; he was a rebel, a loner, and outsider, an outlaw, in fact—not that he committed crimes precisely, but he demeaned them and all their little social conspiracies to get him married. He would not have it. Not even with Elizabeth. He kept firing up as 'they' inwardly, outwardly, pulled at him. What they worship is nothing but 'cock-coocoo,' he was sure that was the correct nonsense name; even if she doesn't love me, or I don't love her, this villager-religion, which presses them to marry me off is all about nothingness-- letters, words that fade away.

He would turn around all weak in the knees and climb over the rocks to go back to town. All this, he said to himself, is undoubtedly a sexual thing. In the end, I have to accept this self in me, this newness, the foolish vertigo, the doubt, and the insistence of sex, but I can remain distinct, refusing to bow down to their images and sayings, their holy book, their babies, their pathetic fight against nothingness.

Catherine came down the mountain to see Katrina—she had met her in the market and had been invited, after five years on the island, it was inevitable-- and Katrina was worn out with isolation and curious. The subject of their conversation turned momentarily to Nico. A solitary man, said Catherine, sympathetically. I believe he is looking for a mate with his intelligence, said Katrina, who spoke in a tone devoid of feeling. He was born all out of sync with us, you know. That is not to say he isn't a good fisherman. But there always seemed to be something on his mind, ever since he was little. You could tell in his eyes that it was something pressing, but he spoke so guardedly; he never let spill any of his thoughts.

Is there anyone to whom he may have been attracted before—I mean a young married woman? Is this a broken heart? Catherine was sitting in the parlor, leaning her elbows on the white kitchen table; behind her a large window, the only one in the room, let in the late afternoon sun. Katrina's parents were sitting in their day seats by the window in the living room.

Oh, I couldn't say, said Katrina, standing behind her, taking her sweater and hanging it on a hook by the door. He always seemed so remote to me. Katrina didn't want to confess that she had the typical middle aged spinster's periodic cycle of indifference and intrigue when it came to young men's sexual attractions. Nico she had a smothered attraction for at one time. Being sensitive herself, she couldn't believe that Nico was untouched by the attractions of the females of the village. Even with summer gone and the women no longer walking about in filmy skirts of red and yellow and white, there were bodies that a man would find. But he was at best that odd fellow, good looking for some… and at worst, an impotent who thinks he is smart.

Katrina told Catherine all this handling the sweater, and setting out some cake with little, light movements. And yet, said Catherine, watching her, thoughtfully, his heart is somewhere else entirely: a bird in a cage, confined forever, who still sings. Someone hears him, clearly.

Best to leave this mystery alone, said Katrina, in a conciliatory tone. The old folks of the village are a little irked; there haven't been any new births on the island for a long space of nine, ten, no, fifteen years, I think! There have been only three new marriages…so they go around saying, he is holding back from us. Doesn't he care about our people? We've been here, generations and generations for three hundred years. There are young women enough; and it is, after all, his duty…We gave him a home from the time he was fourteen.

How odd, said Catherine. So these three marriages…

All infertile so far. Some of the couples talk of going off island to a clinic of some sort. Maybe there has been certain sterility in the air—for the past ten years. There has been a fertility problem for an even longer time—maybe some fifteen years; but fifteen years ago, Michael was born at dawn to cheers after a hard labor all through the night—everyone had been up all night praying and sweating with the mother. She was older, late thirties; her first child had been born twenty years ago. There were whispers that she had to be strongly coaxed into having sex with her husband. There were whispers that the one time she agreed again was after those twenty years. But Anna told me that it isn't so much that they are not doing the act, as they are not consenting to it in their hearts. And not because they don't want the man. There has welled up in our young women a certain indifference to the sweet mechanics of love that spell out the real man and the real woman. Oh they act the same with a man—all the same flirtatiousness, and coyness. I believe that when they are single, they imagine that they do want it very much. But when it comes down to it, the church bells have stopped ringing, and the wedding guests have gone, suddenly, in the dark, they wish to fly away like birds. What is it, I wonder?

A vision of the groom nude, perhaps, Catherine said, facetiously. The men around here are not so spry, slender and strong.

People think we're haunted somehow and thus the seed won't plant—but you have seen our miracles—the fruit growing, the flowers....

The lady who was telling me about the women said that suddenly it occurred to her that this was to be life-- this bed, this matrimonial chain, as it were, and the island looked dim, and lost. She couldn't go on; she was all tearful. Of course, I went through with it, she told me, referring to her wedding night; what was I supposed to do? It would be worse, she said, if all this copulation resulted in baby after baby. She thinks almost with horror about the recent blooming of flora and fauna, how it made the villagers happy because of course they expected...

I imagine, said Catherine, dryly that the men here blame the women. Even this lack of heart for sex.

Oh yes, said Katrina. Some have said it freezes them up. And they talk with the old ones about betrayal.

So I see that Nico could be on the girls' side.

No, he holds himself entirely aloof. He would be blameless, considered a wise man, in fact, were it not for his being young and single, and attractive-- as you might notice, thinner than most of the others.

So there are no little children.

Perhaps in reality, Nico is holding back for love's sake.

Do you believe that?

I wonder about it.

You are so fascinating to me, said Katrina. You see things as no one else. The others all say he is morbid and angry, perhaps deviant, even perverse—doing things out of defiance, not concern. Even Agatha is not sure of him.

And now the developers, said Catherine changing the subject.

It is sure that they are coming with Dimitri. A third letter has reached Agatha in which he says that the owner of a luxury hotel chain will be visiting. I have gone visiting to the houses of the villagers, dropping in in the evening when people are home. Some of them are bored and rude—they don't like me, you know. I have had to click off radios, sit down when everyone has been standing up. Then the argument they don't seem to understand at all. A luxury hotel! They look at it in their mind's eye as if it were a large goat giving bucket after bucket of milk. But mentioning Dimitri, that sometimes elicits a response. One woman joyous, sweet-smiling, distant; one man moody; another woman depressed; a man elated. Some teasing me—unaccountably hilarious. In any case, they all seem to agree that if Dimitri is bringing the luxury hotel owner with him, he must be a kind of gift giver from heaven. And perhaps, said one man reflectively—it will bring girls; and some of the sleeping children—the young men not yet courting will wake up.

So they do not really anticipate changes, said Catherine.

They all seem so far from recognizing the truth. They believe they can go on year after year with their little traditions, and little improvements, their comforts, their farm yard miracles; they strain a little if there are infertile marriages; now and then, they lift a languid finger—they accuse a priest of some vague impropriety—dancing down the aisle in Church, telling a racy story, writing notes on people, they look ever trustingly towards the monastery on the mountain. They weave a nest but they don't see how in the center there is an abyss….Of course, no one would ever listen to me and if they did! It would be as if I was speaking another language. They would laugh, mimic me. I have heard that.

You see things so darkly. Perhaps you are right. I have heard, somewhere, that things naturally tend towards a final crisis.

Then it is just a heap of meaningless fragments left over. Nothing can ever quite be put together again, said Katrina. But somehow I want to stop it.

But there is nothing to stop as yet, said Catherine.

We hear of the world through the newspapers that the supply boat brings. International newspapers, too. There are wars, terribly, dastardly deeds—massacres, women and children! There are crop failures, oil spills, and the climate is warming. There will be greater floods, new deserts, terrible hot summers. It is the end times, you see. And here, on this island, I imagined we could contain human nature, which, when it expands out, through knowledge, becomes eviler and eviler.

You think that if people are kept ignorant and simple….

Yes, it is not a crime; we live a little like donkeys; so be it. We have better hearts.

The priest thinks this is the perfect opportunity—that is, we are—to be on earth as it is in heaven; simple as dirt, as donkey dung; thus, ready—he puts it that way.

For the end of the world, I take it.

If we only keep ourselves from falling into delusions.

And you are afraid of a great business—a profitable thing—something spelling luxury.

I think from reading newspapers that there is a prism, a mental and imaginative prism that worldly people fall into. In this prism they find themselves seeking— wealth, comfort, especially that hazy, lazy comfort that is just not wishing to expend the extra energy, even intelligence…and you ask—what is all this worldliness really? I say, I can't say what it is; when a person's heart is set on it, it is pressing, and urgent, brilliant. But when you try to stand back, analyze, even question its worth—it becomes so many shadows. While what we have—a goat, a chicken, a donkey, a Bible, a few other books, newspapers, a house, lace curtains, a fishing boat—this is reality, and stands the test.

What test? Why?

The test of the world left behind for holiness: Even donkey dung is holier than a worldly man.

I don't understand you, said Catherine, but she was smiling. But—we will be friends?

I believe so, said Katrina emphatically. Whatever you do, don't fall in love with Dimitri. Trust me. Stand against him.

You seem sure he is up to no good.

He went away from us so disaffected. You are here for pure motives. I believe he is returning to take advantage. He is a strange character, highly intelligent, hidden.

A little like Nico.

Yes, but Nico is just a boy compared to Dimitri. Nico is always dreaming. If he makes a mistake, he will withdraw into his own form of penitence. Dimitri is always doing. Tossing aside the way of our island. For example, Nico wanted to read books—so he subscribed to a library on the other island that is bigger with its three towns. He had books sent to him by the supplies' boat. He was content, though they had few books, in reality. Dimitri had no patience with this little donkey maneuver, as he called it. He had to exalt the whole notion: he wanted to study—to go to university.

Nico, clever though he is, is homegrown. Dimitri is a stranger, albeit, sometimes kind. One day, a long time ago, he fixed a bit of plumbing trouble. He could be very handy. The word got around and people asked him—this, that and the other. He must have worked on five or six houses; he didn't ask for any pay. He said he liked figuring out things—problems that have solutions. It relaxed him. Simon taught him the basics, and the rest was all instinct and imagination. But you see, it was the villagers, the island breed, he called it, his scorn is known among us, that he couldn't tolerate: small minded men and women, in the end, going nowhere. He told me this to my face! Don't you see? His free help to us was all a kind of disdain, in the end. Many villagers now would rather pay--.

Perhaps it is the same problem: Nico solves it one way; Dimitri, another. Catherine rose to leave.

Which problem? Asked Katrina, a note of anguish in her voice.

But Catherine wouldn't say. She picked up her sweater from where she had hung it on a hook by the front door in Katrina's house.

You're not going to go away from me? Asked Katrina, childishly.

Catherine came up to her bent down and kissed her on her soft sagging cheek. And then put on her sweater and said—you feel free to fall in love with either of them—our two mystery men. Intelligent, kind, elusive, superior—there's two true men for you. She opened the door and went out. She could just hear Katrina behind, as she walked down the road, softly saying 'but—' like a startled child.

There is nothing wrong with an older woman for a man and Katrina has a nice, familiar prettiness for a wife, she told herself walking quickly; the sun was setting, and although Catherine was not afraid, the steps up the mountain to her home were not lighted and she thought that it would be tedious to find them in the moonlight. She walked through the village thinking, her head bent down. For some reason, her mind strayed to Stephen and she felt a wave of anguish. It was never, however, the grown up Stephen that she thought of; that is she imagined him briefly, but at these moments, remembering him, another part of her mind saw only the child-husband, the lovely boy, the one who had made a bedroom and a few toys, a bicycle, a pet canary, the garden of Eden. It had been all his doing. And there had been that wonderful, sweet, funny person in their secret lives—God, who permitted Himself to be revealed only to children. That was love, her grown up side told her. Something far away, beyond reach now. One continues now, hoping to see it in the world in fragments.

I wish it were all given to me on a silver platter, she said to herself half laughing.

It might be, said a deeper voice in heavily accented English to her left and a little behind.

Catherine, startled, turned around.

No, I didn't mean….she said, faltering; the man had a grim expression but his face was attractive, alert and his eyes were intent and gentle. You see, she said, I just meant that one wishes for something given to one when one is impoverished… I mean all of my life, my grown up life, that is—has been reaching for something—meaningful; I've taken up different routes—study, service, patient waiting, friendship.

The man sighed. It does seem that there are those who are finally given on a silver platter everything….He began to walk with her.

You know, she said reaching the steps that mounted up the mountainside, I—she put her hand to her chest and stopped, straining silently a minute.

You are not very well, said the man, before she could finish, putting his hand around her elbow. You need help climbing these steps.

Thank you, said Catherine, meekly. The steps were narrow and could take only one person, so the man kept close behind, his hands holding her arms.

I suppose you are Dimitri, she said, we have been waiting for him to come, you see; in any case, I am Catherine, the daughter of the Americans who moved to the large white villa just down from the monastery here, five years ago.

Yes, said the man, monosyllabically.

I should have been out with my friend—a jolly person, listens in on all our family spats, but I decided to sneak out without her; I thought I had enough gristle in me to clamber up these steps—just enough. And I so wanted privacy.

Then she said, I rather like this island, though it has its faults. They call you a black sheep, you know, which is quite unjustified in my opinion.

Yes, said the man again.

Since Dimitri wouldn't talk, Catherine lapsed into silence. In any case, the old shortness of breath was plaguing her and she climbed slower and slower. Dimitri did not urge her on but waited patiently behind, holding her arms.

Finally, they reached the top; there was a clearing all lit up now by moonlight and a path to the house with its solitary lamp burning in the front room, which you could see out of the many windows.

This is my house, said Catherine looking at him. She saw that what she had thought to be grimness was merely part of his physiognomy. He was smiling a little now, —and yet his face still looked severe.

You have the face of the just, said Catherine, pensively.

You are angelically beautiful, he said, but your beauty looks like it is about to vanish, he said half to himself and leave behind, he traced her nose with his finger—a flat, doll-like creature that has never known joy. Then he looked at her and smiled a little; I have gone too far.

No, would you care to step in, said Catherine; long ago, she had told herself that she had to die to men; it was not with resentment or bitterness that she told herself this. No, she was rather curious as to this obscure world of sexual death, sometimes found in nuns and diseased persons. And she thought that people, seeing it in her, would pass by; and the blooming would never be spilling over into her eyes and face and thighs with that utter excess of blooming…. Now what was she? Little, frail, the kind of wispy bloom that would die soon and that old women would weep over. I haven't the habit of responding to men's compliments, she said to Dimitri, ingenuously—nor half compliments; but you have been courteous to accompany me. I can at least offer you some wine.

But I must go, said Dimitri. My mother has been anxious to see me for several months, since I told her I was coming home. I owe her my company tonight.

I gather you came home just today.

Tonight. You are the first to see me. He looked away from Catherine, around at the house, at the dark expanse of the sea in the moonlight, and breathed. It smells here, he said to her, of loneliness and of sea wind.

I suppose it does, said Catherine.

We will see each other, he said with a strange sound of effort. Then he turned and quickly leapt down the stairs, two at a time—sure footed as if he had climbed up and down them many times.

Ellen was pacing through the house when Catherine came in.

You weren't waiting for me? Asked Catherine, tenderly.

It's night—I was afraid.

There's a bright moon tonight. I could see very well.

Kali is in the kitchen.

Ellen asks so rarely after me, said Catherine to Kali; she was eating a fish soup for dinner, Kali made a marvelous fish soup—whether I am well, in danger, sick, sad, if she does I always wonder if it is a sudden profound change in her that made her do so. It is in my imagination as mother gone far astray, now wandering home to her child, instead of the other way around; mother sitting off in the fields somewhere, catching a plaintive cry and instead of imagining—a bird, a lonely, hungry animal calling—here there were numerous possibilities—a cat, a dog, a sheep! She comes 'round to the possibility that it is a child, a human child, and alas, she has left behind just such a one. Then she awakens—it is, truly, her child! An opportunity to go—to arrive home, in the old mystical maternal rhythm. Mother-child. Yes, we make a pair. How delightful and mysterious! In such a frame of mind, Ellen looks upon Catherine who made no plaintive cries recently of course, but there is, in mind, softly, a question, always.

Why did she have me? And no answer, Kali, but a conclusion, ever a conclusion, an awkward one, but unavoidable—I must be such a burden.

My mother, Catherine said to Kali, needs the sense of loneliness and infinite space. She really should have been in a boat alone on the broad sea, coming in now and then to market—basic provisions—pens and paper. Somewhere along the way, floating, reflecting, she had made her sole great decision—to marry. And then, not so much a decision, it couldn't have been, perhaps an assent—when her husband wanted to have a child. Periodically, as tonight, she looks at that child, now grown tall and old as a child, and there is fixation in her, a few blind questions, the striving to recall relationship.

Although it is you who are seriously sick, said Kali, you treat Ellen who is robust as if she were the one infirm. You feel that she couldn't live a day, lost among human-ity, in a crowded city street. She would wander, putting herself in peril and be lost, found after a frantic search, in a corner, a path between houses where the cats sit on trash cans, leaning against the wall, oblivious to everything, writing in her notebook. If someone doesn't feed her, she will forget to eat. If someone doesn't call her to bed, she will forget to sleep. I don't think, answered Catherine, that she notices her home much as a home; she manages to keep from bumping into the walls, she is faintly glad of a roof when it rains. It is Robert who is the familiar person, thing, place, all in one, for her. She is used to his voice—it stirs up conversation in her, sometimes laughter. In fact, alone with him, out on the patio under the stars, she can be witty, garrulous, philosophical, complex, simple, congenial, tender. He unleashes the talk in her; it is as if he pushes the right button. He is also the one thing she notices—his body; she has no other treasures—not lace nor china, nor jewels. Of course, it is Robert who has denuded the home of all extra things in response to his spiritual calling. But it is Ellen who doesn't possess them. There is no attachment in her to them, while Robert loves embroideries, antiques, crystal and it had been crushing to his heart to remove them—to make the house something of a Zen wilderness, or a gaping wound of plainness. Ellen has Robert; his body; she enjoys watching his body. It is not sexual even; it has long ago gone beyond that. It simply brought her happiness to look at it like automobiles do for some men. And Robert is a machine and a feast and a place to her—a lovely bit of mechanics, a sumptuous meal and a country with a smell, and a culture. She has established herself there—stopped there permanently. And she has with Robert, almost as much as romantic love, even, the childish sense of coming home.

Catherine said to Kali that she, their child, was the alien creature. Long ago she had sensed this; it hadn't hurt her because she didn't think it was her mother's fault. It was not Ellen's intention to hurt her. Besides, she felt that as a combination of nurse and cook, she could make herself useful. Robert was grateful to her and apologetic. He would have loved Catherine dearly, but his concentration was all on Ellen. When she was a little girl, he was tender and protective, responsible for her outings with her little friends, her getting to school on time. He came alone to school board meeting and people looked on him sympathetically, imagining that his wife was dead. Many people did not know that Catherine had a mother. Robert accompanied his daughter everywhere, and people considered him a good father, loyal and attached. But Catherine didn't think it was more than an apology in the end. She had odd parents, serious, remote from society as she knew it. And she didn't quite know in the end what they did—what it was all about. Robert was practicing spirituality, a brand that he made up entirely on his own. He had no church, no group. She didn't see a discipline --like morning prayer; although he did get up early and stand for hours in the kitchen, drinking coffee and thinking, staring at the white-tiled floor. Ellen wrote copiously from dawn until sunset and there was never a publication; in fact, it seemed that she resisted such an idea—she was writing a story that no one would understand except herself—half biographical with real names, half fictional. And even she, a few years later, would look at the skein of language thrown in neat print across the pages and say here is nothing, nothing at all. And yet she was compelled to write.

Catherine, unlike her parents, was born healthy emotionally and socially. But physically, she was weak. She didn't have the strength to grow up in the normal way. She had had Stephen, a strong person with a brain; when she was four, and he six, she had imagined in a childish way that they were married, that is, married as much as anybody was married. But then, he had gone away and left her to handle mother and father, to wonder painfully what it would have been like if she had been able, like him, to disappear out into the world, to lead a life of her own choosing.

Having parents of this kind and being bound through ill health to remain as an adult among them, led her to internalize all her feelings; the retreat of her parents to the island, in which she was obliged to accompany them, had made this more pronounced. For a time, her day consisted only of getting the groceries, cooking dinner, reading a little, and watching the sea. She had accepted her role of nurse, cook, aide to Robert and Ellen and had learned to hide, though not from them or anyone in particular, the different little adventures in this tightly circumscribed world that she did have and the painful pondering about her 'fictitious' life in the world, as she called it.

After soup, she went and kissed her mother who was out on the patio and sent her to bed with perfunctory comments on her uneventful walk in the night; she said nothing to Ellen of Dimitri, his having helped her home, the slight arousal of interest in her, the little bit of wonder about him. It was just a tender, childish thing. He must be to the villagers a bit like a rocket landing again—traveling as he is from that infinite and infinitely unknown world. I wonder if they will marry him off. I am sure they will conspire to.

And he is not a bit like Nico, she thought that night in bed. Nico is morose, inflammatory; Dimitri is deep and kind. I imagine he could be the life of the island—dancing, talking, making everyone rich; somehow I don't see him as superficial. There is something a little lost, I think, and found—just a difference with regards to everyone else. I wonder what sort of portent it is that I met him first—perhaps I am destined to be the old spinster that he tows around for some odd reason—out of sympathy. Well, I'll continue my study: how people love. If he tows along after me, I'll do a good piece of scholarship on him.

Agatha was at Leo's house all day the day her son came home. She was patching up the heart of this old cavalier who had missed her as she spent so much time with Anna. At first, he would not be mollified. Imagine, he said, bitterly, if I went out as I used, before I reformed, courting woman after woman, keeping not one, for one could forgive that, but five, ten at a time.

And how you did it all those years, baffles me, said Agatha, laughing—and not one pregnancy, not one misstep!

You act as if it is all as unserious as fantasy, the fantasy of a decrepit, fat old man. I tell you once—I had ten; so much coming and going—and the husbands never knew. I said to them to say that they were going to the library—a new library at Leo's house, that I had devised a way for Max to read more. In fact, it was not an untruth. I had bought a number of books. Only once or twice, after Max had gone up to that old priest and turned saint, did the husbands suspect. I suppose he had to be on the run from something to go so far! But it was too late. I had stopped, converted. I had become pious—notice the icon in the corner. Ah, you know, the female is like cream. You must use her in your cooking while she is still fresh before she goes sour.

But it is strange—you are the first person I tell the truth to, besides Max. Oh, there were the women who knew, yes, but they never told after. That is what a good shaming does. No, to them, they encountered, physically, brute truth. But you I open my heart to.

You are such a child, said Agatha, so in need of pampering. A long time ago when I had young children, I would have been angry. Ruffling people's morals, disturbing the peace, hurting feelings, corrupt old man exploiting women. But now I realize, you are a breed apart.

So is Max. We are seekers, you must realize. Max finds it preaching heaven and Jesus Christ. I find it looking up women's skirts. Found it. I have changed.

Did you find it?

Yes and no.

Agatha was making coffee. So you are disillusioned, she said, putting the coffee maker on the burner.

That no. I think when one finds what one seeks for so entirely in this life—it is bound to be a delusion, perhaps a lie.

So Max will not find heaven?

Max, poor Max—my beloved son. Of course, I don't love him as I should. I tire of thinking about him—his condemnation of me for my cruelty. Sex and death are cruel. Savage, savage survival of the fittest is what is left. And yet, what is sweeter? No Max will find half a heaven—the side of escape from. What most pious people find. I suppose I will have my half now that I am reformed.

And the other half? Asked Agatha, she lifted her skirts above her knees and laughed.

No, no—said Leo hastily. I think along other lines. You are not a chorus girl. You are indispensable to me, my star in my house; you come in with the evening and you listen here to me, a tedious old man who loved once like a dog, and now loves like a child.

I only half believe you. She took the bubbling coffee pot off the stove and poured coffee into two little porcelain cups.

Do you know, said Leo sipping absentmindedly, that I have acquired of late a slight incontinence problem. Yes, I wonder now as the body breaks down imperceptibly at first but more and more who will raise me out of the shit and pee in my bed? I think of it you see in Christian terms—the raising from—the dead. It is the same thing. One is raised, you see, not incontinent. And who then will see the glory—the body that once was...

Yes, love sometimes never even comes close to that knowledge. But when it does and remains love....

The other half.

Agatha departed from Leo's late that evening and went home. Jason looked at her with a kind of new old weariness. That is, he himself had never worn that expression, but Agatha somehow knew it well. And she knew too the reproach that was coming. Do you think, said Jason, sulkily, at your age...?

He has changed a lot, said Agatha, reassuringly. Besides, these things are like games that we play....

Why do you do it? Cried her younger son. First Simon, now Leo....

I don't know. Perhaps you are right. I am fifty-two and should avoid all such ideas. But it wasn't meant to hurt. I never seduce. Just a little nonsensical banter.

But she had set off an altercation that lasted for hours.

Late that evening, Dimitri arrived. Agatha had been waiting for him since she had received his letter, sitting up late, praying and wondering, but she hadn't heard the door in the hall because she was busy arguing with Jason. She saw him, going out for a breather, standing in the living room, and gasped and cried. He was more than she suspected—the most beautiful man she had ever seen. Of course, this had been true ages ago but it shocked her to see it again, to know it. He took her in his arms and held her closely, saying in a little broken voice—Mama, Mama.

That Dimitri was home changed everything. The nuns were right—those attenuated, ghostly women who lived up on high like stars or planets. The heavenly bodies were in the right position once again. God had let go of the leash, and there was freedom, kindness, joy.

Agatha had long ago made his room ready—his old room that she had not touched since the day he left. She took off his jacket; she remarked looking at him that he had grown too thin; she promised him that she would put some meat on his bones. She told him of the different things that she would cook for him, of the new things that they could buy now, of the eggs and goat milk in miraculous abundance, of the new priest, of Leo's cooking—then she crouched down as Dimitri sat to pull off his shoes. But he cried out—stop, Mama.

You do too much for me. I am a grown man. I will be cooking for you.

Cooking!

Why not? Of course, Mama. It is natural for a son to.

Agatha smiled. You have always had a different mind than the rest—like I. In fact, Leo does a little cooking for me too. One steps out of the line to dance his own dance.

Or her own dance, said Dimitri, tenderly.

They talked about little things for a while. Then Agatha rose to get her son a towel to wash before going to bed.

Mama, Dimitri said—who is that woman up on the mountain? What is her name?

Which woman? Asked his mother, coming back with the towel, smiling at the sight of his severe face and dark thick hair—beauty that brought her body back to her.

A woman who lives in the big villa up there.

Oh—she's been here seven years or so. Didn't you know about them? They are an American family.

Strange, said Dimitri.

What?

So hidden, so shy. Oh, well, and he took the towel and left for the bathroom, his question unanswered.

By the way, Mama, he said, pausing at the door, catching sight of Jason, coming in from the kitchen, you are a lady. Ladies play. Enjoy yourself.

Jason looked at his older brother, bristling. What do you know? He said, shortly.

I overheard an argument when I came in earlier, said Dimitri.

Agatha was too happy to think of that now. You are brothers, she said, encouragingly. Kiss each other.

Jason held up his face to his brother. Dimitri put his lips to each cheek, solemnly. Then Jason faded away to his bedroom something of a look of justifiable anguish sketched briefly on his face.

The next morning promptly at four, Jason was seated at the kitchen table, and Agatha, who was usually silent as the grave at that hour, was singing an old love song that she had learned years ago in her childhood, not knowing what it meant. Dimitri was sleeping.

Jason drinking his coffee and brandy, usually silent as his mother, suddenly began to speak. Mother, he said, there is a way here. Don't disturb it.

No, said Agatha, stopping her singing, not at all. Why what did you think? If you are talking about my being at Leo's so long—why I was just doing a service for the poor old man. Cleaning up, a little. It is a good thing when one can get out and do services for people at my age. It gives one a sense of meaning.

But they will talk, and if you have in your head anything else... said Jason, dismay written all over his soft face.

Not everything is so serious, she said kindly. There is no reason for them to talk.

Jason swallowed his coffee in a gulp and left the house bent over as if confronting a heavy wind.

When Dimitri came in, Agatha said to him, sadly, I tend to think he doesn't want me at all.

Who? Asked Dimitri.

Jason.

Mother, on this island people are highly irrational. There is one set way—although no one says so usually—but you know, fishing early in the morning for the men, the women cooking, lovers marrying, making children; I come back to take the villagers beyond this simple life—to intellect, business, profit, delight—a life where the core meaning is pleasure. And from there we can go on—to schools, libraries, exchanges. To bring in computers, conversation with the world.

To give the island life of the mind, and spirit.

Leo spoke of computers. I am sure we will be getting one. As for spirit—.

You too are holding out.

We are simple, she said, but if you change us like that—you realize it will never be the same. We have our dignity—we are separate from the world—make use of little, unembellished things. We lived by food and faith—you know, the ancient way. Jason is right, she said, sadly. I was wrong. Once you go down the world's road of change, you cannot come back. We are here because our forefathers came here and we carried on almost as they did, a little like the nuns. Even the Americans in the villa have left the world behind. If you bring in the world, Dimitri, what will we be but a ball of dust in the desert? We are distinct as things are, a little like our own planet. We are men and women of the old style, the old love and truth: what makes fishing, drinking apricot brandy and heaven somewhere in the night....few machines, little electricity—love.

Ah, but that is foolish, retorted Dimitri. One progresses, modernizes— has no need for...to stick to little electricity; I don't say it maliciously.

Perhaps not, but it is insidious; you will creep into people's hearts. We have hearts— private hearts, here—maybe not pure;—but private in that a small group, not an individual, knows the scope of our ambition and desire.

But that is the whole problem. Look at how Jason won't even permit you a little breathing space; you are forced to be so private as a different woman, you are buried alive.

He cannot articulate it well, poor thing, but it is as if he hasn't forgotten the vital thing.

The backwardness here is bestial, said Dimitri, all the worse because it is chosen. One can't learn or think.

Well, I trust you. But I can go against you. Just because you might be less than cautious, said Agatha filled with love and obstinacy.

Cautious? The folks here are children.

Ah, hum.

What do you mean, mother? I know you stand apart.

There are some children that have an eye that pierces right in; and they know things too.

What things? How to squabble with each other; peek into each other's houses. Inform on one another to the priest. Accept rarely, despise, habitually. Live in such a tight circle—as if the world even knows of their existence, much less has an aim to destroy it.

I lived here nineteen years and there was nothing. Some old men gathered around a radio at the single tavern. The women with buckets of water and soap washing constantly, cooking. You want to stop progress, modernization; you simply make yourselves abnormal—a case for the shrink to handle.

No one precisely wanted to stop anything, replied Agatha. People just were used to their way; they never thought, never made a move that was their own doing... and there was always good food, usually good weather; we're out of the way even of the sea paths, you know. Besides, no one thought of us as you say. We have instead a tradition.

What tradition? What tradition worth anything?

Agatha stopped, aghast. What we've always had, she said. You have grown bigger than us. We have our foolishness, our little good, our little evil. But you are part of something—how can I call it-- full of meaning, of wickedness, of bigness and fondness and lostness.

So you think I am wicked merely because I want to lift people out of trivializing simplicity and ignorance and give them life—vital, fabulous, worthwhile!

You are not wicked intentionally. You began to think things beyond the scope of happiness and then you trusted these mad thoughts.

Whom do you want me to trust—the priest?

Agatha stopped a minute. No one exactly trusted Father Isaac; they were a little afraid of him now—since coming down from monastery mountain, he had transformed, become from an earthbound thing, aerial and light filled. He was like the weather on a good day—limpid, floating, brilliant. He has brought miracles, albeit of an ordinary kind—kitchen miracles—a sudden abundance of dairy products and fruit.

Impossible; the earth simply flowered.

He is very gentle and sweet, she began, and the tears welled into her eyes.

What is it, Mama, asked Dimitri in a low, soft voice. Have I hurt you?

You don't understand. I stood by him, believed in him when nobody else…of course, now they all accept…

Why now?

The signs. He did the honorable thing. And she told her son about Father Isaac's penitential trip up the mountain, his transformation—golden, beautiful—you can't help but give him credit, and then the signs!.

But all this has nothing to do with…but he would naturally be against a change.

Why do you say that?

Ah if you cling to such notions…then only miracles make sense. There are people in the big world even, Mother, who believe that all modernization is of the devil.

But there is one thing, she murmured, hastily in answer; you would not find him like that.

My friend, the rich hotel owner whom I wrote you about, is coming over in two weeks. He will stay with us—or, will you accept that?

Yes, yes, of course.

I thank you. This place could be developed as a tourist's paradise. So many of the island's beauties are unexploited. The forest, the caves and subterranean lake, the mountain. Even the monastery could serve lunches.

But we are not a finger of the world, said Agatha, suddenly.

Ah, you don't want to participate. But there would be good money involved—such that if anybody wanted to make a move away—they'd have capital.

Never mind.

But I mind. I will go visit the priest.

Dimitri left his mother's house in the afternoon, the second day after he arrived, slamming the door; he knew that must have shocked her, rattled her a bit; she was used to his being gentle in all things, footsteps, door closing included. She had always called him in pride to others a 'gentleman' and she meant as in a man who is gentle.

He felt as he walked that his footstep in fact was heavier, ruder in a sense; and there was a certain other sense that he had acquired living in a city—haste, impatience— a deep fundamental impatience. But these were things that he had learned almost unconsciously; sometimes he thought that the seeds of them were in him ages ago; or that the world around, consisting of the hotel where he worked, the busy street, the restaurants, night clubs and bars had insinuated as much as it strung him along.

He wanted to think that the 'world' that is what they called 'the world' on this holy island, he called it that—had not claimed him quite. That he stood apart and could still make the final decision as to which side he would be on. It was a wonder, after an exhausting twenty hour sea voyage in a small ship, and a two hour taxi ride, to walk into a fifteen story hotel with a sign in neon out front and to say to a footman dressed in green and gold braid that he came from a place that had no automobiles and just had electricity installed four years ago.

I think it is all a matter of necessity, the footman had said. In the city, these things are necessary. But in a little place out in the middle of the sea—he had shrugged.

Dimitri tended to agree; and he couldn't help noticing the way he said 'the city' as if it were ponderously important, while the other something insignificant—a speck of dust floating on the waves somewhere. But as time went on, the footman, who was a college student at the top of his class, grew very confiding with Dimitri, and it didn't seem like he wanted to offend. At first it seemed that he knew so much, great stores of knowledge, which gladdened Dimitri, electrified him, in a sense, along with the visions he had of the city; but then it seemed, in that distant, reserved part of him, that while he remained detached, despite his enthusiasm, the other was sucked into anything new, modern—and technology convenient or just intriguing to him.

When the time came for his visit back, this friend-footman declared to him, I suppose now that you have worked and studied here and gained knowledge of the world, you could be president back there.

It is not the way they are, he had thought to himself then and thought to himself now. He raised his head; he had a habit of staring moodily at the ground when he walked; and he saw Barbara and Stavros. Stavros hailed him; Barbara smiled slightly.

I hear you've come to make the world turn in our direction, said Stavros. There may be some objecting old men but the women are always enticed by shining, glittery things like gold and neon, glass doors, swimming pools. I have seen many pictures of luxury hotels. Give the old men a share in it financially—then you will have it secure. The island will be a great rich man's getaway. The kind that are photographed in the magazines.

Is this true, Dimitri? Barbara asked innocently.

Dimitri looked down. A man will be coming in a couple of weeks—a developer. One thinks of making use of this island's natural beauty. A kind of contribution.

Come, wife, said Stavros, sternly—before you bite him. She has gotten biting since you've been gone. They passed by, talking in low voices.

Dimitri turned down the single road leading through the village and up the hill to the little white and blue church. It was a road that he had walked along for years with both hope and sullen defiance. Paradoxically, the church, which kept them obscure and backward, was one of the few places where there was learning to be had. The priest had been regularly educated in the world. Father Raphael had known mathematics and biology, history and poetry. Dimitri had swallowed down everything that could be squeezed from this half-sick, half-brilliant brain. But there was also to be ingested the incorrigible piety and conservatism of the Church, as well as the patronizing sense that one was being denied because one was a child so many things. And it wasn't a matter of age, as Dimitri had first thought when he was eight, ten, fourteen, but the strange necessity-- that was part of the teachings of the holy fathers-- to remain "child-like" in mind unaware, even of the injustices and truths the worldly contended with, in order to avoid corruption.

Dimitri had thought this premise of Orthodoxy tacky and false. But there were many who revolved around the priest when he was sane and bright with life, wit and knowledge and were in awe of him and remained his devotees, obeying him unquestioningly, until he had so vulgarly failed them. For his sake, they had voted away developers, and modernizers—happy that they were to be pure in heart, proud of their tradition—that of seeing God. Wasn't that in the end, Mother Dora who had been reborn—flesh of God, blood of God?—who had the Light, which you could see in her footsteps even at night. So they had remained fishing, embroidering, making lemon curd, their quarrels strictly within their houses. They had, with the help of Father Raphael, looked upon the world as the beginning of the end, Holy Island as the best alternative—and they had savored there eternal life. Wasn't it eternal life to sip that apricot brandy on one of those endless summer afternoons with the sun blazing, with the cool winds blowing in from the sea, sweat and then pleasure, a pleasure so profound—few knew it. Teeth rotted. Livers, hearts failed. Once, twice, three times there was a midnight call—someone had to be taken to the other island in a hurry. But they each had an icon in their houses—the Virgin Mother of God. They knew that owing to her protection, the worst had passed them by. They carried a burden; life was a bit raw-edged. People held their breath when babies were born. There was one midwife for their island and sometimes she didn't make it, carousing as she used to be, stewed. But with two exceptions in recent years, deliveries had been easy. Those two exceptions nobody had forgotten. In one, both mother and child and striven for hours; by the time they had been transported to the hospital on the other island-- the midwife rinsing her hands, calling on the Mother of God--both were dead. The other was Max's mother who had contracted blood poisoning after the baby was born and had died quickly and quietly—slipped through the midwife's hands—who had fallen asleep in a chair by her side—before anyone could even think of calling the boat....

The village folk went about whispering and nodding: she had always known her destiny. Dimitri had said angrily—destiny, my foot! This death could have been prevented. When are you going to come free of your grandmother's stories?

But there was also an undeniable hope that resurfaced as he walked towards the blue-shuttered, white church. This hope was not connected to the scholarly studies he remembered; it was something he had repressed in the city where his impatience with backwardness was so respected and nurtured. He hardly knew what this hope was all about, nor the joy that went along with it. He felt alive and free. Maybe it is just that I am so used to these parts, he said to himself. And the sun is brilliant, though the day is cold—a quality of sunlight that makes everything seem ethereal. That tree there: why does it tell me nothing? That rock? Is it because they belong in half to another world that I have dismissed with such arrogance?

Max was in the church kneeling and praying as Dimitri came in. It was an unusual sight —people didn't often come to pray when there wasn't a service and they didn't have the habit of kneeling. He stood back, respectfully. He had thought when he had left that Max was a poor, torn, odd boy, ostracized for some unaccountable reason for he was unquestionably beautiful. He was one of these people, like invalids, whom folks sympathize with but rarely want to spend time with. Perhaps he had some rare psychological disease—all that crouching and grimacing; but the priest had gone and taken him under his wing. His head was bent down and Dimitri could catch the sound of murmuring; the sound was hollow, deep and sad and gave him the sense of wind in the depths of the forest, or of a bell tolling in an abandoned village.

Dimitri went softly through the back of the church to the steps leading up to the priest's quarters. Father Isaac was standing in the doorway as he came up—as if waiting for him. You expected me? Asked Dimitri.

Yes and no, said the priest, smiling at him. I thought you might amble by out of curiosity having heard of the goings on; I had heard of course that you were coming. Then I thought that after all you despised the faith, thought it an intellectual burden; I thought perhaps I'd be the last one to see you and wish you welcome. Then I thought again that maybe it wouldn't turn out like that. Maybe an old sense of pity...

But it's just that that I wanted to speak to you about, said Dimitri, hastily. May I come in?

Yes, by all means. Take this armchair, the wicker one by the window. Sit carefully. It has a wobbly leg.

Dimitri eased himself down into the chair, which creaked and swayed under his weight.

He looked around and half smiled at the painful sense of disorder—not that the priest left clutter round about the room, but rather that nothing had a perfect place, a fitting position in the little room, so that the result was a crazy attempt at neatness with everything in some kind of an order but a little askew: the jacket hanging from a lamp nailed to the wall, the dishes, clean, but piled crazily on the stove.

First off, tell me, began the priest lighting up at Dimitri's softened expression. Did you have a good time while you were away?

No, not at first, said Dimitri, unexpectedly. At first, I was miserable. I thought I was traveling towards the light, going into the big world, he continued surprised at himself and his sudden outburst—and I found myself enveloped by a dirty cloud.

Yet you never thought of coming back, said the priest, smiling with understanding.

No, that was not an option. I thought I had severed myself from this place; in fact, coming back, it looks so pathetic, so impossible. Perhaps I made a terrible mistake. And yet, I must say that the sight of the blue-shuttered church on the hill, the old familiar sight, brought some incomprehensible desire…a sweet free feeling, the first I've had in years.

How did you find yourself on that boat coming here?

I'm not sure. There was a proposition—an interest. I thought it really mature, a sign of progress in me, as a man, to take it up. I was made excited like a child at the same time. I thought I could come back without really stepping foot, live without really planting roots, pass through without really seeing; I thought—just a glimpse-- but that I knew it all already—it was boring, nondescript, an awkward fit for me now.

Of course, said the priest quietly; he sat down on a little plastic stool that Stavros had just given him as a gift.

When I arrived, it was as decrepit as I thought; everybody I met seemed painful, sad, slow. I thought I'd be driven mad. Yet at the same time, it was as if I could take something in me to completion. Perhaps it was all the sun, I don't know. There is an incredible sun on this island. But perhaps shortly I will have over and done with this island, that is all that it is.

So you will stay a short time?

I doubt that I will ever live here again. It is so little, quaint, but on the whole rather badly done. I myself build better houses and I only know a little carpentry, learned long ago from Simon when he was working.

Didn't Simon build most of the dwellings? Inquired the priest.

Strangely, no. But that is just the thing around here. No one organizes their skills, competes in the market. People sort of do things by inspiration—their bare hands. Simon had a workshop and now and then he'd lend a hand. But others took over the main work. They thought he was funny—odd, or half mad-- and as a result no one would listen to him. I liked him; stayed by him. Long ago when I wasn't talking to anyone, he'd take me by the hand into his workshop and teach me the basics. But I know I can build a house, do repairs. I look around now and see that the building is so inexpert, painfully so.

Didn't you notice that before? Asked Father Isaac, smiling and moving to the stove.

Well, I thought, despite my skill and knowledge—that it was a matter of just a style, island style of building houses. In a funny way I had the idea that well—you know, the island is called by some of us 'holy island;' I knew of course that it has to do with the monastery on the mountain above the village, but I thought that it was somehow related to the funny houses and the fact that people around here take things unwisely into their own hands—and that it shows. There is nobody who knows better, or they won't accept one who knows better—to guide them, to set examples of expertise and mastery. I think sometimes they believe that every tilting wall that they build is God's doing.

And yet, said the priest, musing, they are not tractable on matters of faith. He poured water into a pot and lit the gas.

I thought most were sheep, said Dimitri.

Well, even there they think they know better—what a real priest is.

Yes, that is true, although they wouldn't dare acknowledge that they pick them.

But never mind all that. As you say, they have no direction, that's all.

I didn't say they had no direction, returned Dimitri, a little energetically. They have as everybody has—desires, ambitions, dreams; but they have no freedom from their little cramped life.

How do you know they want that freedom? You say yourself that you found freedom walking on these little shores.

Yes, of course, but don't be preposterous, exclaimed Dimitri, half angry, but restraining himself. You know what I mean. They are body and brain; I, he said, a little grandly, am also body and brain.

Some of them thought, with body and brain, that you should be disowned for leaving your widowed mother.

Dimitri was silent. He found the priest different, he wanted to say difficult, but hesitated to use that word. Suddenly, he ejaculated, what a beautiful fragrance!

It is the infusion, said the priest, laughing lightly seeing the delight on Dimitri's face. This, you see, is Eden, he gestured around the room, although you might not believe it.

Eden, said Dimitri, this is something I can't fathom. But I know if it is so, trouble will come.

Well, said the priest, sighing. I have a son, a made son, not a born son—you know the story.

Max, said Dimitri, yes. He ran away from his father, the devil, my mother wrote me about it. And he will betray you.

Yes, said the priest, eventually, one way or another. His kind always do. There is nothing wrong with him, he went on, quickly; he is not evil by nature, though born of a devil and a witch, but weak, incapable, and ashamed.

In the world I felt as much, said Dimitri, compassionately; but one learns to flaunt it—to become the child everyone wants to teach.

Perhaps I pamper him too much. You see, he does not know himself at all and so I indulge him. It is a mistake. Why do you think God put that forbidden tree of the knowledge of good and evil in the garden?

Ah, said Dimitri, smiling—so that Jesus Christ would come.

To permit Adam to know himself in one way or the other; to encourage him to grow up! For Adam didn't know the essential: He didn't know that he was good. God, you see, never said what was wrong with that tree, only that it would bring death. Adam became a death knower, with knowledge of and from death. He had to make the decision. Self-knowledge, a death image, or knowledge of God. It was as it were unhealthful—thus sex as well—good, evil. There is a thought along those lines about sex. Sex is not considered good to someone dedicated to God. And yet sex is quite obviously what He intended. And yet this duality lays us at the tree's feet, back in Eden, paradoxically, at death, close to God; this time the tree is the cross, Christ's Blood, eternal life, soul soundness. Self-knowledge sublimated, coming from manhood, broken open to the core, and the fire of preference for God through disobedience— a mature knowledge of self and the world.

It is curious the way you put things. said Dimitri, smiling.

But taste this tea, the priest, finished, anxiously. Perhaps we have talked too much.

The tea was delicious, fruity and sweet. Dimitri looked at the priest as he sipped, smiling for the sweetness of the drink. He thought Father Isaac had a kind face, marred by some kind of indefinable sorrow. Yet it was not a sorrow that was sadness; in an uncanny way, all contradictory to everything he had ever thought or known, it was sorrow that was relief and gladness, a shadow of having left those old terrors behind. What astonished him even more was that the priest was quite normal as a man. At least, he was logical, was not insane, as Dimitri had at first imagined he would be. And he talked as someone would inquiring about things from a little known acquaintance with whom he was merely trying to be friendly, such as one would who had a well-meaning mind.

He was reflecting pleasantly, sipping the tea—it had been years since he had paused and reflected in this way—and it made him feel somehow manlier...but everything was slightly odd, wonderful and pleasant with the priest—when he happened to turn his head, and he saw Max in his deacon's robes standing in the middle of the floor, looking at him with straining eyes.

Dimitri had never looked Max full in the face before. At least, not since he was a grown man. And his first impression was that his face was not quite in alignment, that his eyes were hot, and that the whole business of the deaconship rather shocked him—that it was entirely painful. But he had heard numerous stories of Max's sadness and the cruelty of his father, whom privately Dimitri thought rather a farce of a Casanova, but who, he had to admit, had rather provocatively stepped on people's toes. Here is one, waiting to explode, thought Dimitri as he held out his hand to him. No wonder. Confined here.

You have quite a job, he flattered him, aloud.

I know what I do. Without faith people turn into blind walls. They don't know what they are doing. That is why the Lord said: Forgive them Father, they know not what they do. Even while they were mocking Him on the Cross.

So the ultimate cry of Jesus is to forgive the unfaithful.

I didn't mean…

Ah, but you said…

Father Isaac, appealed Max; and then stopped.

There is nothing wrong with that thought, said the priest.

Max made a movement with his hand, as if this answer was pointless, looked at Dimitri with hot, fierce eyes and then flushed and looked down.

What was Christ, Dimitri asked, pursuing him with his eyes, intently—naked on the cross or did he have a little panty?

Max put his hand to his chest and didn't speak.

Naked, replied Father Isaac, sorrowfully. People always ask.

Dimitri looked down; I am sorry, he said, genuinely. I am not a Christian but the thought is very sad and tender, for he lost to a rabble of men like vicious dogs his most intimate self, like a woman raped.

He was there, our Lord, said Father Isaac, on that cross like a newborn child or a young girl—pure, thinking no evil. We tend to think of babies born on soft beds, cradled against warm breasts full of milk, but the reality is that some are born to cruelty and pain, young girls too, often they are helpless and tortured, and exist in the midst of something also helplessly cruel.

Max moved across the room and knelt before Father Isaac who was standing by Dimitri. Dimitri watched him look up into the priest's face with a strange high look of adoration and mania. The priest put his hand on the young man's head and softly blessed him.

You see, he went on, speaking to Dimitri, why I chose to adopt him. He is the one most likely to make mistakes, the most weak and vulnerable. He is such that if he were Abraham, he would have gone ahead in his zeal at doing God's will and slit Isaac's throat. No restraining angel could have stopped him then. But oh, how he would have carried that blood cross after!

Max rose quietly and looking around at Dimitri once again, squinting in the dim light, casting at him a strange look half fury, half curiosity—looking the way a child might who peeps then looks away then peeps again, distrusting and fascinated at the same time. Then he said to Father Isaac that he was going to buy chicken at the grocery store and left.

He has not grown to full manhood, said Father Isaac to Dimitri when he had gone.

No, said Dimitri lightly—they none of them are. He finished his tea and sighed. The enjoyment of the beautiful fragrance was gone. Somehow I think I have more to do with Max than I would like. Destiny is not always cruel, he said to the priest, as it was with Jesus. But it is rarely, I think, what you would prefer.

But as he went out he noticed once more the sweet taste of the tea in his mouth. Outside, the fresh wind from the sea filled his nostrils and his body. For a moment he thought of Catherine standing in front of her house on the cliff. There is one natural thing in this place, he thought, besides the trees and flowers. I suppose she thinks of me as she does the others. Rather base, elementary, and rude. I suppose she's seen men enough.

Then he thought of Max—poor, poor child, he said to himself. Half insane by the look in his eyes. It would almost seem as if the priest had wanted me to do something about the boy. I goaded him; yet I didn't goad him. My question was sincere. I have always wanted to know if Jesus was really naked on the cross. And Dimitri went on down the hill towards his mother's house talking to himself.

It was only back inside Agatha's dimly lit dining room--the lamps were hung so beautifully by the windows, that the reflection of the light on the glass made the room inside look like a little gem—she had done the best thing possible with reduced electricity—that Dimitri remembered that he had not talked to the priest about what he had gone to talk to him about. But for now, he said to himself, it doesn't matter.

What matters, he said aloud to his mother, who looked at him joyfully each time she saw him—is you, only you.

Oh well, said Agatha, things have been topsy-turvy since you've been gone. The little village has changed.

Not a bit, returned Dimitri, heartily, reassuring her.

Well, but there are things going on as never before. For one thing, she turned to him, suddenly serious, Anna is very ill. There is no question but that she is dying; for her, thank God, it is slow, but she says crazy things, you see; she is losing her mind, I think—all about how love is the one thing she never had in her heart! Then there is Leo who says things to me—you'd think we were young and romantic and you know the stories about him, the cruelty and pain he's inflicted. I think sometimes he's deceiving me, other times it is just some unnatural alteration in him.

Dimitri laughed. Come, mother, you are having some fun with a man. And you can't have it both ways: first you want it to be deception and then, it might be good, but oh how unnatural. Some old naughty men love in the end, he said.

But I will tell you a real puzzle even you won't understand, said Agatha to him ingeniously. Nico is acting very strangely. He pretends that it is perfectly normal to be without a wife at his age and shows no interest in the young ladies.

It sounds perfectly normal to me, said Dimitri. Refreshingly normal. I have never been interested in those childish women that are bred around here; even Jason who hasn't a thought in his head to bother him, doesn't give them a second glance.

You know your brother is a loner—he grew up without a father. Nico is different. No there is some antagonism towards, towards sex.

Perhaps he is dedicating himself to God, said Dimitri; I visited the priest today and he informed me that sex was unhealthy for those dedicated to God.

Hmm, Agatha humphed. Everyone knows he sets himself above us; they say you do too, but—that is not true, now—is it?

No, no; I don't set myself above you. Rather below you, Mother. But the example of faith around here, no offense intended, Mother, is blundering, even stupid, and in one case fanatical. That sort of thing wouldn't count as faith.

With Dimitri, sure as she was of his error, Agatha was content, excited, to put aside her guilt and painfully slow attempt at reconciliation with Christ, and swallow down his fun, his strong, ringing voice, his masculine beauty, the knowledge of no wrong except that which was violent and foreordained for sins unforgiven. She felt the way a child does when its father picks it up and tosses it in the air, catches it and swings it in his arms. The universe could be danced in, flown in and it was controlled, safe and kind. There was just that momentary gasp of something wild and free, a sky that was a little wider and higher than one thought thrown upwards, before the strong arms held her again. She would almost forget her bad prayer that was her usual recurrent thought, the painful toil of asking forgiveness, the cruel puzzle she had that she should suffer more, now that she was eating and drinking and cleaning china, embroidered sheets, dancing…and that dancing and seeing her son again could not be the cross. With Dimitri, life burst out of her chest—she said she loved him, he laughed, he was beautiful, oh he was beautiful and she was a queen, and there was no realm more glorious—than that little house with the windows that always needed fixing, a realm that consisted of coffee and brandy at four in the morning for Jason, Dimitri coming in at seven for breakfast of fish and wine, and then the dancing around his suitcases and boxes that a man had brought in from the boat before he had arrived.

Mother, you are sweet, exclaimed Dimitri, catching her dancing about—like a young girl—with your eyes clear and sparkling. How your toe goes high! When did you become a dancer? How is it with your energy that you can stand it here, in this stagnant place? And to think you've lived here never budging even so much as to the other island on the deck of the supplies' boat for—how long? Twenty something years. You are more beautiful to me than the young women even; there is life in your eyes—and how is it so? A miracle.

Dimitri, said Agatha stopping a minute to breathe—I am too happy.

But that is the end and purpose in life, said Dimitri, taking her in his arms.

No, I doubt it. There is always a curse put on the happy—here or in the next life; we have to pay—the happy do, the dancing ones. At least, I'll have to pay, dancing on tears, dancing on them so that the teardrops don't break, leaping and coming down lightly as a feather.

I don't believe it, said Dimitri. What malicious old pious crone put that into your head? Of course, even the birds and animals have dances, have mating dances, but forgiveness' tears' dances?

I sometimes believe that if the Son of God failed to bring me back from the dead on the Last Day, you could.

You are too odd, Mother. You don't belong here. But if you have to stay—why not let me make you a new and better place—

Oh, you can't build the whole village over again yourself. What are you talking about?

Architects, planners, fine finishers—a beautiful luxury hotel with a swimming pool and hot tub, tennis courts. And as a side thing, we'd have a better school, a library, a scientific laboratory for the children. We'd build up to something beautiful and workable.

Your friend put you up to this?

He is thinking generously for you and the others—not wishing to take advantage.

I have learned that left to themselves people change very slowly; but if there is an impetus, a leader, a manager of their affairs… You and I know that people here don't understand the mind, the human spirit. A way of thinking that is slightly off from their old worn, worn out road.

You and I are almost blasphemous at heart, said his mother solemnly.

And so, considered in the old traditional light of the times, was Jesus. Dimitri went to his suitcase, unzipped it and pulled out his laptop.

Yes, we have them even here, said Agatha, watching. Leo ordered one; it arrived on the supplies' boat a month ago. But he hasn't shown me how it works.

But it doesn't work, said Dimitri, smiling. You are not wired on this island. Must be the last place in the world. Do you know even places like Papua New Guinea… But look see how it is turned on. He plugged it in and pushed the button.

It lights up like Christmas, exclaimed Agatha.

It is Christmas, said Dimitri, excitedly. It makes the world one. People can exchange messages in little more than an instant anywhere in the world. This sort of thing is going on in the world—amazing things, things that bring light and life to humanity.

The way you talk, smiled Agatha, but standing apart suddenly in a kind of daze. You know we are taught that Christ…

Of course; but in this world, Christians from all over pay lip service to God and in reality depend day and night on little machines like this. Who wouldn't? Only a fool.

Well, this island is…

Full of backwards thinking, obstinate-minded, sluggish-spirited people.

No, but we have our own little lives…perhaps even generous, well-meaning people have no right to fool with them.

Mother! What is it with you? You know the world is even here—you can't avoid it. Electricity, gas, motorboats, a motor scooter or two. It is just that you are sixty years behind. Even if you creep at a snail's pace, ultimately, people here will have to change and the island will be developed. Besides people here just think they don't want it; yet the children see airplanes fly overhead—they dream.

And the old ones dream. But other men have come, even when you were a boy and when I was a girl too. I watched the old men then gather in the tavern, and the arguments, hot headed and fierce; the priest would join in, the priest at that time, and I would watch him lose his cool, smash the table with his fist. He told us that our culture, and this beautiful island, which is all we have, would be lost forever. He told us our children would go and come back changed, corrupted, and insecure and godless. He said that as a group of islanders, we had a chance—a chance spiritually and a chance even regarding the world. For we could maintain our pious lives, our traditions, the rhythm of our existence, and also we could in time, offer on our terms something to the tourists, to the seekers of little untouched havens in the world. If we gave up to the developers, he said, we'd be nothing but a spoiled Eden in the end.

That is a myth, said Dimitri, hotly. The whole island is rag tag and funny and useless as it is. But you could make it a place of pleasure. Then it would be Eden.

You are mistaken, said Agatha, sternly. Then, she sighed. You left ten years ago, and although I see that physically, you are just as I remember, inwardly you have become something so difficult to understand. You might think I am just childish—that I can't see yet as an adult in the world, your world, but there are things, lowly as they might be, that are nevertheless in the end what counts, the dignity, she went on dreamily, not of kings but of the king of kings who lie low and grotesque, as ex-fornicators, old crones.

You have no experience even in argument, Mother, said Dimitri. You are being obscure. State what you mean.

No, no, I can't. She left the room.

How odd; I have these discussions with a strange, beautiful girl, with the priest, with my mother, said Dimitri to himself and it seems that I am saying things clearly, and yet they are not what I want to say at all. Is it that I can't come home? That in this place where my mother is, my family—I can't talk anymore? Language is all wrong, somehow. These people are so rude and crude and foolish that I actually have to communicate somehow other than language.

Interesting, my mother is like me; Dimitri picked up a hammer that Agatha had left on the table and a screw and began to fix the windows that were askew. She will ultimately come around, I think, although—he began to take the window out of the frame—she is just a little off, obstinate and backward, the way I am not.

Dimitri, you are doing my job, said Agatha, coming back into the room.

Oh, I can do it slightly better, Mama; one thing I learned here—how to build and fix. I have a builder's heart.

. . .

And you know, said Agatha to Anna, later; my Dimitri came back at last and did the windows for me. You know the ones I was having trouble with? They are all back together and working! Opening and closing.

After all those years, said Anna. She was hunched up, in bed like a little ball. She looked white, transparent and sweet like a pearl.

How do you feel? Asked Agatha.

Always the same; I begin to wonder though if it matters. A single, elderly lady who's had three marriages and been content, in good health, well fed, all her life suddenly complaining that she has never loved. Do the sea gulls hear? The winds? The water stretching out to the setting sun? I think there is a God and He picks out for His own pleasure, a strange pleasure—who it is that will love; and who will simply wither away and never know…Then there are any number of people who imagine things.

So now you are a believer.

Oh it comes over me now and then. Old age, you know. I get tired of gazing out into a black sky at night. I want to think—oh, of another reality, light only light. It has to do with the retina in the aged body—gets clouded.

We have our huge sunlight, murmured Agatha.

Yes, I don't see it the way I used to. And then there are signs—signs that the body is well not the only thing. But ah, I am so content—with weddings and feasts, faces, chit chat; I also feel like I have no need for God. I just want to sit at a dinner party and serve crabs and lobsters to a round of pretty people.

And you so close to...

To the grave, I know. How do I know that it is not a beautiful experience, dying, that is. Shall I not go to it smiling if I can? And then it seems that after all this there is only a kind God, a gentle God, if there is God. I see it like music to end the feast. The movement is not harsh, discordant, but like the turn of the sphere, perfect and beautiful.

It would seem you are right. It would seem logical. Agatha couldn't somehow express the age old battle, the talking with, the hairy wild Jesus asking now for a hairy wild woman with purple ribbons in her hair, who kicked her hairy wild legs up high, grinned and leapt like a monkey—to come away for a sweetness beyond sugar; the One who knew the sweat, the purple flush between the legs and the draining of all feeling, all sense from the body, the coming away with the fat gone, the flesh crumpled like paper crushed into a ball then spread out again—her life. The slow rebuilding had consumed her for years and years. And when one day she had lifted her leg high at an acute angle from her erect body, body like a sentinel, the way, she had realized stretched out infinite before her. And this hadn't seemed like the way, so much, as necessity like food and water. The body asked to be stretched, the limbs wanted above all to leap higher and higher. The brain wanted spinning, erect and beautiful, with the leg slightly bent behind. There was taut resistance for seven years and then the going to Simon the wise, and the spreading out before her at last—ability, sweet ability. All this was is Jesus, the true Jesus. And yet not. It was only the long purple road to the delicious Jesus. And yet not. Agatha lived like this—certain, uncertain. And now Anna, an atheist, who had never battled like this, who had eaten and drunk sweeter than anybody, looked at the earth and said—oh God, yes, in my old age—perfect, beautiful; it is only logical. As if one could have and have for nothing.

Finally she looked at Anna and said—it is the heart open, utterly, outrageously joyous.

Is it, said Anna, her worn eyes glittered. And I am beginning to feel the pain, now. It would be alright, I have gotten everything from earth and men that one can possibly get. I have had families; I had a son, grandchildren. I have sat and feasted and drunk. But you know what I complain of—you know, I have not loved.

Of course you have.

In the world's way—family affection, erotic pleasure, coziness, a bit of under-standing here and there. My husband said to me: I will make you walk on velvet, and wear gold and there will even be diamonds. I saw myself as beautiful as a clear night covered with stars. Seeing it in the mirror. What can be more fulfilling? I had a good heart. How could I not? If there was ever an argument, my last husband would present me with a Godiva chocolate after no matter who had won. I feel now that my life was like the cat got into the cream. And for all your weary millions, the poor, the sick, I say—that isn't how it should be. Your God who calls on us to give it up in favor of the painful feet and hands, the penitent thief with his back breaking deliver-ing the homage to God…it was all to me as if we had to be punished somehow. It shouldn't be punishment. So I delivered myself of God. It is interesting how now through a dim and hazy eye, not the sunlight, alas, not you, but his image comes to me as an earth perfectly made. But it is an earth that I don't quite recognize as earth from those astronaut's pictures; in my vision it is something even more mighty and awesome, and perfectly, beautifully, in line, you see. Now suddenly I think to myself what more splendid next step than God! But I want more than God with all the beauty and perfection—I want to see it, to walk it, that is, to love.

In a way I have you—in a way. I've stood by you, my Agatha—it amused me to. All the island in an uproar over what? Our quiet depressive, our blue bruise girl with gypsy blood. Of course, they don't like you, they like straight-backed women with fathers who have bibles in their bedrooms. You were bent-backed for years, a picture of misery; they blamed that Koran that your father read; they blamed the brownish-ness of your gypsy face; above all they blamed you, contaminated creature. I laughed. The holiness of this island, says Paul, still rankling from the way you used him be-cause I know that though he thought to have the upper hand, something happened in that room long ago where you stole from him the taste of victory, through sudden unexpected laughter, mockery at him, though you almost gave it back, broken as you were, and then, though they blamed you for wearing your brokenness in your spine, read—still retaining the eternal victory, for it was eternal victory, in your odd way, the whole village would rankle for your rising up. And Paul just as he was to ease out the whole victory from your hand, as you turned weary, doggish! How he looks at your walking erect as insolent. And imagine how evil the villagers are! For secretly the whole village enjoyed your bow-backed posture—hated you for it, yet relished it, as it went on, and get lower and lower like men with whores—they want whores for unbridled sex, to see them degrade themselves, and hate them for it too, as if hating makes them superior. They had free license to hate you too for being an unbeliever. But it was when they tried to come at you with fire—no one knows who, exactly— Paul called them off, for sure he knew the men; we know them too, of course, any one of those faces, sitting with body with coffee, casting an eye down the road going from the tavern all aware that they are being looked at—showing the sides of their faces as if they are to be engraved on coins—then I thought yes, well, I will love her. And I looked at you in that face of yours that sometimes seems to me to be the color of light, brownish, whitish –how is it that I can't quite see—and said but it is only solidarity. I have a long way to go to love.

I loved my father as a child, said Agatha. He used to put his hand on my back, it was always straight then, of course, gently and kindly. I was barely able to walk out the open door of my home, though, when he left us. There was something extraordinary about him; he said to me once all that is is music. What is not music, is not. How do we know music is? I asked him. There are no words for this argument, he said. But where there is no house, no country, no life even—there is music.

I thought because of statements like these, he knew everything, and more—that there was nothing, nothing, evil in our home because of him. When he left, I went out squinting at everybody; the sun was suddenly too strong for me. The men and women raw and crude. I thought his sayings were lies—here was the world, it was glaring, tearing, mindless, heartless and there was no music. Yet his sayings could not be lies. I knew from the tone of them. But this was what was left. I understood your going off, Anna. And I felt that I was growing feebler and feebler, paler and paler, that I was diluted until only a vague flavor of what was me remained. The words of my father sometimes came back to me. I had gotten to the point where he was half liar, half son of God, when he came back and he was only tired worn creature, so worn that all his sins were just sort of rubbed out. When I started dancing—woman gone mad, Barbara must have said—I felt his hand on my back again, mystically there, mystically correcting and healing straightening vertebra after vertebra and on up to my neck and head, perhaps something in my imagination. When someone's talk cannot be lies—there, that is love.

You know what they say about him, mused Anna. A Muslim in the midst of what was once a pure Christian world. Little world to be sure, but Christians with their little church. Some looked at him like he was desecration itself. There were a few, like Simon, who were kind. Most were curious and condemning. I was young then, still Christian. But I thought he could teach us a thing or two about faith.

He was a Jesus lover, said Agatha, pensively. It was he who told me first about Jesus. Madman, they called him, but he loved the despised and outcast, he said. Looked like a beast, he said, but had a heart of honey. Always singing to God. Love of God is singing and dancing without cease—not that you don't sit down, but you sit still dancing. Men and women were afraid of him because he was pure. He didn't care about anything except this singing to God, and dancing (he minded purely anything else, even the slightest word that was not singing, or dancing) not about clothes, or food, cleanliness, shelter or things—went around with broken sandals, got so thin his clothes fell off, not much in the way of clothes in any case, and there he was with his unwashed butt exposed. Went around tenderly raising the sick up to God like offerings of incense merely because He was so perfectly music and crucifying the proper people, hateful, pompous, dried up people! And he laughed as they all jumped off their crosses and went home, grumbling. But the Christians made me afraid of Jesus and slowly the old ugly mug, the bestial looking man with the only heart for miles, and the high and mighty picture perfect King with the eye of power and judgment mixed somewhere in my broken brain.

Those vultures, said Anna, coming to tear living women, seeking the dead—angry to find only living. Ah, the pain, she suddenly gasped—in my chest, ah. There it is gone now. If that is all it is, I can live through many cancers. But it was heavy for a minute. She paused.

I must not complain, said Agatha, half to herself. All that I told you, of course, you are not to think of it as anything but the roving fantasies of a half mad woman. The other side of the coin is that I love you. I 'd do anything for you.

No, no, laughed Anna softly. That is the time when you loved for sure. That time with your father. Tell me more.

There is nothing to tell. Basically, he thought Jesus was not someone to turn people on. Very few wanted him. That's all. And do you think someone enormously beautiful in soul would be so rejected? He not only didn't play the part of the Messiah who would liberate his people, he didn't look the part. Thin, stinking, ugly. But the kindest eyes. No one, said my father, would fall in love with him except the poor, the pathetic, the abject. Now and then the sick. And yet he gave His heart to the rich, the self- satisfied, those who tortured Him and His children: How could He not? It is the dignity of a king to give His last bread to His torturer, not only give, but to gift it him with blessing.

Ah, don't tell me. You expect a miraculous conversion here in this mansion of red Turkish carpets, silk dresses, paintings, chandeliers, crystal—as I come face to face with what is it the Christians call it—spiritual poverty?

It is lifelong sickness that I am talking about, said Agatha—that my father was talking about. Those who are lifelong sick—when the sickness is in their bone, brain, in that essence of person sometimes called soul. But I read in the Gospels about false Christs who are damn well able to sway imaginations. One thinks that the worshipping masses are running after them. They are always clean, with their beards trimmed. Some work miracles, gush over babies like politicians!

When one feasts and feasts and doesn't listen…Anna paused and then said, I too wonder if Christ wants all of us. There are some pointed comments about those who are dead, those of whom he asks –how are you going to avoid the sentence of hell? Yet it would have been hypocritical of me to go to Africa and work for the poor, to come so close to disease, poverty, pain, death? I wanted so much to sail away dancing, covered with pearls, to see the cities of the world—London, Paris—to buy the perfumes in one, the expensive teas in the other. Ah—it's the pain again.

I don't know. I can't know. I just know I love you.

Sh, sh. Just a minute. Ah, there, it is better. Love me? I who have never loved. Poor heart in me dry and brittle as—well I don't know as what. It is not what I dreamed of, of course, when I was little. When my first husband came I dreamed of love like mountains covered with the red dawn. New, glorious. It wasn't that way; it just wasn't. So I quietly set aside the dream—for a while it lived in its own world of little dreams, the child helped; but the child turned out to be an unimaginative, selfish type. And so the dream died and rotted. On a different subject, did you know I have hired a nurse and she is coming tonight? Kali's cousin. Your services won't be necessary. I am not sending you away. But don't you see? It is not a question of good, evil. We are all old carcasses, good for nothing but to fill our bellies. It is a question of love. Who loves?

Love?

Yes, you may well ask. All those lifelong sufferers in Africa, are they really angels and saints? Would they not in different circumstances be the same wizened old carcass as myself? Why when God knows that in one solution the soul will rot and die and in the other live does he not take us and make us—that is put us in that lifelong solution? In any case, this little cousin of Kali is coming for the money but they say she is a simple loving girl. One of the many whose hands are scented with disinfectant, hands that the unspoken terrors of death of old men and women, their unsung and uncared for and horrible pain, the abandoned hearts of the old, the deserted wizened carcasses—pass into. I, suffering devil, pass into her hands too.

I can't imagine….

What me in hell? Anna paused, and then said with a sigh, no— there are times I can't imagine it either. Of the good and infinitely delicate God whose reflection is in this awesome, exquisitely fine earth so precise in its orbit. But you run along to the good race, Agatha, leave me alone. This little Tia is arriving soon.

It was the second time, since the rainstorm, that Agatha was letting herself out of the glittering mansion; she had a sudden inclination to snoop around a bit—to see, the rest of the house that Anna had never offered to show her. She thought she tiptoed, walked feather light to the other room opposite Anna's bedroom but the floor boards creaked. Anna called out; it sounded like fear. Agatha felt a stab of pity and apprehension. This huge old house and Anna somewhere in it dying alone, she thought, and in her heart of hearts felt it to be unfair. Not unfair to Anna, but unfair to the human race. Despite the evils, and the mere faint traces of good, one was flesh and blood; it was only natural, yes natural, the ladies who gave themselves over to dancing, drinking, feasting and sex, it was almost as natural the rapes of the men, the drunkenness, the murders. She would come out and say—but it is natural, to God. And no she couldn't accept the moralists and their clean notions of themselves and moral good. What were the Pharisees but the moralists and again and again hoary, hairy Jesus had disputed with them, raised his voice into a warning shout mingled with joy--discarded their petty ideas of the law—even the punishments, the trials, prisons, executions that she knew were common in the world. Ha moralists! No, rather the toilers, the laborers, and those who when it got to be too much drowned their pain in drink, drugs, sex, suicide.

But Anna was what? Just a beautiful woman who had lived it up; a beautiful woman who had had all the luck! Beautiful even at ninety—like a crystal. She was glad, despite the fact that Anna insisted that she had lived a life of luxury without love, that she had kissed her on the naked breast. For Agatha wanted she too to taste this life of luxury with its perfumes, lobsters, silks, gold, diamonds if only just on the withering flesh of it—of one of its old women dying. It was really curiosity not jealousy or desire. Agatha breathed in the corner just next to the glass door of the bedroom opposite Anna's; contrasting to Anna's room, which really had only a bed, a chair and a coffee table book of some kind in it, it was a bedroom elegantly furnished, more luxurious than she had ever beheld. A splendid table of oak, polished until it shone, as if tables were there to reflect light rather than to be eaten off of or worked on, lace curtains, fine and yellowing, but real lace, that is, hand crafted; the bed was the same size as in Anna's room with a red cover on it with embossed roses.

Anna had once told her that she was a stumbler, and a bungler in the rich person's world. She didn't know how to decorate properly and there was something simplistic and gaudy about this room; she imagined that it could have been more elegant: there were no rugs here, no paintings. But Agatha recognized Anna in it, severe, yet smiling—the beautiful woman who like all beautiful people was something of a mystery in the end—coming up with, from the depths, this cry—but I have never loved!

It was enough Agatha thought to have seen one room. She was not an intruder. She wanted to call out to Anna, saying: I am still here. A call of love, fearless, despite the fact that she had gone into the other part of the house uninvited. But for some reason, despite the fact that they had after all been friends for something like twenty years, she didn't want to call out with love. She thought of the kiss that rainy night; the warm flesh was still in spirit on her lips, she could taste it with the tip of her tongue; Anna, she said to herself; Anna—stranded, beautiful, all of humanity—never to die, no. And then she crept down the stairs like a thief making a getaway and out.

When one of us is dying, we make the provisions for their souls. We stand on our history—we are those whose ancestors abandoned the world and its pleasures to dedicate themselves to God. We all have lapsed of course; and there are those who fell prey to great temptation. Anna was a girl who as a child delighted in all the sweet things—ribbons, jewels, perfumes, music, dancing, laughter. And we all do. Of course, we all do. Along came a handsome man—relatively handsome. She was young, very young and wearing a big dress. And he said…but here we remember that it doesn't matter what he said. He looked and smelled like wealth—what Anna knows now, she says as rich hotels, the opera, the ballet, paintings, fashionable stores in Paris—then it was just freshness, not quite of the air but of gifts wrapped in tissue and silk like the box he gave her; in short there was this supreme ribbon, a jewelry box, with a stone and a perfume of rare quality wrapped in tissue and off Anna went dancing, throwing her head back in his arms, laughing before and after the wedding. Who can blame her?

She came back with her third husband twenty years ago. He died here of a cough one winter, one cold, windy day; the phlegm got into his lungs and there was no sun that month to dry it out. Anna smiled thoughtfully when they lowered him into the sea. There was no room in the graveyard. She said all sorts of things that weren't here or there—like never was a great companion. But I will miss him—like a chair I use often, suddenly taken away—and the other chairs won't do; for some reason don't bother buying another. Laziness. We didn't listen to these outbursts. People grieve in different ways.

She gathered herself up, read, walked, swam for twenty years and suddenly, oh, perhaps for the past two years, she has been calling herself an atheist. Nonsense, we said. Why, you are always at Liturgy, at the charitable activities! I'm well enough without God—who is he? What is he? So far you haven't answered that. And she says all this nonsense looking at us as if we are the children, little ones who are telling her tales and make believe.

She said to us one time the most preposterous thing: It was Christ's job, destiny, if you like, to die on the cross. My job, or destiny, is to wear jewels and lace, promenade at two in the afternoon, dine on grilled red snapper and sautéed mushrooms. Why should I feel guilty? I have breathed a sigh of pity for him.

Of course, this is our Anna, although in some ways it seems we hardly know her. Cleo wanted to simply knock her down, she was always carrying her head so high. But we, we didn't believe it. We think she simply wanted to show us that she was better than us. We want her to believe in the God of our fathers. But she laughs and says, and who am I if the mothers don't count?

Most often, we can't be bothered by this argument. We don't question Anna—she has the same blood in her as we have and came back so glittering and good humored. We are told she helped families for a while, although we know nothing of it. But we wouldn't put it past her. Our Anna, intelligent and beautiful, even when she was dressed in that plain big dress—looking a little like a classical statue—is no real atheist. Besides we believe in our hearts that no real atheists exist. How could they? We all want to go to heaven. And on our island? Anna is just funny. Of course, we don't believe in the flat out literal interpretation of Anna's words. She with her good humor. It is all a kind of poking fun.

Of course, recently, the island has been a bit different. There is Nico, moody like Dimitri used to be, unmarried, talking of his unbelief. Here and there the old strain of faith has gotten fainter. Zoe found herself wondering what it meant to be the Son of the living God, suddenly. Did God descend in a cloud to a dead earth? Did it mean we were so entirely reprehensible in God's eyes? Accused, accursed: dead! She sipped several black coffees thinking this through. We had thought ourselves part of the living light of the risen Jesus, embracing us, drawing us in towards him in love. Perhaps, Zoe, even, once, affirmed, that is a lost illusion.

It used to be that the light streamed down on us into our souls straight from heaven. Now there is fog, clouds, blindness in us. About fifteen years ago, Simon came down with a peculiar frown on his face from church where he was sitting; he used to go there to study the 'miraculous' blue of the fresco—an undying, delightful, immortal blue, he says always; so down the hill he came with his mind in a fix and said to Cleo a shocking thing: Our holiness is gone. The blue is faded. About five years later Agatha cursed herself and the babies stopped coming. We could see that we were suddenly getting old, drying up—it was as if we couldn't hang on anymore.

But our Anna did an odd thing in addition to all her talk. She started hanging around that Agatha, with her gypsy blood and her Muslim bible. No good can come of it, we suspect. And Agatha now rearing up like a snake twelve years later proves it. Of course, we can't blame Agatha. Who can blame a child for its father? Her mother was a rotten one—who would forget herself and marry a gypsy? What about the children? To have to be cursed with that wretchedness— to be flesh and blood united with a people who sell their own children for money. Yet she wouldn't stop mourning him when he left; seems she mourned him when he was still with them as if she had lost her hold on him. A man, we can hardly remember him—nothing to remember for he wasn't strong --all grey and brown face, a cloud of dust, not a man, playing music incessantly, weeping in our streets, hanging his head in the sun. No wonder Agatha thought that hell was not far away. Having done nothing wrong she thought perhaps heaven was held out to her. But considering—unbaptized, half in church, half reading that Muslim book...and then the story went around, just a suggestion mind, but God himself sometimes comes just as a suggestion—that Agatha's curse was our unholiness. That it had started then with her—we suddenly could see bits of human flesh—fingers, noses, fat hips in what was supposed to be our supreme otherworldly light. Human flesh, pig-like, too. Suddenly even the roses look as if they no longer have an ulterior thought. This was the curse material, living and breathing, permeating the island. Of course Anna said that was sheer foolishness. It was nothing. The only curse was hatred, our hatred, not God's—hatred of others, of life. But what are we to think and do? We have always given Agatha everything. But we have our history to consider—a chosen few, after all, were gifted—to see the resurrected Christ himself! And how is it possible to corrupt this same bloodline— this bloodline of light and even if we graciously, compassionately let pass that very corruption, in name of the faith, why then what of this lack of conversion? Is it not wrong not to insist that all be converted? Agatha has made no attempt...

We consider, we murmur amongst ourselves. We don't deny that there has been some feeling against the poor woman. We sally forth, we let her know that she may at any time be baptized. And she stops what she is doing, her face turns sad and serious. But to be baptized one must be prepared...she said. And the same thing the second time.

We have to indulge her sometimes. Agatha isn't ungentle. For a mother to have two quarreling sons is an extreme hardship. Now that Dimitri is home what will they do? And now it seems that Dimitri is bringing someone to set our economy in order. Therefore we fall back gently tenderly on toleration. She, we— all need a certain straightening out of our financial situation. And though it irks us a little that it should be she with the son who had a head on his shoulders, still—who knows the outcome? She did baptize both her sons. And now that Anna is sick, she is the one most treasured at that bedside. By hook or by crook, she has always been the one— that we have looked upon with a kind of pity, indulgence, love. She has wormed her way into our midst—and so into our tenderness and toleration.

Agatha is not exactly one of us, since her mother of her own free will, consorted with the others—those of a different Bible—but we have always taken into consideration, her children, and her misery. Through baptism and the Bible, she may come to be a decent enough dweller on Holy Island. But what is this—other way—this sudden queenliness in posture and gait? They say she is dancing. Of course, she could never dance—it was one gift that was taken from her by God in punishment—but now? Ah, her son returns, so she takes a few light steps, kicking one, two, three? We have heard rumors from Barbara who has seen her, peeping through her window, outside in back at dawn on the sandy drive-- it is more than kicking one, two, three.

We are not to be put out. No, what can we say about people who are so antagonized by the sight of a mere woman as to take torches to her house to burn her and her son, a good fellow who is quietly reading his Bible at night? Ha, bah—evil, violent creatures! And yet it is true, says Cleo, with all the wisdom of her eighty-five years, that when one creature comes bringing evil, others will be inspired! She meant of course Agatha's father. But wait, says Zoe—didn't he actually only play his instruments and then leave the island? Leaving his wife and little children, says Cleo. But It was cruel and intolerable for a man to stay here the way he was treated, said Foti. Ha, treated! Why did he come in the first place? Didn't he know the name Holy Island meant island dear to Christ?

We are not going to bicker. We are a peaceful people. Wasn't there a tourist, yes, we believe so, more than one, who said that the peace that is not of this world is enjoyable on this island? Let us keep it that way and let us go about with sealed lips over this Agatha question.

Anna is dying. We are planning a little trip to the top of the cliff to the monastery. They know those last minute remedies. They are skilled in prayer and the practice of herbal medicine. Why if the Mother was convinced of Anna's need, and we believe she will be, down she will come like the drop of a hat, in her poor black veil and sit by that bedside until Anna softens and accepts Christ once more. One of our elders, Timos, his name was elder Timos, not the present one-- who had nightmares—visions of devils as he was living out his last days—was utterly cured by Mother Andrea. She came down looking a little ghostly herself from a bout with pneumonia, but her grip was strong—no one living could deny it, and warm. She bent over him with her smidgeon of face, all delicate eyes with an Oriental fold at the nose and freckles and whispered to him prayers that would make your heart sing. Oh these were prayers that were songs themselves, lovely, alliterative, singsong prayers. She brought the heart back, you see. It is all a question of the heart.

Some of us can't believe that Anna is dying. Impossible, says Cleo; she was the pillar of life, I think, says Foti. Besides the steps are hard and steep to the monastery. And who is to say that they are saints now? We know that has all disappeared from Holy Island. What are they but olive pressers and wine makers, milkers of goats and bee keepers. You'd think if they were holy, the mere breeze would waft down the blessings of God on us and we'd have our children, people would slip into the old ways. What was all dusty would become clean and the general focus, a blur now, with the white white light of the sun in a cocoon around it, would come cool and clear again. My vision is clear enough, said Cleo. I didn't mean eyesight, said Zoe; there are two or three million visions in us, but when you ask—what is Holy Island, it is all fuzzy like a desert with everyone leaning on their staffs, thirsty and half dead. Only the new priest brought us any change and that was to our kitchen gardens and our goats. Something in the weather too. But he didn't get to the hearts of men where the desert is.

Anna lived like she would have a million years of dancing. Ah, as for that...Those types of sinners are always pulled up short.

In the end, we went up the steep stairs of the cliff—some of us with our staffs. They say the old men and women on our island have immortal life in their bones. We passed the rich man's villa and Catherine obliged us by coming out to offer drinks. It was one of those warmer winter days, cool breeze blowing; we decided not to stop. Then we followed the road that curves around and goes on upward. We could see the black figures of the nuns on the side of the mountain.

There are only six nuns left. One is our Elizabeth—the youngest. We were of the impression that it was a dreary place with no protection from the winds and the storms that sometimes lash us in winter. Mother Andrea seemed a pleasant person, though, who often said Hum, instead of talking. We don't think she was thinking so much as meditating as if she could find for our satisfaction the perfect answer in a serene and ordered mind, perhaps, a slow mind.

But is she asking for a spiritual guide? Mother Andrea asked at length.

Oh well, you know she is asking, said Zoe. I mean the sickness has gotten worse. She gasps a little for pain. She has only Agatha, and Agatha, well—you see, we permit Agatha at our circle, even though she is, well, unbaptized and rather young...Zoe drifted off; Mother Andrea had entered a quiet realm with her mind and it seemed that no word or sound could quite penetrate.

Cleo would not abide this sort of treatment so she picked up where Zoe left off: There is asking and asking, she said loudly, addressing the nun's calm face. For one thing we are responsible for the funeral, and the liturgy and you see Anna has always said funny things—not quite religious about God.

She says she doesn't believe in God, said Foti, unguardedly.

And yet it is not quite true, said Cleo, firmly. She is being unconventional, yes, because she has always been a little irked with the slowness and oldness of our ways. She has a modern streak in her. It has to do with a different interpretation but one which I am sure you could accommodate.

Ah, said Mother Andrea.

We are here, resumed Zoe after this pause, at the request of Anna's soul, you see; at the request of every soul faced with—faced with…

Yes, said Mother Andrea, and no.

No? we all asked in wonder.

No.

You won't come? Said Foti, she had a kind of baby face in her sixty odd year old body that quickly registered whatever was passing through her brain—at this moment, astonishment and fear.

No, said Mother Andrea.

Very well, said Zoe rising in wrath. We were of course indignant but Zoe was bristling. We will not bother you anymore. We find your response abominable but typical of the direction in which our island is going.

Mother Andrea signaled to another nun to show them out.

We have tried and we are on our own now, said Zoe.

We were of course depressed a little about the state of our holy monastery. It did not seem to be at all the sort of place one could count on. We had grown up with the idea of the sisters as our intercessors and helpmates, spiritual of course, of the soul, but still—when they refused to attend a dying woman—it was the last straw. We swallowed down the impulse to accuse them of loss of holiness. But we wondered what in the end did what they did amount to? Paid for by the Church, but supported to some degree by us! But we were also afraid. Had they spiritually, of course, moved on like the sea eagles that visit and then unaccountably disappear one day? Had we ceased to be for them home, friends, children? Were they one day going to rise into heaven and lose themselves there? Or had they lost holiness and with it our last hope?

Perhaps if Anna asked, said Zoe later, stiffly, when we had gathered for tea.

Anna will never ask, said Cleo, and she sighed and folded her hands. We felt all of us old and weary, perhaps deflated. We felt also, secretly, condemned. We were left on a rock in the middle of the sea, deserted, abandoned. Life now seemed so little, frail, insufficient in so many ways. What had it all amounted to? On the best days, the drinking of sweetened coffee, the rich imported coffee that we made by boiling water and throwing in the coffee grains and then straining them out. And the sampling of the delicate apricot candy.

Ah, said Cleo—we haven't had a really good nun since Mother Dora. Now she wasn't this type—cold and quiet; she was tender and kind. Every step she took, they say, light sprang up behind her like a cloud of little flowers. She was one of us, too. Our blood. This one is from abroad. I hear she is a converted Catholic.

Do you know about Elizabeth? Zoe put in; that is what makes me really indignant—not this pettiness on the part of the Mother. Elizabeth is as thin as a bone. Not eating, whipping herself, and absorbed in reading the Fathers of the Church.

Perhaps she has found holiness, said Foti, mildly.

We wondered about this. We thought that perhaps the priest would know. But when we asked him he said he had little to do with the sisters beyond borrowing a cell for his own conversion. We came away a little chagrined. Surely he should know—and then we thought: conversion did he say? And what was that? Weren't we all converted? All, that is, by baptism, excepting Agatha.

Agatha was selected as the one to convey Mother Andrea's 'no' to Anna. Ah, said Anna, gasping a little in pain. On the grounds that I don't believe in God. Well, it is just as well. We would not have gotten along. My desire is not so much to be forgiven in any case, but to love, right now. And I don't want to escape death. Just to love going into it. Just to love.

God is love, said Agatha, softly.

And you know I was thinking, God must be sparrow-headed to the sparrows. I am content with that. To shrink down in myself to sparrow. What good did a man or woman ever do? Usually our heroes come to rectify the damage men and women have done. Sparrows belong to a world that is little in the midst of that big glare made up of men and women. I hope that it is written on my epitaph—laughed and danced no end until, she shrunk down like a sparrow and died. But I find that even that, an easy enough thing, is difficult.

Perhaps more difficult than anything else, said Agatha.

Is it the first sign of love or am I being hopeful?

They say He comes without condemnation.

Ah, your 'He'—how can I face him? What is there to say? That I believe that God is sparrow headed?

I have often... Agatha stopped.

What prayed?

I can't explain. It seems I am always...

Praying?

More of a give and take. Jesus, you see, not the handsome one but…

The one that has the head of a serpent?

One eye is sorrowful, one eye makes a cruel study of me. He looks at, doesn't watch; but suddenly, he has seen— there is a suspension of all knowing/catching and God is with one—having fun. It is an odd thing to say but even suffering—.

With all the tragedy in this world?

I can't explain it. It isn't gleeful. He did put his own son in hours of agony. Took away the fun. He is ultimately only and absolutely serious. And I don't begrudge him. But there is a kind of ta-da at the end. Ta da! But it is only us in our vanity and narcissism who would think that God wouldn't set aside to some degree stiffness and severeness or wouldn't ever be intrigued, letting go of everything, wobble with his creation. And from, you see, a perfectly joyous perspective. How can one be ever only Spirit and never even enter into a conversation with? No Jesus came for that 'wobbling of God'—even in agony: brains-belly! What beauty this our imperfection and darkness!—he wanted love—in the human sense—even no matter pain and agony-- to see it, touch it, to know what it is like, hunger and feeding, the tastes that we long for, and last of all he wanted, yes wanted, pain, where the body puts its self utterly into it, a kiss, or the experience of death—joy or the grip of ice in the bosom. God wanted oneness with us, physically too. And how could it help but lead us to him—the center of our making, now our birthing, not creation? Enfleshment is knowledge –of course, you would say God already knew; well then, he sent abroad the sign of his knowing in whom he was well pleased—himself among flesh! Ah, what delight, intrigue and joy to him. To be helpless, afraid, in pain, despairing—then surging up to heaven—from the void to light, from nobody to Godhead.

You sound as if you are intimate.

Everyone is. It is part of our creature-ness. It is, in fact, the inheritance.

Then you too have been having fun, as you call it.

Not I. I haven't always known how to talk to. I am no great Christian. I don't know what it is to believe, really. Mine are just ideas, and my talking to is musing on.

You of all people! You've borne a cross.

What kind of a cross? Painful, cruel, you'd call it, yet here I am with my toe pointing at the sun in the dawn. There are those who bend lower and lower until they die in the dust. To be something of an outcast on a nothing island is to be something and nothing of nothing. Why it would be joy except with me the human flavor is stronger than the angelic. I didn't die. In the midst of the agonized Body, I tasted sweet.

A saga that might whet God's appetite, mused Anna. She was sitting up in bed; she had been reading one of her many books in English. It was a novel about a respectable business woman who falls in love with an accomplished thief. Now she, this character, she said to Agatha indicating her book, The Hidden Pearl, is someone who changes from insipid to profound, and thoughtful. The salt, he said, must keep its savor. Seriousness! For God couldn't have fun without our being serious. A little child, for example, is serious. Once past that age of seriousness they are no longer the kingdom as such. But seriousness about the job at hand—even if it is picking tomatoes!

My Dimitri is serious. His mind is the deepest, broodiest, kindest kind of mind—seems like his eye is on something difficult to attain, impossible to put into words. He is sharp, a good businessman, so they say, and you understand my drift, the man is honest, I feel it in him—the more so since he is my son. They say I am prejudiced but I would feel in him the slightest discrepancy being closer—him being of my veins and genes. His birth was a drop of blood from the crown of thorns—horrible, I must confess it. Almost lost my reason; but for this, I know him through and through. Shut down into a machine I did to feed and clothe, feed and clothe; the same when the other came, although that birth was easy, almost pleasant. But about Dimitri I was easily alarmed. I would wake up one night and someone would come, a messenger, face ghastly-lit—to tell me he was dead—that was my prevailing thought later when I had come to love him. In fact, when I began to have these nightmares—it was the way I discerned that I loved him, perhaps hated him too. He grew, you see, into such a handsome man. I was proud, curious, attracted all at once. Like a tide that comes way in over the sand, into every little pit and crevice this handsomeness enveloped me; and then there was that taste, talk about salt—his seriousness. It seemed to me that he knew what the poets know early on at eighteen. Then he rebelled against the Church—but there was also always something of a smile on his face for the priest, a kind, soft humility in his eyes. I didn't know, nor do I know now, what he really thinks.

It is unimportant, said Anna, gently. I have often thought—what does it matter what we spout forth from our crazed minds? They seem to me to be like windows that have come unhinged, all askew, hanging there, impossible to close. That one grain of salt in us—is worth everything.

Seriousness, said Agatha, softly, he never lacked; she bent down and picked up Anna's hand and kissed the back of it, and the veins protruding on it. Then she touched the knot in the vein with the tip of her tongue. I will keep your saltiness in mind.

Yes, said Anna. And I, and I—nothing. Nothing! She smiled at her a little sadly.

The much awaited boat pulled into harbor among the little fishing boats. It was a passenger vessel that came regularly once every two weeks or so. There was a little, rotund man at the front of the vessel—the first one out. He pulled an expensive black suitcase on wheels and held in his other hand a man's leather purse, the kind that used to be carried in European countries by well-to-do men. The purse had been restored several times by a highly skilled tailor and although worn, looked elegant and durable. He had on a white Panama hat over a less than memorable face, thin lipped, but fresh cheeked, wore tiny spectacles that gave his gray eyes an expression of constant thought, sported tailored, costly jeans, a white shirt and athletic shoes. People, walking by, cast an eye in his direction as they did to whomever came to the island, not one of theirs, but walked on. The man disembarked and waited, looking right and left, took out a cigarette from a silver case, lit it, and stood smoking and watching, still as a cat, with its tail twitching. After about a quarter of an hour, Dimitri came walking hastily to the dock; he looked handsomer than usual, dressed in dark business clothes and a soft slightly misshapen hat. Michael was passing by with his diary and noted that they shook hands, Dimitri took the bag, and that Dimitri seemed to bow over the other man's hand with a kind of affection or veneration.

So this is the island, said the strange man; Michael heard him say—yes, more or less what I imagined.

It is not hard to imagine, responded Dimitri. In the world, the great advances are made—astrophysics, space exploration, cyberspace…here our triumphs include electricity, refrigerators.

And yet there is significant natural beauty—unspoiled qualities. I am sure the people have the same.

They are a little stubborn, explained Dimitri; they think like children. But once you find the key to their imaginations, you can simply turn it in the lock and enter.

Do you find that to be true of yourself?

Dimitri smiled, uncomfortably. He felt suddenly that he had been pounced on like a mouse, called a liar; he looked at the unperturbed face of the little man; of course nothing like that had been said. He then felt guilty for the imputing to his venerable boss' comments such ulterior meaning. That the man, the hotel chain owner, of which Dimitri was the manager, was precisely the same-- imperturbable, aloof and perfectly business like, clean of all passions-- in London as he was on this tiny backwater island, in a village where there was no hotel and where it was hard to find a telephone-- Dimitri saw immediately. Dimitri was slightly different on the island than he was in the big city; here he was slowed down a little as if he had drunk half a bottle of wine, his analytic thinking less sharp, perhaps, but his spontaneous philosophy deeper. He felt he had to suddenly change gears, quickly—that it was imperative that he be as he had been in London with his employer, courteous, professional and smart as a whip, a character that he felt, in these last two weeks that he had been home, was as meaningless as man to the islanders as a paper doll or a marionette. But he thought in frustration that this meaninglessness was all a physical thing, a matter of too much sun, gazing at length at the blinding reflection of the sea in the noon sunlight, eating the traditional heavy noon meals, sleeping a little too much in the afternoon. He thought that even his mother's sweetness, the sudden attraction to Catherine would all wear off him if he were suddenly transplanted back to England and had to thrive again in the colder London climate, drink the larger cups of coffee.

He had learned in the world off island to have intellectual and nervous control of his machine; now it seemed there were fits and starts in the controls themselves, that they were running slow, and that he didn't quite understand himself. He found after a short conversation with the hotel owner, whose little neat baggage he was towing to his mother's house, tidied up and perfectly clean in anticipation of the guest-- that his mouth was talking, speaking what might have been gibberish for all he knew but sounded like the sort of thing that would please the rich man.

Finally Dimitri confided a strange thing despite himself: You know I am glad to see you. Too much of my hometown makes me more of a monkey than a man—a clambering beast, a grinning member of a lower species.

The rich man said coolly—we all know what it is like to rest and recreate. It is enjoyable, relaxing, but unwinds the intellectual machine after a while.

Do you think the intelligentsia, the business man, the elite of Paris could sit here and vegetate?

Oh communications would have to be stepped up. I hear they are building an airport on the next island. Here, perhaps a helicopter pad. I think it would be glorious to hop over here for a weekend with the wife or girlfriend to eat a meal and climb the cliff—maybe to hand glide off it. Of course, Internet access would have to be installed.

Dimitri was silent. There was the fact that he had been the one to encourage the idea of a resort on this island. Now the resistance, which was all childish, had to be quickly buried; a little like burying a body alive, though! He thought of Catherine for a minute, for some inexplicable reason. Could she give words to his feelings? Maybe she wouldn't. and maybe it didn't matter; she didn't matter. Who was she? But when he tried to discard the thought of her, he found he couldn't. It seemed in just an hour talking to his boss, he realized that he was not the same person and that it would be imperative if he wanted his job to choose that person over this person—a 'this person,' whom he thought no longer existed for years. But that person implied life over on the other side, and this on this side. How had it happened? He thought he had physically crossed over to his childhood home but had left the essential self, which was the whole new self that he prized above everything even love, back on the other side, on the world's side, that he could smile a bemused smile at memories of Holy Island. Now there was some new emotion…viscous and entangling—but oh so childish!-- of that he was sure!- and it made it seem somehow almost impossible to go back, suggesting that the new self was superficial, although intellectual and refined, and that the old self, physical, animal even deep and enduring. Yet all was, he thought—one of those crazy rambling thoughts—solely an effect of the sun.

This is my house, rather my parents' house, said Dimitri, suddenly, after they had been walking five minutes—the door is down this little alley.

Rather quaint, said the rich man studying the blue and white exterior, large windows on the ground floor, smaller windows above—where the bedrooms were.

My father rebuilt this house when I was a tiny child. When I was born, my mother and father were living in a shack. My paternal grandmother managed a little dry goods store and put by some capital. They didn't want my father to marry my mother. Her family was frowned upon. But my father insisted. And so they paid in part to tear down the old ramshackle dwelling or most of it and build this house for them when they married. So that at least they would live in a clean looking place. My father got the bug to earn money, a lot of money; he had an idea to start a real fishing business—to sun dry and sell the fish on the mainland. My father was a bit of an entrepreneur-rustic fisherman combined. But the idea died out quickly for want of knowledge, money and encouragement. And my father died bitter with the heart, my mother says, of a lost child to whom she had to spoon-feed hope.

That is, I wouldn't say the idea died, exactly, Dimitri said correcting himself, suddenly; there is still talk of it going around. People here are very slow to make changes and there is a feeling that these local fish wouldn't transport well even dried—a sense that, of course, this is senseless, but in any case, just to explain—that the fish are an extension of themselves, the islanders who couldn't be themselves in any other part of the world. You see they don't kill fish so much as—well, suck them into their souls, dance with them, catch in the net with them—make feasts where they eat and are eaten with them, themselves, and there the trouble starts, they say. Who is to eat? Who to be eaten? At least, it used to be like that. In any case, as the Holy Spirit slowly moves and changes...Dimitri grinned.

I like to see a place with its own independent culture.

It's not entirely independent—ah, here is my mother! Dimitri pointed to a smallish woman with thick, muscular thighs, and shoulders and with long abundant silver-brown hair falling loosely on her shoulders, in one hand a glass of wine and water, the other shading her face from the sun, which was setting and brilliant on it.

A very great pleasure, Madam, said the rich man in English and held out his hand.

Dimitri translated and Agatha shook hands with the rich man. Agatha, she said, bowing a little.

Mr. Cours, Dimitri introduced him. Please, said the man, call me Connie. Your son has been of genuine assistance to me in my business and personally. It is rare to see in so young a man the qualities of maturity, astuteness, intellectual tenacity—I have often seen inspiration, but the inspired ones come and go—Dimitri has the kind of good, honest persistence that goes with the lifetime careers.

Dimitri translated and Agatha smiled, pensively. He has his own mind, she said at last. When her son had translated again, Connie Cours said— he has always used his intellectual independence well; he has made good choices governed by clean, rational-analytical thinking, yet I think remained sensitive enough to the feelings of clients. In our business, one becomes esteemed only in one way.

Dimitri rendered the English into the island tongue in a way slightly depreciating Connie's eulogy of him. Agatha only smiled again and looked sweet. She took Connie by the hand and wrapping it under her arm against her bosom, led him into the salon where she had already prepared on the dining table two plates full of little fried sardines with hot pepper oil sauce and sliced tomatoes, basil and salt. Near each plate stood a glass of white wine and a warm roll. She smiled across the table at Connie, bowed again, and turned and drifted quietly out of the room.

My mother, said Dimitri, realizes that she is close to really big business. She is somewhat unaware of all the implications of this business, but she is impressed with its significance. You see, nothing like this has ever happened here.

You have a virgin island for a home, Dimitri.

In a manner of speaking. People have in the past turned down developers, foolishly, I think; but then there has never been one from the inside to plead their cause. The developers couldn't understand, the islanders have, of course, refused to understand; there has never been a go-between to arrange the marriage, so to speak. And there has been the sense on some other islands in these parts that I know, quite a distance from here, that the developers have beguiled, constrained, used a kind of force… Whereas I think we could encourage a relationship of trust.

Of course, of course. We wouldn't make a move without trust.

They are very simple, said Dimitri not intending his voice to grow so soft and sad.

It would all be opportunity, said Connie—for them. And nothing would be disturbed. A few trees would be cut down, a few electric cables laid; there would be some building—our own builders, naturally—but you do as much for yourselves.

And the hotel?

First class—TVs in every room, room service, refrigerators, Jacuzzis, double beds; there would have to be room made for parking in the harbor for personal yachts.

Dimitri looked down at his uneaten sardines.

You are silent, said Connie cutting a sardine with his fork and taking a bite. Ah, this island cooking is delicious. Simple, flavorful. I wouldn't be surprised if your mother's was the best.

She is rather in demand, said Dimitri a little absentmindedly.

So your mission is before you. The island will be developed; it is a matter of who gets here first. I would say that following us the Excelsis resort hotels step by step development procedure –which takes meticulous account of the people's needs and desires—the islanders have a better chance of controlling their destiny.

Some would probably rather kill themselves…Dimitri blurted out softly, suddenly.

What? I didn't quite catch that!

I said that with a little talking to, they will probably see this, he said aloud. They are obstinate, as you know, but when they see a man of the world embracing like family, understanding them, wishing to grant them only more freedom and well-being…

I can see now, how the poor, rude, helpless folk when it was too late rose up with knives and forks, inarticulate, crazy…Dimitri said to himself in a low tone, meditatively

You know, he said aloud again, they wouldn't know what they'd be protesting if they did protest—which is so much as to say they will, they must consent.

Connie smiled, which made his thinking eyes pleasant. I too have family that I must always oblige; it's always a toss-up whether I will finally content them. But my conscience is clear—everything is done in their best interest. You can take a horse to water but you can't make him drink. We only need a margin of go ahead here; after that, it doesn't matter so much. A signature, and we're in by law, you see.

After dinner, Dimitri showed his boss to the guest room. Agatha had carefully cleaned every nook and cranny of the little room at the far end of the house over-looking the forest. It had once been the study of her slightly intellectual husband and so was furnished with a desk and a library, a small bed for the nights he was up late and didn't want to disturb his wife and a tiny bathroom with a toilet and sink. She had laid embroidered sheets and a heavy knitted woolen blanket on the bed for there were winds on the island at night and it could get quite cold in early November, though the days were still warm. Agatha had also laid out soap and a towel, and a small razor and bottle of aftershave. She had perfumed the towel and the soap was molded in the shape of a hen. Dimitri saw these little decorations and comforts laid out and arranged with greatest care so that they were both aesthetic and useful and the room looked warm, hospitable, colorful and sweet and thought with pride that there was in his mother some latent talent for something such as greeting cards, gift boxes—oh if only she could be put to use! Perhaps in the end, this was the way, as Connie suggested. And people would own businesses, go professional! Instead of burying themselves every other year-- having lived half lives. He said goodnight to his boss and went to his room, thinking.

Of course, it was just a moment of excitement and pride. Connie had noticed and smiled again. Island hospitality, he has said, contentedly. After, Dimitri thought bit-terly—she'll be folding colored napkins at most in a hotel dining room. The world is like that—really, deep down, one has talent, imagination, high spirit—but in the end, it is smothered rather than put to use—for it is not quite what is in demand—not the sort of thing one can be completely proud of—the new, the superior. Then it is all our fault. One lives and dies too timorous. My own grandmother, robust enough, a beautiful singer, in the last five years never spoke above a whisper. It is rumored that when her gypsy husband left her, her songs died in her; but that is the way of things—one who sings, dies drowned. And all the singing dissolves in vast silence. Here we have silence that is different—the island silence. I can see my mother folding those napkins quietly, not complaining—not one word. Somehow never speaking. There is no use—that other, the talent, the embroidery, perfuming, cooking, lace making, designing of hospitable interiors—she'll carry with her to the grave despite all the new opportunity. But she knows, despite the colored napkins folded all one way, day after day—what does she know? Island silence with a personality like a huge, tender, close, but mis-comprehending god. It wouldn't be Connie's fault; his way is just the way the world is. And that, in the end, is the only thing we have, so—even on the island...

The next day, Connie emerged from his room in a pair of white cotton shorts and a tee shirt and proposed to go hiking up the mountain and later walking on the beach. Dimitri felt obliged to offer companionship, but his boss declined it and insisted that Dimitri 'do his thing,' which Dimitri could only suppose to mean his work of convincing, persuading, molding and manipulating his home folk to agree to the hotel owner's plan. So they parted after a breakfast of fruit, bread, butter and yoghurt with coffee and brandy and Dimitri wrote for the morning on the computer offline.

You are convinced, said Agatha quietly coming up behind him and putting her hand on his shoulder at around noon.

What do you mean? Asked Dimitri hotly and crankily.

Of what the rich man says, she said, primly.

He told you to call him Connie. It was a gesture of great friendship, Mother.

The rich man may be friendly in his own way, she persisted. We are friendly in ours. But a true friend doesn't presume...

A true friend pushes and prods a person to do what is best for them.

Should I tell Anna to go to the other island where there is a nursing home, or take her there by force, a form of powerful persuasion, by guile and cunning? She might easily become a bit cloudy in mind once she begins to use painkillers—I could trick her—for her best interest.

You told me Anna wants to die at home.

Yes, but—

Well, there is no question then. Besides, what does Anna have to do with...? He picked up his hand from the keyboard and let it fall in his lap, slightly exasperated, his mother now, suddenly so typically holy islander, crude, childish, bringing up analogies that don't really make sense....

But I will have to serve her, persisted Agatha, to help feed her along with Kali's cousin, to wash her and help her to the toilet. And we are two blundering, and weak assistants. She could be cared for so much better, without the embarrassment of bothering us—in that little pretty nursing home on the island just across—where her son is.

Yes, but she doesn't want that, said Dimitri; why are you talking like this?

Oh well, I am her friend but it is so inconvenient, so anti-modern, and so like an islander—it isn't progress, efficiency…just old donkey work. She smells sometimes when she doesn't make it to the bathroom.

Well, of course, it is awkward and foolish of her in one sense. But Anna is Anna, Mother; I remember her as a child—she was the same way stubborn as a mule, but so sweet; and she enjoyed life; it seemed that although she followed all the traditions of the island, the cooking, the gardening, the embroidery, the faith—she did it decidedly in her own way with a kind of zest and deep feeling; on this little island where there is really no opportunity for women or for men for that matter, she lived life to the full. I can't imagine the island without Anna. I believe everyone feels the same. We don't like to think that she is dying; we believe just that she is so old that she has gotten frail in all the human senses, but she is still living here and will continue living on and on because you see living is a spiritual thing.

I suppose that all makes rational sense, said Agatha, looking down at him, coolly. But I am not sure.

Mother, why are you talking like this? Do you mean you don't love Anna now that she is old and helpless?

Oh, I have so little time. I help Leo and Jason.

Leo? What is this about Leo? He is a philanderer.

Remember—you told me to play, and to enjoy myself; laughed Agatha.

Did I? asked Dimitri; Oh yes, but that was in jest. And I didn't mean…

How terrible—you will be the talk of the village. And to think that at your age…

I am fifty or so, said Agatha. I still have a sex instinct.

But this is criminal, criminal! Said Dimitri. Here I am trying to sanely work out this deal—to craft a proposal and you break up my concentration, stab me through the heart with your talk.

I hear that they say women are melodramatic most often in relationships. What is criminal about my sexual liaison? I am not married.

Your what? Shouted Dimitri, hearing only the question.

You wanted this island to develop, to become part of the world. Well? I have a head start on you. I have affirmed my freedom. I sleep with a man who is outcast, rejected, despised. I choose him. Perhaps it will one day be love.

Dimitri stood up red in the face with anger. Perhaps I shouldn't be living under the same roof with you, he shouted at her.

Calm down, said Agatha, smiling a little. You are the one entirely irrational. Then again, not really, she said stroking his cheek. I did say it only to provoke. But you consider, son, that we are very ignorant. We read newspapers, up to date novels, texts. Our minds know things. We cling to a way of life, old perhaps, but lovely to us. We have our traditions but there is freedom here too. We are not slaves, rather pickers and choosers. We have faith.

There is my mother again, said Dimitri sitting down, exhaling. Yes, mother, of course Connie is different, he began to explain a little condescendingly, but if you could only understand as I do, having lived in London, Paris, Athens—you would see that he is being very reasonable.

Yes, you see the world, said Agatha, but you see your home, and your mother, with what they call 'sentimental blinders.'

Dimitri had recurrent thoughts about Catherine, but it was days before he managed to climb the mountain again to knock on her door. Ellen opened the door and seemed, Dimitri said later to Catherine, blind, unseeing somehow, although it was clear that her eyes were good enough. Ellen left him in the empty waiting vestibule where there wasn't even a hook on the wall for a coat, and disappeared into another room to call her daughter. Catherine came and Ellen left the room without a word, a little impatiently, Dimitri thought—she had other things to do.

I am glad you came back, said Catherine as she shook his hand. She led the way into the hall that opened on to the kitchen. Here there was a vast room, Dimitri supposed it was a dining room but it was devoid of furniture except for a little table in one corner.

I am trying to get some business done. I would have come earlier. Have you had good days, good nights since I left you?

They have been the usual—that is, if you are asking how I am—well, nothing painful. Catherine's face took on an unpleasant yellow tinge under the dim electric light. It was evening and the house was dark enough so they had turned on the lights.

Is there ever pain? He asked, looking intently into her eyes.

No, that is, not now. There again, that flash of loveliness, almost like a burst of indignation, passing away, leaving her pasty.

Perhaps, he said, still gazing into her eyes—one day, you will tell me about then.

Yes, said Catherine meekly; but I have not been a complete invalid for some time.

Does this island do you any good? Or have I intruded…he put his brown hand on her slight, dry, warm, white one.

It is a good enough place.

When I was a little child, said Dimitri eagerly, I thought it was glorious; I thought God came down at night in the deep of winter and checked if we were warm enough indoors. I thought one day, I would catch Him opening our back door, peeping in.

And it was wonderful.

Yes, yes. Simply to be was a gift of God's. I had forgotten; now with you I remember these things. What it was like to be joyful.

Then, you gave up belief?

I became angry. I thought that perhaps Christ had not covered every aspect: For here on our island, I saw our poor hypocrites. Our folks marching off to church because they expected that in church their narrow minds would be upheld, their prejudices...There was hatred and prejudice against us, you see. You see my gypsy face, Muslim too! My mother says it is like my grandfather's. He was not an islander. They say he was one of the Rom who embraced Islam, and we still keep the Qu'ran—his book. Up until the age of ten I thought that something was up of the devil in the village; I was taught to pity the creatures who hurt us, sang out angry insults, because they were driven by the devil. So my father told me. We were told we were going to hell. And my father said that the devil always threatens people that way. But they also, at times, seemed to be without a thought or care for us. You see, we were free too. Freer in a way, condemned though we were. We had the wrong book, the wrong words with which to speak to God, so people left us alone, largely. That at least was my experience. Though I would often see my father weeping. Not tears, such as my mother used. Shadows fell from his eyes, not salt water, to look at like autumn.

When one isn't poor enough—I mean the islanders, said Catherine, warmly.

Do you think so?

For some it takes no possessions and only bread and water, for others illness...

For what exactly?

To feel. To feel.

Back in the other country, on the mainland, I would have disdained your argument. All a kind of childish narcissism, I would have said. But even this, one step away, and being with you—it is all different.

The old saying is, said Catherine, that here it is a kind of Eden.

That Eden is—the pleasure of...

Love—as it used to be. The pleasure, the luxury of love—of feeling. You see, here one is fed—the lemon trees bloom, cream blooms in the goats' udders, hens burst with eggs, vegetables bloom in the gardens—tomatoes so red, squash, yellow and green, potatoes—there is nothing lacking. People learn to relinquish other desires and eat and eat and so taste, touch, feel…

But they do not, said Dimitri, looking at her as if catching her at a trick; and you know they do not.

I hear that the priest, Father Isaac, tries to awaken them. To let them see the naked reality. All that counts is passionate love. But they take it in the wrong sense, turn in on themselves, burn the priest's truthful books, and then attempt to burn…but I am not going to say it.

Dimitri looked at her curiously.

It was just an accident, a sudden aberrant pathology. Not even real, I don't think. The isolation, the sun…it crazes the brain.

I am trying to find a way to make them independent minded; to give them the ability to think…

Of what? That they don't have a swimming pool? But she smiled. Tone and face, thought Dimitri, as if this was elementary stuff, this rebuilding by steel and concrete, an old, neglected little place, half run down.

How do you know that they don't have ambition? Fishing is all well and good—but…

They can go off island and study.

It is hard, Dear; it is hard. And then the sense is here that one has abandoned something precious; that one has changed. And there is a reason for staying as long as they have in mind that they are closer to God. You see, they are not all God-fearing but scratch the surface and down deep you see fear, distaste; we have a strange population—proud, obstinate, and down deep clinging, primitive, soft and savage. Fed on goats' milk and goats' meat-- fed to the brim—vicious for their goat's milk and goats' meat—their godliness, he didn't laugh; they love their living for their feasts-- that are all holy as long as no one pokes a hole in their bright altars.

There is a saying among the folks that everything growing here is smiling—the animals and the flowers.

Ah, said Dimitri, smiling and then sighing—I would give anything to come back not physically only, as I have done, but in that other state of mind.

As a child?

I don't know. It seems only that I was content—even though there were times I was maddened by the place. There was infinite depth to it. Now there is nothing to my madness only absurdity; the island is no more. I've been robbed of this depth that was once mine and everyman's and I was everyman. A fragment remains and one looks out at the world-- wants admiration, wealth and finds that perhaps one can get it.

I have ceased to think of what I want, said Catherine. She put her hand out and he took it, swung it gently.

You—you are like an old woman and yet beautiful, and gentle, extraordinarily so--and sad.

I am what I am.

I thought in the big world over on the other side of the sea that women were always a little resenting of men; they had all been so seriously disillusioned, some abused; some so hurt they drowned themselves in alcohol or drugs. But when I left here, I thought the women were foolish, without a heart—that is without ambition except for their absurd marriages. I defined heart then: I thought to be intelligently heartfelt one must want—that is, inside one's heart—to conquer the world. But here I find someone—I don't know exactly what to make of you. But I know that it is sweet, so sweet. Yet so slight, so negligible.

But you wonder if I am free? She still held his hand and talked to him with that slight trace of condescension.

What do you mean? Laughed Dimitri, nervously. You are married? You?

No, of course not. But it is not impossible.

I didn't mean it that way, he hastened to say; it is just that you are so modest, so remote. I thought you looked down on men, somehow—one feels so blundering near you.

Not at all; if I am enclosed it is because I am sick; I have heart disease, this time there was no condescension in her tone. It tires me to go out and you see, I feel for the men, their routine—fishing, drinking, dancing, making love. I don't find them obnoxious, overly crude, or half intelligent—although they could be on first glance. I have never seen a single man drunk—only slightly high, a little more boisterous, dancing the Easter dance all out of step—but it would be a burden to be a wife and painful to be a lover.

I, on the other hand, find them dead somehow. And I have seen drunkenness, if you haven't. But I admit one thing: I thought as I grew disenchanted with my teachers, yet continued loving them a little for they were to me both obnoxious and pathetic, the way they put so much store by being faithful to the same old ideas, clinging to them thinking that put life into them, and at the same time, some of them intelligent, reading the new journals and so on—I thought that there was something unutterably delicious in it—because something convinced me that they couldn't be evil; that a crime would never happen here, despite, despite... No one would ever get killed. There was innocence, if also lack of depth, in the very air. I believe people stay on for this deliciousness and for this innocence. I was bright at the time, seventeen, erotic and wordless. I didn't speak until I was initiated into sex. I wanted a woman, I wanted the sea like I desired a woman, I wanted to fly as I dreamed of making love—it was all the same act, the same sweetness and the same fire. I could never find words for my feelings. If I could have I would have been a poet and perhaps contented, deep, exhaustively contented, I would never have gone anywhere; I would have lived like Thomas, the fisher-poet in his two roomed white house with the three windows, with his old wife, old enough to be his mother hymning to her body turned Aphrodite equal to songs of delight.

You can't do that in the big world? Asked Catherine

There it would be corruption and lust. She would be a laughable old woman.

Has that affected you?

It hasn't affected you, said Dimitri. Or else, these old, simple ways have been a kind of cure. But what do you mean by 'free?'

There is the body, you see; sickness has been a cure because I know my body well; and then well, the simplicity—one senses a different species and is content to leave it alone but not with hostility. There is none of that as far as I know. Thus, I am free.

Perhaps, you don't know everything about us, said Dimitri, thoughtfully. So, I am a different species. What? Monkey? And he began to jump around playfully, letting go of Catherine's hand swinging his arms around her. Bird? He waved his arms running in circles around Catherine. Fish? And he sucked in his cheeks and made little fish-motions with his lips; Worm? His body undulated.

Well, which am I? He stopped laughing in front of her, hopping from foot to foot.

Something unknown but akin to bird, said Catherine, laughing.

You mean I have wings, said Dimitri, looking at her seriously.

I wish I had—as you. But I think I am closer to the very dull, armchair-sitting homo sapiens not the avian variety. My breed exists in some uninteresting places on this planet that serves no apparent function and lives to sit, watch, breathe and make odd noises.

And so if we had a child, said Dimitri—we'd have a bird-boy, or bird-girl. A creature with a body like yours only wings instead of feet. While you were pregnant, you would feel instead of kicks from our small progeny, the whir of wings.

Catherine was silent.

I have gone too far, sighed Dimitri. Looking into her face, he saw tiredness, and dullness.

Catherine looked down.

You know, I have never seen someone I liked so quickly. But I feel as if I'd just made a horrible mistake.

It is not that it is repugnant to me, Catherine said. She sighed and lifted her head, looking him full in the eyes. Again that mysterious wave of loveliness crossed her eyes. It is just that I wonder if you often jest like that. One senses from all that has ever been written on the subject that one had best conclude yes.

My species are indelicate although bird-like. I will be indelicate a little more, perhaps rough—because, as you know, there is always so little time; I will approach you, take you by the hair, firmly, though gently, and insist…here Dimitri with his hand around Catherine's neck and a tress of hair wrapped around his fingers, came nearer, slowly, and finally, kissed her—one kiss, softly. Then he let her go, and stood back.

Catherine sucked in her lips, looked at him, blushed, looked down. When she looked up again, she saw that Dimitri too was looking down, blushing.

I didn't think you'd kiss me, she said, naively.

I didn't intend to at first, he answered. I must now revert to my monkey form and get down off this cliff.

Why don't you use your wings? Catherine spoke seriously.

Because, Dear, I have not used them yet—not for flying. I am afraid—so high, to test them. I will go but soon—see you again.

I am here, Catherine looked down, thoughtfully; then said, softly, sadly—always.

As a bird-man, said Dimitri, I too. Unfortunately, I will now after I leave you walk into the village a black sheep. So many species transformations…he smiled at her and left.

He is, nonetheless, half believable, though he might be, intriguing, Catherine thought. And he seems to make such a distinction between the world and this little island; I see nothing of it when I think of the two. The difference is here we live without, and there somehow seems to be… but sometimes just sleep, gentle and undisturbed. There in Washington, we lived with—was it gadgets, machines, teeth cleaning, hair sculpting and there was never quite time enough for a thought in the old armchair sense, or a careful sentence. And sleep was broken with bad, hellish dreams.

Here there is miracle, magic, gods and goddesses. There a half-sentimental, half-prejudicial insistence…and yet it is the same thing always, she broke off. The song of our irrevocable obstinacy; they have the same thing here—but the love airs are older and the obstinacy that of the less informed.

Could there ever be a humanity that doesn't cling to one old system or another? A nation that just opens itself to the reality—without preconceived notions, an idea that must be sustained at all costs? Whether the world or this tiny, old fashioned, remote island—it is all the same. But here one is content to be. Ideas, like words just float by and fade away. There the idea or word means action.

After, coming down the mountain, Dimitri decided not to go into the village as he had told Catherine he was going to do, but to take a ramble outside of town in the forest by the cave that led down to the subterranean lake. It was four in the afternoon, the men were coming in from fishing, up the hill on the other side from the church, the tavern was open and Maria was serving wine, talking, jesting with the men; there were rumors about the girl—that she was by night a prostitute, that she 'taught' men, explained things, and made it sweet. Dimitri thought—a different species, I have learned this—let well enough alone. But he didn't want to be seen by the little crowd and put to the test, as crowds do, when someone different strides in. He wanted to be alone, deliciously, and in the forest with the sun coming through the leaves white as spun honey.

There were no sure friends on this island except for his mother, and maybe, just maybe Catherine. One was alone, though, and there was a certain safety in being so. No but he was almost sure of Catherine—she was simple, yet understanding. She had no ulterior motives. One comes to a point in life, he thought, where love may or may not be; if it is, it is to life like frosting on a cake—just what can make it flavorful and good, perhaps to make it perfect, but not in the mysterious way of things, necessary. He had once thought love was meat, or wine and had then learned the hard way. But there is much one can do with frosting. Frosting, for one thing, is far more philosophical. And the sages were aware of this; and he thought whether something came of it or not, he would keep this relationship frosting. Gone were the days when love was desperately needed, when love had to be. He had had a broken heart; worked day and night to 'work it off,' studied, worked some more and walked away, smiling, gaily, with money in his pocket—vengeance!-- and prospects for earning more.

Now Catherine—oh but she was a bit odd. Of course, there was the sickness— but such resignation! He could see that she did not long for the world one bit, nor perhaps much for love, probably would not jump at the chance he was proposing; well, so be it…. He had managed his life so that the different components of it— work, love, play, and even fantasy all fell into separate categories—separate times, demanding separate parts of his brain even. And because he didn't confuse the different components, he had clear command over himself engaged in each different one. No one project affected a different one. The men on the island he thought a little inferior in this regard. Fishing, love, dancing—it was all the same thing—village life rolling around to a particular time—at three a.m. fishing, then in the afternoon drinking and love making, the evening dancing and closing up shop, as it were, to have their backs rubbed by their wives with oil and herbal infusions and everything a little confused, one thing with another. For if loving didn't go well, then neither fishing, nor drinking. And all these activities were manifestations of the same confusion year in and year out—the same mixing up of categories. Where distinction rose up as in Thomas or Simon—in the making of things—rhymes or frames for beds—the talent just adorned the village, and no one took much notice of it, not more than to stop sometimes and in the same way as smelling a jasmine bush, remark with a certain poverty of language that that was a sweet poem or a swell bed frame. There was no rising above, no perfecting. For that one needed the ability to divide from other things in life, pour one's energies into an endeavor; one couldn't do village life at the same time. But Thomas and Simon were not complaining. And Simon had now a broken foot, his mother told him, and there was a lot of pain for an old man. Anna was dying and the doctor who had nothing but a little pocket book full of medicines could do nothing. Of course, dying was part of living but it seemed in the big cities that there was more action and hope, machines, different combinations of pills; and therefore one died more reasonably—when different sciences employed in saving your life were shown to explain why you had to die. And dying was separate from living in a hospital with the wrong kind of light. Here people just died in a muddle with life however nature would have it; perhaps, here, yes here he could believe it— God walked in and took you by the hand—pulled, wrenched, some of the people here—they were particularly hardy—away to heaven. There was no reason for it. But that was typical village life. Nothing was allowed to be answered. And yet this was answer. In the real world a word was a word; here a word was not a word—and yet here there was somewhere, somehow an answer.

Dimitri was sitting at the entrance to the cave, thinking these thoughts, when he heard footsteps. He looked up and saw that Nico had come—apparently had had the same thought—to get away from it all. Dimitri sighed—his golden hour of solitude was over. This boy was an odd one and they said a little like him—intellectual, brooding—and that he had a secret.

Oh you, said Nico, looking up and seeing him.

Are you averse to sitting and talking with me? Asked Dimitri.

Nico hesitated—no, not at all.

When I went away last, you were a child, he said. They say now that you are—a loner, a misanthrope, unmarried like me.

The island has a shortage of babies, said Nico, morosely; they are trying to get the young folks to breed.

You naturally have no interest.

Naturally.

I see. Of course, men and women are animals, breeders in the end.

You think so?

I was saying it jocosely but well—what do you think will last until Judgment Day? Many other things we do will fall by the wayside.

Jesus cursed it.

Did He? Yes, I seem to remember now. But not sexual passion?

I don't know. I am not much of a believer, Nico said moodily.

Ah, like me—a doubter, an atheist.

I've learned faith—that is, a kind of waiting without a particular end in sight—unless death...

To live on this island!

I don't notice it.

You have a secret that absorbs you. Let me guess—an illicit love of a woman, or else of a goddess.

I have kept to myself these more than five years.

Ah, a love affair that you have carried with you alone, burning, for years. Tell me, perhaps I can bring about a solution. This is an equation, no more nor less.

Nico looked into Dimitri's face, scrutinizing his eyes. Dark, serious and unromantic, he thought; I can tell, yet if I tell...perhaps it has been futile, yet there must be some last trace of love, of passion...will he reach out to destroy?

No, no, no, said Dimitri watching him in his turn, patiently. Don't be suspicious. I only build; I don't destroy.

Since you know already...she is a sister—one of those that live like eagles up there.

I take it, she once loved you; perhaps still...

We were male and female in that sense. Her name is Elizabeth.

And despite it all... she must have a will of steel to be up there, leaving you behind.

Leaving me behind, trailed off Nico, hollowly.

I say that she has not forgotten. And you have left everything behind too—they say you are excruciatingly chaste and celibate.

I am mad, mad, mad.

Both hot and cold; no one sees or knows. I was once the same over, pardon, a prostitute. I covered her with gold. I admit I was a bit acting a part—young practically—not technically, but still—virgin boy falls in love, first love, with a whore. I was grandiose, I strove to write poetry, submit body and soul to the law of love in this free, implicitly illicit zone where I felt it could become anything. I must have read all this somewhere. The affair lasted quite a long time—some seven years. I was patient about her business. She preferred the crueler sort of love—taunting me with her clients--she on our bed, under my nose. I grew old and longed for a gentler life with a woman. In the end, I realized it was just as well—there had been little understanding on my part for her as a woman in a cruder sort of way, mind here, body—needs, flaws--an every day way, there had been little beside love of an ideal, because one can make of the prostitute a sort of saint even if one is not religious—the genuine soul and that sort of thing, and the sense that a wanderer like me would find few refuges, and she had been one.

So you didn't have many women?

I am reserved with women. Few interest me. But when one does—I am expansive, huge with her—a Gargantua of eros and madness.

I feel foolish sometimes, hanging on. But one plays the fool, I think, once in one's lifetime. I ask only to be allowed to grow fully, freely. That is, to manhood.

It is more than just the matter of Elizabeth; yet, it is somehow all wrapped up in her.

And she has expanded or contracted, I imagine, said Dimitri moodily. She is either at this point divine, in which case, she looks upon you as inspired by the same light, though unaware yet and so craving the sexual discourse still, or else she is human, tortured and miserable and the nuns in their black drapes, somber as the grave are obscene as the brothel. I propose the latter.

When she left, she seemed so above it all. Nothing could touch her. All my prayers—that is my shouting, went unnoticed. Yes, divine or horribly tortured.

Those were prayers. Ah, that was show—a kind of sacred theater—the body seized by the talons of the god.

You don't believe at all in—in what they do up there.

I accept God. God is a metaphor, an end or an 'outside' – to the rational mind, to everything. Anyone who thinks science is the same thing as reality is a fool. I see God's hand here—hovering around in the mulish stubbornness of the people, the blind adherence to an elementary way of life, the fertile ground for tragedy or ecstasy. Yet science might come in and describe it as all derived from the sense of smell. The folks are so ignorant, so sure of themselves; knowledge will bring pain—a little difference will bring trouble, anger, and sorrow. But I don't believe, no, in fantastic rituals, magic words.

There have been situations where the crowd in the village has seen anger and sorrow—for example, with Leo and his seductions of married women.

That sort of thing falls into their categories, rather too neatly, though-- among their sins; there are other things that fall into uncharted realms.

But why when we were happy…?

Human nature is only navigable, like the sea, not knowable. Use the old wisdom of these (said facetiously) foolish villagers—if there was a grain of truth in her love, it is growing still in her heart. Assume it, and argue her down. Argue her to your feet. She too, you too are tied to the old village. She will see the light.

I can't. Whenever I look up to the monastery, it's as if my body falls back in exhaustion. Every man has a circumference; she has gone beyond mine.

Yet she has eviscerated you and taken your guts with her. Look, I myself will go to her. But tell me—if in the end, she only toyed with you…

Yes, I know. But it is impossible.

Then you must see some human equation that would still make it imperative for her to have you if she is warm, you know--warm. Not cold. One can only be cold or hot in the end. God and a lover both demand hot. And in my faith, God gives preference to the lover.

You will go? Yes, I must go into the village first. My mother expects me; but this afternoon.

Nico shook hands with Dimitri; thank you; I feel as if you have removed a bar of lead from my chest. You know I barely know you—of course, I knew you as a child—but I didn't know you were like this—a friend such as I imagined men could have. Rational, and sympathetic, comprehending—and you are right, there is nothing but confusion with the others—foolishness and confusion. Of course, I couldn't court their daughters—to wind up impregnating a hen and having to crow and cluck with her for the rest of my life!

Yes, well—there is that.

Never.

Goodbye. Give me a week.

Yes, said Nico. Dimitri walked away through the forest along an invisible path that he had known since childhood towards the village.

Dimitri was seated with Catherine on a plastic chair in the huge empty container--what passed for living room in the big bare villa. Robert was in the kitchen bungling making coffee and Ellen was seated as usual out on the patio writing in her notebook.

The thing is, said Dimitri to Catherine there are men, here, men and women—Nico, Elizabeth—although she is impossible, my mother, even Anna in her day and something makes them stay here. It is inconceivable that they should not desire the world. Every child of fourteen wants to save it. He was smiling, his foot was resting on his knee, he looked as if he had grown younger; his cheeks were fuller and some of his severity seemed to have softened.

This is home life, said Catherine; I have heard of little differences with the island life in the past, transferals—Anna's son left and so far has never come back. But one can be a man here too.

Ah, they are not men and women for the most part; little hens and cocks.

They have human sized passions, said Catherine.

Well, the ones who are men and women, yes. Why-- do you have other experiences? Take my brother, for instance—a strange humdrum hater of humans; I don't think he thinks. He won't go near women either, but I am not sure it is sexual preference for men. I honestly think he doesn't want the depths of sex; he is content to be something like a sea urchin with a prickly temper, living the same old life over and over every day. He never gets bothered by the older women about his loveless life.

Not like Nico, said Catherine. You talked to him—what did you discover?

More than talked, said Dimitri reflectively. I went on a little mission for him, a voyage of discovery; he has been holding to a chaste, passionate love for a woman in secret for the past five years. And the woman is a nun—cold, passionless, aloof. I would say that with flesh on her she would be sarcastic, snapping back at you with superior intellect each time you opened your mouth. At least, that would be her intent.

So you talked to her?

I failed in argument with her.

You mean you went to the monastery to convince a nun to elope with you for Nico.

Well, now that we are open with one another…he laughed. Yes, I was to bring her down to him.

What did she say?

I don't remember. She was skeletal, horribly so—a bone with a brain.

Poor child, said Catherine, thoughtfully.

I thought she was all violence, said Dimitri, quietly, looking at Catherine. I imagine it is because they had a hot-headed passion she can't forget and she is whipping it out of her with the cruel pain of starvation.

In love there is a spiritual science, said Catherine. Perhaps, she does not know, like he how to further it; she knows only feelings, poor thing; raw emotion. Perhaps she simply can't eat, since the truth, which is to be her feast at the Monastery, is Nico.

I would agree with you, but the spiritual science that she knows, or thinks she knows, requires her to fast at length. Though the others it is true seem to make up for it on feast days. But no, she is not pining, Catherine. She is at war.

I don't think you saw her. You saw, as you said, bones—and what is hateful to you is that what you call cruelty.

She is at war with sex, with the body.

Yet he has been chaste, sacrificially so.

Some foolish dream…as for science, there is biology, it would serve her better.

The world out there and far away—that is natural science. Everything labeled, and abiding under laws. What if the world was so close, you couldn't see it—just had to believe it? The sphere so shoved under our noses that it looked flat so it took a long time to challenge the vision? And what if it was not only a world but a person and began to behave as if in contradiction to all the rules?

Who her?

Yourself. What do you honestly perceive?

Strange, extraordinary…

And I a woman who is so unhappy, said Catherine softly.

Dimitri started and looked at her intently. He noticed that Catherine's face changed expression rapidly like light on the different facets of a crystal; for a second, there was that white in her dark eyes that spoke of intellect, clear and cold; then the next moment, she was tender and sad. It seemed that looking at her, Dimitri couldn't pin her down. And yet he had thought, continued to think, that here was a woman made simple, actually intelligent, but essentially soft, obliged to be, to resign herself to an island prison far away from civilization, interest, and delight, and from real men and brilliant women. He was glad, nonetheless, that he had found her. She was lovely especially in the evening with her long, pale face, and shadowy; shadows starting with her eyes seemed to surround her. Now and then it seemed as if from the depths of still, dark waters, an expression swam up into her face that was sweet, honey sweet, newborn and sexual all together. It's a wonder, he thought, that mind and soul don't atrophy here—that she doesn't become old and bitter with a sardonic smile, so habitual that it merely plays across her face instinctively without any thought behind it. Instead—a gentle girl, kind and intelligent; it's as if there are inner resources entirely independent of one's environment. She would stand out in a concentration camp— steady gaze, steely thinking, tender words. I don't think electrified barbed wire, or commandants with cudgels, or even gas chambers would move her.

What are you thinking?

I am thinking of you. What makes you tick? I imagine not only an extraordinary machine that is you, but also an organism which year after year goes about its little routine.

As you know, merely going down the mountain and coming up again fatigues me. Here with my parents, I help out in little ways—too little for my liking; I'd like to be of some use that is more distinct.

Why not go to her—the girl in the monastery;

The nun?

Nun implies that she is actively participating in the monastic discipline. I believe she is like the Monaca di Monza of Manzoni—imprisoned.

If she doesn't care for the life, she can go.

There are perhaps inner constraints—the village that won't take kindly, in all likelihood, to a nun of the mountain un-transforming, de-transfiguring—to become an ordinary person; to marry of all things—adultery of adultery for a nun—for they expect her to get them into heaven with all their fallacies and foibles, their awkward misshapes, their stinks—can you imagine, among the angels?! There is here a sort of inner life, not the same as the more peaceful exterior—and it is obdurate, poisonous, cruel. People murmur things, excited rage, hate flies around like wild fire; you don't see it often, but periodically, even here, they will do things.

They made Father Isaac burn his writing.

Yes, that is part of the inner life—suspicion when someone breaks a tradition, writes a book they don't understand.

And I believe a child couldn't quite cope with it. Michael: He went back to the priest, asked forgiveness for the files they burned, goes around now, flaunting a sort of diary, tries desperately hard to be intellectual.

It will get to him, unfortunately, after a while; mark my words—the frowns, the disapprobation; the spirit in him will shrivel down and become hunger in his belly. The beautiful flight, the high vantage point in which to see things, will become nothing more than a headache and he will fish day and night, dreaming of grilled snapper.

Your imagination is crude, Catherine said. They are not as educated as you, but there lingers in them a kind of threadbare poetry.

It is the same for me; who said differently? I think I was attached to a long elastic sailing-away fifteen years ago. I thought I was entirely free of—of home; but then, you know back I came, impelled.

You mean with your rich friend to make the proposition.

No, said Dimitri not noticing the insinuation. I mean not so much when I physically arrived as now. I am falling in love with my little, extraordinary mother—something has happened to her; it's as if she is saying little? Little? I am tall. And she is you know, taller than I remember, brilliant, one of the bodies in the upper atmosphere; and she is, you know, I have to contend with her. Our house that is so small and rickety is no longer so much of an eyesore. There actually seems to be a deeper truth here. I breathe a sigh of relief to leave traffic, fashionable people, modern technology behind, now. And at the depth of all my criticism, there has begun to burn a warmer instinct, a kinder interest in the islanders. I guess, you wouldn't believe it. I have postponed traveling back to Athens, London, Paris, Rome. I am manager of the hotel chain, you see; now the owner wants to branch out into more remote places, places the potentially would bring rich people to vacation. Since this is my home, I have been given some margin of rest and vacation myself. I walk in the forest now, quite a lot, and there are times I wish to vanish, be enveloped in the forest mystery—I don't know how else to put it-- like a wild animal.

But still you do not quite accept them; perhaps because they are your flesh and blood. They say that relations as you grow up are the worst, the most unforgivable.

I see I must talk clearly and profoundly with you. Yes, there is anger; I didn't want to be born in a goats' garden-- especially out there in the world—goats for their prejudices, despite their beauty, their inability to have a mind! But there are times I weep over the beauty of the goats.

Would you like me to try to convince Elizabeth to come back to Nico?

He is so dignified and idealistic.

Do you weep over them?

He laughed. They are made of one mind like all lovers.

When Dimitri had left, Catherine went into her bedroom, changed and gathered a few things together in her purse. The girl might be totally assimilated into the life of the monastery by now, she thought, with no desire at all for Nico—except the flash of memory now and then. And maybe, as happens sometimes, he is even repugnant to her.

Catherine decided as she left the villa and climbed the little incline towards the wooden box-like houses, plain, and awkward looking that constituted the monastery, that she would simply put it to Elizabeth in an even soft voice that she could hear or not hear as the whim took her: true or not true?

It was the question that crept up in her when she thought of Dimitri. Love then, she thought grimly, is a little like God—living or not living, absolute, or nothing. The origin of all things or something utterly laughable. There was a step one took—a reception; and it may all be a false run. For the devil could imitate God so well that the very elect could become dizzy trying to see clearly. Best not to be overly passionate, and yet that could be the distinguishing mark of truth.

When she came up to the clearing in front of the monastic dwellings, the wind was blowing in great gusts and she could see little figures in black robes bending into it among the goats and stunted trees that stood here and there in what appeared to be a garden; the forest crept up the mountainside and stood in a thick mass behind just at the edge of the top of the mountain. There was a pool and several cultivated plots; it had a certain attractiveness, but on the whole seemed bent and little; where the village was simple but lush, the monastery above it was plain and Spartan. Here one had in one's mouth day in and day out nothing but salt and dust.

An old, bleary-eyed, half bald man leaning on a stick hobbled past and smiled at her, the smile strange, one-toothed—a smile, Catherine thought, instantly, that would appear eerily and without malice for whatever—because it was not a smile at something or about a thing; it was the smile of nature that appeared, Catherine thought, like the glitter of light on water, because of life that shone like the sun.

A little wrinkled old nun came hobbling towards her, hailing her. That is our elder, she explained to her; come in and rest, you look tired. She took Catherine's hand in her rough one and led her into one of the boxy houses to a sitting room of sorts with an old plush divan embroidered with a purple peacock on a red background. We have visitors sit here, she said. Unfortunately, just now the Mother is busy. But I can entertain you; I am second in command. We have lemon curd, aged goat cheese and bread and wine—all very good. Before Catherine could protest, the ancient nun had brought everything to her on a tray and put it on her knees.

She said a prayer, solemnly, blessing the food, and then insisted that Catherine eat something before stating her business. It is a tradition here; all visitors must at least eat a bite before saying anything. Catherine dipped her spoon into the lemon curd. It was delicious, very faintly salty, but also perfectly sweet.

Do you taste the little salt? Here, the nun went on before she could answer, there is always at least a little salt; they say it is because God weeps tears of joy when we cook, it is so delicious.

I thought you fasted, fasted quite severely, said Catherine.

The secret to fasting is to alternate with feasting. We consider that feasting on the proper days is just as holy a duty.

What if a sister fasts but won't feast?

Yes, there are some of those. One waits, doesn't presume. Waiting is part of holiness—patient, gentle waiting.

I imagine these sisters are interpreting very rigorously the injunction to mortify the body?

Yes, the little nun, sighed. But you see, they have free will. Nothing is imposed.

But what if a sister imposed something, let's say this life, in its entirety, on herself for the wrong reason?

She would be anathema, said the nun smiling, but of course not in the old sense. We would not send her away. Here there is room for anyone.

But you would not mind my visiting such a sister to try to convince her that what she is doing is wrong?

The old nun sighed again. You may, of course, see the sister, she said, gently. People think that a Christian society, such as at a monastery established for the following of Christ, is a place of utmost rigidity, an imprisonment, a tyranny. But yet we have no violence in us. The world can come, eat our lemon curd, talk to our sisters and convince them, of course, to go away. We only ask that if the sister refuses, one, two, three times, that her wishes be respected.

Sister Elizabeth lives in this house—the most comfortable with rugs and a soft mattress on the bed. Go down the corridor, two doors down; you will find her.

Catherine walked down to the door pointed out to her and knocked. A thread of a voice answered, Come in; and Catherine pushed open the door.

Elizabeth, she said; the girl was bent over a book on her desk; she raised her head and looked at Catherine; it was a gaunt face, a face that looked like it had been 'beaten' by harsh living—what she had assumed was the face of the usual monk or nun.

Looking at her, Catherine saw that what she thought must be sadness was actually just fatigue from long concentration. The girl, looking at her, was curious and attentive, but not excited. She also looked as if she was waiting for something.

Dimitri has already talked to her, thought Catherine; she guesses why I am here.

Elizabeth, I have come on the same errand as Dimitri. I realize you assumed so. And I will respect the monastery's wishes—apparently if someone solicits a sister— that she leave the monastery and she refuses three times, her wishes must be obeyed.

Elizabeth sighed, but remained silent, looking at her book.

You refused Dimitri when he came on Nico's behalf. That is once. I have come to say this. I do not argue for Nico. There are plenty of men in the world—if you were to be inclined to marry, you may or may not choose Nico. I am not asking you if you are desirous to marry even. Nor pushing that you, as a woman, should of necessity want a man. Perhaps you do not. Perhaps Nico is odious to you now.

Elizabeth lifted her hand in protest but was silent.

Perhaps it is better not even to mention such things. But this is not about sex or marriage is it? This is about a quest for the truth, isn't it? People spend their lives overlooking that and thus die and perhaps are damned. In any case, what root do they have?

Elizabeth was looking at her more intently now. Her weary face had lighted up a bit.

I believe in the strait and narrow as do you in this quest, narrow and strait until quest becomes goal, said Catherine. And there is only one way. But there is a route that seems to be it, and over time one learns that it is not it, yet strives along it because what the hell—one cannot be blamed for striving, mortifying, torturing oneself in the name of truth. This route is the anti self, no, I don't say anti-Christ, I am not sensational. But it is the route of self-torture; sometimes, soft self-torture; it is the route where unlike the true one, nothing, no spiritual practice will ever become nature, God's nature, through Christ, in you. The true route is the route of selfless love, an entirely different thing from the anti-self and not self-abnegation, but the gift of love flooding self, so that self is dissolved for love's sake. The Christ forming infinitely and eternally out of the lover within the small minded grudge of the human. This route I too wish to learn. It involves self-mastery and fundamental honesty. But there is a passion, His passion instead of your own—that you must yield to to arrive there. Some people can't give something up—in your case—it is an idea, I believe.

No, said Elizabeth; I don't want to go.

Well, you have refused. I will leave you. Perhaps someone may, perhaps not come again.

Catherine got up to go her face slightly averted from the girl from embarrassment. Elizabeth was watching her closely. Catherine turned and left, saying faintly—well, it is over in any case; Nico will perish or find another.

She was just proceeding down the little corridor when she heard a broken voice—wait! And she turned and saw Elizabeth standing there, holding her emaciated body with her thin arms; as she looked at her, the girl bowed her head.

No, said Elizabeth, her face struggling, dark, tears falling—I mean yes—yes, what you are saying it is true and good. She stopped and panted. I will go with you.

Let me hold your hand, she said—I don't need my things. I brought nothing. I take nothing away. I go like this, suddenly, half dressed, without anything—or, not at all. Don't tell them; they will know. One surfaces a minute here in this place and then falls and dies passes into a desert of blightedness, and of insignificance. I am dying now, but it doesn't matter. I'd rather this this lovely ripeness—the other life, then this dead pretext, this 'science' as they call it, for trying to draw miraculous water from the desert wastes of their small-minded grudge—which is what their Jesus is.

Her hand in Catherine's hand, was cold, rough, and sharp.

It was to be the desert itself, withered, barren and dry, wasn't it—so as to be life in Christ? Entirely without love, or attachment, specifically mortifying the lushness of the heart!

She lifted her other hand in front of her face. I thought I'd find the life, the Jesus-life in me that existed before him, before myself—that is, not as time, but as space—because yes it was him all the time; not of course the way he is, but some ideal— but him; it was not only before in time, before I made my vows, but before in my body—for time is printed on the body in its changes…and I thought I would at last find the true Jesus and wriggle away from that terror…. of joy through extreme piety and asceticism! I would be the daughter of the Cross—miserable, ashamed, alone, finally arriving at my spiritual goal—weeping the requisite warm tears kneeling with my forehead on the ground, prostrate before the Lord.

How can a person re-enter their mother's womb and be born again except through the Cross and tears?

Yes, you see, but he seemed to me to be in the womb, seemed to be the womb. And I seemed to weep for him. Every cell seemed to write his name out in me. There were times he was so pervasive I thought he was the devil. You see, I thought I was especially cursed, double cursed, because I had been a great adulteress—with Paul of all people—I was fourteen!—I was good at making it secret—but then when Paul had thrown me over, it was he not me who ended it, I was that slavish about sex—he was not even sex but it was still going on; the same slavishness—only love with Nico. I didn't know who to talk to. I just knew to punish, punish body and mind—that perhaps, the great God, Christ Jesus, seeing me punish and punish myself would hesitate to condemn me.

I don't think one is condemned by Christ for not punishing, or for punishing. But how can you follow an idea when you are so terrified? And how can you come back to slavery once you are free?

I feel so ashamed; said Elizabeth, not answering; he must not see me.

Come and stay with me for a while. Gain some weight. Re-possess your ordinary body. See what you think then.

Tell him from me that I am coming. If he can stand me, in my old age…

He has waited, passionately and chastely for five years. He can wait some more. But I think he would eat you up if you were ninety and wrinkled with white hair or no hair and go away thinking he had found immortal honey.

Catherine didn't need to obtain permission formally for Elizabeth to stay with her family and recover her health and strength. It was taken for granted with that indifferent, half helpless compassionate gesture that she knew well in her parents before her schemes. She put her up in her room on her bed, and slept on a cot with a sleeping bag in the drafty impersonal living hall. Elizabeth vigorously protested and so it was decided that after two weeks or so of eating well, she should be moved to the cot. In that time, Catherine mostly cooked with cream and butter, cheese and oil. She made chowders of fish and cream, butter sauces for fish fillets and salads of herbs and goat cheese. Elizabeth first drifted about in a semi shock. It struck her that she had understood something profound and devastating—so much so as to alter the course of her life forever. But her brain refused to think what it was and so she felt as if she existed in a kind of limbo, floating about, so to speak, in the knowledge that she was changed, but not realizing that there was any enlightenment in this change. As she, finding her new root in fish fillets, chowders, butter, and cheese, gained flesh, she said to Catherine that she felt that she was not so deeply plunged in the old depressive agony. A kind of shadow had left her mind; she was franker, firmer. She sat with Catherine and argued with her about the need for God in the world. Catherine said meekly I can see that there is a God—in that "God" means something and certainly has commanded our attention for centuries. But Elizabeth argued—It is not a matter of God's existence so much as the need for God. I love the need for God—that God, you see, not the proven God. Argument destroys people's hearts. And it's when you prove something beyond the shadow of a doubt that faith is most absent. People should be simple and profound. No proof should ever be given. Those people believe in God because they need Him, like the dying.

Then is He invented?

Assumed.

You go back years and years, centuries and centuries.

To the early Church. When one is just a product of sins but not of presumption—and the sins, clean sins, themselves bring the thread of salvation. For 'while we were yet sinners, Jesus Christ died for us'. Salvation of course being this death of God because of our sins, and because He is God, rising to uncontaminated life, with us clean despite our sins that killed him. Jesus, you see, rose as pure life to ascend to heaven as the Son of the living God and to open the way as Christ for all. What does it matter death, life, guilt, love—the Lord chooses life, love, and things turn like the left cheek. Between St. Peter, the rock and St. Peter, the Satan—the Lord chooses the rock...St. Peter leads the flock.

And prior to the Crucifixion—Jesus was?

The same: "In the beginning was the Word, and the Word was with God and the Word was God"—the resurrection and the life. The one who can turn envy to light gaiety, malice to kind, consuming interest in.

What do you think the cross is—beyond the two beams of wood?

Actually, perfect labor. It always struck me that we are in need of God. Not because we can't find other ways to explain the creation of the world. But purely sentimentally, yet this is most high; comfort over all is needed, extended—who would say they didn't need it--to frail humanity, which can't grasp going beyond the self—that is, what makes sense to it, and which lives in and out of delusions. The robust ones they toil for love perhaps, for love is the end of labor; they sweat and die making lace, or fishing. Perfection, you know –soul. You can in lace making and fishing. You say for the sake of intelligence, which is so limited, you have come to something, and for this reason… but before God you say look here, at this and that, this and that, and even the reason behind your perfection becomes shaky, blown to bits by this and that; perhaps even in the last analysis, not reason at all, but an intellectual form of belly rubbing, or lice picking, still apish…

As for me, I just study love, said Catherine. If there is a God, isn't it better to take this approach?

And what have you come up with?

At the risk of sounding unorthodox—for me, the fixing of old machines. I do it now, regularly. People's fans, stoves. I make them run! I am not sure that it is good; it may be at times evil. I know though that if I don't, I become morose, depressed, live deeply in pain and that despite the finding of others to comfort.

Is that a fair description of you?

I have tried embroidery too. But I spend most of my time seeing love in others—and feeling satisfaction at the implement fixed. Nothing but satisfaction now. As a matter of fact, I am a bit of a ghost, you see; I've lived past death.

What is your ambition?

What is yours?

It used to be to practice the Gospels—night and day, rigorously—little sleep or food—for the acquisition of the Holy Spirit.

And now?

To live, to heal; to die death in the flame of life, to live, I suppose. Just to live and allow myself pleasure in bits and pieces through the exhaustion that made my life.

I, too. My ambition is simply to see another happy. I actually enjoy that. I guess it is just as well that I am sick. In the world the kind of weakness I have would never permit anyone to esteem me or even notice me. But here, if I fix an electric fan I see smiles and sighs of contentment for the summer days made a little cooler for someone.

I love you, said Elizabeth. I know that you mean to see in me genuine happiness after a long struggle. You are like a mother to me, yet I am a perfect stranger to you. But how odd you are so tender! And it is entirely instinctive! You are a bit like the old fashioned ideal of a woman only cooking up a restored electric fan instead of a sauce.

No, not really. I am not interested for instance in marriage, or comfort the old fashioned way. Just in love: how people love.

To be a lover? Would it ever occur to you?

Oh yes, now and then it does. But I am weak physically. No the love I aspire to is a general thing—physical, sexual also maybe—but mostly a matter of intellect, of which kindness is the first sign. Lack of envy, the second. Love as in love of people in large crowds, or of the isolated fisherman fishing at dawn; love of the naked girl among the goats, love of the miserable old/young woman, love of an instrument like a violin or a flute; love of the leaves of a forest, love in one who is waiting to die.

It is a grand thing to have love. I don't think many have it.

One is recognized more by fish and fowl than by the human animal, she smiled, but recognition may not be what a lover wants, using the word as I said—broadly.

Elizabeth moved from her chair to sit at Catherine's feet.

Master, she said to her, tilting back her head and closing her eyes. Teach me. She curled her fingers around Catherine's ankle and swung her foot back and forth, opening her eyes, she smiled up at her. Catherine looked down at her shaking her head. The things I know are so banal, she said. How to cook so that it pleases. A little elementary engineering. How to feel genuine interest in the conversation of another. Many people are only interested when they talk of themselves. I notice this with a certain pain. In it is the inner life of the exploiter, the desecrater, the profiteer, the picnicker who junks the park and the beginning of hatred all around. Yet with a kind of servitude, I see the fragility of that person. I want to pin them to the ground by their shoulder blades as we do to the wings of butterflies and make them give it up— until they turn tender and industrious as worms. But as you know I am particularly boring. I have to sit in a chair a lot. I move exclusively in this space, this barren home, from dawn until dusk. I go to bed early to breathe quietly for an hour before sleep.

Elizabeth had been a guest with Catherine for over almost a month. It was January; the month of snow and rain. The island climate had become hotter taken as a whole. That year, there were still warm breezes late into winter. Two years earlier, they would have been wearing sweaters under their raincoats and sometimes to bed.

Elizabeth sat with Catherine on the door sill leading out back where there was a little wooden railing, looking Catherine always said like an old person --rickety and frail, and it was supposed to catch you if you were to suddenly fall over the cliff. The monastery up above had no such railing. Elizabeth said to Catherine that she had often gone out at night wandering in the direction of the cliff with no light other than the one for the ships.

I don't know if I was hoping to fall or not, she said, picking up a stone at her feet and drawing in the dust with it.

I can see death like that—a semi consent, said Catherine. I have always wondered if there wasn't that to all deaths. One ceases to struggle. One gives an imperceptible nod to the angel of death. Sometimes it is extracted from a screaming, terrorized brain, it seems. But then again, the nod might have been given earlier. You hadn't consented. The back of your mind was on Nico, furious with him—for he had interfered, violated, almost raped—and you hadn't forgiven him. You couldn't let go. So I believe.

He didn't actually force…

Oh there are rapes and rapes. He forced your mind open again when you had closed it up after the affair with Paul.

Elizabeth smiled and said to her—how like a little owl you are full of wisdom. What shall I do now Owl, in any case? I can't leave here and go down into the village. I would feel a little like a raped woman. It would be all shame and torment. They would think the worst of me, you know, especially Paul.

Why do you mind him? He is the one that should be ashamed.

You don't understand. He made a 'mistake' she held her fingers up to indicate the quotes. He has a solid marriage; solider I hear since the little adultery. He rules Ella with an iron fist. She wilts, too frail to conceive of standing up to him. Marriage as long as it lasts is a holy institution—that is within its precincts you are sanctified that far. He has remained within its bounds. I was to go to the monastery—with my free wheeling sexual thing. Doesn't it remind you of a brightly colored kite up there, soaring. There, you see—taken care of. Confined in those quizzical little shacks to spend my endless years of penances. I was not to come back and live open to other men. He was part of the category—'neither do I condemn thee'. I have failed, turned back from the plow.

Is that how he sees it?

Yes—he is forgiven-- the more since I am back, will be living flagrantly, that is, in full flesh. He conducts himself now with utmost propriety. I, I was to be forgiven-- provided I repented. But then this breaking off for... Nico—instead! You see it is all soft and quiet here in a way, nothing is said--but holiness is serious with the islanders. I feel ashamed to go down among them.

When you were all bones?

I would hardly have minded walking naked among them. She put her hand on Catherine's shoulder. Look at you in black, she said—a black shirt, black skirt with only a red wool vest and a white wool cap. You can't say that you aren't yourself in- fected by some of our traditions.

I don't want to stand out.

And yet it is strange, went on Elizabeth in a soft, musing tone. The whole thing with Nico—the affair—grew out of a kind of need for perfection. Real body with its tenderness against the wood—of the monastery where I was headed. These things are not so childish, not just random thoughts. Wood is house, home, forest, cross. The sacrifice and boundary. The end of limitlessness and still the beginning of wis- dom. Body lover, feaster, drinker. There is a kind of magic when body meets wood. I don't know if you've felt it. All the little petals of the body opening, then dropping one by one from the tree like a snowfall.

What is left is a honey of a fruit, said Catherine. Perhaps you are right, you needed that time in the monastery—the time for Nico was not yet.

No, you see, there you are wrong. I was not worthy.

The two women remained sitting for some time in the dust. Catherine looked at Elizabeth in her old intense, scrutinizing way. She had beautiful hair and forearm bones; they showed so elegantly, sharply through the soft, hairless, brownish flesh for she hadn't gained much weight there—the new flesh had all settled on her hips and thighs. Her expression such as it generally was, Catherine couldn't quite under- stand-- slightly open mouthed, wondering, hostile, a little repelling. She guessed that all women look and act and feel in some inexplicable way like Woman, the archetypal breeder, erotic, tabooed sister; but with Elizabeth, there was something about the wideness and sway of her hips that made her enter the wanton and wayward category more easily. That was the impression. She thought that a lover could transform her easily in the metamorphosis of love—but it returned her really, rather than made her something new—to the Shape: what was more like fish in water—found body, swimmingly in eros when all the subtle hundred directions of her wayward hips slipping and writhing in the drunken, agonized land dance would be focused into one seamless movement. From here to there: it really was from birth to Nico. One single glorious movement; love was essentially simple when in its element though not rude or crude. How few people recognized that.

Elizabeth was talking in her low, slightly guttural voice, but Catherine was not listening. She tuned in and out her thoughts sometimes taking precedence over her attention. She finally heard:

When I knew him, he was just a boy.

She realized that Elizabeth was laughing that little half-tragic laugh people have sometimes emerging from agony and looking back at their own unsuspecting minds of before.

And so, said Catherine—there was bound to be in the end the test. Is that the real reason you went flying up the mountain?

But we didn't feel that marriage… Elizabeth said anticipating what Catherine would have said had she given her half a chance.

Catherine got up. No you see, she said looking down at Elizabeth whose mouth was open in a part smile it seemed in the evening light, I don't blame you. You are right. They are wrong.

She walked into the house. Elizabeth continued sitting, her mouth still half open in a little smile. It was that excruciating time of day for Catherine, when the illness announced itself subtly but strongly, going on to overpoweringly. Ellen was in her room reading; Robert was in the kitchen sitting at the table in a plastic chair under the dim overhanging light. Catherine felt a kind of heaviness overwhelm her, sitting especially on her chest. She struggled. It was that odd sensation she had periodically of dying, just dropping down dead at someone's feet, suddenly. She felt that she lived on a breath; one breath, two, three breaths would see her—if she just used her old horse strength as Robert called it—to her room, to bed, where she could breathe lying down. These struggles that happened more or less every day went unnoticed. Perhaps Robert and Ellen knew. They had been told a few basic things about this type of heart disease. It was and wasn't serious. She might just experience the natural dizziness people get sometimes rising from sitting. She might actually have her heart stop dead in its tracks so to speak. But Catherine was grateful she had parents who stood, as it were, a little farther off than some do. She was able to have her pain in privacy, to keep her dignity; to develop her world, and although it was a world around pain, still it was a coherent world, not something blasted open, shredded and sent flying in all directions. Her parents were those familiar strangers who sometimes engaged in a kind act; who appeared suddenly, leaning in the door, smiling a little with embarrassment with a plate of garlic chopped in oil and salt and fresh bread—a dish she relished; and sometimes they even appeared at just the right time. She had learned as a child that it was not that the food gift had anything to do with solving the riddle of pain, nor of all those wasted years when she could have had lovers, skiing in the mountains, something other than lying in bed! It was more that this food gift was the gift in her life. To be able to eat even when there were no hunger pains—just for the luxury of eating!

Periodically, she would take time to rest –that is, in addition to retiring in the afternoon for a nap, spending whole days at home under the blankets. In any case, it was too cold for her outside. She had rested with Elizabeth; they had holed up together. There had been nothing of any kind of extraordinary communication, no exciting intimacy. But there had been the gratification of knowing that Elizabeth was healing, that Catherine had led her on to the right path, that the path was love and food. She had, she had told her, looked so ungainly skeletally thin. All out of joint. Cold, bloodless fingers. And now it was all smoothed out and carved out and all open mouthed and slightly repelling but with beautiful hips and forearms and thicker hair, thoughtful hands, too, rather than bird's claws-- she thought that could pick out the tiniest screw of the machine of the body and set it back in place perfectly, that pulled apart and put together again, it might work as if it was never created but only begotten—Elizabeth was now to descend to Nico.

And she, oh she, would rest in one of those inscrutable ways of illness, the cure of food and love had some effect on her too—health-wise; it had made her happier and with that happiness had come fatigue, and more illness.

She told Elizabeth after, when she had rested in her bed and recovered from the 'attack'—that she was allergic to happiness.

Not such a tragedy, said Elizabeth, munching on her fish. Happiness has its dulling side. Never quite what we want.

Catherine smiled. You are going to marry?

It is what I am here for. Elizabeth blushed.

It seems there are times when it rolls round, the great pointer thing of the universe and points to you.

No one particularly noticed that Katrina had kept inside her house for the most part since Dimitri had arrived. She was retiring and most people thought not smart, though not disabled like Martha for she had, had had, Eve's cleverness with men. No,

Stavros explained jestingly to his wife, if a woman doesn't in her young age receive the man in marriage, she becomes atrophied in spirit and mind no matter how clever. It is the man who awakens her in the end… if not the falling off the far side to the dragons and monsters.

Stavros had said this about Katrina because he knew that his wife would believe him and he liked to sow discord among women; essentially, too, he disliked Katrina who seemed to insinuate now and then that she was nobler for having sacrificed husband and children, although he sensed too with his deeper intelligence that this was a bit of a sad, bitter pretense. But there seemed to be something in her consciously creating an ideal-- of single adulthood, carved out for her day after day; he began to suspect she had actually much more of a mind than other women, and so had battles within himself between admiration and dislike, secret wonder, public condescension. He didn't like her sweaty, muscular, aching toil of love—watching over her sick aging parents, changing them, washing them, putting them to bed; it was tedious, bothersome, low work, ugly, despicable work. But the fact that she didn't complain ever not like his wife who annoyed him over every petty thing—and showed her strength in arguments at their meetings made him think she was unusual and had character, that is, he begrudgingly conceded that she had mind in between the stink and the slops. And because of this odd combination of admiration and dislike without the usual sexual titillation he thought normal in the assessment of a woman as a woman, he ruthlessly disparaged her to his wife—as good for nothing, old, dumpy all of which epithets were patently unfair. For Katrina was useful and efficient, loyal and strong; and although she had a paunch, she was still agile, muscular, and although often sad, her eyes were deep and thoughtful.

Father Isaac had taken her side seven years ago when she had made the sacrifice—she did not 'grab life for herself', he had said to Anna, understanding that self-sacrifice was the beginning of the eternal path. Katrina herself thought out her act in different terms. She was more instinctive, more like an animal guarding her parents whom she conceived of as wounded, as they sat there, half asleep, without thought or reflection. She had no principle. She was as driven to it, as a person might be to make love, but not out of tenderness of desire, but out of tenderness of cruel pain and fear. She wanted to control the deterioration of her mother and father; to witness and mark every detail of the slow transferal of authority from them to her. And she wanted to watch the slow encroachment of death with notwithstanding anger and yet still aloofness, despite misery, still calm.

She had her thoughts, kept very much to herself. She had ultimately discovered that Father Isaac was open and kind, not judgmental, an incessant listener, though liking, in the way a chef likes cooking, his own talk-- feasts of his own talk. She told him almost immediately that she would never dare not to come to church; it was the proper thing; that is what they did on this island; and yet, she had read enough here and there, in science journals that made her understand and enjoy life as manifested totally mechanically in physical bodies, not evidencing any soul, but one after another different machines, which fought and raced against death and sometimes almost won. The universe, she said was a beautiful mechanical game. God let us say had set it up that way for his peculiar reason. If there was a soul and eternal life, then, perhaps, a different kind of game, more abstract, and general was played.

Father Isaac had mused about Katrina's statements for a long time and had written a long piece on her entitled "The Machine at Play", which was burned along with his files. He told Max that what it all boiled down to was the high distinguishing mark of the body—whether it was, in the end, machine or soul, and thus, an entity unknown— to be resurrected and revealed to us in its mystery at the end of time. But he added to Max, that Katrina had no joy! She had not allowed herself that in conceiving of her duty towards her parents. And there was a selfish part of salvation. You mean, said Max, in an open-mouthed, childish way, that she could have sent them to an institution? It is not sure that they would have suffered more, replied Father Isaac. We have on this island a number of pretty images in our minds—the elderly being cared for at home by dutiful, tender children is one. The reality of that image is back-breaking, cruel, and mind-crushing. And yet the image is so powerful like some works of art that I too bow before it, sinner that I am—for I can't espouse it as a rational man, only be in awe of it, irrevocably in awe of it, moved by it, cheer it on. This type of inner duality is what sin thrives on—old enduring prejudices still in command, no matter the new science, new science no matter the old, enduring love.

But you talk like an atheist.

I am thinking a bit like an atheist. But that is only thinking, Max, he said gently. Sometimes I think that the Holy Spirit presses us there Himself. Again, it is only thinking—but what if we are obliged to it, pushed, encouraged, coaxed, imperatively to it? Out goes our inner conversation like an elastic, the dialectical mind stretched and then back it comes exhausted and we return to old prejudices, but also soft waiting love.

Can we come back? Asked Max

Why not? Maybe we are a little bent out of shape, stretched out of shape, rather, different in form but still the same. In any case, Katrina is a woman as old as the hills in some respects when you come back to center—but a new woman: one is a little different in spiritual shape after getting to know her.

Cleo --who had lost her husband in her sixties to pneumonia and had moved beyond love, she thought, to the realm of wisdom, although ever one step behind her sister soul Zoe-- was a little in love with Paul. She thought this justified in that Paul was young enough to be her son, was in fact the son of the island, the apple of its eye, like all sons are, and thus subject to the adoration of mothers, such as herself. Cleo's own son had died at age five owing to a cold winter, she said in which some fluey thing got into his lungs. They had thought it common enough, nothing to worry about, but he, with his soft, sweet smile had taken to bed and had begun to cough and then to frown and then one morning was found dead. Just like that. Ah, one could live and die between minute and minute. It was not that big a difference. Finding her son dead in his bed, Cleo had not shouted or wept; but inside her womb had 'dried up' instantly, so she explained it, a little mysteriously, but effectively she had had no more children.

At seventy she had a little fantasy about Paul. Her womb "warmed"; she felt that she was fruitful. It was a strange, out of place fruitfulness. It was as if a terrible sun and bleached and blanched and dried up the territory, and in the midst, like a fetus in a little-bellied pregnancy, lay a tiny, soft, forming, throbbing love. The whole thing was so anomalous, so alien as to be extremely pitiful, and spoke of a weak, dumbing down universe with a febrile little vein of blood, rather than of something strong, and beautiful.

Nevertheless, in this pathetic, attenuated, fetal way the love thrived, although Cleo didn't talk about it. She mooned a little when she saw him, she thought he was a handsome man, worn, she thought, with the care that Ella gave him. The pallor that Agatha thought was cruelty—she saw a different man entirely, but we thought that was just resentment and jealousy for her 'punishment'—what happened years ago when Agatha went to his house and he gave her something other than the marriage, the betrothal—but a woman should never be so forward, so violently, crudely assertive, breaking all the natural bounds for...and we bit our tongues at this point; perhaps he had been a little cruel—in any case, that pallor Cleo thought was owing to the kingly thinking of the brilliant man who was, when it was all summed up, more sinned against than sinning. It was, to Cleo, lovely, endearing pallor—not at all the brown of the face of Dimitri, an earthy, sensuous face—some people said he was like Paul! —Not for a minute, said Cleo to himself. Why half a mile off you can see that they are unlike not like—the difference between a crystal vase, that was Paul, high minded, refined, reflecting light and a terracotta one, opaque and vile, almost villainous in its presumption to vase form, though attempting enlightenment, and putting on airs. Dimitri had learned big words, had gone into the world, but Paul knew that true intellect lay in following true faith, the one way, the old faith of the island. Didn't the Athonite monks despise the so-called 'intellect' of this world? The usurped Reason. The Reason that drove men further from the faith? What does cruelty matter at this point—if one is intent on following the faith and remaking Holy Island to be again holy? St. Paul was cruel, St. Peter; they wanted a thin, perfectly carved path in the wilderness of sin and if one had to die for it, or be tortured...And Cleo thought, yes Agatha had been almost burned alive but hadn't Paul saved her? What a severe and proper warning that had been for those who profane a holy place, and yet what mercy...and seeing him almost as Jesus, she became a little tearful.

And now there was a lack of proper, just support for Paul. The island was not exactly violent, but lazy. They were lazy in mind, not taking the extra step of intellect to see Paul's light and beauty as she had. Easily giving way to sins of the flesh, not seeing how Agatha, the reprobate, was among them as traitor. Paul was the one that knew. And then as some pathetic, weak, fetal lovers do, Cleo's leaped to a grand and terrible idea: Paul would in the end be crucified! Paul! That is what happened to just men who hungered and thirsted for righteousness under threat of treachery. But she would be behind him. She would be by the cross as Mary had been for Jesus. And they would be reborn in heaven, she thought deliriously—he with the crown for dancers, that Agatha could not take away, for he was a true man, and a true man danced. Wasn't it after all a sign that he wore the dancer's crown on earth? Didn't the prodigals come home to singing and dancing?

Max entered the little narrow doorway of the priest's house bearing lace curtains from Anna one day. She made these for us, he said, bowing to Father Isaac as was his habit. She said better to be useful. Of course, said the priest, putting the curtains to his face. So soft, and the work light and beautiful, delicate as foam on the tip of a wave. They even smell delicious; she must have scented them because they were to be a present. I will hang them myself.

Max looked down, sat on the bed and then murmured—you will hang them all askew, you know you will.

Perhaps so, said the priest sharply. But that is the first time you have spoken up like that. Just a few weeks ago you were so delicate and careful not to hurt my feelings. Not that it does, not that it does, he said, hastily, gently. Well, then, little one, you hang them.

Max obediently took the curtains in his hands as well as the curtain rod, offered him, and began slipping the hooks that had been sewn in to the edge of the curtains on to the rod. When he was finished, he said, quietly, but distinctly, I think this is absurd. Everything in here is broken—the chair, the window—it doesn't open without half hanging off its hinges, the stove—only one burner works, the bed sags in the middle, I sleep on the floor on a mat; you told me this was the way of Eden—the ascetic way; I believed you, thought it looked proper to have those stark, naked windows, and now, all of a sudden, lace curtains. Are we going to fix everything up—make it work now, forget Eden, live decently?

No, no, of course not, said Father Isaac, laughing; but then suddenly serious: yet you know we live perfectly. It is only that I have a great weakness for lace curtains; I thought it might be a little touch, feminine and sweet in the boys' garret.

This is all just about you, not about principle, not about holiness. I once trusted you with everything—my mind; can you believe it? I too was absurd.

But I have not done anything to violate your trust! I have taught you to the best of my ability and followed all the old traditions. It is right to a degree to mortify the flesh, to fast, but also at times to feast, to follow the delectation of the senses. There is celibacy and marriage in each soul: abstinence and solitude and then also nuptials. Christ Himself endured the trial of the cross and then rose and feasted on honeycomb in this same world—in this same world!—and in less than a week--now a world of crucifixion and honey. Why endure the cross if you are not to feast on honeycomb after? Labor that is so profound merits only divine pay.

All I know is I have followed you trusting and you do not know me. I came because I was helpless and afraid. And you made me believe so much. That life would happen, love because of these 'fasts' and 'mortifications' as you call them. And I have seen nothing and then our wonder of wonders, he said half sneering—lace curtains. what will it be next the overeating of apricot candy, the tippling on that sweet brandy until you are on the floor? Sometimes I think you are the worst kind of human being. One with pretensions to holiness. I can't even call you a hypocrite. Hypocrites sometimes are trying, vainly, stupidly; I was a hypocrite and it was all innocence—I only loved you who taught me. You believe yourself.

Father Isaac quietly examined the curtains; he noticed with a little smile that they were a little askew. His protégé had followed him even there.

Max smiled bitterly; I think you do it on purpose. I was a child before; I thought everything that you did had one meaning or other. I would have spent hours trying to see in slanting windows, messes of books and papers piled up at random on the floor, a higher understanding of things. You talked to me endlessly about perfection. But it is you, you who lack perfection. Even the least among us responds sincerely to the truth in their heart. I mean Martha, for instance, who periodically blunders in. The other day I found her half naked with a goat in her arms. She demeans herself but she is Martha and we all accept it. But you, you conceal who you are and pretend in all sorts of ways—in untidiness, seriousness about trivial things.

I am glad that you were kind to Marta, said Father Isaac.

If you want to know the truth, said Max, flushing hotly and shouting a little, I was not kind. I told her that she was engaged in bestiality—that she was ugly, stupid, sinful; that no one but she would do such a thing. Even the clods of villagers, I said, who were no better than donkeys themselves would never stoop to such filthy degradation.

Why—said Father Isaac, truly shocked; you said yourself that you accepted her?

I had to scold her. She is the kind of dumb creature that can't learn unless thoroughly humiliated.

Poor thing, said Father Isaac, heartily. You are quite wrong. She is somewhat mentally unfit for this world, but her depth of feeling, her natural trust, her tenderness are full-fledged humanity.

She had a goat's head on her bare breasts.

Well, she was feeling, said Father Isaac. I am a little surprised at your own lack of it.

Max was silent and lay back on the bed with his hands behind his head. I am not kind, he said, at length; I do not wish to be kind. I owe you, I know. I owe you. That is why I am here. Waiting to pay.

Father Isaac sat down in the broken armchair by the window, pulled the new curtains so that they blocked out the sun and studied the view through the sliver of window remaining. He could see into the brilliant light down the road from this window into the little knot of houses, yellow, white and blue and then over and on to the sea. He could see even as far as Michael's house. Michael had recently received from his parents the gift of a little motor scooter. His father thought himself relatively advanced and that there was no harm in living a little more—that is, through noise and luxury. Father Isaac studying the little red bike, reflected that now there would be a few more purchases of motor scooters. And the island would pass from being a place of little three-wheeled trucks and donkeys to a place of scooters and three wheeled trucks and finally to the motorcycle, the little car. Inevitably, the island would modernize, even if only relatively little. And inevitably people would ask what was the good of this miraculous way—of visions of heaven and fertile, multiple egg laying chickens, abundant milk producing goats. Even Max's frustration—did he think he could have gone on and on having it never occur? What were lace curtains in a shack to a young, depressed, abnormal, entirely soft and sweet, but also somewhat violent male? And it must have seemed only entirely alien and futile to him—meaningless, a mockery of things as they really are, perhaps even of himself at the deepest level—to live with Father Isaac and bear this instruction that started with the tale of Eden and looked like an old ascetic's craziness.

So they sat for a long time—the priest near the window, thinking; his protégé on the single bed on top of the blue coverlet; and in the heat of the day, the priest relaxed and forgot Max's antagonism and Max fell asleep. After a time, it came back to him—Max was agitated—perhaps something should be done? And Father Isaac roused himself and came over to the bed. He looked down on Max—there was a softness in his face—full, open lips, rose-color in face, freshness in vivid black eyelashes-- that it seemed no amount of the man's anguish and anger could efface. He looked like a child when he slept; he completely abandoned himself to sleep, as he did to anger; things come over him, thought the priest; he can't help himself. It must be this childlikeness that he is ashamed of—something he is half aware of, can't help! How easily another could exploit it—man or woman, although I think in his case a man.

Max woke and smiled a little, sweetly, drowsily at the priest. We were talking just now, he murmured, something heavy and harsh. Then, he remembered—I guess I was angry.

For no reason, said the priest, smiling reassuring him.

Yes, there was a reason—those absurd lace curtains. But it seemed there was more to it than that; he thought a minute. Oh yes, the way you are different. Yet it is the world that condemns you, not I. Shall we have tea?

Why not? said the priest, smiling and sighing.

There is so much to be done; said Max sitting up. Listen, you make the tea; you are an old hand at it. I sometimes think that these things can become significant in the life of a religious person—simple things, little barely noticed things. I wanted to gain some expertise in making tea, sweeping the floor, making the bed. To start from the beginning. I wanted to start over. I still want to start over but not with a frivolous person. Can you assure me that you are not frivolous?

I often wonder, began the priest, wearily…

No I need a direct answer, no prevaricating. If I am going to do this job with you I need to be serious.

You have come a long way, said the priest; you are no longer so hurt, so tied to the memory of your mother.

What do you know about my memories? Said Max, frowning.

I just mean, said the priest, gently, that it seems you are not so confused, so anguished, so burdened.

Make the tea, said Max, a little sternly; talk later.

The priest filled the kettle under the spigot over the large sink and put it on the burner turning on the gas. Then he took an old bent spoon and put a spoonful of chamomile and a spoonful of black tea into the teapot.

Max watching, suddenly asked in a shrill voice—why are you not making the infusion, the sweet one you usually make?

This concoction is sweet too, the priest said; we need calm and energy both of us.

There are things I just can't understand about you, said Max half to himself. You are so outlandish sometimes, this place is so small. There is a funny smell no matter what we do to keep it clean.

Father Isaac smiled slightly on one side of his mouth, then peered over the water, watching for the bubbles.

Why don't we have a dialogue? Isn't it better that way?

The water boiled and Father Isaac poured it into the teapot, smiling to himself. He brought it to the little table by the window, sat down and motioned to the seat. Max walked over and sat down carefully. He was still secretly in awe of the priest, and he knew that he could as it were say anything he chose—that he was free in that sacred nook, the altar of freedom the priest had called it—precisely because Max was free there and still loved and accepted. And the priest still kept him wondering.

You have your ideas about lace curtains, the ascetic life, spiritual father and spiritual son; but you are thrashing in these ideas; you have to learn to swim.

Max savored his tea. Then he said—yes, it has changed. Everything has changed. I don't know who I am anymore. I am lost, yes, lost but found too. There is my mother, yes my mother…he drifted off. But those old memories constrain and constrict. I have learned to almost discard them. You see now I am older, wiser, deeper than you thought I'd ever be. It's something you have to learn. I won't have superficial training. I have been with you one year and I think I have the right to expect the real thing. Of course, if for some reason you are not up to it…

Up to it, murmured the priest. Who is up to it? For sixty years I have lived with one thought—love of God. For twenty-five of those years I was scandalous, rebelling against God. I loved women, one after another; I was a libertine of the first class. Violent too, with other men. I could use a knife in a fight expertly. And would you believe it? All along I was learning, learning, learning love of God. I too had a sacred nook—a place in the basement of a hospital, would you believe in a big city—with rats, traffic, fire trucks—and there it was always cold; it was underground and I brought in a mattress and a candle; I went there alone, to think and mostly to try to keep warm and sleep; no one else knew about it for a long time, until a vagabond moved in, a real vagabond, homeless, and part thief, who used to make things with a knife and wood and string. But I would pray. Can you believe it? I was embarrassed to pray in Church. Here was my closet with this stinking, filthy man watching, holding a knife in his fist. And I would pray one thing: I don't want to be this way. Make me different. Make me the way you want me to be. No I was not up to it.

And now? Asked Max, in a little childlike tone

You see, God is humble. Very humble. When I confessed up on the Virgin's mountain, I found that it came to me; very tenderly, the dance was put into my heart, and although I couldn't walk—my mind was one thing—a true dance of joy. And I thought and prayed—let's start with Eden.

You don't know all that much, said Max, crossly and uncomfortably. You're no saint or dancer—either would be fine, but you are nothing.…

No, a child. Even now, I find I have no great thought, no profound interpretation of the Crucifixion of our Master.

I am finished with the tea, Max said, suddenly. I am going out for a walk. Everything is in order, yes? You don't need me now.

Did you enjoy the tea? Asked the priest, softly.

Ah leave me alone. It is one thing you never learned to do.

Dimitri and Connie were seen in the village walking arm and arm; Connie with dark glasses, Dimitri with a cigarette; Barbara remarked to her husband with slight resentment that it was like a movie they had seen on their honeymoon on the other bigger more modernized island fifty kilometers away. They are going to take the island by storm, said Stavros; pretty soon we will be rocking.

They are both crude I think, said Barbara; but she said it under her breath. The fact was she was a little afraid, a little exhilarated by the sight of the two men. By the time they had talked to Simon and called a village meeting, complete with Father Isaac, she and Agatha and Katrina were as excited as young girls going to a dance. Agatha wore black dresses now that her sons were home in honor of her dead husband, but she put on a sky blue headscarf. Barbara wore a gray silk dress with a green leaf pattern and a white headscarf. Katrina, who had a habit of hiding her femininity owing to her embarrassment over her paunch, put on black trousers and a red shirt. They went together separate from even husbands and Stavros said if anything can defeat the arguments of men it is these little bands of females.

Simon's house that evening was a lively place; people were gathered together talking the way people talk when they are anticipating something of a celebration, although no one said anything about a party. But it was a village decision that Dimitri in bringing this rich man from the city, had brought rich things, improvements, answers to wish lists—and that in short, although no one could give more than a vague reason why—soon the little houses would be all lit up; there would be dancing in the streets, wine drinking night and day. People carried it further in their hearts: there would be, inevitably, after these festivities, new romances, love makings, weddings and children, finally children—sweet blessing on the island like rain in the dead of summer.

Anna was unable to come and Martha was sitting by her, instructed to run immediately for help to Agatha, should there be need. The girl was capable of watching for a short while, though Agatha knew she couldn't be trusted more than a few hours to sit and when she had to walk, she would undoubtedly forget Anna, the house, her duty everything as she followed her ambulatory urge and roam out down to the beach or around the deserted streets.

So Agatha sat watching both watch and her handsome son, swelling with pride to see that he had made something of himself. For now, she had laid aside all her private fears about this stranger that her son was indebted to for livelihood, and that he put so much trust in. She tried to think that the island could be brilliant, new, modern, above all open and tolerant—and that they could all be much happier and she could put to rest certain fears that were there under the surface. Already Michael had a motor scooter that frightened the chickens. It was a good change. Father Isaac, who sat smiling in a corner, had brought talk of heaven, eggs, and milk as if they were all one. But it was, in Agatha's opinion, not altogether trustworthy. Modern meant logical, rational everyday living. The machine but also the world of machines—predictable and controlled. Not this wave of irrationalism that pervaded island life, this waiting for a miracle. It was getting too chaotic in the village for the villagers own good. Things just happened and one didn't even see the reason why. Dimitri, like all great men, was going to give them the solution to themselves; he would overthrow the overthrowers of the strange nightmarish evening when they had come with fire in their hands. Once there had been revolutions, he said and civil wars in nations. Now it was just a luxury hotel for the tiny, remote island.

For some reason, Agatha didn't know it, Max and Jason were absent. Otherwise all eighty households showed up in full. Dimitri was sitting at the head of a short exquisitely polished table and Connie, the rich hotel owner, was sitting beside him on the left. When everybody had crowded in, Dimitri looked around, whispered something to Connie, took off his watch and rapped on the table with it, saying --Silence!-- in his low, beautiful voice. Thomas, the poet, took out a harmonica and played a little introductory waltz, which Agatha thought was typical of how out of step the villagers were with practical, modern things. But soon everyone was quiet and leaning forward in their seats to catch the voice of Dimitri who was talking in slow, carefully enunciated words but without trying to project his voice.

Speak up, said Simon, gruffly. No one hears anything.

So then Dimitri began to talk in a strong voice that seemed to stress him and leave him a little out of breath.

Agatha caught these words: Completely new island. What we actually want here is not to live the same old life year in and year out but to develop in the way we ought to as viable members of a larger world. This island would make, for instance, good use of tourism—economically and spiritually—here there was a loud murmur—economically and spiritually; there is no point, he explained, in pretending that ignorance is really some kind of deeper wisdom, division --our kind of love. We need to press boldly towards a future where we live with others and in knowledge of the world. Also, with a viable economy. This means greater material enjoyment with the advantages of material wealth, including medications, heating systems, communications. We are not donkeys but men. When babies are born the mother is in danger for her life. Two hours away by boat there is a doctor, a little hospital, a nursing home. We need something besides a slow caique to get women in childbirth to these facilities. When our parents are old, they linger in pain, or unable to make use of hygiene. We need to give them the care they deserve. They don't want to go away? Build something here. Dentists don't exist. In Athens, a person might visit the dentist once a year. Our old people let the teeth fall out. We are small but we could have some of the amenities that make life endurable even when we are not physically what we once were.

There was a stir at the door, Catherine asked in a quiet voice in the language of the island—could she come in? Simon pushed his way through the crowd with a plastic chair.

Dimitri looked up and saw her, looked down and was silent a minute. It is disturbing to think that the problem of wealth, he said, distinctly, is so easy to solve and no one wants to solve it. Money would mean to us a more livable life. Yes, we have food, it seems we have houses. But what if a drought were to come, an animal disease? Money generated by a viable trade with the world would be our surety. I went into the world to make money. It simply did not make sense to remain poor and obscure when I wanted to make changes for the better. If we generated income here, village wide, it would be a start. I am talking about a real change. I am talking about worldliness; instead of magical, backwater religion. I have nothing against religion, but on a more philosophical level. We can't depend on miracles.

Here I have a man who is rich, yes, you all know that; Dimitri said pronouncing the words distinctly. But do you know how rich? And how he got rich? He has over five hundred million dollars and he got rich by his own labor. He was only a footman once—a servant in a hotel. He worked his way up. He is answerable to nobody for his money. It was not a gift but sheer toil, his own. As Adam, in the sweat of his brow he earned what he earned. He has chains of luxury hotels around the world. He is looking to make getaway resorts—that is hotels, fancy, beautiful hotels on remote islands for the rich and famous to vacation. And the rich and famous bring commodities. I have worked with him in the small capacity of hotel manager for three hotels. Thanks to him I can consider myself a man of business. And business means making things better. Thank you.

The room was silent. Nobody applauded. Then one man with a wool cap who had been chewing on a piece of bread in the corner asked—and the rich hotel owner? What does he want to do on this island?

Yes, said a plump young woman with thick black hair. Is he really going to make us rich? Or is he going to make money off of our island and leave?

Someone clapped to this in the corner. It was one of Barbara's sons. We live a simple life. We are religious. We know that the world is full of rich men. If we wanted to change and become businessmen we would leave like you did for money. But we, long ago, our fathers and grandfathers, and great grandfathers, chose a simple religious life: on earth as it is in heaven.

Never mind, said a thin, blonde nervous woman. Here we all are. Let us give this hotel owner a chance to speak. He too is a man no matter how rich. We have shown him hospitality. Give him the opportunity to tell us what it is he wants of us.

Dimitri motioned to Connie. And Connie cleared his throat. Dimitri said: I will have to translate; he only speaks English.

Connie spoke a sentence and Dimitri translated. Essentially, he said that he was happy and honored to be a guest on the island. It was everything he had imagined when Dimitri had described it to him—charming, beautiful, relaxing, sweet. He hoped that they would share their hospitality. Great people from Athens and Paris were looking to take refuge from the traffic and the whirl and hubbub of the world—oh you cannot understand the whirl and hubbub—it makes one nervous, though it is indispensable too for the very refrigerators in your houses, the telephones, the TVs, the motors on your fishing boats. And so these great people would come perhaps for their honeymoon…he smiled, and ended abruptly.

Who are the great people? Asked Katrina suddenly, in a loud murmur. She was astounded by the speeches and overwhelmed by the ideas, clearly; the truth was she had had a clue that this was what would take place at Simon's meeting, and she had resisted, as she said before to Catherine that she would. She considered Dimitri to be thoroughly bad; but it seemed to her that he and this rich man had a tremendous secret and with the others she had become curious and a little impressed by Dimitri's grandeur, the easy way with which he said he had become a businessman, his physical beauty which had heightened over the years; she had suddenly had the thought that wealth, the world, makes one intelligent and beautiful. And she had suddenly felt like someone carried downstream by a strong current reaching out for a branch from a tree bending towards her hand.

Lipingo, Connie suddenly pronounced.

I know about him, said Michael from the back of the room. A contemporary film director—makes films about fat people; wrote a book about why. I read it—it was on the best-seller list of foreign books.

I met him, Dimitri quietly announced with Connie in London. He said that he was looking for an island—quiet, no cars, no signs of modernization—but a good hotel, a decent hotel with room service, refrigerators, TV, swimming pool, Internet access. He liked the idea—Holy Island—ah simple people among their chickens and goats, he said, with icons and at prayers; he wanted to see our forest, our mountain monastery, and taste the lemon curd, and apricot candy—yes I told him even about that specialty. These people stay a week it is true but they come with their retinue, with a girl or two… Dimitri smiled at his inadvertent rhyming.

A fat girl? Someone shouted.

The quiet crowd in the room began repeating Dimitri's words; all eyes were on him in wonder. At the mention of the candy, usually reserved for weddings, a number of people smiled slightly.

Of course there will be cameras, Dimitri said, large cameras, a boat brought over specially, filled with equipment.

Yes, said Michael, exultantly. We will be in the films. I've read about films—everything is glorious…

Glamorous, corrected Father Isaac in a soft voice that was distinct, however.

Glorious, went on Michael, ignoring him, and stunning like the sun. And people live covered with jewels, beautiful people with glorious faces.

Let them come, said Simon laughing—I know a great dish of fried shrimp—invented it myself with my own two hands—lemon, pepper and a special kind of oil; I could open a restaurant.

These things and more could be. We needn't be so stagnant, in any case, as we have been, continued Dimitri; we could have our own identity but that would mean some effort, a kind of interpretation, participation in the world scene.

The villagers all began talking suddenly. There issued from quiet murmuring, a steady, increasing roar. No one was quite sure about one's neighbor, but on the whole after that rather startling night they had somehow agreed. Dimitri's plan would be put into effect. The island would be reinvigorated; for a few days after there was dancing in the tavern like never before. Even Simon got up from an iron chair where he sat with his usual drink of brandy with a few almonds on a napkin, and twirled perfectly looking like a man of twenty.

The streets were more crowded than usual in the week after the meeting. Women wore gay colored skirts, white, sky blue, and carnation red headscarves—the village looked decked out as if for a wedding. It was a soft modest kind of costume for the Veil, as it were, with the Body shy and excited beneath. Agatha was rather silent, and pensive but donned her best mourning, a beautiful black silk skirt that she had sewn for her boys' wedding ceremonies.

Simon unable to wait, actually did cook up the red snapper dish and brought it on a silver-colored tray to the tavern to be tasted. Maria, the tavern waitress, handed out free cups of wine and coffee that day and the village women crowded around on the grounds usually sacred to men tolerated because by island tradition, women were the best tasters, though men were considered to be the finest cooks; these women judges pronounced in Simon's favor and it was decided there and then that his dish would be served to the film stars and to this strange director who put fat people in the pictures. Then they will need to eat, laughed Barbara; Stavros smiled ironically; it was rare for his wife to laugh. Everybody stopped a minute and looked silently at her. She flushed and frowned but then laughed again as if filled with joie de vivre.

You are forgetting duty, God, Christ—he admonished her in making those raw jests. I am full blooded, she said in return; Jesus saves sinners first, before the just. Indeed, said Stavros smiling then I suppose we must certainly sin away.

Agatha overhearing took Barbara by the hand. You look unusually well, she said to her encouragingly. The point is that you are so gracious and hospitable. Of course, if they are fat we need especially to feed them. And I am sure the film people will enjoy all that we have to offer. We still have a surplus of cream and eggs. She went on murmuring gentle things to her companion as they walked along the street, Stavros ahead of them. At the end of the street, Barbara suddenly caught sight of the rich man in a white Panama hat and jeans and an immaculately white, pressed shirt. He was standing looking uncertainly down the road, the only road in the village that ran along the shore in front of the houses towards the mountain. All the other byways were paths and alleys. The crowds of women in their best were marching to and fro along this main road paved with dark flagstones. Barbara thought to make connection with this amazing man as Agatha had, and she stood on tip toe and waved vigorously. A thought formed in the back of her head that perhaps he would stay in her house next, grace her presence and somehow by transmission of aura, almost, Barbara would find herself more glorious as Michael had said. Because he, the writer of that divine book—Michael had explained something about the diary being the search for the divine self but Barbara in her simple mindedness put it that way—he knew words—while the priest was—well, not particularly intelligent.

Connie, a little figure down the road did not see Barbara waving. But he took off his hat and waved it to the crowd of ladies in general. Then he turned his back and walked to Dimitri's house. He was to stay another week with Dimitri and then the plan was for them to travel together back to Athens where Dimitri would end his vacation; a promotion was planned; he was to be executive director of Excelis' getaway hotels as Connie called them. And would spend his time island hopping, visiting one remote island after another in different parts of the world sounding the territory and the people for the building of a resort hotel.

Dimitri for some reason unknown to himself avoided Catherine but encountered Katrina quite a bit. He said to Agatha that he had something to hammer out with Katrina, a playmate from his youth. She I know is hard to persuade, he said. I don't want to force anyone in the village. Although, her opinion is treated with very little respect, I need to know her mind on this—for old times' sake, for the fact that...

Go, Agatha put her arms tenderly around him. You know in your heart what is best. What do you mean by that? Asked Dimitri suddenly angry. What does this have to do with heart?

He went out without another word. He had begun to wear a hat, not white, but his sort of soft black felt hat, an old, very cheap hat that he had bought when still a worker in Athens. It gave a more casual picture to onlookers. He went to Katrina's house with a cigarette hanging from his lips, the black hat on his head, white jeans and a dark blue shirt. He walked in without knocking as was the often the custom among villagers and found Katrina boiling milk and stirring in honey and crushed almond blossom.

He called from behind her—Katrina—do you remember me?

She looked around. I think so, she said, turning around. She smiled at him a little askew and then asked briskly—and why do you wear that old hat?

Ah, the old hat, said Dimitri, not answering the question, and looking down, reflectively.

You seem to be trying hard to impress someone, she said, a little sourly.

No, not I. What do you think of the proposal?

I don't bother myself about it. The island won't change. You'll see. It has its own mind made of ageless sand and sea. They will try to build and try to change but...

Perhaps you are right, Dimitri murmured looking at her. You have not changed.

Katrina looked down; one has time to think when one is occupied as I am. I guess the world is where a person never has time to think.

Yes, it changes things, said Dimitri, stiffly.

Everything changes, life, feelings, even language. They say you are leaving soon—going back into the world with that Mr....I don't know his name with the white hat and a lot of money.

Yes, that is my destiny.

Well, you chose a path.

I realized myself as a man, Katrina, what did you expect me to do? Remain here, your little boy love running on the beach, walking hand in hand in the forest?

It was just an innocent little thing in those days, said Katrina; many people are happy to have such a memory. And some people here act on these little things, build their lives...

I wasn't willing to marry; I find it a cramped, foolish, vain institution. We could have had a real affair gotten to the bottom of our attraction for one another, enjoyed its sweetness thoroughly and then like mature people, realized that there was an end to it, had to be an end to it. Or, it may have been that you would have come with me.

You never suggested that.

It was always implied, of course.

Of course, Katrina said sarcastically. Of course. Only a real lover would make an honest offer.

If you had wanted me to be your real lover, many more things would have been articulated. Love means certain things are in fact said.

Do you mean sex or love?

As you wish, Dimitri answered, sighing wearily.

In any case, sit down. I have become good at making sweet, delicious things to please two old people who don't know any other pleasure.

I will gladly.

Katrina poured out the hot milk and served it to Dimitri in a little porcelain cup. He put it to his lips.

She suddenly laughed. Most people take off their hats when they sit down.

Forgive me, I was embarrassed, not thinking.

Do you like that hat?

It is good enough. I got it when I first went to Athens. I wore it for good luck.

It is old, old fashioned—it is a nothing hat.

Dimitri was silent. Then he said, what do you want out of this proposal, Katrina? Ask and you might get it.

I don't know why you wear an absurd hat unless it is because maybe that rich fellow also wears one sometimes.

You are the same, said Dimitri a little annoyed; you toy around; why not go to the core of things, now? We are on a different footing than we were ten years ago.

We were always on a different footing from what I thought; I didn't know the footing until you told me you didn't believe in marriage, said Katrina. And now you come in absurdly dressed as if to extend your compassion—that is what it is really all about, isn't it? The hat means, of course, that I am not here with any manly intentions. I'm here as a clown—but as a serious profiteer who combines compassion…—here you too can get a bit of gold.

Well, alright then. Wouldn't you take it?

Katrina winced a little as if in pain. Why? She asked him.

You live with your two old parents. They might need something. And you might want some help. If you could hire someone, pay someone to come in…

Look, I can hardly stop laughing about that hat. Do you expect me to believe all that?

Dimitri was astounded at this reception. He had expected, half hoped, from vanity that Katrina would be a little adoring; he remembered that when they had walked together in the woods she had quite outwardly shown her physical attraction to him; and he had been gratified and made little advances, even sexual caresses. She had lifted her skirts and his fingers had slipped into her vulva, fluttering there, and she had gasped for the shock of the wonderful pleasure. She had gotten a little high after imagining a wedding and had taken him into the woods dousing him peasant style with all her body and soul and he had been with her—she had thought to no one else would she permit! and they had met in secret a number of times, and laughed for no reason in public places. It had been enough to inflame him with desire for more, but Katrina had proven to be of island mentality and refused to be, as she had called it, his mistress. And so Dimitri, unable to impress his girlfriend with modern ideas had gone off angry and rebuffed, and rather naively expecting women of Athens, Paris and London to try to entrap men into marriage. He had emerged on the scene timid, angry, suspecting, ignorant and wrapped up the problem by soliciting the attentions of a call girl who stated her business in honest terms, he said to himself, and with whom he had what he called plain sex, but actually a rather passionate entanglement on his side for years. And so he had formed an 'elastic' approach to sexuality, at the same time, gradually, disdaining what he called the call girl's graphic availability and lack of refinement. In the depths of his heart, Dimitri had changed his ideas about matrimony. He thought that over a given length of time in a love affair, he could even marry, although that was a very private conviction, not his public opinion—and there had to be a plan from a level headed woman in which he could participate spirit and body, and he thought she would also have to deal with this elasticity, this independence.

Katrina had also developed sexually, unknown and unnoticed in the village. She too had been violently aroused by Dimitri had howled literally all down the forest walk when he had left the island and in secret and not so secret had passionately adored him for a year. But, unable to wait, she had eventually found another nineteen year old who was led by her like a little dog round about. This was only discovered after it had been going on for three years.

Since it was supposedly the second affair, the villagers judged her heavily but with a sort of leniency. Simon thought to himself, well, if an old woman is a whore in her heart what does it matter? She'll be the teacher.

After a while, Katrina could pick out the virgins among the lads. She knew their walk, smell, look. But except for this one teenager Romni, whom everybody knew to be her great adorer, Katrina kept to herself. With Romni she had a mad love affair in which her mind was still entirely on Dimitri. Romni was a hulking boy of twenty with sandy hair combed over one eye and pimples who flushed for nothing in and was unaware that his one desire was Katrina's sex, or rather he was unaware of it as simply sex, and thought it was more god—and therefore that he was commanded, created by that pink flower. The villagers themselves saw the whole thing with some laughter and pity. They had set high hopes on Dimitri and in their hearts, through a kind of osmosis of feeling, they knew that Katrina pursued him still. Romni eventually found that there was in effect another god in the area with ash blonde hair, which he never found out was dyed, and so long she could sit on it, wide hips and a narrow waist, and so Romni drifted away from Katrina. And this Katrina tolerated well, almost coolly. It had been seven years since she had had the affair with Romni and she was panting still over Dimitri. But ten years of fending for herself, showing herself that she could find pleasure independently of him, made her a little brittle. She sensed that he was worldly from the way he used his body. And she was both intimidated and in awe, both of which she desired to cover up. He was still Dimitri—how could she not know it? The same attraction, the same voice. A certain familiarity and love slid into place in the pit of her stomach. She thought of the forest, how could she not? But this time not as an ignorant girl and it occurred to her that he would never again accept her as that.

In a way, Dimitri was the same; the hat she hadn't really noticed but it appeared to her flirtatious to pretend that it jarred on her somewhat. It wasn't part of his old aesthetic that was very apparent and she wanted to just laugh it off. She remembered that men, even young men, often wear hats because their hair is thinning, and she resented being attracted to, pursuing a man whose hair was thinning, despite the fact that she was as old herself as his mother. She convinced herself that the whole pre-sentation was of something odd and futile in him. She thought that this would give her power over her feelings.

So she said to the astounded man, I am really grateful for your hat, and laughed, and thought it was over. She thought herself very much in control. And she imagined that she would carefully weave a web about Dimitri, not because she was so desperate as all that, all that, being what it had been, but for the hell of it.

Dimitri didn't want to marry her? Who said she wanted to marry? She had learned to play and to enjoy when she could, when she could. But where had she heard, or had it arisen out of the natural knowledge in her—that sometimes men on their return to their homelands, single men who have had love affairs— because she was sure he had had, ongoing love affairs and knew sex in all its dimension—suddenly, out of the blue, marry?

Of course, it wasn't for her with her care-taking responsibilities. He would have to drag her away by force. She thought if this were a novel or a film that in the end; ah he would have her by the hair and she naked and he…and then there would be a hot romance, something full flesh and blood, and finally the old devil of prevarica-tion would dance away down a road of hot coals and the new determined man would step up to her side, drape her in white. The new determined man—that was in effect what she wanted. Dimitri, the new man! And hadn't he come back to show them all that that is what he was? Well, she could be a new woman. But the old faded hat was out of place. Now a new beret, the artist's kind. Perhaps she would go to the other island and buy one for him.

Dimitri left in a bit of wonder. He had not quite gotten out of Katrina all that he had wished. It seemed that she was trying desperately and in a quirky way to get personal again. He had let slip things, which he shouldn't have. He had wanted her to benefit by his plan because he had a kind heart, reached out to everybody. In ad-dition, she would always carry for him the scent of a full, mature love affair that was never quite fulfilled and that intrigued him a little still. But no, she had a large, funny body now. She was not that sylph—a sylph with buck teeth and greasy hair, but still something in the undulation between wide hips and waist, she had a flat belly then—and that sylph had once walked with him in the woods, laughing, talking lightly, mak-ing him think of butterflies and open flowers. It had been at that time, in his morose nineteen-year-old heart, all hot rebellion and sex—an ecstatic sweet paradise.

Katrina had written a letter full of imploring once—she had wanted to come as his wife—it was right, it was just…He felt that her flesh spoke and was satisfied. But the thought of her had changed in him. As his wife, she would pull him backwards, and they foolish, naïve, sparkling forest virgins as he called them from a remote isle—they would be swallowed up in the mad rushing crowd, drowned in the depart-ment stores, supermarkets, amidst the traffic.

And so the love affair remained dangling in them both. But they had begun to look at it with a more philosophical air. Dimitri with his call girl had prophesied a new era of full sexuality—a bloom of the sexual flower latent in a man—a rediscovery of innocence through sexual love. The call girl had been everything generally fantasized by young men—long silky legs, ample bosom, a nature inclined for sex at all sorts of times, man sex. Dimitri thought this the best thing under heaven for some time; and then, subtly, he began to tire of it. They had read the Kama Sutra together sixteen times, had traveled to cloud nine together; one would have thought orgasm after orgasm would make the interest endure. But there were the weeks of fading inclination; Dimitri suddenly felt that he had had what he had come for; that she, he supposed was very obliging; he realized he didn't know much of a she at all. He even envisioned that she was a little like a machine without a heart. He tried to talk, deferring to the fact that they were living together—that she might become his only--, and found himself rebuffed. He talked of love, and she burst into tears. But when he took her in his arms and questioned her, it seemed that it was not him at all that had aroused her passionate melancholy. She had fallen in love—would he forgive her...? Yes, yes, he kissed her hair, of course. Yes, yes, it is natural—you're beautiful and young. And in reality her confession of loving another man, after the scenes of her sexually enjoying them in their bed, after a certain recoiling, made little impression on him.

They left each other actually shaking hands. Then he had struck her lightly on the side of the face—for good luck, he had said and thought he had meant it. She had looked at him a little strangely and said: you owe me—about four hundred pounds for the last couple of sittings; and Dimitri remembered that despite the fact that they had agreed to be boyfriend and girlfriend—that they would go out together, travel, eat together, sleep at night together, he had agreed to pay her for the sex, which she called 'sittings', so that she would not lose her income. And he in fact felt that it wasn't so very strange to write that cheque; and so with a cheque and a slap, he had left her.

He wanted to feel that he was robust sexually, open-minded, kind hearted. That he had compassion on the human instinct for sex. He himself had experienced all sorts of sexual positions—erotic games, books, movies—times out, and times in; he saw the restraint of the man or woman inclined to marry as rather lower in consciousness, and the giving up of sex of some spiritual people, as a drying up of the human mind and heart. Yet now he himself was seeking something spiritual. He wanted, he said—a path that was 'robustly' human beyond the besotted. The Church in the city was an irony—worldly itself while preaching poverty and asceticism and suffering. Strangely, he thought of the Church as he had known it as a boy back on the Holy Island—a combination of sorrow for mankind, tenderness, practical wisdom and magic and foolishness. Long before he ever knew he was going to be sent on a mission there, he had begun to nurture in secret a belief that his island home was closer to his spiritual path. And thus he had begun to conceive that he was himself a kind of priest to a Christian Church that the world was far away from—a simple Church that had compassion on the human animal.

But all that had vanished for the time being. When he had come back to the island, he had felt like he was in a cloud of loneliness and separateness. Meeting Catherine had made him feel as if his hands had grasped something real, tangible, sturdy. And yet she was so pale and slender, almost grotesquely so, had floated from him almost; it must have been what they call 'vibes' in the American circles that he had encountered in the hotel: That emanation of a man or woman, which can conjure up all sorts of experiences in the brain while at the same time, on the periphery, reality registers a difference, the ordinary difference. He didn't think her body healthy yet he loved it somehow. He had come down from the sky, come up from the depths of the sea with her. She was, he thought, a high priestess of a temple that he had never quite seen and yet been dazzled by. And flesh with her was like an elusive flower with a light but gorgeous scent.

Katrina was the old earth, the old road. Dimitri vaguely wondered if it would ever open to him again.

Agatha was humming and singing when Dimitri got home. The house was dark, Agatha didn't turn on many lights in the evening, since they were so dim. Better to get along with natural light, the reflection of the luminescent gray, the sunless, hanging on of light in the evening. She was bending over the stove, stirring something with a spoon in a pan. There was a delicious smell of fish and tomato and basil.

I got some more olive oil, she said, as Dimitri entered—from Leo. He and I share now, recipes, tomatoes, goat cheese. It is quite a congenial love affair.

Mother, tell me the truth, said Dimitri, sternly; are you really doing that with Leo?

Well, well, said Agatha. What is 'doing that'? Oh, love affairs are love affairs— right now we are doing cooking, outdoing one another at the stove. He has a good hand for some things. Said he learned to make apricot brandy at his mother's knee. She was an old sot. Reeled and swayed around the village when there was nothing here but paddling boats and oil lamps and people hauled water from the caves in the forest. They used to think of drunkenness as close to joy—but only for the men. When women got drunk they beat them. So she got beaten and kicked and this drove her more into the brandy. Her husband beat her too but only a little, mostly he shouted. He drank only a little and used to complain that because of her he issued forth smelling of spirits so that people would eye him askance. And the children smelled too. People used to demonstratively put their fingers to their noses walking by, especially the woman. Leo's mother fed her son sweetmeats constantly as a sort of easy way of providing affection and covering up for the smell. He grew up weak, fat, and alcoholic, like an unwholesome plump prune stewed in brandy, and driven to become the Casanova of the island out of spite for the women around who disdained his family and because he wanted to laugh away the pain of his mother reeling and staggering and making herself ugly and stupid. He was bowled over by Magda. He is only just now getting to love a woman on his terms.

So you are the answer to his history of woe. Come now, Mother, this is all lies. He wants another conquest. Mind you don't get into trouble.

I know much more than you do, son, about trouble.

Well, what is it now?

That rich man has aroused a number of people; he is in fact like a love elixir here. What does he really intend to do? Stay here, understand our ways or…

No, I am the one that does the understanding. It is a matter of a new island now, Mother; a viable part of the world—a contributor, an island perspective, Dimitri was calm, clear, intellectual to fight off the memories of the woman Agatha was talking about. Someone who would stop, holding herself rigid to try to stay upright, then suddenly stagger behind a bush and pee. He was fighting island memories right and left. You'll see, people here will have something to say—clear, undeniable, and the world will listen. I don't believe that anything new and luxurious will be made here. And the rich and famous if they come will see—what you and I see: colorful, quaint houses and people who fry fish, make apricot brandy—and they will go away again without a word.

But you want change, Mother, as I do. You are a skeptic, you are not quite sure of things as they are given to you without explanation—things that, as one might say, rain down from the sky. Not that you wish to harm—merely to ask: What is this, what does it mean? Where does it connect?

That rich man will give us no answers, Dimitri.

Perhaps not, Dimitri said, frowning.

You went to see Katrina today? I saw you at her house. Are you fond of her, Agatha asked anxiously looking at him.

Inevitably in this village one becomes a poker and prier. I went to her only to ask her how she feels about the new hotel.

Then it's nothing.

One is reduced so reduced in this village to confessing to nothings. I kissed Katrina a total of twenty times alone in the forest more than ten years ago.

And so?

And so nothing.

I thought you had a flagrant affair.

An affair of mostly kisses and caresses.

Then it is that woman in the city.

What woman in the city? Asked Dimitri astonished.

You said you were living with…

Oh, no, mother, that was a prostitute. There is a limit of time on affairs with prostitutes.

Agatha experienced a strange kind of elation. Her son was a handsome man, and not a weak, foolish boy. He had gone to the city, found work, risen in his profession and he had at the heart of it all his own mind. He had found his manhood and yet not quite divided… There was something reassuring about prostitutes—they didn't take the man away from his family. There had been one on the island, Patti, she was called, quite a homey figure, rather pathetic and really a warm-hearted lady, longing to be part of the wives, to talk and gossip. No one held it against her that the husbands visited her now and again. It was really charity. Then she had drifted away, or died, or something. And now there was Maria, the tavern woman with a large bosom, slender legs—they say she had a bed in the back room that she called the broom closet.

Now Agatha's son had grown big and handsome, physically radiant, intelligent like no other man and of course he had to have an outlet. It was natural. He had had a woman, of course, given his depth of character, his development, but no woman had had him. Agatha almost wished with a possessiveness she was ashamed of that Dimitri would stay confined to prostitutes and that Jason would have a prostitute to make him a man. But she imagined that in the eventuality they would marry—just to be sedate and calm. Perhaps Dimitri would take up again an interest in Katrina whom he had left behind with the memory of twenty 'kisses.'

And she would commiserate with Katrina, a little chunkier but still with her passion for Dimitri, she was secretly sure and secretly proud of this—how a man had to be a man but still could, you know, not quite have a focus on women as women.

But thinking about Katrina, she realized that she couldn't rid her mind of a certain image of defiant bitterness; ah, but a man would change all that, she thought.

You know, Mother, said Dimitri watching her thinking—I don't intend to stay on. I know you think I will, now that I am here and don't have a woman possessing me back there in the city.

I came for work only, Mother. In a week, we are leaving, Connie and I, flying back to Athens, then on to London.

Ah no, said Agatha, with her head flung back looking at him. You are destined to stay and marry.

Well, well, alright, said Dimitri in jest; who?

Why? Who else? Said Agatha also in jest, not knowing what would pop out of her mouth but just babbling on—the American girl on the mountain!

Dimitri flushed; that is absurd. She is not that kind of woman, I don't think.

Why not? Now that the sentence had come out like a baby with no one controlling the thing except God, Agatha thought she might as well defend it, nurse it...

You don't know her, said Dimitri, shaken. She is a profound person—one who needs solitude. Besides, she is not like the others you jest about, Mother. You don't understand. She is strange and meditative. Removed. I wouldn't want to disturb...I wouldn't want anyone to disturb her the way she is. In marriage I suppose there is a constant jostling and jarring. People change, bits and pieces of themselves as people fall off and get lost. I wouldn't want it to happen to her.

You make her sound like a fish that has jumped above the waves at night and whose silver is caught in the moonlight. One of these visions for a lonely person. But if you leave her alone too much, she will disappear you know.

How? She is up there to stay?

She will sink down into the depths and swim away—your will never know her.

Love is knowing too, Dimitri. Not knowing is to make a person end, like a house with rooms might end, but knowing is to make a person continue, boundlessly forever like the sea in its rhythm seen from a window.

Is that the way it was with my father?

Early on, yes. Then we got a little stuck in the house of frustration and it became not knowing--but cozy, sweet, at times, all games. It was easier thus. But when he died, and a little while later, I let go of grudges, there it was again, the knowing:—I saw him framed by that unbounded place. I still do.

By the unbounded place! I am glad, Mother. Yes, I see a number of people framed by the unbounded place. You for one.

And that girl, or Katrina? Asked Agatha;

That girl or Katrina? What does that girl have to do with Katrina?

They can't both be in that vision.

Mother, promise me—you won't refer to either of them...

Then it must be that woman in the city—prostitute though! I never knew that a man could speak endearingly of a woman that way.

Mother, uttered Dimitri, aggravated—this is really not your sphere at all. A true man keeps his intimate affairs to himself.

I've heard that mothers always get to the bottom of whatever happens with their children.

How long does that last? Asked Dimitri regaining his humor.

Until, until...

Until, said Dimitri taking her in his arms, they forget jealousy and reconcile themselves to the fact that no matter what happens their boy is in love with them forever; he kissed her softly on the lips.

Then would you listen to me? Asked Agatha, smiling up at him.

Not about women.

No—but –about this island. We need you. Stay here. Don't go back to that city.

Stay and do what? It would be an unthinkable sacrifice. He let her go and turned away.

Not really—to build the island. Surely this Connie would understand. And if there is going to be a hotel with all that luxury—there will be a lot to put in place.

You don't understand, other people under me would do it.

Strangers? Alien to us? For all these years we've held on to—to our ways…only to be forcibly changed for the whims of some rich people—this Mr. Lipingo with his vision of fat people who wants an island retreat. Why, son, should we have to change? Don't you think that if you were responsible for destroying…

I don't destroy, said Dimitri, interrupting quickly; I build.

But life would be lost—maybe not to death, exactly—but the old life.

It is odd, you—talking about the old life. What is in it for you? Hasn't it mean years of hate, the islanders cursing you? What attachment can you possibly have to this dried up old island?

Don't talk like that. It is my home too, although a bit like swallowing bread with sand and stones. But, what can I say—it is still home. My father played his music here and I went with him to the dances seated on his shoulder and the music was the sweetest I have ever known. My mother half the beauty god, half the bitter, wild, tearful woman hugging us when we came home—all this is in here, in my heart, and in these stones.

Well, alright; I will ask about an extension on my stay here to smooth things through.

It's more than smoothing things through. It may be smoothing out Mr. Lipingo, as I see it.

You are an old fashioned fuss budget. Expand your way of thinking. Enlarge your heart: Mr. Lipingo is actually unprejudiced and sweet. His films are comical and sad about society—that is, a room full of more than fifty people.

You think so highly of this island, Mother, and so distrustfully of the world. Why, the world is only a thousand of these islands. Bring together all the islands dotted around these seas and you would find the same evils; it is mankind in a sardine can instead of a dollop of jam in a glass of ice water. Here one can be cool and breathe and go for walks; there, one is rubbing elbows with one's neighbor....

—and therefore, hates him, brings charges against him, tortures and kills him, interrupted Agatha. I never said the island was morally or spiritually superior. I only say that it has the right to be unmolested, with its little old ways if they're peaceful. That I somehow am not so much a part of—and yet I am, I am! More than they for the bread with sand and stones. Agatha added in a quieter voice. She went on: I realize you think that we need help, as you might put it, but it is a little like trying to help a bird on the ground. It molests rather than cures it. The bird never gets over the touch of the human hand. Even helping, it somehow hurts. You might secretly resent this, but understand it—you too, Dimitri, are the bird, the island bird. I feel that the more you become attached to this Mr. Cours, the more likely, you will suddenly find yourself alone, deserted, incapable of coming home again—and dying out there.

You speak as if out there is a big dark margin of nothing, Mother, an abyss. But the world...It was just all about the island, Mother; the renewal of it, the reasonable renewal—the making something where there was nothing, a heap of old things—refrigerators, old, rather stupid houses. Ignorant, suspicious, even violent people.

Of course, there is nothing to attract one such as you...to your own home.

That is not true, Mother. To prove it I will stay on longer—getting to know the place again. In the world, I was somebody it's true; everything seemed to work there—my intelligence, abilities. Here one rolls through the day, he laughed. But it may be that I am mistaken in my judgment.

Agatha turned, went to her room and closed the door. She thought of dressing herself up a little, a black skirt of course, but a green blouse to go out—she had triumphed in little over her son; in reality, she didn't want to go through that terrible waiting and misgiving for letters that were late, weeks late. She thought she would celebrate his staying on—go to Barbara's house, just step in a moment, talk to her not about Dimitri exactly—except to mention that he was staying on, but about Martha, whom she had so sorely neglected. Martha now refused to go anywhere and hung around her parents' house but she couldn't bear to wash so they made her sleep out of doors in the back where they kept a goat. She had gotten considerably thinner last time Agatha had seen her wandering around. It seemed, she thought that if they were in fact, the holy island, they so proudly claimed to be—then they must love this vagrant-neighbor who was going to wrack and ruin. Not that she could be helped in any real way—but to entice her to wash herself and plump herself up! It was not the picture of their ideal to have her so gaunt and wretched in a place where the vines were heavy with purple grapes and the goats yielded abundant milk. Of course, Martha's family made a habit, a lifestyle of wretchedness. Matrona who walked now with her hand on one aching hip and her face set as if she had to endure beatings in an old flowered skirt where the mending showed. Oh—if only Dimitri could introduce some little improvements so Matrona wouldn't drag herself around so much; having a falling down house made it seem as if life were impossible; she envisioned Dimitri repairing the roof that leaked, and the walls on that house that tilted crazily.

Agatha went meaning to mention her son only in passing, but ended up in an argument with Barbara about him. Barbara was a stiff-faced woman who had little tolerance or tenderness for viewpoints other than her own. When in the company of other wives or widows, she always looked to remember, if she could, their marriages compared to her own, for this inevitably flattered her vanity. Her bartering point when she had been husband-seeking had been what they called on the island her purple hair. From her teenage years into her thirties, she had been famous for it. It was a lustrous, thick mass of dark hair that had a mysterious way of seeming purple in the evening light. In those days she smiled and sang a little walking home or through the forest. She developed a grand manner, conscious of this great mysterious beauty that she possessed piled up in thick coils on top of her head. Now that amazing asset, her dark 'purple' hair looked damp and wilted. Now she was always black haired with grey clumsily streaking it here and there and the evening light didn't reflect in that same wonderful sheen that had made her such a catch. At the same time that she had lost the beautiful point about her, she turned from a little faint but still perceptible joy in mind that thrust her into marriage with one of the best men on the island, to heart-felt disgust at the world. But she kept the grand manner. She was still a lady of the village. Agatha was a creature of rejection; look at her, she thought, not in the sense of the material presence at her window, but in a deeper, more holistic sense, her worth as a woman:-- Alex had come 'round almost for pity—nothing but a decent figure in those days. Now she was rearing herself up, parading with her fancy son.

As far as the hotel was concerned, Barbara secretly thought that it was a little exciting, but she told herself that Dimitri would let them all down, sooner or later. He is not to be trusted, she said, primly. A bit of a loafer, and opportunist, he always was. He will turn us down for the next offer and leave us dangling—you wait and see: a better island, more money to be made. And this film director for some reason won't create a film on our island and moves to the next one down. For it is not about our island for Dimitri any more than it is for the rich folks. It is about money, film—the picture, in short.

Barbara had her head wrapped in a white turban and she was red in the face. She was dicing tomatoes and garlic for a fish sauce to be eaten at dinner, when Agatha came in.

You think, she announced, that Dimitri is some kind of hero. I am sure every mother thinks that of her sons. But you, you imagine it in such a grand sense. You imagine that he has come home to help us, and solve our problems. In reality it is all as my husband told me—a husband that she never failed to point out, was a good, solid catch (unlike Alex had been, although she didn't say it)—exploitation is what this business is—a kind of cunning trickery deep down. Don't get me wrong. I accept the hotel. But I will be glad when Dimitri leaves. Yes, glad. He has no real feeling for this island. I am sorry for you. Everything in your life went off track. But you have to wake up to the real situation; you can't always see things as if in a dream. Don't you see how Dimitri pretends—gives us long lectures, walks alongside us whispering in our ears…

But that is not true. He stated everything in a very straightforward way. You said yourself that you liked the idea of a hotel. You were all for the changes he proposes.

I myself can engage in a bit of trickery. Barbara put the tomatoes and garlic in a frying pan with oil, turned down the gas, and wiped her hands on her apron, stared at the wall a moment, and then slowly turned her face to her neighbor and frowned.

You are being foolish, said Agatha, tilting up her head for dignity and looking at Barbara defiantly; she found herself pushed into the position of defending Dimitri's project of improvement, constantly, even though in her heart of hearts she knew that the villagers were only somewhat enthused. But where was inspiration? Where was youngness of spirit?

You know perfectly well that we are backward, burst out Agatha in frustration, talking 'the language' that she knew had nothing to do with them. This is an age of modernity with machines that talk to one another in the sky and we have our tiny old refrigerators, our light bulbs, our pull-chain toilets. It is a matter of seeing the truth, Barbara, she said, finally, lapsing into a slipshod 'translation'. What do we know when all that we have, our entire world, is a memory out there and a silly memory. There is room for the great old days of ladies and princes like in children's fairy tales, but there is no accommodation in men's hearts for something as ugly as an old, bad refrigerator and when it is a hundred years old, even a thousand years old and discovered in the sand, it will be nothing but an eyesore from primitive civilization just as it is today. You see, we have accepted a little bit of modernity, the old discredited type with our old and odd appliances, but because you imagine that it is somehow closer to holiness not to, you won't go forward modernizing. You imagine that the delicate things of the past, the lace making, the embroidering can rule because the refrigerators are not too big. But in reality, we can't help but go forward modernizing. There is no room in the world for a slow, dull amble along. Imagine if we treated fevers the way my grandmother did with suction glasses and burning matches? Now we could invent that we had adhered to a holy age of grace and beauty. But there –in reality, we want aspirin--we cover all sorts of ailments with aspirin—and in a sloppy way adhere to modern medicine; and in a sloppy way we are modern with our old refrigerators, light bulbs. But they gave aspirin to our old Lero, Thomas' father's cousin, who had diabetes. Well, here I think Anna gave him aspirin, what did she know, poor soul, and he went into a coma and died. We are blunderers and dullards-- going half way on the route to modern civilization and stopping indecisively to look around, prolonged stoppings and waitings—protracted considerings—a little just a little, we say, because we are so old and cannot help ourselves: So the question: would a high powered boat that got someone to the other land in half an hour instead of two be worth the while instead of a little motor? Saving lives vs. tearing to shreds our blessed silences?

And what do we do with our blessed silences but conceive of how to tear to shreds another person's mind and heart. But we step back and protest: a little just a little. Is it within the scope of that little?

Ah, we are alright on the whole, said Barbara; but what does that have to do with Dimitri and the hotel?

It isn't going to be a little brightly painted house, Barbara. It is going to extend through the forest and down to the beach with all the latest equipment and a swimming pool. Communications—what do you think he means? A helicopter pad maybe, high- speed boats, Internet access—you know, on those computers. Just think—for a toothache you will be able to jet speed across these waters to the hospital on the other land.

People will arrive, my son said, and do business with a film productions company in California. Here, here! They have already done such things—even in the jungle.

But here is not the jungle, said Barbara obstinately. Here we evaluate people for their hearts. We do not seek them out among the animals. As far as the refrigerator goes—mine works well and I am grateful to God for it. I don't need a refrigerator that can communicate with other refrigerators through a machine in the sky. I, for one, need just so much and no more.

Agatha threw up her hands in dismay and went off to Leo's. Here she found the man dipping a teaspoon into the honey and sucking on it. He was sulking, reading the newspaper and sucking alternately.

I thought you had forgotten me, he said. In any case, you will forget me now that your glorious son is home from his wanderings.

He is kind and good, said Agatha, simply.

Another holy man, I suppose, said Leo, only half sarcastically. And therefore you would rather marry him than me. But although he is holy, marriage with him would make him unholy in the extreme, and therefore you are stuck again with me—unholy but not that unholy and where there is relative joy and goodness in life one takes it.

Dimitri is more done with religion than you are, Agatha said a little gloomily. It has long been my fear and I have to confess my curiosity. I think he believes in the spirit of man as man, she said.

Something spiritual, said Leo, thoughtfully. No one quite resolves it all in flesh as I do. I thought that was beauty.

Agatha smiled softly at him. You are not such an old rogue in the end, she said. A blunderer more like—but we are all that. But you would not really marry me?

There is no saying would not. It is more a question of could. Could I lift my head up again as a respectable man when I have had so much fun being disgraceful? Now I walk down the path along the beach by the main road in my sandals and breeches and

I hear the lads saying—that is what I want to be—a seducer of married women like Leo. And even though I give them a stern look, they go away like the young—gaily, light-stepping down the road. Ah, they haven't a clue of the suffering, of the toll of philandering, the superficiality of cruelty and deceit. It was like being in a cage. And although many a pious woman thought I laughed at women, it was really that I was being horribly mocked. I—attached to the end of the devil's tail, swinging with every flick of it. And then you come along and with such perfect fingers extricate me; it is as if you have magnets on your fingertips that pull me along out of the trap…But as you see, I can't stop talking with guile.

And I wonder—are you really…? Or are you not. And if you are not—why then, you are really—what makes it so exciting.

What is that?

A liar and seducer.

So, said Leo, rubbing his finger along the edge of the table, you would take the devil by the horns?

Quite a foolish, old devil—a seeker of tenderness, a sad, faded sensualist.

There is no getting around you, said Leo with admiration. You have intellect.

I went wrong in the eyes of the island. I cursed myself. And though I never sent my son away—I must have bred him wrong; not only not to fishing, and marriage, but not to contentment; I suffer now for it, having lost my peace.

Is Dimitri going away again?

Yes, he intends to—that is, eventually. He has agreed to prolong his stay for my sake.

An admirable man, you know. I thought passionate once. Perhaps the world, which he wanted with all blood and brains got in the way, you know. Gave him the cold shoulder, offered him money—repayment—not love.

But Mr. Cours said that Dimitri's plan for the resort hotel here would be used; Dimitri at last got to renew his home island—to reform it.

Perhaps it was Paris that he wished to renew. One wearies a little of the wrong sort of reward.

Agatha looked at Leo with a new kind of interest. In a little less than a year, feeding on Agatha's cooking, he had grown even more robust, his face rounder; he had little features, fine, small eyes, a delicate nose, little rose bud lips—a face that would have looked pretty on a young girl but was rather comical on an old man. A wisp of soft gray hair rose straight up into the air from the top of his head like the root on top of an onion. She had kissed him a few times on the cheek and it was soft and humid. He seemed always to be sweating, although he did nothing but sit and the weather was cool. Agatha had become intimate in a very unromantic way as helpful women often do with slightly immature older men. She had seen all the stains on his laundry, washed the pee stains on his underwear, the sweat stains on his shirts. She knew his dirty clothing well. From knowing his excrement, feeding him, and from being the only person in the village he looked forward to seeing—in fact, the only one of all, including his son-- to whom he pulled back the heavy iron bolt on his front door after peering through the key hole to see for certain it was she, Agatha had simply ceased to be afraid of him. If he had told her he was a killer, she would have told him to hush—that that kind of talk brought too much stress to the brain and heart. Although, their relations had never gone beyond the kiss and the peripheral caress, Agatha felt she could have touched any part of Leo's anatomy with the knowing of a mother and the exquisite exactness of a surgeon. Her attraction for him was a little of both—maternal tenderness and an almost medical curiosity as to whether or not the old notorious flesh still burned, still could burn with desire.

There was a lot of laughter between them. And Leo felt himself strangely reconciled to Woman—as a good friend, and for the hilarity of it. For sex was no longer an action drama in which there had to be war, a tragic, grisly duel. Now it was coming round again as a comedy. And Leo was coming home to his own house where he had been waiting, a foreigner, for years.

In any case, Leo understood things in mind and heart. He was straightforward and wise. It was as if he had himself been in the world—but it was all an imaginative thing. He had grown up here, a dusty, flabby, weak boy, Agatha remembered, with a mother weaving in and out of bouts with apricot brandy, and then piety, a father such a faded man, gray before his time, seldom speaking, a slow, slow mover. Now and then an outburst escaped him—scorn and invectives against the island, the inefficiency of the Church: there were young people of twenty who didn't know the Lord's Prayer. What was the priest thinking of—all that muttering in his beard didn't help! But then Leo's father would relapse into silence slowly walking away. In what seemed like the blink of an eye, he went from an erect posture to a stooped one with a cane. And then as suddenly, he died. And Leo emerged with his mother, now a young man of twenty, somewhat fat, obviously weak, staring often into space. He had somehow managed to crawl into the beds of two girls—sex as an experiment. It was his main achievement, of which he boasted in a nebulous way. His mother still in an alcoholic haze, encouraged him to marry—she was alcoholic-sweet and pious, arguing that Christ came for the sinner—which he was planning not to do when Magda moved through the fray—six or seven young animal men—and picked him, pulling him along by the arm. He was terrified and relieved; not knowing what he was saying, he agreed to marry. His after-the-wedding infatuation with his wife had charmed and slightly angered everybody—acting in broad daylight in their new home as if it were a hideaway in the forest but that too was an island tradition from sometime around the time of Christ –the two eloping lovers. And he had emerged, after her death, first the Casanova of the island, immoral, laughing at the irate islanders, the sometimes doting father of the infant Max, a both radiant and reclusive child, then the newspaper reader, now the man of worldly wisdom, the pet of Agatha, the scorn of the villagers. How it had all happened was something of a mystery. He said in order to flout the villagers that everything good was the result of love: Hers and hers and hers etc. and now the final?—hers! as it had always been.

Agatha picked up the plates, for they had cooked and eaten lunch in the midst of this conversation, and began scrubbing the olive oil residue off them with a sponge under hot water; she said and it is my delight—there will be children, holy people on the island.

Leo moved over to her and put his hand on her hip—you are beginning to sound more and more like you have imbibed my philosophy. I thought you were a student. Soon we will have to be, not just Socrates and neophyte but between the sheets—an old man and his post-virgin knowing and known.

But there is still one point! Said Agatha, putting down the dish that she was scrubbing and picking up a glass—do you think the island will change profoundly with this hotel, the new building that my son is preparing?

Ah no; there will be a few rich people, some money in our folks' hands—but the whole plan will be to keep the place backward so that the rich film makers with their lovers can enjoy the forest, the mountain and the sea. What would be the value of a spoiled Eden? Why do you think men like virgins? And why do you think the Virgin Mary in our religion is called ever-virgin? For in her womb lay Eden. In the womb of a virgin, pregnant but still virgin—beautiful, mysterious to men, bringing forth even God—the before the sex act—pristine, sacred, and the subject of any number of sex dreams—should men dare. No one dared spoil that, he put his hands on his hips and bowed at her.

But we are not quite that inviolate, Agatha said. We keep to ourselves, it is true and we have that little vanity—but people have come, workers to lay cables, plasterers, electricians from the next island, tradesmen with fabrics for our sewing and embroidery, with lines and nets for our fishing.

We have been penetrated insignificantly by the lesser part of civilization—and you see we have our lamps and our refrigerators, electric fans.

Not quite a love affair. But there will be—even if a little forced.

You are saying that it is inevitable?

People believe in the desecration in the end—they think this is the way things must be.

And we have had no babies for ten years, said Agatha—so maybe, out of despair, thinking that young men will come....

What has it been so far?

Oh, everybody acts excited. We are to have a helicopter arrive if all goes well—that is the latest news; it will carry the architect, planner, a forester, and engineer. I have worn my best dress in the streets, but I feel handled.

Oh, that will pass. And a new restaurant, and a bar where they play music will give you some chance for joy. You see you can have a major shift, a new creation here, a different thing entirely from the work of the forefathers and still have your tastes accommodated. If it is a question of taste…but here Leo stopped and looked at her with an upturned face under half closed eyes.

I've never quite had my tastes accommodated, said Agatha, smiling at him, a little rising excitement for she knew not quite what audible in her voice.

It's all puff and play, said Leo waggling his head at her. You will see; whether they do it with steel or wood or stone, electric fans or automobiles; some people think there is desperate need—they turn to the gun, the bomb, some kind of law. But now we think we've fulfilled this desperate need with a single contract—and we will have footmen, swimming pools, helicopters; men and women arriving all gaudy and photogenic, the writers and cameramen with their machines. Soon someone will speak of a spiritual path. But I will bounce soft as a lady's powder puff between your delightful waist and ankle in my other self, which is I think actually no more than a powder puff, given over to beautiful perfumes and puffs. All delight is my other self.

And what am I?

My other's other, lady-self, fantastic fellow joy-seeker, near mistress and so love forever.

Agatha lingered on with Leo, washing dishes, windows, dusting tables—working up a sweat and he continued talking, what she called his half babble, watching her with one eye on the newspaper and one on her hips. When she had put his house in order, she came over to him and curled an arm around his neck, affectionately, and seated herself on his lap.

Why do you come? Asked Leo, in a low, half whisper, kissing her neck.

You have no one, replied Agatha. You'd live in a trash heap among mice, excrement and flies if it weren't for me.

You think I am so helpless?

Not in certain matters—in what you call puff and play. Why weren't you with us at the contract signing? Your vote is as good as any.

I was there, in hiding. And I don't remember any vote. There was just a unanimous ah!—something the villagers rather couldn't help—I've known many a lady in that same position.

Agatha stayed on until evening, leaving tomatoes, onions, shellfish and crumbled goat cheese for Leo who was cooking up a storm and would save some for her lunch tomorrow.

Simon—wise, foolish, prophetic, babbling Simon --for whom all the world was a wheel of fire, said that they were making their virgin flight to the sun with this Mr. Cours and his luxury hotel. What did it matter if they were to come tumbling down when the wax melted on those foolishly made wings? Now was the time to rejoice! He was out in the streets dancing, a white handkerchief in his raised right hand. For they would be a place inevitably a place of champagne and beef steak; the swimmers would be amongst the idlers, loafers and lovers, the executives and the narrow waisted, long legged blonde girls, and they would dive down into depths dark and sweet, body disappearing in the fold of the huge mass of water, human organism somewhere in that mass that looked more and more like relentless infinity then surfacing, quickly, the being again alive having had something like a mystical experience. This is what Dimitri went around talking about—a word here or there; God knows how a few words suddenly convey a picture that it seems the villagers had been carrying in the backs of their brains for years.

To many of the villagers as they congregated at Simon's, it was a new way of looking at the old island. There was no question about it; the door had been opened a crack on the vision of this sun-voyage. The village had come out of doors at lunch to stare at one or two or maybe more each year—business men of a certain age, known by their paunches and frizzy hair, or bald heads with the skinny women-girls, looking like little wreathing vines of flowers, coiled around them. Imagine—these would come! At first, the answer had been no. Absolutely no. They had their own women. But the non fertile years had crept up into their imaginations. The villagers had seen themselves old, with hanging lower lips, red-rimmed eyes, skeletal looks and thought that second life would come in the end… this was after all inner nature, the first and last desire.

Dimitri was not looked on with favor. But he had come laden with imaginary gifts that were soon to be real. Electricity back full force so that Holy Island would look like a string of brilliant pearls in the night from the bosom of the sea instead of dim with one light on the monastery up on the cliff, high powered boats, yachts, motorcycles, film makers.

The priest had come and was sitting smiling looking frail as a moth, and like a thing of winter as if a little cloud was about to come out of his lips. But he said in his usual slightly annoying nasal voice—so the world has touched base. Modernization. Things working efficiently and properly, and decently. A superior level of existence. At first, running water, then the refrigerator, now film making. Brilliant, brilliant. I genuinely applaud it.

But what are we to do? Asked Max who was standing by him. It will destroy…

What will it destroy? No, it will simply not answer all the original questions; it will silence them. And some will fall asleep over the original questions. That is the way of science and technology. To offer distracting evidence, beautiful theories that make up a brilliant puzzle, but still do not answer the original questions.

Which original questions?

Often not articulated; people live and die them, love them. Most and best expressed in a little child's incessant why? I think these questions are the most meaningful. Nevertheless, I applaud modernization and each new gift of brilliant minds in science and technology. I applaud refrigerators, washing machines—he kissed his fingers with enthusiasm, and now motorcycles, jet boats, helicopters. If it weren't for this blasted three feet of rock in the middle of the sea, if it were six, eight, five thousand feet, we'd have had limousines for the rich people.

Limousines remind me of millionaires rolling somewhere in the night, pressing business, a meeting with a Mafioso. They are the new version of the old carriages of kings only lacking in the aesthetics—all that gold and horses. Now, I have a question for you, Max, said the priest in a lethargic tone: Which do you think our God will adopt as a vehicle of triumphant return?

Max smiled a little despite himself. I don't know.

Obviously, he will walk, barefoot with the wounds fresh. People still don't know what come again in glory means for Christ.

Sh, sh! The whispered command went around the room. Dimitri had entered and taken his seat at the head of the table. Barbara and Katrina suddenly sat up erect from slouched positions in little plastic chairs. Everyone leaned forward looking at Dimitri. Paul looked at him from one side of his face and a frown of disapproval. Peter imitated Paul from the other side of his face. But it was clear that everyone had forgotten for a moment the village-wide dismissal of Dimitri as an errant son, a vagabond gypsy-blooded boy bound to come to no good. They were mostly spellbound now because they were out of their depth. He had come to them with depths and they had been unable to find footing, and he also had handled them neatly so that they would not drown. A luxury hotel—but not something overpowering: just a getaway lodge, as the rich man had called it—a few people would come, maybe thirty, maybe fifty. Quiet, of course with their cameras, maybe one day a film crew. It was almost as if he said to them—if you are good! Faces—maybe Katrina's, one of Barbara's sons would be in the pictures, and there would be the old white washed church in the leaves on the hill, the blue sea, the forest with the millions of butterflies in summer and a woman in a white dress in a pair of those beautiful sandals, slender, leather thongs with gold sewn into them walking along by their cave, here a little catch in the breath, where there fresh water came from—and meeting, a dusty, shadowy man, talk, the kiss! And it would be their soil, their water, their sun blossoming on film. A brilliant movie. A flower in the world as live and mysterious as an orchid. And one could just hear the mothers saying—you see, it is a real place, across the sea, far away for people to say—to their children: Who would sing without attaching the these Hollywood words to the picture of blue sea and millions of butterflies, a far away place for children?

Their brains filled with such ideas, the villagers had accepted Dimitri back into their midst. He had eaten richly and drunk deep with them. He had danced a few steps. And he had encountered Paul who asked him—are you going to make us rich? In a very serious tone.

I have no intention….began Dimitri, hesitantly…

Then you intend to deceive, said Paul, quickly strident. Dimitri looked at him, open-mouthed with the kindness just turning to amazement. Paul strode off.

But now Dimitri had the floor. He had a list of houses, which Connie had offered to buy at large sums; this included the grocery store since it was in the piazza, a prime location for the hotel. The other houses were in the middle of the village spreading part way up the hill to the church in back. Dimitri read aloud the names of the owners of the houses and store and the price offered. There was consternation. Peter's house was included, and Barbara's but not Agatha's or Foti's. Cleo's house and Nisos' but not Timos' and a few other houses of anonymous figures in among the crowd. There were stirrings in the crowd; people shifted feet. Paul sensed with a certain definite relief rising indignation.

He rose to his feet and addressed Dimitri without a trace of emotion. First things, first: We must talk to the rich man about the selection of houses. And about the people who would be selling. It is true that they would be getting this good money but on the other hand, they would have to move away. They would have to build new homes, maybe off the island. They have wives and children, pensions to consider. They can only work at fishing.

They merely have to move to the other island, said Dimitri, or to build another house here.

But the island belongs to all of us, said Foti, pensively. It seems unfair that seven or eight families should suddenly get this deal and all the rest…because in a sense we'd all be selling.

That is not the point at all, snapped Barbara. What I want to know is why they think they can buy us? I have lived in my home for forty-five years. It is all of what I am in this world. It is my childhood, marriage and my motherhood. And they think they can simply give me a cheque?

But the terms, my dear, said Stavros, are entirely reasonable. Just think—we'd go to Paris, Milan!

That is the way the world is, said Barbara; they offer you money for something you put your soul into. And then after, the answer is don't complain. You got an amount of money! And my house? What would happen to it?

But if we had that money… said Stavros.

I don't want it. I want life, said Barbara, unreasonably. I think if they were to give me money, it would have to be three times that much to show them I was not to be fooled.

I think, said Stavros, smiling slightly that my wife in her confused way is saying that living in the modern world would be pointless without a lot of money.

Tell them, said Barbara, her nostrils slightly dilated with rage, that if they are offering us a million, we are asking for three. It is reasonable, considering that in Paris we'd be fish out of water. You'd have to look around for proper employment, she said, turning to Stavros, and undoubtedly you'd be treated in a very inferior way at first and have to by dint of hard labor and perseverance work your way into the esteem of some company or other to finally bring home good pay.

But I can't do something like that. I am a fisherman, said Stavros, suddenly taking the opposite tack to his argument of Paris, Milan.

The other women eventually caught the drift of Barbara's argument, unreasonable and clouded with fantasy as it was as it came floating around the village and they too argued with their husbands nights. Even many of the women who were not to receive anything for their houses, still argued, shrilly and angrily with their husbands. And the husbands countered them first one way and then another. They stated one thing positively but then all got to contradicting themselves without even realizing it and the arguments became almost incoherent. But the upshot of it was that they joined together in asking for more money.

These creatures, said Anna, sweating in her sick bed, to Kali's cousin are so bedazzled by the idea of having their houses bought by men who promise the island a helicopter pad and swimming pool, a fully equipped hotel and private yachts arriving in our little harbor that they imagine they can just ask, like children asking for a cookie, and receive from them. She had heard everything from Agatha at two in the morning after conferring with Simon. Agatha who had come over to lie down near Anna, kiss her hands, and tell her everything undisguised.

I say to them, said Anna to her, accept the terms if you are going to, if not—then know that the developer will eventually come in, buy somewhere else, and you'll lose all chance you have of cashing in on that rich hotel.

Simon sat back after the flood of people had left his villa that one night when the houses that were to be bought had been named and the numbers the actual amounts of money offered read aloud. They will not sell and he will not buy, he said to Agatha, who was standing near with her arm around his neck.

Dimitri says it is a process, said Agatha. Negotiation, he calls it. The villagers only think that the rich man has prized Holy Island highly, as a kind of priceless treasure, after all isn't it here that a light brighter and softer than the sun blazed in Mother Dora's footsteps? But also in their heart of hearts they are thinking: what if that really is true? Holy Island has lost it, lost its holiness, but we have to go on living. All it is is a handful of dirt in the middle of the ocean. Some would say best move on, then—Paris, London! But they would need more money. But they think—ah, we won't tell the rich man that Holy Island has lost its holiness. And so we will jack up the price and jack up the price. Who can after all buy us out of holiness? Whatever price offered—it is invariably too low. And then they think in a kind of panic—what if they find it again? What if in the middle of the jet boats zipping over the quiet waters, the helicopters coming in, the giant TVs, the computers, a new saint walks in the forest, or pops up in the monastery, and someone witnesses the light, inevitably without a camera…and then they in Paris or London, fish out of water, running out of money, cursing their luck, think were not there now and curse it all we didn't even ask enough. Those others think they can sit and sit, fish and fish with that unfathomable value under them. So they think—we will ask a little more and then at least we'll have the money. With the money we can do anything—like Anna did—live it up in the glittering nights in Paris--come back as often as we like. Be buried here in our waters. We could even surprise them all by buying a little down the road and staying, pension secure. Of course, we'll ask for more. What do they think we are? Fools? To stay where a bunch of old people lose their teeth over apricot candy! Where people turn ninety without ever driving a car. Where the children, when we had children, used to creep to the church to school and the priest used to make them recite a little poetry, count, add! Where everything is so slow that it has almost stopped. Rockets go into space these days. Scientists study the sun. What are we? Donkeys? Eating, sleeping, fishing. And yet one imagines that the holy saints are frightened away from rockets, as well as private yachts and jet boats like certain fish or birds.

Simon smiled, nodded and laughed his old man's guffaw. Every tool is given to these people, he said; life is not so much to be constructed as to be taken apart. They won't find it with the rich man.

Nor are they really sitting on the pearl of great price, said Agatha, a little wearily.

Ah, said Simon. If we all just waited, meekly, working, tending the sick, feeding the poor, loving the despised…chances are…

Chances are what? Asked Agatha.

God would look with favor in on us—like the sun on a winter day.

And dance? My dancing? What would happen to it?

That is work. For with work, God brings bread.

What is bread?

One chews it and it fills the mouth with fragrance, the heart with relief, the mind with gladness.

I have never left off dancing, not since you first instructed me. I dance until I ache and my muscles announce themselves, sore and weary. I have yet to eat this bread. It's just toil and more toil.

It is an expensive bread, earned with sweat said Simon, dreamily. Perhaps you still have not near enough drops of sweat…

After ten years!

What can you do? What can you say for yourself?

Very little. Some other creature though is doing the grocery shopping, the entertaining of Dimitri and his friend, even the tending of Anna and Leo who are helpless for different reasons—one sick, the other fallen as usual into a funk; I, little i, am dancing. The rest, the big gloomy I—that is the one here and there, the other species.

Ah, so there is some music in you. You are one of the few.

Do you ever notice, said Agatha, catching on to Simon's dream, how it wells up from behind, emerges from down deep in the flesh?

And the bones, which you have broken—rejoice, said Simon—made whole as they are…the bones, which you have broken…

A woman, man, anybody was made to dance—even breathing on their bed alone.

Anna that was mother to this Anna, said Simon, was the kind of person that could turn around in her kitchen with a dish dripping in her hand and make you think of the goddess of love rising out of the sea, taking her few, dainty, diminutive steps naked like a pearl. I think very few ever noticed her when she danced. She kept the rhythm for all the rest, guided them, glided noiselessly and lightly in the line, effaced herself all except her little feet and invisible pearl nakedness.

And I have broken off from that.

You had a vision. This is a dying island. No one wants to acknowledge it; they don't want to be the ones dead. If someone has a vision, the very atoms of dust rise up and shout—out of the corner, on with it, out with it, show us the path.

And in the world?

It must be the same thing. Why would you not think it? But there, you know, there is a certain amount of money making involved, more than here. A certain mind that turns away from—all this seeing.

This kind of dancing. They must dance like steel rather than sunlight and sea.

Anna always said it was the bigness that was offensive in the world, bigness that had 'lost contact,' she said, mused Simon, smiling and looking down; whereas her mother, old Anna with the jet black hair, dyed with the old type of dye they used then—an impossible black, so that no one ever knew her age—though a big woman herself, breast and midriff like a four post bed, a man once joked, she was very little, tiny-toed when she danced—little as the breath taken in when you're concentrating. Calm, deep, barely noticeable as the ordinary Anna. The very breath of the music—even when she turned.

And I wanted hugeness, cosmos after cosmos balancing on my knee caps.

You had a vision.

Yes, you said that. Dimitri says that this Mr. Cours, the rich man, who barely says a word, goes around looking and looking—he has a vision.

This island must die, said Simon. It must become a beautiful view off a yacht; a postcard with an old, toothless, smiling face, or a picture of the little fresco in our white washed church. It must become tourist's haven. And our little life, embalmed now…the old infinity eaten away by a definitive speedboat.

It is my fault, said Agatha, pressing her face against Simon's. I should have known, should have left. But I was young, you know—just sixteen when I wanted—just wanted to dance a little higher, brighter, wider, as if the whole cosmos was really mine. I came to be crushed. Then the years married and raising children. Then hell itself, I think, then love of my son at last and dreadful and good—and then the wonderful man and woman covered with hair in my dream. Adam, Christ returned, in the midst of the shocked faces; and the hairy woman tying purple ribbons in the massive hair on her head and emerging kicking her leg high. And you told me—as you know… and I went out almost without thinking to work at it at it through dawn 'til late morning. I went through it all with a dream behind my eyes. It is still there—otherwise I couldn't. How often I have said to Jesus—Master, the dream is behind my eyes. I couldn't do anything about it.

Come now, Simon sprang up from his chair, snapping his fingers, and turning his waist. Agatha lifted her hand and barely touched his, flung back her head a moment, then lifted it again as if she had a crown on it. Swept up her leg high, opened her arms. Then brought it down and pirouetted, her leg cocked to the side, her knee bent and her foot behind her. Then she crouched down and crept across the floor on her toes, at the far end of the floor she jumped and spun around landed on her toes and crept back. Then she snapped her fingers jumped high into the air and split, landed, stomped and pirouetted across the room, stomping at the end, and raising her hands and clapping.

Ah said Simon who had stopped dancing and was watching, I could live in your dancing. It is all muscle, and a tiny bit of fat. Delicious and fragrant! Cooking that leaves a steam of the most beautiful odor in the room!

Agatha looked at him, the sweat running down her face. What am I dancing for? My son has come back and with him a man who is going to buy us, change us, make of us—what do you call it? A commodity. Take our soul.

We are not to be fooled. A rich man of the world has stepped into our lives. He has lived, of course, at Agatha's, of course a friend of that Dimitri; he thinks that he will give us what amounts to him as pocket change in exchange for our lived-in houses, for generations lived in! And here our mothers made their lemon curd and lace. So much for these stones and white wash, he thinks; so much to wave in the face of a grizzled woman like Cleo with a number of black whiskers on her chin; so much to pluck away the ground beneath her feet and send her-- with her one white satiny purse and her hair net, her black dress that she has worn for the past fifteen years since her husband died-- away with a suitcase and a man carrying boxes on a boat. She has three children all on the other island but she insists she won't disturb them. No, with the million she would go to Paris, calmly, flying in the serene azure sky in a glistening silver airplane and ask them when she landed there in the midst of what they call traffic flashes of steel –red, blue, black in streets that go like whistles into long stretches of space like we see on TV—where might I buy perfume? She has a mind of her own. So much to bedazzle that mind. But we ask a little more. We demand a little more. Just a little. We are not greedy nor unreasonable. Where it was a million, a million five. Even Barbara hot under the collar as she is, came suddenly to a million five, nodding at us as if it was right. Yes, it is right, although it could have been three million.

We don't see it as a transaction—an exchange. We are not the world. To us, this land is holy. This money is an offering—righteous and beneficial. Even if lately, yes, it is true, we have fallen under a cloud, a shadow. The light of holiness has been obscured. We are getting old. Children have not been born to us in fifteen years. We wonder and shudder our worn out wonders and shudders. Odd things have occurred for the past fifty years. For half a century we have felt ourselves fatigued in a way that our foremothers never knew even when they were ninety. But the mind plays tricks on us. Perhaps this is still normal fatigue from the heat of the sun; nothing serious. Yet there also seem to be signs: our former priest died of an overdose of illicit drugs—what happened? A robust priest, face like a lion; died like a rat. We have crept around asking—what was it? And there is no answer, none; but some of us think that the presence of that Muslim bible, the gypsy who owned it…We can't tell. Of course not. What does that Muslim bible change shape and fly through the air to Father Raphael and disprove or prove something to him that makes him despair?

Foti thinks that it was the newspapers that did it. They are full of horrible stories. But the newspapers tell us of the world. And how are we, ignorant and still tainted with sleep from our afternoon naps under the blazing island sun, the white sun of winter—to go into this world? A million might be a lot for a start—but isn't it after all, a start? We need at our age, something more secure; one, two, three steps down the path into old age.

We creep and creep. For many years we find Agatha miserable, bent, and sick in mind. We conclude that it is nothing particular; just loss of holiness. Quite literally, although this we can only whisper, the Holy Spirit was taken from us through her, through the presence of that other book. For then out of the woodwork emerged the unbelievers. Anna, but she is only joking; but then Nico. Even our Stavros has been on the fringes of doubt. Now suddenly Agatha is erect! It is very mysterious— she has on her face glad tidings too. She says she dances. Next, her son returns and with him this offer. But we know better. A gypsy is always a bit of a thief. It is a deceit nothing holy.

For now the world stretches out its hand with its pocket change in exchange for us. It thinks it can—what is the word? Bulldoze away our spirit. For we await, nothing less, yes—Father Isaac has gone up to the monastery on his knees—yes we await the return of God. It is at this crucial moment, when we are poised, heaved ourselves into position—some of us have prayed on our painful knees, and we are just beginning to believe…

If they want us, they will have to pay a little more. We are not asking for anything unreasonable, unsound in the business sense. But we think it makes good sense to spend a little on our people. We have spent so much of ourselves, waiting. An offer of, shall we dare say it—even in the business sense—honor and charity. To line the cloud of old age with a silver lining. Look at how Katrina, poor soul, has to cope. More than that, since nothing in the world can repay us for the loss of our home!— Make the world bringers pay!

Dimitri getting the drift of our discourse was amazed. It is you who are receiving, he said a little sternly—for almost nothing. Mr. Cours has no interest in your little homes that are all badly built into the bargain. He is going to demolish them and build in their place a well-built little hotel with tasteful design. You are behaving shamefully. What on earth do you think is being taken from you? You would only be in communication, would benefit enormously by the world in the form of a few international tourists with good money coming to visit. There would be something called economy. What you have now—your savings stuffed inside your mattresses, sometimes a little profit that allows you to buy a table…But already you are well enough off. Granted. You can eat and drink and send your children to a remote little school on another island if you wish. This would just be a chance to live a little more as you have always dreamed. Most of you have relatives on the other island or elsewhere in the world. Why—go to them with your

newfound wealth.

We listen, yes, we listen. Dimitri speaks like a voice from far away-- from those big cities, like big city music. It drowns out all our thinking, all our careful discernment. It's as if we are worth in fact so much and not more. But we ask: Are we not the proprietors even now of this island? What about our say in the building of the hotel? What about our people, our treasured people, once, maybe even yet, treasured among the angels? Yes they have failed, fallen; perhaps they lie crushed in the dust. Leo despoiled marriage beds. Peter keeps company with a whore. Even Paul once or twice…But can it be true that Christ would forget his children? We should say categorically no to this rich man. We have lived for years, Dimitri can scoff and scorn us, but he knows well—we have lived with our tradition, our one and only hope. And now the world in the shape of one Mr. Cours, who thinks he is tremendously important, to buy us and not only that to pay a fraction for the real thing. For isn't he proposing buying all of us in a very real way? Holy Island as a tourist resort is our Holy Island altered entirely. Perhaps, dare we say it—is Holy Island dead except that the light of the resurrected Christ can never die. And then there is no going back. For this we need to be paid damages. We need to be paid but not so that the world then is at our feet. We don't ask that. Not so that we become kings and queens. Not even so that when we go back to our crosses, we can send a million, no less, to the poor orphanage on the other island. We need to be paid just a little more. We barely can afford to collect a relief fund for our poor monastery on the cliff. Don't the nuns' bones ache with the cold? We wish to buy them woolen sweaters, heavy coats. We need to be paid so that we can repaint our church, and restore the fresco. Don't think we can be just pacified and forgotten. That our ways are not to be taken seriously. We have been after all doers and shapers and movers for Christ.

We want to do several things: One is to build another church dedicated to Mother Dora, who has been canonized. And in this church we want to commemorate the hundreds of saints who have lived and died here. Oh, we will put the money to good use.

Another thing we want to do is to preserve the island butterflies and birds. Have a scientific institute like they have on the other island built, which studies the species, watches for disease or change. Another thing we want to do is to have a fund for the elderly that they might receive proper care. We could continue the list of things we need. But of course we are not asking for very much. Just in addition to the houses bought, a little charity for the island. Why, it is not unreasonable! Are you not planning to build right here in our midst? To join with good will, we imagine, our own community?

You are being so very irksome, said Dimitri. This was a transaction that could have been smooth. Nothing here is going to change and you can't just ask a simple developer to hand over all the money you need for the care of the island.

Our clamor was louder than his conniving talk. All of us were in agreement. We would only, that is, anyone of us, sell if it was going to benefit the whole community. And we needed more money. Not much more money. But certainly a little more money. We remaining would still wait as we do for the coming of God. Of course, we would. Sometimes we have dreamed of being kings and queens rather than poor fishermen. There are kings and queens who are saints just as well as poor folk. Think of King Constantine or Queen Theodora. Well, then money if you like, and changing the character of this land, but we still wait for our island invisible in the midst of it all, in the midst of your jet boats and private yachts.

Finally, we congregated at Simon's house again. It was about three weeks later. Everybody pressed into the house talking at once. It was noisy and despite the cold winds of January outside many people were sweating. Dimitri came in looking tired, but smiling. Mr. Cours was to join us later. We could see the women especially look half disdainfully at him, half flirtatiously. We had high hopes that he would come to see our point of view. He was after all, an islander. Surely he didn't want us to become mere rubble underneath these rich people's feet. Everything that was Holy Island to be sold as a few postcards and sent around the world!

Dimitri suddenly turned to Simon and asked, what is your opinion? Despite all the chatter, everyone heard this question. All heads turned in the direction of Simon, who stood with Agatha in the corner of the room.

We are perfectly comfortable, said Simon, slowly, in a high old man's voice. We don't need more money. We don't even need to sell. What would we do with jet boats? But I suppose a little hotel would do. Let the people of the world come to visit. A little hotel on our terms.

I suppose you want to build it? Asked Dimitri, slightly sarcastically. In a similar manner to these homes round about?

If they would let me build I would build, said Simon. But little. No more than twenty rooms. Bathrooms with hot water tanks. A kitchen serving fried octopus and red snapper, French fried potatoes, tomatoes, goats' cheese, oranges; a place you could get tea and instant coffee, apricot brandy. A place to eat and drink the way we do.

A septic tank. Electric fans.

Old idiot, said Zoe, indignantly. Hot water tanks, septic tanks, electric fans! Why we could have running hot water, heated instantly, a sewer line, and air conditioning. I see you just want to build us another donkey stable.

At this the whole room suddenly was full of heads talking; people began to stand so as to shout louder. Dimitri at last was the only one who continued to sit and he put his head in his hand and sighed.

It's a simple thing, he said in frustration, raising his head, but the voices were louder than he. Then there was a sudden hush as the figure of Mr. Cours was seen in the room as if he materialized out of nothing at Dimitri's side.

They want more money, said Dimitri. All of them? Asked Connie curiously. It is you know such a last ditch honeymoon island. True, the waters and the forest are untouched but that you can find almost anywhere in the Aegean. I was drawn to it by its name—I thought there would be relic upon relic. Ancient texts, footprints, pieces of the true Cross. But here I find just your ordinary old clown upon your ordinary old clown; the kind of person I remember sitting on his front porch with his wife, next door to me—slowly going deaf; I used to think is that what life is about?-- sitting there—when one can be a doer and a maker? Tell them I am not a hand from heaven simply scattering gold in their direction for love. We have painstakingly appraised the properties. They wouldn't get anything more for them on the market. But then, perhaps they can't hear.

Perhaps we want to sell, shouted a voice; it was Cleo who was looking carefully at the rich man talking. She suddenly realized—a feeling like Christmas, that had been made into a great festival by the presence of the rich man, but now it was just out of reach! For they had, of course, offended. But still, they could reclaim it. We could, of course, sell, she said to the others. It is our pride and dignity—what we do with it. The rich man need not know of our lives—our intentions to go to Paris or to stay with our families on the other island. He has left it beautifully—what is the word—impersonally—our choice. There is a kind of justice in these money transactions that belongs neither to us nor to him. It is better than when we take it upon ourselves to make it just, right, and proper. We have had so many troubles, so many problems. The island has changed—right under our feet. The very soil is different. Sell, move on, I say. And she saw herself for a moment bowing reverentially and in despair to a great purse full of money.

Just, proper, shouted Nisos. You know nothing about business. It is by its nature inclined to cheating, to betrayal—the whole point is to deceive you. Only God is just and proper—and He is neither you nor I. I will not sell. To Cleo, her own soul was lost.

If one took that position—to remain as it were doing nothing because it is not quite clear, not quite out of the hazy area tainted by sin and corruption—then one would do nothing, nothing at all. Even sitting at night in the tavern with a glass of wine could be considered... You know Maria always makes us give her a little more over and above what we paid for—she says it is for her pension, and seeing as she has no family...And it is not only that but the decisions that one makes even simple ones—to kiss one's wife, may when you look into it, break it down into its infinite components—animal, intellectual, emotional, imaginative, moral, be filled with sin and injustice, said Stavros.

Oh, oh, said Simon, smiling as if enjoying a hearty flavor in his mouth.

Or, perhaps, thought Cleo, not quite.

How do we not know, finished Stavros, grandly, that this is not a blessing, a sign from God? Yes, even this—an exchange benefiting us financially. That we can go now. We are freed from this curse as we call it. But the old island is dead, as all things must die, you know. We can take the scraps of our material lives and set up comfortably somewhere else. There we can go to church and follow the Christian life.

This is utter defeat, Peter murmured. He was sitting beside Paul who remained during the whole of the rich man's stay, studiously silent.

We need some time to think, said Barbara, in a harsh loud voice. Perhaps for this man, she gestured at Connie, this is all in a day's work. But for us, it represents lifetimes…

Mr. Cours nodded at Dimitri, after he had translated— of course. Well, then we meet again in a few days, announced Dimitri—three days. At this time Thursday. Mr. Cours leaves on Saturday. You have to have your minds made up. He is not going to pander to your indecisiveness, or to your selfishness, he said with strong emphasis.

Selfishness! Katrina, who was standing near where Dimitri was sitting, threw back her head and walked out with a humph. Catherine followed.

Dimitri looked after them with the expression of a child wary that he might be in trouble having tread somehow in all the wrong places. He wanted to extricate himself from his obligation to Connie to stay and discuss the matter of the sale, and the eventual beauties of the island built up if the islanders should comply.

It had taken an age for him to work himself into this web as he saw it now—silver and glittering and perfect as it was, spun by not only Connie, as he had thought at first, but by a host of other Connies that all understood one another, talked the same language, even walked the same walk. And the point was, Connie had once told him, as if reading his thoughts—because he had found himself transparent, helplessly so, to Connie like little children are to their parents—the whole point was to be the spider, not the fly, in business. Step by step you weave the web and devour competition. Yes, there was a certain cold heartedness, but then again there was beauty too and what was it about nature, even in the animal world—cruelty and beauty, they go hand in hand. Connie said to him—even you—you have something of the old island home about you, perhaps you will never shake it—an instinct to tenderness, even innocence. It's as if all this, in the end, somehow, is not the serious thing. The flavor of an ice cream is more serious to you than a transaction worth millions.

Dimitri didn't know how he had come up with this metaphor since he, Dimitri, never went near ice cream. He had thought himself respectably jaded, something of an intellectual, a sneerer at anything not of modern tone, and scorner of sentiment. Business meant money; he had come simply by industry and hard effort, by energy and will power into this position of confidence with his employer; for at first it had been of course only a question of survival but with it had come freedom—material wealth and choices-- then what he would have called 'mind', then the glory of being a cut above others. He had at first not thought of money seriously. He had paid his bills. And, in fact, he was still not earning anything, which put him out of the bracket of economizing on everything he bought in the big cities. But he was, after ten years, slightly past the initial wide eyed, eating of bread and scraps stage, and a little used to his boss' company. He could congratulate himself that he had, what the world called, 'talent' in the area of business.

Connie had told him—if you turn away now, it will all be worth nothing. Going home may make you turn your back on us.

He had protested: But how? Why? You don't know the place. A miserable island with a cliff and two rocks sticking out of the sea—no cars even, no doctors. What do you take me for? May as well think I'd go and live in the bush in Africa. And it's all the more primitive because what with a refrigerator or two, a TV set, and reduced electricity at night, they have the nerve to call it Holy Island. The women and the men are gawkers, pot-bellied, head waggling types who think that their trinket crosses will save them from disasters and invasions. And you think this place will lure me away from Paris, Athens or London?

It's not so much the place. If the place was to be taken alone like a dead body in which you could just itemize everything—hair, eyes, brain, tongue, skin, ribs, liver—and come out with the person. No you know well the island is more than the sum of its parts.

But what you don't know is that the place is dead.

Ailing, old, but not dead. There is something more—a way, a truth. That island is an island on the one hand, but what St. Paul called—a cloud of witnesses on the other.

Dimitri was taken aback. I didn't know you had read the Gospels.

I am an educated man. For a short time, I was an art dealer. I majored in art in the university and of course, with it came the obligatory Christian education.

But I have done everything to remove myself, to reshape myself; I am not a Holy Islander anymore; it is as far away to me as a black hole in space.

And yet, said Connie on one occasion, thoughtfully, not every question has been answered for you in this business. You are a malcontent in the world.

And Dimitri was shocked and looked at his employer from a different perspective, learning that in business, like in love, the rhythm is the key.

You know they believe in blasted miracles still, he said to Connie.

And so? What is a miracle? Something which science has not yet caught up to to explain away intervention by God; a miracle is really just the most beautiful thing—shocking, deliriously perfect—a man come back from the dead.

What are you talking about—ghosts?

No, living. It happens.

Dimitri didn't quite know the next step as it were in this case and so let the matter rest. But he had a vague suspicion that his employer thought him as still tied by many strong threads to his old island home. At first, he was annoyed, irate. He had done so much to change. But gradually he realized that his employer would seek to put this old attachment to good use. It was not at all a handicap; rather Dimitri was to be the leader on a series of island tours to establish getaway hotels amongst the natives. And he was to know them inside and out and to come to them with a certain genuineness and freedom precisely because his home was and ever would be Holy Island, a place set apart from the world answering to the need for peace and seclusion for holiness if not quite of the religious type, of the worldly type—a place to be whole, free, alone—to cultivate one's own world. Dimitri therefore felt himself ready for the job—he wanted a rest a getaway himself; and by the time they set off for his home island, he was anticipating a beautiful retreat, and he had in the back of his mind a vague idea of reunion. For the islanders need not be as he thought them originally—from the perspective of having to escape a mad brother, a bent backed tangle haired mother with misery in her eyes, from the perspective of having to answer back to those who would take away the natural freedoms and settle him down with Katrina and let the years of nothingness and boredom, empty, mindless years imprison him. The islanders could be as carvings and sculptures to a sculptor—the worst, curious, the best, full of intrigue and passion—men and women in a state of being released from this island earth.

But the thing had not flowed smoothly. He had thought to work from the inside out. He had come—back to his mother—and he had settled inasmuch as he could settle, given the time restrictions. Then he had gathered the villagers and told them in his simplest words that there was a golden egg within reach—unavailable to them before. He thought: Was that not also their miracle? Miracle at last of living—that is, of all having full electricity, washing machines, better refrigerators, air conditioning, all the latest inventions, doctors and surgeons at their disposal, good ones, travel, luxuries. To be able to live comfortably, decently, even sweetly—rather than to have husbands arriving home smelling of fish and knowing that one would have to wash out the clothes tediously by hand; or to have the refrigerators break down, the food begin to smell, no air conditioning on those intolerably hot days! Worst of all to be sick, or elderly and infirm and not have the proper care! Wasn't this then their miracle—a better economy for all? The miracles of the Gospels sound good as stories but one knew better than to believe that if you have only six or seven fishes and a few loaves of bread you could feed five thousand people; or than if you have water you can somehow transform it into the best wine.

No one didn't live by God, beautiful as He may be, but by air conditioning on the intolerably hot days, washing machines to get the stains out of clothes, doctors to handle illnesses. Everyone knew that. Everyone accepted that. The villagers were no exception. They wanted their electricity back full power—not an angel of God announcing good news. At least, he knew in his heart that that was what they wanted. And so they had to recognize the fact. He was sent, the messenger—not from God, but from the world of comfortable living, real living, decent living, and the world that looked reality in the face. What provision did God leave us for someone with acute appendicitis? Laying on of hands? No, and so the world, education, the best food and comfort for a would-be surgeon so that his hands don't shake; if the weather is hot, air conditioning so that he is not distracted. Clean clothes from a washing machine-- make no mistake about it—hand washing does not sterilize and disinfect.

This seemed to be only an expendable thing—a hotel far more for useless pleasure than for anything else. But see what it would bring to the island—ease and comfort and that same ease and comfort would go into the education of a surgeon—the funds necessary, the living, all the materials, technology and instruction. And that was only the beginning.

Holy Island as a little enclave where people really awaited the coming of Christ was history. Here one was facing the world of every day. This was the world of men whereas Christ so eloquently explained it is impossible to follow Him. He had asked himself: What other world is there? He had considered Christians on the whole to be hypocrites, wanting both worlds as they always did. Consider even toothpaste, a product of factories where Mammon is set before Christ. But who would go without? Not Timos who had a horror of toothaches. Not Paul who brushed and brushed hoping to achieve a whiter smile, if his could be called a smile. They wanted the world, with utter, absolute wanting, and they depended on it, followed it more and more in their tacit sort of compliance with it. Why not just leave that world of the Gospels on the shelf instead of dragging it constantly into heart and mind. Beautiful as it was-- mythological like the world of the Chinese dragons and immortals.

Dimitri knew and was frustrated with the islanders that they wouldn't just let go somehow. In a sense, they hadn't exactly died away spiritually. They were just on the verge of modernity and they held back out of old prejudice and resentment. There was nothing left of the old self that actually was caught in the net of otherworldly light that Mother Dora had cast. True they had resisted; but they were in a sense spiritually like desperate men whose hands are found clinging to the rigging of a drowned ship when they uncover them as dead skeletons under the sea. Dead to Christ or at least to that old holiness of Holy Island, they yet clung to some half-hearted memory and they clung spasmodically, irrationally, out of an immense will power from the land of the dead.

But there was a little change. Oh, just in his mother. But what a change there! He looked at her standing by the window peering out into the night. If ever there was meaning to the word 'soul' for him, she looked like it. How had she done it? Fighting them off, all of them and getting up at four to dance? What did it mean, exactly? That she had let life be taken from her—that it had flowed away, the mystical river— and that she had somehow diverted it, caught it, brought it around to her in a circle? The image made him smile.

At the end of the meeting, thinking of this, he caught up his mother in his arms and lifted her and kissed her. I am thinking only of you, he said; it doesn't matter to me what happens, he said unexpectedly to himself more than to her.

Of course not, said Agatha, feeling a rose of sweetness in her body and heart. If there were to be a hotel on this island, Dimitri, it would in the end be as Simon said—a little marginal thing. Everything here is little and marginal. What do you expect—heroes and fantasy creatures? Film makers?

You might begin to consider, said Dimitri laughing, that you could accept good plumbing, electricity, washing machines, and air conditioning.

Bah, we get along, said Agatha, as she came down in his arms. It is the tour de force of our people, she said; we have nothing, we pretend nothing—at least the wise ones don't, we are nothing and what we do under God is simply to offer littleness of stature, and simplicity. The one or two machines that make you realize you don't have enough—the refrigerator that slows down on hot days when you need things to be cold; the electric fan that barely circulates the air.

You! You! Dancing every morning. I have seen you with your leg lifted high, like the wing of a bird.

It all came from wanting to leap high. Body in the blue hollow above. Then it became new body after years of effort. And all that came out of living the crushed life, you know. Crushed until, she looked at him; there was a sweetness to it.

Everyone had left Simon's house except Dimitri, Agatha and Simon. Simon was clearing away the chairs. Dimitri went to his mother by the window and watched the old artist in the reflection in the pane of glass; he had a little smile on his face as if he knew something, or had realized something suddenly. Dimitri suddenly felt that the old island was rich and beautiful, unfathomably dark. The candles that Simon kept burning in trays on the side tables by the walls and in some cases under windows because of the dim electric lights—made it somehow limitless.

His mother noticed him looking at the candles.

Candles, said Agatha—yes, we use them like they did in the old days. They were for the 'wedding feast'. We believed in this rich man down under, you see. We believe in all rich men. But he was to be our bridegroom—even if he didn't marry one night or the other. And you were to be his friend. Or I suppose, the other way around. But now little things have gotten in the way. The villagers come along like the elderly do when they are most insidious and ask as if helplessly for that little more of sugar. They always think that a young man, young men, must oblige. They hardly realize that five hundred thousand can't be just handed 'round on top of the one million that they believe this Connie owes them. No, they think the extra is after all in his pocket where the other candy came from. Nothing to him. These candles were supposed to remind them of that festive joy we are about to receive as an island, and we thought it was to be our eternity, a wonderful room of treasure, but instead—ah, they are standing on the road going nowhere, except perhaps that it leads to Christ, a cross, painfully irate person, and they whisper at Connie 'sugar?' It is like they deserve pity before they arrive: as if a wedding is about a sugar coated man not God. These candles were put out on purpose. Simon meant to remind them how to behave: The wedding feast! But they so absorbed in their greedy desires, their arguments, and their pettiness thought only of how to get some of the sweet.

I've heard it said that the damned think only of heaven and not of the Cross.

Curious, said Agatha, her eyes staring a little past him. Anna is forever thinking that she never loved. I, of beating my way through the wilderness of despair.

I see the marks of sweat on your brow, Mother, said Dimitri with a frown and stooped and kissed, one, two, three, along the line where her hair met her forehead. Then he gathered her into his arms and pressed her head against his bosom. To me, it is you, Dimitri, said Agatha—you, the bridegroom.

I? Worn out old shoe that I am, Mother?

She drew her hand up his left leg, over his groin, up his belly to his breast.

Dimitri looked at her as she did so without flinching; then tenderly took her hand and kissed the palm.

You, she said kissing him on the lips. All my beauty.

Simon watched in the shadows. Ah, ah, ah, he said softly. A woman is always reborn with her children—half with the female, all the way with the male. And what does one do, if one is half in the womb again? And if one is all the way out?

Croaking against women are you, Simon?

He looked up with glittering eyes. Mother, new and born for once.

You old mad hatter, said Dimitri; I remember you. No, but he's right, Mother—psychologically, philosophically speaking—men and women are reborn through their children; he looked at the window, musing. Then he woke from his trance, his arms still around his mother and looked down at her and kissed her again, three, four, five times softly on the lips: come Mother, shall we go back to Jason?

How to describe Dimitri? Agatha was lying alone in her double bed; she couldn't get to sleep. It was well past midnight now. She had gotten up once to make herself an infusion of chamomile for insomnia and it had lulled her but not quite stopped her mind from the wide wakefulness of midnight that it sometimes had.

He was an innocent—believed everybody, even this Connie person; but not quite an innocent. There was something that was gloriously innocent; he believed that with a little industry, industriousness—one could make the island flower again. Tourists? Yes, of course tourists. It was a kind of trade—they had thought the trade of blue pigment seventy years ago was a holy trade. Why not a people trade? Yes, there would be still, the waiting folks—sitting on their balconies, cracking nuts, sipping lemonade, eating apricots in syrup, watchers, commentators on the passersby. They were so worn, so old, so dilapidated some of them; the newspaper on the coffee table, the slow movements that took them around the house, out into the street, down the street dragging little carts with cloth coverings to put the vegetables from the grocery stores. Even an insect did more and more meaningful things during the day. But they? Oh they—waiting for God! Once long ago it had been. Every taste in their mouths had been God. Every beat of their hearts. Now Dimitri in sheer innocence and without irony had said to them: Tourists. (How she loved his lovely rubicund mouth.) Tourists to take pictures and record this one place in the world where most people did almost nothing but wait for God. And unlike the blue pigment trade which set their eyes on heaven—its wonder and glory, that one of their sons had said 'tourists' had made them believe their life was over. Similar to the Egyptians battling with locusts. But Dimitri had thought, bless his soul—more money for the island— better housing, the electricity restored. The hand of comfort and consolation—his hand rather than God's. In all this, Dimitri was merely innocent. He didn't imagine that the islanders could want anything else. He thought like a child that his beautiful plan, and yes, he thought it was a beautiful plan, would simply be what everybody wanted. Nor did he, would he, ever suspect them of any fundamental cold hearted- ness or antagonism to anybody least of all to himself. He didn't see, as she, that the islanders didn't want beneficence, kindness, gentle restoration—the best for their community—that they weren't united in brotherly love. They wanted each one of them wealth for themselves. A chance to move away. To spend the rest of their lives looking out of a different window, stepping on to a bus in London, walking with a perfume in a little satiny bag in Paris and to hell with their neighbors with their goats and lemons.

What else was Dimitri? He was open, flexible, warm-hearted, comprehending. If the islanders wanted something different, he was content, although he couldn't necessarily provide it. He loved them nonetheless. He wanted to love away misun- derstandings. He saw them as winter coming to spring in some ways—there had first to be the thaw—the acceptance of a beautiful new world. He saw them as people in this phase and would see them as such even if they did send him and Connie away. If they had a long thaw, so be it. But Dimitri was an optimist and believed that with a little patience on the part of his employer, warming them like the sun, they would be brought 'round; until they found that in fact the winters weren't so very severe on this island and that down deep the islanders were amenable.

And this was his innocence, his open, warm heartedness, his flexibility and his comprehension. He was the son she saw in the white light of summer, standing up on a high edge of the cliff she had yet to reach, standing there like a golden flower. All sorts of things said inside her body that he was not quite, could not be quite— that. It would take some adjusting, some minutiae of change. Comprehending was not the same as discerning. Warm-heartedness was not quite love. Flexibility was not quite reformation. Openness not quite purity. But on the whole Dimitri was closer, much closer to being a true man than was Jason who had taken it into his mind that he wouldn't move except by the Bible.

So satisfied, she slept a little and woke thinking joyously that whatever might go wrong that day, her son would be in the kitchen for a breakfast of fried fish.

Her dance that day was easy, and perfect. She didn't totter once on double, triple pirouettes with her right knee bent, and lifted. She arched her back and tilted back

her head and it was as if rapture, at last, rapture. She felt at the end of her movements that she had been on the tree, as it were, long enough, and that it was time for
the ripe fruit to fall. And how it had been a ripening in every detail! The long sour
years after her littleness, that flower, was gone; there were times she didn't know that
it was a matter of coming to fruit. She thought the misery and bent backedness after
the unspeakable act, that half bitter companionship with her husband, the pain, the
friendship, the sometimes love, the hard, relentless hours with him and the relief,
yes relief when he was gone was in any case all futile, all meaningless; it meant two
children that she had looked at out of misery-fogged eyes, willed herself to take care
of, often wished she had never had. Dimitri especially—the odd, mute child, horrid
offspring, he was— to her before the advent of his beauty, and the secret tenderness
she felt even in her viscera when he left— obliging Jason, her legitimate, who wanted
the house.

And perhaps the death of her husband had allowed her to breathe, and in breathing she had conceived, yes conceived in her heart by her own child, Dimitri, and it
had rubbed off too on Jason, the right to smile at her son's handsomeness (it was
her 'son' as opposed to her 'legitimate'), to see his body as beautiful, to imagine that
he had brought back to the island the gift of manliness—that is, to live by beauty, as
she. And then, her dancing, was it this joy or another? The lifting of her leg at last,
high into the air, the tilting back of her head at the same time, the raising of her arms
had brought with it a living dream, freedom and love at last; then there had been the
talking to—who was it she was talking to? God, Dimitri, Anna? It may have been
all three rolled into one. And often this talking to went on without words. Often it
went on with the words that only God knew in the depths of her mind. For at last,
she realized that this, all this, had been ripening. For what in the end was all this for?
This beauty, joy, love beginning, which was only drinking in the sight of her son's
eyes, or lifting her leg high—nothing. Yes, there was that. That nothing. Inescapable,
unavoidable. She would go down in the dust as one whom the air remembered if
the air remembered at all, as one who loved to look into the dark eyes of her affable,
open, yet reclusive and mysterious son, briefly handsome like a light on a little unknown island, and as one who could lift her leg high, with the toe level to her eyes
and arch her back and tilt back her head. Ah a man, a woman was the ocean and the
sky, and also nothing.

She brought down her leg. Perhaps one day, she thought raising her leg bent behind her touching her toe to the back of her head, I will be a saint. One who, with the
cross shoved between her teeth, found, miraculously, and logically, the savor of life.

The talking-to began: What then did it come from? Surely it can't be born out
of nothing? Love. Are you sure? Dimitri was, was—the beastly thing, then the mechanical child, the mute child, that furtive little animal child, in the end eighteen and
stinking of Katrina's cigarettes, dark electric joy…but it wasn't Dimitri. What then
was this love? A mystery; a secret code discovered in her mind. I didn't really think
when I cursed myself. Though that too was for embarrassed love:—excuse, World,

my blood. But I knew it wasn't that way at all, at all. Was it the vision? Was it what Simon said after all? Was it rhythm? Was it dance?

It was throwing a hiker's line up on to the edge of the cliff, that is, what it was if you want to know. I thought I just might get up there.

Dimitri is up there—a golden flower, you said.

Ah, only one of the beautiful things. And even he, not quite. More an image of what he might be.

Perhaps then love is made of energy, hope and faith.

Is it love? Continue talking.

You know the commandments. Love…

I think in the end, to love is to make life. Make life between you and God between you and your neighbor, and that is why the poor and the sick and the despised.

Do not think Christ lightly. For if you have consented and not turned back, he will not come in the shape of the golden flower, you know; but in that of the cross. Be advised. Unendurable pain.

Agatha faltered. She stopped dancing and sighed. So all this has been merely the ups and downs of life. I haven't come upon Christ, haven't endured the cross, haven't come to the glory promised after. I am too weak; my mind is too scattered. I am just a simple mother with a son come home for the first time in ten years. I have just lifted up my head, she said, half piteously.

What is it you want?

Now it is six o' clock; my boy will get up at seven. I will shower and cook.

You want Christ, the beauty, the truth.

I will offer him figs, apricot marmalade, toast, butter, coffee and fried fish.

But you don't want the Kingdom.

What would you have—all my bones broken? My soul in agony?

I see, I see. And the talking to ceased.

Soon Agatha showered and fresh, smelling of scents of jasmine—on the supplies' boat they had jasmine soap—was in the kitchen sweating in the steam of the fish frying and the coffee bubbling. Outside of the window facing East it was just beginning to show light.

Dimitri came in in nothing but a grey sweatpants and threw his arms around his mother smelling her in a loud sniff.

Beautiful as heaven, he said, and sniffed again. Little one, little one—he said; I know it has been hard on you. Maybe it was wrong of me to stay away so long with you here with only Jason so taciturn and unhelpful.

What could you have done?

Given up the hunt for more money. Come back, been content with the lowly life—fished.

Lived like Jason?

No, never. Been your good boy. Helped you out. Picked the tomatoes in the garden, fixed your windows, white washed your walls, rebuilt your fence.

Jason does nothing but fish and sit.

You would have been tired out too at the end of the day, said Agatha. He gets up at four, comes home at three. Eleven hours out there fishing, part of the time in the dark.

Dimitri pulled out one of the old wooden chairs at the kitchen table and sat down. He looked down and sighed. So you have one boy who does nothing but give you a little pittance of his pay and makes you work for him—keeping the house clean, cooking his food, all the necessary chores that go into maintaining the place so you can live decently, and in addition to all of this injustice, provides no company to speak of, and you have another boy who leaves you in the lurch, goes bounding off God knows where only to come back ten years' later as if he is always the favorite no matter what with ideas to change radically Holy Island where you are sitting still praying not to disturb things and hoping just hoping that you will get your holiness back so that God will return.

Agatha said nothing but carefully removed the fillets of fish from the pan and set them on a paper napkin to blot the excess oil. Then she went to the cupboard and selected a blue china dish and took out of the drawers her best silverware, a cloth napkin and a glass and deposited them on the table in front of her son. Then she brought over the napkin with the fish in it and flipped them on to the dish. Then she filled his glass half full with apricot brandy. Finally she took a white china coffee cup from the cupboard and placing it near the glass beside the plate filled it with coffee from the pot on the stove.

I'm not sure. Eat, she said. But there is nothing unholy about finding you home safe.

You have changed, said Dimitri, taking a bite of the fish, and smiling—delicious, he said in an aside to her softly. Yes, you have changed, he went on thoughtfully chewing. You walk like a young girl, erect as a sapling; if you were a tree, I would say you had found a new root somehow and that fruit are in the making off your boughs. Or if you were a fruit I would say that you had turned from green to golden.

What is it, Mother? This dancing! Some new love? Is it really Leo?

I dance because I want to live, retorted Agatha. Leo has nothing to do with it. Or I dance because it is in me to dance. Because often bruised, lame, crippled things dance.

And that is all, marveled Dimitri. A cliff rising out of the water on a sandy beach, two rocks, a few goats giving abundant supplies of milk, lemon and apricot trees, tomato vines, grape vines and jasmine and a woman who dances like a dream before the sun comes up. You, he said turning to his mother, must be rejoicing. I wonder for what?

For the sun, said Agatha. She sat down at the kitchen table with a piece of fried fish on a napkin and a mug of coffee. She began to eat with her fingers and sip the black coffee. Then she got up and went to the bread basket on the counter and brought back a piece of soft bread and broke it in half, giving one to Dimitri and biting into one herself. They had been silent all this time.

I think you grow tired of it, said Agatha, at last.

Of what?

The day. In the big world where you are—what is the city, London?—

Athens, now.

In any case… you see the sun each day or the sunlight at least and you feel a weary sensation in your head, even though the city is frantic with business.

For me I had a vision of a wild woman dancing on the cliff sticking up out of the sea and there were purple ribbons in her wild hair and I believe she was dancing for the sun, no other reason, the absolute joy and beauty. She lifted herself up, bare breasted towards the sky. It was all joy. I saw it, Dimitri, all joy. Wedding joy. For a while I went around without telling anyone. Who was there to tell? Barbara? She who half hates me, constantly hopes and prays that you will not stay—you make me too popular, you are too popular—could I tell her that I had found, despite it all, you and Jason quarreling and you going off… No. I know that she wanted me down, conforming, maybe not entirely in ill will. Anna—she would have laughed at me. Now you see, she would have said, what you really are. And she would have been right, but she would not have told me the next step. So I went to Simon—you know he is wise. He told me dancing. Just alone, you know. For no reason. And I applied myself day in and day out. I couldn't do much at first.

Not much, yes like the dancing women do around here, Mother, said Dimitri, frowning at her, not much!

No, said Agatha. I dance man dancing. I am happy with it. I can lift my leg, and twirl and leap. I don't go very high, but high enough.

You'll beat all the men, exclaimed Dimitri.

It is just that—you see, it lifts me up and it makes me see. It isn't a waste beating them. I could go now to God and say to Him, you see I practiced lifting my leg to Your sun, the glory of it!— will you forgive? I split my legs towards earth, the beauty of it. I twirl with my foot marking the cosmos around me. I have sung my song of praise, body and soul to all.

More and more beautiful, shouted Dimitri, laying down his fork. He sprang up from the table and started cavorting, kicking his feet, jumping, turning. To think that I would at last learn joy from my mother.

Agatha smiled at him. It is a serious thing, joy. It takes labor, sweat and pain, torn muscles, hearts. But everyone loves dancing. And it was Anna who, after she found out, said to me—why not?

What is incredible, Mother, is that you have been working now at it for ten years. You are forty-eight—fifty-one by my calculation and you are able to do things most twenty year olds can't even dream of.

Don't talk about it, Dimitri. There are people on this island who would rather see me bent-backed, cursed, as they call it, miserable. There is an infection even deep down inside, Dimitri. That I have done something illicit somehow by raising my head and lifting my leg to the sun, bursting through my chrysalis of pain. They can't actually pin it down as illicit, nor criminal. Yet, it breaks some very sacred law for them. Of course, they all strive to do the same thing, all except the women who were made, they are sure, to uphold this subconscious sacred law against leg lifting, wings' spreading; and there are some, thus, who would rather see me burned to death than carrying on.

Who, Mother? Who? What are you talking about? I too am a man. I can protect you. Who are they? Give me their names.

No, she said, soothingly. It is nothing, just a strange little fear of mine.

I know there are some that do not love us, Dimitri went on, more calmly, but here what I am going to do—this hotel that will bring money, because a real industry, a tourist industry to the island—will patch over differences that arise when everyone is living in this miserable uncertainty. There will be peace, joy and the neighbors will smile at one another even at you. Even you will be able—to sell those beautiful embroideries you used to make all the time, the lace…

Yes, said Agatha dreamily, I suppose so.

Perhaps they will sell—Connie will grant a little more money for their wretched properties. It will all go well, Mother. I will be here and there—your wayward son come home at last with gold for you.

I can't believe that the curse will end.

What?

Did I protect you from that too?

Those were just old wives' notions. The majority of this community never believed...

People thought, people thought, said Agatha, warmly.

Well, they will have no more time to think; they will be buying and selling. You know the devil plays with minds that are not put to good use.

You believe that?

I half believe in the devil, so I guess in some roundabout way I am believing in God-- half, sometimes, he said moodily.

And what is the antidote?

To the devil? Oh, you know that. Of course, you know. Love, wouldn't you say? And money.

You say it as if those things grow on all the trees. Agatha said, chewing thoughtfully. She finished her fish and drank the last of her coffee. Then she got up and picked up the plates and napkins and coffee cups. Dimitri standing, finished the last of the apricot brandy in one swallow. Then he listened intently.

I hear Connie stirring. He usually gets up at eight. Put all these things away quickly, Mother. He doesn't like messy rooms. You know, he has already talked to me about cleaning up some of these old rickety fences and gardens, and fishing boats. Pouring in money out of the goodness of his heart to clean things up.

Oh, well, if he is so good he can wait. I will wash after I finish cooking for him.

Mother, now Mother. You absolutely must comply. This is not a family affair. I am not Jason compelling you to work unfairly. You know that Connie is bringing something immense to the island considering. Just clean up and get ready.

I was just teasing. Of course, I will clean up. You are far too nervous though. We don't need this gentleman nor his gentle offer.

But it would make all the difference in the world, retorted Dimitri, irked. The islanders would be forced to loosen up. Tourists would come and tourists change old habits and prejudices.

Agatha quietly washed the cups and plates.

Connie Cours entered the room. He was in his usual fresh jeans and white pressed shirt, polished shoes and warm dark blue wool socks. He also had on a light red woolen sweater that smelled of clean wool. I slept well, he said, warmly, body and soul. This is a very congenial little home, Mrs. Binos.

We live well, said Agatha, shortly. Would you care for some fish for breakfast? I have flounder, a kind of bass...

No for me a light breakfast; some yoghurt would be best. He sat down and lit a cigar. Agatha rummaged around the kitchen quickly for an ashtray. She had never permitted smoking in the house, thinking it was a dirty habit. But one made exceptions, she found, all the time. There were scarcely going to be any hard and fast rules in her house when it came to the rich man.

Do you enjoy eating light? Asked Agatha, anxiously, with her head in the refrigerator looking for the yoghurt.

Most of the time, said Connie. I take joy in little things. Yoghurt, the vision of the water here, the smell of the sea on windy days.

I see, said Agatha depositing the jar of yoghurt in front of him and finding a silver spoon and napkin to go with it. She was warming to him in the kind of friendly, artless way of the little woman who is genuinely glad when an important man likes her. I myself, she said to him, do something to welcome in the sun each day. I lift...

Mother, interrupted Dimitri, I am sure that Connie is not at all interested in your morning rituals.

Yes, that is true, said Agatha, blushing a little.

No, on the contrary; I am quite interested.

Ah, said Agatha, but they are nothing. Nothing at all. I live a little like a bird, Mr. Cours; I just lift, and she giggled senselessly.

Connie, said Connie smoking, pensively, and swallowing down yoghurt alternately. He seemed, Dimitri suddenly noted with a rush of useless indignation, entirely accustomed to these affectionate displays of the poor and insignificant of the earth he had induced to dream of riches, and responded to them with a familiarity born of lifelong condescension and contempt.

But that is what, he went on, Dimitri translating, to a rapt Agatha, we all do in one way or another. One has to get the sleep out somehow. The sleep, you know, is what deadens us, damns us. When one of my enterprises doesn't work out it is because somewhere along the line I was asleep. Here I have slept too much, too much.

You have had by my calculations only six or seven hours, said Agatha, mystified.

I didn't mean that kind of sleep, he said. I have been asleep in the mind. He finished his yoghurt and stood up. There are places to go and things to see, he announced. I have been very hospitably received here Agatha; the visit on the whole has been a chance to reflect. You know the famous detective who talked of everything being a matter of using the little grey cells. I have used them this morning.

He picked up his coat and headed towards the door. Dimitri followed. In less than an hour Dimitri came back for Connie's suitcase, which was sitting packed near guest bedroom door.

He is leaving, Dimitri said.

Ah, said Agatha, and you?

No, that is the thing. I am staying. We have had a difference. I was told that I had to work on presenting an offer to the inhabitants of one of the towns of the other island; not here. Not anymore. I declined. I thought that he owed it to us to at least host one more meeting. I had in mind a renovated Holy Island, not just business to be conducted—all the same anywhere. I guess deep down I was the loyal son returned. I will have to stay for a while until I can see my way to a new life, Mother; you don't mind? Jason...?

No, that is precisely what I wanted. Who cares if we have a hotel or not? The thing is we have one another. The thing is we have one another. Everything went by so quickly Agatha was a little overawed.

We have had a difference, Dimitri said lightly; I just said I would have to iron a few things out here and so stay a little, he looked sternly at his mother.

Yes, of course, said Agatha

No well he asked me all sorts of funny questions as to why. I would think...

It is nothing.

He asked if I were in love;--as if I were a schoolboy, said Dimitri annoyed.

Ah, said Agatha. But it was all a test, from the beginning, she said, angry now herself.

What kind of a test?

For you to see if you— you!— would renounce us. Not grandly, but in a little way. Flicking away the fly, the moth...He never meant to buy or build.

But you, you did not renounce us. Something held you back. It was in the wheelings and dealings—you saw that we were true people. We believe from the depths of our greedy hearts.

Connie left on the caique unobserved by all except Michael who came around the town like a flare with the news so that everyone poured into the main street in confusion. Barbara so furious that Stavros told her she could walk on water after him, mere anger would prop her up, boil her up, as it were, like so many bubbles. But there were others who reeled in the square in a kind of drunkenness brought on by shock.

Of course, he is coming back. He is a business man, a man of his word. He promised us. What do you think in the middle of a lucrative opportunity...?

Where is Dimitri?

Gone.

No just not here. Bring him here. Get him. Hold him. Don't let him follow.

Dimitri was dispatched for and brought with Agatha behind—saying what are you thinking of? My son had nothing to do with it. Connie just decided...

Oh, so it is Connie to you? Little Paul sneered at her. He had appeared out of nowhere.

But you don't know, said Agatha surprised to see him. He had been so quiet, so quiet. He had been that boy with strange fair hair and freckles that she remembered with the innocent lips as she called it, slightly cherubic, but not fat that had kept out of all the usual adolescent trouble, fastidious, she had thought him, one of the clean ones; but secretly, for some reason, she had feared him too. Now all this came back to her looking at his distorted face—half disgust, half hilarious violence—strange, ugly, agonized mix.

But it is not because of my son, she said, fearing to say his name as if fear like a white cloth covered him, made him impossible to discern—fearing that boy that had now turned into a phantom man, the kind that appears out of nowhere. For some reason she thought that all those years of 'not being there'—at meetings in Simon's house, in her spectrum of people encountered during the day, and just at the center amidst a throng of people and so inaccessible, almost invisible in Church, sometimes not at all in Church—had piled up between them and had somehow filled him with deep brutal anger. For what she was not sure.

But Dimitri stood in the center of the crowd. She saw that somewhere along the line he had put a tie on and a white shirt. The tie was loose and his shirt sleeves unbuttoned. He said to the crowd in a harried voice—you see, he would not wait for you to make up your minds, to argue and bargain for a little more money. Men like Connie Cours come out of the world for curiosity and for good or evil; but that is not the point. You buy from them when it is to your advantage—never waiting... But he looked at them with love, Agatha saw. This Connie had come and gone over-looking something. And he, her son, accustomed as he was to the great world and important people would not.

What is good or evil not the point then? Said Timos with a quizzical look at Dimitri, peering, in fact, into his face. It seems to me that we are not at that level. We still mind that something be offered us here on Holy Island that is good.

I suppose, said Paul who had come into the crowd also in a white shirt and a jacket and a tie well tied—that you would take us beyond good and evil.

What is beyond but nothingness? Asked Barbara who found herself wedged between the two men. I am not going there.

Yes, said Stavros behind her—the falling off place on the other side of the world, filled with meaningless men and women and meaningless corruptible men and women. A place for would be heroes, mad men and suicides.

You have made us all mad men, said Nisos; look at the crowd. They don't know which way to turn now that their golden plum has been taken from them.

But isn't this fellow coming back? Asked Cleo. Why not? I was just beginning to think that a little hotel on Holy Island would be cozy and that a packet of money would do me a world of good.

It is Dimitri, hissed Foti, she had fallen prey to the growing rage and was suddenly prone to dislike what she had always loved—what the world called handsome men. He made the rich man leave us and go away. Who knows if he will ever come back. We are like a grain of salt in the sea.

Nonsense, said Nisos, angrily. Anyone can find us. We are quite distinguishable on the map—right next to the other island, you know, that has three towns and a hospital.

Anyone could miss us too, said Stavros. Not geographically, but in the worldly sense. What are we worth?

I could try, shouted Dimitri above the crowd. I could try to get Mr. Cours again but it would take some time. And at that time you would have to be very sure that you would sell for the price named. It might go down, you know. He is trying to tell you that he doesn't need you. There are other islands equally beautiful and there are other opportunities to erect hotels, getaway lodges for rich men to come with private yachts and spend a few nights in the sun. (Dimitri didn't tell them, for sadness, that Connie had said something to the effect that in a few more years, the island would be up for grabs anyway—so many would have moved away.)

This fired the villagers with fury to the boiling point. Bastard, one voice was heard shouting. And who are you to think you can come into this island home and tease us. We who nurtured you—we who brought you up; what have you done but waved millions before our eyes? We are poor people; we have nothing but fishing, lemons, goats. We are fishing-lemons-goats people, hissed Cleo angrily and in disgust; her eyes were fixed on Paul—surely he would save them from themselves.

I meant it for your own good, shouted Dimitri who was getting pushed by one furious fisherman and then another.

Our own good? It was a cheat nothing more, a cheat! Supposed to make us see that you were better than us, I imagine.

Let me go, returned Dimitri, his indignation rising, at this point. I know you as well as you know me. I remember my village home, your nurture—the way you treated my mother and family. You're the ones who are the absolute disgraces in every respect. Greed and envy rule here. And that is why the perfectly honest business transaction failed.

Little Paul came up to him with his fist clenched and punched him in the jaw. Dimitri wobbled and reeled backward and then fell in the midst of the crowd. Little Paul came up to him and kicked him in the face.

Agatha who was next to him began to scream and tear and Little Paul's hair. With one elbow he shoved her in the stomach and sent her backwards gasping for breath. Michael shouted I am going to get Father Isaac.

Father Isaac! I don't give a damn for Father Isaac, and little Paul kicked Dimitri in the face again.

Peter elbowed his way into the midst of the throng. Stop, little Paul, he said, all weakness and fat.

Why is this person, said little Paul, allowed to come back—to sully our island with his business prospects, his money and maybe more money taunts, his lust?

Oh, oh, said Cleo, seeing the blood on Dimitri's face.

Paul burst through the crowd to Dimitri's side and seized little Paul by the arm, struggling with him. My son has lost control of himself, he said, apologetically. This is really what happens when….the whole thing degenerated into a fistfight. One knows that it is really of course, in saner moments…the young have a tendency… but I would say that when people come to cheat us, anger flares up. And then you know neither God nor man can stop what happens next. In the struggle with his father, Little Paul had had a vision of an old lady in utter, helpless shock with a round mouth, round eyes, looking at him imploringly—it was his mother, Ella who had somehow drifted into the crowd and looked at forty six as if she was seventy; he succumbed to his father.

He took Little Paul by the shoulder; the crowd opened up and father and son were allowed to leave.

Simon with his fingers touching his face and a look of horror written all over it was watching Dimitri spitting blood. The priest had arrived with Max who cringed slightly as he followed him; Father Isaac elbowed his way through the crowd around the man lying on the pavement and crouched down beside him and began to wipe the blood. He asked Michael and Max, whose face was contorted, to help Dimitri up.

They got Dimitri home to his bed and the priest went to work with his herbs and concoctions.

Agatha said to him—don't you think that it would be better if we had him treated at the hospital?

He has wounds but they will heal, said the priest. Keep bathing that left eye it will be a ghastly sight for a while.

But what happened, Father? They seemed themselves not to want Mr. Cours' offer.

You know that this is not about Mr. Cours, said the priest. When violence starts doing the talking it is never for the reason apparent on the surface. The key lies deep down in the heart. The priest shook his head and gathered his things and left.

Dimitri turned in bed and groaned because breathing hurt. Agatha kept bathing his eye and crying silently. She whispered to Dimitri, this is all my fault; I should never have let you come back. The villagers didn't want the island renewed, and reborn. They are old; they want to mumble their prayers and to sleep. The young ones on the island like little Paul are resentful of those who went into the world adventuring. In a sense, this is an island of not fitting in, not an island of sane, rational, discoursing human beings. It is an island of half beasts. Inasmuch as one needs to be reborn to face the world as an adult, this is an island of half reborn people. You and I, we are different. You grew straight in my house, proper, handsome. And everywhere in the village there were eyes watching, hating as well as admiring. You looked like someone—even next to Mr. Cours. A person who had confidence, faith in himself, intelligence, ability, wit and discourse, carved out of light. The others half mad, or full of fantasies—they are not persons! Worn our flesh they have, and the young ones raging, crazy, flabby, idle! For a long time I believed that there was a curse on me. How was it I couldn't regain my light? I was plunged in darkness. Preferred the dark corners to cry in. And then I saw that oh no the curse was on this island. I thought the place was gentle. We have our history—the resurrection of Jesus. The coming back from the dead of our live god. We believed he was ours. Our own flesh and blood way back when had seen him. I thought it was enough to ensure that no one would ever profane the earth here with human blood. I thought no one would ever kill, my child. Now I am not so sure. And something told me way back when Jason and you fought and he put that razor sharp fish knife against your neck that there would be trouble for you, my own darling. That no matter how far you fled, how you walked abroad so to speak, back you would come and together we'd end up facing the mad crowd.

On Holy Island? Asked Zoe. She had not been in the crowd.

Kicked him in the ribs and the head, said Cleo, she was dabbing her eyes with a scented handkerchief, clasping her white satiny purse to her belly, recovering from the sight of violence right before her eyes.

That is an outrage. We agreed. Of course we believed that try as we did not to believe it there was always some sort of trouble surrounding Agatha. How was it that she ended up at the center of some sort of fray with fists, and violence, even fire, and we hesitating to breathe a word about it. We thought there was some mistake. And yes there was the strange little affair years ago between her and Paul. But one grows up and forgets or remembers only in passing these adolescent missteps as it were. Agatha was a poor creature, a little muddy in the face, but she had been beaming over her new dancing, Leo, Dimitri. For a while she looked like someone had lit her like a candle. What happened now? The old man had seen her back, erect as a baby's; they were old gabbers and fornicators and they babbled about her hips and buttocks, but at heart they even meant well. She is after all quite a woman. All these years she has sort of kept to herself. She didn't need anything from us.

The island didn't say anything when she had gone off unbaptized twenty years ago to celebrate her wedding in the town hall on the other island. We are all of us married in our little church with its jasmine bright whitewash and our own dear fresco the only one of its kind in the great old world that thinks it is so much better than us. It seems to us that she felt that she could just use the island a little—inhabit it, grow her tomatoes. But we are not just a territory. Oh no, there is something far beyond. The place that we live in is part of a great puzzle of God and we are a piece of it body and soul. That hasn't changed. Of course, it is our Christian duty to love Agatha—to love the stranger is a great command of our God. And can we help it if she chooses to be a stranger? There were always opportunities for her to blend in, to come to us, to join us in our get-togethers. Even in our charitable concerns, Anna is so good there, Agatha seems a little indifferent. Agatha said once that she would like to establish a school for gypsies. Wild idea. As if gypsy children could ever be taught! As if the little wild men and women would do their arithmetic when they could be out in the sun running barefoot, and stealing gold watches out of good people's pockets. She is a little like a gypsy—outcast for her own fault. All that misery that sent her into dark corners, alleys, under the cliffs, walking alone at night—what self-indulgence!

But the last thing we need on this island is any kind of physical violence. We are going to put it to Simon to put it to Paul that this kind of thing has to stop. Dimitri's beautiful left dark eye is quite disfigured I am told. He looks monstrous. Agatha is beside herself with pain and distress. We need to consider that our little street and our alleys, our piazza and our cliff, our shores and our sunlight need not harbor ugliness of this kind.

Ah we want the beautiful, brilliant shores with that exquisite white light that we get on this island that in the summer has a soft, sweet fragrance, a holy fragrance of heat on stones. Yes, our faces like faces in some of those postcards we see now and then of other remote villages in the world –ancient but lovely, profound, full of that wisdom of life, wisdom increasing a thousand fold for every wrinkle, so that the aged man or woman could climb a hill and proclaim to every person around for miles the good news of life. We have our lemons and our goats—they think perhaps in the world that we have very little. But ah, yes, we know how to live. For in the end, because we have remained steady, all except Agatha, our holiness will come back to us. We have lived after all in simplicity. We have done our charity and loved one another.

Zoe decided with our approval to pay a visit to Agatha and Dimitri.

When she stepped with her firm step despite her antique, shrunken, skinny frame into Agatha's house there was Dimitri smiling at her from swollen split lips in the entrance corridor and in a second he had wrapped his arms around her.

Auntie Zoe, he said holding her against his bosom and kissing both of her withered cheeks. What brings you here in all weathers? See I am fine. You needn't concern yourself about me.

Oh, said Zoe, extricating herself; she didn't particularly like being embraced by a half-ugly Dimitri. Ugh! That eye! What a hideous sight! She turned her head away. Her lips moved and her voice mechanically said: The weather is fine today. There is a blazing sun.

I know, said Dimitri smiling jovially. It was just so as to say. But in any case it is still winter. You'll catch your death of a cold. And then you'll cap it all off by blaming me. Now that isn't being the Good Samaritan, is it? He said, touching his eye.

I see you are in good spirits, said Zoe, still looking away. I am glad that there was not more damage, she retorted, wrapping her black wool shawl more tightly around her grey dress.

Oh, no. Little Paul came by with his father. They apologized. It is rare to see them under this roof you know. I was always convinced they thought they would contract something fatal if they came into our home.

What did you say?

I said something to the effect that we had fought together as boys and that I had won on a number of occasions and that maybe it was all one thing in the end. I lost this time. And so, I said to him, we also could call it quits. You know there is only so much proving that you are a better male and that now that we were even we could grow up and eat and drink together instead.

And what did he say?

Well, his father nudged him a bit and he smiled a half smile; he was pale too; looked half alive. He was as I remember a little obnoxious to me as a boy. There were many times when he hissed out nasty insults, a number of times to my mother. But you know he was so stupid in school, that I easily got my revenge and justification. How could such a stupid boy speak the truth?

Agatha came out of the kitchen and ushered Zoe in and sat her down in a chair by the table. I have made some wonderful fish stew, she said. All sorts of seafood and fish. Everything is tender, spicy and tomatoey. I was plentiful with the potatoes. Please help yourself.

No, I couldn't.

You are not going to just sit there and say a few words to us? Agatha said looking at her.

First of all, said Zoe. There really must not be any more of these physical outbursts. She squinted at Dimitri's blue black and red puffy eye. We have an island to consider. An island that is and ever shall be holy no matter what other people have to say about it. Uprisings among the young people may be natural but they are not what we ever do here.

But, of course, said Agatha, mystified. I can assure you; I saw it all with my own eyes. Dimitri was just explaining something—why Mr. Cours had left. I don't think anyone expected…

Although Dimitri appears to have been the victim and Little Paul the perpetrator, there are times when extremely clever people subtly rile up a perfectly honest person by tricks of argument, a person who may have a little problem with his temper, but we all have that in a given extreme, so we do not know where the real fault lies. Dimitri would try the patience of a saint.

Auntie Zoe, said Dimitri, if it is my fault I am sorry. Look at my eye and see my punishment. I only thought that this island could use some renewal.

We are new enough, said Auntie Zoe. New in the world in our oldness. She looked away.

Auntie Zoe, look, a new, viable economy is what you need. The factory on the other island could even shut down your electricity altogether. They want big contracts, not monthly fees from seventy families. People, rational people, whether they are from the real world or just from the periphery of it, from the other island a hundred and fifty kilometers away, say what are you doing here? Paddling little boats? Drinking a little brandy? Saying your prayers? I am the one who is asking: Who is going to defend you from their indifference and scorn, their harmful decisions? Who protect you? Little Paul?

There is Michael as well and Nico and you know a few others.

They might well leave, said Dimitri. Michael is young, the only young boy on the island. He is seventeen. But what is he going to do here? Be the island's message bearer all his life?

I believe so, said Zoe, stiffly.

Come, come, said Agatha. Aren't you hungry? The fragrance of this stew fills the whole kitchen. She put a wooden bowl in front of Zoe.

No, really. Said Zoe frowning and pushing the bowl away with a little violent gesture.

I came to say that we have reached a head on this Agatha, Zoe went on, standing up and shouting angrily. We have seen what your family does. If anything like this ever happens again, she gestured to the eye, you will not be wanted here.

Agatha picked up the bowl quickly, and looked at her, staring, rubbing the bowl with the dish towel she had in her hand spasmodically.

I have never been wanted here, she said in a low harsh tone.

We gave you every opportunity to become one of us.

We were shown that we were outcasts in all sorts of ways. It may have been only a gesture, a look, an insult as Dimitri said. There were acts of violence, threats as you know quite well…yes, threats and acts. She stared into Zoe's face.

Oh, said Zoe standing up. How ludicrous this is. I came simply to tell you that this kind of thing is not part of what we are. Our island home is gentle, kind, known for its simplicity. You and your son would have naked blood stains on our soil. Now anyone who had half a heart would see this. You want to protest, to prove something by living here. What do you do when you cause a disturbance? Not that a single disturbance would in any way alter our feelings of good will towards you. But one, two, three…

Agatha was silent. Dimitri said, one, two, three—what?

It started long ago when your grandmother refused in the end to baptize your mother. Of course, it was not her fault then. But as she grew older, and before her marriage, she should have taken it upon herself to…but in any case, she didn't. She rebels against the most holy sacrament that would make her one of us-- one that waits for God.

Mother? Asked Dimitri, confused like a child.

But God, Jesus, is not to be pleased by rites, not to be loved by baptisms. It isn't a magical ceremony where the sins of a lifetime are gone in an instant because of water and invocations. Jesus is to be walked after, to be danced on water. One's soft foot in his clear leaping footprint.

Oh, shouted Zoe. So now we, Christians, know less than you—a –a free spirit! about the resurrected Lord! Of all the effrontery. You see, you have no shame. Now I see and know.

But you were always so good, said Agatha, conciliatory. What has changed you?

Ah, don't you know? Didn't I tell you how prepared we were to accept anything almost?

Zoe came back panting and sweating. I have been through the very worst. I have stood at the cross and seen the Lord mocked. We all gathered around in consternation. But this can't be true.

She said that baptism was unnecessary. Yet that is not what it is.

We all had something in our hands, sewing, embroidery, lace. And we all put it down. She must not be allowed to continue in this way, said Cleo. We must force her to attend catechism. Otherwise, who knows. The devil could be rampant on our island. Our poor little island—where once Mother Dora walked with the uncreated light in her very footsteps...We cannot let this continue, said Cleo again.

We gathered together that lunch huddled over stuffed peppers and pieces of stewed goat's meat. We are so old and feeble, complained Cleo. Can't the men do something? Raise the outcry among them.

The men do nothing sane or conclusive, said Zoe.

Why not tell Father Isaac, said Foti, her eyes wide with terror from hearing that Agatha had brought the devil rampant among them.

That priest is too clever, said Cleo. But it is true. This sort of thing might sway even him. What about Jason? Is he of the same opinion?

Yes, Jason, said Zoe, I forgot him. There are differences, we must not be too general in the way we handle these violent races; Jason is not at all like his brother Dimitri. A quiet boy, a sane boy. There is a possibility that we have marginalized him because of the flamboyance of the other one—a false person tends to be flamboyant—and he might be completely in agreement. I have heard tell on good authority that he dislikes the rebellious ways of his mother and brother.

So in the end, said Foti, one of Agatha's sons is going to heaven.

Why always, lamented Zoe, the most miserable—unintelligent, unhandsome?

We thought like Zoe. She had been harsh with Agatha, upbraiding and cruel. But we knew deep down that given any other situation, our Zoe would have been the most gracious on earth. If she hadn't seen that eye! She was like some mothers who take out on their children their pain and fury for seeing them so wounded. She let loose on them fury unbounded for that reason and that alone. You see long ago our little group had repudiated violence of all forms. We had lived together rather to love one another. The thought of someone having broken the covenant...Little Paul was a weakling—everybody knew that. He could hardly get out from underneath his mother's skirts. At the same time, he liked to swagger and to pretend he was a perfect copy of his father. To see them together when business was to be done—was like seeing the prime doer and maker marching ahead, and then, as if you hadn't had enough of him, marching again behind. A duplicate! A replica only littler, tackier— yes, we must say it! He had the same zeal too about regaining holiness on Holy Island only it was a little pseudo. And the same weakness, only more so, than the real Paul. But the Pauls would probably be pacified if only the situation were slightly different. We were old, said Zoe, incapable of arguing 'round people. And it would take genius to turn around certain personalities. Besides one didn't know the deep inner side of a person. It seemed that the Pauls were prone to taking certain harsh measures. Zoe acknowledged that she had been cruel to Agatha. She was prepared to go 'round and apologize. They were all of them a little rough on this island these days.

Of course, what little Paul did was most outrageous. He must be tamed, stopped. If there was vitriol between the two, this must be overcome. They must embrace like brothers. She was sure it was possible for little Paul. It was the whole project of the island—the renewal that Paul was always talking about. And he of course, had always offered himself—the first in line for the rebirth. Of course, if not with Dimitri, Jason.

Dimitri was in the right, of course, to complain, not in so many words of course, people like Dimitri are always outwardly gracious, but in gesture, in silent looks...! But Dimitri had gone away, a rover, an adventurer. Little Paul was one of us. He had settled here, grown roots and if he had become a little thorny—it was only like us, the same essential; those bonafide island thorns. It was natural that he should resent this grand coming home of Dimitri but only like a brother would resent—enough to prick him here and there with these thorns. We have our passionate side.

If one could only understand, we thought. But who was there to understand? Our half thoughts, phrases, we understood. But something in the end was not plain. Blood is blood. We had seen in all over Dimitri's face. It just wasn't quite the whole argument. We had been here, aching for years. Dimitri, the shadowy, half-dancing son of a gypsy-blooded mother, who had yet to be baptized, high toed it across the seas to become a hotel manager. He ah—had come back with his hands open, full of persuasion, reaching for us—our homes and, we knew, our hearts. But we are not to be had; we are not to be coaxed and cozened. The idea of asking for a little more money—why, we are not greedy at all. That was a ruse, a trick to see if the man was in earnest, cared about us, and if Dimitri would fight for our cause. Because our island, our community of Saints, the ground where Mother Dora had walked with the uncreated light at her heels—this village, was worth a little more. Just that extra that would make a rich man, a man of worldly mind, weighing the value of every penny, sweat a little. For he was to have bought, bought, mind you, with money in the bank, stones and sand that once had like a thread running through them, like a snake sewing it all together with his tail, the uncreated light itself. Who talks of selling? We weren't selling; we were testing. But where was Dimitri with his gifts of oration, his ability to talk as if his heart was hanging on every word—to tell the rich man of the world before our eyes and ears what Holy Island was and is. If he was a son of ours, returned for love of us, where was his passion for us?

We could understand the silent fury of the people. We knew that blood was blood. That the world analyzes that blood the same for the worst as for the best. But let Dimitri know that blood, his blood, is island blood. Let him disavow that if he dares.

We were silently amazed. We had witnessed a war, essentially. It was a war between our homeland and one who had sold out—was ready to give up the island identity, the very flesh and blood that had pressed saintliness to the very bone; the flesh and blood that could walk on water, raise from the dead—for air conditioning, jet boats, tourists buying our own labor—embroideries and lace—as trinkets to look at and place among the other trinkets from Africa or Tibet. Of course, we had been attracted. One thinks about it; mulls it over with a glass of wine. What is the problem here? Are we not always too hot in summer? Are not the waters peaceful and broad for a fast boat? Would not embroidery and lace still be a pastime among us? We can think of no argument. There is no argument but the one, the single, solitary one— that of prizing, treasuring our little nook in the Aegean sea, our three rocks and every single particle of sand on which walked living saints who had nothing but God... and this was not done.

What is blood on the face of one person compared to the betrayal of mind, heart, spirit and soul of many?

We had witnessed a war. We were ready to march to Paul's house in silent rebellion. We wanted no bloodshed. We wanted to live peacefully in our old age. We understood the anger. We felt the anger. But now that Dimitri has lost his job. Live and let live. Let us love one another once more.

A few of us bowed down in consternation and fear and one or two we know prayed to Magda. She would understand this thing impossible for us to understand.

It is not possible to say that we are not weak. It is not possible to say that Cleo would not have relished getting on an airplane, soaring through the sky to Paris where the most lovely perfumes are to be had for a little more money. But Cleo is also homespun, a delicate person, a bit of a fool, perhaps, but exquisite and rough at the same time, profound in her way. With the money, her liver and stomach and spleen would have been in tip top working order; but the Cleo we knew—who would prize her? The old complainer and sweater with the little white glossy handbag that went so well with her lace shawl. For we had a way with us—with us the delicate, rough, foolish people who sweated in summer, the people who sat with us and groaned, drank cold lemonade and gossiped.

God put the sun in the sky above us, near us, a white blaze in mid-August. One could hardly open one's eyes out in the streets in midday. We were people of this sun, people of God. And when our illnesses came and death came, it was as if we were still living, but passed then, on to a heaven which outshone the sun. We are people who labor with our donkeys and our little crates of fruit. Toil is good for us. And the world would make a mockery out of all of this. Cleo would have come back from Paris scorning our little foolish ways. We would become to her too small, too impossible. Or, if she loved us, something else would give way—as for Anna; the faith itself.

What did this faith come from? From the blazing sun, the donkeys, the lemons, the fish, the goats. We are not a tourist's trinket, but the way. When our Lord was hung naked on the cross—there: He had pointed to the way. And to sell not only our own land but our waters, sun and faces as if it was worth only so much!

Ah, but no wonder; we have lost our holiness. We speak from ancient times; the dead speak in us, perhaps; as if we were still following Mother Dora. But no, on the contrary. No wonder Little Paul kicked Dimitri in the head. A horror. But blood speaks. There is not one of us who doesn't have a relative who has been on those airplanes, flown high in the sky. And back here nothing—we have even lost that nothing, that holiness for we are in demand now; the developers demand us. But blood also speaks on our land now. What is blood? We have learned in our children, the ones that had the grace to be born, that blood is white blood cells and red blood cells. So the world would tell you. But we know something different: Blood is a trumpet of justice, blowing loud and clear. Whose blood is it? Our blood. What is it blowing for? Our souls.

Ah yes, how can we forget? For we love Dimitri; and yet it is right that he shed his blood. Poor son of ours. To go out and to come back all faint and robbed of what was once....it is like a fish swimming down deep, and then, dead, floating up to the surface, belly up. Come and see—see that eye. Zoe has proclaimed it. We understand her even if the world does not. He went away, ah yes, and we thought—now then, there was one of ours who couldn't, didn't fit. Agatha will just have to get used to the idea of having one son. We blamed nobody. In fact, Jason, of all people, is quite tolerated by little Paul. We say tolerated because who is to know what is in the heart of a man except God? But they are fishing chums inasmuch that they prepare the nets together in the early hours of the morning.

But Dimitri had left one spiritual leg on the island. He stood with his mother. Both of them other types. With all the possibility of becoming one of us, through faith and reform, both of them, other types. And how we loved them, as if they were one of ours. Agatha says she isn't wanted. But that is only her old rebellion talking. Because women dancers, dance together with long skirts and don't kick their feet high, or do flips in the air—she is distinctly not in line. But are we not all of us bound to the same tradition? And in any case did we say anything when she began to kick her feet just behind her home so that we could see, in the red-gold light of the dawn—feet flying upward, legs like wings, long hair trailing almost on the ground?! Of course, we only smile and pass on. She had youthfulness still in her, we told ourselves. We didn't blame her. When she came out of her shell, insolent and impertinent—it is the impertinence, not the dancing, that gets to us—not of course in what she had to say, one could never quite catch it anyway, she talks so low, like a murmur, but in her back and hips—no wonder there were some who got riled up. A woman is after all a woman. We must at least make a show of it-- a down turning of the eyes, a little weariness in the gait. And for years, Agatha—of course, she overdid it, which indicated that it was all show, but in any case—she stooped as if she had the real cross on her shoulders. It was however more correct and might have led to baptism, through a gradual unbending, catechism, immersion, purification, and then an ever- modest downward turn of head and neck.

Instead she popped up, an arch in her back, her shoulders thrown back, her chin high, as if to say—see here, I have some strength. And strength whether you win or lose gives you grace, dignity, pride. But Agatha wriggled along as if we didn't have anything. But we also have dignity, grace and pride.

And Dimitri had something with Katrina. Island trick of pride, love.

It is always something a little different with Agatha, something a little off. She simply wasn't disciplined. And we privately think there is no disciplining her. But this latest explosion, if you will call it that—this violence: once more we have to ask ourselves—is it not too much? Oh yes, it has seemed to be just within the bounds, always. Agatha with her misery, her stooping, her reclusive behavior, her murmuring— we were inclined for so many years to laugh and call her our 'witch' but the memory of Magda stopped us. Magda we didn't know—witch or saint—but such beauty, and such virtue and the predictions coming true make us imagine something holy... and Agatha? No surely not, but she too was different. And it only shows you how between the wretched and the holy there is such a thin line! Look after all those years of stooping and muttering, she just picks herself up! Is she not, after all, like Magda in the end who just picked herself up when she fell off the roof, physically, and then later, metaphysically, as it were, when she knew that the baby inside her was her death and she smiled, played, smiled again? In any case—this is just within bounds. And Agatha too married and had children. Dimitri, almost exactly nine months after the wedding night, and then Jason. Of course, she didn't die. The wretched never do. They deform, they complain, they spit as Agatha did. Strange things happen:—all that blows up with Alex, those uneasy circumstances in which he died! The poison was within her reach! And then those blasphemies and Father Raphael saying that she had gone beyond the pale even in Christ's terms! But she—oh she didn't despair. The wretched never do. She had fallen in love, she told us. With whom? A little with her son. And mothers do fall in love with their sons. But oh, somehow, she tipped over the top, spilled beyond what is decent and right.

Calling to mind: To see her passionately kissing him in the late morning when Jason is out! That is what Barbara has told us. Her own son—on the lips, nose, brow! On the very breast! She said to him, we heard it, holding him in her womb had changed her like a chameleon from misery to love, real love like wine. Birthing him had replenished her where that conception had taken it all away. Oh but she meant years later than the day he had come out of the womb.

We are beside ourselves! Of course, Little Paul knows what he did is wrong. One talks things out. One reasons. Man was given a brain for this purpose. But Dimitri, Agatha! They seem to be strange and terrible...

We visited Anna to seek her advice. Anna has gotten thin, skeletally thin, her hand is simply a translucent web between fine bones. She can barely balance herself on her leg bones. We sat at her bedside breathless. She lay cocooned in white—white sheets, white wool bedstead. Of course, we asked her if she really wanted to hear these foolish petty gripes of ours; the escapades of our sons and daughters. We didn't tell her about Dimitri. But we began about Agatha: To say, just to suggest, that she was doing something dreadful. And we hinted and delicately detailed…

And Anna laughed the soft laugh of the sick and said to us—well, she is the only one of us who lives.

Zoe rose up stiffly at this. We murmured to Anna—yes, yes, we knew you would say something ironic like that. You so beautiful, severe, intelligent and worldly. But we have an entire Christian community to think about. We can't afford to lay aside everything for one of us who 'lives' as you call it. As if one can avoid living when one is given flesh and blood and Holy Eucharist. No, no, we said to her, as she struggled to sit up and talk; in any case, we know what you have to say. We toil too. We have our feasts and fasts, our hot days, our cold winds. Our hearts beat and we suffer. No, no. That is the sort of thing clever people of the world have to say—that one, that different one, the strange one doing the outlandish things, every outlandish thing you can think of—that one is alive, they say. We know. We have children and nephews and cousins in the world. But we have to handle this situation. This live fish that can't but live but not in this our air, so to speak. We are not cruel. Why not let her go free?

What? Said Anna. You would do that? Send her away?

She has brought blood, shouted Zoe, bending over with the effort. And then unavoidably, it all came spilling out. Anna listened with her eyes closed and chin lifted, her face going white, as we described the crowd, little Paul and his savage beating of Dimitri, even kicking his head when he was down.

Ugh, said Anna. Healthy young delinquent growing up to be a murderer. His father too was a criminal.

Do you mean little Paul? articulated Zoe, slowly.

Of course, I mean little Paul, big Paul, oversized Paul, the lot of them.

He was born and bred on Holy Island—they are islanders, down to the last drop of their blood. Never left. Never showed the slightest interest in abandoning their homeland for the world, for money and luxury, for strange religions, atheism, natural and Indian inspirations. Followed the way of fishing. We are simple people. They have always eaten our bread, drunk our own clear, pure water from the middle of the forest. They have entered into the blood stream and heart-beat of this island for better or for worse, continued Zoe, romantically.

And Dimitri?

Son of a half-breed with some hocus pocus notion of our Lord.

Anna had an ugly look on her face made all silvery by the white of the pillow and her hair, the shadows from the blinds and the white sunlight of the winter sun. This is how you refer to Agatha!

I tell the truth of the blood.

So it all comes out, said Anna. Curses that I am sick and cannot kick you all out myself.

We have always loved Agatha, began Foti, trembling with the anger of the weak. We simply have not known what to do. She has always been so much her own person.

I have not loved Agatha, said Zoe, in a harsh, low, guttural. But I have tolerated her. I thought that with a little more time, a few more years, a new understanding, a life with Jason, the one son that is in our midst, one of us, and no, we do not even count his blood, his breeding, he is adopted through faith, we are not prejudiced, nor irrational—I thought that Agatha would follow. Didn't she see our own priest go up the mountain on his knees? Repentance is a serious thing. It is conformity; severing oneself completely from the old rebellions even those buried in the heart, no matter the pain.

Ah, but you hated Father Isaac for his repentance.

We wondered if it was show. That is legitimate. And we asked ourselves why since Agatha was seen talking to him, intimately, fixing his meals sometimes, sewing Max's trousers—he didn't take a firm line with her. Catechism. Baptism.

You know perfectly well what we have always said and we said it loud and clear to the rich man: We are not a playboy's paradise; we are a particular place where our Lord walked in the form of Mother Dora; we have lost but we will win again. We are bound together by our way and traditions. Intimately and unavoidably bound together. We have no room for the dancing of the world on our shores because they are beautiful, the swimming in our waters because they are pristine. We see no possibility of jazz on the island and the women kicking their legs high and free.

You are sad and foolish, said Anna.

You don't understand. We toe the line with the angels. For the true freedom lies in ultimate and absolute obedience—and so the Lord visits us once again. Makes us part of Him until we are not ourselves but Christ. Not flesh but God.

But even Agatha in her own heart loves our ways, said Foti, yielding to her soft nature. She is not worldly. She simply can't help herself. And she needn't go far away.

Can't you see, said Anna, leaning back her head into her pillows helplessly. That what you think about yourselves and about Holy Island is a myth. The Jews of Jesus' time also had a myth about themselves. This led to the near stoning of the woman taken in adultery. They imagined they lived according to the commandments of God. Jesus showed them they were nowhere near the commandments of God. In fact, they were living in such rebellion in their pseudo righteousness that publicans, harlots and Samaritans, Canaanites and others whom they despised for their sinfulness were living closer to God. What do you have here that makes you close to God?

We live with only our fish and our lemons…

What do fish and lemons have to do with God? Do you think that He is sitting down to one of your fried fish feasts with you? Where you overeat and tell salacious jokes, gossip savagely about your neighbors?

We are but sinners, but we try...

Feebly, said Anna with disgust.

We crept away. For one thing Anna had a certain smell about her. For another, Tia was beginning to agitate and to motion us away. Apparently, it was time for Anna's painkiller. What we had said to Anna was indeed feeble. We tacitly agreed—if only we had a true priest, a man of the Spirit who spoke eloquently and could put the words in our mouths to use against near atheists like Anna. But there was no use referring to the church. Imagine—we couldn't even bring it up! We had had to resort to our simple life—our fish and lemons, as if that was better than some rousing argument with words that so twisted the mind that there was a kind of check mate of logic and no getting out for Anna. We decided to try a tactic—maybe unusual, but it would show good heartedness. Zoe was the one who initiated it. Send Agatha, she said in a weary voice to talk the whole thing over with Anna. See if they can come up with a compromise. It was feeble, though.

Months had passed since Dimitri's beating. One after the other, bright, brilliant, blazing winter days with the cold winds and blinding sun, alternated with shade, the beautiful sky here blue, there with patches of shadow-colored clouds. There were dull mornings when the sky was a blanket of cloud. And these would clear later and the same thing—the sun would come out, glorious as a king and then the winds would start up and the clouds would move.

The siestas melted in us all desire to talk about what had happened. Paul and little Paul had gone to Agatha's place already. So it was settled. Our digestions continued good: We had eaten all the feasts of the recipes we had devised for the rich man. We were reconciled to his leaving us; it was after all all the same to us. We went back to the life we had always known. Of course, even now, periodically, someone humphed a little. Cleo, Barbara, Nisos—whose homes had almost been bought and who had almost gone abroad and almost become world travelers smelling of different fragrances. But what is it in the end, said Cleo—eating fish in a restaurant in Paris instead of here...not as good even. For all that the world has its trucks and airplanes. Nisos said—but oh, the ladies. I see a congregation of ladies in hats and dresses. Color and beauty and kicking high the legs and dancing.

So you would be an old hornet among the flowers, said Timos. Drink your brandy. You would do as little good there as you do here.

The truth is, said Zoe, sans a few machines, we have everything here that the world has.

That must be impossible, exclaimed Cleo, raising her hands and eyes to the ceiling, as if to say, this idea should be raised in utter deference to the mind of the Absolute. For such ideas had been rankling in their minds since—the beginning-- that is, the time that was only a vague notion--the epoch, the year just before the loss of the island's holiness.

At that time, explained Zoe, when it was again referred to, that time of holiness, we knew perfectly well that the world had nothing. We had everything. Then the change: Now we sense that the world has, in fact, a little more than we do. This is our tragic change. The sign itself of loss of holiness. Yet we live, we live.

Ah, said Foti, as if she had said something very profound and as profound things go, tended to be secret.

At that time, said Nisos, speaking of before the end, wives were the most beautiful of women.

Cleo batted him lightly with her handbag. What are you thinking, you old fool?

Only of waking up and finding a violet by my side, instead of fat flesh and smell.

And you a stink hole? As if any violets would grow by you, you old garbage heap! Nodding and jeering slightly, the women passed through the crowd of old men like water through fingers. The men thought that they could hold them back with their banter; for there was even among them—seventy, eighty years old with hair so thin— on Cleo's head it looked like it had been blown there with the pink cranium shining through-- and Zoe who would braid what was left and then curl it up in a bun, with her prominent nose and once the smoothest skin on the island that she doctored with moisturizing lotions morning and night—Foti truth be told, the stupider one, but who had a face in a perfect heart shape and even now she had hair, hair, which so endeared the boys when they were younger, they were so embarrassingly sentimental—a chance for the suitors. What does a woman need brains for? These were the women that sat on the balconies and in the kitchens, tasting the apricots of the year, passing information, making pronouncements, leaving fragrances; it seemed ridiculous but what they determined on, what they had in mind, and muttered all together in their powwows, this parcel of hags, that is what usually came to pass. They turned the winds—these jabberers from North to South and East to West. It was a saying among the men. And when you tried to hold them—perhaps it was just that one's old magnetism had died away with age—they flowed away as even now. And they left behind a slight residue on the old men's flesh for they were oil and water, not just water.

Agatha was something else. Young and electric still like an eel in still water. She moved with the little group of ancients just because she had been unwanted elsewhere and before (the end) had been prematurely old. But she had been reborn at the end, they said, the old men did. To some she was as fascinating as a snake… Nisos saw that her hips were loose, moved almost as easily as branches in the wind, yet clung all together like a ball of electric fire at the end of a wand—her spine. He dreamed of spring nights on the beach with her—naked skin like melon flesh—and eating and eating like on midnights, midsummer, when you can't rest for the heat and go down to the refrigerator and pull out something cold and wet. And he woke from his dream stupid; he went around proclaiming that this was true holiness not anything else—wet, cool melon flesh- nakedness of man and woman, that is, Agatha and he. The town slapped him; he sat at his slapping post in the tavern with Maria weeping and raising her fists, but she couldn't stop them coming around and slapping his face.

When his face was swollen and hot, Maria ran to Agatha's house and she listened to her and came quickly and knelt by Nisos's side, with his face blazing red, weeping like a little girl. If you touch him, she said looking up from her kneeling posture with blazing eyes, I will call the priest. What foolishness! To think that slapping someone would restore their sanity—that is, change their minds when their minds had discovered something. They might have laid hands on Agatha too—for they believed in their heart of hearts that she started it all—standing erect in such a way, kneeling erect too, as if defiantly, and Nisos now meekly crying, tear after tear!—but up came Dimitri from the street with his eye and down came Father Isaac with Max from the little church's hill and somehow we knew that we were doing wrong. Father Isaac asked us whether we knew about what he referred to as Adam and Eve before the Fall, perfect eloping true lovers, for this story shows you why, you understand, why, authoritatively, in spiritual science, you may have redemption in Christ Jesus.

Why Father? said Michael who had relished slapping old Nisos, despite his age—the young man in sheer insolence-- and now hypocritical, toadying at the priest's feet!

Father Isaac merely responded to his question: Because of that nakedness before God that this man that you have desecrated for so-called madness talked about. Because you were created naked in God as man and woman. This is love. This and only this. And so Christ said to us—give up, give up to it. And who would give up to nakedness but an old, retired fisherman who sat all shrunken and impotent and saw heaven move on the axel of a woman's hips. Where do you see heaven—suspended in midair? Is the soul fleshless?

Nisos sighed, and got up from his chair, wandered off. For a month he sat still at home, barely eating and drinking, his eyes with that look when someone is kind to you, so kind that it draws tears. He had traveled to another place in his mind, his wife said.

Everybody began talking at once, and after a short time, they were gathered around, Paul too. It is despicable to see the young slapping their elders, he said. It has become clear, however, that the elders, venerable and dear to us though they are, have been foully tempted.

The priest was silent. Dimitri took Agatha by the arm and tried to lead her away. But Paul stopped them. Perhaps you don't understand, he said to them. The new-fangled way of living in the world is fine for out there, he gestured towards the sea. Here we want our peace back—just that.

Peace and a little money would be helpful, peeped Cleo, she smiled softly, unwittingly in Paul's direction.

We watched a little shamefaced. For we should never have subjected Nisos, one of our own, to such a wretched violation of his dignity. We thought, it was almost funny—to bring him around. We thought he was in a stupor of sorts. But we clammed up and listened to what Paul would say to Agatha. Aye, she was the cause of it all.

It is logical to the uttermost end of logical, said Paul; time and again we have asked you—conform a little—and instead...

You don't understand, murmured Agatha, despite Dimitri trying to silence her and surreptitiously creep away with her. It is a gift, a gift to all of us.

What—a mature woman, who ought to be remembering her husband, off on tours around single men's homes—Simon, Leo—with food and a back like that...?

A back like what?

Don't play the innocent. You know what I mean. Growing straight up, swinging and swaying, arched in the middle and lifting her buttocks, and full of self.

But don't you see you are ridiculous, put in Dimitri. Why should she not stand tall?

You are distracting us from the main point. There is something unfeminine in Agatha at this point. Male and female God created us and right now there is something decidedly not female.

But it seems that Nisos here was tempted by her femininity.

Not so. It was an evil temptation. Agatha expresses, yes, expresses in her walk, her physique that she, not God, is doing the deciding. You see, men and women, Paul presented his argument to us, there are ways and ways of subtly trammeling people's minds. St. Mary of Egypt when she was so gaily promiscuous knew that it took just one look, that it was not a matter of lengthy discourses, convincing people by words. No, the quiver of a thigh was enough, the slow walk with the buttocks displayed to an advantage, a shift for a shirt falling down over a plump breast. One excuses almost sexual savagery when one sees the way women have of twining the man by all his senses. How can we live except by our senses? What do we know except what our senses tell us? We become helpless. Of course, the saints, like St. Mary, when they were converted, mortified by fire in all their senses for years and years wandering in the desert without food or drink, burning in the sun. And that was a light penance for she had caused so many others to sin.

For a time I thought, we thought on this island, that Agatha would go the way of the chastened—sober and firm in resolve. Instead, she turned her heel on repentance and lifted herself up like a snake, and came down the paths of all our days coiling around the men.

I am going to live, exclaimed Agatha, hotly. Yes, I am going to live. It is you that are violent and evil. You. Inciting your own son to acts of violence against another. Murderer at heart. I don't blame an old man for thinking thoughts. You too have thought thoughts. But you are something else—not a thinker of evil but a doer of it.

You see, dearest Saints, said Paul sweeping his hand around to the crowd. The vice and folly in this woman. Maybe in the world she has a place. Here we can hardly call her a woman. For the women we know, the women born and bred on this soil are one and all the Woman of Christ—abject before him, soft, withdrawn, a true listener of his words. Not a kicker of legs high, heels in his eyes. Look at her passionate, furious. We know the true fathers prescribed for us dispassion and meekness.

Mary Magdalene flung herself in Jesus' arms and kissed him often. We know that because on the day of Resurrection, he told her not to touch him in that kind of a tone.

And it is the resurrected Christ that we preach here, said Paul, sternly. She fell at his feet and worshipped without touching. The tone you speak of comes out of your own imagination, deformed because of sinful thoughts.

We all of us were stirred a little by Paul's words. We knew that Zoe who had taken one look at Dimitri's eye and been thoroughly disgusted had been conferring with Paul for several days. We knew that Agatha was being severely tried and we thought that maybe the upshot of it all would be that Paul would compel her to go and that in the course of time when Simon died, he would be our chief. But we felt that Nisos had been in this instance the fool and Agatha had been exceptionally gracious. Simon and the priest said that they saw in Agatha only grace and kindness. It was difficult for us to sort this kind of argument out. But seeing as she had the priest on her side, maybe Paul's arguments would be set aside. We longed for arguments as arguments to be set aside. We wanted only one pronouncement: the utter, absolute pronouncement of truth!

Was it our fault that Nisos had been whipped? He had sat in the corner not resisting, hanging his head like a dog. Was it Agatha? We considered a minute. Our minds changed in a little light confusion that we rather liked. We rather thought that it would be sad to lose her. What we liked was this kind of rousing debate that then ended in nothing at all. We all went home to drink our red wine—a glass in the winter is so cheering and Nisos would recover his senses and his wife would give him a tongue lashing. For whatever the priest had to say, our half-witless priest, as Paul secretly called him, but it went around the village, you can't live without your senses. Nisos looking after Agatha had crawled up the tree of desire like a cat. Perhaps, as the priest said it was in the end the tree of Knowledge of Good and Evil, but he had been stranded on it, stuck up there beneath blazing sun, and cool moon and not able to come down. And from that perspective, of course, even nakedness was holy.

That Agatha's father had come to our island as temptation became the theme of Paul's discourse wherever he sat down. Whether he was among the fishermen with little Paul, setting out hurriedly in the dark with the tackle and gear, the little flashlights and the lanterns that they set on the prows of their boats, standing around, arms folded, reminiscing about how he used to be the first one out—or in the tavern sitting by Peter who would be busy fondling up Maria's leg as she sat with us as she sometimes did, he would mention it, sometimes just casually, in passing. But it was all one tune like father like daughter. Both had refused baptism. She had that slightly muddy gypsy look, and she had held on to the Muslim bible. This island was intended to be for Christ.

Once Maria had said to him with tears in her eyes—but I know that she loves Jesus, our Savior. I have heard with my own ears, seen with my own eyes.

What is that? Thundered Paul. What have you seen?

Well, that she—wouldn't give up, that she loves and helps others in need, that she talks sometimes to…to him.

What has that to do with the price of beans…began Paul disgustedly. Mind that you don't enter into this again, Maria. Or I will call the police from the other island to put a stop to this nefarious business of whoring.

We began however to listen with half an ear to Paul. We all of us privately considered that he liked very much the sound of his own voice. He wanted it ringing in everybody's ears like holy bells calling us to church on Sunday.

A month went by. Nisos came back from the journey he took in his mind to a gentle place far away where they had healed his dignity. We were glad to have Nisos back with us. He was still a little stupid; he would drift off while talking or remain very silent sometimes and tears could gather in his eyes. When we asked why he said that he had within him a voice of truth—that he knew, just knew things. What it was he knew he couldn't tell us. So privately we laughed and left him alone. Agatha had knelt down beside him that day he had been whipped in public. And she had been shamed by not only Paul's words. Men have a way of looking. Paul didn't look at her, we noticed. He averted his gaze as if she was contemptible. When she spoke, even full of fury, he looked at the hair of her head as if he was going to sweep by like a storm wind. For the moment, she was free but he would be back. There are spoken and unspoken messages.

Dimitri with his eye long healed but still looking different since that day it had been so disfigured, had awakened certain disturbing thoughts in us. Paul seemed now supremely to disregard that violent episode of his son. We thought well and well…. It was true there was violence and blood had been shed; but we were men, Dimitri had to stand and take what was in the line of a man's life to take. The women were all fastidious and squeamish about what for men was obvious and living reality. Even Nisos got to laughing at himself after a while, squaring off with Timos, feigning punches, wrestling a bit. Yes, the thought of a little fighting was not so bad in the end. A man living all his life without once testing himself that way was hardly a man. Michael, our youngest, because he had been swimming and running was muscular in the sun like an angel. He and Little Paul or Dimitri or Jason or Nico should wrestle in the sand. It felt good to strive against a body. What was the body but a door of flesh that one had only to ram through.

Dimitri found himself sitting with Katrina on the beach one warmer winter day. He had asked her there in a humbler tone than the tone he had used with her when they were last together, months ago. It was not in order to get anything in particular done, he had told her. It was just to do that most delicious common thing—waste time with an old friend. This time Katrina had been low key, not so hilarious as before.

And Dimitri had honored her—pointing out that it was noble of her to sacrifice so much for her two aged parents.

Katrina had said—it seemed that it was put in front of me to do. I never thought of it as a choice. And if you are going to ask me—how could I do it? It isn't the doing of it in the global sense that is so impossible. It is the everyday, minute by minute and you find out that you have had enough, that you can't bear it anymore, when you can't find a scissors or a spool of thread to mend a jacket and your burst out in a roar, something you never knew you had in you.

Even for me, it would be hard, you know, to see my mother go into a nursing home. But if things got to that point…I like to see her in my home always, busying herself, now dancing—but…

Does she really dance? Asked Katrina; it is said that she dances as men dance—freely, leaping, standing on her hands.

She dances seriously, said Dimitri. She takes big steps. It is natural for her having the big feet that run in our family, he said jestingly but soft-voiced.

I would have been enthralled, said Katrina, years ago. We all know such things as duty, and obedience, but when you come down to it, following your heart is the most beautiful thing.

But if your heart discards people who are helpless… My grandmother died shortly after I was born, but I should like to have thought that my mother would have cared for her night and day as you are doing.

Ha, you want someone to do it, said Katrina morosely. What about when you yourself are tied hand and foot, almost physically, I mean?

Yes, that is true. We always think ourselves honest until the old back to basics woman comes in and rubs our dishonesty in our noses.

But you would still choose dishonesty, hypocrisy even and be out in the world.

Dimitri put his hands behind his head and lay back in the sand. He looked at Katrina, her thick hair still dark and lustrous shining down to her waist, her heavy arms, the fold of fat around her waist, and in his mind's eye he saw the way she walked, stiff as a board and the calf of one leg stretched out, the knee at an awkward angle with a slight rustle of dress. She was a year under his mother's age, but she behaved as if she were older. He had never thought her ugly, although he knew that that was the general consensus, and had respected her flaming eros, thought it right and natural, intelligent and good. But one thing she lacked was body.

It wasn't that she wasn't slim, she had no give, no sweetness. She didn't conjure up that delight that is only most beautiful, nothing less. It was not ugliness physically; but it appeared that locked into her body were years of anger and frustration. If only, someone had taken her out of the line of women dancers at the festivals, years ago and said to her kick your leg up as high as you are able. Make that a goal to kick above your head towards the stars!

And then if, every day at four, she had gotten up just for that purpose. Didn't the priest advise them to pray—to rise and pray every day, he had often told them in Liturgy—well, so, better even than prayer—kicking towards heaven—and then one joy, physically is released from a body. And then maybe you'll become a body.

If you are thinking about what I was like! If you are remembering me years ago… That is all over, Dimitri. You left. I fell into whatever family life I found.

It is true I left you, said Dimitri. Yet you were loyal. But you have done something to yourself that I think is unfair.

What is that?

You have not permitted yourself one thing—the real joy in you could shine through, he said pleading, the real love. I am not talking about what happened between us. Of course not. I was young, you were infatuated. We both didn't know what we were doing.

What one thing, asked Katrina, astounded. She looked at him; her face was that of an elderly person, open mouthed, perplexed, despite all the years of wisdom— here was something she had never beheld held out to her as if it was life.

I don't know, said Dimitri, half smiling at her, half sad. Anyway, it is too late for it.

I have found that the universe is a great machine; we are all just parts, cogs…it is not more our fault about our decision—things that happen.

There you are wrong. There exists sweat for some higher purpose that is life too, said Dimitri. For that sweat is the sweat that produces fruit.

It is really all a vain exercise, said Katrina. But a part of the machine—this expenditure of energy as the lights flash, and the wheel rolls around.

She looked at him and shifted her legs stretched out on the sand. Katrina still felt something of the old flame for Dimitri; he came back even more handsome than he had left. She was not at all a participant in one of Paul's little lectures; she snorted at Paul and little Paul, despising them for what they had done—even resorting to kicking Dimitri's face when he was down at their feet. It was odd and horrible. She had exulted when Dimitri had pulled through. And would have thought it just if he had beaten little Paul—wished he had. She felt that he would not be the one to do so. She felt in fact that she knew him better than many people—knew him a little like his mother knew him except in a different depth where men don't go with their mothers. She felt she was as she put it to herself 'old flesh' with him—there was something whether or not he approved now of her body—that was one body between them, even though this was part of memory and imagination and nothing more. She felt she knew what Dimitri was talking about, and like him she said to herself but that one thing—what is it? I don't know. And for years she had felt dry as dust.

She wanted to open her mouth under his gaze and say to him—but that sweat is less and less now—even that; for although it was meaningless, it was refreshing. And she would have done so, only he anticipated her and said: But that sweat can again be conjured up.

Look at you, talking of sweat, said Katrina. I sweat. You don't even have a job.

Not for the moment. But I have plans, said Dimitri, airily.

Katrina felt her heart sink—of course, youth was on his side. Females, fun. And she? Who was she? An abject creature—forty-nine, worn out, thick with food. And even his mother, a year or two older than she, lifting up now, leaping and running the way she couldn't even dream of. Who was she? It had all passed her by. And she felt a tightening in her throat.

Of course, you have plans. You are young; there will be women who have slim waists. Isn't that the regular theme of love poetry since the ancient Greeks?

It is your fault, Dimitri raised his finger from the sand at her and shook it. For getting old. But you and I Katrina are two jaded lovers, in reality. You from frustration; I from use. I don't know which is worse.

They sat until it began to grow too cold and Dimitri said he had nothing to offer Katrina except his poor shivering self to use as a blanket, and looked at her with a jocular look. She smiled and shook her head.

Ah, you have refused me utterly, utterly, he glanced down with a look of concentration at the sand. Let us go, then and spread our woe 'round about so that men and women know how love is friend and foe.

Katrina laughed, scrambled clumsily to her feet and held out her hand to Dimitri. He kissed her hand. Katrina's hand was a commonplace hand, the kind that are always a little too big, not particularly soft, the kind that in fact you don't find often in literature or actually even on women in romantic situations when hands metamorphose and transfigure and become more akin to birds of dawn or the material of nightingale's songs; but this was not a romantic situation—just a blundering middle aged woman with an old lover, younger lover who was looking at her without any unkindness but with a certain amusement. For she had done something 'right' this woman. And the world rolled by and saw no more than a thick knee under a light coat kicking out in the uneven, awkward walk of the pudgy. There must really be in her, thought Dimitri, getting up, some electrical charge—getting her up in the morning, telling her, yes, and you will move up to the next level.

You have lived like a nun, said Dimitri to her; I mean it in admiration.

Nothing like, said Katrina, looking at him uncomfortably.

Perhaps you have found the one thing needful, and in that case, we rush by like phantom creatures—immaterial to you.

Don't mock me, said Katrina turning and walking awkwardly in the sand. She was carrying her shoes but had on stockings. Strange, thought Dimitri to come on to the beach in stockings. He was behind her with his jeans rolled up and his thin brown ankles visible and perfect feet. He felt he was properly attired for the beach but somehow behind her in some vital way—the march to death—was it that? But if I am going to believe such a thing, he thought to himself, half my intellect would have to be buried alive. Still, he thought, something about absurdity and truth—that she for all that she appeared to be an absurd figure…

Dimitri raced up coming up just behind her. I want to see you again, he said.

See away, said Katrina. She was irked because although he had left off tantalizing her the way he used with his loveliness and intelligence, he still exuded a kind of huge knowledge and she expected something from him—an answer, recognition that what he had done years ago, reduced her to begging, was wrong and some offer, some piece of that beautiful mind asking forgiveness, but really offering it to her for making such a fool of herself.

Of course, she forgave him; that was not the point. He had had to go and she had had to stay. She realized that the carving of destiny in each person is what it is; he hadn't meant to use her at all and she was equally responsible having started it the way she had started a number of little passions in young men, as if magically, for she was not beautiful nor romantic, never had been. No, of course, he had had to go. But to remember her and not to offer her to that piece—that forgiveness--to raise her to his level by a word, and initiation into that fabulous knowledge that he had acquired over the seas and that she could see in him like a bright storm cloud! And what was this 'one thing, the one thing needful?' It seemed to her a way of holding her off that she was again held just out of reach of so much.

Father Isaac looked at Max in the fading winter sunlight of the afternoon a week before Christmas. Max was lovely, he thought. One doesn't usually think this about a member of the male sex. But who would know it? Many a novice in the monastery had also been lovely, lovelier than the most lovely women—come to them as if carved out of innocence and joy like little birds. God had an eye for physical beauty. Appearances were not disregarded in heaven. Father Isaac privately thought that both John, the Beloved, and Nathaniel in the Gospel were physically lovely boys and that in John's case his beauty was thorough because it went along with a certain purity—read honesty and zeal. Nathaniel himself was seen—for the beauty must have attracted even the eye of the Lord, and then of course, he knew that Nathaniel was without guile—for outer and inner corresponded.

Now Max was too elementary to hide himself or to obscure his real meaning in any given expression of his. Out it would pop like some embarrassing sexual proclivity given the right environment. The priest thought in his endearment of Max that his heart was too full of natural vigor, that of love and faith and hope, so that the evil tendencies, the wicked emotions would all burst out of it when they arose instead of festering within being unable to keep company with this natural vigor, this inborn health.

He hesitated to say purity. Max was obedient and God-fearing, but he had not reached that fearless intimacy with God, that stepping over the bridegroom's threshold, that last moment of self abandon, abandonment of the small configuration of prejudice and complaint that is the abode of all those who rejoice. He cringed and turned in his deepest mind to his dead mother and even away from her sometimes and looked with an eye of intolerance at the priest and villagers.

What is it? He had asked him. Not in so many words, but in little movements, gestures, tenderness. Surely, you don't have a deep dark secret or do you? And even if you do—what of it? God knows where you are sore. He is a healer of broken birds. Aye, they die and go where they are counted—a blessed place that is light and flight, sun and oneness that they can only approximate on earth—or they heal and fly again. And if the birds—where we see it simply—how much more us created in the very image and likeness. But Max cringed back. It was too painful. The finger and thumb of God too heavy.

Ah, so the priest had kissed him and let him alone. Periodically, now, after a good seven years of serving, Max would burst out but all irrational, almost bizarre. You have fed me for years, he said once; who do you think you are? As if I ever asked. Who told you to do me a kindness that night I came to you? As if that sets you into a place of mastery. Oh yes, you know it all. Eternal life and all the tricks.

But Sunday morning would find him praying, preparing for the Liturgy. For Max was soft, almost entirely meek and ultimately childlike. He had worship and passion for the great and wonderful as children have; he believed that there were whispers of the saints during the liturgy that the great and wonderful was yet to come. Surely nothing on earth has been or ever will be that. Until the great and wonderful, we are nothing; and we will be shown, shown up in some cases…So Max still went around the village ringing a little bell to gather people around him and he had a few even now—old Simon, sometimes Nisos, sometimes Agatha, Michael, a few of the elderly widows who prefer to be anonymous and stand in headscarves their anonymous backs set against the cold sea wind—and they would listen as he described the King-dom, quoting from the Jesus' words and showed how it was to be in the glorious return of the Son of Man. Then there were the funny parts of the lecture—Jesus was to sit not on a golden throne, but on a little stool with the angels round about. His crown, the crown of thorns, now not causing him wounds but still bloody. And he was to say—come you gentle and obscure who loved the poor.

And he would watch Agatha smiling. She often smiled at him. An encouraging, gentle, lifted smile. His heart held out a little, delicate, soft hand to her heart. She knew although he had never told her that she was the one person who could stand where his dead mother stood—in that same light. He once said to her—ah, you too, are dead, for what happened, women never live beyond such things, but you are liv-ing. If you believe that Jesus is the resurrection and the life, even if you are dead, yet will you live. And Agatha had believed. He had seen it in her. She danced and not only--. She had looked at him dainty, soft, so unable and seen in him the greater per-son, the one walking confidently in the way of Christ, along the strait and narrow of the Lord. And she had gotten a glimpse, set her foot in the footsteps once or twice and nearly dance-fainted, as he, Max had, and she had believed, come to life, danc-ing. But going back home she had realized—the house, Jason, the electricity bills to be paid; the old grasping nude bone had come through the soft hand of faith—she could not let go.

Father Isaac was there and not there. No one noticed him when Max spoke in that sweet coaxing voice. Max, everyone noticed, was actually rapt when he spoke. Around him seemed to be a cloud of light. Father Isaac knew that he was as a kinder-garten child only able to speak to express all the fervor for the Truth. There would be no listening to him in the world of men. He would be squashed like a beetle. Few ever had compassion on a beetle. There would be not a moment to talk in a city street or auditorium. It was only here in this funny, scarcely populated island where they were obsessed with the idea that they had once been apostles of Christ, having seen Him resurrected-- that this little beetle of the light was allowed to crawl, because this baby sparrow peeped about God, brought them news of the far away dwelling of the saints.

Father Isaac took up his position behind Max when he preached and bowed his head. Ah, the world had a way of considering it somehow wrong to believe, to love God, and to dedicate oneself to poverty. Love of neighbor was often overlooked if it was not dramatic, heroic. And it could be love even of the beetle for love sancti-fied any creature. This love-configuration of faith, God, poverty and neighbor is the only path. Max knew it. Everything else no matter how loud it sounds, how bright it looks is phantoms, ghosts. The world is to be whirled away in its frivolity and loud impatient sound.

Yet even now—could he say that he was poor? He had had those lace curtains made. His heart had sung in the sun at the sight of those lace curtains framing their one window. And they were hung slightly askew. He had wasted time longing for them to hang perfectly but somehow they hadn't gotten around to fixing them. So was he poor? The Church fathers those dried out, tasteless bodies had said that even if you give away all your possessions but hang on to one spoon with love and desire, that is, one set of lace curtains!-- you are not poor. Ah, the tricksters.

But no, he would not do it. He would hang on to those lace curtains--deliberately. For he had Max who came when he called and whom he loved and those lace curtains that lightened the room with their beauty were for him. A true love gift.

Faith in Christ—did he have it? Each time Max opened his sweet mouth, the priest fell back on his wondering soul. Faith in God—what was it? That if he did his bit, the Lord would give him heaven? No. It was more a matter of come hell or high water, God would not let him perish. No reason for it--the simple act of putting oneself into the great hand. And that came and went in him. And yet the Lord said: whoever comes to me I will not cast out.

Love—alas, so little. A lot of food. Nothing could detract from the meaning of loving your neighbor. Many many had come in holiness into the world, Father Isaac knew, on purpose to stir up hatred against those who were different. Many were bitter with him for harboring, that is, loving, a gypsy family with a Muslim bible. And yet, he thought, what better testimony to Jesus' image and likeness in a man than such exquisite tenderness as love of an antagonist?

Yea and there are those, like himself, he thought sadly, so ready to see the mote in the eye of another. How little he had loved. Compassion yes, on the trees, the insects, the birds, on Martha, on Agatha—he had offered food and had loved, yes, gently, opening his home and what little he had; but love, the divine fire: that was still elusive. One had to burn sweet in one's heart—that was the Christ passing. Passion at last, the beautiful truth but some thought that pale insipid shadowy thing sex. And yet in secret, a secret sign in the body, known only to a few—sex was the sign of Christ's Passion too. For eros was a form of deep suffering-- encoded in this act of the flesh was the whole absurdity and deep pain despite the pleasure!— but people didn't believe that life on the whole is God. That physical things, men, women, even children by one gesture here or there, were, in secret, heavenly signs.

And sometimes he, yes—neighbor, God—sometimes he: He wandered far from faith. The neighbor was ugly and didn't give anything to him, God was God damn it! far away.

So Max made him feel so close and so far away. Max whom he held to his bosom, whom he kissed on the mouth and forehead, made him feel as if the crowned Jesus was looking at him with his head on one side, half in rebuke, half in sorrow. He, Father Isaac, an ugly old man that had presumptuously stood before Christ as if he had done something for God.

Now he knew that Max had something on his mind. He knew too what it was. The stirrings of an adolescent desire to burst out that he had repressed growing up with his father who had not only beaten him, but who had instilled in him a horror, horror of himself—that he might be capable of corruption and despair and pride masquerading as little jokes, on-going hilarity; this clownishness had appalled him. He had tried to make himself little. He had grown super sensitive, dainty-fleshed. He knew that his father, were he to watch him and see him for what he was, would flay him alive, emotionally and spiritually. And so he hid in corners, one day bursting out against the cruelty so commonly found in his father towards one of his mistresses. And then he had fled.

Even when Max knew that Leo had changed, he had hesitated to approach him. It was settled and decided, the priest was Max's new 'father' and 'mentor'; he was learning something; he was following a way that was hard. For poverty outwardly is merely the most elementary level of poverty. It was necessary to a degree, but from there one passed to poverty inwardly—poverty of ego, of anger, of lust, of envy. One had, in short, poverty of self, nakedness of heart. One was as Jesus—meek and mild. There were difficulties— for carnal natures such as Max's always demanded richness of spirit, cloth of gold over love.

Max was an apt pupil. But there had been something unresolved. A tiger waiting in the wings when he had been on stage, as it were, as a sparrow. Father Isaac sighed and thought. This is not something I am going to interfere with. Let it come.

And the boy had brought out one evening when they were eating an omelette with goat's cheese that he had cooked-- wrath. All accusations, self-accusation, garbled arguments, passionate nonsensical proclamations; it got to the point where the man couldn't speak, he was burning with such unjust anger, and yet it was just. Father Isaac hadn't considered the man that was Max. He had only thought of the soul that was Max and not Max. The soul of which Max is the sign.

Max rose from the table, stacked the dishes in the sink with a loud clatter, and went to pick up his things. He had packed a little bag.

No, said Father Isaac, imploringly, no.

Why shouldn't I go?

I love you. Yes, yes, it is nothing special. Only an old, ugly man who has sinned against you. But—here is where it will all start, if you only have patience.

When will it start?

One waits—sometimes even after death, one is still waiting. There are Catholics who believe in Purgatory—souls being 'finished' and made ready for God. They believe it is a form of punishment and thus very terrible, though they have the hope that it will end. I don't believe in this punishment but what I am saying is that the soul is still evolving in some cases. There is a craziness in Christians that make them wish pain and suffering—on others. Hell mongers, and now Purgatory mongers. But me and you, you see, are working out the finishing with God. Gently. I don't mind that you blow up at me.

I was going to go to the other island and live as a beggar, preaching in the streets.

No! I mean only gentleness—stay here and share my simple food. Bread, eggs, fish, when we can afford it. Be well. As a beggar in the streets you'd be sick. Endure what has been worked out here. God is slow to come. Work out a rich love—as you have been given, give. I know that I was wrong; you never really came to me to live here and abide with me. I cheated and stole you. But you see, it was love.

Max was standing with the light on him looking for all the world like a carving of a saint or an angel. He was stooped slightly and his hands were cupped together. I didn't want to come. I didn't want to know.

Yes, I know, sighed Father Isaac. It is just that here was such potential when you came that rainy night. And then if you remember the next morning was glorious. I thought it was a sign.

But I am not what you think I am. And I can't be myself here.

As you wish, said Father Isaac sadly.

In the end, Max didn't go. He lingered and loitered, imagining that he would get the idea, the inspiration—that he would ultimately know what to do for it would be put inside his mind and heart. He went to bed on his mattress on the floor—something Father Isaac had made sewing together in two sheets bundles of rags;—he went to bed thinking and woke up thinking. That Father Isaac loved him never seemed to him to be of any importance. He would say that. It was natural. He was a priest who had raised a young boy. But he wanted above all to be honest and clean and more than even this he wanted his spirit.

An odd thing? No, thought Father Isaac. It is a conviction in the human bosom that the spirit will solve, make beautiful and fulfill, give life. And with it comes the devils. Yet let them come. There is energy in devils that comes quicker than God.

The priest after watched Max as much as he could. He didn't quite think that Max would come at him with a knife but he wasn't sure. For Max had screamed, stampeded around the room a number of times since that day he had threatened to leave, but interestingly, after about five minutes, he had suddenly calmed, and without having destroyed the furniture or smashed the crystal—what little there was of it, he had leaned against the wall with his eyes closed, had lain down on his bed with his head on his arm, or drunk a glass of water.

Father Isaac felt that Max's whole body was saying –and it is all for the cause of nothingness. He wanted to take him in his arms and say to him, no—no! The machinery is defective here that is all. What we might call in our impoverished way: the machinery of the soul. There it is perfected when the soul is in Christ. But there were times he too began to doubt. What everything for some future date? Why not now? People live and die and this thing is still in the future. But the future is as real as the now. For in the future the now will be counted more than it is now. Every gesture, every thought. And either the Lord justifies or one is cast out. Even these days of sickness with nothingness all around us, are recorded—on what, how? Ah, are you so elementary, his one half said to his other, as to believe that God needs a notebook? That God needs what we call physical reality at all? Yet it is written, is a sign as well. And he began to wonder if Max and he had their names written in the Kingdom of Heaven.

Max, he knew, was suffering this sense of nothingness. It wasn't so much a lack of material reality somewhere or at some time, such as the end of the world, it was more the sense that nothing could help, nothing at all. That he had fallen into his own configuration, a trap of sorts, but of just being, existing, and that he could not escape. This configuration was and wasn't him. This nothingness formed and shaped in a certain way all around him. Here was the dilemma of the damned themselves, Father Isaac thought, for he knew Max's thoughts. One is but one is not. Whereas the blessed have left that behind. They were Christ's own Body—that is substance and in that substance one detected yes the configuration that however was transfigured. Just as a corpse and the corpse with life coming back to it are two different things.

So far away on a little ignored island in the blue Aegean sea, lived a man who was angry, afraid, sick and deliriously joyful—who lived, in short, partly in this world, and partly in another. In his little ramshackle room where he lived with the priest, Father Isaac who was wafer thin, white, had once been fragrant was now somewhat smelly, he moved around daintily and delicately so as not to disturb his mentor, and periodically, blew up at him. That was the only difference now—he blew up, he stormed and stamped. Then he flung himself on the bed for ten minutes or so, turning fitfully; then got up, and moved around the room again, leaning against the walls, or on the stove. After the age of several hours passed, he went out into the streets, Father Isaac following almost as if spying on him, creeping behind, and preached the Gospel to a few stragglers. During this time, he lifted his eyes and looked out to sea and seemed to see beautiful things, golden thrones on clouds and what not. He seemed to perceive the very gentleness of God on the sea when it was calm.

An insight came to Max when he was talking later to the priest. God fathoms rather than judges as we know it.

Fathoms said Father Isaac. And that evening he put a tape of opera on the old tape deck. Fathoms, he said smiling with his lips pursed as if drinking. Then he began to sing in his dreadful voice.

Slowly, without words being exchanged, and with more omelettes eaten, Max was reconciled to Father Isaac. Father Isaac said to himself half sadly that the human animal wants to be a war hero, a Leander, a Columbus, an astronaut! He has finally resigned himself to living in this inner room. It was not even my intent that he do it. Yet I am the one that told him no don't go. Don't explore the streets of a town far away all cut off from house and home. Here you will find it. Am I so sure?

Max didn't want to become public; and this the priest knew. He was a private person; he suffered Father Isaac to stand beside him, hold him, kiss him and to instruct him and sleep in the same room with him. But if he had had his way, he would have lived in a corner by himself.

Father Isaac fed him company; questioned him, teased him a little, made him talk. He had become sociable enough to respond sometimes more than monosyllabically to the intruder/accoster, the one who met him on the road and said things, and asked things. He was a fantasizer, he was; he held pictures in his mind. The picture most often there was that of heaven—a golden kingdom, light despite the weight of material gold, light as gossamer, as goose down and he raw and sick beside it. The visions of his unfitness for heaven made him sick too—a painful, disturbed kind of sickness—disturbed as a person, personality-wise, disordered in character. And yet the beauty of heaven in his mind was such that people did stop to listen to him talk of it and after the discourse made them wonder if such a thing was a gift from God. In other words, if God had set him in their midst and if God had set him talking.

Whenever he appeared on the road, it was always as if the sun appeared too, at that moment, making him brilliant; and he would begin—lambs and sheep, wayward ones let me tell you: there is a Kingdom finer than other kingdoms, golden as dawn light; it is the dawn and comes out as if floating on a white cloud when the sky is still un-blue; and God, the King, rests his chin on this cloud and his kingdom grows in his elbows—red gold as the dawn light. Light, momentary—I have seen it suspended like a breath in winter. In this kingdom the poor are kings, the despised, the pure, the well-fed pious ones clean out stables of oxen and smell excrement, and all gather together at the table and there they feast, an elixir of joy, a meat of love, and they are all suspended as a breath in the cold, frosty air.

Of course, there was a certain distaste that led people, Zoe and Cleo especially to wonder—this is the product of too much beating. Poor Max! His head was beaten so often that of course the brains are scrambled in such and such a way. For they, considering themselves the pious ones, didn't want to clean out stables and smell excrement for eternity. It seems we have suffered enough! What is this? Isn't God proper? Of course. Why a despised person, pure? And so on. But they would come back to listen. Max's voice was like a lullaby and soft, soothing and light. And it was apparent that he really did see things that somehow struck home with them. Besides, they secretly liked him. He was beautiful without that rather annoying and yet titillating odor of masculinity that Dimitri carried about with him. Max was pleasantly untouchable, celibate and correct; he would be just the perfect person, they often thought, to be priest. They felt they had had one too many fallible priests—first Father Raphael whose brains were eaten by drugs and now Father Isaac who yes had produced perhaps a miracle in the kitchen garden, but was such an awkward person, a little, how can one say it—carnal. It made them think that God had blessed them independently of Father Isaac. He had, as it were, just stood in the way as it was being done. But Max had a real bloom on him, a spiritual bloom. His mental eye was fixed on truth. Yet how strange he was. A child who hadn't matured, but just saw things and opened his mouth and spoke. They pitied him, liked him, listened to him, although they would have preferred to say they didn't.

Once they had cornered Father Isaac and asked of him: What does this mean? You surely can't believe that this is proper preaching—what Max does in the streets, that is. Shouldn't he exhort us to love our enemies, that sort of thing! Father Raphael used to say if someone were to steal his wallet, he had either to go and pray for their eternal souls or risk the displeasure of God! There was an outcry at the time—someone found it and returned it. One thought, among us, that the thief was Agatha. Gypsies will do things. And when the priest had come by their house, the father had come in waving his hands and shouting—don't you bother! It was a shock to all of us. But the wallet had been discovered at the tavern. We found Father Raphael at prayer in the little church! That saintly man. Though he took back the wallet, he said so sweetly—I am glad that a poor man had use of this. It was a beat up tattered wallet too, for he had hardly any money. And he, a just man, went down—so terrible, terrible. So what is this fancying on the part of little Max—that he can just dream and do no real work? Nothing honest, no honest words.

Father Isaac had said to them in return: You waste words yourselves. No matter how uncomfortable it is, he at least, sets your minds in order. Do you think that all this talk of the priests did anything to you? Are you holier because of it? Perhaps you are not because you never had any vision. Do you think it is possible to adjust your behavior here, alter your thinking there—if you have no vision of heaven—the core and rapture of all the saints and what made them who they are?

We tiptoed away with all our dignity, although our minds and hearts were bursting. It must be spiritual elevation, said Zoe, to feel in the midst of a cacophony of voices inside and outside and to be able just to be silent.

Silence, said Cleo is closer to the real heaven; that is written, I believe in Revelation.

It was only for half an hour, I believe, said Zoe—one of the terrifying seals. Then we talked again.

This priest is useless in any case. What did he say to us? A lot of nothing. There is still the very real side of the issue—why is Max, the preacher, not teaching us from the Gospels and from St. Paul? We are not here to be toyed with. To be fooled by a lot of childish dreaming and fantasizing. We do not doubt that Max is a dear, we come down expressly for that reason, and his delicacy and tenderness, we must respect. But there is something quite wrong with loosing someone to preach to us the Word, who is obviously a bit of a disturbed person—not quite, well, not even quite a man.

The other parishioners who now and then heard Max, and yes, there were some that couldn't abide him and would walk quickly away, felt as Zoe and Cleo. Cheated, insulted when they thought about it after, but somehow gently drawn when they actually saw Max and heard him speak.

It led us to say that we turn and turn like the weathervane.

Paul said it was all about degeneracy—that we were, mark his words, nothing but the dissolution of holiness. People talk like Max when the last vestiges of holiness, the rags of faith are slipping away and it weakens and weakens. It would be better, he said, to start a riot—burn a house. But he quickly said—no, he was being facetious.

There was something in Paul we feared but also revered. He was a doer and a shaper. He had energy and mind. If only he were a little less...we didn't know exactly what. He was near violence sometimes—but hadn't heaven to be taken by violence? It seemed he had a plan for our rebirth. No one else came forward on that score and to tell the truth we were desperate. And Paul had won the Easter dancing competition time after time, he had the figure of the old time men, and he was a fisherman and thinker, a husband in the old style.

So here was the configuration on the island: Paul and Little Paul, and the priest stood in opposition. How it happened we didn't know—but the man, Father Isaac, was stubborn. Agatha and Dimitri were living in one little sore house, it looked like a little sore house, in the middle of the village, illuminated every night and although dimly, all through the night. Perhaps they meant to send a message. Simon and old, sick Anna in her bed, in two large, dark, watching houses on a little path perpendicular off towards the dark sea. The rest—us elderly women and older women, the ones Zoe and Cleo spoke for, in a cloud that moved all around the village, and the old men, who peeped and piped through Nisos and Timos, scattered here and there like rain when it seems to come hesitantly. And this configuration seemed like it would fall apart somehow—that there would be trouble, agitation. We couldn't quite live shoulder to shoulder. We were sore, agitated.

We went to Father Isaac in a body and told him before he started talking and baffled us and made us forget what we had in mind to say—we aren't peaceful; we have lost our holiness. It seems Agatha and Dimitri...Can you reconcile with Paul? What is going to happen? Can't you be more priestly? Paul and little Paul simply want the old perfection, the old truth. What is going on in our village? Agatha and Dimitri have come in and destroyed... Cleo put her hand to her lips in anguish.

Women, said Father Isaac with a certain sternness that we rarely associated with him. You know that Agatha is in the right and Paul and little Paul to blame. I have never seen such viciousness in the ten years I have been here: to kick someone in the face brutally, to offer to burn someone's house while they were inside…!

But he apologized. Yes, yes, little Paul and Paul went to Agatha's house and apologized in person. And it was Paul who called the thugs off when they had cans of kerosene in their hands.

I wonder. Certain things were not apologized for. And is an apology enough?

But it is really better for a priest to be above these things, Cleo said, fanning herself with her hand.

A priest has to be at the heart of the matter of the congregation, said Father Isaac frowning.

And we all withdrew quickly. There was no use. We sensed and knew Paul's response to this. A priest should be a leader of our spiritual lives. But a proper chief would lead our minds and hearts. We thought to ourselves that here Paul and little Paul wanted peace—yes, they had made a number of mistakes, but now they thought in terms of peace; the Lord's peace, he had said, not the peace of the world. Our priest on the other hand was one of these worldly creatures, all opera and science, who told us that we were to live together as one family. Peace as in laying down knives, fire.

We went back to our lace making and our embroidering. We sat out on the balcony of Zoe's house, sipping a little apricot brandy for the cold winds, wrapped in our shawls, working the white silk threads with our fingers. Cleo was fastest; we thought she could make lace in her sleep.

Suddenly, Zoe broke the silence: It is all foolishness. She said; it is what we were all thinking. The priest sends out Max on the streets to plant in our minds of vision of heaven. But he worse than anyone stirs up the disease of hatred and antagonism. Not so much by anything he says or does but by what he does not say or do. Why hasn't he been to Agatha's house, to give her a good lecture? Yes, she tries, poor thing, of course; and what happened to her is wrong. No violence should be done another man or woman. But it is obvious that she cannot go straight.

To me she seems kind, murmured Foti.

Kind or not kind; she uses her own head for all things—even, God forgive us, to understand the Lord. And I have always thought that we should just tenderly help her, tenderly pull her towards the right path, the path of the heart—the old ways. But the priest refuses to teach her our ways. He lets her flourish in what is not our ways. If we are to be family, we need certain things to be established: Our faith, for one. It is fine for a visitor to claim a different sort of belief. If Dimitri had gotten his way, we would have had all sorts of unbelievers on our shores. That is of course something we have to expect from visitors. But one of ours—a child…

You mean baptism, of course, said Cleo.

Yes, of course. Why won't she be baptized? We are not ogres, monsters of hate. We roundly condemned the violence she and Dimitri suffered. We, in our faith love the outsider. But can we have this rebellion when we want to form a community based on our own faith? We are not hypocrites, although we are weaklings. The priest would strike down all our objections—citing the fact that Agatha is one of the most charitable people on the island. And there is no saying that it was right for her to be subjected to rough thugs. But there is no way to teach her. And if she does not want to be with us, why then there is every opportunity for her to move away.

It is such a little thing, huffed Zoe. Maybe it is a sacrifice, although with Dimitri's earnings she has plenty of money—but to move off the island would not hurt her and would bring a world of peace to us, she sighed.

I didn't like the sight of Dimitri's eye after the beating, said Foti.

It was monstrous, monstrous, said Zoe. That will not be tolerated ever again.

Cleo said: The priest is not perfect. He doesn't make peace but stirs up Paul to a passion. Doesn't our Lord tell us to be wise as serpents but blameless as doves? Our priest has some wisdom that we don't dispute—but is he blameless? Already he bears a grudge, no doubt has seen that eye himself.

But I know where to put blame truthfully, said Zoe. This is a delicate, intricate matter. I heard Dimitri from his own lips confess to having gotten the upper hand to Little Paul quite often when they were boys. Little Paul is not what you might call a thug. His mind has been damaged you know by Dimitri. She sighed. For years I have opened my arms to Agatha and her brood. We have tried. Even when there were suspicions surrounding Alex's sudden death and she had the bottle of sleeping drops and a man she had violently quarreled with lying prone drinking water from her hand; but no we overlooked all that. She lived among us for years. And even though Father Raphael quite rightly brought her to task for that horrible curse on herself, although I do think like any curse it would have vanished away in baptismal waters, even so we embraced Agatha.

A long time ago she went to Paul's house and…

Well? What was she doing there? Can you blame a man when a young woman shows up, offering herself…

Agatha has not killed in herself that little rebellious worm that lives and thrives in all of us. That is my personal opinion. And if we were a worldly village, that would be fine. No one could say anything. But we seek a peace that the world does not know. And I am afraid that for the Holy Spirit to confer that peace, it means absolute conformity.

Ah, said Foti, she had begun to remember her attraction to Dimitri again, sipping the yellowish brandy slowly and swirling it around in her mouth, you are so harsh. Why I can remember Diogenes and I, little children looking up at the moon and saying that we would be our own people—moon people and live our own ways, that we didn't have to listen to anybody. Of course, he married someone else, Rosa, and I, Symeon and they ruled us --both of us; we always liked to joke with one another --until he died. Agatha just preserved that moon gazing, in my opinion. Why make it out to be such a reprehensible thing? Perhaps really God only asks us to behave justly and lovingly, to be humble. I can't imagine that being in his image is anything else.

Don't you know, said Zoe, irked now, and almost turning on Foti, the word 'fool' on her tongue, and suppressed with an effort—that love is not that sentimental thing you mistake it for. Real love is not rose colored and certainly not moon gazing or becoming moon children. Real love is harsh, sometimes even cruel. But it is as God wants it not as men do.

I think to myself of Dimitri and I want to laugh in his face, said Cleo. Of course, he would end up with that bruised eye. But I would have ended up and a few other people lost—yes, lost.

In Paris in the traffic? Asked Foti, wonderingly.

Lost in a far mightier way than that, said Cleo, rearing herself up. These were the temptations of the world. It was not that the rich man had left that was so awful—it was the legacy…glad I am that it ended with just a bruised eye. It could have gone on, you know. With people just out there looking for hotels to come and be built, with people being paid off and going to the middle of Paris where the world has converged and all of the Holy Spirit is lost in speed boats and jacuzzis…that was the legacy. Now Dimitri is quiet you see. I doubt he will pull another one of those tricks on us easily. He seems inclined to stay. Well, whatever our little island offers, let him enjoy it. Our three rocks can't interest him for long. As for Agatha, the chances are if we wait a little longer, and we have waited a long time already, she will follow her son to another location where there are people of all beliefs and imaginations—America, perhaps! And then we will be rid of this problem. We were always wont to open our arms to the stranger—well! Let them live with us as long as they need to. They will find nothing here but simple people fishing, lace making, lemon and apricot growing.

Foti stared at Cleo's yellow dress sent from Paris by mail. It had a lace collar and was thinner than what was wanted for the weather. She had heard her words but thought them useless. Zoe was convinced of one particular thing and that that was the whole dire situation in a nutshell: Agatha's rebellion. And they thought Agatha a visitor simply because her father had come from the other island. Foti just couldn't contemplate it right then. She was embroidering a pillowcase with golden flowers and a dragonfly in green and blue. She had a knack for original embroidery they said on the island. The gold thread that she pulled through her fingers she loved. It shone in the air. Somehow she seemed to sew together much more than a figure on a white pillowcase. There was something, she thought a minute; there was nothing. These moments of wisdom, she called them that to herself, jarred her now and then. And she was considered the most foolish of the lot. But she thought that she might have in mind, with the thread running across her hand—golden on the soft pinkish flesh—she might have in mind a great philosophy, something far deeper and wiser than all physical science.

Cleo put down her lace making. You think that staring at me in that indecent way you are going to find the truth? She asked Foti.

I was looking at my thread, responded Foti, turning her heart-shaped face downwards.

I decided to wear yellow today, since winter is upon us full force. Do you know, at seven or so, Kali is joining us. Cleo stood up, leaning on the table because of a painful hip. She attends the girl on the mountain.

Zoe said, well, we'll hear what she has to say about her. She had put on glasses too heavy for her sensitive face to make her lace. And as she looked up, we saw in her a fine woman, delicate even, slightly in pain; her eyes were slightly murky too as if with sadness. We thought that Zoe had been thinking hard about the island's troubles. Perhaps she didn't want to die in this state of confusion. Death was frightening for anyone of us; only recently we had felt the dead alive and near us. Now it seemed that what with Dimitri, Little Paul—a different spirit pervaded. And the dead were now sometimes quite dead and as far away from life as lead. For we believed that the dead couldn't stay alive where there was such aggravation in us or where there were foreigners who offered to take our island from beneath our feet for a paltry price…We don't know if anyone can possibly understand but no, now the dead were dead often.

Perhaps we too had killed these dead of ours. But then one can understand as Dimitri brought us to this— the assault. Assaults serve where there are no words, or where there is haste and time not taken to conceive of the words. But it was in our heart of hearts that Dimitri had come in and killed these dead of ours. For they, with us, would never have allowed Cleo to become so mad and outside of herself, or for Zoe to rear up and behave with such harshness towards Agatha. Magda, beautiful Magda—like a child of the ancient days had laid down her life and we periodically raised her back up in our souls. She would have stopped this underlying cause of violence and agitation. For she too had raised herself up—even on rooftops, had risen up where women were supposed to walk a little bowed on the ground—fixed them, jumped down. She could jump! But in the end, who was more of a woman than she—dying for her unborn child?

Magda would have come to Zoe's aid—she was soft spoken, a deep voice that reminded us of memory and love. But when other forces were at work, these dead of ours that longed to protect us, to rise up inside us and show us the way, crept back to the underworld where they became again bones and dust and the silence of the sea.

Zoe suddenly had tears in her eyes. We thought it was because of Agatha, but she said—I remember just a few years ago the youth on this island—faces like holy candles! It is not a matter of wishing anyone ill…One wants this place of love, where you used to be able to smell holy love…she looked out into the withdrawn sunlight of the late afternoon, for a moment there were no winds. It was beautiful, she sighed. We had, moreover, certainty—we were doing the right thing. It was not harsh or cruel as it seems it must be today. We almost had knowledge. I mean, of course, knowledge of God, of that one perspective in which everything is sorted out—into its little order and logic. We don't find anything overpowering anymore, nor even ourselves-- for most of the time we overpower ourselves. Agatha is, of course, a beautiful woman. We should prize her, she is half daughter. If only she would see what it means to be with us and not against us. The hotel was an attempt I believe for Dimitri to just spread his wings, boasting, in front of us. It probably would never have gotten off the ground with that rich man presiding. No, we are a little nondescript in the eyes of the world. They expect more out there. We with our million butterflies and little shred of forest, in the cup of a limitless sea-- are pretty but not worth even an overnight. One can go to the Himalayas, the great rivers of China. Now there was an attempt to overpower and with Agatha I feel it still. She is like a great rock covering up something. One must move it aside. I don't say she must go, but she must be moved—moved out of that self of hers that rears up, that walks in front of the old men as if knowing, knowing that she is above all a jewel under heaven.

That whore! said Cleo softly, amazed at herself for using that language. Then she put her fingers to her lips and looked down at her lace sternly bending a little over the table.

I think, said Foti, that it is time for some lemonade. We've had enough brandy. It will go to our heads. Besides, something cool and refreshing…

I call no names, said Zoe in a crabby voice, more her usual self. But when the place of love is suddenly usurped; you see, differences arise. I would say it to the mother of God herself.

I will get the lemonade, said Cleo; she fixed her purse so that it was planted in the middle of the plastic chair, and then moved, slightly bent, inside to prepare the lemonade. She and Zoe were often in and out of one another's houses. They were just down the road from each other—one blue and the other white. Often Zoe came in the morning and stayed all day ostensibly to help clean, but in an hour or two just to sample cooking and to gossip. She had left behind her hand cream smell so often, and Cleo her scent at Zoe's white house that the territory pertained to both as if one house existed, rather than down the street, within the other. And then again, the fragrance of Cleo in Zoe's house faded away within a night and morning, the fragrance of Zoe in Cleo's house might last a little longer—no one was measuring, just living, just remembering. But it was clear that each would have to be continually refreshed. And that was the system among the ladies for with Zoe's and Cleo's mother it had been the same—what was it, hand cream for the one, a perfume for the other. Cleo at her mother's knee had smelt it on Zoe's grandmother sitting by, the hand cream, that is; and she had been like a sister to Zoe—that is, one within the province of that fragrant hand cream, a smeller of Zoe's grandmother's hand cream and sometimes a visitor into the secret recesses of Zoe's grandmother's bedroom. When it had come to be Zoe's mother, they had luxuriated together in their family lives—husbands, children—but now and again, leaving all that behind to enclose themselves in the perfumed nook—and talk, and talk. Zoe's mother would be close—somehow Cleo always associated her with white—white hair, white hand cream, white lace shawl, pearl-white—and she sat in the corner near the window watching that endless road, the main road that went from one end of the island to the other—endless if you looked at a fragment of it for years and years. Then she was gone and Zoe was the heir of that hand cream, not quite the right fragrance anymore, but still, a fresh, clean thing. Even though Cleo could see how Zoe was a little off, and no doubt she could see Cleo didn't quite come up to the same perfume, the same exquisiteness of her grandmother, then finally her mother—but perhaps that was yet to come, they had something indomitable—neither man nor God…not man because he was such a blunderer, even when he knew the timing, didn't understand the hot and cold of a friendship, not God because he left one alone…ah, but they had soul.

She came back with a tray of lemonade and a little dish of fresh apricots. I have discovered something! She said. The soul is a ballet in pairs—moving in, around, down among all the little nerves…

What? Asked Zoe, yawning and languidly picking an apricot with fingers that seemed permanently curled at that moment, although Cleo and Foti knew that was just an illusion for they would spread flat and straight and she could point and gather the threads across her palm.

The soul is two, not one. And Cleo decorously moved herself around the little group with the tray. Something most cannot understand; she looked at Foti, and thought briefly of Ella.

Foti looked at Zoe helplessly; she knew she was the odd one out and therefore had not the right to speak over much. She had always been slightly too fat, at one moment on the dance floor, slightly too pretty for the approval of the elderly ladies—not a brain in her head, not a useful brain, said they—too weak as a woman for her husband. She plucked up her courage, which she did about as often as the wind blew northerly and said—why not three?

Oh well, said Zoe, sighing noisily. I suppose you could say—why not forty, fifty, eighty, seventy-nine? You can't rationally mind what Cleo has to say about this. It is only an opinion about one of these things that you simply can't know anything about.

But in any case, no. Agatha is not one of us. She is only one.

Am I? Foti squeaked in terror.

Oh, of course, you are not only one. We are not talking here about slight differences, she said, taking off her glasses and wiping her eyes with the napkin that lay at her side. Without slight differences, where would we be?

Yes, said Cleo, thoughtfully. There are slight differences. Enough for a person to say—one! And another –one! And she thought again of Ella and then of Paul and blushed slightly. Perhaps one and a half, she murmured, but definitely not two.

Yes, went on Zoe in a little huff of disdain, thinking of Agatha, for she really saw things in a much clearer light than Cleo. So there are differences, slight differences. But when one takes up what has been offered and rejects it in that incomprehensible way…And the question that revolves around my head as often as the earth spins 'round the sun is—why here? I am sure there are unbaptized people in the world, people of curses, people who walk around as if the sun has crowned them—and I am willing to grant that these people have their beauty—yes, she raised her curled hand, opened a little now like a claw; but we don't know them.

They are, said Cleo, roused to Zoe's discourse—one without. One and zero. And that is a terrible thing.

It is just, said Zoe, a different fashion. We have our little ways, our community mind. One doesn't strike out as if one lives in a little hollow all alone. And even then!

And at fifty, said Foti in astonishment. It is as if she had no contentment inside herself.

No, I wouldn't say that, said Zoe; I'd say rather that she was all content with herself. It is as if she is advertising the whole thing on her hips—that is her contentment with herself.

Cleo was going to say that whore once again, but suddenly thought of her discovery about the soul and wondered and remained silent.

Well, it is no use talking about it. There are certain things that over time make themselves known and felt. I almost feel as if there was a possibility once, a hope, a design sketched in the sand—if we had only looked at it, taken it to heart, remembered it. It is our fault too, you see. But who could understand? It is too much for us. The Lord himself does not require us to understand our neighbors. I have said what I have said. Agatha must be moved out-- of that particular way of hers. Baptism would solve everything. But we can't have everything. Just the formalities. We can insist on the formalities.

Because of ill health, Catherine had remained in the villa on the cliff for months. She had not heard, therefore, about the savage beating that Dimitri had endured, nor seen his swollen and sore, half-closed eye. When he came up to see her, it was months later; he had been healed as best as nature could and wasn't disposed to talk about it.

Catherine was an inch thinner all around. She looked gaunt to Dimitri and that haunting, about to fade beauty, which had attracted him and made him pity her, now appeared like the faintest glimmer in her, the daylight in the depths of the forest. Ah, but he wanted it to be light—fresh, unbelievable sunlight—not a lesser shadow. He walked up to her and kissed her in the half faith that they would suddenly be lovers and full of light. She put her arms around him and kissed him sweetly, hesitating to let go of his lips with hers.

Then she said to him—you—you've been a long while gone! Did you intend not to see me again?

And it all came out; he hadn't all intended —working, changing, smashed up. I was busy. If my eye looks different it is because I got into a scrape—something very ugly, he was smiling as he told her, but Catherine stepped back, looking at him in horror.

Look, said Dimitri, taking her hands, I deserved it. You see, I didn't for a minute understand my old native place. It was my job and bounden duty to understand it—them. I thought in an abstract way about the whole thing: To bring televisions, air conditioners, computers, Jacuzzis. I thought the point was a better life. You see, it isn't. Not exactly. What they want is something different. Something I can't give them. They want their little ways to make ultimate sense. It doesn't make much sense to me. It is like someone in the city insisting on walking when they could get there far more comfortably by car. It is a kind of stretch of your muscles, work your bones thing here too. I honestly believe they like to sweat in the summer.

But how can you possibly excuse violence? Asked Catherine. She had stepped up to him and was seeking out his eyes that shifted away from her.

I don't excuse violence. I excuse it on me, he turned away.

You or anybody, she murmured. I wouldn't subject my worst enemy to…

It was my worst enemy, said Dimitri. I had just forgotten him. He gave me a betrothal gift in terms of enmity. A rose and a violet of a broken eye—perhaps also a yellow chrysanthemum. A veritable bouquet of enmity. And a message of soreness and swollenness from the depths of his soul. And in truth, my dear love, I love him as I love you. I do love you.

You see, it is not that I came home innocently. I came home to change, shift, tear apart, redo. He sent this bouquet to tell me that he remembered me from the early days when I talked and talked—they thought it was nothing but talk—of the need to reinvent, tear apart, and redo. My family were of course the ones that the island had semi cast out. He, angered that an outcast would talk in these 'big' terms, wrestled with me, and we beat each other. I usually won in those days; I was an old fashioned village boy body and soul— although in my head I was an exotic and brilliant foreigner—pouring myself into my fists. People thought that I was letting off a lot of heat, resentment, you know; they didn't believe in my talk. I thought I would make them believers in the end. I went away and by sheer determination as the old saw is…I thought now that I had proved it they would have to be reconciled; and I didn't take them seriously—a little pet home, a home that would yield to me, a home that was cute to me. He came to set me square in the dust to fight it out again, to tell me some things haven't changed, that the home has a deeper root after all, and to claim the victory long denied him.

Now there you are, you, an angel in your sweetness, saving me; but him, oh him, an angel too, you see, an angel too. Besides, Catherine, for a man, a good fight is natural, even humane. I don't say that of wars but—what if individuals from either side could go at one another, one, two, three personal fist-fights and the country abide by the outcome? Oh, my head must be full of clouds today, seeing you. Dimitri kissed her again. He paused looked down and then raised his eyes to hers as if some indefinable guilt pressed him on and said you have such a sweet tasting mouth. What do you live on, syrup?

Catherine put her face against his and said, I'm sorry. Sorry for what happened. I heard of course that the rich man has vanished.

My mother pampered me day and night over it. Should have left me groaning. Then Auntie Zoe came to visit and…his face darkened and he looked out the floor length window from where they were sitting at a little plastic table to the sea.

What happened then? Asked Catherine grimly.

Perhaps you are not aware of certain things, he began in a lower voice. My family chose to be a little different from the community. Saints village had their ways; one of them was a rule unquestioned—the baptism of children. It was of course not forced but still required… My grandfather was a Muslim, a gypsy, that is, of the Rom people; playing instruments as easily as breathing. He was a fabulous musician. You would think he would have been forgiven out of the sheer joy of hearing him play the flute or strum the guitar…but no. They had their signs of crosses, baptisms… well, he left the family because it was not to be endured but his wife, my grand-mother, an islander and a Christian, remained behind. She did not, would not baptize the children not because of the Muslim father but because of the way the islanders had behaved. She wanted to show up this community. It might have been revenge. My mother has a different idea. It is for the precious Christ's sake that she won't be baptized. I think this still holds. They call her obstinate and stubborn. She sits in the back of the church-- I hear she has even ingratiated herself with the priest—and will not accept the sacraments. Do you realize? Even the atheists here take the sacra-ments. She has an idea that she must encounter Christ first and, well, make sure He wants her.

But I understand that, said Catherine, earnestly. I myself am not baptized and the priest said—what need? What need? I was myself as shocked as if I had been a whole army of old Church ladies.

It is the army of Church ladies and I am afraid Churchmen who have rallied against us. Of course, nothing dramatic. I haven't seen stones. They came around to apologize about my victimization. I heard stories though, which make me shudder. Apparently while I was gone there was a threat to my mother.

Catherine looked down and bit her lip. She decided she wouldn't break the news to Dimitri of the hallucinatory but real near burning of Agatha's house.

You see, it is and it isn't a matter of what I call real violence. No blood shed, that is murder, has ever taken place on this island. Nothing. Isn't that remarkable? He smiled at her and his face sort of cracked in Catherine's estimation under its expression of tenderness. She looked up at the top of his head and her insides opened out like honey and dripped. She saw that he was slightly shorter than she, and that his face was wonderfully innocent and intense—also familiar, though she had only known him a short while. Someone on the voyage in.

It is odd you come to me, she said looking down.

Why odd? I'd think you would realize how natural...

Catherine shook her head. It is not natural. For me, natural is lying in bed recovering my breath, looking at the sea, wondering how many days I have to live, watching other people in their usual lives—walking, talking, free, not even thinking. Imagine a heartbeat that you don't even notice? It is as if the heart in me, the raw, quivering, spasmodic muscle with all its bloody meat torn from me, touches my lips, this last she murmured so that he didn't hear.

You have worked commendably—even loved your neighbors and enemies, I have loved indifferent passersby whatever they are, goats, sheep, wolves, sparrows, people and I give them seeds, meat, crumbs, tea, ice water and syrup to celebrate the life in them. Did you know I housed Elizabeth, Nico's flame, for days here...she flushed and put her hand on her breast for a minute, caught her breath and continued. Yes, she came down from the monastery. I was glad. I felt that I had caught a fish, a woman-fish. She is gone—oh, she loved, yes. I enjoyed kisses, caresses. But fast away, leaping down through the clouds to the village and her love out of my life where it stands bleak and blasted on this little ledge. She didn't think she was indifferent. No, she even believed in me. But I always thought it would be like that—one or two that I pluck up hold and feel the beat in them for a minute and then...

The rest of your menagerie said Dimitri looking at her with a pensive smile, moves on despite your love except your pet monkey. In any case, I heard you played the Good Samaritan to that poor lady. She and Nico are other people, you know; very elusive, immersed in themselves. I don't see them. I think they frequent the loneliest shores on the other side of the forest.

I have learned to love people—despite the fact that the majority are light hearted, jolly themselves about and return with their wives and husbands—living in some other world of which I am not with the comfort of many things that I don't have—

can't have, despite my father's money. And if in all that jollying I am caught, like someone half in a picture, someone not supposed to be there…or if I catch one and they throw me in the end a radiant smile…

You say you love people—what do you mean?

I remember them. Yes, I have a startling memory—even of people in my life for all of two hours. Poor, rich, despised. I have a startling memory even for leaves, roses, birds dancing in the garden, butterflies fluttering, bees drifting near grape vines, even of flies zig zagging lazily in summer, of ants scrambling across the kitchen counter carrying bits of food.

And so?

And so I have been carrying them around with me; it is as if I dug myself open and planted them inside. Can you imagine what love looks like? Take a person, man or woman and go down to the depths of them, plant a tree there whose fruits are this person's face, that person's face—people that came into their lives and then passed on without thinking much—long ago gone on and forgotten them; the leaves of the tree are a white or yellow butterfly, a gold finch, the leaf of a rose, a pine tree branch, one little patch of the grinding sea, the blue ethereal bowl of the summer day whatever they saw in their prime—and this tree will grow and bloom in that person so that one can scarcely make out who it is anymore —their identity, the face, the vision of self, will all be other.

You are cute, said Dimitri, laughing. Why have I even brought up my unmentionable troubles to you? Why, here you are an original! A once in a lifetime woman. Do you do anything during the day? Or do you just sit languidly on your rock and prophesy?

I breathe and think.

Good, Do nothing but breathe and think. The world needs such thinkers as you. What do we end up with? People who try to encompass big things—like oh, the beginning of the world—and for what? I don't believe we understand anything more about ourselves by serious theories like the big bang than in funny, odd, whimsical notions.

But what you said—how strange and funny. So we are not lost. No, as long as the big thinkers think and say huge bombastic things, we are lost. But because of one who has from the perspective of breathing, and that is all—thought and loved, up on a mountain, deep in that hole of a self—we are not lost.

It is you who is strange, said Catherine smiling, and turning her head on one side.

I am staying on now, said Dimitri—until I think of what to do next. I don't want to leave my mother; I will have to find a way to make sure she is alright. My brother doesn't take her side. He sits like an immovable stone, obstinate, mute, deaf it seems, that is, not physically, but he hardly responds to anything. He is waiting for a magical materialization out of thin air—of what he calls the Kingdom of God. I think it will all end badly. I think he has been swayed by the villagers—that he was always rather soft in the mind and that he couldn't resist, poor thing…He too tried to kill me once.

So, said Catherine, in this very peaceful village you and Agatha are living dangerous lives.

You know, in that tree that is growing inside of me, one of the branches has a fruit that is uncommon. For it is not only you, and there have been others, but you face on. The others I remember in profile, or in pieces-- thigh, breasts, nose. But with you frontal picture of your thin face, beauty almost fading away in it, but still delicacy around the nose and eyes—as if an artist had sketched that bit. Then there is another fruit—he twisted his mouth in bitterness and looked down. Bitter sweet but this one's fragrance I have had in my nostrils-- That of my mother with her slipshod body, bent over like a witch, like an old crone for years; of course things are different now. But I still see her as she was then-- I don't see a face, only a veil of misery—blurry eyed from chin to hair—as if the eye space covers the entirety, perhaps from toe to crown of head. What she is now, God bless us—I don't know. She has achieved liberation!

She is dancing, said Catherine. You know, oddly enough, in my opinion the dance flourishes, like poetry, in two situations: One is in an environment replete with comfort like majesty, the other in an oppressive place where you are being watched, where there have been threats—even to your life. It has to do with how a seed is planted.

What was that?

I would say of Agatha that it has always been there; she allowed it a little space— saying, what the hell…

Yes, that is what I want to protect—her 'what the hell…'

I see, said Catherine.

Yes, that is what I am back for in the end—to protect that 'what the hell' in my mother.

I must go before it gets dark. Do you know I would say that far more momentous encounters with women have befallen me, yes it is true. I have been, you might say, using holy language, rapt! I have been a desirous animal, responding to a bitch in heat. I have been a sot driven out of my wits by women, wine, moonlight. I have taken on the devil's face and seduced a girl who I then found out was the talk of the town for her courtesan activities; I found that it was she who had laid the honey and laughed when I in my big-headed new boy in town way imagined that I had overthrown all her resistance. And she had Joe and continued to have Joe and then it was Tom, all the while that I was rapt in her nakedness by the light of the moon. But you, yes, you give me the feeling that I am rid of all pretenses and deceits. Or, at least, it's as if they don't matter. They say those who believe they can be honest in love are either fools or…but in any case; I must go.

I suppose that it will be flavorful—that is, the dish that I will eat tonight; I wonder if after—if it won't seem like punishment.

A war widow already? He smiled—if I am fool enough to die on you…!

He kissed her and got up from his seat. No, don't show me out.

Agatha turned around from where she was fussing over some chicken frying in a pan, when Dimitri came in, and she saw—a bejeweled prince; of course, she knew it was just a dream. He was dressed in black and not only did he look like a fairy tale, but also like a charcoal sketch, but a great artist, gestures, strokes of black traveling where words could not go. And not only did he look like an artist's stroke of genius, but also like a web spun in the crevices between the stars. Soon it was her son, her baby, she was looking at and she was not ashamed that she had permitted herself these effusions; he was man cut out from something other than clay, perhaps from crystal. And when he was clay, for just one memory, then did the earth rear up like a serpent with a jewel in its mouth.

You are late, said Agatha to Dimitri. You have been out courting.

Dimitri smiled, and lazily picked up some basil leaves and put them in his mouth and chewed them slightly with his front teeth. Mmm, he said, softly, kissing his mother's ear.

You make the basil smell sweeter, said Agatha, taking his face in her hands and looking up at him earnestly.

Mother I am a good for nothing and the equivalent of two and three good for nothings. I am in short the very sum of good for nothingness that has ever existed in human flesh.

Why? You were in business, you made your way?

I had instinct and a few friends. It was just natural. He began to poke in the pan. You need the gas on higher or this chicken will never cook. He bent down to examine the settings on the gas knob and then placed his hand over the pan—yes, this is the right temperature to cook in hot oil.

How did you manage without me? He asked his mother turning to her. You can neither cook, nor clean house, nor fix the windows that are all askew, nor I believe even mend a shirt. Ha, you too are a good for nothing. Goes to show, I inherited something from you at last. I was wondering what it was.

I do quite well on my own, and everything is clean and fixed, Agatha retorted. The windows….Oh, Mother, I was teasing you. You're going to have to learn to be teased a little where it hurts while I'm around. He suddenly picked up the pan and screamed with pain dropping it back on the burner. I didn't realize it was hot, he said bending over, his hand above his knees.

Dimitri, Dimitri, cried Agatha.

Cold water, he said. Agatha turned on the cold water in the sink and Dimitri held his hand under the stream. Not a good sign, he said to her. Right hand. Flesh is tender. Fire is hot. I tried not to drop the wretched pan. I didn't put two and two together.

Agatha was looking at him with fear.

It is nothing Mother, nothing. Can you imagine, someone who supposedly has a few brains in his head doing a thing like that? God this hurts; thing is the hurt won't go away now for days.

Dimitri, said Agatha nervously, walking up and down in front of him, I think this was a sign.

Of what? It means nothing. Under the cold water it feels much better. Watch the chicken.

It all happened, Mother, because you didn't propitiate the kitchen god. Get me a pan of cold water and I will hold my hand in it for a while. Ah, this is a bad burn. There is no doctor on the island is there?

No we live like outcasts and wanderers. But you can go to the other island. Agatha filled a plastic tub used for washing with cold water and set it on the table.

No, let it be. It will just heal, I think. He looked at his hand. The flesh is eaten away a little by the burn. Cooked. I think this place is lethal. First my eye, then my right hand. A place to go blind and helpless—a place withering away, losing all love.

It isn't the place, said Agatha in an aggravated tone.

No, no, of course not. But I just wasn't so awkward and blundering anywhere else. I come home to my dear mother, infinitely dear mother, and start somehow falling into scrapes. And to cap it all off I then require tending and caring when I came expressly to tend and care for you.

But Dimitri, these things happen because of me.

How because of you?

Agatha took the potholder and seized the pan and shook the chicken parts in it. She prodded the flesh with a fork and found it cooked, a little over cooked. Then she turned off the gas and dumped the chicken on to a plate. She had some leftover rice salad and a sliced tomato with fresh garlic. With these she laid out the table for dinner, moving around the plastic tub.

How because of you? Repeated Dimitri, in a harder tone.

Agatha moved to the counter and found the saltcellar and the pepper and brought them over. Then she set out dishes. Finally, she moved over to the door of the kitchen and called for Jason.

Jason had been, if possible, quieter than usual following Dimitri's return. When Dimitri had been thrown down and kicked in the crowd, Jason had slit his eyes and watched, following his weeping mother as several men escorted Dimitri home with a look of sleepiness and detachment.

His face had drifted by Dimitri's as the latter lay in bed, seeing with one eye, and Dimitri had felt, despite his injury, a sibling superiority—the wounded one, the war hero. All of the old antagonism had passed from his organism like a foul pus drained off. And he knew that Jason saw him with bitterness and he thought also with that kind of indifference that simple-minded people sometimes have about the great findings of science or the truths of history. Somehow, years ago, he had penetrated that indifference. For a single instant, Jason had risen up and because it had not been truth and intelligence, truth and intelligence for years and years—because scoring over Dimitri had been impossible, because it had not been beauty, old beauty coming out smiling so sweetly that any injustice is passed over and repressed for her sake—so take away all things, which even in this closet of a world make a person person, and he had resorted to murder, then indifference. Blood because there was no talking. There were no words for the way Dimitri had stolen personhood out from under Jason's nose. Almost murder. Agatha had screamed and cursed; Jason was a believer. He had paused, removing the razor sharp blade from Dimitri's neck, looked at his mother, turned away, became impassive and stone mute.

But when Dimitri had come home with a bloody eye, swollen and half closed, he had felt no triumph, Dimitri thought. A strange unreadable face had dangled over Dimitri's, once or twice. No words were spoken.

When Agatha had served the chicken on the plates and poured the sauce from the pan over each serving, Jason came in. He looked briefly at Dimitri with his hand in the cold water; his mouth was half open, his large white face tired. He bowed his head, prayed a minute—a short rote prayer, and then began to eat.

Do you know, said Agatha, smiling a forced smile at Dimitri, Jason helps lay the table now, usually—when you aren't here. I never thought, she swallowed hard, that one of you would help out at all in the kitchen. For many years it was not the rule. But now that you've grown, you both do so much.

I can't speak for Jason, said Dimitri, shortly, but I think I make more of a mess than I'm worth as a helper.

Jason had his eyes on his food and was eating quickly.

There was relief for Jason, thought Dimitri, glancing at him, in not having to talk or think. A certain blessedness, yes blessedness, in being cut off from human interaction. Life consisted of fishing, eating, sleeping. The subtle and quick little details of living, the expression on someone's face seeing another, the hints and gestures in which all the meaning of humanity, Dimitri thought, was stored, were inexplicable, indescribable to Jason. He was willing to concede that this stone that he had for a brother was actually by mere existence without cogitations, and contemplations— closer to the truth. (Dimitri believed that there was a truth, single, utter, absolute); but how beautiful it was to have thought and intelligence, and who wouldn't serve beauty to follow trails—the explanation of stars, the origin of the sun, the enclosing of all of poor sad humanity into an ape waving its little human like hands, deftly picking the lice out of the hair of its infants.

Jason asked none of these questions. Perhaps, thought Dimitri, he was a Zen monument.

I have long ago, said Dimitri to his mother, quietly, eating with his left hand, ceased to wonder about my brother's inner life.

Jason finished his chicken without saying anything and stood up, making a loud scraping sound with his chair.

Agatha looked up at him, a little timidly. The silence that pervaded in the kitchen, that seemed to hang over them like the light bulb dangling from the wire was a hard silence. It was the kind of thing that said to her, you have failed as a mother—perhaps, she thought the overmuch preoccupation with my own misery when they were young. No wonder there is no love lost now.

Jason looked at his mother from his narrow eyes. Dimitri said—well, I sense that Jason would rather be off. And all the midnight moonbeams be with you, said Dimitri to him as he turned away. Probably thought of spitting at me, he said to his mother. No, why should you think that? He has become much calmer. Don't tease him.

Do you think sometimes he is unable to speak? Asked Dimitri, I do.

When it comes, it comes in fits and starts. Yet something tells me, he picked up a piece of bread with his left hand and sopped it awkwardly in the sauce on his plate, that he is not so off track as I.

Agatha got up and removed the plates. No you sit, she said to Dimitri who was about to help her. I'll just dump these plates in the sink and get you a rag soaked in oil to bind up your hand with.

Dimitri watched his mother moving around the kitchen. He had always thought her a homely woman, with little or nothing to say for herself, but also someone absolutely irreplaceable. It was not the usual affection between sons and mothers. Truly if he could have stayed in Agatha's company forever, sitting in a chair beside her as she embroidered, hanging around near her as she cooked, he would have done so. For beauty too, he thought, she had, periodically, a perfect quaintness and in portrait photos, he had one of her, it came across as tremendously sweet. She should have been outfitted in lace. When he first made a little money in the big city, he had contemplated bringing her and parading her around, giving, just giving anything she should desire. But he had also forgotten her. Not forgotten in the sense of ceasing to care for her. He had forgotten her in the sense of keeping her away in his consciousness from the daily job and daily actions, from all that goes into being a man in the world of today and that had seemed to him righteous. His mother belonged, of course, to another sphere, a place of his incorrectness. And to tell the truth when he came home and found her dancing, he had a little misgiving about his own enthusiasm and her wonderfulness.

Would this salute to the sun, this dance that she practiced at dawn—mean a different woman; that is, would she be more of a woman—because for ages he had not thought of her as a woman at all, but as the perfect woman. But he had seen the fierce joy in her as she stretched her arms wide, lifted her leg high, knee bent and then straightened it up, the running crouching over bent knees on her toes, the leap, the pirouette, the split, and he had felt awe. And after, perhaps it was a result of that strange feeling of sunrise, he had taken her in his arms like a lover would and said to her—you are most beautiful, and meant it, and he had crept in as if his being there was illicit and it was only illicitly that he could see beauty like that. Now throwing down dishes with a clatter in the sink, and finding a clean rag in the drawer under the sink, she looked her old quaint self—big hipped, slender waisted, the old woman whose skirt he wanted to crawl under.

You used not to be able to dance, said Dimitri, reflectively. You are beautiful dancing of course but—you were perfect without it.

What all hunch backed and slipping along on one weak leg!

I never noticed. You had your sphere of light. I always thought that if grace was true it would be exactly as you understood it. A kind of talking to. I used to hear you, you know. You would relate how human nature defied easy explanation, how love started with the cross, how you couldn't have a faith in a Church that taught you to dry up, that one could only be faithful by being a full fertile flesh and blood —with the nerves, the anger, the passions, the sorrow. You had an argument once about meekness; you said it was more unsuspectingness, rather than lack of passions.

Agatha poured olive oil on the rag for Dimitri. She brought it over and bound his burned hand with it. All this you loved? I thought you didn't believe.

Ah, unbelief—what does it matter what we say to ourselves? There are times now with you, you know, that I make it up with God. The great talking-to-er. I find I've never quite let go. It seemed to me as if the scientists seek to end mystery, imagination as reality, to heal it, put it to death—as something defying our ability to know through science rather than to know as science—like a health official would try to end a disease endemic in the village without understanding the loves and weaknesses that planted that disease in the first place. In short, closing up the window of knowledge about people as science, shuttering it—ceasing vision to the human mind and heart;

science tries to know the brain cells and heart muscle in every detail and the scientific hubris claims that thus it can know all things. Science postulates the extraordinary notion that the human brain can comprise truth and so end it, freeze it to death! Truth itself as a chemical in the brain of an evolved ape! Ah, Evolution: but what is changing from ape to human? Purely physical, science argues. Yet a metamorphosis in its way as miraculous as the resurrection. Now contemplate beast to human, think: From pride over one's mate to pride in a more subtle, clever way of torturing people? Surely the ape is far too intelligent and decent to behave in this fashion and would never-- confining himself to family and friends, feasting and swinging. What inner logic would make an ape rise up to torture children or stone women? Even if we consider the true and good in being human—what ape would come to say: "Give me your poor, your huddled masses;" or, "I am the rose of Sharon?" Which ape could ever come to have anything like the mysterious human ego that some people think is God—a psychological creation yet physical—I see it all bones and dressed in bridal finery. Or, how could an ape's inner eye appealed to by some overwhelming beauty in the sacrifice, choose selfless death over the all-comprehensive ego? And then see the healthiest, fittest apes hanging themselves on crosses or dashing themselves off cliffs like the Greek women before the conquests of the Turks? How can an ape possibly evolve when he must be able to choose beauty above life to be human? For what reason would it? For it seems that it must on some level be conscious choice. And evolution can be only for superior eating and drinking—that, at least, is logical!

But there is still a mystery, an open window. Humanity is far more than science makes it out to be or can ever make it out to be. I even believe that explanations and interpretations cover up for supreme ignorance, that by following science we are fast and cheap with our souls. Better to delve into religion, any religion, which is, at its origin, song and dance, and ecstasy. Steer clear of the chemicals that will unlock sanity or health—that turn once more the ape into humanity, its evolution machine. Learn disease, dying, death. Learn littleness, lostness, love perversions.

My son, my son, groaned Agatha at the close of this tirade; you are ill, you ramble-- the island with its strange, angry people, the burn on your hand....

It is true, Mother, I am not like myself. Hold me.

Anna still lived; she was like one of these trees, which, colored grey like dryness, continue to produce little green leaves here and there, as if life can cling even when death has come to abide. What happens is that the knowledge seizes you at the core; the heart and mind are always at bottom prophetic, she said to Agatha who came to visit. Her firm voice was still evident and periodically, though with pain, she got up and walked and sat in the window seat in her bedroom and looked out at the fig tree. This year there were many figs, and she had even insisted, despite all that Tia could do or say, that she dine on figs and honey and tea. Her face was discolored by fatigue and pain, but her back was still straight when she walked holding on to Tia and she smiled in her old lovely way, and her severe, silvery face, for all the encroachment of the end, was beautiful.

It is Dimitri, she said seeing Agatha. Your face doesn't look like a cloudless princess' as it did just many months' ago.

You heard, said Agatha, about the mix up.

What are you referring to?

The plan last year and then how it all collapsed on us. For months I didn't want to tell you.

The islanders wouldn't have the terms and conditions for the hotel, said Anna; yes, I heard. And it is funny too; all over the world prized places—beautiful for lakes, forests, seas, mountains, are being destroyed by developers and it seems that no one has a say about it and yet our islanders, the Holy Islanders, the Saints as they call themselves, just managed to bungle their way out of it. They actually preserved their little treasure, Holy Island, this tiny land, by greed and pride. Surely the Holy One is looking after us.

Agatha sat down beside her on her bed. The room was darkened but it was a brilliant day outside, and the sun that afternoon shone full on the windows, and through the slats on the shutters light came in, projected in rectangles on the wall opposite.

What about you? Have you loved yet? You said it was the thing you hadn't done in all your life.

That is true. I was stuffed to the gills with sugar and spice—gallivanting here with one husband, settling and eating and drinking there with another, mothering, making friends...I couldn't have been more pampered; my bowl was not only full but replete. No I've rolled around in sugar and smiles—ever successful, brilliant, and monied; no, I have not loved. I suppose it will happen here as well as anywhere. Anna began picking at the woolen blanket covering her.

You were always friendly and kind to me, said Agatha, sadly.

None of that, said Anna, looking sternly at her and shaking her finger. None of that. I think I was merry and obscene. I came ploughing into your life half looking for material to gossip about, you know, half amused by you toiling like a drudge, like you used to, subjecting yourself to the village 'rules'. Seven or eight years ago when you started to look and act a little differently, not so much like a fish in a soup of misery, but like one that could leap out of it at will, I was genuinely glad that I had befriended you but only then. But I have often been this way at heart. Merry and obscene—prying open other's private minds to jolly myself over them.

Tell me, be honest now, you too wanted to know—what are Dimitri's present relations with Katrina?

I don't know. Dimitri is not himself. Not like himself. He burned himself on the hand handling a hot iron skillet; before that Little Paul punched him until he fell down on the ground, kicked him in the head—he had an eye that I think will never quite heal. He is thinking and talking unlike himself, Agatha repeated.

Ah, he will heal if he finds a woman.

He holds on to me like a little boy.

Our villagers are magicians in a little way, said Anna. They metamorphose grown men into children. Tell him he is home, again and again.

I have trouble myself thinking of my home as home. There are, as you know, folks who never wanted us. Oh, yes, I hang on. I see something to cling to like the red rose bush that grows near us, a little way down the road, that hangs over Barbara's fence. I think her heart clings to that rose bush. You know it wasn't planted recently. It's been there a long time. And it is one of these plants around about our village that grows just like old times, or so we think, abundantly. There is a wisteria over by Simon's and a jasmine outside right here but they have fewer blossoms and in the old days, well, thirty years' ago, I remember them in full flower…so many flowers! Well, as that rose bush outside of Barbara's house that isn't really hers, not her production anyway—so my heart clings and it isn't really mine.

Your heart? Whose is it then, Leo's?

Leo's! Well, why not, I guess. Leo's. But I was going to say—but those are just old memories.

Which memories?

Child born wild, to two outcasts. Big-footed child, high-minded, proud wanting to swing her legs high in the dance in a little place in the middle of the vast sea; —or on a fistful of earth, some few staring people, men in old, worn jackets, women in bright skirts—beautiful profound days and she, this wild girl, wants to stretch her legs to the sun. Just that, nothing more.

Ah, her heart.

Yes, savage and pure, it was. Seeing God.

That is the story of youth. Come, said Anna, get into bed beside me. Of all people in this village, I most want your arms around me.

Agatha climbed across the little body outlined under the red knitted blanket and slipped herself under the covers that were drawn up to the soft white pillows. She kissed Anna's chin and smoothed back her hair, brought her body close to the sick body and put her hand on her shoulder. What is it, she asked in a murmur that stops you from loving?

To love is a very high aspiration. Most people will settle for affection, family tenderness, or sexual joy. not the high-born notion of love. What am I to be so favored?

Agatha and Anna lay together silently. Both were peaceful. Anna smelled for once, less of excrement than she did of lemon perfume. Tia came in from the other room where she was faithfully keeping watch to see if they were still together, bringing pills and a glass of water for Anna; she watched her drink, and then went out. Agatha stroked Anna's grey hair periodically; it was soft and light not too thin. Then with her fingertips she caressed the now putty colored face that still had the light of beauty in it. She put a strand of Anna's hair behind the right ear that faced her, softly drew her fingertips around her neck. A cloud must have blown across the sun, for the rain started. Agatha and Anna heard it. They lay together listening to the rain; for one hour they listened, and the hour grew into two hours. Agatha went in and out of sleep like a swimmer going in and out of the sea. Anna in the end, slept soundly. Agatha even after three hours felt too lazy to get up and go. It was warm under the woolen blanket, the wind had started to blow outside, the rain continued. From the corner of her eye, she could see the room, bare except for a large coffee table book on Peru on the armchair, an old lamp that must have been on night and day, and the little wooden chair for Tia near the bed. Anna had had the room rearranged and everything taken out, refurnishing the room with these things. Peru, why Peru? It took Agatha three tries to get herself up, move to the side of the bed and out.

She thought as she moved towards the door treading softly that she would have another peek around the house that had been closed to her—for once Anna had drawn this line in their friendship—while she had always allowed Anna to drop by anytime. But Agatha thought that all that she had asked of Anna—the first thing: What to do about Dimitri? The second thing—Anna's lost love? As she called it, playfully to Anna—hadn't solved anything.

The next afternoon before supper, Agatha toiled up to Leo's house. She found him in a blue funk, sitting outside the door in a plastic chair, smoking. I didn't know you smoked, she said inhaling the fumes with satisfaction—she rather liked the smell, second hand.

Sweet decadence, said Leo; it starts and ends with cigarettes. I'm on the ending side. But the reason is—this package of cigarettes was the only thing left to consume. All the food is gone.

Since when?

Oh, I believe since yesterday. I slept instead of grocery shopped. I have become a little shy of going down into that muddle-- he gestured towards the village square, bowed his head and smiled.

I will run down for you, said Agatha. What sort of groceries do you want?

Oh, but I wouldn't dream…

In fact, you were waiting for just such a pleasure. One knows there is a God because people like you, thoroughly unjust as they are, simply wait like little mollusks in a shell and the food bearers come.

Yes, it has always been so, said Leo, heaving a sigh and closing his eyes. How I would have rather have been an athletic doer and getter.

I will get you chicken, fish, cheese, vegetables and rice, said Agatha moving off.

Don't forget, if I may persuade in my humility—the wine.

It had come to our attention before that Agatha was doing things for Leo, and that Leo who had been the riot of the village, the seducer of married women and young chicks, had suddenly settled, as we like to call it. He had become something of a loner, the old man on the hill, perhaps mad... in any case, saying nothing to anybody really, except Agatha. We imagined that he had just drawn himself in as it were; there comes a time in life where one feels a little disgusted with the ordinary goings on of life, the eating and drinking and making love. Just suddenly, just like that at fifty-eight, sixty, said Zoe. It happens, said Cleo.

We were not so surprised that Agatha frequented his house, and we thought, after all, why not, one and the other—the loner and the lone; we thought perhaps they will be a configuration. Whispers went around the island. You see, Agatha was walking like the dream women walk, the old men said she had a full moon on each hip, something to gaze at. And what did she do after all in Leo's house—but Zoe said: Bend down and pick up things—trash, discarded clothing, furniture.

Before she came there were months after the last girl left when we heard music, Michael went by one window and peeked in: There was an odd assortment of junk and a man, as far as he could judge by an arm and a foot, lying in the midst of it. The worst kind of mess. Agatha whom we alternately wondered about, and grew quite angry at—what was she after all, something that we were not? Agatha went into that house. She stopped doing what she was doing at her own, went up the hillside along the dirt path, through the patch of pine forest singing like a bird, and opened the door, entered and began to clean. Leo clicked off the tape recorder, Michael, our spy, heard the click. We thought when he told us—ah, so these two now; and there was, of course, a kind of disgust. We thought he had reformed, or wearied himself. We were sure after the months when the last girl left and there was silence and we saw him shuffling about, his trousers held up by a bit of string, that there were to be no more ladies.

And yet Agatha went up that dirt path as if she knew something about the end.

The old men wrinkled their noses, thinking about it—a wedding? They cackled. Timos said: Someone should rape her first.

We would not hear of such talk. Michael said they had not gone near the bedroom and that when he bent over little Agatha, it was to smile in a strange, interior way. We heard Agatha protest to Barbara—we are friends, Leo and I, cook together. Oftentimes, he cooks, and spends his mornings, savoring different sauces.

Is he different? Asked Barbara crudely in a harsh voice.

No, said Agatha, although she calculates on shocking us all. He is not different. New! A new creation out of the same meat, the same man.

Of course, we were too fed up with the both of them in their separate lives to care much ultimately if they joined forces and however they joined forces.

Some of us said, but Leo, if you remember, once won our hearts just after Magda died with his tender loneliness. It is such shame and degeneracy now—and to cap it all off, Agatha! We flickered in our hearts: the house came to our mind in and out of light. Shame, profligacy or friendship, purity. For some reason we were more furious about the idea of friendship and purity. For they have abandoned the right, said Zoe. First they shock a mild, settled, serene community, stain themselves and us, although in Leo's case there is some reason, for the death of Magda drove him mad, then they think they can just reach out and take up the holy light in their hands. We thought in particular of Agatha's brownish hand, gypsy colored, or discolored, Muslim tainted.

Simon said and what if we all stand before the Straight Gate and she passes in? What are you going to do? Bring out your baptismal certificates?

Nonsense, you are babbling, old crack pot. How can she unbaptized, half Muslim, and now freely, freely...

We didn't know exactly how to end our sentence. But it was about this new relationship with Leo.

The fact is, we were perturbed. We had considered, yes and no, the fact that Agatha must go. Just that it would be easier, as you know, or perhaps were never told, but in any case, as Paul had sometimes said. Purging the island, Holy Island, would be gentle, kind; there would be no suffering. Oh, there were people who believed that she should suffer. Rearing up like that, serpentine as she was, gypsy, dirty.... She was the bad tree and the fruit, although Jason had tried, poor thing, clammed up, accepted us; we don't think he even could help the situation at home; there was that time he had held the knife to his brother's throat—well, he had understandably gone mad; they had driven him—the way people drive you mad with their obstinacy and confusion over certain clear undeniable rules. Obviously, he shouldn't have held the knife! One wonders if he would have held it to his own mother's throat....But she and he, Dimitri, who grew more and more like his mother, were two peas in the same pod. Over in their dark corner—it seemed dark to us, where they lived; it was more noticeable at their house that the electricity company still would not provide full light.

But we felt along with Paul that we could settle with dimness outwardly at night, if all was clear as day inside our minds. Someone, perhaps Nico, now that he was getting married—oh, yes, Elizabeth had told us, laughing—that he had at last chosen the day; we said nothing about her having changed from nun to bride. Of course, it wasn't often done, but in these latter days no one was holy. And she who had had such expectations…but Zoe said, of course, she was such a meaty kind of girl, a member of the feast not an initiate of the fast, one could see her finally failing at the discipline, the all-night watches, cruel hungers of the sisters. Someone, perhaps Nico would buy Agatha's house. It was the one near the red rose bush, the roses like beauty and life itself, the only ones in the village --and the house had blue shutters. Made us think of peace at first, and then how did it happen? That a dim, dusty faced man should enter in, hardly talking, refusing to go to church, squatting down to pray like a heathen; someone Simon said who was lost in music. In any case, he was not part of the fabric and there the trouble began. Making as he did a rebellious daughter who stayed on with the mother, while he and the little boy left us, to flout us with her hard, fierce looks and wild hair—cursed one. Witch, Paul called her, when he was hardly old enough to know what it meant to say such things. But we are non-contentious, not so easily offended. For years we have walked slowly savoring the lunch smells at three, been peaceful in our afternoons, we have dozed, we have sometimes gotten up an argument, and sometimes gotten up to dance, but we have not had violence in our blood. An argument, a heat on the brain, yes, but in the end, nothing ugly.

We have grown and grown with Agatha; and now in her madness, she has lifted herself up as if she had something like the sun to offer us. She walks as if she was wearing a crown. And her son comes sidling in with money at his right hand, in the form of a rich man, developer, who is keen on building a luxury hotel for tourists who wish for a night or two in peace and quiet, away from the world. Ah, no. We don't have light at night but we have the sun already. Our sun: Brilliant, blazing even in winter, making things float, the sea itself floats in a mantle of fiery stars. And we don't like taunts and insinuations.

No, we won't argue. It is too maddening. We will be gentle. But this island is not her island. She cannot flaunt her way, as if her vagina, smiled Timos, has coiled into a king cobra and been let loose here to rule the island.

We think back to when Agatha was just a tiny child. She had a shock of thin brown hair and thin legs. Her face was never clean. That mother of hers was so overwhelmed—yes, that is how she appeared in public, overwhelmed, with two dirty children and a perpetually open mouth, sad eyes—one thinks she was a bit slow in the brain, one thinks, says Zoe, that she never paid proper attention to her duties as a wife and mother! Even so, even though it was clear she couldn't handle anything at all, we were surprised to understand that she didn't want any help at all. She was jealous of her household and especially of her children. She would snatch away Agatha's hand if the girl reached towards someone else. We think that Simon once touched the child, held the little hand between his thumb and forefinger and looked up at the mother as if she were a wild animal, cautious, quiet, gentle—for two seconds she suspended action and then she swooped down and separated the hands.

We could see from way back is what we are saying: they, the Agatha family, were not fit for the island. All caught up in themselves—that is, their difference!

All very well and good. Be whatever you like. But you cannot build another island, another Holy Island in our midst. For one thing, no Muslim bible is holy, and for another there is one Holy Island just like there is one Jesus. We cross ourselves. We remember that the Lord's Name is holy.

We cannot live where the Lord's Name is taken in vain. Of course, she says nothing. But Father Raphael, the last good priest, that is, half good, for at the end of his life he went insane, said so well and wisely that it is not just the word itself uttered from the mouth. But the word written invisibly on the walls of the impious home also. And we know this is the case with Agatha's family. They are a blasphemy—not only do they not baptize their children, they talk of Jesus, we cross ourselves, again, like that! As if Jesus were a dancer, a feaster, a muddy- faced, laughing urchin king of the gypsies, laughing that some gypsy thief had stolen a diamond ring. As if he wept when a poor Muslim wept, slept in the bed of a rebel woman abandoned by husband, with her boy taken from her, and put his arms around her and held her to his bosom.

We don't say that Agatha has said anything exactly but we know. We have ears at the windows—not that we listen; we just hear. We have eyes like sentinels, guarding 'round about. Not that we look; we just see. The holy home does not have brother against brother, a knife at the throat; a virtuous mother does not curse herself to hell. Nor rear up after as if you could throw penitence to the winds, and kick your leg up high, arch your back, lift your arms, as if welcoming the heavens. Now we know, of course, that the world does not share our convictions. Surely someone may be unbaptized…we must say, though, not in our midst. The American girl—but even she, lives apart, and so quietly; she makes less disturbance than a mouse. And she is sick, and delicate—a heart ailment and it is said that she does well in the weather here. Warm except for the winters, and always the sea air that would refresh the blood of anyone. She, we close our eyes, and wave our hands, as if to say out of mind, out of mind. She is an exception high on the cliffs. And we hear they have hardly a curtain or a carpet indoors for they believe in simplicity. Yes, we have all colors of faiths.

But Agatha is different. She has our blood in her. Even there, we have made our allowance. Yes, even our children grow up, following a different path, and decide to move off. We hear of them in France, Italy, Greece. One or two became bankers, prominent men, involved in politics. One was reportedly discovered, house penetrated and found with another man, a friend, he insisted, and would you believe it? Holy icons all around the house, in living room, and hall. The other man came toddling along behind our informant, explaining in a high falsetto voice: this is the holy

Mother of God of the black face, this is the holy Mother of God of the monastery of N….the house was littered with icons, our informant said.

We said nothing to all this. This is the world and its strange deformities. We know all about this world. Even a little glimpse tells us volumes. So we said nothing, even though we knew whose son it was. But Agatha wants to bring change to this island. She wants us to open our circle, the one circle that is our hope to regain our lost holiness. We know that if we are strict, if we purge our hearts—once again we shall be pure. We shall see even Mother Dora's footsteps lit with another world's light.

But our people must be our people. If not, well, we gently let them go. We believe we are fair-minded. We are not against anyone. Look how we handled a rich man. We did not believe in his promises, nor his offers of worldly wealth—no. We teased him away. We have our own minds, certainly, but all of us know Dimitri, Agatha's boy, the start of it all. Cleo, Barbara, they pretended to want more of a deal, a little more money, that would have been only just—to see what happened. Ah, the rich man went away—we knew he would, yes, we knew.

It is time for us to rise up as a body, the body of Christ, Himself—and should it be joined to a harlot? God forbid. Should we be joined to the demon of laziness, or money or any other demon, and refuse, because she has lived with us a long time and is, of course, our daughter, to set her straight as we fight to be on the straight path?

Here we have the light and what is not of light…it cannot exist here. Yet what can we do? How can we say it to her?

…

Dimitri one-handed wasn't so useful around the house and his mother thought that getting out, going for good long walks, talking to Katrina or climbing the mountain to that American girl would be good for him. But it was not without a spasm of jealousy that she watched him go. If she had had her way, she would have kept him in bed, fed him, dressed him, all day long. A son sick was like having the son a child again and it was a beautiful thing to come to him lying half asleep in bed and kiss him on the side of his face, on his hair, on his hands. He would smile, invariably, he was never moody when he was waking up, and open his arms and catch her in them and toss her from side to side between left hand and right arm, avoiding the wounded hand, as if she were his bride. But there was pride too in letting him go among women to see if they would vie for him. In her heart of hearts, she believed that he wouldn't marry—it was just not his destiny. With a mother's foreknowledge she knew that he wouldn't be long with a woman. Perhaps there was too much of a bond between them—a secretive, slightly guilty, unspoken pact between mother and son-- deep as blood, close as breath. She felt justified in one way: We have always been on the outs with society, she thought, and it would be a rare thing for Dimitri to find a woman to marry--who could fit in in that higher sense, other than being simply passing sexual fulfillment, possibly mother to his children.

So Dimitri, after an omelette with tomatoes and onions and goats' cheese for breakfast, and sitting around for a good hour, chewing on bread, drinking coffee and babbling of this that and the other with Agatha, rolled more or less out the door with his jacket thrown after him to go where he would.

He did not go to Katrina's or Catherine's but he went up with a look of intrigue in his eyes to the white washed church with the simple cross over the door.

He entered the dark little church with the strange, joyous fresco above the altar contrasting so blatantly, he thought with the gold and the heavy cross, and sprinted up the narrow staircase in the back to the side. He found the door to the priest's chambers open and the priest in the straw chair propped up by pillows, reading a little book of Cavafy's poetry.

You didn't come when I expected you, the priest quietly said, putting down his book. Now you expect to come and go when you choose, pop in and pop out.

Dimitri looked at the old man, smiling tentatively. The curtains were drawn and the room slightly darkened. The priest was sitting in the middle of newspapers thrown down all around him and a dirty coffee cup on the table in front of him. The room smelled stuffy and a little sour. The priest appeared cross from his words, but his tone was gentle and his look simply curious.

With respect, answered Dimitri softly.

Ah, well then. Where were we?

The garden of Eden.

Yes, people think of it as a beginning, you see. That is where all the trouble starts. The story goes backward from the end. Not forward from the beginning.

From the perspective of the end of time?

From the perspective of paradise. Where Jesus walked with the thief. Adam and Eve were thieves, you see. We are thieves. We want life, which is God's. And not for that, which God pardons, Himself, 'erotically tender' with us, the best way that I can call His love in language, but for the way we go about it—killing, ego tripping, hate mongering—all of this is wanting when we fall short and taking in despair, thieving from the world of worlds. Alas poor soul so as to be decked out in the gold and diamonds of your vain imagining, you would desecrate even God! Sometimes sub-consciously imagining that it is God in the end that you'll be getting. And Jesus says yes, yes—take! Take! and forgives the murderer and thief who come to Him, the pain and agony of the blood writing on their faces. The thief on the right side had the good sense to confess that he deserved to die; he was in a rapture seeing His face of sweetness and fellow pain. Remember me. Sheer love. No more beautiful way to be saved. You'll be with me in paradise tonight. The Omega, Eden, is that paradise of love. And Alpha—perfection through erotic passion (that is, of His blood) passion for Christ of all creation for it.

I suppose it is pointless to ask where Eden is, said Dimitri, after a pause.

Better to ask how it is, said the priest. Surrounded by nothingness, what can we be? Evil hearted madmen.

Violence and pain —is it any different than pleasure and love?

I suppose there is a world, that is the world in truth, where one loses all such distinctions. People have suffered even in pleasure and love, sometimes less in violence and pain. I have myself suffered pain and though it is unbearable, there is something almost to my liking about it. I don't seek it out, of course, I am not a masochist, it hurts, I fear it, yet in the end, there is still something to my liking. It corresponds. I believe this is what the thief meant when he said he deserved to be on the cross, seeing His face.

Christ deserved the cross too, not in the sense that he had done wrong like the thief, but in the sense that it was only through the cross that he was able to penetrate like a lover all flesh. Suffering is not popular. It is when you think of it as a labor, great labor, that it begins to have meaning.

There are people who would consent to five hours of pain, even a full day of pain, to receive something in return, something they have always wanted. There are people who would gladly suffer to go to heaven. Not suffering at all costs has encoded within it great spiritual sacrifice.

We don't want to suffer, exclaimed Dimitri.

There is that problem. And one is sorrowed to see those who suffer. How God plays out. Considering which of the two he will leave us with in the end—flesh, spirit! If flesh only, lethargic, deceived as in the Eden story-- to eternal death, that is separation from the one thing needful, and this will torment us like a hot flame. If, with spirit without flesh, then we are much less for the sore profound beauty is gone and we suffer ceaselessly with regret. Many torment themselves thinking—how is this God to be, this God with whom everything is possible? How is Spirit, where is Spirit? And there are some who recite formulas as if we can invoke him in the old sorcerer's style. Even I myself at the altar, proclaiming Chrysostomos' words: making the change... so that—this is truly the Body—what nonsense. I feel I should be beaten with many stripes in order to feel at least the blood.

You are always the same, Dimitri couldn't help exclaiming. Making us think, saying outrages...Don't you realize that the people want answers from you. Do this, and you will go to heaven. What do you imagine they want?

Yet it is unclear what heaven is, murmured the priest. I can certainly see where some are better off in hell if heaven is as Jesus—myself for example. I see myself —my soul and body-- diagram of greed, arrogance and lust. Some of it spreading into my yesterdays, and some spilling into my tomorrows from this foul core, which is my today.

Yet, you are joyful.

For one word, one mute spasm of self-abandonment in love for another human being, for God, Christ gives himself, utterly. A saint is no more than this—a brief lover, whom no one sees or knows.

It all comes from the heart, said Dimitri, smiling a little ironically.

The priest smiled too. His thin white hair hadn't been cut in several months and hung down like a wispy fringe along with his tuft of a beard. When the light shone around his head and on his balding pate, he looked as if illuminated, a sort of Christmas ornament, Dimitri imagined, light weight for his skinny legs, curled up like an insect's underneath him on the seat. Half-crawling thing, half-transcendent beauty, he looked, Dimitri thought. Yet in the end, this kind of life and thought make us nothing. He is content to sit and eat dried apricots!—the priest had a napkin in front of him of the dried fruit and gestured now and then to Dimitri to partake but the latter refused—sit and sit and eat and eat and do liturgies. What kind of a priest is that? What kind of a man? What kind of a holy man?

They are sweet, said the priest, gesturing to the apricots again, and bring a little water to the tongue.

There was a sound of footsteps on the stairs outside—the walls were thin as paper, said the priest—he was smiling, a kind of gloating, gluttonous smile. These footsteps he said, still chewing an apricot, I know well.

In came Max, fresh cheeked and sparkling eyed from the cold wind. He had that stern and yet fragile look of a man who's reached his full manhood in total innocence. One would have said he didn't know day from night. In reality, Max was a twisted, anguished child still—anticipating violence, villainy, still sometimes clinging in his mind to the idea of his mother—stronger than life in him; she was an ear that heard, a heart that forgave and he had the idea that he was entering into a world—on this slip of an island in the middle of a vast sea—that was cold and hostile; that would above all turn him upside down and hell itself would become his heaven. He had an idea vaguely that the priest was to blame. Yet he clung to the priest for he had washed his wounds and healed them.

He imagined the priest knew all about this. The horror, the horror that was in the back of his mind every day and entered into his dreams at night. He saw Dimitri, sitting in his usual chair opposite Father Isaac's, and he gasped. It was a jolt, something strange about that black clad figure—the very form of man was startling, violent and cruel. But then Dimitri turned his face to him and Max saw, the thinking in his eyes, the peace around his lips, and thought—no, he is beautiful, and breathed in relief…

Beautiful was the word he used when he wanted to say something that transcended the horror. That was and yet was not. A man and yet a god. For that is how Max saw people and the world—in shocking contrasts, and even more violently startling unities. Of course, he was childish in his perceptions. Beauty was beauty like a house is big to a child, when that same child, later on, grown and worn and jaded, returns to the big house to find it small. A certain awe took hold of him, seeing Dimitri, who happened to have more manliness than usual about him probably for having suffered, and still suffering his burn. Also because Dimitri with a quickness in his own brain that was characteristic of him saw instantly that Max was overcome. He saw it really before it happened. He blushed slightly. And then he felt a little out of place. He felt in fact as if there were many little seedlings growing underneath his feet and he had or would trample on them hideously. He got up and began to move awkwardly towards the door.

You can, of course, stay, said the priest in a languid voice. Max has little sudden ways of moving when he is surprised. It doesn't mean that you are unwelcome. I feel that this place is holy, said Dimitri speaking in a rush and not thinking about the words, and, and, I am not.

There is not so much difference that sets holy and profane a world apart. A little hesitation to kill the living thing…a beautification of an ugly thing.…the connection of love and beauty. So that is the difference, even just that. And I can see you hesitate even to tread heavily across our room.

Max was standing hunched over his arms hanging down, his face down for embarrassment. Dimitri came over to him and said—well?

Max looked up at him and nodded.

Dimitri smiled, breathed a sigh of relief and sat down on the bed in the middle of the room. There is something tender and warm in this room, alive, yes, you are right, alive. It is in the air, mustn't kill what is in the air, here.

It is in the air, it is in the floor, muttered Max. But it is old man's live, like worms and butterflies. Most of me is closed up in a book, called the Liturgy of St. John Chrysostomos, and when I emerge I am a liar that tells the truth, a worm in a chrysalis.

No liar, said Dimitri, in a voice that was low and soft.

I tell him that he doesn't have to serve if it eats him up like this, said the priest, but he hangs on to the chalice. And you know, if he wants to hang on to that golden chalice of the Eucharist, he has to suffer the terrible pomp and majesty of the liturgy, which is only beautiful to rapists.

Why the chalice? Asked Dimitri, turning to him—ignoring the last strange utterance.

Max had his face lowered again. He was standing as if frozen over the bed. He didn't answer.

The book plays with people, he said, in a low angry tone. One goes by the book to become what one is not.

And yet the intent, said Dimitri, the heart and soul of the matter, is not in the book. It can't be. For the Word was made flesh and dwelt among us— not book, as I understand it.

Max walked over to his seat by the window and sat heavily and noisily into the chair. Flesh, it gets us nowhere. I preach in the streets, people stare, and then go home to eat and drink. The bread is the same, and the wine.

Ah, said the priest looking at him with affection and nodding. The bread is the same and the wine.

Why do you repeat what I say? Max asked the priest angrily. You are not learning, not thinking about it. Didn't the Gospel say to get rid of fathers? You can see why.

Poor child, said the priest, gazing at the floor. One is so humanly uncomfortable with life often, growing up.

But the chalice! One sip and one's meat comes back to one. Not of course the profane meat. But the meat that is the will of God in one. Is that it? Asked Dimitri, looking compassionately at Max.

People don't understand the meaning of the will of God, said Max, looking across the room at Dimitri; his eyes were serious and sad; he had recovered from his 'shock'. And then he seemed to wrap himself into thought. It may be he said from a remote place just to fall into an abyss singing beautifully.

Dimitri thought that he and the priest went on murmuring like bees around this figure, beautiful in an uncanny sort of way with his freshness and his sparkle. He dreamed they all opened up like flowers in the first spell of spring and their voices, disembodied from their bodies, buzzed and buzzed; and somewhere in the dream there was that light, soft touch on the down on the small of their backs. The priest laughed and smiled with his carnal mouth and said something down the line about dried apricots.

Dimitri was dreaming and talking and carrying on all together. The back of his mind kept alert ever to catch what the priest was saying, in the concentration part he held that figure, so thoughtful now, lovely as snow because he had both that virginal, childlike terror, and that age-old thoughtfulness stamped on his brow. He looked at Max out of the corner of his eye and though he knew about the island's tradition of silence, sudden silences between people that lasted one, two hours as people thought, or chewed, or washed, or sighed, or simply sat and waited, he was amazed now that Max could sit there as freely as if he were alone on a high hill, and breathe and ponder. He sat as if he were indulged frequently in this sitting without responding, breathing, living a life that was in hermitage where he alone bloomed like the moon at midnight.

Until people come around again, I am afraid we are rejected stones, said the priest, his voice breaking into Dimitri's thoughts. The stone, which the builders rejected, murmured Dimitri, still fascinated by the thinking figure, hunched a little as Rodin's statue, but not posturing-- yes, but the cornerstone of what? Said the priest, warmly. It may be that we find never a place on earth to set our weary bones down in peace and trust…

In this way, the conversation came to a close. Dimitri hardly remembers how. Just that the priest pulled back the window curtains and looked out, as if he was cutting himself off from all company but the usual, and Dimitri found himself stepping as quietly as he could out of the little room where he no longer belonged—yet it seemed a long way to the door, maybe because he was in a little agony about his harsh steps—one, two, and another and another…When he went a little way beyond the bed, he turned and bowed at Max, a bow of respect, and tenderness, a way to 'give up' a little; the idea came to him after…

Give up what? He asked himself like a child, persisting, even though in part of him he knew to talk about it was to ruin it. The way I have things all settled, locked into place. That man who seems sometimes less, sometimes more than a man, knows things I don't, is things I am not.

When he thought back on it that night on his bed, it seemed in his memory that he saw Max through a great fog, the kind of fog where things are suddenly upon you out of nowhere, out of the blind atmosphere—and there is no help for it, you will run crash into them, and he thought, miserably, destroy all their fine filaments.

Katrina couldn't help feeling a deep satisfaction since her date with Dimitri to go to the beach and sit on the sand, right on the sand, that had been the agreement, with nothing in between and get sand in their clothes like they used to when they were children. And with sand dripping from her, she had come back from the beach to take care of her parents whom Kali had babysat during the few hours off that she had had that day.

Kali knew and Kali saw. She smiled and thought –ah, the handsome man comes to the village—like a purple fruit on a tree that has been nothing but leaves. People stop and exclaim. In my way of thinking, my lady—she called Catherine this, affectionate, and formal—had best be on her guard. I hope and pray that another man will come. That man Connie was better, an American too, but he had no heart.

She heard Katrina singing and saw her twirling on her heavy legs as if she was six and going to get ice cream, and heard her voice artlessly say—I am going for two hours to sit with Dimitri and talk about old times, can you possibly watch Mother and Father? Kali had pretended blindness, deafness, and almost muteness. She had nodded her head, and said briefly not to worry in a low voice, almost extinct, like a whisper.

When Katrina had returned, Kali had just given supper to the old folks. She was wiping their faces and the front of their sweaters with her napkin. Katrina's father was sitting perched forward, his eyes staring into nothingness, her mother was reclining in a crumpled heap in the chair, looking as if she had shrunk down, half dissolved away, her head bowed. Katrina kissed her parents and her mother lifted up her head and looked at her with narrowed eyes. This day after day with the slowly dying no longer seemed so brutal. She felt she had enough spirit to 'change this world', to make it lift its head—to make it not so meaningless, she stroked her father's back. For even these suffer, she said to herself, and if they suffer, so they remain alive.

She thought of her own suffering in poetic terms. They had ceased to think of her as anyone in the village. She was Katrina the childless, the widowed before she was married. All this she could have slung out at him, didn't he deserve it? He was familiar enough to hear the truth, the core of the truth down in her belly…but seeing him, she hadn't wanted quite to sling at him. He had come back like the only companion in the world for her. If only, she thought in the depths of her soul, he could wean her away from all this; yet at the same time, she corrected herself, this was what she had chosen. Some people do, she imagined she was telling him, pick up the cross, because life is…and to be in the truth…They were father and mother, could one really abandon them to a sterile nursing home-- a place where people one has never seen before, nor imagined, are suddenly fluttering in your face as if they were your children, but who are nurses, paid to zoom around you in and out on a hot summer's day like flies?

She thought she would keep her parents on the balcony a little while longer—the fresh air did a world of good bringing to life people, the old, bowed and sick. One tended to sever the relationship in one's mind and heart but really she was blood of blood, sinew of sinew of these fading two. She was a meaty girl—stocked herself up as a defense against that decrepitude. Ate and ate, meats, vegetables, goats' cheese, milk. Sank down, she thought, on seeing Dimitri, into a lower level. The level of the primitives who were at their core, fearful beings. She turned to Dimitri when he came, recoiled knowing her guilt—she had just allowed herself to be pulled down. And she thought in a frenzy after he had left with that absurd old hat on his head, how she ought to be reading science, philosophy, at least the latest novels. She had looked at herself in a mirror and seen her meaty body. Ah, he would judge and condemn; he who had kept slim as a pencil, and had sailed the seas, had cleverly crafted with his mind, lost his religion, she presumed—for that was for the foolish—and made enough money based on the wisdom of his brain. She, on the other hand, had kept to her family, performed the duties of filial affection, for which there was little regard in the world and had grown fatter and fatter, lost her grip on the old fire of intellect.

He didn't seem to judge or condemn at all, though. It was her impression that he came back to her without condescension and with the old un-permitted familiarity of a brother and the reprimand of a lover. What had she been doing all this time—he seemed to ask her accusingly. As if she was supposed to stand on the beach for ten years straining to see the boat with him on it sailing in!

In the cross fire between them, sometimes spoken, more often undercover of little jests, strange hilarity, grumpiness, a flash of the old love, Katrina felt that they were essentially the same, exactly the pair that came wandering out of the forest on that afternoon when she had stolen his virginity and had danced off with a whipped flesh and a blood of honey; the difference was that he had been then five steps behind her and seemed now to be two steps ahead. But they had been defaced, torn, tangled, both of them. With him there was a certain smoothness that made her want to stand up and shout at him—so this is the way of the world, is it? Go away, go away, in the village, we hump along. She would stand there all unblushing for the reference.

He had said to her a little sadly, except that he was too dry for tears, when first she saw him, ah, it is mostly conceit and deceit. Katrina wanted to yell at him, you know, I too can't see religion; the whole thing runs like a great machine—but I too stand with them, you know, the old folk faithful; I insist on being among the foolish. Where there is a potato, I eat it. My mother sick, I nurse her.

And the old tender voice came back; once it was reserved for her alone. He said, but I too, Katrina. The old machines jingle and jangle in the sky.

Which machines?

The ones you saw in your dream.

When had they had this conversation? Katrina didn't remember. It was time to change her father's diaper; he always defecated after a full meal. Kali was standing in the hall dusting the mirror and a little inlaid table they had had for centuries. Katrina called her and together they picked up the old man who weighed just little enough for them to get him off the ground. They brought him to bed and Katrina raised his skinny legs.

She used a sponge to wash him; he always sang a little garble; it was a song of agony, Katrina thought, when long ago he was aware that his own daughter had to wash his feces off his anus and penis—he had once been a private man. The smell was pungent and sick. The awareness, mercifully, had dimmed, but the song an agonized chortle had remained.

Years passed, and necessity and time had taken the edge off this operation for Katrina. She felt she could handle anything now—an eye operation, brain surgery. And in her waking dreams she sometimes came upon life in him-- and in her mother too, the other little witless duck, as she sometimes privately called them--as a thread, white, gluey and very frail; it would stretch just a little before snapping. She often thought—for them, for their dignity…But then another idea blundered into her mind: let them live, this is life—a kind of caricature, a sad, tragic caricature. This is the end of the machine. I watch them, meditate on them, she decided she would tell Dimitri, like some monks meditate on a skull. I have no desire to throw it away.

And they? Came Dimitri's voice out of the shadows. Wouldn't they have said— better kill me.

But they are not they, said Katrina, in answer. This, you see, is life. This—a hideous deformed agony.

But he would not eat the potato, nurse his mother. No. He would keep her on a long rope—somewhere in a pleasant nursing home. Reel himself in to kiss her, to coax her, to cozen her into thinking that he was the loyal son. Katrina knew this about Dimitri, as a wine connoisseur knows the difference between a fine wine and an ordinary one: He was fine.

And so there was no real mixing of him and her. No miracle was going to change her to the kind of woman he would accept as a wife. The old dream, although burning away like the perpetual flame of Christ, had to be let go of. Somehow, she would let go of it. For ten years, she had been tending that flame. The village was harsh. She had been Katrina with the hot vulva, taking up with any man that came her way. Men had drifted past. Usually they were young men that had those knowing eyes and deep down didn't know. One had asked her—are you going to marry me? And eventually, she had said yes, yes, but not until the young man had come to his senses and realized how old she was, how much of a buffoon, and wandered off, coming back only once, able after all this propping up on her part, to pity her. She for her part, had let them go after a few necessary tears. Eventually, she had thought of them with loathing too. And this had come along on the wind to the old men, who had laughed and said to one another—the old hag thinks she is going to make a good match.

As Katrina's upper arms and thighs, and belly swelled from oil and meat, she saw herself more and more as a kind of warrior buttressed up by fat to take the wounds from the derision slung at her. And over time, her lust died down, she became known in the village by many loud praises of the priest, as the one who had sacrificed in a Christ-like manner. It didn't matter that some of the old men astonished and old women indignantly asked sacrificed what? They always saw it as Katrina incapable and unwanted, staying at home and being naturally the extra hands there. But her toil gradually became an acceptable village phenomenon. It was very much the village mind and heart, obscure and rough and bitter as it was, to have the children tend the aged and sickening parents. It was, it appeared to them, one step on the path back to Christ, one whiff of the incense of their lost holiness. Begrudgingly, slowly, but surely, the village began to find a place for Katrina. It was always as the lesser, the inferior type—but yes, she was in.

Another year rolls by. Christmas is coming. It is a time when the priest instructs us to pray and fast under no uncertain terms. We are instructed that the Incarnation is the first step to the Resurrection: that God became Man so that Man could become God. The air is colder, and the sense between us solemner. It is the time for confessions on our island although we hear of the world making merry, eating and drinking and dancing.

At Agatha's house all is quiet. Dimitri comes and goes on great rambles by himself. Little Paul has seen him at night climbing the cliff to the white villa, finding his way by moonlight. We wonder at the Americans, but we don't say much. They are out of sight and out of bounds, keeping to their house on the cliff and coming down to the village only to buy food. Peter wanted to go after him and challenge him, but Little Paul said what is the use? You know nothing, you can't prove anything against him; he is allowed to climb the steep cliff's stairs by moonlight. Peter went away grumbling. We pressed Kali for details about Catherine, the American girl, and Dimitri, but she remains mysterious. All the more reason, we say, to conceive that they are lovers although we confess that to us the lady looks ready to fall over.

We whisper about the priest. While he confesses us well, we shudder in horror to find that he isn't in the least concerned that Catherine isn't baptized. Our shudders are not for Catherine whose family lives peaceably enough—she is not one of us perched on the cliff as she is; the island is for her and her family a landing place not a home, of course; rather we shudder because this non baptizing is extended as a general way, and the way Father Isaac goes on about it, you'd think that Christianity is more of a matter of feeding bread crumbs to the birds, which apparently Catherine never fails to do, or of dancing which is the case of our Agatha.

Of course we have our feasts. We believe that a man is not a man without dancing, and the women not women. It is right at the feasts to joyfully be—for the music and the dance. It was ever understood to be part of a context—the Christmas all-night vigil, the next day feast and the late night gossiping and laughing, the cracking of jokes, the coming round the great dinner tables, the drinking of wine with Maria, the visiting Matrona and her worn husband—for once Martha has on a new vest and shoes. And then we dress for the dance and it has always been that the new ones, girls and boys, should find themselves there, courting. It was good luck when long ago Paul won the crown, for there are two coronations—Christmas and Easter, and carried off Ella—proper good luck, island good luck. But over the years, as Paul has won the crown again and again, we fade even there. The other men blunder; Michael is all arms and legs. They don't know the first thing about keeping rhythm and time.

Agatha though is dancing up a storm at her home. It is a new kind of dance; it isn't part of the blessing. It transcends feast and festival. When asked about it, she said something once about it 'getting to be' an invocation of the Holy Spirit. She has gone mad, we said; but no, we saw her sail by, stepping so smoothly it was like sailing, cool as a cucumber. We start; we stop. That is all very well, we think. But what irks us is that the priest, who should remember the traditions, goes entirely along with it. And so, Paul almost sneered at him one day, apropos of nothing, you are going to anoint her with holy oil for it, bless her in the Name of the Father, Son and Holy Spirit.

Ah, said the priest, why not? He seemed to be waiting just to say that—why not? Not only to Paul, you see, but to us all.

I can hardly go and see a dance, complained Barbara to us; I can't return to our festivals—not with what I am forced to see morning after morning.

We thought this exaggerated. We could, of course, just welcome it, said Zoe, judiciously. Except that it seems as if she is dancing in a sphere of her own, as if it means something more than…and all the time the feeling about her as if her presence itself, before when she was miserable and now mean something more than… One thinks she believes that the Almighty God takes a special interest in her.

It feels, said Cleo, just as you are going to open your arms to her that she is saying to you, wait—I am higher than you, infinitely more important!

You must admit that as Barbara puts it, she is 'taking off', said Foti, wonderingly.

I said the same thing to the priest once, and he said, a person can do that, said Cleo. Just as if it didn't matter that we are left in the dust. And dance was always a great joy to me.

You never put your mind to it, exclaimed Zoe. No, it is just something aside from what we do, she said; the only thing I disagree with is using this island for one's own space, in order to take freedoms, to enlarge oneself. She can dance as much as she pleases, but it is such loud dancing. And her goal is not to contribute to our feasts and festivals, I think, but to attract the attention of the whole village. If dancing is going to be her career then I think she should leave, all the more reason to go, and live somewhere—in London, Paris or New York. There they have people come together not as quiet community, but as loud ones, great people, talking, as it were, nose to nose with God.

But one should be allowed, said Foti. A human being is not a human being until she lifts her heart! And there is Simon, who paints as he pleases. No one ever said a thing about it. And Thomas, he periodically goes mad writing poetry.

Simon is half fool, said Zoe, irritated. This is his little garden where he is kept quiet. Thomas is likewise kept from harm.

It was Simon who started Agatha off, you know, said Cleo. He had a prophetic dream.

No, she did, said Barbara.

In any case, it seems almost obscene. As if Simon didn't express himself enough already with those strange pictures, said Zoe. Oh, she waved her hand as if dismissing the whole thing, I predict Agatha's dancing will just wither away. It's as if the sun on this island drives us all into a different state; a kind of sun god is what we have here. It clasps us all around in a fiery embrace in summer, still a blazing white fire in the sky in winter; it whitens things, blooms things, dries things. Perhaps Agatha came out into the sun once too often and it caught her—down to the soul as our sun does. But it is not anything to consider. At Christmas we will have our feasts, our dancing, our music; the island will continue. The only question we have is whether Paul can keep on dancing as he used—that hard precision of his feet, the perfect stunts, back flip, one handed hand stand, leap—he wows us every time. The others you see, the contenders, haven't practiced.

They start about now, said Foti.

Too late, too late, said Zoe.

It was dark out as we sat in Zoe's kitchen chatting, one of those cold, dark winter nights. Thinking about Agatha's dancing—Barbara said it was all high legs and leaps, toe stands, splits, twirls on the toe without shoes—we felt feeble, weak—as if all that we wanted to express, the choices that we had once, had been drained from us, crushed from us, in fact, like a lemon squeezed of its juice. We were rinds, dry rinds. Thomas could make a poem looking at us—cast aways, we felt. Not because anyone had literally cast us out of our homes and island, but just because time itself had come and shoved us aside; it was as if one is walking, walking, day and night to get somewhere along a harsh, stony road, dirt and gravel path, ruining one's shoes, and ultimately cutting one's heels, going at a fast clip nonetheless pell mell to get there despite the aches and pains in one's feet and along comes destiny or death and pushes one aside. And this was inevitable as Sisyphus' stone falling away from him just as he got it up to the peak of the hill. Now it entered our minds that Agatha was somehow getting the stone up that hill. She was using all the technology of the body—the sinews and nerve connections; that her whole body was engaged: and we would see her, right under our noses—actually push the stone in place and crawl out of hell.

We wanted and we didn't want to see this. We pretended it had to do with some grave offense she had given us; but really it was an agonized why? When each day we had put ourselves to the task of continuing and had darkened our dreams of triumph, and not only triumph, but the ultimate right to look destiny or death or time in the eye because we knew she had made beautiful the work, had succeeded, that is, in setting it in place in the world.

And to cap it all off, we saw Agatha, up there, in the brilliant sun, softly turn her head, lower her gaze, look at us as destiny come clothed in rags and drinking nauseating wine to oust us, and gently say—but you too…and we knew that this love came too late, although it was our fault as much as hers, still, considering she was far more, she could have done something…we knew that she was just embalming us, making fragrant and beautiful what would soon be bones, according to the will of God.

Foti was the first to say—well, I never enjoyed dancing all that much. Some pour themselves into one thing, some into another.

And you, snapped Zoe, we knew that Foti made her seethe with anger, although she kept that secret for the most part, what did you pour yourself into?

Other things, whispered Foti, looking at her fearfully.

What a horror, said Zoe, although she had looked away from Foti. The great waste. I would almost rather hell.

Zoe! screamed Cleo; why? Why? She burst into tears and cried for some five minutes. Then she dried her eyes and said: I, for one, dancing or no dancing, think that Agatha has tried our limits, and the limits of every sane, rational person on the island except for Dimitri and the priest. We are told to love our enemies; we have fulfilled that commandment. But no one said you couldn't fight a little when the enemy wants to drag you down into the dust and to put your face in it. And perhaps we would have anticipated this, and allowed her in a Christian fashion to do it, but then to tell us in no uncertain terms—you are dead, you are dead! I believe we can protest.

Ah, she like a serpent, we like God's children, said Zoe, recovering.

But, but that is brilliant, said Foti, forgetting everything; she had a certain innocence that expressed itself in an artless love of another who impressed her no matter that they hated her for it.

Yes, said Cleo sitting back. She looked around at the members of our little group, Barbara was present this time but she was knitting, quietly; she had looked up only momentarily when Cleo screamed. Barbara for whom the idea of obedience that is emotionless continuance of her activities—as if some master had set her there out of time and place to accomplish some task, like knitting—had an idea that was paramount now that her marriage was on the brink of real catastrophe. She 'obeyed' in scrubbing the floors, cooking the food, washing the clothes…she was not going to rise up and protest, no—but keep the faith, that is, the old old faith of our island.

So we sat in silence, island fashion in the now late evening, each one of us looking around, taking note of the single dim light hanging down over the table, the yellowing, fading room, the weariness of our eyes in this light and the rise and fall of our bodies, breathing. Zoe was a good housekeeper; the silverware is sorted out on the counter, forks, knives, spoons, the dishes are piled up in the corner, lovely dishes with the edges in pink and flowers painted in the centers, crystal turned over so as not to collect dust even for such a short time as between lunch at three and dinner at nine. She has two windows she gets Michael to clean with the new window cleaner fluid they bring over in the supplies' boat and they are so transparent almost seamless with the space except that one can see in fragments the glossiness of the glass. The curtains around them, soft tan-colored curtains that turn the sunlight to gold in the morning give her kitchen a warm feeling that no other kitchen has. And we can say that Aunt Zoe made a space—island style, a space for warmth, heart, intelligence, in the end. One does these sorts of things out of sanity, kindness, and the proper kind of hospitality.

We are included in this sphere. And the little path laid out in front of the house is for anyone. Zoe can hear the crunch of footsteps on the stony path even in the kitchen. And she can look out and smell the salt in the air and see the visitor. She has even seen Agatha and opened her door.

But we know that to be included means of course that some are excluded. Truth excludes the lie. The heel comes down like a hammer driving in a nail. Something is boarded up in us. We understand that we cannot, no cannot accept those elements that would oh—turn upside down the tranquility, the sweet nothing of our island; yes, we call it sweet nothing; our island is like lover's talk-- beautiful and wonderful when you have the faith; and in our summer sunlight, our winter sunlight too, the faith often warms you. But without it, and we suppose despite the sun, people lose it, it is just little and tacky, silly—something that will float away in a minute like an unmoored dinghy.

Nevertheless, we are secure in our faith in our island. But what if someone comes in—what if, with proofs, as Dimitri showed us, that our system may run better if—and argues in jet boats and computers, helicopter pads, film production companies—shakes us to the root? Would we be wrong in throwing them out? Untruthful? Unscientific? For it is love and truth that is at stake. And just because you can factually arrive in a helicopter at our doorstep, does not make your arrival truthful to us. Perhaps nobody did arrive in a helicopter but it all added up to the same thing when Dimitri proposed it. The jet boats that he insinuated belonged here as they did elsewhere were not truthful, nor the computers. And yet we know they are factual, that they exist in this world and could be driven here in our peaceful, radiant waters. They could get you to the hospital, he argued, save lives! What are we—on a battlefield, in the city dense with noises, with screaming sirens...? We die when God arrives like thief in the night; and we in this place sit so still that we hear his tread but do nothing, nothing.

What is this news we hear, this little noise? Agatha left her door ajar and Simon walking by—oh, he's wily one, neither for that side nor on this, a law unto himself... one day, a grey day when we pulled out the extra jackets for the weather, he walked by in just a white shirt and vest and said to Zoe: Dimitri and Agatha are not thus and are not so. Just like that and then faded off before she could lay hands on him and make him sit down and brighten her kitchen. Later Barbara flew into Zoe's face practically as she was going out—knocked on her door and opened it before she did, and said all red-faced and her voice coming in little squeaks—she and he like lovers! I saw them because my kitchen faces on to their kitchen and she was pressing up against him kissing him repeatedly on the lips.

Zoe went back into her kitchen with Barbara and set down her things—her purse on to the little white wooden table. A mouse ran across the floor and Barbara gasped and looked at her and said—won't you do anything about the mouse? Zoe leaned against the tile wall with the blue sailing ships design on it and said—the mouse at least is innocent. How could you enter into this place—this one, in particular?

Absentmindedly she began to eat crumbs of bread that were left on the table and drink from a glass of what looked to Barbara like wine and water. Barbara helped herself eventually to a chair. Zoe went to the refrigerator a little mechanically and took out some cheese and butter and cut new slices of bread for her guest.

What do you think it means? Asked Barbara in her old low harsh voice. Zoe sat down and folded her hands on the table. I once had the occasion to talk to Agatha on matters of faith. She said to me she thought full-bloodedness was key in conversion—full bloodedness! St. Peter was a full-blooded man, St. Paul was. She is practicing full bloodedness. That is what I think it means. But calm yourself, no doubt she is expecting that we expect the worst of her. This is probably nothing but a little charade.

But she does not believe.

Oh she says she does. That is what comes and sits on my stomach here like…like too much mustard. She says without baptism without the sacraments—she believes, in other words, better. She is no atheist; she walks with the Lord. Of course, I don't have the slightest idea what Dimitri thinks.

To think that people can be so perverted about the one holy thing.

What I don't like is that she does things full force and frontally. She must of course kiss her son in this hideous way right under your window.

Yes, shouted Barbara, I looked out of my own window and saw evil.

Hush, said Zoe, commandingly. We would never condemn without thoroughly weighing the evidence and then not even. She had her eyes half closed and one finger pointing to the sky. She looked sunk in profound thought and since Barbara never managed to, she accorded her the privilege of deepest respect. But after ten minutes, Barbara couldn't help bounding in verbally and asking—but when do we condemn?

She is already condemned. She will leave us—watch and see. But it is not I, nor you, who condemn her. It is sad to think and yet it is true…for there is an inner condemnation and a place where there is no escape. Many who commit suicide suffer from this inner condemnation.

And this 'full bloodedness', what is that? How dare she?

Let us just say that she is seeking in her imagination for a reason other than baptism, which is not a reason that would justify her.

Barbara went out with Zoe, was escorted firmly out the door after about half an hour; Zoe for one thing couldn't abide Barbara she was too meaty in the face, too prone to shout, a person whose ignorance was, according to Zoe, a kind of insanity. Of course, she was harmless, religious wise, but a real trial in every day get-togethers. Barbara sensed that she was not altogether welcomed and came irregularly.

Somewhere along the line Barbara got a hold of Revelation and went around after this little affair or vision of Agatha saying that she had seen the moon become blood and it wasn't the moon at all but Agatha. And Agatha at last came to her,

Barbara thought, ludicrously, we know, that Agatha was going to go down on her knees and weep on Barbara's foot as the sinful woman had done to the Lord, and was surprised to see her standing erect and talking to her calmly. In fact, as it turned out—Barbara came to our little circle at four when we were sitting in our shawls and making lace with glasses of apricot brandy and hot water—she, Agatha, 'announced' the end of the world. She said it was here amongst us and that people knew, yes they knew—in their hearts there was a kind of scales and they weighing too much, had become those which were all flesh and heavy bones and therefore dead. Didn't we know, Barbara said she said, the flesh-bone configuration 'talking and rearing itself up' within us.

Of course, she got our goat. Cleo humphed and made a snag in her lace making. Foti swallowed a few gulps of the yellowish brandy and water and coughed and spat. She was old gristle even though she had her softness and timidity—her fatness, Zoe said unsympathetically. She couldn't be pricked by a pin without screaming and imagining torture. Zoe remained aloof. Finally, she whom we looked to when we were in this kind of trouble, found the sense in her head and spoke thus: Why should we get angry? Of course, this 'rearing up' is true—true of me and you, true of her—but she, I think trusts to something called her heart. And we, wisely, look upon that fiction as unreliable.

Our Lord Jesus spoke of the heart, said Foti in a tiny voice.

Did he? Asked Zoe in a firm, loud tone. Well. Then he did it for good reason.

He put the kingdom of heaven there.

As well as lies and blasphemies. Let us never mind it, in any case. Whatever it is beyond the fiction in our minds, let God take care of. Our job is to above all follow certain rules, though mind you, not without discernment. It seems to me with a good head on one's shoulders one knows right from wrong. And one goes nowhere without baptism.

Is it the end of the world? Asked Foti.

I don't believe, I won't believe, said Cleo, angry that Agatha would announce it.

Anyway most are a kind of turned inside out people, said Barbara gloomily; our souls are shadows and salvation is impossible for us. She said 'us' on purpose.

I would say that that has been true for most of the world since the Holy Roman Empire expired, said Zoe; that is why our island is so important, taking a different tack.

We all remained silent. Zoe knew as well as we did that the general consensus, no, our knowledge of the truth, told us that we had lost our holiness. Zoe knew like the rest of us that we were spiritual waste—dead carcasses lost in an immensity of darkness; that perhaps, although not wanting to become histrionic, we were rot itself. Just rot. And yet there was something that ran through the whole thing, a kind of sweetness, sweet smell to this rot like there is to dead leaves—and we snuffed it with a new hope and asked ourselves: what does it mean?

Yes, said Zoe, looking around the table. What have we to do with meaning? We sit here on this balcony drinking sips of apricot brandy out of little glasses, Cleo with her white gloves on, Foti with her hat with the blue ribbon and all of us in grey and black dresses, propped up by some idea of making a good impression. All this we get up in order to prove that there is, still is, life unalterable in us. And we go home and stand before our icons, sometimes thinking all is at an end, other times that there is, yet there is…and we ask the Holy Mother of God—what does it mean?

Don't you see that we are innocent? And think how we have fed Marta—all those scraps, the good chicken, the goat, the cheese. She has eaten heartily because of us. We have knitted her wool socks, and sweaters. As far as Agatha is concerned: Here is a case of loving our enemy. She has come among us rearing herself up as if she is truth itself with that Muslim look in her eyes, and we—we have welcomed her. Of course, she ought to be a little more circumspect and not come to church but those are simply rules. And if the priest chooses to ignore them, we swallow down the bitter savor, the reminder of the lost holiness on this island, and we go along with it. For at all costs, our innocence must be preserved. We must not be guilty of judgment, at all costs, at all costs.

We all sat silently. Cleo sipped her brandy and choked. Foti and Barbara handed her in unison a white napkin. She took Foti's and dabbed her mouth with it.

And yet we must be on our guard. We must never throw pearls to swine. For there is something inherent about Agatha. Again and again, we have offered her baptism. She has remained stalwart against our pleas, entreaties, our suggestions and our advice. We must consider, just consider of course that there is an innate, genetic difference, something as deep as species itself. For can a beast become a man?

Yes and one sees, said Foti, mesmerized by Zoe's strong insistent voice—in her hair it is so frizzy, such a bush. She is a wild woman.

Thrown here and there, said Barbara—by bestial energy to commit atrocities. In the spasms of the demon! That dance she does in the morning is not dance but a mad rite honoring the sun god, or something like that. License is what it looks like, not the old dances that we knew and revere. And she has such big feet.

Have you seen her eat? Asked Zoe, smiling a little coldly. What never? Oh, I have—ten years ago when she was bent backed and lame, misery itself. Told she had sinned against the Holy Spirit by our old priest. I gave her some of my special recipe for stewed goat—I told her it was lamb and she ate it readily, saying that her father had once brought them lamb from the other land and it was so wonderful, a perfect meat! She didn't know the different—ate practically with her fingers, hunched over the dish, her face almost in the mess of meat and sauce.

Yes, I pitied her. I didn't see the way of eating, the ugliness itself of her body, bent and lame as a sign. We have become a land of throwing pearls to swine.

In the form of good goat meat to Agatha who doesn't need it, said Cleo, snorting.

In the form of love, said Zoe, simply.

But we are to love, said Foti, fearfully.

Yes, said Zoe. But you must all understand now what I have learned over years and years: Agatha is inherent. This is not a case of stubbornness. There are signs that this is a case of another—that is another species, another will, call it what you want. She cannot be what we are anymore than swine can be princesses and wear pearl necklaces.

For it is by firmness, when we cannot love that we come to God. Firmness is not sinning; nor when we see through our very own windows evil itself, is turning away.

I will always try to convince her; said Foti. My heart will be open to—to her change, she said meekly, seeing Zoe frown at her.

We are not to fear those which lead the body to death but those which kill body and soul…said Cleo, paraphrasing the Gospel.

Yes, said Zoe, decidedly.

Catherine was climbing down the steep cliff with Kali to go for a walk along the beach. It was too cold for a swim. She half hoped to meet Dimitri and half hoped not. There was longing for him, terrible longing, for not only had he rained kisses on her face and bosom, day after day he had told her things, which only the companion of one's heart tells; all without knowing her heart. For she had held back—not out of lack of desire; more because she was so used to being alone. No question that he had 'brought her body forward'—her expression, to herself, at if her body had been a long way back—inside a tunnel, in the dark, alone—and he had taken it and pulled it towards the light and all that the light included—the honey of the day, blooming flowers, spring, although spring was a long way off yet like the bell of the church when it tolls and leaves a faint resonance in the air. She confessed to herself that he had acted as all lovers act —as a savior. She had not known how far gone she was— starved for the love that he gave her; but all that, she thought, would not do for an affair that was to be serious.

It was as if, she thought, that even without knowing it for years and years, she had been waiting, her whole, poor, sick body had been waiting for the sound of his footstep coming towards her room. That he had, that he inevitably had because he loved her—the one right word, look, smell, motion. She began to think that she was like someone trying to patch up a roof or wall all alone. She simply didn't have enough strength. And he? He had the strength as needed, the expertise, and the intelligence. It was a light going on at last.

It was a little as if he was in the end, the roof, part of it, or the wall. He not only protected her, but he saw her on the inside, and did not condemn. He had the eyes of an eagle, but whatever it was that he saw and saw anew when they were together, it only made him open his heart; he was tender, kind and sweet. Sweeter for seeing the truth. And it was a kind of sweetness that lifted her –as if feet off the ground—for there was no reason to root herself in the old loneliness anymore. And he was teaching her patiently to follow him.

Catherine held Kali's hand lightly on the beach. Kali had that usual inscrutable though smiling face. Catherine knew that she probably eavesdropped on them when Dimitri came. She guessed that the desire to gossip was paramount among the ladies, especially the old women. Besides which, she had told Dimitri, you are like a fragrant apple in a barren place that smells of dust usually. I mean that everyone sees, besides me, that you are amazingly handsome.

He had dismissed this shortly and with good humor. But she sensed that he was thinking about it all the same. He said in the end—I am in the position Jesus was in relative to the crowd: They'll love me and then hate me.

And Catherine had said, some. He had said, alright then, some will love me. Many will hate me. Yes, I believe that.

More and more when he had left each time she felt that here—at her feet, by her side, was where the true man came. This made her feel overwhelmed with joy. When the true man comes, it is so beautiful. Perhaps there is no greater beauty except God.

Kali and Catherine walked on the beach. Catherine knew that Kali wanted her to talk of Dimitri and was angry, or at least irritated, when Catherine began talking in an off-hand way about the day. They watched the little waves swell and break on the shore.

Do you know, said Catherine to Kali, swinging her hand, that Leonardo da Vinci made studies of nature, things like ocean waves, using geometrical shapes? I think that he thought that he would find through geometry and painting the secret to the design of the universe. But if one fragment escaped from this geometry, you see, the whole universe had eluded him. I think generally it came in and out of his grasp. There are people who want the whole thing mathematically, said Catherine. I hear there are people on the verge of obtaining it.

I know the design of the universe, said Kali, gruffly. A man loves a woman; the woman she says many things, asks many questions as if to say—I don't see. But then at night, when she is all alone—ah yes, then she loves him, only him.

Catherine laughed—yes, Kali that is very good. But then there are any number of people out there and they can't love for whatever reason. What about them?

They sing and dance for the lovers, said Kali, readily. Because one never knows. I always think that when there is enough singing and dancing—something happens.

It is the sign of heaven, said Catherine. Remember the singing and dancing in the father's hall when the prodigal son returns.

Ah, but the great sins on earth! Nevertheless there is a certain dispensation when we sing and dance to usher in the bride and bridegroom—even to hope in our souls for the bride and bridegroom.

Agatha dances; Dimitri's mother. He seems a better man for it, Kali, although I think he doesn't quite approve. I think deep down that he doesn't quite approve of his mother, but there also is a huge love for her in him. He wanted to escape the island and its pettiness and he did for a while, but he came home to protect his mother because things aren't very good for her here. His brother doesn't seem to… doesn't seem to…well, just doesn't seem to. I think there is hatred, resentment; I'm not sure why. At first Dimitri blamed his mother too, and then he pitied her, feared for her. It sent him paradoxically running away at first; then after ten years and seeing her again—of course, knowing nothing about that terrible night…in any case, life brought him full circle and to the point where, willy-nilly he feels he must own up to being flesh of her flesh. I don't mean genetically. I mean in that kind of sense of self first. Of course, everyone does that. What does it mean, I wonder? One almost feels as if Agatha and Dimitri were called by some deep conviction that is more than selfish.

Kali stood by smiling down at the sand. It was a silvery sand, Catherine noticed, although it seemed yellow most of the time. A hidden silver in it, she thought, like Kali's hair, which was dyed black with that black that Greek women use but was in reality auburn and grey mixed and sometimes in the evening light, silver appeared. It was interesting to do little experiments on Kali: You could see that she constructed and constructed, but this was everyone constructing—the hair dye, the smiles and then when it was all stripped away—the fear and bitterness. With Dimitri and Agatha, it had gone beyond fear and bitterness. She herself had thought—what was out there? Nothing? And had returned from the long journey sweet.

Dimitri had reared up manly and protective, wanting, desiring, treasuring. Agatha had, as they say, reared up—but when she saw her, she thought ah militant to some ultimate joy—her son in love! Although with Agatha she was uneasy; here was the mother and there were bound to be border skirmishes—on what side is Dimitri still son, on what side lover?

It was Agatha who believed in that ultimate joy and Dimitri went along because his mother had led the way—just a few days ago, it's true, but he had never trusted in anyone else.

Hidden silver: the possibility, she thought watching Kali move around the beach with her folded arms for the cold winds, bending a little impatiently—that it was joy. And joy would then be at the essence of—what—life? No. of the expectation of life. Which meant that joy was encoded in the fabric of it. In the bride and bridegroom there was joy.

Agatha believed this. Catherine believed that Agatha was a great Jesus person. Not Jesus this, Jesus that. More Jesus the flesh, dawn-gold flesh of light in their midst, His mother silver flesh of the moon. Flesh meant dancing.

Kali bent over the incoming tide and Catherine watched her. The folk on Holy Island, which was a tiny spit of an island, really a rock or two emerging from the sea with some stony, sandy soil in between, sometimes acted as if they hardly knew the sea was there. It was what was all around this little cup of human habitation—vastness, infinity, or suggesting infinity, that is mirroring it—a great blue green grey swirl with its own other world in the belly of it, and they toiled up their hill concentrating, singing, sometimes, forgetful or purposely forgetful.

Agatha too, although one sensed in her that the forgetfulness was more of a sizing up, yes, even a sizing up of infinity, or this mirror of it—and great appreciation. She had only seen Agatha a few times, greeted her, and she had nodded her head vigorously saying yes, as if it was about time and natural that the lover of my son should come down from her high residence over the broad outlook and greet me. She was not in the least arrogant, or rather, her arrogance was a kind of kindliness. But Catherine wasn't sure whether all antipathy had been as it were swept away.

She imagined, briefly, Dimitri and herself huddling up beside Agatha, in a kind of cave, the mother-cave; and Agatha saying calmly, and it will be thus and so. Coming out with a kind of relief—so Agatha knew all along the end of this, though not really. But people do know—only Dimitri and she didn't know. All the male and female of mankind did know what would come of Adam and Eve wandering near the tree of Knowledge. Only Adam and Eve didn't know and huddled, frightened. They were innocents, the rest, including God, already had the taste of the fruit of death in their mouths.

Kali was gesturing to her to come and put her feet in the water. Catherine always obeyed Kali. She obeyed her whether or not it was sensible or ludicrous for her to do so. If anyone asked why, she would simply say—I don't obey her, it is just that she must be pleased and I like to please. Everything would go awry if I didn't please her. My world is so shrunk down, you see, there is only Kali and Dimitri, Agatha and death.

She was surprised at death. Death was a newcomer and also and old timer. She could see herself in a kind of flirtation with death.

She went to Kali; took off her shoes and socks, rolled up her pants and stepped into the water. It was freezing but it felt good. Kali beckoned her to wade a little further in. Catherine usually loved the feeling of the waves jostling against her legs—sense of the material—it was a beautiful thing; but this time she felt a little crabby about it; the water was too cold for one thing. Then she felt a sharp stone in the arch of her foot. Suddenly, she was down in the water, and a stone scraped harshly against her back.

Kali cried out. At first, Catherine couldn't get up. She was gasping and writhing a bit in the water. Then she dug her heels underneath her and rocked on to her feet, put out her hand on to the sand and pushed herself up. Kali ran over and offered her hand; Catherine took it and Kali pulled her out of the water.

So sorry, she said, so sorry, in English. Come let's get you home. She wrapped her arms around Catherine. Catherine was shivering violently. She put on her shoes— thinking, hey, what of it? I got wet. If I was a fisherman, she said to Kali…You know it is nothing. Nothing whatever.

I thought that you looked so young again these days; I thought that perhaps stimulating the blood…said Kali.

Well, yes it is stimulated and so there is no need to worry, said Catherine. In fact, I kind of liked it. You know one gets bored pampered and indulged all the time by the parents, by the over protective lover.

They climbed back up the beach towards the cliff. Catherine favoring one leg, crouching for the cold in her because of her wet clothing.

The way to the cliffs was isolated and it was late in the day; only one person was out—one of the daughters of Peter; she turned and stared at her. It isn't the day for a good Samaritan, thought Catherine, moodily; in any case, I am alright. It was just a dunking—a kind of baptism for big girls.

The cold got a little more tolerable as she moved. But her heart was throbbing and Catherine was worried. She thought more of her heart these days; there had been fewer symptoms on the whole of the disease and she had wondered if love had improved her health. There were times the old machine or old marcher as she called it, had moved into the background; she told Dimitri that its tick tock was less noticeable to her—just like in normal people who pass the day forgetting…and he had been overjoyed. But Catherine had thought all this joy and made her less of a watcher and early riser. She no longer flashed awake in the night, put her hand on her left bosom and felt and watched and waited.

Now it was apparent again. Strong, warning beats. And it was in her throat. She put her hand on Kali's shoulder; Kali adjusted it around her neck and they proceeded up the hill, slowly. Catherine stopped and Kali waited. She bent down and let herself breathe. Then she said to Kali—it is better. We can go. I mean, after all, I swim until late October when the water has a nip in it.

They climbed the cliff stairs quietly, Catherine preceding Kali and climbing without pause as rhythmically as possible. There were times when Catherine did her own doctoring—although she knew it was hardly what worked. What worked was medication. But she knew that rhythmic movements, coordinated breathing all helped. She theorized that she could in this way make the right environment for the heart.

Climbing the stairs, although she was quiet and in control, she had a thought that she would not last much longer for her shivering. Then once up the stairs she would go straight to bed and in an hour, when it was possible, take the medication. She had ceased to think of how terrible the cold was; she thought only of her heart. And she thought of herself as bringing up the ultimate treasure to the peak. A last and most noble effort. She saw herself with her living heart cupped in her hands...

Once in bed, with Kali sitting by her wringing her hands a bit, for show, Catherine thought, and feeding her chamomile, Catherine thought it was all for nothing. This solemn procession—the bringing of the heart. Yet she continued to feel that there was, after all, significance: the bringing of the heart, the heart, not her heart, to the top of the cliff. The last act. And yet not for she lived on.

Her father came in saying, what's this? What's this? You took her into the sea in this weather? What are you doing?

But he didn't go further. Catherine motioned to him. I am quite alright. What do you think I am made of china? But Robert went down into the village and had the doctor from the other island sent for.

He came late in the evening. Robert and Ellen were sitting in the kitchen. There were half attempts to love, half words of endearment. Each time they were refused. You know it has come to the end between us, Ellen said. What are you talking of now? Answered Robert, our child lies in there gravely sick.

She has always been gravely sick, said Ellen; and if we are responsible, we were responsible way back when we conceived her. Perhaps it is this responsibility, which I am asking you to face...

The doctor was a short man with a bald head and round belly. He spoke English perfectly well and came into the little dimly lighted kitchen with a jovial air. He was fond of the Isolets, thought them ignorant and eccentric, generally at a loss and it was clear that they had been at a loss since they were married. Ellen said to Catherine that she felt like he was always patting her on the head.

Falling into the tide was a shock, he said, to Catherine's system. Nothing more. She will calm down again in a couple of days. Make sure that she stays in bed, quite warm; it is drafty in the villa—a little too cold, although one doesn't feel it moving around in a sweater.

Ellen's voice rang out loud and clear. An entirely unusual phenomenon, thought Robert. Maybe we are coming near to the end.

She sees a young man, said Ellen to the doctor. Is it alright to bring him?

Oh, there is no problem with love, said the doctor. Just make sure she stays warm. I think I will go to see her, said Ellen. Robert showed the doctor out and Kali started to prepare dinner.

Ellen sat on the bed beside the prone body of her daughter. Catherine looked up at her, smiling a little. Ellen, she said, and took her hand. I am glad that I got to know you. Ellen responded: How do you know that I am going? Daughter with uncanny insights. The world inside these four walls is the same every day, no warnings, no signs.

She looked at her daughter who was still smiling up at her. Recently, her face had become more material—a lovely material, blooming around the lips and eyes, soft material, soft and evanescent. It was a material that seemed to float in the air. This was in her face, her flesh. Ellen saw her one day and said, so I've been wrong all these years. She is so beautiful, so graceful, so perfect. This is more than brains, this material, a spasm that makes the whole thing tick and I see it now all naked. I see in fact the Catherine world, now, and that it exists—that is, the Catherine perspective.

Undoubtedly, she said to her one day, you have an argument. What I mean is that you have a way with you—of seeing things.

What can I possibly have? With all our rootlessness, and losing Stephen.

It was the first time she had spoken sharply to Ellen, and Ellen drew back, afraid. But that had been the end of it. And the daughter that had blossomed like the rose for a man's love was, she thought, sick and all, living half in her bed and all, running away with it. Ellen had said to Robert then that despite it all, despite the mysteriousness of the love that had coiled around them, opened its lips to reveal Catherine in its mouth, and then uncoiled itself and slipped away into the emerald forest, one could see clearly that there was something eminently good in what they had done, how they had been.

They were in the end, three people who did not know one another, but beauty had come of their relationship, beauty had. And now Catherine was running away with it.

She could only bow to it. She had long ago suspected something of the kind. And it wasn't only beauty; for ultimately, she realized although they had reached out and reached out like Tantalus for the fruit, she had come and whisked it away—all with love. What was it life?—life, indeed! Although not so much the machine—more like the shine on things and the little infinite connections of mind and memory. She had come with her blue, grey, dark eyes like the sea sometimes just before dark—and love, had done the talking. The old Catherine who was so obscure, unnoticed and unnoticeable had finally whirled out and it was found in her—the sum total of life and love. All, all that Ellen was looking for in those endless hours of meditation and writing.

I am being selfish, said Ellen, leaving you. Horribly selfish. But you will have Robert. There is enough money for you to hire people too. I think you are beautiful. I think you are love itself. But staying here brings it no closer to me. Perhaps one day I will be a convert for beauty's sake and return to you.

No, you don't have to Ellen. I am not beautiful. I just knew that you would have to go. I just see, that's all—that is, into you and your intimate self. It isn't so hard to do. Robert is blind because he wants to be. He thinks that is the way to love. You see, it is really his fault that you are going. If he just let himself take one peek, he would be all sorrowful and penitent.

Of course Dimitri, the picture of the hero in the novel, as Barbara said once, would bound up the steep steps of the cliff side, hearing Catherine was sick from Kali, explode into the little blue blanket room with its white cold and bareness and pick up his beloved wrapped in the blue blanket and sheet and hold her in his arms. Robert and Ellen blanched by winter and passionlessness wilted and faded to the sides of the room, out the door, and periodically peeped in. And of course the room for a moment as mute and hard as a stone, though with some beauty, maybe because of all their Zen meditations, would suddenly blossom into love. Secret, fragrant, new born walls…breath, on her ear, on his, and against her lips…the cherishing of her wrist and the watching with a sort of anguish the little pulse near the blue vein. The blue blanket suddenly took on a life of its own like a magic carpet except that it was still, thrown here and there.

Even though in reality Catherine was longer in body than Dimitri, he made a little lover's pretense that she really was a tiny girl and that he was going to envelope her with himself, hold her, like a warm, captive child in the night. She protested the kisses, of course, she protested the kisses, saying that really he could catch something… and he kissed and kissed and acted as if she was talking a language he didn't understand, meanwhile he was teaching her the one language of truth, smiling at her as if she were a little child. Of course, Catherine awoke body and mind several thousand times over. In the days and nights that he wouldn't leave her, his tenderness was so agonizingly sweet and brought her to almost plead. How did it happen? How could it not have…? Body against body, the utter relief…the sting and swell of in-ness, oneness, unfathomable openings and depths of body, the ecstasy and the 'swimming upwards from the depths'-- soul gifted with skin, returning to the Bosom.

Catherine conceived in the throes of what they presumed to be some terrible shock to her heart and in the end turned out to be only a mild cough on the fringes. Dimitri of course went away on the seventh day harboring it in his chest. Robert and Ellen had said nothing; they had fled the little nook outside Catherine's room. Dimitri cooked for five or six nights for them in a kind of love delirium. Huge omelettes, and fish stews fit for an army. The big bare villa became a kind of beautiful hallucination for him—a palace of dim light in which he kissed Ellen's queenly hand, bowed to Robert's kingly immobile head. He said some crazy words along with the general reverence to his lady's progenitors—such as, that he was as this fish slathered over with such a delicious sauce. And he brought the platter of fish and sauce to Catherine who lay deliciously in bed all this time convalescing.

A few days after the affair, Catherine knew she was pregnant and informed Ellen.

You could have been more careful, her mother said, crossly. You went all out making love without giving a thought to…so irresponsible!

It is the turning moment in my life. I am no longer a daughter to you exclusively. I am Dimitri's wife.

Did he propose?

Not precisely.

Then what you have said is imprecise.

But we became husband and wife by the way things went—I mean this love is the stuff of marriage. It is what marriage is all about. It is marriage.

Robert, who was sitting reading a book, spoke up. I don't see that what Catherine is saying is untrue, he exclaimed, quietly. Why are the formalities so important? Isn't how a body feels against you, yes, in fact, the way it feels to make love to a person a better test of whether or not you are man and woman meant for each other—that is, husband and wife? Never mind if it lasts thirty years or seven days. She is his wife. Eve was Adam's wife and there was no wedding ceremony. They made love before God. And so? Haven't Catherine and Dimitri done the same in her estimation? In this love affair, they were naked before God. Why should one try to take away by snide remarks her hour of glory?

Ellen said Oh—and faded away. But Catherine had never seen her mother look so sour. In fact, she was surprised: for Ellen generally never entered in to Catherine's private life. She would even say that her mother didn't know her, not in three dimensions—outward, impression of, private. She was to her a face floating in the air—recognized, approached, talked to, sometimes for there were attached ears and senses, outward, but never grasped. Suddenly, she was emotionally grappled with, untenderly grappled with. And this sort of thing was done in the name of truth.

It is not impossible to understand Catherine's 'revolt'—her crying out that Dimitri was truth and siding with him even down to a veritable mythologizing of their relations. Her parents were dim shapes in the dim light. There was a lot of foreign space around them. Sometimes one would swim to the other with sudden knowledge, intimate, secret knowledge about the other. And she, oh, the usual—in a corner, lurking. Now it was different. She had found the one she could swim away with—same pace, same rhythm, same wave. Why should she not reinvent the whole process of intimacy: Call Dimitri husband from the very start in her head? They had swum through the same darkness, surfaced at the same time, jumped, gone down together. This by all accounts was what a human being was made for. At least, this was what the soul was supposed to be. Marriage got down to the soul. This giving away in marriage in churches, this waiting with white carnations in one's buttonhole, this wearing of white veils—what was it? Old signs and symbols that people in their lives did not support to make of them meaning. Husband was not a legal category nor a show of a suit and flower and ring, but a holy name.

And she knew, or believed, the same thing it seemed to her, that just when he buried his seed in her and one hit inseminated her ovum—that he had murmured something like 'wife', or 'life'—she hadn't heard the murmur distinctly, for it had come just after the ejaculation and the loud, unstoppable Oh, that sounded like joy and pain; and whether the word from his lips so over used for kissing her had been 'wife' or 'life', she didn't know and thought that it didn't matter. For they were in this mythology, the same word.

She was life and he was lord! Something like that. Whether he went down and kneeled before her feet and kissed the narrow, yet dainty toes or whether she went down and kneeled and kissed the beautiful arch of his golden foot –what did it matter? There was a mutual holiness, now it filled her with joy and now it filled him. She mirrored him; he mirrored her. She with flesh and he with fire. For they were flesh, blood and fire—golden vein given to golden vein, and body greater than they.

On Catherine raved, all of her body still revved; her face looked awakened and beautiful; it was as if the sun had come out for the first time. Robert looked and looked away, his eyes full of tears. One expected only a cloudy day, every day. And now here the sun—brilliant and strong and the little growing things springing up. I never knew, he said to her, that you were Aphrodite. All around us there is beauty— the sea and the forest…but I never saw beauty until now. It is a riddle how love changes us.

Oh, father I need him, was what Catherine wanted to say. Instead, she laughed, tossed her long hair and said, well, Robert, he's cooked enough food to last a week or two.

Agatha saw Dimitri come home panting and sparkling. Ah, in love, it sprang to her mind—sure, though she had never been. Curious, the fear, almost panic. She hesitated, but in the end took him by the elbow and pulled him to her and kissed him. You have woman written all over you, she said.

Catherine and I like each other very much, he muttered. Her name is beautiful, isn't it? I think that she is the only Catherine; other Catherines have been misnamed. This is Catherine; I have found her. When you find someone named the right name…it is the ring, the gold ring here—he pointed to his breast.

You are in love, said his mother.

I belong to a secret society now, he said, smiling; Agatha saw he had gone without sleep…it has one other member, a lady, a dark and most beautiful lady.

It will eat your entrails away.

What need for them?

You will rot, she said half jestingly.

In golden wine.

Agatha calculated, began to see with a narrowed eye—the future: a daughter in law, thin girl, very polite, retiring, apparently a thinker from what she could catch from Dimitri. She sat in the kitchen expectant. Bring the child here, she told her son. But the next day he didn't go to Catherine's. He had business in town, he told her.

And he went and came back from Katrina's.

What are you doing with that poor creature? Asked his mother. She still holds the torch for you and you just go and tease her.

We have an affair. A business affair to see to, he said. I have decided to try to build a hotel on my own and engage her as assistant, secretary—whatever you wish to call it.

In reality, in the back of his mind, Dimitri felt that Katrina was the old music that linked him to the island. This music ran in his head whenever he felt that he was an islander, that it was after all his home. He felt freer now; freer to go to her to show his 'new' self. In his heart of hearts he believed she was the most compassionate of islanders. And she was a shrewd girl after all, she knew also her limitations whether physical or because of circumstances, read the old situation. She had built a life after, admittedly a sorry and sad one, but yet charged with a noble nature. Her readiness to give, and to sacrifice, could also be exploited. Katrina could be redeemed, he said to himself—made to seem the smart one in the village. She was the working girl, he thought. It was time she shared in profits rather than only the noble idea that she was doing the right thing. He could introduce her to the world of economic justice. He didn't doubt that she would have a good head not only for figures but for the sense of it all. Why poverty? Why not pay commensurate with toil? Why not give the girl a taste of something truly fair?

After they had talked—she had just let him in with a tiny shrug when he came calling, --he realized that she was intelligent in ways that even Catherine didn't come near. Katrina knew when to cease to 'understand' a man. A long time ago, when there had been a shadow of relations between them, she had humbly taken, although she had been the seductress of a virgin boy, only whatever was offered in the end and had not sought more. That is, she had accepted his gift of a harsh fling, rather than love. She had humbly, dumbly thought they should have married because that was the proper thing. When he had waved her away, she had retired, taking boys to appease sex, spelling out what the village thought of her, but not of course what she was, what he might have said, had he not been tenderer than all that, but she continued holding the torch for him—the one lover whom she had admired, and had always imagined marrying. (After all Thomas had married an older woman). But she had never tried to fathom mind or heart. Dimitri was customary in her way of thinking and made love well—and Katrina thought that marriage was making love well and eating apricot candy together—and even though it had been years, he was still customary.

She knew about Catherine, according to Dimitri. He told himself that she knew. She wouldn't cross boundaries. And he told himself that she didn't really think that they would ever again start up the old affair. He told himself that he would be circumspect and respect the feelings that may have lingered on. But they talked both seriously and lightly like good old friends as time went on. Catherine was the holy of holies: she was first for him. No, no one would ever come near them in their retreat together. That was the beginning of the world, he told himself. But this, with Katrina was a daily, ordinary, going on of life. With Catherine he was a soul—truly, a sun at dawn, a rare being. With Katrina he was the good old door in the same old house that he had known since he was a child. No matter it looked plainer and plainer as he grew older. He had never quite had an honest to goodness home, so he felt; she was what he knew—the one who had opened that door to him so many years ago. Of course, it was still there.

He came to her very jocose and joked about her needing to lose weight. Same little harshness. They gabbed a bit and then he proposed the project. It was to be only a house, you understand. Big as a brothel. He was in a rare humor.

Katrina said that she had enough to do. And after all that had happened, you'd think hotels were the last thing....

Oh, Connie was all wrong for the island, said Dimitri. As he warmed to the subject, he could see that she shifted and moved under his gaze. This body, he thought to himself, within all that fat is sensual, wide open for sex. Katrina as if sensing what he was thinking, looked down, smiled sourly and looked away.

But you, he sort of swooped in on her intellectually, with the intense, electric gaze of his rousing up her entrails—and she knew the rest. You are the one who could make it work.

Katrina thought of Dimitri sometimes as a vulture, hanging around seeking out the dead meat. What was it that had died? The old spark, the old faith...and now he had come back to despoil precisely because that initial life was dead.

But not dead! Said Dimitri, the vulture.

Ah a trick! He would weave delusions. Back and forth again and again he came— each time for what he called the Katrina, not dead—that is so intelligent, so capable, with recognition long overdue.

Katrina began to think of him as lord of her door; it was proper for him, she thought, to walk in as if he almost owned the place.

When he saw Catherine looking like a gem in the sun, brilliant as the sea on a summer morning, or as a garden in spring—as if someone, the West Wind, the god

Zephyros, just breathed and the flowers sparkled in amidst the softest rain—this was life, sweet life all around triumphant because it takes over and becomes proprietor of all the dead spaces—when he saw Catherine, at first joy and awe plucked his heart from the center to their song and then a strange, incomprehensible guilt pulled it back again. He walked beside her saying, on the one hand, you are the bride, my bride?—incredulously and joyfully-- and on the other, you know I don't have the youngness and inspiration I should have.

Neither do I, said Catherine.

You have been reborn, he said; you are a joy to men and women.

Dimitri would say things, Catherine thought that were all humility and tenderness. She felt like she was a little thrush on a tree branch singing its heart out because ah, what glory to be on a tree branch in the middle of a tree!—this was existence. One simply walked out in the sun—a winter sun, but so what?—and everything around spoke of blossoming in the midst, a little line of life that brought to a point of light, all energy and joy! This was hallowed. This tenderness and joy. And it quivered in her entrails.

They, in fact, were light to one another. Dimitri knew he was going to be a father and that Catherine had said in her own little wriggling way: don't you think, don't you think that this time it is what it is supposed to be?

Yes, of course—he had said without using the words. It was all such a surprise and delight. He confessed to her that he hadn't felt that love was such a jewel ever before. The modern world, he said to her, in one of his drunken moments, drunk on her, the light in her and the joy in her—has its sadism. We've never quite grown past desecration of altars, and the sacrifices of innocents. We are not lost in the jungle, you and I, we have not devolved; but what we have become—oh, I don't know, more pleased with things of existence—air, water, earth—utter beauty dwells in them.

We live for beauty and yet not quite for beauty, said Catherine. There are no words for what we live for. I feel almost like we are on a crusade, a quiet one, without violence, except for the violence that rises up naturally in our minds and hearts against the usurpers to the throne of love. You lead down the path; I convert. I speak the language of conversion. Particularly to the poor, the weary, the sinner. I perceive that many will come and bow to the throne and say to us—please heal me. Ah, you know, I am so besotted. The sight of your foot, golden foot—reminds me of racers, dancers, princes, even warrior angels. I suppose the good God built in beauty to our configuration and it keeps dragging at me.

You are silly, said Dimitri. But now the beauty in you, so extraordinary and so swiftly melting away before has come to stay. Yes, I believe it. I love you more now for your ugly duckling origins—how you couldn't get your beauty to stay before. It was like a flickering light about to go out. And I would have loved you, Catherine, if it had gone out. You know that, don't you? And that would have been beauty—that going out.

No, you wouldn't have loved me gone out. Why you?

Because—I love with a blind eye-heart of your heart; not with my seeing eyes of flesh. You bring out your treasures—your new found, new born beauty, your intelligence. Yes, I am happy. Happy that you have a little hoard. But what I love is you, dear. Something of queens and kings. It is almost pathetic to me the way the little body struts its loveliness, its love in so many vain postures and pulsations. I love you, a highborn lady, a princess, a queen. Don't you know those words? It means forever.

Dante Gabriel Rossetti had a wife with long pre-Raphaelite hair. She died and he buried her. And one day on a whim exhumed her to find that her golden hair had grown longer and more beautiful.

But I, I love the little bare skull of you, dearest love.

Yeats said to Crazy Jane that only God, my dear, will love you for yourself alone and not your yellow hair.

But I am one with God. We have been in union since I met you. What is the true lover if not Man? The true beloved if not God?

Catherine squinted and then smiled at him. You know, I thought love was in the little leaves....

You think I am an egomaniac, Dimitri said, looking her in the eyes. God is not the spirit of lightning bolts and earthquakes, wars and illnesses. He pulled her to him and kissed her softly. These are our prayers. You know, I loved my grandfather very much although I never knew him. It shocked me that he had suffered so much simply because he chose to read another book about God than the Bible. It repelled me to think of the hatred in these few people, this little holy island—because as a child I thought of course it was holy. Holy for the utter whiteness of the sun, the kindness in spring of the blue sky, the smell of goats. Holy for Aunt Zoe and Aunt Cleo who circled around my nostrils with their scents and made me think of cleanness and gentleness and faith. Holy for the little leaves, the subterranean pool where the water was always fresh and sweet. Holy for the vast sea, which contained us and stretched to infinity, and to far away lands, which were brilliant with palaces of kings.

Little hints dropped during our childish play by the adults made me question my mother about my grandfather. The answers made me freeze up and turn away from the communion of the Saints. Curious, though, my mother believes strongly in Jesus. I was told that he was on our side. That my grandfather who simply played music that set us all dancing and singing all day and every day and lived on bread and wine was blameless and now reposed in the bosom of Jesus, the Christ. He, you see, was only poor, gentle and kind. His Muslim Bible a gift for the dreamer of God.

I loved him—he was the one, for me, for many years; and then before I ceased to think of him, I swear it to you—I saw him in a vision. It was a vision of light, gentle, evening light and he was walking away down a path of dim light. I saw his back and then he turned and I just caught a glimpse of dark hair and a worried brownish face, stopping a minute, smiling a little at me. I guess I didn't really see his smile, just felt the light, the blessedness. He had a look—in appearance. He could have been the son of my grandfather. Son of Man, He said, Man being an old Muslim gypsy who plays music so accurately.

I have carried that with me all these years down deep. Funny, I had almost forgotten him in the other land of modern life, the world, Athens, London, Rome where I did all that men were doing, are doing, but coming back, being with you—brought it up again.

Perhaps, said Catherine, your grandfather is a saint.

He was despised, played his music, said not a word to anybody about God. Kept to himself, uncomplaining about the way they treated him—but wept, yes wept. You see after that I hated God, but not the truth or love. It came slowly to me that the true Christ is God, that is, God, that angry spirit in reality does not exist, but the divine One does. There is no pompous raging figure. A gentle, tender, curious person, Jesus, the lover who is believed in through tears and dance, Dimitri went on in a little rhapsody.

Have I been too strange?

You simply improvise—given your love and faith.

Yes there is a tune and I come along and jazz it up.

Are you God?

No, I didn't mean that I had everything sorted out. And yet I love your little bare skull. You see it is all sorrow too—that my grandfather put in me through my mother's tales of him and the half hints, the spiteful remarks.

I kiss you little grinning skull, your lipless mouth, your bare teeth. I gather your bones in my arms and say bones, knit together flesh, and let me sleep with my Catherine once more deep in the mysterious earth.

And I don't believe we die. I believe God is a kind of director or composer saying to us—get the music right.

Slender hands—too thin, signs of sickness. Light on my hands, lighter than spring rain. The old pleading in your face. What is it, what is it? Catherine, I want to tell you, not to keep you in the dark about me. I love you, you are my dearest friend, my bride in my mind, but I have an expansive heart. There may be a time when I share myself more than I ought with another. It seems right and just to me, although I can't say more than this—I am only a man—we have in our heads only our thoughts. It seems to me that if I was not expansive, as I choose to put it, I could not be as I am to you. I could not love you, nor wed you.

What kind of expansiveness is it? Asked Catherine, guardedly.

I don't know. I cannot say. I am not asking you for license to destroy what is built here, to profane the love. But this love is something that deepens me as a man and yet does not possess me and I can only say that I fervently desire it to be the same for you. I am not saying that we should indulge in group sex or sleep with anyone who comes along. I am merely saying that there exists still although it is rare a tenderness and a trust that says you may be the judge, you may decide; if it is right for you to love another…

Catherine was silent.

Not with the same love, not with wedding love, he added urging.

You mean said Catherine looking at him with shadowy eyes there might be a time when you say to me that it was right for you to make love to another.

There might be.

If you wish, said Catherine seriously. She sat down in a chair in the big bare sitting room of the villa where she had served Dimitri and herself a glass of wine, and put her elbow in her hand on her lap and her fingers against her lips and thought. But what you are saying is, she said at the end of a few minutes of pondering, you don't think you'd leave me despite that eventuality.

Despite it, said Dimitri with a faint smile. You are eminently companionable. I would marry you naked with nothing, dying, sick—in any shape or form. I adore you. My will is to adore you. I don't give a damn for what you say or do. But, he sighed, I am not a possession.

You have seen my inner being?

For once I believe I have come down to the mystery. But making love can be just a lighthearted thing, or a moment drunk with passion. With you it is always, has to be, always, serious, body and soul.

Yes, said Catherine.

Are you angry?

Not at all. You seem to me to be more and more beautiful even as you talk about your possible faithlessness. My head reels with your beauty.

It is not that. It is the expansiveness that I have told you of. I am sure that it is the wrong word but at the moment I can think of nothing but you. I tell you it is as if I have a dancing partner, that is you, and we do the waltz a hundred times and other dances, then suddenly, walking down the street I come to a jazz club and can't help stopping in and dancing a few steps with another; what can I say to the inquisition that follows: I am a dancer, that is what I do. But I have a partner who is perfect.

And I. said Catherine.

Besides, we bond here, in the brain, said Dimitri; let other happy couples tie the knot in the groin. Do you really understand?

I believe, said Catherine, the words coming slowly—I do. I believe you are saying that you want me as core to your life, the center of the circle, but that there might be other fleeting encounters…

One knows a person only over time.

But you said—'I am a dancer that is what I do.'

Ah—my mother creeps in I guess. I meant every gesture, every motion that brings with it joy or love or life or tenderness—is my business. Singing and dancing!

No longer the making of money?

I've made enough. Now I can live and work on what I always thought should be. Once I nearly married a courtesan. It is not that joy and tenderness, life and love were lacking altogether; it is just that these things were confronted daily with cruel sneering and scoffing. I too learned sneering and scoffing. The killing of gentle honesty; the dissecting of truth. I learned that the lie was probably the one thing you could count on in human beings. And yet, I was not that. I didn't sleep around. One time I made love to a girl who washed dishes in a dinghy bar. Her boyfriend had left her, with traces of his fists on her body and face. I went home to abuse, myself, of the most insidious verbal kind. Yet I stayed on. I loved my courtesan for the wrong reasons. For her legs, her hair, for her delicate, pink vulva that was of extraordinary beauty. We made a lot of love. And in a shadowy place, here, he pointed to his head, in my brain, I was forming. This time, that is, when I left her and thought of love— for something utterly sweet.

But I must be scrupulously fair. Do you accept me? You have the right to reject me.

I too love you utterly, said Catherine from her heart. You are all life.

Think about it, Dimitri said gently. Perhaps this was just a mad whirl. Perhaps we are not made for one another.

You said you would keep me no matter what.

Yes, I mean it too. But in your thoughts everything must be clear. In your mind it might be very different. In your mind there might be doubts and division. Hold on to it for a day. I'll be back tomorrow and we can decide.

And if I say no? What will you do?

Go fuck my mother. He laughed and laughed at her shocked face as he left.

Yes the ice cliffs had fallen around about as she had flown with the rich southern thought in her head—marriage with Dimitri, companionship with him, they as compatriots in a mini nation. She had to fly through the ice regions before all this—she had known, and the cliffs had fallen around her and still, still and silent as a dreamer, she had flown on—thinking those wings shall never die. Deathless wings. They were not even of her body, not entirely. Wings joined her from the outer reaches of the sky…they were the wings of flight itself bequeathed her for passionate love. And she still, like a mechanical thing when there were such signs and indications—the unstable earth, the ice cliffs fallen went on; she had to go on. She would have gone on had they told her that someone would inevitably shoot her down on that course and thus she had better for life's sake choose another. She had flown on with that sunwine in her head, the best, the most beautiful she had ever known. And the gentle, compassionate bequeathing of the wings to fly with. For her strength was gone and yet she flew on through the crystal gorges. Mechanical thing her body—another thing those wings!

All around, she realized—friends and family would betray her. Subtle betrayals, knife stabbings in the back—yet merely a matter of: ah no, you shouldn't. You are merely infatuated. You can see for yourself he doesn't want marriage. One would not at the very beginning, said Ellen to her in her mind, commit to a man who may not under any circumstances be faithful. Thus attempting to snip through the threads that bound her, to blow away those deathless wings made of light and flight. To reduce all things to the mechanical, predictable—marriage is because marriage was so announced, like the readiness of the machine, by the bride's rosy lips, to be one's exclusive amour. The machine in a rosewood cabinet, the only place for it! That was marriage.

Catherine stood against the world: But I understand him! We are hand in glove. We are companions. We need no words to talk, do you realize that? That is what is exclusive. But for the mild enlargement of the engagement, he says to me, I don't know if I will never again feel love for another. I only know that you are core. The other loves, they will be on the periphery. I might spend an hour making love to a butterfly… I might just waste myself one day with a ladybug, a beetle, a cloud, a she-goat, a she…Now there you have the whole of me. I don't think it is evil.

Ellen, however, lived in a world where none of this could happen. The rules had been clear from the first day—Robert would be an everything, and all minutes of the day husband that she could slip away from, return to. He had once protested—but that little notebook of yours that you are always running away with—it is adultery. Catherine remembered the squeak, but she had always been slightly infatuated with her mother, although loyal to her father. Her mother told her frankly—but you know, at least, that adultery is grounds for divorce and if you get tired of his once too often straying away, groin grinding with little girls, or long-legged blonde beauties, you can always separate and the paying is on his side.

Despite having lived for ten years on a remote Greek island subjected to Zen and Russian Orthodox asceticism without a television, without videos, Catherine's mother had spoken like a character in an American movie. Why this sudden sardonic humor, this letting go of all things that lifted the spirit, all things that moved the heart? Why this sudden cruel invective from the ice empress who stood the most horrible thing in the midst of the massive ice cliffs falling: you are a machine, to machinery you are bound. If the machine cannot fly, then you will not fly. And in parenthesis, whispered in the breath-bated air—you will die, will die, will die.

She thought suddenly of her mother's world and saw—darkness welling up on all sides and a little flimsy glimpse of blue, like the blue gas flame on the stove. That was her love, her life—notebook, Robert, and the big, bare, white villa on the cliff. She had had her breathing. A fact! Catherine now in her body had a breath that was a cosmic wind. Groin-grinding groins faded into bones and floated away like prehistoric birds...the modern blue sky expanded, breath filled it, everlasting possibility breathed in with every breath; for she was not of course merely Catherine, the light-walking, long girl with slim hands and shadowy face that climbed laboriously up and down the cliffs, rested in bed, calming her heart, wondering how long this heart disease would go on until it killed her. Now she was everlasting possibility-- EP! A woman in love is magical, said her father, understandingly for all those years of Catherine's faithful attendance. You have just undergone metamorphosis. Of course, love making is no longer groin grinding. More like roses meeting and kissing, candles melting down to swim in each other's wax.

No, Catherine knew, she was no more breathing but wind pouring and becoming—new wind wings lifted, filled her...She didn't move or walk anymore; she floated. She said to her mother: I consider it joy to be with him even so. What else do we have to live for? I trust him, yes, he was open and honest to me—only that. And so she flew on giant wings of light, only slightly grey for the long, long shadow of the ice empress cast beyond the ice cliffs in the cold still air.

At breakfast in the big, bare, white villa, Ellen arrived when Catherine called, having made muffins and coffee, eggs and fish, grim white face, an expression as if she had a stiff shirt on buttoned up to the chin. Catherine knew without taking more than one look at her that she would have had the baby aborted and the marriage called off. It was not what she would call a marriage, although it was Catherine's marriage. Of this, Ellen grandly took no notice.

How easy it is to misunderstand, to overlook the significance of those words. Catherine's marriage—on one side—Ellen, suddenly realizing that her daughter had been for her all these years a rather pathetic figure; Catherine knowing this, but seeing things differently—as in the interpretation she had the right to present to the world.

There were the usual comments—what did you put in the coffee? Not that Ellen said this every day—for today Catherine had put cinnamon in the coffee, but there was always some little disgruntled snort. Catherine had always taken it with equanimity. She had been, as it were, asleep in a pearly world of the distant but well-meaning mother, the kind, bungling father. Now she woke with a start. The pearls were scattered. There were she realized more from Ellen's tone than from anything else, grounds for enmity between herself and her mother and as is usual when there are such, it was slightly unclear as to why.

Yes, Ellen, cinnamon. Why she had never called her mother! Dimitri is coming later today. I think I am going to postpone the wedding until after the baby is born. I enjoy our togetherness, our companionship; if we find that all is in place for a wedding we can go through with it. Otherwise, remain friends.

You mean for once you are not quite sure, given that he might high toe it to another woman's bed on any given night and leave you holding the baby.

I don't think she means that at all, Ellen, said Robert, softly.

The words wouldn't quite come for a minute and he took Catherine's hand in his. It is love, she said. I just want to know him. To come closer like two little mice in a storm might huddle. I have no doubt of him. Or, at least, I have doubts too of myself. And they are not all about what you call groin grinding. One just wants to consider, to savor, really—the question is it real? For a good length of time and to be with the joy, to come and go with the joy, to do nothing against joy. I am quite assured that he loves me deeply and the baby. He will be a great father, whether we are friends or relations.

Ellen snorted. Ellen! Robert gave a loud groan that ended in a shout. Isn't Catherine thirty? Isn't it high time she had a life outside these walls? What about someone to care for her in her old age?

Ellen let her fork fall on her dish of egg and got up abruptly. She pushed back the chair and walked away, holding her head high.

There was the burning of her notebooks, I admit, I did that, but this ash taste is from a different kind of fire that has burned down to nothingness. It was a fire I thought and had no right to think, of course, I would be warming myself near until I died, Robert murmured.

Catherine suddenly felt a different kind of god than the cold wind that had given her wings, the expanding, limitless wind. This god said to her—you stand in the position of one who can make or break. Your poor mother and father: one so brittle, but awfully frail—about to die dust instead of love; the other so meanly depressed, gazing up in awe as the great hands tear apart the world in front of him. Shall you not with your white, fixing hands, slim precision-making fingers, readjust things so that your mother can come back to life, your father to his steady ground and gaze again, thankful to you, up at the clear and beautiful stars?

Oh, you know, said Catherine sweetly to this god—the baby. There was guilt eclipsed in an instant. The baby will bring roses to their cheeks and dearness to their hearts. Who can resist—a baby?

...

So you have decided! Said Dimitri. You know my monkey legs have gotten swift. I nearly flew up the cliff steps. I think the little one will be a climber and a flier.

I am so glad that we are having a baby, said Catherine. But I thought we might put all thoughts of marriage out of our minds and just concentrate on—on our friendship.

Ah no, Dimitri encircled her with one arm and put his hand under her chin; no. He kissed her softly, long. I want to marry you. Absolutely. Completely. You are unsure of me—afraid. What I told you—

No, I have accepted you. From now on, I consider that my life, my path has two people on it, and one day soon three. I don't negate that, the joy, the love. It is just that the institution of marriage means a certain guise in society. You see, I will be not quite me as your wife, and you not quite you as my husband. Of course, the words can be used, why not? For their spiritual significance. Already you are husband to me. Or perhaps the word husband should never be used. Given the way it sounds and means in so many people's minds. Perhaps we should be red rose love 1 and red rose love 2. And that would define things more accurately.

It is the one act of possession and entitlement I wish to allow myself. I wish you to be my wife. Perhaps I am like a Turk with a harem in your eyes. But you are the princess, not for your wealth, or beauty, but for the sheer love I have for you, the nearness I come to you, mind in mind; the rest, the others, are slaves. Oh yes, there are slaves in the world, many, in fact. And if not slaves to the world, then they are slaves in terms of sex, love, relationships, that sort of thing. And there are slaves that pull themselves together and get quite clever and put on the lady's dresses and strut about... From my perspective, the world turns around you, no one else.

I wish I could only tell you, said Catherine suddenly. It is me, I think, that would marry you at the drop of a hat, no matter what you say or do.

Years later, Agatha would savor the words of her daughter in law, whispered to her at the wedding and again after the baby was born: he is pure, he is holy—even though things hadn't been, according to the way the world mutters, squints and nods and says in a righteous tone —what would be considered pure or holy.

But when Catherine decked in a light blue silk dress with a white sash over her ballooning belly, white hat and white gloves appeared all soft and joyous at her side and kissed her and told her these things, Agatha stepped back open mouthed. She said to Dimitri standing near mirroring Catherine's joyful smile, I never thought you'd marry, nor find so pretty a bride.

You told me to, said Dimitri kissing his mother. You remember. It was April, just after Easter and the air was still fresh. January had been the month that Agatha first heard announced that she was going to be a mother in law, and, not so incidentally, a grandmother. Agatha went down to Anna's to get the momentous fact off her chest.

There is going to be a baby, she said to Anna. Anna looked like a spider. She was emaciated and her arms and legs seemed to billow about in bed. But she was still walking. They had expected her dead months ago. She smiled about the baby. A little gleam came into her eyes. And so the village will be blessed with your children and grandchildren, so far...Little Paul didn't quite manage it. The curse, you see, Agatha, is over. Tell me about the bride.

Oh one would never have thought of her as attracting Dimitri, said Agatha, conscious that she was sounding like a stuffy old woman full of old fashioned pride about her son. Not that she doesn't have her beauty—odd beauty sort of now you see it, now you don't. Befitting the recluse that she has been on our island. Of course, they would come down in the village, and I remember when they first arrived, her stopping by—oh it was all politeness then—could have fooled me! But I knew that what she wanted was a way into the island life, strange though that may sound to some. Unobtrusive, always polite, perfect comportment—all that yes, but I would say that she lacked a certain spark, you know. I always thought Dimitri would marry a thoroughly unconventional, modern girl with great imagination. This one—what did I hear her say she was good at?—fixing old machines. Literally! Her father has taught her certain tricks—ways of figuring out what is wrong exactly with any given machine that is broken. But this is pedantic to the extreme—why anyone can do that; machines are merely diagrams; you have to look at one, understand it, and then catch where it doesn't quite come together—where one part is off, quite off.

Catherine, thought Anna, breathing audibly. What do I know of her? Very poised, little head up always up and body narrow without shape like an eel. Some steady idea or inspiration in her grey dark eye—not to be shaken. That is what I remember. She reminds me in fact of grey days—slightly magical, now it is and now it isn't but that little eye remaining, piercing steady, calm through it all.

Strange how you seem to love her, said Agatha with a hint of resentment.

I? How odd! I was sure I loved nobody—that I have never loved, in fact. Didn't I inform you of this? I am lying on this bed waiting for love. It is the reason I don't die, didn't you know? I lie here and painfully don't die! The works have been stopped; the grind of the machine has been held up. I await love—and you tell me Catherine? Why? I suppose she is as good as any other. But don't you think you and I should be closer? Hasn't it always been you, when I've been sick, I, when you've been miserable? Wasn't it to be us, the two peas in a pod? Catherine I see through you, your unjealous side. You put jealousy somewhere over there, and yourself in here with me; and who knows? We may even arrive at love.

What is it that you want?

Nothing I can pin down. What was it in the Gospels after the resurrection of Christ? Jesus was walking by some of his disciples and they didn't recognize him. He talked to them and said to them: Fools to mourn Christ's death. Ought not the Christ to have suffered to come into his glory? The disciples did not recognize him. It was his will that they should not. But he left his sign—after when they had discovered who it was and were marveling and wondering that such a thing should be, they said as a way of knowing the true Christ: Did not our hearts burn within us?

Did not our hearts burn within us? This is the sign; this is the love I am talking about.

But you have gone all this time not believing.

Let's change the subject. The island for Christmas had it usual roll of festivities. The feast at Simon's house—was he quite up to it. I hear that he went a bit bats—that sometimes he seemed to see someone disappear who was standing right before him.

He is alright—meditating mostly—in a kind of rapture. Agatha seemed to drift off. I go up to him rarely; he doesn't seem to like to have me underfoot—washing, cooking, mending—he manages all for himself. And so I spend my time with Leo, only he cooks you know. He had no lights for his house for Christmas, our lights are dim in any case on this island—its hardly worth putting them up; but he put up bits of shiny red paper all around his door—little curly cues made by pulling a scissors along a strip of the thin red paper. It looks funny, soft and pretty. He really made a little curtain of these curly cues. I jested with him and said it suited him—his greasy grey, curly hair has grown longer. His face is puffy and he wears spectacles and to see him peeking through the shiny, red curly cue curtain…it is strange and quaint enough to look magical —like some fairy tale, you know.

I came in to the house one day and it was all steam. He was taking one of his never-ending showers that I had heard about from himself, of course. He says they last half a day—and oh the hot water and bath soap and bath oil and fragrances that he uses! Then he emerges, he said, light and clean as a snowflake.

Well that day, when I opened the door, there was a whale of a fragrance, steam and heat that puffed at me, surrounded me, filled my nostrils. I called him, looking around meanwhile at the usual mess and clothes strewn all around as if they had flown off his body into the various awkward places—the sofa, the floor, the table, soiled underwear over the back of a chair as if placed on exhibition on purpose. He has a thing about clothes and nakedness; one wears clothes for a festive reason only—for color, jollity, prettiness, fun but really only for the occasion, as it were, although he did wear clothes, at least when I saw him. Nakedness is serious—the real, everyday statement about one's existence. So when he jumped out of the showers and waggling-walked all around me, shouting hey hey, in a perfect, rhythmic beat, I knew he was just expressing his most serious, ordinary self. Nothing shocking or extraordinary. He walked round and round in a circle waggling and hey heying and then slowly moved back to the bathroom, leaving a trail of wet footprints—all with the greatest of solemnity and ease, no embarrassment whatsoever.

I felt a little thrill—that is, that whatever he felt towards me, he did not hesitate to do the usual with me—to expose the heart, as it were, that daily, steady, same life inside him. Odd, I didn't find it outrageous—perhaps I thought to myself—leaving an imprint—a way of not forgetting? Hey hey—

I brought into the shower fresh clothes—sleeveless undershirt, shorts, white shirt in soft cotton, baggy light blue jeans held at the waist by an elastic, slippers, a red woolen sweater and left them on top of the toilet. He was behind the shower curtain but heard me enter. I will emerge from my cocoon of hot water and steam shortly; he said. Beware when I come fluttering out, the butterfly!

Summer seems so unreal in the midst of winter, he said; but you know what is unreal now will be reality later.

The shower eventually ceased and out popped my genius—I call him that; I don't know why. He did remind me of a butterfly, soft and light on his toes, bouncing a little weightlessly up and down though he has a belly and thick thighs. In fact, he is no good for anything except for cooking, talking, walking around and laughing. He lives in a world where all one does is sample delectable dishes and laugh. But it is not cruel laughter, rather a child's laughter. Soft and elastic. Reminds me of a sling shot with a tomato, or a broccoli, a fish in it hurled up at the stars. That is about the extent of his evil today. So he would protect me, he said, hurling tomatoes and raw eggs at destiny, at the evil one, at little Paul, laughing when they hit.

You are a new creature, said Anna and your son is the one that married. Weddings are always about the old folks. I've known two types of weddings: one where the old folks limp off to welter in old age and infirmity, wither more and more when the children are gone. Another where the old in laws marry in essence again and the old weds outshine the newlyweds. I saw that with Barbara's mother and father while they were alive. Bright as two new buttons, they were, at the wedding when she married Stavros. They looked like they belonged to another world, I can tell you—allowed to sparkle a moment here. It was all a kind of sparkle in them, nothing more. Beauty. They were the most impossible of folks in the day to day. Full of complaints. You, instead—someone to live with—blameless and wise. Fortunately, they died young.

The village blames me for straightening my spine, said Agatha. They wanted me to become an old hag, witch, anything for an excuse to throw fantasy stones at me.

Ah yes, and they have lost their holiness, and now you come out as if wearing a divine crown. Not because of any visible 'sign' from God—any moment at prayer, where you were on your knees and the heavens opened. (The heavens that were by the way going to condemn you.) But because you wickedly went and stole joy—you lifted your leg, you danced! Ah so they are after you, hating you, utterly tempted. Mind that as auntie Zoe lifts the silver dagger of moral outrage to plunge into your back, you don't whirl around and in doing so, whirl her so that she tosses away her evil weapon and dances. The one with the wrong book—the book of strange utterances and gibbers, beautiful and magical made the village dance like the true book could not.

Perhaps they will only become angry in the end.

If they attack the dance, they attack God, said Anna, solemnly.

I remember that night when they all came for us with torches. Surrounding the house...actually there were only a few men, cross-eyed, creeping, laughing, a yell now and then: But at first I thought I saw the whole village there. Old, wizened folk, hardened in hatred. My soul whirled up to the clouds, I became dizzy, confused. I wanted to walk out and offer myself if they would not touch my son Jason. In a minute Paul came, the priest came, they debated between themselves; strange and fearful thing: although they spoke our dialect I did not understand their language. And then howling slightly, muttering as if casting spells on the air, looking at us with hard black eyes as if our fate was sealed, they dispersed. Paul had dispersed them it seemed when I thought back on it. At an order from him, they were gone!

Paul, the mighty. Damn him. That is why I say leave poor God out of it. He's had enough of our village letting Paul be born. Turned on his heel the day he was conceived. And you, little Jesus lover, are the antidote.

Well now there is a new family with us, you see. A new fruit on the old branches. I am in awe. It is a matter of weeks and Dimitri is already gearing up to be a father. I don't feel quite safe; not quite. I will talk to the children—Dimitri and Catherine, about moving away. He can go back to London lickety-split. He has contacts there. I feel it may be better. You know he has his modern ideas and here it will not go over. The best scenario is that they ignore him. That he lives abandoned with wife and child, a recluse family. The worst I don't even want to think about.

But you've always lived with a toxic cloud hanging over you. You've always breathed in its fumes with lungs fit to endure all kinds of poisons and survive a million years. What has made you worry now?

You know yourself.

The baby?

I've always felt I was up to them, a passionate Fury—for if they raise their hand against one of the mothers—ha! Beware. Horrid hag with blood streaming from her eye sockets, and claws longer than a man's arm unstoppable by any weapon, saving justice, justice. You see I had them bound by their very souls, the joint seat of madness and ecstasy. I almost didn't mind dying at their hands for I knew I had an afterlife in them. Also the very poison of me—the curse itself—would spread to them, be inhaled unavoidably—an ineluctable transmission that would damn them, damn them. I tell you Anna it wasn't kindness or compunction on Paul's part that made him cancel the planned immolation of my house, myself, my son. It was real fear. I am not quite human to him. I don't end in flesh and blood. I metamorphose into a hell hound.

No it was just that I wanted to go to a place that was all softness and sweet world. I wanted to be helpless. An infant again, a virgin in love—a tiny girl perched on my father's shoulder about to being joy and justice so much joy and justice to the world.

I did not, I could not rise up for war—you see? The hellhound, the Madam Fury, shrunk down, losing fur, claws, blood-dripping eyeballs into a little bloom of chamomile, soft, sweet, crushable. And emitting only fragrance if crushed under the heel.

Ah, ah, Anna gave two sweet little cries of delight. So you want sweet air, she said. The toxic cloud and the chamomile don't quite go together.

And this dread, Agatha said, and Anna felt she continued the one thought—this dread is what makes me nervous. It isn't a game anymore, she said suddenly, incongruously, but Anna perfectly understood.

One is helpless to the dread. I don't know what it wants of me. To swear my allegiance to God? Too pedantic. No, the divine is something else. I know it is coming.

Well, you will find it. Here is Tia now—she had gone shopping in the interval, while Agatha guarded Anna, who was all bones, against slips and falls. I have just renewed her with all sorts of thoughts—and unburdened myself a bit, as friends do.

As for me, said Tia with energy, putting down the shopping, I think our Anna is fit for several crosses. She has a robust temper, and opinions that wrestle with you like my brother—he throws everyone down; pins them to the mat. Uncontested most powerful wrestler in my city. That is our Anna with her opinions.

Salt that has not lost its savor.

Go away, go away, shouted Anna, but she was smiling. Have to swallow down these pills and then, oh luxury! Sleep. Take care of the baby. You know you are bearing it yourself.

Catherine round enough to look like her belly was a large ball and Agatha were sitting at Agatha's kitchen table looking at one another. Catherine was explaining that it was a most unpleasant pregnancy. There was constant nausea, dizziness, swelling of the ankles…She felt that she was sick most of the time. She had had to stop her heart medication. She said Dimitri generally made sure that she only walked two steps a day. Today she had eluded his watchful eye—he was asleep in the villa—and she had come down the cliff, carefully, step by step alone. Just wait, said Catherine, he will come raging down the mountain like a lion after me. But it was really intolerable.

I felt that I was imprisoned with a guard who shed his handsome self all around me and kept me in a stupor of sex from which I would come out only to vomit.

Come, said Agatha, I will put you in Dimitri's bed and bring you a tea that I know will give you strength and put you to sleep for a bit. If you can't climb the cliff with me later, because I wouldn't let you go alone, you will sleep here for tonight. On second thought, sleep in my room on my old wedding bed. I've slept alone there for many years, it is only right that my children—son and new bride should occupy it now.

Agatha walked with Catherine to the bed, knelt as she sat and took off her shoes—tennis shoes and thin socks. Her feet were cold, April was gusty on Holy Island, so she made a hot water bottle that she wrapped in a thick, soft towel for them at the foot of the bed. Then she lifted the sheet and heavy woolen blanket and wrapped her well.

Catherine, lying there, still bright and chipper and for once not nauseous, said I always remember the lifting of the covers over me in bed. My father used to do it. We thought that it would stop when I came to adolescence—off I would be to all sorts of hours getting into trouble, growing smart—but it didn't work that way because of my illness, and he was still covering me with cool sheets and soft, warm blankets until I was thirty. Now Dimitri would do it, but I insist on doing him. There have been so few things I have been able to change and to do from that perspective—overabundance of love. And so it gets boring. As if I should have left off—years ago.

The front door slammed and a voice cried out in despair and fury—is she here? Is she here? Mother, is she here?

Yes, yes, said Agatha, her light body, turning and leaping up to meet him. Right here and totally sound, almost sound asleep.

Dimitri barged into the dim light of the bedroom where the shutters were pulled to block out the winter white day and one electric light was burning. He looked drab to Catherine, his face a little bloated from the good meals and overmuch sleep that he had had since the start of her pregnancy. But there was something so pathetic in him, so strained and drained, as if he was lost in another world entirely and didn't know which end was up, a singular example of a different species and she was exhibiting to him a forest of womb and placenta in which he looked around fearfully, although he pretended wonder and delight.

Sit down, said Catherine comfortingly but also unable to disguise a sort of mischievous amusement.

Oh, thank you, indeed. I am to just sit down and relax while you have just now willfully, and willingly—you were not dragged by the hair down the steep cliff by a wild Indian, I presume—horribly endangered your life and our son's. I just want to know one thing—you wanted to escape or to have a day to yourself or to fly abroad, or to swim and dive and be free with your hair floating in the ice-cold sea—something of that sort! Who am I? Yes, in all this, who am I? I am allowed no margin for my feelings as a husband who cares for you and as a father to be who wants to see the live birth of our child.

Yes, I have been selfish.

Selfish? Dimitri, sat down on the bed beside the prone body of his wife. I would say possessed.

Dimitri, said Agatha, she was feeling a little cooped up.

I supposed you would consider me King Kong if I just grabbed you now and forcibly took you back up the mountain.

You know I am a lady of sorts and there should be a kind of sense of awe or reverence when I lay down in bed pregnant much like a pilgrim might feel at a holy altar, replied Catherine, her eyes twinkling.

What if the man you married is not a pilgrim but a crusader and simply seizes the goods, holy and not so holy?

Catherine sighed and closed her eyes. They have bad reputations on humanitarian grounds, those crusaders.

Humph. So here she will stay, he said to his mother.

Until she has a little rest.

You are responsible for this. I am sure of it, he said in a sudden totally irrational fury to Agatha.

What?— that she wanted a breath of air, to walk and to use her muscles like an ordinary rational human being? Even if she should not, the answer is not force, son. Perhaps it was all a moment of ambivalence. Haven't you had the same? What if the difference is that you can walk quietly away, or meditate, or practice some other form of withdrawal and communion with a celestial body, she has her own body and a body enveloped within to think about to dream about—she is invaded, she is subjugated—don't you think now and then there are moments a woman, that is, a mother to be might want to wake up, get back at the whole idea…

Ah, so when you were pregnant with me, you thought of killing me—getting back…

Yes, there was that. Was it my choice to have you? I didn't want children. There was something on my mind more beautiful than children.

What? What is there more beautiful than children?

You are such a tender chicken, said Agatha, laughing—why, getting back—and she whirled around on the toe of her foot. Then she planted herself under the frowning face of her son. It seemed the bedroom where Catherine despite their altercations was sleeping peacefully had an ominous look. It was in the walls that seemed to say—ah now, you are going to catch it! Agatha continued her talk, it was fast, uncaring talk. For years what she had to say had gone unheard, uncommented on. If she had ever raised such an issue with Alex alive, he would have hushed her as if she were a child with his soft, slightly flaccid hand over her face nose and mouth. And the children would have thought likewise—it is just mother talk, something that goes on and on, the mournful cry of the sea in the night; one closed windows on it, and opened windows to it, it was ceaseless, solitary and alien. But one continued because in the end it was no human thing. There was no having a real talk with it.

No, I would not have had you, would not have loved you, had I had my way. But then Dimitri thought—so it is with mothers, for his ear had caught Agatha's mourning. And somehow new life sprang out of a dead thing, or not dead exactly, but alive as blankets were alive—all mute and still life.---then he looked at Catherine and thought with a chill, oh so she has her own mind about this whole business! And she can, quite without my being able to stop her if I don't use physical force—walk about in the middle of the night, down steep cliffs, into the sea.

Agatha saw immediately what was going on in the head of her now beloved son; she had grown so possessive in her heart and brooded her mind into such a fine point of understanding of Dimitri while he was up in the villa making love again and again to Catherine that she could practically see his brain working. She dressed in a huge sweater in her solitary bed, and said to her son in the morning: The answer is love, Dimitri. Not love as in love like some form of jam slathered all over one's sensory apparatus, she said from behind the sweater. Love as in honesty; love as in kindness. There were times I talked to you, you know. Perhaps you don't remember.

The mute, still bedroom, the sense of the mourning and stiff apartness in his mother, the perfect poise of his wife asleep in her own world in which there might be death or life subject to this hilarious will of hers, which led her on the fine edge between—down the steep steps of the cliff in her condition with her heart!— were too much for Dimitri to bear. He tore out of the bedroom uttering a stifled cry. Soon he was out of the house.

Agatha wandered into the kitchen, still in the massive black tight-knit wool, her nude heart beating madly underneath. This was the son she had once hated—when he was still inside her, when he was a baby—whom she had once thought of drowning like one might an unwanted dog or cat, along with herself, perhaps; in any case, she was already dead, in those days, killed by misery and torment. And then one day his black eyes and the flash of his mind in them, dropped a drop of pride and attraction. She suddenly fell in love with Dimitri, it was a year or so before he left, and for pity's sake then, the in-lovedness fanned out its rosy wing and almost but not quite included Jason. So it was Dimitri.

Perhaps Father Raphael had seen who she was, the almost incestuous love song that filled her heart like a balloon and burst and the spine straightening (later,) the looking with eyes clear as crystal down into the depths of people through their eyes, that wild sweet will that came and conformed only to the dance. One can imagine that this did not fit in the rosters of the Church's heaven. And so she was a demon, her soul burnt black by hell fire, but amazingly sweet. Nobody knew or cared that her hate had changed to love, that this sexual flame of dance enveloped the earth with passionate compassionate adoration. They just knew above all that she was to be avoided or treated as one would refractory servants with harshness, shortness, if one was a countess. Worse, as one in the fires of hell, loving her son, here one spat— a harridan with a face like an Easter candle.

It seemed to Agatha that she had breathed in, one sharp breath when Dimitri left and never breathed out until he returned—as he had now, in the fold, permanently. She liked to see that there was an umbilical cord connecting him now; it was useless to try to tear it she knew. It only caused him pain then, and made him utter those tearing cries. Catherine was the binding force, she knew; but it was just as well. For effectively now they, that is, he, was at home with her and dependent on her. She knew that he would come back all a-whimper wanting everything fixed up by some magical hand, her hand, with herbs, and peace—infusions of even temper and all going well. And Agatha felt that she now could achieve this. She had the magical powers.

Over the next few days, while Catherine lay, taking every precaution, in Agatha's old marriage bed, and Dimitri appeared and disappeared like a magician, Agatha worked up a sweat in the kitchen, a real whirl from which soups and infusions, chickens and herbed potatoes arrived at her daughter in law's bedside as if borne by waves of steam. Steam filled the house, with smells of tomato and chicken, garlic and oil and flooded their nostrils. The clean steam and the beautiful odors worked as a purge on their air passageways; all the impurities—the residue left by the breathing in of soiledness of other people, of their breath—were pumped out and the blood was purified, the brains circled round, strengthened, though dizzied. In this rarified atmosphere of boiling and bubbling, frying and simmering Agatha moved closer, physically and emotionally, to Catherine who ate and drank everything she was offered with real joy. In fact, the chicken and the fish stew gave her such delight she began to hum, and the garlic in oil on soft warm bread unleashed waves of love and sweetness in her so much so that in a kind of rapture, humming and half singing—a whole song if only Agatha's name—and Agatha told her to call her 'Mama'—all sorts of confessions overflowed in her.

Dimitri, ha ha! Catherine positively tinkled with silver laughter. What a terrible man—what a horror—I am exaggerating, of course—but you know what I mean. Always the lover...She held out her hands for the sweet lemony tea. Whereas you and I know, she smiled impishly at Agatha, it isn't that kind of sweet nothing that makes the baby grow. Oh, I suppose, he has to stand by like the wall here, she pointed to the wall of the bedroom behind her; he has to hold the room up in some capacity with what it is—I suppose masculine fervor—protecting and defending. But that is all the stuff of myth and legend. One look at me and the people here will step back to let me pass. Down the road, down the steep steps to the grey-blue endless sea. They want babies, and I am bringing them one. I!

You know I was in love with him first—Dimitri, the father! And now I think of him as a sort of wizened old sage sitting outside mumbling trying to make the clouds break up and the sun shine again. A little shred of a human being, hardly part of life at all.

Of course, he is holy—one can tell by his passion. I don't believe in holy people who are just smilers without that old stern passion that makes flesh and blood flesh and blood. It is not so much passion for me as a woman, but passion that his principle, his wisdom, call it that, should out rule everyone else's vain, fragmented objections and take the day. Even I am subject to this passion of wisdom and knowledge, righteousness, you know; but I wiggle and waggle my way away. Driving him mad. Ha, ha.

He'll be back, said Agatha in a soft conspiratorial whisper for Dimitri had just stepped out.

Then I'd best get it out, said Catherine, before he comes in like Last Judgment. Where was I—yes, I was in love with him first, I believe. When we made love I was sick but in a rapture all the same. I think I thought he was the new sun rising, or some such nonsense. Then we came together, a little like animals having bouts of one another, mating bouts; I even remember his teeth on the nape of my neck and my growling. Then the marriage and smiling all around, a little, sugary celebration for what was desperate and mad in us. A new level of knowledge, a transport of the senses and mind. Dimitri wanted to be sun and earth to me, water and air. And at first he was. It is true. I lay under his ray, I walked on his body with soft bare feet pressing into his flesh, I drank him hot and cool, I breathed him, his moist never foul breath—that is one thing, even in the morning, his breath is always tolerable. And then I just filled up with him. Enough for the hour. I reminded myself that I had legs and that I had had my fill of love for the day. One has a quota of sweet whisperings, tender touchings.

And he has not, said Agatha, drawing her legs under her. No. One imagines that he has never found love until now with—with a woman. He is curious, driven mad, lustful as an ape, tender as a little chick. He would do anything for you, she said, softly. Yet you haven't seen him, she said, suddenly grave and incomprehensible as new mothers in law are. Do you know the story of Cupid and Psyche? Cupid, the god of love, falls in love with Psyche, a beautiful maiden, against his mother's jealous wishes. Venus discovers it and tells him he must never let his bride know who he is or she will murder her; so he comes to her at night, hidden in folds of darkness for the most glorious love making. One day her jealous sisters come to call and they advise her to shine a candle on him when he comes at night, to find out who he is for there is no telling he might not be a monster. She, all curiosity and trepidation does what her sisters advise, and as she sees him leaning the candle into his face, illuminating with fire, the beautiful god of love, a drop of hot candle wax falls on his body, burning him, and he wakes and must leave her. Mournful Psyche follows after seeking him for many years, seeking the abode of the gods.

Catherine too wise to answer what was clearly supposed to be secret passion spoken aloud by chance remained silent.

He is your true love and mine, said Agatha, openly, and we will find and lose him, she murmured. But as yet, you have not shone the candle....no one has.

He hasn't promised me fidelity. He has not done that exactly, said Catherine nervously, tangentially, he's sort of asking me to take him all on trust, even though he may wander. But that is his latitude in the sphere of our relationship.

It isn't that so much—it is raw delight and a kind of pity that comes of seeing, Agatha said. He is beautiful, she finished, looking at her daughter in law in wonder, I mean beautiful, the way the dance is beautiful, in intent, …but he doesn't know

Catherine said: Not how beautiful he is nor how it may affect people.

You don't see it, said Agatha to herself.

In the warm cocoon of Agatha's home, enwombed by cooking smells, smothered in a wool blanket that kept one warm in the coldest of temperatures, Catherine became, she told Agatha, because with Dimitri she was silent, though laughing periodically into his solemn face, a soft, springtime laugh, which he, all winter, didn't believe in—she became like a harp string, like melted butter on warm bread, like an insouciant daisy, a little trumpet of sex and all, as Dimitri complained—in his face! She had that 'way', he said, of taking his balls and going, on the run to never never land where he supposed he would inseminate witches and fairy queens. And he would sit, the holy man, she mocked him, emasculated, growing old beyond his years in the ageless sun.

He sat by her or walked slowly around with her. There was no more afternoon absconding, slipping out, pouring down the mountain…for one thing, the mountain was behind them. They were by the sea in the village and for another, Agatha had made Catherine utterly content. She accepted her ins and outs, dark sides and light sides, laughter, and seriousness, watching, waiting without shadowing her as Dimitri did. It was all joyous, a chorus singing constantly—Agatha made known there were others in the village watching and waiting for her. They were humble, little, and bowed before her—speechless with surprise, then as if they had long expected it from her raising their glasses of wine to her health. Dimitri was morbid, helpless and full of wonder all together. He was convinced that someone would die of all this. He looked at her as she lay asleep in bed with that kind of concentration frown as if he was trying to solve—just because life itself drove him to—an unsolvable absolutely impossible mathematics problem!

He sat by her or walked slowly around with her. She had a kind of light spilling down over her bosom—seriously, he thought to himself, she shone, or, rather, she possessed this light, a platinum light. It was as if she was dressed in an angel's scarf. Tossed it carelessly around her. It was the kind of phenomenon that had he not known better would have caused him to bend the knee and worship. Instead he argued with her, because irritated over nothing, and the irritation traveled all the way down to his genitals. She tended to speak to him in the old, low, measured voice that had won his whole heart, the way a child's whole heart is won by love and seriousness, but her whole being was laughter light. In fact, another odd phenomenon was that as she grew heavier by weight, she somehow simultaneously grew lighter. Yes, simultaneously as she sunk, she rose and floated. The bed creaked as she sat on it and adjusted herself and then seemed to raise her up on a froth of bubbles and present her to him, talking seriously, laughing in every pore, lightly like fairies, angels, magical immortal creatures that live in the wind.

Who was he making love to? The old Catherine who had pumped love out of him like water out of a well more and more—one would think he would run dry…or this new double creature that seized him like an eagle, mated with him high up in the sky, and in this coitus ignited him so that as they turned around each other, cartwheeling through the blue, they burst into flames, flying, spinning, a new sun. And just as he wondered—where on earth are my wings? And made ready to fall, he parted from her body, looked into her love-glowing eyes and became earth. He became earth after love making with her that was new creation.

The worst of it was, with him sitting by her and walking with her, little steps but endlessly, that she seemed to know the impossible mathematical problem inside and out, backwards and forwards and had ready another impossible philosophical solution. Like it appeared that they would need three houses, not one. Her house, his house, and their house. But no, everything had come in a rush, he said, meaning her swelling body. He had his savings, they amounted to much—he would build her a house, a better house, a bigger house. Nonsense, she answered, every time—then riches he had and knew he had, all calculated were nothing and now more with her eyes, than with her tongue—a little dwelling on the cliff—her land, his house. And then a friendly get together—her parents' house, his parents' house interchangeable yet so unlike. Already they had shaken hands, Agatha, Ellen and Robert—Agatha firmly as if in solidarity, Ellen, slightly disdainfully, Robert in agreement with Agatha.

Catherine noted after to Dimitri that it was as if they were all confirming that they would tolerate this completely preposterous notion of two grown adults making a little moveable home under the very roof of their elders. Agatha said to Dimitri—it is necessary. Don't you see how the village has drawn back from the old abuse, the usual torment that it used to inflict on us, now they creep around softly; there are a few smiles. The old women—Cleo, Zoe and Foti are coming by soon with knitted caps, blankets and sweaters for the baby. Father Isaac grins from ear to ear. I must say he looks a bit like a clown. Yesterday there was a little line of well-wishers at our door. I gave them some biscuits I made with lemon and honey and shooed them all away. No, we have come into our own, Dimitri. Catherine said, of course, in a serious tone. Except, said Dimitri, finding his voice after what seemed like days of letting the women have all the say—you are American; it doesn't quite count. The child is half only.

After all these years! Said Agatha who was, as usual, busy bringing Catherine things to eat and drink! They will just rejoice like Christmas. We haven't had a baby on this island for fifteen years. Even if you and she were foreign visitors and she conceived and bore a baby on this soil, people would be dancing in the streets as if you were their own children, grandchildren!

They are quiet, said Dimitri; not dancing.

You will see, said Agatha.

But Dimitri continued half grim and wouldn't be shaken out of it. The other side was pleasant and sweet enough; that was the side the women sucked in—his mother, and the insatiable Catherine. In fact, when his mother held him in her all-around embrace, and Catherine made love to him, Dimitri was like new baked bread, sweet, fragrant, warm and soft. Go a few hours, however, and he got stale, bitter and dry. This was the half that wouldn't let go—that is, returned to him not matter what the women did.

He went for a walk one April morning to shake himself loose, he said of the blues that he had, but also of the women in the house, letting down their hair, talking incessantly about nothing, shining the light of their bosoms and have himself a think. Without really noticing it, his feet carried him down the beach and up an alley towards Katrina's house. And when he arrived there he thought—she is a friend, after all, perhaps a glass of apricot brandy, or one of the infusions she likes to make....

Katrina spotted him from her kitchen window and opened the door. She had a pile of washing in her hands.

What are you doing? Dimitri asked her with a frown. You wanted another life.

Katrina said nothing.

You wanted another life, he said more loudly.

Katrina still said nothing.

Curses, said Dimitri and went up to her, tore the washing out of her hands and seized her head violently and kissed her hard. Then he drew back, panting. You make me mad.

He tore her blouse and her skirt, the prim, large underpants; and her fat underbelly came bulging out.

Come, over here, he said to her leading her to her bedroom. In the living room near the balcony where they sat for the sun came the imbecilic cries of her mother, and the sound of her father coughing and banging his spoon on his chair. Dimitri pushed Katrina on to the bed, mounted her and began to make love to her, hard, pushing himself into her warm, wet flesh so deeply that it hurt her. When he ejaculated, he waited, panting and then he began over again. Katrina screamed for pleasure, opened her legs wide, her large, melon like breasts bulged on either side of Dimitri's body.

Then after three ejaculations, Dimitri flung himself down beside her. Emptied of his rage.

What was this all about? Whimpered Katrina.

It was what was needed. We had gone years wondering about one another—we had broken off mid-love making, without even saying goodbye. I could not marry you, Katrina, you are too different, to un-companionable. But you, you wronged me and yourself and all of humanity. You closed down, you became a machine—functioning by some kind of duty. Duty is not organic energy like love. You made a life for yourself based on duty. And with this, the machine might run for a while but the soul in you will deteriorate and decay away. He caressed her face with a face of sternness and total deflation—so much hidden anger, fury, bitterness. You have in your bosom cruelty.

And you? Your wife is pregnant.

It is not the same kind of cruelty. We have, in any case, discussed the whole thing, he tossed off to her in a voice reflecting lifelessness and drear.

Ah, I am disgusted with you, said Katrina getting up. And will always be disgusted with you. Not only do you cheat on your wife, you don't do it honorably, as there is honor among adulterers as among thieves; instead of creeping off and making a good jolly secret of it, you tell her beforehand. You are no more than a fornicator through and through—and I got my pleasure from you, I did! Ha, to think that I once thought you a lover—who out of despair, the honorable way, came looking for me.

In fact, you wanted it so, retorted Dimitri. But the lie is yours. I simply follow the dictates of the spirit of love in me. You knew that living here in this abominable slavish fashion was totally intolerable for me. There was a time I loved you and defended you before the sneers of the island men—old hag, they called you and other things that I won't mention. And you thought because I married and now lived in a realm of beauty, love and higher thought with my American wife, I would have lost all passion for you. Not so. How can I forget my first lady with her bubbling cauldron of sex underneath that brutally prim, foolishly prudishly, old fashioned lid of a mind and heart, he continued as if without life in him he would go on and on.

But to torture your wife...said Katrina.

She is what she wanted to be knowing full well from before our marriage all that I would do. She is my wife, I her husband. I did nothing but what was ardently desired by the both of us.

They struggled to get up. Katrina felt beneath her rump on the sheets for the damp spot of urine. She would pee slightly whenever she was aroused and told her lover so. It is old age, she said.

Dimitri stuck out his tongue and bent down to the damp pee spot and licked it. Then he licked her wet vulva and her pee place again and again. Ah, said Katrina—you are on the brink of convincing me of everything.

But despite his antics she knew Dimitri was a crawling thing without spirit.

Finally, Dimitri stood and started to put on his trousers. I am not saying that I will come night after night, he said. But there is something wrong about leaving you in a house that is too small for you, he said, waving his hands around, with a job that is not your job. You too deserve to blossom and once long ago you had pity on a lone boy who didn't want to court the usual narrow-minded, prejudiced, village maidens. You who had thoughts of your own deigned to make love to me. Remember? In the forest near the cave. I was ruthless and cruel, it is true. I didn't give you my body in love. But there was always solidarity, Katrina, and as you can see—I didn't forget you.

Katrina pulled out of her drawer another shirt and skirt.

Ah no, said Dimitri, put on your marching jeans—the oversize ones. For this once pretend you are a revolutionary, a worker in a factory, a coal miner. Not the above board, always prim and proper lady who has ladied out the boiling cauldron of sex inside.

I'll stay for a glass of tea and a cookie. Talk a little, Katrina; tell me that you, the old woman who unzipped my trousers and gave me a real man's makeover as it were are still alive despite your death.

Still alive? Katrina said casually, impassively. Her hands began to move across the stove; they had somehow moved into the kitchen—perhaps crawled, perhaps flew. Dimitri felt that he was more in her hands as a man than he was in Catherine's. Catherine's savor was that of a girl, hilarious and joyful in sex and pregnancy and perhaps somewhat high from that old repressed fear that women have. Katrina knew the mechanics of a man. She could handle, push buttons... And he thought he was entirely self-willed, an independent man making his way! She made him into an ironic little genie, seeing himself.

Katrina was the mother-prostitute—the one from whose side he would have to be torn in the end; Dimitri knew that. He drank the infusion and a little wine and watched his old girlfriend—rosy, flesh transformed now, more liquid, graceful—like water despite her bulk. He was himself with her—that is, the old home self. The island man that had carved a niche or dug a hole in this damn land; but it was a step down, what he had feared, what he now welcomed—gave himself another half an hour with; he was man-animal with Katrina—what she had herself produced years ago. She knew him, tamed him, that is, left him, thankfully, half wild.

Katrina had said nothing to him all the time he drank. She took off her jeans as he watched and pulled on stockings. She lit a cigarette half dressed like that and smoked, looking at him through half closed eyes. Then she roused herself, put on her skirt, and went to check on her parents.

They are asleep, she said coming back.

Kill them, said Dimitri.

What? Said Katrina.

Ah, got you there. You see, he said, gazing up at her, I am in the soup as you are. I love my wife, but it is precisely this love that led me to you. I wanted to know, see, feel again--especially the one who has sacrificed life and love for my sake. You know all that.

That's alright, said Katrina.

I suppose the wound will heal. If not, come in the night and kill me with fucking.

You are still a boy, said Katrina, calmly. What has passed between us—it could have been anywhere in the world—am I not right? The above board life, the underground old history. But it wasn't just for the sex that you came?

No, not at all. It was for myself, my identity: the little corner thing I left in the woods near the cave, naked with you on your knees sucking me. I have been since skipping across the water and then coming back and marrying an American, an entirely different person. I left behind a creature stranded in the middle of the sea. I remembered a poor, older woman with no looks crying her eyes out, writing me letters. Deep in your body, I remembered. I want change, yet I don't want to cut. I am afraid, you see, of death to that person. That original. That is death, I think. An active terrible person-obliterating thing. The other, the ceasing to breathe, is just a cease of eros.

Ah, I asked if it was just for the sex out of simple curiosity.

You should wear a skirt more often; Dimitri had changed his position on Katrina's attire. You look, I must confess-- like a lady. And as a lady, you know the truth. Don't expect our normal every day relations to change. We had an affair, I am not ashamed of it. I knew, you knew, we had this root together—fated, circumstances made it. We were cast into the stew together. I am, of course, there for you. Should you want money, should you need me…— of course, I don't have any! Call yourself my lady if you like—my dark lady—dark for the underground, old history that you so aptly named. History taking place in the inner outer cave as it does. You did, you see, have something with me. I believe no matter what the match is there is something immortal in it. All lovers have that. But I am of the old island school.

My American wife perhaps does not agree in her heart of hearts. She is my king, my empress. The only thing she cannot do is make me stop exploring, touching upon all aspects of my humanity. Otherwise we are seamed together at the hip bone.

. . .

When Dimitri left he had a headache brought on, he thought, by talking too much and the heavy wine Katrina served him.

It was late in the afternoon, the sun had already disappeared; there was a glow in the sky. The cool breeze made him feel better but his relaxation, his solitude brought on a sudden melancholy that led to tears.

He felt that he was of neither this world nor that. He was not an island man; he did not love Katrina, the island nymph of his. He was more of an Athenian, or even an American. In this grotto, people would never understand, half magical though they were. They were busy, yes, with their Christmas story of having through their ancestors seen the true Jesus. How they beheld a man child of golden fire, of divine life. Now what they did was to repeat form prayers, cross themselves, confess their sins—be ashamed of sexual wandering. And he entered in dark, steady with an argument: it was not something to be ashamed of. Not with him. It was part of his lungs or his kidney—it was a disease that was spreading—the disease that was him, the disease that was humanity. One went in with the knife—sex, cut it out, examined it. And knew that if he cut it out entirely he would die. One can be only so much God.

They had their serene, golden-skinned Jesus. He, a wild man that hovered near breathing on his neck, saying: I want the reality, the truth of mankind.

He made his way back to Agatha's house, tired and hungry. Catherine took one look at him as he came into the bedroom and said to him in her old voice—we have already started the great experiment?

Katrina, he said, he couldn't help but smile a little at the way she penetrated him life, mind, heart, body.

I won't say you could have waited until the child was born. I feel all organs, foolish, helpless.

Dimitri sat down on the bed beside her. I will not go to her again. It was not about love or sex—it was about the old self.

I don't make it live?

No.

Catherine looked neither weepy, nor angry. She looked at him innocently—nothing in her face, but a slight frown—like the angels, he said to his mother later. He leaned forward and kissed her on the hairline. There may have been an improvement in the lighting, perhaps the electrical factory was supplying them with more light, in any case, the one lamp in the room cast enough light so that Catherine looked all light—hair and bosom and eyes. It is you, in the end—that I'd protect from falling off the cliff. Given that there are two women on this day. She—I let go. In any case, die or live, she is the same—a survivor. Part of the sand and stones here. Part of the wild forest, the old bones. But you are the new life. Slowly the dragon turns into a man, the fire-breath still coiling around him.

And I am not quite the dragon woman.

There is only you. Do you understand that?

You smell of smoke. There are times cigarettes tell more than words. We tend to use words, however. Perhaps in the yin yang configuration words do not really fit. Come sit down here beside me and let's breathe together. The little baby is asking something—what is it? Are you really my father, are you he?

Am I? asked Dimitri hardly daring to breathe.

I will have to consult my calendar. Well, I have to admit, I have a preference for you. I have been lazy sexually myself and cooked up only one dish.

Yes, Catherine, sighed Dimitri. You too are free. We've discussed this.

Well! Perhaps you are right. Katrina is miserable. And perhaps she has never ceased to love you. I am not scorning it, but I hardly know how to proceed. Are there to be two wives?

I've told you—no. But you must understand, you are my dearest companion. I have nothing at all against you, no grudge, no failing. It was—when I am with you, I hardly know what it was—but it was an old, miserable side of me—the island side.

I love you. I can see where not everything has entirely changed. You went abroad, you fashioned yourself; but you left something behind, a root, a smell—something. You married someone who reminded you of life abroad....

Of life, said Dimitri a little sadly.

And this other—was the old thing.

My death.

Catherine looked into Dimitri's eyes intently and then softly caressed his hair and face. It's alright, she said, gently. Dimitri remembered Katrina's same words and shuddered a little.

No it isn't alright. It is unfair. And yet, if you could see it from my perspective, it is entirely fair. You are bound to a single man and I to a single woman in one way. Not in every way—it wouldn't be possible.

Strangely, I love you for this too. You are not so much a polygamist as an artist-lover who must break the rules and conventions. But what is your art?

Life. Of course, life.

Mine is love. This love. One gravitates towards an art eventually—don't you think? Although for me—it is relatively sooner—an oppressive thing; I've gotten older sooner although it hasn't hit in white hair and stoopedness.

You're the beautiful woman. You know that, Catherine. There isn't anyone who can hold a candle to you. But there is a part of me—rather ugly, simian in this case.

Yes; nevertheless—you have a very firm commitment to something different than the norm. I don't think it should be repressed. I realize it is not wanton adultery; there are times I feel that even murder can be justified if it fits into a human quadrant. Not as a welcome thing, never that; more as a fated intruder that left in the course of the incident, a mark of blood. Adultery too. It is sort of similar. I know and am profoundly sure that you would not want Katrina over me. She was destined to be part of your configuration. She has something to do even with your staying here on this island. I do not. As far as I am concerned in your life, we could be anywhere and may one day move away—Paris, London—isn't this true?

Yes, as always, you are right. You don't belong here and you know it, although you try to creep in sideways, as it were, loving people, helping them to fix their little old machines, wandering on the beach, breathing in your high cliff top roost. You are a loner and an alien. And I love you utterly; I too am a loner and an alien with one difference. I belong here in some hellish way—to the crude farmyard. As a greasy demon haunting this place where I must be by high decree of the angels and where it tortures me to be, I needed to copulate with Katrina, a hen. That is the long and short of it. I love her as a tortured demon loves the earth mother who bore him, her mouth on his member. I am a bit violent with her, a bit abusive—and the man in me says no to her constantly. She knows this. And precisely because it says no to her, I fall into her lap.

Catherine caressed his face again. You're still my husband if that is any consolation.

That is something my soul prefers. He kissed her hands as if she were a queen, brushing the tips of her fingers with his lips.

Catherine looked and saw—shrunken man, dark and bitter eyes. His voice was slightly harsh, steady—always as if a little angry.

She thought with gratification that she was, must be, free from certain chains. He would not be an ever there dandy proving to her muscle, intellect something that made him select; she would not ever make him so familiar that he seemed like a pet to be jealously guarded, or a piece of her flesh over which she had jurisdiction. No more like a wild animal that had its own territory, raw will, senses governing it and she would wake up each day with a little cry of joy to see it beside her but not begrudge it its straying. And deep down under without force, coercion, any kind of female rape, she would know that they were one —even if only for a flash; she perfectly understood him, she thought—but inarticulately, without words to this understanding. This understanding was a place in her, a crevice in her body in which she sat and looked out on the world—a refuge built for her alone no other woman would come near it.

Come, go if you must, she said as he curled up against her and put his head on to her breasts; I love you, you know that.

I love only you, he said hoarsely. There is love, love, and love—I defy all that with you. If only there were a different word. Something harsher, rawer—like the wind in winter. One doesn't want to use the same language all the time when people only think of sweet April, the roses, the adolescents who want straight off to sell their souls for sex with the beauty and to swoon forever holily, always holily. It's not that with us: You and I are like the two rocks under the cliffs that stick straight up, pointing their needle points into the blue. We've been there too long for it to be an escape. Something like geology brought us together, the earth crust shifting, breaking. Something metaphysical but not sentimental. Man, woman—a little like earth's crust and core. People who think it was the hilarity of a midnight party under the moon, see us whipped up together like egg white and sugar sold, as one single thing— only sweet! Arbitrary laws, cruel and pretty party laws. Yet we have separateness, blessedness. I mean by that merely a poor person… yet I know you, you me! Yet it is not necessarily so, no not necessarily so. But you would not want me were I not a follower of that which makes me genuine, tender, passionate and free.

I want you with every fibre—nerve, sick heart, weak lungs, electrical spine…said Catherine.

I am not a cheater, said Dimitri. I didn't play a low down trick, deceive you, become enamored clandestinely with some barmaid's bosom in the toilet. I said goodbye to a woman who belongs to my past, who rescued me; I had to end that past with hope and tenderness, sex, a little savagery.

I trust you on that.

But do you trust that it is not she? I brought her to bed almost forcibly to jolt her because she was wronging head, heart and all mankind—growing fat, dissipating muscle, mind, dressing with a corset, when damn it she had wanted me like a cannibal for years and years. You can see it—her asking me to marry her in a pathetic letter, the psychosis that followed my refusal. I have stepped out of one hole now. A hole that I found waiting for me when I came home.

There is a path here also, murmured Catherine; he was sitting beside her and she leaned towards him and her tone was grim but kind—one must be courageous. I have chosen that path.

What is that?

To be alive to a real man, or woman. I confess that I never told you of all my loves. The men went badly, but there was a woman….

Dimitri smiled at her, a little congratulatory smile.

I can see that we are not bound by the foolish intolerance of most of society. Catherine sometimes I think we are the only two, Adam and Eve, or perhaps two of the few that are chosen. There are no more Pharisaical laws, rule abiders, trapping life, killing it. We know who we are. We have the courage and the strength to be man and woman, Christ like alone, and sinless. We live before time.

And what do you think the child will say?

Nothing. He will solemnly whirl through the sand, spinning until he drops. He will begin a new creation, creating beasts, fish, fowl, trees, water, stones as babies do when they come upon them, naming them baby names, and christening them.

In my heart, I don't believe he is really ours. He is the winds', the sun's, the water's. Tell me, wouldn't you say the same?

Despite what Agatha called their wild babble, Catherine and Dimitri behaved like normal parents when the baby arrived. It was a relatively easy birth for a firstborn; Catherine was in labor for four hours and Dimitri anxiously walked up and down the whole time saying scream, scream let them hear you in London and New York, God almighty—Catherine! In the end, the sweat was rolling down both of them. Dimitri's eyes and mouth were three Os—as if he didn't expect a human being would emerge from between his wife's legs. Catherine was tired, sweat-dripping and happy.

I am ready for the second one, she said to Dimitri, kissing him.

You should make it a hobby, this bearing of human children, he said. For a while, the way you were carrying on, I thought some sort of monster, a gargantuan lizard with a long tail would emerge from there, he pointed to her crotch.

You haven't quite degenerated to that karma. As long as you are fully human you can bet that we will have human children.

The priest uninvited and of his own accord came to take a peek at the baby. Agatha told him first, and when the villagers saw Father Isaac sneak in with a smile all over his light-filled face and come out looking as if he had seen something utterly intoxicating, in they went, also uninvited, one by one—for certain secrets, said Simon, can't be kept even for a little while. And round about the village went the news and Michael ganged together with Simon and Max who was looking as if he was trying hard to understand, and they built a bonfire in the village square near the grocery store at Michael's instigation.

The fall sun again. The summer sun with its overflow of blaze, wrapping the island in a ball of brilliance with the blue sky shocking and the cliffs gleaming gray-blue, the water dark and full of fire stars had come and gone. Now the light was restrained, philosophical, old; the island was often wrapped in meditative clouds. Dimitri and Catherine walked regularly with the baby. Barbara had given them a pram; it was plenty big. They had had a little baby as opposed to Barbara's, way back when, her two robust eaters, heavy, with many flesh folds. The new baby often turned fastidiously away from the breast.

Agatha could usually get him to eat. She took out her old plastic bottles and boiled them, cooled them, and gave them to Catherine who drained her breasts into them. And while she and Dimitri walked out together and immersed themselves in the forest, by the sea, kissing one another in a tragicomic way—half as if it was for the last time, half as if this was only a glorious run through for an even more glorious eternal finale. Catherine said to Agatha it's as if his skin has passed on to me and mine on him. We've made this exchange so that we know one another thoroughly. So the baby would be for whole half days forgotten while in the forest and on the beach they became incorrigible lovers.

But in all villages there is someone who peeks in a window at an opportune moment for mischievous talk. Soon everyone was whispering about Dimitri's 'visit' to Katrina and looking with knowing disdain at Catherine and he. It was a relief to Zoe and Cleo who thought they might in the end have a real romance on their hands, produced on one side from Agatha's unblessed loins. There it was shocking them at every turn for how perfect it was—how purely one blended into the other, how utterly the bodies in one soft unison, like a kiss, gave way to joy.

All this is nonsense said Zoe to Cleo and Foti reassuringly. He is not faithful to her. This is just a kind of flirtation for him, and he, a father too! The way he carries on—and she doesn't have the nerve to stand up to him. This is not true love but an absolute farce. They got married in church—Catherine baptized expressly. But this is Agatha's son and no wonder.

It is called selling us a bunch of goods, said Cleo drily. A picture perfect romance with a hag's son! Ha, and in his spare time he is laying Katrina out on the bed—Katrina who once made the mistake…but anyhow has paid the price for her impetuousness; that was all youthful blood, understandable by anyone's standards. This is cleverness, a kind of jesting with holy sacraments like matrimony. Well, we are going to tell him that this jesting, this cleverness is simply not allowed, not here. The whole world may be jesting but here we are serious. My husband practically wore a chastity belt when he was alive. Never touched another. Then he wasted away with cancer—but an absolute treasure here, Cleo pointed to her heart. That is how one goes to heaven. No matter how old and tired we become, we cling to that promise.

Foti said, they say your husband was tired of living—said so; despised life at the end; she shuddered.

We all say things when we are in pain, said Cleo majestically.

The three ladies were sitting on Zoe's balcony around her little black iron table. Zoe was crocheting a pearl white sweater for the baby—it was mercy that made her do it. Actually, she had nothing to do and wanted an excuse for a visit back to

Agatha's as Catherine and Dimitri were living there now. Zoe wanted to poke and pry—to feast her eyes on the beauty of dark-haired, brown and grey Dimitri, earthy enough to leave the taste of salt on your tongue, and the gracefulness of Catherine, who walked around as if she contained all of heaven between her bosom and her back and would turn the screw on them a little, say a few sharp, penetrating things and leave them writhing inwardly. This outward beauty, she said to herself in her heart, would not conquer her. They were contemptible. Shallow, foolish, degraded as dogs. Smiling like simpletons all the time. She would point out and she would point out. In a subtle, sly way she would not exactly say… She was too smart for that. And the dig would be sharper; the win absolute. For she was seeking an absolute win. For they were not right; they were wrong. Especially the woman. For how can she walk around so peaceful and gentle, sometimes with a look of inward joy knowing that he had—oh, it was so disgusting. As if flesh was a kind of salami that people at a party took slices of, their fingers all dabbling in the tray. The only answer it seemed for Catherine then was a kind of slavery. How obnoxious and renouncing of all dignity. She was casting her pearls, every one of them, before swine.

But no matter how she put it to the others, growling, in whatever degraded light she chose to show them the truth, that truth always seemed to shine beautifully as this sunlight now. Why was that?

They are genuinely in love, said Cleo to the silent other two. In fact, the matter had been dropped for days but still everyone knew whom she was talking about. Foti moved about uneasily on her full-flanked bottom.

We are not arrogant people. We would bow to the passing stranger were he to demonstrate an accurate worship, a true holiness in Christ. Even now we simply stand back and wonder—what of it? Simon has wittily said something about the Mary and Joseph of the community…(He likes to be provocative and clever!) For this island was in fact drying up with old age and these two just out of the blue, such are the ways of God, came up with a child in their marriage, first thing. But it is not as if this child is the Savior, for heaven's sake. Although old Nisos came out of the house when the boy was born with his eyes gleaming looking as if he had been refreshed by mighty cool, pure water!

We have seen the child. Zoe was the first; she crept into the house one day at lunchtime, a few days after he was born and caught the baby feeding at the breast of his mother. He was a red, wrinkled little dumpling as all infants are but with a kind of grave expression on his face, as if he was just finishing serious business when he looked away from the breast. Catherine buttoned her shirt with the same grave look. Mother and child therefore had the same expression, exclaimed Foti. It changed when the baby went to sleep. Then, like all newborns he looked like perfection. Catherine all tender and rosy. Everything resolved, he looked because of that sweet breast milk.

Zoe wanted to say something like—what a little cub, so precious! But on second look this looked so different—intellectual somehow. Zoe had forgotten that aspect of birth. She remembered the rosiness of mothers and the perfection of infants but she had forgotten this aloof sphere of the mind in the face of babies. She bent over the cradle and the baby, like a little sun smelling of milk, beamed back in his sleep. What is his name?

Tock, said Catherine, for the clock. Zoe was properly shocked and indignant. Tock! That isn't a name! It is just a sound.

All names, all words, are sounds, said Catherine. I wanted a name that suggested that yes we had lived—another minute—and chances are we will live one more minute. And to me it seems to mark the very beat of life in us.

Couldn't you --baptized and all now-- have named him for one of our saints? There is even Joachim, said Zoe, she had not herself had children but was ever ready with various unique sounding Scriptural names to distinguish a baby just in case.

I simply did not want to name him after someone. I was thinking more along the lines of River or Eagle. Then I decided why a name with meaning? Why not a word that sounds like?

I have never heard of a baby boy named for a sound. How very base, said Zoe, however more to herself and us than to Catherine. Imagine, she said to us later, if she had named him 'quack'.

Or quark, said Foti, sympathetically.

That is a scientific word, snapped Zoe—it means some sort of thing in matter that is very very small.

It sounds like an odd kind of noise, said Foti, defensively.

But in any case, can't you see what they have done? Exclaimed Zoe. They have gone and ruined the institution of marriage and family as it stands in the tradition of the elect. For one thing she stands by and lets him mix himself up in various love affairs—I always knew Katrina to be at bottom a shameless hussy, old as his mother, loose and provoking men, but he, you know, is the instigator! She stands by as I've said without a murmur of protest. On the contrary, as serious as ever, joyful, tender, rosy—as if she has found the very gem of love with him and now this baby with the preposterous name. As if Tick Tock will get him to heaven instead of a name honoring a saint.

Oh you never know, said Foti, a little unwisely. It may be that the boy will bloom like a rose in the desert here.

Cleo rose grandly and furiously. You all know perfectly well that this is a purposeful provocation. And the point is this: Say we go to the priest, the head of us all, and say to him Father such and such: Look at this time bomb that will explode on our island and cause it to disintegrate such that we are never holy again. We lose all thought of our obligations, our respect not only for marriage, but for the very Holy Ghost who threads into the true marriage our own souls at the end of the world—the marriage between God and man! What will he say?

I will tell you: He will say—I see nothing. There is nothing there. And that is how all true revolutions start—with the idea in the world that there is nothing to be concerned about.

We were sitting on Zoe's balcony at the little iron table with our crocheting. Zoe had delivered the baby sweater—for which they hadn't even been properly grateful, gypsies never are! Foti made her little iron chair creak by sitting forward and sitting back in consternation as Cleo spoke. Zoe was nervously fingering a glass of apricot brandy. She had taken to drinking a glass around eleven o' clock in the morning to relax and stimulate. She had taken off her glasses and her eyes looked a little smaller and you could see they were watery. She always said that she was getting old at the edges, fraying like a piece of cloth, and fading a little, getting thinner but she was still whole. The doctor had told her yet again that she was likely to last a century. She was dressed in grey, conservative grey—and she had taste and style, making all her skirts with a little flair for design. Her blouses were the expensive kind, imported from Athens, scented and very fine. On top she had a heavy wool jacket that kept out the sea chill. To Cleo she was obviously proper, and possibly the last truly proper woman in the Christian sense: demure feminine dress, with a hint of the grace of being a woman—caught in a woman's body, she had once said mysteriously to Cleo. Cleo looked at her now with admiration. She held intact in her figure, the very stuff of the island.

And she said, said Zoe, at last, as if sensing Cleo's thoughts, that we were simply rule abiders. That we have no heart.

Who said asked Foti, who was falling asleep. She had on a heavy grey wool jumper, wool turtleneck and socks and a fur-lined black jacket.

Catherine, said Cleo. I always thought it was a mistake to let her family come.

But it isn't her, said Zoe, warmly. She is poor, deluded—like Katrina, the rest of them whomever they might be. You know it is him—the serpent. The adultery and the way he cozens his wife about it, all this is just a sign of end times; you see the true nature can be either good or evil. Often evil comes under the guise of someone frank and sweet. And now evil in the guise of good in a woman's house! Auntie Zoe, he calls me. Others it is true want to just ignore things, let them go by. I am not one to stir up the waters but this is a question of our dear island. And I am not too old to stand up before everyone and say—this is what we stand for.

We are not viable in the world? Who cares for the world! Do we not in the spirit of our God seek to overcome it?

Foti was confused. Was not the conversation about Catherine and the baby, rosy and sweet smelling like all mothers and infants just a minute ago? And now to overcome the world where apparently these two were somehow discarded. Suddenly her mind skipped to another thought: She was not sure she wanted to give up the world. She looked in the mirror and she was still live Foti with curls and a dimple on her chin. She had joined Zoe and Cleo because they were strong ladies, of a long-standing tradition on the island as her mother had been. But that island had been a rather jolly place and little picturesque scenes of a mother strolling out with her newborn in a pram were things treated a little like angels descended...All that had been right and proper and it was never possible for anything to be other than heavenly. Now suddenly for certain reasons, which she agreed were deplorable!—but nonetheless... could they look at the mother and child in any other way? Here on Holy Island where God had willed that the rest of them should wither and dry up and not produce offspring? A rose had bloomed. And with it the island. To simply choose the way of drying and withering because there were some discrepancies in their family—secretly to herself she called Dimitri, Catherine and Tock 'our family.' And could it be that the rose of them was evil?

Foti got up from the table and went into the kitchen to drink some cool lemonade. She was sweating with all her woolen things on. She stayed in a nook by the refrigerator, in a corner looking into the middle of the kitchen, which was suffused by afternoon light; she stared at the table and chairs where the light seemed to gather and let her mind go. More and more she felt that her mind was very constrained, stiff, almost unusable in company. She felt that she sat there like a large doll. And she knew they said it behind her back—that she was less than able mentally speaking. But she had another capacity, a deeper one, she thought. She could see things like light gathering, call things by the right names like 'our family.' And at some point in time she would collect all these bits and pieces of reflection and exert herself a little and see—the work of her lifetime—the vision of the center, the meaning.

To Dimitri she had had antipathy—he was a handsome man, perhaps thought himself better than the usual on that account. What would he do, being so clever and smart, but come here and make a baby. Ha, ha, laugh in their faces. She thought that sometimes about Dimitri. But there were other times when she saw them walking together, frail, sweet, slightly arrogant—one couldn't help but adopt them. All the life was in them—in their young limbs, their eyes of knowledge. And there was a little tendency to adore them.

Our Foti has a little crush on Catherine and Dimitri. That is what they would say. Appearances make all the difference sometimes. But Foti was convinced that she was seeing into. That she had begun her seeing into with Catherine and Dimitri. What she saw down deep inside them was a solid door running from her to him and it was firmly shut. This vision made her feel weak. She felt that her flesh was disintegrating in fact. Her mind was getting stupider. On the one hand she revolted against the world of Dimitri/Catherine; they had taken, just taken whatever they wanted. All the impoverished folk ran about aimlessly, missing their world—for some reason Foti saw Aunt Zoe in her underwear—everything cotton and huge and Zoe in them billowing in the wind… On the other hand, she thought this is the one, undeniable way—perhaps it is spiritual to just take people's worlds. And she made with her inner intellect a great leap to think that.

Therefore she set up a difference between herself and Zoe and Cleo. They were unyielding and, she knew, very angry. It was useless to say to them—we were drying up, disintegrating, rotting away and they brought us a baby. A baby! Ah but, they would begin—they are unconventional—what is this—Dimitri goes and has a love affair with another woman and the pots and pans don't go flying in the kitchen; the woman (they called Catherine that) humbly, gently accepts, walks out with him as if he is worthy of her! Then she names her child a humbug of a name. They would squint at them, even spit a little after seeing them as if coughing up phlegm caught in their throats. About the other woman we are not so surprised. A poor creature—sex even rough sex is her one consolation. This island you see—our very own island is degenerating terribly; and yet we have tried. And they come along—he and the woman and mock and mock. There is no letting up from this suffering.

God said to Ezekiel prophesy to these bones. Prophesy to these bones and say to them: "Oh dry bones hear the word of the Lord. Thus says the Lord God to these bones. Surely I shall cause breath to enter into you and you shall live. I will put sinews on you and bring flesh upon you, cover you with skin and put breath in you and you shall live. Then you shall know that I am the Lord." And the bones were knit together with flesh. These are our ancestors' bones settled, floating at the bottom of the sea. And the Dimitris and Catherines like phantoms, shadows of death drifting by.

But they are so full of life, and we--, said Foti, objecting, to her own thought.

Deceivers always are, said Zoe. When Christ was tempted in the desert, when the devil goaded him to make stones into bread—do you think he showed him sand? No, no, feasts with meat dripping sauces, he could smell the herbs and oil, see the reddish stuffed tomatoes just out of the oven. All through his ministry he tempted him with a fine life—silk clothes, colorful wool caps—What is wrong with wool caps? Asked Foti

Of course, nothing, said Zoe. But that is the point. To distinguish, to discern—a simple yearning for a red wool cap and the succumbing to a fine life.

We have always been simple. We are the dry bones. But we would have succumbed. Just think that Cleo was about to take the offer in the end of a million for her house and go off to Paris. Then she would have been as an idea that melts away to nothing. Not bones to be covered with flesh.

That is different. Cleo is not the son of God and today in this day and age we have to make these little bargains with the world. Besides, what would Cleo have done in the end? We all know Cleo: bought maybe one expensive perfume, eaten once or twice in a restaurant that serves wine out of the price range of this village; but you know well how it is with Cleo. Once she had just sampled the goods, then away she would go to live a quiet simple life. How can you find fault with that? And the million—well you know, expenses here and there. In the world today it is not counted so much.

And we who live a relatively simple life—what happens? Asked Cleo rhetorically. For all our toil we are brought to shame: we are mocked, we begin to rot; the island is corrupted by a baby.

But I wouldn't put it quite like that, commented Foti, hesitantly, although she saw that the light, that was not of course the light around, but the light which gave light to the light could be taken by them.

Zoe said: No it is not the baby. Tick Tock Tick Tock we are that baby—the heart in us. I just don't like the idea the parents had—when they could have been more transcendent in the island tradition to reduce us, metaphorically, to batteries wearing out.

She paused; it is all a kind of joke that Dimitri is smiling at—behind the scenes you know. Don't you see Katrina, Catherine. The dark and light? Both on and on about machines. And bones are not machines.

But she didn't mean…Catherine fixes them, murmured Foti, disjointedly. She fixed my toaster oven; but Katrina—what does she know about machines?

She insists that we are just like machines—that the universe is a great machine.

Foti: But Dimitri's smile is not a joking smile at all. Granted he smiles, but it seems to be because he is thinking of something beautiful. Perhaps not bones, but…

What can be beautiful in this situation?

Why his wife, Zoe, said Cleo and his little baby—that much is true.

No, I think you are wrong there, said Foti. I think it is something for himself and the world. Something like, what can I say—manhood!

What do you mean 'manhood?' All our men are men.

No, no I didn't mean the being masculine. A woman might have in the end manhood too. I meant living by the truth, exclaimed Foti. Living by the beginning when we were men. You see, Catherine loves it in him, and bears it.

She certainly does. And all you are doing is justifying polygamy.

No, no. Why is he here and not in London? You see? It was the ability to give up, to yield, to return to the soul. It is all tenderness, strength, intelligence. Mark my words the hotel will be built, the electricity will come back on, our pensions will be secured.

He has little ability, said Zoe with contempt.

But it seems to me, said Cleo, thoughtfully, that all of us here, even the family are twisting and turning like blind men caught in a trap—that when we finally see straight…oh what is the use? I only blame him for saying one thing and then another to us like he did to his wife.

They say, said Zoe with a dark frown that he told her about his unfaithful streak all beforehand.

No, said Cleo peremptorily; that is an attempt to make a justification out of a lie. A marriage is a holy union of two souls—there is no place for a third even should one party rationalize it that way. You see a lie isn't in the telling at all. It is in the being. The double being. It requires a shift; an uprooting. The old man must die—the liar—the one who permits doubleness— must be exterminated.

Foti came away half drunk on Zoe's apricot brandy thinking the old women and the violent old men to be one and the same. They had the same gristle and the same cold sneer. She had become a little afraid, terrorized for some reason although she had drunk the brandy and eaten their candy as if she were one of them. Hadn't Cleo said the soul is two and meant her and Zoe? Wasn't she, the third, a kind of adultery or granted, since it was not a sexual thing, blasphemy at the very least? Wasn't it true then that where there were three, there was even worse evil, division and strife? Tripling. But what did that make of the Dimitri, Catherine and Tock, all parents and children, the Holy Trinity? Perhaps it was Cleo who was philosophical. And Cleo who knew that all their problems arose because not everyone was divided up into twos.

The priest was worried about Max. The boy was too innocent and he thought rather foolish. He did not rebel against the teaching of the Gospel by so many stories of heaven. And he threw tantrums about all sorts of irrelevant things. The priest of course handing out the prescribed day of activities and lessons from the Church had secretly hoped that Max would respond in a more deconstructive manner---picking apart this nonsense until the bones of it flew in his face and all over the floor of their chambers. The whole portrait that the Church painted of Jesus Christ was silly. And most people suspected this. Imagine if the Lord had behaved as some of the Church fathers and gone off to sit in a cave and eat bread and write these obnoxious treatises on whether holy love belonged to the heart or the head! What would the Lord have been then but a withered nut cursed by God and man? But Max instead of applying his intelligence and his youth, his very ripeness to the question he faced every day, sailed off on that flimsy vessel of fantasy—put all his treasure into these dreams.

And the priest, besotted, kissed his adopted son's hands when he came home in the evening, sat him down in his chair lovingly, made the sweet infusions, and looked in awe at the bright and beautiful cloud of rapture that was Max. When Max woke up from his dreams and looked around him, then the crankiness would start and the arguments—the priest-father hadn't given him this or that proper to the holy life—he was degraded, corrupt—why should anyone listen to him? And the priest like a holy love slave to this seed that would bloom for Jesus held the door open, but beseeched him not to go. Max would complain of a trap. Perhaps it was so. Other people were saying the same thing. It used to be that the island was a refuge; now it was a trap.

The priest began to think to himself that even the obligatory monastic prayers were a trap. One couldn't help the tendency: to slide into quick repetitions with the mouth, and the thought that one has gotten that necessity of connecting with God 'over with'. Where was the voice coming from the wilderness—that cry like a knife, like a serrated knife that could saw through the bone of death between the divine and man? For that one had to put the soul into what? Sand and stone? High birds, animals, prowlers and leapers? No—into misery, human misery. There was no more sin now. There was only the wound—the eyes falling out, the teeth crushed to powder, the screams, the agony, the severed limbs—and there was death corpses, crushed and horrible; there were the sick sitting in silence, tortured. And there were the desperate, the torn, the starved, the dying. There were the lonely and those without hope. From here one prayed. From here. Jesus was in the thick of it—eyeless, tongueless, having lost all limbs- a mangled cube of meat. Thus he was in heaven. Even the single cry of help uttered with all one's humanness was a better prayer than repeating the psalms. This island, Holy Island, was built on the notion, floating far away from the world, that somehow those who beheld the Lord's face were superior to a child that has lost its eyes. Yes, a Muslim, Hindu, Buddhist, African child! This was Holy Island –a place where people thought themselves in Christ for repeating prayers, for baptisms, for weddings in Churches, for sacraments. A people who still believed themselves to be the chosen few, provided they could get back to shining whitely with holy light. Ah they had to see it—like the novice had seen St. Seraphim—the uncreated blaze in the very face of flesh! But the light God sees is not that. He would see in that muted love-brown child's face more glory…and in the woman who loved him, broken hearted more too. For God didn't work by signs and miracles but by love and truth. Why, then, wasn't he at every train wreck picking up dismembered limbs, holding the heads of the dying? Or at least with the poor and the sick? He who knew the truth!

The prophets that ate nothing, and lived in the sand—who are they? Romantic images? Brain soothers. The far away who fasted, went mad. Heaven is far closer. To be where the suffering is. That alone is heaven. Empty the churches—to hell with sins. Come back only to love. Leave all else behind.

This rang in his ears as he performed the Liturgy. He felt it was almost unnecessary to invoke the Holy Spirit. Eat and drink Christ by action not lullabies, and only by the violent and also sweet beyond anything imaginable, the erotic offering blood and body, wine and bread. The softness on Holy Island was human decay and not God. It was the sickly perfume of erotic absence. There were times he would almost have preferred the stench of corpses, of rotting flesh that makes one vomit by merely inhaling it, to the 'holy' smell of frankincense. At least in the one a body mingled with the pneuma—the poor person suddenly sucked dry of living, mingled his remains with breath and the sorrow perhaps a kind of holy nausea, the bitterness of the belly that the saint in Revelation experienced after eating the book! At least, the gut, the viscera! In the other—what a laughable artifice! Those things never go to God. Eat and drink—this is what it meant: the sweet taste of work, good work—the pages of the rule book that gave way to void—bitterness at the shiftiness, greed and hypocrisy that had divided and killed man's spirit.

Feeding them His body and blood, His sweat, tears, bile, nausea, blood, gore—the Savior Jesus Christ fed the apostles a life of sweat and death for the flock. That is what this eating is. Not justice, not righteousness in the sense of the rule book—but erotic sweetness, mad falling in love with the bitterness of viscera turned ineffably sweet. 'Compel them with violence to come to the wedding banquet!'—this eating and drinking was the violence referred to—a rapture, where one is wrenched away from the hunger of life.

Yet if you do it right you see the beauty and greatness of a poor human, crumpled like a dried leaf in the agony of poverty, illness, shame, pain or dying. So many on Holy Island didn't understand; the priest knew Christ would pass over them sternly, but he felt a pang of pity at the lost in delusions about God. Not that he himself understood all the ways of God, nor His thoughts. But there was certainly a closeness, a reality that God wanted that the poor and suffering have. And there was nothing else to do. Ring the bells for prayers and then get back to work—feeding, succoring the sick, clothing the naked, sheltering the homeless. Of course, they would laugh at him had he proposed such a thing. Why they were a handful—none was poor excepting Martha—and she had his house, and was fed by one and all. Could they not go to Christ Jesus on His high throne of Judgment and say to Him: Where were the poor that were hungry? And He: Over there, equivalent to here. You did not remember me eating my tears in my belly day in and day out.

They had no thought that they might have to travel across the waters to minister to the wounded side of Christ. They had no thought of rekindling the ancient fire of God—passion for healing and bringing joy to the desperate. The one fire they stuck to was the fire of the apricot brandy that was sweet and burned in the gullet—a substitute for that living passion of the Most High.

Now that brought them a belly full—contentment, and easy conscience. Damn.

He ejaculated this last just as he was rattling off the blessing before Holy Communion. He thought let them swallow a little hellfire this Sunday morning without pity. He looked at their faces, ignorant, foolish; what? They would say; we have only our little houses, our fishing salaries. We are little, unimportant, gathering around our families. Stiff and dried Zoe and Cleo looked on with attention and disdain. They hated him. And then there was Agatha, the only one, the one who covered Martha with kisses and went and cleaned Leo's house, who listened to Maria—who would, he thought, go away, one day and dance with poor children bringing them joy. And she, they hated. Paul standing stiff as a ramrod with Little Paul who put great store by the Holy Eucharist—miracle of miracles Paul told the story of his sick grandmother who would not eat and was starving to death—how she could only swallow the

Eucharist! Swallowed it at last through the gentle intercession of Jesus. Ah, perhaps, who knows? But the branch of the old tree had withered. What was left of Paul the priest knew to be cruel and hard.

After swallowing stories of miracles down one after another as a monk in the monastery through the teachings and readings until he was up to his gills in miracles, the priest decided suddenly not to believe much in them except for healing. Signs, perfumes, stigmata, which blessedly they never had any of on the island, he thought was all for the dogs. Living poor and sacrificing your two cents—the entirety of what you had—that was worth ten thousand miracles. This was living in Jesus. Nothing else. What were they clutching? Diamonds, some of them, blue stone—the old blue-schist of the island, some of them still had—fragments wrapped in tissue, especially Simon who had a little wisdom still in his addled old head.

They still came to him: Zoe and Cleo and Foti, Nisos and Timos and Paul and they looked a little helpless at times; sometimes they stared vacuously like dead fish. He wanted to say to them: Do you know what God would say: Give your gift and shut up. That's all. What Jesus called making interest on your talent. He doesn't want your tears or your shallow bickering. He doesn't feel sorry for you in the least. Spring into gear. Go to the other island and kiss the gypsy children. Sell your houses and give them the money; they don't even have laundry soap, soft mattresses.

Max had the chalice in hand and gazed at the congregation with his dreamy, abstract look. It was all nonsense of course—heaven wasn't all those golden angels and purple clouds that Max was seeing in his mind's eye, his imagination on fire! But the fact remained that the boy looked himself solemn and beautiful, austere, perfect. Dimitri saw it and Father Isaac saw out of the corner of his eye how he trotted over lovingly and bent his knees a little before Max and opened his mouth for the teaspoon of blood.

Suddenly Father Isaac saw Max, as he slipped the teaspoon between Dimitri's red lips, lovely as never before. No, it was not beauty; not the eyes and mouth, the hair. But he saw the etching of the human—like you could see in anybody, he supposed. But it was what the Lord was talking about when he said –sheep. Sheep have that face on them, an etched one-face. And Max had the face then, not the jewel of eyes and expression that he had sometimes in the sunlight or in sleep but a face not put there by his own will or genes at all. The face tender, beautiful, knowing, sweet—a face of knowledge put there by God. Where does this come from? Wondered Father Isaac. Suddenly, for the next communicant, the old Max precipitated out of this wonder suspended somewhere between earth and heaven. And the old grind continued— servant of God, so and so receives the Body and Blood of our Savior.

Periodically, thought the old priest after, sitting in his wicker chair by the window, Max washing lunch dishes in the corner and rattling annoyingly, we see something— revealed to us, unfolded from the bosom of the air. Of course, one might pass it over, one might pass any number of things over that are not part of the science in one that belong to what we term holy—or proofs of God: it happened so fast…still, for once I saw Max humanized—Max who has gone around with his head in the heavenly clouds, thrown temper tantrums, crouched in anguish, called secretly on his dead mother with candles and lamb's blood. He read somewhere in the classics that ghosts have to drink blood to talk…Max thrown from one thing to another—from living poor for Jesus, to whining in my ear about his fears, to secret rituals.

Strange boy! Should be a man now but isn't quite. Fastidious, virginal, sharp intellect but blighted. Can't quite manage life. Rosebud, I call him sometimes. It doesn't seem to bother him. But he has other accusations—no end of them. I think to size it all up the accusations amount to one thing: I haven't protected him. In other words, I haven't given him enough knowledge about the world. This is what he wants—why he tried to leave me.

And it is true—on this foolish island with all its old traditions—fishing, hoarding, making the sign of the cross—I have squirreled this man-boy away. I have been grateful for the little plenty, the lack of misery although I know that one of these days I too must come out of my nook and give and join the ranks of the poor christs, the ones with faces 'beaten' with misery and pain. Otherwise no. I am no priest of Jesus Christ. But I have held back too for Max's sake. He is like a rare species that finds refuge in few places in this world, this being one. But I haven't given him knowledge of himself. On that day, the joy, the innocence, even the hope might be destroyed.

I have been entrapping him. Purposefully—catching him up in a cloud of ideas— the trumpets of the archangels, the burning bush, Jesus walking on water, and we noted time and again how in our stupendous fresco behind the church altar, the Lord has his heel high up behind him, almost kicking himself in the behind and his hands raised as if for balance. How often we noted this. And puzzled and puzzled about the face that has decayed away a little—is that a smile? A gape? Laughter? What? Strange expression and yet undoubtedly Jesus Christ with the elements around—for in the painting the clouds are low and grey, the waves one would say growing higher.

Do you ever think of it, Max? asked the priest, with tenderness in his voice. Max stopped washing dishes.

What are you talking about?

That Jesus is dancing on the water in that fresco. He is letting it all out. His spirit, his soul! One needs only the women to clap for him.

Oh you would think of nothings as if they were important.

But the painter must have seen something in his mind's eye quite clearly—that is, something true. You know the Gospel is written in a very sparse way. Walking that is rhythmic, flexible, light, almost flying would be the way one walks on water, and the wild joy of Creator in the midst of His Creation—Jesus felt that— stepped that, danced, He must have!

Those things are all tales—you told me so. All the gladness happens in heaven. We are to remind people. They are to live the gospel to get to heaven.

Ah if they did—on earth as it is in heaven.

We are poor.

Hardly—we live simply. But we hoard and we gripe. No bring the gypsy children from the next island over here and clothe and feed them and teach them to dance. Don't preach a word. Don't ruin their raw young health feeding them those insipid, saccharine, or violent artifices the Church calls Jesus. Feed them Jesus-dancing in the Eucharist—the fit of giving a little more goat's meat with abundant tomatoes and oil, the soft soft blanket to the cold gypsy girl going cold yourself for it evermore. Yes, that is the meaning of that fresco.

You have preposterous notions.

But the human being as created by God, listen very carefully, Max, is not just a product of food, clothing and shelter. A human being is also gladness and wild joy— also dancing and singing for divine reasons. One walks on water because one is the dance, one is the song. Dancing and singing is walking on water.

Max put his fingers on his mouth and smiled. I wouldn't be surprised if you started dancing and singing in the streets, he said, following me, and, in the background as I preach, dancing and singing. It would be like you.

The priest smiled and relapsed into thought. Max was used to these long hours of silence, longer even than the island silences that happened between people old and young in their homes as they sat together. Max would watch the priest, and sometimes Martha too, creeping in and kneeling and swaying back and forth humming; he was white in the sunlight, both diaphanous and earthy; he thought there was something perfect about being with the old man even in all the confusion and intellectual riot that passed from his lips. All the thoughts of our Savior so strange and wild. And there was a strain in Dimitri's house, he had once told him when they had talked—what was it—two months ago?—Dimitri had stopped him in the street with a warm smile, and engaged him—after the preaching and Max had listened and invited him to Liturgy—and Dimitri had said there was a peculiarity of his mother about Jesus. She had her own mind on him. But she did call him Lord and knew he was coming. And it seemed after that that Max had pieced together Father Isaac's mad sayings too. Something in the air on Holy Island about the Lord. Strange three visitors maybe—Agatha and Dimitri and who, Father Isaac himself? Leo?-- the commentary she invariably left behind among folks—she was a visitor the way she was different-- and this priest bringing slightly discordant calling—even to her, to the dark 'thought' of Agatha—left with the others, and Dimitri who had stirred them.

Father Isaac was thinking: But he in reality—he was a traitor. Wasn't he as a priest singled out to administer the Word made flesh to people? Shouldn't he say go out and work your asses off in the gypsy encampment on the other island. Don't stay here puttering around your homes. Don't take communion. Eat and drink the Lord by working, working, working and not for gain but for the alleviation of pain and despair. I could have said that. Instead of telling them to think of their sins, their angry moments. That is not reality. Deny self. And what I tell them only brings them back to their apricot brandy—savoring, stewing. All of them are drunkards, gluttons. Drunkards even if they don't drink the brandy—Paul doesn't drink—on their self-righteousness, which they savor and stew in, fat tongues lolling in their mouths in the stew.

Max thought: I see him dancing and singing—a beggar who has suddenly gone mad—alongside of Agatha who has made a profession out of madness. A long time ago, they say, she was raped. For twenty years she nursed the wound—married, gave birth and raised children mechanically. Dimitri thought she didn't have a heart until he found out. And then she gave birth again, loved her children, found out they were handsome, especially Dimitri-- this time something inside her was born—mother then woman…A dream it was, and Simon who found her in the throes…Her loins woke up once more. She started to practice the dance, the man-dance; her body became a medium for the pain and the sweetness—the vision of beauty in Dimitri. She was content to be a rough blundering girl melting away like snow into beauty that began with him—the rape. She had gone through it so many times after, and now she was content to go through it—for now it was eternal beauty. It is in Agatha's loins that I, oh I—

Dimitri told me without my having said anything—I agree, she is mad but I won't tamper with it. And wouldn't it be better in the end, even for the Church, for us all to be cartwheeling and singing and giving meals to Martha, cleaning Leo's house when he lived in such a depression, reconciled and loving than to be sore with one another and taking the sacrament? Or, sleeping with Anna out of courtesy of comfort and kindness? She has never once forgotten to bathe Martha, to slip sips of rich goat's milk into her mouth, wiping it after, to rub perfume on Anna's naked breasts.

What was the sequence--how does it go from misery to joy?

Perhaps the answer was as the priest said—the other island. One could work for the poor, build a nation for the gypsies. Here for sure there is nothing.

Max got up quietly and tiptoed to the door and went out, shutting it softly behind him. He wanted to take a long walk and rid his head of all this talk—Father Isaac's, Dimitri's. How often he had thought his own tale of woe was enough. And here the news poured in through the cracks of this perfect little egg in which he lived with the priest. Ah those cracks—hadn't he made them—pecking away at the shell the priest had erected around him to be born himself? For the priest didn't say anything of consequence to anybody, though Max sensed that he thought and thought. But what was the use of this thought? One didn't become anything by it—not man, nor beast, nor angel. Not conscious, nor free, nor glorious.

He walked down the hill dreaming, slightly rebellious, and yet at heart the most ardent believer. He was so lost in thought that he didn't see his surroundings, nor really note where he was going. He walked by the sea that lay before him like a flat grey dish in his consciousness, although it was really opaque, dark bluish with waves. The sea! The whole meaning in it—but that he would put aside for another time. Instinctively he turned to the forest that stood in the young afternoon like a golden lamp in the midst of pine leaves and grey branches—a redundancy this lamp—but there were two or three--the sun made them, lit them with fire—here and there, the surface of the sea, the snow when it snowed, in between the leaves of the trees.

Max too was lit; he himself was vaguely aware, he too was a lamp. Lamps draw beings to themselves—they emerge from the forest, sometimes slightly suspiciously, but drawn inexorably like moths in the night drawn to light. They cast their bodies against light bulbs, fluttering to escape against lamp shades, diving ecstatically into the well of light. And they fly around and around periodically hurling themselves at the light. Max half wanted to be an opener of the eyes of the blind. He thought himself ensconced in the light like the Buddha in the lotus. There were times he thought himself similar to Christ resurrected. Of course, he was not physically glorified, but his heart and mind floated in heaven while his body was on earth. He didn't despise the body; no, Father Isaac had made sure to teach him against that trend in Orthodoxy. He had that ease about himself physically that comes from innocence, manhood formed under the tenderest eye of a father. He had no suspicions and other than fear of his father, his heart was sweet as honey towards the world around. The cringing he had almost conquered. And he was standing at the brink of love, profound love, as if he was at the brink of a great sea. This love was for the world, for mankind, for the earth; it was the kind of love God has—innocent, lost in its own fulsome sweetness, and extreme; it was the very substance of God. Max in fact felt that he was 'lost' in the contemplation of God.

When the old priest admired him, Max turned away in secret disgust. This sort of old man's love he believed to be an inferior trait. There was nothing at all deep and thoughtful, careful or meaningful in it. And it led to a lot of useless babble. People didn't know Father Isaac. They thought of him as a repository of wise sayings. In reality, how much waste of talk on different subjects—the curtains hanging to keep out the sun, the sweetness of the infusion, the sagging of the bed, the need to keep up intake of oranges and lemons…It seemed that all this verbiage lay cluttering the room he shared with the priest. There were times he had to escape, sink into his profound heart far away.

He came to a halt under a pine tree in the forest and put out his hand and leaned against its trunk. Trees had a beautiful feeling about them—they were old sages knowing all about the business of living. The priest and he had discussed how the tree of life in the Garden of Eden, banned to Adam and Eve after their sin, was in fact the cross glorified; then one day the Christ would hang upon it. This fruit this meat of God was permitted; it was essential now to eat it. And it was the strait gate to Resurrection—this eating.

The flavor was described in the Beatitudes: blessed are the poor in spirit for theirs is the kingdom of heaven. Tears, brokenness, dust. Then again blessed are the pure in heart for they shall see God. Psychic tenderness, soreness, lack of all antagonism, bitterness only towards one's own faults, this is purity. Blessed are the peacemakers for they shall be called sons of God. The taste of smoothed out life—clarity, forgiveness. All of this described the savor of that fruit of the tree of life. But each piece is in the context of the whole. For the Beatitudes is one person.

The priest said the whole purpose of the Christian endeavor was to eat that fruit. But all meditations come to an end and shifting his gaze, Max suspended his a moment just to gaze at the sun coming through the bare trees and the pines and he became aware of another figure standing a little way away leaning with his hand against another tree gazing at him.

Dimitri had come for a walk to clear his head of baby. Baby had taken over everything. One ate and drank baby and slept baby. Catherine was catering endlessly to baby. Her voice had become different; herself had changed as well. He felt a little out of place since he couldn't keep pace with her baby talk and new outlook of baby. Not that they didn't have their moments together. But these also were clouded by baby. Catherine wasn't comfortable leaving Tock even with Agatha for long periods. She really was now a devoted mother-- that is enslaved to things like baby socks, baby bibs. He felt her horizon had changed: Where it had once clearly been him, it was now Tock and vaguely in the background him. He was a now and then remembered reference. It was as if he was not considered even the author of this baby anymore! The baby was 'larger' than he now, in the sense of life's perspective; and somewhat magical. Its little wholeness was its own—that is, perhaps, it had another origin. Catherine called it God. And now Dimitri at loggerheads with God went into the woods to lose himself and find himself—what he was or what he never was but is, somehow—hiding in some self or other.

Half angry not knowing what to do, he had leaned against a tree and then looked up and saw a sight that made him smile with sudden joy. Max startlingly brilliant in his manhood like a flame.

Dimitri smiled. Max saw him and approached; he stopped in front of him, trembling and looked at him with a darkness in his eyes that seemed to announce that he had something vital to tell him. Dimitri laughed slightly, nervously. They began to talk in short bursts, having no idea what they were saying. It seemed to Max that Dimitri was hilarious somehow, about what he didn't know. He himself said little and it was as if he was dreaming. Then in the midst of a golden fire, Dimitri put his lips on Max's lips and Max pressed his mouth against his, welcoming the tongue that slipped in.

Max after found that he was in a cave, the cave that led to the subterranean lake that fed the island with water. He was naked, and Dimitri was covering him with his coat. They lay together and the down on Dimitri's chest brought such delight to Max. But Max was like a little child and clung to Dimitri. He had brought everything—the uttermost, the overwhelming, absolute delight.

I didn't know, he whispered to Dimitri. And I didn't think you... And yet I knew, and I did think.

It was brewing in us, responded Dimitri. He leaned over and kissed Max again, five, ten times. And it was the sweetest thing I have ever experienced.

It is who I am. You that is, inside me. And if people hate that they hate me.

Yes, said Dimitri, rising and putting on his clothes, people hate that so much they are willing to put to death you and me in some countries for doing it.

How far I had come, you know, down a false, false path.

Which path was that—the path of the Church? Of God?

No, it wasn't. It was all a false Jesus. I thought righteousness was only rules—instead of real self, and love—knowing in your heart who you are so you can love. I was a nonentity.

And I am a nonentity now, said Dimitri.

You won't go will you? Said Max, fearfully.

This was not meant to be, said Dimitri to him, tenderly. It was a dream in the forest.

Max put on his clothes quickly. He was shivering. He turned around just in time to see a shadow move away.

He ran up and grabbed Dimitri by the arm as he was turning away. There did you see? Someone saw! Someone saw us!

There was a slight hitch in his voice as Dimitri put his arm around Max and said it is nothing. What does anyone know? We will simply stay away from one another and go about our usual business.

But said Max faintly, he wondered later if Dimitri heard—I love you.

Come, said Dimitri, calling; the story is that we met one another in the forest and talked and walked together.

When Dimitri got home to his mother's house, Catherine was putting the baby to bed. She had a look of relief on her worn face. Dimitri kissed her abstracted in thought. There is something, Catherine said to him—isn't there?

Humans are mysterious and unfathomable. Their beauty catches you unawares, unprepared. Is there no religion that celebrates the depths of man? Or is it always a matter of editing out things that are vital and profound?

It is not the sin, said Catherine, I don't think. But why the sin. It wouldn't make sense and it would make God so arbitrary otherwise.

Ah, suppose it was for beauty's sake?

Catherine leaned over and kissed him on the brow. Of course, greedily I wish it had been me. But that sort of thing is in God's hands.

You! You're the one that loves me, cherishes me. If it was just possession of the infernal sort that so many women on the island feel, you would not understand, bear with me, stand by me. I live for beauty, though because I live for life. Not you understand, only the physical type. You, child, are a dove—for you the building of the nest. I met a seagull and a spectacular eagle—ah, Catherine, my heart went away—high up, this time. Oh God! Dimitri brushed his face with the palm of his hand.

I believe, said Catherine putting her hand on his shoulder, that there is nothing at all sordid about you. You want to live really and not by rules, arbitrary, senseless rules, prejudices and fears that flatten and dull the vital taste.

I thank you that you don't degrade me, whispered Dimitri hoarsely.

Then he said in a low even voice looking down at her waist: It is not that I want to live life to the full wallowing in love affairs and champagne by candlelight, daring exploits…It isn't all that. I am content with you and the baby. I had intended nothing other than a walk to clear my head because it was a bit claustrophobic, it always is with a new infant. I was taken unawares. And the thought was with a bursting brain—ah Christ, this too is me. I wanted that dimension, to see it, savor it. Catherine had you given me the fruit of the tree of life—the pleasure! It could not have been more absolute and profound. It was not some skirt, Catherine, out to intrigue me. It was a man, he raised his head slowly. Beauty like Jesus!

Hmm, on this island, though…

But you said you too knew love for a woman.

Yes, but it didn't go far. A kiss or two on the lips. You know that when you married me I was practically a virgin.

Ah, so was he. And I had a sense he wanted nothing but heaven. But when he saw me, Catherine, he came, like a little rabbit suddenly let loose out of a cage—except that he was glorious—an eagle of fire.

No Catherine if there is no place for this kind of experience, then I don't fit in this world. We are not the sordid ones. Those who deny us are. With their little mechanical God who when a sin flies at him lifts his hand automatically. That is not Man, Catherine. One knows simply knows what is dead and what is alive. The Word of God is a flesh and blood thing always never a book. A man is love, Catherine, for mother and father, and then for wife, but it doesn't stop there. A man is love like a mighty river is water pouring down into the sea, bursting its banks in the rains. Join me in this. I don't say you must find a lover, but be your full self, don't stint. Think of Sappho and Shelley and Byron. Don't shrivel and waste yourself. That is the lie.

Yes the old soul in me says yes. My poor mother wafting about with that kind of fire in her memory! I wouldn't be surprised if she leaves at last—frustrated, worn out with pacing with bursting against the bars of the prison—not my father, no, just the only thing to do—to feed, to wander up and down halls, not to do but to have moments, inner shifts, yearning after the sun. It is so glorious over the water, leaping over the water! House in the back faces west, you know. I wanted often to dance down that trail of fire on the water—possessed, of course, with the god. For her it isn't that simple. She wants language—at least, one facet of its multi facet shape. One thing that it can do. So she scribbles and scribbles with her pen, planning to type when she has found it. But I think life gets to her at the same time, particularly around the time of sunset. Little Tock is meaningless to her. To me, he is like a memory: All that you are talking about at the very beginning. When it wasn't pale, twisted and lying to talk of purity and truth. And perhaps these sorts of words were absorbed in the being of them. One didn't talk. There wasn't language. What need? One grunted, snorted, sneezed, chortled, wept, laughed. One was language far more brilliantly than one can ever produce it.

I've often thought, said Dimitri—what use is this poem that speaks of trees or snow or dark seas? Here in this essay, language goes to work. In the poem, rather it reclines, looks at you, reflects, casts shadows, lingers, bodies a moment in you.

It is that it is, said Catherine. First and last lesson of the day.

Yes as God. I am that I am….You don't mind that love touched on Katrina and Max? That I, in love, different kinds of love, that mystery, touched them?

Do you mean will I still sit on the bough waiting for you? I have told you yes. I guess it would be a kind of listless envy to hold your passionate encounters against you. No, I feel instead rather honored to have as a companion one who wants to live full- blooded life. I feel rather we are two of a kind. But I seek with virginity, God, in the end. Such a thing in the world beyond these waters is scorned. And in this island, it is not thought of in the full-blooded sense.

Ah yes, you have merely called me to come inside the cave. I have penetrated, but not intruded, despoiled. The call of love of a woman is always a virgin call. Bring little Tock.

He is sleeping. They moved over to the child's bed.

What a perfect baby, said Dimitri, looking down at him with a smile. If something happens to me, tell him I love him.

Of course, you will do it yourself. Change diapers, feed, blanket him; put a cap on his little downy head and take him for a walk.

I?

Why not? You won't hurt him. Bring him out to meet the folks. Aunt Zoe, Foti, Cleo, Uncle Nisos, Timos, Simon. This is his world: let him preside. He is the island's little prince! We have had no babies in fifteen years.

So taking her advice, Dimitri bundled up Tock against the chilly weather the next day that arrived with a morning like a ghost over the sea, and went around with him in the used old fashioned pram squinting for the glare that comes when the sky is cloudy. The passersby on the street town side that ran next to the sea, ambling along, on their way grocery shopping, poked their heads into the pram and beheld him, a little ruddy baby, soft and moist in a pile of soft crocheted cashmere blanket. Simon was the first to encounter father and child walking up and down. He was in his black britches, which exposed his hairy legs and which he wore winter and summer, and a light blue sweater. Ah, he said: Blow a trumpet, rouse the sleepers: We have life at last. He looked at the child and then at Dimitri and blinked his eyes, which Dimitri thought to himself looked golden. He went on talking in a low voice, periodically raising his tone and looking around smiling. But Dimitri, day dreaming looking at his face, didn't catch all that he was saying.

Here is what we will eat and drink! Dimitri heard at last. Little feet, soft lips and breath that is sweet. Doubtless it will do us some good.

Foti came by in a faded purple skirt and rather shyly sidled up. Her hair was thinning so she spent some money on mouse and cream that would make it curl and frizz. Her large heart shaped face framed by this frizzled grey hair seemed to Dimitri perfectly grandmotherly and she made the proper little baby noises as she bent over the pram. And then scolded Dimitri for having the baby out in this weather. The wind is still blowing, you know, she said. Winters on this island are a little raw. Easy to get a chest cold.

She picked up her head from the pram and saw a well-known figure in the distance. Cleo, she said—look, she's always a little prickly; Don't mind, don't mind.

Cleo came up: Foti and Dimitri were standing side by side talking with smiles on their faces, which infuriated Cleo. She grabbed Foti's arm with both of her hands and said in a loud stern voice—I trust you have reprimanded Dimitri for taking the baby out in this weather. No good can come of it.

A little outing can't hurt. He is so adorable, Cleo, he must be shown.

Babies have been known to die in weather like this, said Cleo. Her anger at the joint smiling of Foti and Dimitri had not abated.

Why must he die? Asked Dimitri in a gentle, innocent tone.

When fathers are so irresponsible, and villainous and violent....Dimitri looked all around. There is no one here who has been..., he began;

There are men who have strayed far from the path of virtue in my sight,

How odd, said Dimitri, affably; there is only I.

Murder, Cleo responded suddenly and without warning. Murder, that is what I call it. And it is murder not only of a child, but of a woman, and of many others on the island—people who expected a decent family, good people who sit and wait and wait, who ask for just a little.

Cleo I believe you are exaggerating, Foti piped up. Dimitri may have disappointed you in some ways, but here he is just taking a stroll, blamelessly. One must consider the actions of a person irrespective of other actions. Just as we do individual writer's books. One is good or bad, and the next good or bad independently of the other though written by the same author.

You never read books, said Cleo severely; and it is not the same. Once blamable always blamable. You see the ineffable core of humanity is a person tainted like bad meat. One tastes the rot.

Cleo! Said Foti, desperately.

You know it is true.

Yes, but—that is in cases where...and now we have a baby! Foti said this latter almost shrieking.

You can, if you don't like us, said Dimitri meekly, simply move on.

I will, said Cleo—and Zoe will hear of this.

Hear of what? Asked Foti, who was being tugged at by Cleo.

The general state of affairs, said Cleo. Murder! Yes, it has come to that.

. . .

Father Isaac was the one person on the island in the end who most doted on the baby. He would come by with little gifts that he had bought through the supplies' boat from the other island: Tapioca pudding, bananas, cereals. And although Catherine herself had a good supply of these things and Dimitri went regularly to the supermarket on the other island to stock up, still she recognized an old man infatuated with her baby and accepted his gifts and laud with a sense that it was right, such that all mothers have. It was Father Isaac who dandled Tock on his knee and sang to him all sorts of strange, rhyming songs about animals and magical folk, kings and queens in caverns under the earth and in the deep sea. Catherine didn't know that Father Isaac possessed such a store of fairy whimsy in his memory. She herself would listen to some of these songs and half- chanted stories and the baby would sleep on Father Isaac's bosom.

When Catherine put the baby to bed, Father Isaac would stay on, nibbling a little cheese or drinking half a glass of wine and talking to her seriously about the island. They have no notion you see of forgiveness, tolerance, love, anymore. They think these things should come their way, of course, bound to since they all support each other's narrow mindedness, bad habits, even violence—this they think is their forgiveness—or their latitude morally. But it is fueled by hatred and not by love, where the latitude is fueled by love—even man and man or woman and woman …And you have that to face.

For what they won't forgive is you—you, an American, and a woman who forgave and abided by a husband who is an adulterer, infinitely adulterous, because he loved a man, and he a gypsy rebel, with Muslim blood, so to speak, and because he cheated on you a rich heiress and beautiful American woman—and you had his baby. Because, you see, you did. You went and had the baby—of course, they are not for anything else, but then they must all hate the baby, hate the baby with a passion; not abort it, just kill it, after it is born, with hatred. They thought of course that the baby would have belonged to Nico and Elizabeth or more properly to Little Paul when he got married. But wonder of wonders it comes down out of heaven on crooked wings, so to speak, to you, a foreigner, and to Dimitri, a gypsy rebel. God went and planted his seed, Dimitri's.

They are mad enough to kill about that, continued Father Isaac. There is of course some excitement, some curiosity. One wants to see a rarity—you know—sort of like standing out for an eclipse. But at the same time, this baby has taken away their light. All in innocence of course; they used to wait satisfied that the right person would have the baby—because of course though they have lost their holiness they are still—as it were, a chosen few. And merely a few weeks of penance—didn't it work for Nineveh? Just a few days, in fact. So they imagine, a diet of beans, songs of praise of the Lord, prayer, reflection and sorrow—for what? Well for having judged Little Paul for his outburst against Dimitri…Then they think ah, we'll be back. And since something tells them they are not, they are all up in arms. And then that baby, the baby arrives at the door of the family they secretly and not so secretly hate—the family that riles them up with a Muslim book, and an aging mother, who should know better, kicking her leg high above her head, twirling on her toes.

Of course it isn't God to blame—but someone, someone…you! And though they are too frightened of themselves to actually kill—notice how they abandon you after the first inclination to rejoice. The baby now whom Zoe crocheted a sweater for is looked on as that child, a tainted gypsy Muslim child, a problem in their midst. And mind you the fact that she crocheted a sweater for him and will probably do another will loom large later on as her proprietary rights—a piece of that poor infant in some way will be hers, her little patronized urchin of urchins. Conveniently, the baby born into the family of the Muslim book is not forgivable. Why? Precisely because it has done nothing wrong to them—a wrong would forgivably spell out their logic! If the baby grows up a criminal, then it would be—ah, their lost holiness! Only God can forgive the Muslim book. And Zoe thus has a handle on God for his human interest in a baby. And so they can grow with license to hate and despise—to teach that part of it that belongs to them cold heartedness and self hatred with God's latitude.

I dance down the aisle to spite them all during the Sunday liturgy. They wish for solemnity, gravity—as if we are really and truly changing wine into human blood! I give them childish lightheartedness, gaiety—an idea like a spark in our midst that we should dance like Agatha, wander and eat like Marta, be passionate like Dimitri ecstatically in love with the One. And ultimately that we should walk over water to that other island where the poor need help. Change our wine into their blood, feeding the most lovely wine of wines to them. And now that there's a baby—how much lightness we do need—softness, tenderness, sweetness. We should have had practice with Martha.

So the title of my next sermon: Practice with Martha. And this time they will get what they desire—a sermon full of advice on tending and caring for a gypsy Muslim American baby. But there are other babies. You see, I had best not outlast my welcome. I am one who has a mind, thoughts, opinions, imagination—terrible things in the Orthodox Church, among the Orthodox faithful. And I tell you, he said to Catherine, chewing his goat cheese thoughtfully, that we are all wrong. That it is not at all the meditating ascetics, fasting and repeating long prayers, the bell tollers, the sacrament givers, the wearers of vestments and the people who cross themselves and ask the Lord—oh please, forgive, heal, whatnot who go to heaven. Father Isaac looked full of mirth at Catherine who sat silently in front of him looking down and thinking. No, no, the people there are the comforters, like the Holy Spirit, the givers of life, and true love, joy and tenderness, and the hungry, sad, sick not just full but softly replete now with healing with healed love. That is truth.

I am afraid I'm not very near to heaven, said Catherine, meekly. My life has been rather selfish—I've enjoyed a good day without sharing it. Now there's Dimitri and I bask in what I conceive to be his beauty. It really isn't sacrifice, if that is what you are thinking, she said, hastily. I love him; I've loved him in his scrapes as well. I believe he has enthusiasm, ecstasy and joy. Where I have it, timidly, among the newborn leaves, he goes all out—yes, women, men—the feast of life: and there is not gluttony or lechery. Just peeking in, stealing a taste of the beauty, returning to me with the thievery written all over his face in love with me. How can you live otherwise?

As for our Martha, she has always been treated tenderly at Agatha's and in your house. She comes and sits and rocks the baby. She is quieter now and doesn't walk as much as she used to. She conceives of all sorts of things—imaginary pregnancies—one with Connie whom she believes to be a great movie director. And we pamper her and prepare her dainty meals that she can eat to help the baby grow healthy that will keep her strong too. And then the hush hush near her parents, for they are still in the dark. I think the sight of the baby inspired her. She has asked us for lodging when she begins to show and we have said yes, of course. But other than this little charity, that is, again, I must say, stealing a taste, you know—of well, a different life—I have no experience with loving my neighbor.

But Martha needs a proper house; my poor little room is hardly big enough for the two of us let alone three, said the priest; her mother and father harbor a lot of resentment against her, and they are full of meanness, small-mindedness even in the poor, broken down, ratty little dwelling place. They are poor yes but he loathes to work, hides in the house, comes home early from fishing to drink, hide, and to be pampered by his wife who dotes on him, despite everything. They tell a load of stories about how they are so victimized, and driven nearly to despair by Martha's being ill. Then they spend all their time trying to lay the blame—Martha's grandmother who was weak in the brain, Martha's aunt who committed suicide, and at last they come around to Agatha and the curse on the island, and Martha's father cozens Martha's mother to believe despite Agatha's exceptional personal goodness to her. You see that Martha has to be rescued.

And brought to Agatha's yes of course, which means that Dimitri and I have to move out. I think it is difficult on Dimitri being the husband of a sick person that can't help much in moving, living, doing.

An Elder of the monastery lived in a shack on the other side of the cliff. You get to it through the monastery and down some steps. It is a one-room place but it has a little corner kitchen with a gas stove and wonder of wonders it has plumbing. It could be a temporary arrangement until Dimitri builds you a house.

We are lazy-bones, vagrants, visionaries said Catherine, smiling. And yet we could bring such joy I think—we are such comrades as have never been—in this little time that life gives we have actually claimed the leisure to love one another, despite it all, the leisure to love one another for our person, character, beauty! We could be kings and queens with the luxury of it. And now little Tock like the jewel in the crown. It could have been that we had nothing but a desperate hope of bread or freedom. Could have been that we loved whatever came our way, like most here—fast engagements, marriages in the old style without much love, a little shyness, a little hope. Instead we have this rampant, luxuriant love. And they blame us for it because Dimitri is not what they want him to be, secretly, of course, they're happy because justified when they call him renegade. So you see it works out on all sides. We have brought just the kind of misery that people are happy with.

Are you happy just loving? Asked the priest.

I fix old machines. If you are asking me whether this joy, that is, the basking in it is what I delight in, the answer is no, of course. But there is something to it—I can do it, see—I can be his companion. And out there in my jeans in the village fixing an old fan, an electric typewriter—useless things but well, you know, something to set my hands on, give them a go—I feel at once that I am companionate and handy. It is not precisely being an insider. That remains elusive.

Ah, salt and apricot brandy—a kind of squeamish cocktail, take it twice daily—then you'll know. We used to think they had such hard lives that we had to tell them, Max tried— give them news of beauty—way up there on high—a place you could get to by dint of a strenuous climb. The dream let them rest at night. Then we found, Max and I, really I knew it right away, but hoped against hope that they were corrupt, savage and sterile. They are now entirely cruel folk. Of course, one could see they had an argument having somehow lost something precious—the blueschist on the cliff side, the footsteps of Mother Dora—in any case lost in a little patch of dirt and stone in the middle of the sea, it is something. They had a reason for being here. God was here—there in that glorious blue, in the light on Mother Dora and maybe there was an extra glory. And they were rapt little pupils. But something went wrong; it was years before I came—Agatha raped, Father Raphael ill with overdoses of cocaine. Evil never comes in bits but it comes wholesale and nearly knocks out the extra inner light in the bright bright light. They became so savage—how should I say it? Language lost its high referent, clear, crystal meaning.

This island was supposed to be a little enclave, murmured Father Isaac, having finished the goat cheese, he was leaning back in the chair with his hands behind his head; it was where we all were honest toilers, giving the neighbors a hand, soft down under like children, never suspecting evil. When we ate apricots we made great joyful singings with our mouths—I talk as if I was there, a dream of beauty, of course, yet this is real history. And God gave fish, goats, apricots and the blessed sun who leaned on us not too hard nor too light. Everything and body was a person, you see, in a magical story—from the sun to the pine tree to the eagle to a stone—all worshiping God and being worshipped for the dwelling within of God. But from the first, something went wrong. There was anger, envy, hoarding of apricots and goats. And after a time, Mother Dora walked, the uncreated light like a pearl on the sand under her feet. She looked back and said with joy—you see there is still, for you, if you come. She didn't lie to us. But then quickly she was gone. And again, instead of love, hidden crime, cruelty. How can it not end in death when God ceased to forgive to send one then the other, an eagle, a woman with light in her footsteps, a girl full of magic, a dancer.

Well, they are so lonely, out in the desert sea; perhaps they think they have a kind of calling to be the offspring of the few who on the night of nights saw the abiding giant star, only dressed in flesh, the Lord resurrected. Then you see they feel they are, how shall I put it, brethren, and they seek to do God's will, not seeing at all how a Muslim bible fits. And also seeing one Paul so revered, polished, and looking clean, winning, of course, all the awards, should have introduced that element of sin; and since it was years ago and no one dared at the time speak, it is now only with difficulty spoken of—like something conceived to be arcane, rather a bother, but nothing relevant, although indicating a time when all fell apart.

Agatha would never talk about what really happened with Paul many years ago. It was right after she married then nine months later had Dimitri. I know she couldn't love for years. Alex was a compromise. There was talk that she had used the narcotics by his bedside, slipped too much into the spoon. But it was nothing like that. She wasn't wildly angry. Broken, rather. Living only because, you know, she is old gristle not tender meat and the misery made her tougher. One had to chew and chew to crush her and not even then. A real dancer is like this delicate, because consummately tough. And around the time she had gotten tough enough to fall in love with her children, up rose the dancing in her and she drilled herself until she could dance us all breathless. So I believe. No one has ever had the courage to ask her.

I know, of course, that she is jealous. Dimitri, she idolizes. You know the stories, that she kisses him like a lover. But more and more I do find that as fate would have it, mother and son are inextricable, character wise. A gene tangle, perhaps. I believe Dimitri tried to run away. Succeeded only in a miserable affair with a call girl in London. But then, coming back, he really came back to his mother, and the mother in the island forest and sea. This marriage would have never happened except that his mother permitted. The rest is all wandering. The peep of a child from under his mother's wing.

There is no time to throw these useless little fits of prejudice. If the islanders knew, said Father Isaac, energetically. There simply is no time. But there is a child. God has blessed once again. But I see not darkness but the end—maybe one more child, then the dying out.

Father Isaac couldn't help but adore the child when he saw it. As it grew, he saw to his private satisfaction that it was only happy. There were no tantrums. The child had only one or two playthings and was endlessly content with them and loved to waddle, and turn around and around. In the village he passed the time staring at one person or another from Catherine or Dimitri's shoulder. Sometimes, God knows why he looked all-exultant. The result, he thought of good feeding—Catherine took care with that—and natural well- being—a grandmother teaching him spinning and leaping. Children with little are happy, he thought. And they know so much.

Father Isaac saw Tock spinning and lifting his leg and falling down, getting up and trying again; he knew that the child had seen his grandmother—peeped out at her from the cold dim kitchen in the dark back yard at dawn. There are two ways that dancing comes, Agatha said to him once in the street apropos of nothing—one is from joy and the other is from sadness and want. Yet it is all really one thing—a tingling vein, you see. Tock is all joy. For me it was utter misery and despair.

You struggled to climb out of the tunnel, said Father Isaac, and lift your toe to the sun. Admirable and primeval as if you were developing an extra lung sac or another artery in the course of evolution, as if all homo sapiens was now going to lift the leg so high that the foot salutes the sun. Of course, the first stage was misery and despair. How can you evolve from joy?

And Agatha responded I think now you understand my faith—all sweat and tears and pain. All for the sake of that extra step.

That is the sign, I believe, of what Christ calls 'having it'. The only saints worth anything were those that actively sought deification, wanted, determined to have everything. They wanted to be God in their small configurations of human. The only difference between them and Lucifer was that they went about with love of God— joy, beauty, truth, love transcendent, preference for this One of gifts —. Of course, you are to want knowledge of God, and despite our betrayal, he gave....Dance, is the only way—as it is both work, love, prayer, the path to deification. The liturgy when it is performed rightly is not prayers and hymns but dance with God.

Agatha became so enamored with the priest after this one short discussion mid street, that she came out with Tock bundled in a baby blanket when he was two years old and set him in the priest's arms—just like giving Father Isaac a gift; a fine object only live! And the priest in her house, coming to visit, genuinely and not to pry, received the gift with utter delight and the beginning of a great three-way friendship started between priest, Agatha, and baby whom Max gently mockingly referred to as the three sages-stages of the island.

Simon clapped his hands when he saw them and said the holiness of this land has returned, the holiness itself.

But Simon spat when he ate, sometimes, spat out whole mouthfuls of food, urinated often in his trousers and in general played the geriatric patient on the loose that everybody humored as best they could but no one paid any respect to. They merely said that he was young to have become so old. And he said it himself. He still continued with his painting and it was said, by Agatha, who visited him sometimes and caressed his bald head, that these latest paintings were uncannily lovely. All about the old island and the dream island—real, imaginary, so that you didn't know where the reality ended and imaginary began. But Barbara peeked in the window once at him at work and saw a half finished painting—Simon wouldn't let Barbara near his place, saying she was crude, half formed, vulgar, a barbarian that didn't know a whit about art—but Barbara managed to see and said after—ha, he is sick with old age. His hand can't paint what his brain tells him, that is your meaning, asked Stavros. He is sick with old age, continued Barbara insisting on her words. And Agatha heard of it from Stavros and said, there is of course truth to it to Simon. It is how a vulgar person would perceive the truth and would put it in language.

Yes, said Simon, clasping Agatha's caressing hand; in the end, you are right. I can't be mad. I am laying down this old body, this diseased thing, and taking on the wings that the years have given me. Rising out of body, you know, is impossible. So there I am stuck wings and all, half down in the dust, half flapping up, catching the wind— not quite able, imprisoned and free all at the same time.

Agatha reported to everyone, including Barbara, shouting it from her kitchen window into Barbara's kitchen window—he is sane! He just has his way of talking.

I never questioned, Barbara said to Stavros, who laughed because Barbara refused to shout back—not after this strange marriage, and the beautiful child that melted in you like chocolate but was not the proper child for the island, bound to be queer in other words, like his father and mother, grandmother and the self-made reject, his great grandfather—; Barbara half seduced talked for dignity's sake to Stavros—and said, I never questioned his sanity! I too love Simon. It has all to do with the tragedy on this island.

What tragedy? Asked Stavros; he put it in that tone of innocent blasphemy as he called it to Zoe later so Barbara wasn't able to answer. We eat enough, continued her husband. Agatha is dancing.

We thought we put it clearly and succinctly for Stavros—Barbara being a little witless as far as expressing herself in words was concerned: our old traditions are under threat of becoming weaker. Why the old priest told us the other day—seemed to have quite gone mad except there he was calm and clear—that all this taking of holy communions was useless. May as well take a swim in the sea.

So you can see that our island is threatened, betrayed—when our own priest... Stavros and Simon glitter in smiles over it; it is as if they know something we don't. But we are aware of one thing—our holy ancestors established these sacraments and they are not to be tampered with. Besides the Lord Himself gives Himself to us on a silver spoon and from a golden cup!

Catherine was at the meeting in which the priest just announced this piece of madness and looked around at us as if triumphant. She stepped forward like a new mother who wants, naturally, to bring peace and said to him: isn't it true that there is a holy grail administered from heaven alone?

Yes, yes, that is the highest experience of man regarding the Christ on this earth. But for that he must seek by giving himself, love-wise to the poor, the despised, the sick. And by doing it with the Christ in his heart—without rancor, with just compassion, justice and fear of God. And for this there must be sacrifice! Agatha at that point slunk away, pensive-faced; she was not dancing then. Ah, the hypocrite. We have seen her openly giving to Martha, fixing up Leo's place, there are flowers there now, all around the border of the front walk! Yet what has it meant besides the few hours she spent? Martha's silly devotion of course but Agatha simply likes to use her—to give her orders, send her around. All quite useless. Watching Anna who stinks and smiles more and more. But Anna has Tia who is responsible rather than that forgetful mess Martha. Ah, we know that in Agatha's heart there is only self-pity.

Zoe has gotten rather abstracted, not thoughtful, so much as not there. She murmurs, and Cleo echoes her—Christ will come with a sword! Then Cleo says—you see, we have begun to disintegrate. Interestingly, Jason, Dimitri's younger brother heard our ancient little Zoe in the market place, I think, and became rather fascinated. Aye, with a sword, he nodded at her. He has come out of his shell and come round to be with us, evidently approving of Zoe. And it is, says Foti, so gratifying to see the son of the old enemy family sitting amongst them. How it has been ironed out after all, and no one is denying or destroying either Agatha or Dimitri, or banning the new wife and little child from joining our group, making the proper arrangements and ceasing to be, how shall we put it, it is so hard because one doesn't have great focus of mind—but, more or less, out of joint, strange, one who walks with head so erect—as if proving something to the others, and kicks her foot up to the sun. And she used to be our Agatha—enemy was just a word. Not really our word; something had happened long ago to cause bad blood between her and Paul and Paul sort of commands, but that is God's will—no, she used to be tenderly considered, by all of us. Now there is this division—and it is made more poignant by her younger son sitting so loyally with us as we sample our brandy and make lace.

Zoe says things now—of course, she is getting old. Touching though how Jason sees these as heavenly pronouncements—as heaven speaking through Zoe's lips. Cleo says that Jason is a real old timer. And she gives Foti little lectures that one should never go by family, race, or some old religion that once enslaved. For in Christ there is a new creation! Cleo seems, more than ever, as she leads Zoe around, to have all the right things on her lips. Leads Zoe around! Zoe is not blind but in a way she is. She is so abstracted that she literally doesn't see what is in front of her. But perhaps this light of Christ has come into her, burned her entrails, so to speak and made her ready. In any case, Jason, uncomfortable at home as you can imagine, seeks her out and sits near her. Zoe periodically touches him on the breast.

We see that the little island of antiquity, the one that cherished the risen Lord is beginning to fail. Of course, we are still here. We are passionate, obstinate believers. But something has shaken the foundation—an earthquake passed imperceptibly, split the rock. There are signs too, and no wonder. Jason, on the few occasions that he is prevailed upon to talk, says wise sayings—like that it is the end of the world. Yes, he says, because no matter our faith and our tenacity to this vision of our ancestors, the flesh and blood resurrected Christ, things of the earth are just things of the earth. At a certain point, all will again become dust, brushed off the heels of the living Lord.

It is sad for us to see Zoe, not exactly fail, but become so remote. We wonder if she is soon to be taken from us? Anna, we thought—and Anna we felt uneasily almost deserved—she used to make us laugh, you know, she who thought nothing but of gaiety—yet the old Father Raphael, the Father Raphael who was full fed and so in God!—before he became wan and sick—now he would despise such gaiety, although he never said anything about our Anna, perhaps because she had a tongue to answer him like a whip. Anna, we thought—but she is still living. She is like a tree in the forest that is dying forever, and still stands and will stand and walk when she is dead, we think, such is her rootedness! But Zoe is like a whiff—of an odor more than anything tangible; she is there, perceptible than after a time, gone.

We gathered together to talk of our Zoe, that is, if we can really get it together without her guidance and direction. She is you understand, and we all understood, so brave; she wanted the life, not not the life only, but the holy life of our land. It is not too much to say that. I think that goes beyond the call of duty—and to think she was so humble, really, although she had a will of steel and if anyone got in her way…she didn't want herself to be noticed in this endeavor. Now it is as if she is hearing something—an inner call? Is it peaceful? Ah yes, it must be, but sometimes in her dreamy silences we notice her face cloud over with pain. Sometimes her poor jaw spasmodically bites.

Foti said: Is Holy Island really going to die? It is as if we never lived. She looked down at her ice lemonade—a chill that was pleasant to her even on a chilly day in March when the winds blew and sometimes rain fell all of a sudden, like pouring a bucket of water out after the washing. I thought, she dabbed her eyes a little, that we would have back a thorough life—with the women having children, the men holy… Zoe was the kind of lady that would say—yes, of course we will…She had a fist like iron, I thought, but of course, how could I? Foti laughed. She had a weak, crushable fist like an old lady. But she is always so white, these days—that white shawl made of cashmere, the white pearl earrings and that look of white.

Cleo replied: You have always been a little lacking in mind, Foti. What on earth is a look of white? Zoe is simply reaching the end. She is on a track by herself. All isolated one comes to God.

Agatha, who was with them, despite Cleo's disparaging looks, out of pity for Zoe, said: It is as if we have never lived. We have been so concerned for the holy via the righteousness that we imagine to be God's! Yet doesn't he say: My ways are not your ways nor my thoughts your thoughts.

You would be clever, growled Cleo, but she hung down her head a little. She was tired and sad.

Foti looked at her and translated the incomprehensible outburst for Agatha: It seems as if she has struggled all her life to do God's way—of course there was living, but chastity, obedience to holy Church; then she had a whiff of money waved in front of her nose, a little picture in her mind of carefree pleasure, buying a perfume in Paris…it was all taken from her in a moment by your son, though I don't say it was all his fault, he is the kind who can never realize—and anyway, back she was a widow in a fishing village with primitive machines—old sewing machines, fans, tiny refrigerators, little three wheeled trucks that puff up the mountain. She thinks it was her fault, no, her sin, Foti ended with a whisper. And that just before her death—the falling down, the backsliding before our Lord's eyes. She ends up you see with the old bundle of bones and a terrible sin. Of course, the first is not her fault…

Cleo picked up her head sharply: What are you talking of now, Foti? Yes, yes, I am an old bundle of bones with a terrible sin—what next? Do you think she is even capable yet of understanding what it is to be in the desert, the very desert of humanity?

Agatha had the sickening sense of bodies, emaciated, decomposing being turned over and over by trucks with great shovels. She shuddered. She didn't want Holy Island to die and be buried as it were in a common grave. To have the inevitable rich man buy it and tear down the little disjointed houses of yellow and red, for the little white washed church with the lively fresco of Jesus with one foot up, walking on water, and a great smile of joy on his beautiful face for it all to be at last abandoned to decay and rot.

I want to stay and fight, she said, softly, looking with great pity and Cleo's tired eyes. And what can you do but destroy? Answered Cleo. Yes, you can suck out the very life, you woman, you can leave us helpless, Zoe unlike herself, me on the edge of despair, but you cannot bring back what you know well we had and had until your family came and ate away like rats at the very structure. She turned away.

Agatha felt no anger looking at her. She backed away from putting her hand on her arm. Cleo stared straight ahead of her and then closed her eyes.

It has always been like this, murmured Agatha softly. You were all I had and I hoped and hoped.

Agatha said nothing to Dimitri about the 'like rats'. It has stayed with her although she thought she was ready to deal with things like that. The old hate, the fierce, bitter antagonism. What exactly was it in the end? That her father had come bearing a different book to the bible, had stayed away from church, prayed at home, but yet taught her Jesus—the one who loved the despised, the poor, those who crept around in corners like Martha, and she had listened and not gone to be baptized. And she was listening now. Her father who lifted her on to his shoulder walked around town with her, bowed his head with respect to each passerby, despite the way they turned away, sang to her in his broken voice—the voice in which she could always feel tears.

Home with Dimitri and Catherine, for they still lived with her part time and part time at the villa in a sort of loosely agreed upon arrangement with the in laws, she did nothing but smile. But Dimitri couldn't stand it: What is it, Mother? Why are you torturing us? That strange smiling face so sick and ugly.

At Easter, said Agatha, I am going to do my one public dance. I am going to dance in the competition. I am going to win.

What is the dance called?

Secret Knowledge of the Sun. I am working on it, polishing it off. My whole self—my very body—has changed, now. There are no more grievances bowing me down. I can be burned in the fire—melted, disintegrated. And in the ash, on the air—only sweet.

It is really most remarkable, said Catherine, as she unbuttoned her blouse to nurse Tock who wouldn't sleep and still was not weaned. Don't you think so, dear? She asked Dimitri.

It has always been remarkable. I look to my mother for hope, you know; in other words, when I am really downcast for being so lousy—ah but there, you have the genes...

No, these are not genes at work, said Agatha; no, no but pain. The pain is evident, manifest—as eyes and nose. How lovely it is to be sometimes blind, sometimes incapable of smelling. Other times, ah, the smell has returned for the fragrance—most miraculously.

But little one, she encircled her son with her thigh—the new spirit pierces even the gene coil, displaces it, replaces it. And you, no longer the old dream, nightmare of once, but the new man whom I love and watch like an eagle.

Catherine, watching, laughed lightly, softly. How like your mother is to your young permanent extramarital lover, your perfect concubine she said to Dimitri. What competition.

I think that is the gene coil, he said. She hated me until we both approached adolescence. She, spiritual, me physical.

Why did you hate him? asked Catherine, curiously.

Agatha sighed and withdrew her leg from her son's waist. She then explained: He didn't seem at all lovable or friendly. For a long time he was mute, saying nothing. He withdrew into his own shell, untouchable, cranky and alone. I thought he was a young boy inhabited by the spirit of an old man, an ill old man. I didn't see him as part of me. Then one day I looked up at him and he looked frowning and virtuous. Almost like a saint. I didn't want to lose him but it was almost a second after I loved him that he left. He thinks of me as a mother, ha! What kind of a mother am I? I believe we are closer to being lovers than mother and son. Hasn't the passion been in my dance, then, hasn't it? Dance where essentially the fire reigns where of course it cannot otherwise. But you see that is true I find even in life, what we call the correct, moral life. Dance is where the fire reigns. In the course of ordinary life it would hurt, kill. But in the dance it is the source, the beauty.

But it seems that here is something, which could be held against you, in the village, I mean, that you have called and made the beginning of life, said Catherine.

What is this girl doing excusing everybody? Asked Agatha, turning to Dimitri.

Dimitri looked at her—you and the baby, he said.

Catherine coiled her hand around Dimitri's arm and pulled him towards her. Tock was asleep in the other arm, one breast was still nude and warm and full. Dimitri turned to his mother and said, we are going to retire with your permission.

Agatha said of course, of course.

You see, Mother, you own me—she only gets me with your say so.

Agatha looked at her son—dark serious eyes, slight smile of mockery. Perhaps it is all as they say—we are demons Dimitri, you and I. That is the gene coil.

I wouldn't be surprised if angels dressed in demons' clothes when living among liars, whispered Dimitri and kissed her on the lips.

Oh, I would say the villagers are only half way there people—their lying is holding on, all befogged—to the golden glow of the past when the flowers shone—minds full of that sort of thing.

The problem is that some of them saw the light—that is actually saw light such as men don't usually behold.

Is that so? Catherine looked seriously at Dimitri, and slowly buttoned her shirt. Agatha whirled around on her feet and stalked into her son's room where she was sleeping now that he and his wife had the double bed in her bedroom.

It is one of our legends, said Dimitri. 'Our', what is this 'our'? The village hardly recognizes me. For the quarter of Muslim blood and the fact that my mother refuses baptism as well as perhaps another thing we are ostracized from Mother Dora and therefore the light of God. But you know, I think I would refuse recognition from them even were it handed me on a silver platter.

The peasant mind is simple on the one hand, homespun, dear, replied Catherine. The flip side of the coin is savagery and prejudice and fantasy. I don't question the light at all. The stuff of legends is serious in my opinion. But their attachment to it breeds only exclusivity, ill will, envy, contempt—all the ingredients of the worst kind of human.

I do things in a sort of unthinking, careless way. But anything to break through the moribund life. Not to get infected with it.

But you love, I mean, love....

Yes. But I, my mother, you, he, Dimitri pointed to the little sleeping infant, will be branded—you get my meaning—with their idea of sin, the black cloud of God's contempt.

Catherine handed him the baby and they walked slowly down the four steps between the kitchen and the big bedroom where Dimitri's parents had slept. Catherine sat down on the bed, looked up at him and ran her first finger across her forehead.

Dimitri put the baby in the crib standing next to the bed. He looked down at him, sleeping with that utter trust of infants. Perhaps, I have tempted, tested, gone too far...

I would have cried, thrown a tantrum, turned my back on you, all the screaming little fits that women are prone to when men stray, but you know, I saw your point entirely. You didn't lose your love for me; I didn't lose mine for you.

Each day, said Dimitri, you grow more beautiful and more delicate in my imagination. I like it when your breath stinks, or you fart, you know, because then I say to myself—ah, she's real—not some snowflake likely to melt away and be gone forever. No, you have a digestive tract, you are a thing of rot and so a thing that is of this life, this life. He took off his clothes and crawled into bed with Catherine. Old half rotten thing for your gases, and also my life, the light of my mind. You know I know nothing of God and heaven. I haven't as you know been very studious in that regard. I haven't as you know followed the Church or prevailing concepts of morality. My aim has been just to be an honest lover, my instinct, no more. And yet something tells me—what is it? You—all kindness, Mother Dora—he laughed, gently—the old light of this island—that it isn't all that sad.

What?

You know—death, humanity's tragedy.

How?

Well, we have to do what we know to be true. That is all I can say. And of course—how could I not love you? You are my flesh and blood, Catherine—don't you see? Dimitri gestured with his chin towards the crib. But you have found a soul that is rude and passionate—an old sailor and deceiver. I who pretended that I was oh so educated, high minded...in reality the same thing between my legs as between Nisos', the same strange old insanity as in Simon—all of them faced the sea day in and day out. I faced it, leapt over it. That was my answer. Yet it was all the same in the end. I came back. Had to. Who knows? Perhaps I have the same obstinacy as my brother.

Oddly, perhaps, it was sweeter to Catherine to have Dimitri now, coiled around her breathing the soft, peaceful breath of sleep on her breast. She ran her fingers lightly through his hair and felt something like tears of pity start up. He was most like a big-eyed child—people had lost that. A child is different. So different. One thinks the child is just an ungrown, unblamed person that has stages to get through. A child is someone who takes delight, sins and forgets his sins, remembers funny faces. Who doesn't read, as it were, the X-rated film that streams and flashes about him—the adult talk, the reading into of adults, the squinted eyes of the envious, the nakedness and offense of each and every person. Dimitri is a child, she thought.

And they would say—they all are children when you love them. All. So Dimitri, looking up into her eyes with that new awakened, puzzled look—why are you crying, little mother? Is it my sins? And her thought is only, someone protect him, someone protect him. It is the early hours, she heard herself say; the birds are not even awake yet. You must sleep. And you, he reached up and held her face with his strong warm hand. I've gotten used to not sleeping so much. If the baby has need…Seems the baby is sound asleep. You, you are going and building the nest, psychologically. Making it safe, high, secure. Are we really going to be a family?

This little talk went on and on, it seemed for hours or was it only a few minutes. It seemed they talked long after they were both asleep. She softly responding, he delighting in asking teasing questions. Are we going to be a family? It was a puzzle. In fact—how were they fitting together? This impossibility of one human and another and another together. In addition, she must have said after pausing a minute to dream, we have no house. True our nest is lovely, excellently crafted—a matter of brain cells though. We borrow right and left for the needs of the body.

Do you have anything left? This was Catherine from the midst of soft sleep.

I thought I had so much. Some I gave to my mother. It is only fair. The rest, the jewels, I thought I'd run with, with you and the baby in tow.

Run? Go where? Catherine didn't understand the jest.

Up the cliff. There is an old elder's house on the other side of the monastery. He died recently. A few years ago. In perfect comfort and peace. The nuns buried him. The bell of our church tolled. He refused a proper funeral. His life was only prayer. He thought that everything was alright on the island. Considered it a little garden of sorts; it was of course. And perhaps in some ways still is. He was so old, he could remember Mother Dora. I think he retired from all service at the time of her death— he was young then, ten, I believe. She had made an impression on him. And he went and how shall I put it—buried himself in a cave and prayed. He built this house at the end of his life; the house is empty now. For one jewel, we'll have a new roof. For another jewel, an additional room built. The day room for our little egg and you.

The rest of the talk was that beautiful murmur and fluff—the sound of love, the visions sweet, intangible, like the softest silk, drawn across the face. The delight of it, and the ease—that murmur and fluff, it might be called, because it seems like nothing is actually said; but in the end something at the core changes. That puzzle piece miraculously fits again. One awakens solid, renewed and yet light as breezes.

In the end, Catherine thought, half delirious with love and sleep in a gentle sort of way— the half made house, the pacing back and forth in the villa where they camp with Ellen in a semi objecting state, Robert silent, worried, both of her parents floating by adrift like two pieces of wreckage in the mysterious, unknowable sea of relationships!

The next morning they were more alert and alive than ever. Dimitri was his old electric self, Catherine evanescent and beautiful for that; somehow they seemed to Agatha to be like shadows around the baby. Something about the family, the parents were not quite reality, but the baby was a little bright piece of flesh. Of course the other side of the coin was that Catherine nursed, Dimitri walked around talking of this and that and they all converged at the kitchen table for lunch—tomatoes and goat cheese, fish broiled, bread and garlic and oil and they all seemed fleshy enough. At one point Dimitri turned to the baby that Catherine held in her arms, she liked holding him, said it was the best thing for a little child—and he, the father, a remote face for little Tock which however hovered near, peeking in, began to sing a song about chicken soup. It was a conspiracy, Agatha decided, watching him; a secret code between the baby and himself to get Tock to remember his father. Make a secret refuge for just them—baby and father—an alien, cut off figure, where without the advantage of the breast, one needs something to bond with. The chicken soup song. And Tock was hearing the words, and had grown teeth to chew and had placed his tongue in it. Chicken soup correctly salted, sang Dimitri; baby Tock smiled suddenly.

Where did you get that song? Asked Catherine. She was all languid, dark hair grown more lustrous, thicker, longer; she had gotten a little thicker, a little misshapen with the fat that she hadn't lost after the pregnancy and looked like something stuffed in her too short pink flannel bathrobe, but still that look of shadow on her, the expressions that wafted into her face and made it appear as if in two minutes she would dissolve, and she, or what he knew of as she, become nothing but a body—worn out, old. He imagined it—forced himself to—He is in one end of the room, she on that same chair and total senselessness in the air. But he smiled at her, she was now so pretty in her odd body, and said: It is a secret code. God gave it to me.

Agatha left the room and went out. When she came back two hours later with the groceries, both of them were moving in the bedroom, passing the baby, swinging the little boy from arms to arms, singing the song.

And they sang it day after day after day. At first Agatha thought it was kind of sweet, though tuneless and somewhat harsh; it had a different melody all the time, a changeable tune if you like. And then it became a sort of quiet chant and Dimitri laughed and made it sound like the chants in the Orthodox Church, half-correct in his imitation, half off. Agatha became annoyed on the third day—when are you going to cut it out? But they went right on singing, sometimes a little dully, other times laughing at one another. They went out for walks, Dimitri went to visit the dead elder's shack, and then he came back and together they sang the silly song again. This crazy singsong with few words other than chicken soup correctly salted was the way they were making a nest for themselves—a sound nest, so that Tock might recognize them by the singsong the one that only his parents sang. Agatha realized this insanity was a serious survival technique a matter of family rooting and communicating.

Agatha didn't criticize after she had realized this and went about her business. Crazy two, she thought to herself though—it will be good for them to be alone, fending for themselves, in that little shanty on the side of the cliff.

In the beginning, Agatha had worried about the baby with those two parents living such a harum-scarum life with Dimitri not the ordinary husband and Catherine willing to accept just anything; and she had worried that she herself might corrupt the baby--she had taken it into her arms with delicacy and fear. Although she was all for an alternative lifestyle, although she took freedoms that shocked others, she had fantasies of the baby growing up in the most regular of households—something fixed, safe, and seamlessly one with the village folk. Despite the antagonism, which she thought in the back of her mind was understandable, she had visions of Tock growing up with many aunts and uncles as it were, the eventual gathering of the village around the baby. She had visions also of Tock alone, a little child in the square and Zoe and Cleo, Nisos and Timos gathering around, and the stiff, ancient creatures, slow moving like crabs, coming up in a non-threatening way, changing to tenderness even as they took his little hands in theirs. It was to be like some species of beasts a question of whether they would attack and kill and eat as it were the offspring, or whether they would nurture him. It was a thin dividing line, and she told in her talking to, the old talking to, which she had stopped a little in shock when Dimitri had returned but now started up again.

It was a thin dividing line. The island had its points. The old consciousness of once— Mother Dora, of whom it was said, she was so tender that it reminded one of a snowflake melting—that she never raised her voice, never rose up for or against either good or evil. The whole island, they said, had concurred then—it was before father came, when mother was just a little girl looking across the sea and wishing… or was it earlier? Or was it that Mother Dora was so bright that her light lingered on, found its way down the passage of dark time when death had come for the best and for her? So bright that several young girls had caught fire from that light and had gone up the cliff to become nuns and the meek and soft nature prevailed on the island. But then when her father had come and taken away her mother to marry her in a civil ceremony—oh then, what then? She had come back to a suddenly (or was it suddenly?) changed island. Stiff, alien and cruel. Yet they argued the same God, they espoused Mother Dora, they clamored and claimed that they wanted that same holiness. But who was prepared to give up the hate and the narrow minded condemnation for that slightly earthy face on her father, his softness, his tears too—that made them so uneasy, the uncomplaining and above all the 'other' book? Mother Dora was white white with lineaments so thin and fine and for her the Gospels, the Epistles of St. Paul, the writings of St. Symeon the New. God was their God not of this earth, but white like clean; not brown of earth. It was awkward, the kind of thing that would bring on a community migraine: Agatha, myself, the other puzzle piece, brought up on the other book that was put away among scented silver tissue paper before a lamp that burned night and day.

Jesus, the Name so tender, joyful, righteous. Ringing in her. "Smiling before God!"—in the Muslim tradition. That is the holy sound. But He is no book. No nothing of the sort. Rather a dance, rather Tock smiling—there are infinite incarnations--all You. Strict and perfect—may walk on water for me, or change water into wine. God tender, playful, sore. Ha, I see now, she went on to her talking-to; that is the only thing. Jesus born and I born again in His birth long ago—a brown gypsy woman dancing so lightly as to leave no footprints— that the shepherds shooed away.

And then Tock and the ringing continues. Surely, surely they will give up the stiff ghost, the bone ghost—suspicion and dislike. It would mean nothing—Zoe will come off her cloud of abstraction, a new woman—because it is after all a child in their midst; Cleo will echo Zoe and Foti and they will all be cooing happily like doves. Life will return to the island, the olive branch, and hope.

But they are not quite doves, said her talking-to.

Agatha had a vision of a claw creeping out under a soft wing and shuddered.

It was this vision that made her decide way back when, when Dimitri and Catherine were still hovering around the infant and singing chicken soup correctly salted, burbling with the infant as a chorus, to take Tock and go far away, one day. Not a real decision, of course; more dream....

Agatha divided her extra time between Anna and Leo. Now and then she stopped by the priest and told him the news.

So, Anna still lives? He asked her.

Thin as a chicken bone. It is as if she has a new style, though. She is still the same—humorous, high-minded. Life in her still strong. She has pain, of course. Lives on morphine. It is a great bother, she says, when it subsides. But she refuses to be afraid even of God. It is not that I don't want him, she says, just that all the language written down about him seems to be so stiff and unnatural. I don't know how to begin to speak to him. So she lies in the sun in the afternoons, just after Tia administers the medication and lets, she says, the sun do the work of talking to God for her. And she says that she won't die; she refuses!-- until she loves.

Kali comes by every so often to gossip with Tia. And they murmur in the background while Anna dozes and prays—that is takes her sunbath for 'God's sake' because she doesn't have the words to speak to God. Kali you know has nothing to do these days that Catherine is with us and so she simply cleans for the Isolets, and runs errands. They still keep her on. She doesn't in the least mind being virtually useless. Katrina came by one time. Anna said she had the look of a struggling child in school. Katrina sighed looking at Anna and said to her we are all of us like odds and ends. Nothing useful anymore. Nothing contributing. I think we will live and die and go entirely unnoticed into oblivion as if we were just lines in the sand washed away by the tide.

Anna had some energy then. And so? She said to her. Mayn't oblivion be sweet comfort? Was all this precisely the right thing? Mayn't oblivion be a new kind of experience? Mayn't it be the answer we are all looking for? Set your life in order, make it beautiful. Oblivion ha! What is that? If the end is beautiful and muscle and energy and intellect has gone into making it so…who knows when that beauty will be uncovered, rediscovered when we are inexorably useless in the dust?

The priest smiled and leaned back in the straw chair. He had pulled the lace curtains and the February light filtered through perfectly bright and filled the room that was still shabby with dirty plates piled in the sink, the soft bed with the hole in the middle unmade, a few books piled up behind Max's chair and clothes on a line tacked to the back of the door. Max was gone—usually gone now, the priest commented and reflected briefly. He comes, he gestured as if pointing out something little and meaningless—to eat, to sleep, to practice one night before Liturgy. Ah, Anna, he picked up on Agatha's discourse; and Katrina! Yes, what are we, where are we? The truth is we come very close to senselessness.

Why not just follow raw impulse? Aren't the little children, Christ so proclaimed—for such is the kingdom of heaven, He said—closer to this low, base thing? So that was the point of the sinners: the murderers, rapists, robbers whoever has 'burst out'—is better than the righteous who remain stifled within.

It would do us good, said Agatha, 'bursting out,' I mean.

Yes, and so, you know, would our leaving this island, this charmed circle that is death and wants death.

The priest got up out of his chair and walked slowly towards the sink. Each day I make this journey, he said, across the floor to wash the dishes. Max won't do his duties any more. It isn't rebellion; it's sorrow. There is something inside that leaves him weak. And so I too….He sighed and curved his spine, hung his head down, stopping in the middle of the floor. Odd how the sweat comes too, he said, wiping his face with his hand. In the middle of February. All for nothing of course—having to wash the dishes.

Agatha moved to the sink—she was standing by the door.

Oh no, no! Father Isaac waved her away. You are a guest; sit down in Max's chair in the sun—just as Anna says, there are things that you can learn just sitting in the sun—things of God if you will.

Agatha moved to the chair and sat down watching the priest. Slowly he rinsed each dish and then squirted some dishwasher detergent on a sponge and washed them one by one. Then he rinsed them again and stalked them beside the sink. He took ten whole minutes to finish. Then he rinsed his own hands and let the warm water flow over them for a while. You see this washing is what I do now mostly. Washing of dishes and clothes. It is the main work of the day. It used to be reading and writing. I thought I would write something original, a priestly work, but imaginative: the characters of my parish. How bold I was; how eager to leave my imprint.

I think I too, you see, in Katrina's tide—washer man as I am, will be finally washed away. Ah, but what to do? Kill, rob? In the torture of living? Anna was right. May not oblivion be the answer?

Father Isaac when he looked at her after washing the dishes, still had that luminescence in his face that had stirred all the island to setting aside its difference with him. Might that not be the same light that was rumored to have lit up Mother Dora? There was that whiteness, but also an earthy look—the lips a little too fleshy above the slightly discolored beard. But then the smile despite two gaps on either side where teeth should have been, like a light. The thinness too, the waif likeness, and the way that smile that shone seemed to come out of him inevitably, as well as the miracles of goats' milk and fruit that continued, all added to her/their perception of him as still in question as to sainthood. Popular sainthood, of course; Father Isaac was one of those unnoticed clerics in the Church, which he had and had not divided from, of course, as was usually the case. He was thin, he was light, he did miracles… the people gathered around despite their many reservations about him. But Agatha suddenly had a hunch that this smile on the priest's face, which was joy was sorrow, the same as sorrow. And she left him wiping his hands, smiling gently at her, feeling like the tears were coming.

Agatha went to Leo and found him sitting in front of his house on the rocky soil with a white plastic chair smoking. The house for once looked clean and neat. She went inside and found that he was washing the dishes, picked up after himself; the floor could have used a mopping but what of that? Leo had turned the corner.

She went out and kissed him on the thinning side of his hair, over the front lobe on the left and they looked into one another's eyes, Leo squinting, Agatha serious. Well, he said finally, is it alright? I think I caught a little fever, didn't know what I was doing. Saw you standing in front of me with a dishcloth and so I took it—from your hand in my dream and went over to the sink. There were piles and piles of dirty dishes. It was a taste of domestic life such as I never had before. Magda prohibited all knowledge for me. I was not only a howling fiend when she died but also an utter ignoramus. Can you imagine the other women slept with me stinking of pee, and on blankets full of bread crumbs, stained with wine and gravy. I have a bundle of dirty clothes, by the way, in the bathroom. Of course, if you can't or won't I would fully understand, he said airily, knocking ash off his cigarette with his finger.

Can't or won't what? Asked Agatha warily.

Marry me, he said exhaling the cigarette smoke.

That is funny, said Agatha, not replying, it makes me think.

To have every day and night your husband's caresses draped over you; you would be like the Greek statues, breasts exposed and pubis and all sorts of useless wet drapery over the rest of you. For of course, I would honor those parts above all and kiss hand, foot, knee before venturing…

I am, said Leo, looking meekly at Agatha's sharp look, prim as a package. I will only be opened on Christmas/New Year's/Easter that combination of holy and profane days when the wedding is.

Agatha found her little prissy, girl-spot in her brain and thought—you were profane with so many girls, weren't you?

But she caught Leo looking at her through half-closed eyelids and the flip side of all that--the big sensualist in her--came and camped between her thighs and she smiled and giggled a little and ached for him. How do you know what you'll be marrying? She said a little coyly, finally.

First the kindling, he murmured, the sudden fire; but that has to catch and burn slowly so that there are still red embers in the heaps of ash when the fire burns out. Leo leaned towards her and touched her neck softly, caressing and caressing the side of her face.

Agatha was alarmed and a little gratified when she felt herself aroused. It was all so lazy-sweet; her body was sound this time around, far better for marriage.

She pulled back. It would be a decent sort of thing for us—to be husband and wife, she said. And she reached up and knotted a strand of Leo's thinning hair around her finger and pulled his face towards her own, kissing him on the lips.

He kissed her softly and then stood up and away, his moon face silent, inscrutable. Don't come tonight, he said. A look almost of tears in his eyes, he said, I am not ready, his voice shook.

Agatha sensed she would have to lead him through marriage like a little child. It will be, she said, not the same thing as beauty, the beauty that you know. But oh, if I had another word—for the fire, majesty, sweetness...

Ah, murmured Leo, more in command of himself, I am too old.

You mean broken in structure, said Agatha, here and there. No. You shall cook and I shall dance. And we shall be happy. It will be as ordinary as the sun.

And there will be those live boring moments.

We'll live through them dallying in housekeeping—I mending socks, you smoking, or cleaning windows. Somehow comfortable, despite it all. When there is a yen to go off—to the forest, beyond this rim of sea, you go, I'll follow.

Or vice versa. Strange, murmured Leo, you came just to help out. I would have hounded you out of my house yelling or obscenely flirting but you were an old friend of my wife's—remember? She liked you immensely. She, I never knew well enough, as a lover says, though I would have died for her—felt I had to, as if she were my country. And she was immensely beautiful in body—but with you it's as if once you were planted in my house for fifteen minutes little tendrils grew around the coils of my mind. I seem to know you more than well. You are so squat and rough -faced by comparison but it is as if—you open me up like two halves of a nutshell, and I find you, like the delectable nutmeat, inside. When Magda died I went after girls. If you were to die, I would sit in this chair, he indicated his armchair, and stare and smoke, not eating or drinking. I would waste, go blind…that living sex instinct dead in me, my body, or my soul, like two halves of a nutshell on a napkin with the nut gone.

Why die? Why not just go away, go a little beyond? This place can be so cramped, barely room to breathe…Whenever I think of moving on, out, it is as if all my bones shift and resettle and then they are taut and lively and in position, as it were, to fly. Were you a dancer, you'd understand. You can fly dancing, you can finally walk properly dancing. The body will actually do it.

So you wouldn't die? Asked Leo gently, urgently.

Not I, said Agatha, I'd fly.

I have to undo in myself billions of years of training. Since the earth began it has been dying not flying. Dying is the great event.

It has been falling, not rising; retreating, not moving forward. As if life is a spasm confined to a little place instead of a mighty movement covering earth and sky.

I am not sure we will only talk, said Leo suddenly looking at her with half closed eyes again.

Indeed said Agatha with dignity and humor. She whirled around her leg cocked behind her. Do you know how long it has taken me to perfect that pirouette? Look, and she did it again—you can draw a circle around me, center on the standing toe, and the circumference by the toe of the other foot. A perfect circle.

You should dance in the Easter competitions, said Leo.

I must go, said Agatha, suddenly.

But you will, said Leo, grasping her arm.

What?

Marry me.

Oh I suppose, said Agatha evasively, that there are chances and still more chances. Interruptions also, interferences. But, she looked at him, at his now white and drawn face, not so bloated as she had once thought: Of course, I will marry you, she said with tenderness. In the ordinary course of events with everything so limpid and fine, like these blue days when the sea and sky seem to be in secret the same thing, I will, of course, marry you, she felt she had to say again. I have nothing better to do —on a blue day.

Then we are engaged, shouted Leo to Agatha's retreating figure.

Engaged, said Agatha, slamming his front door as she went out.

Coming home was sweet; Dimitri and Catherine were amusing the baby doing chicken imitations around his crib and singing the chicken soup song they had invented. Chicken soup, chicken soup, nothing is better than chicken soup. We gather together in a group the chicken soup group. Chicken soup with potatoes and tomatoes or rice. And the two were laughing hilariously at this nothing song as if they were high on champagne.

Agatha smiled at them. It was impossible not to. Adults in their big, awkward bodies trying to elicit laughter and smiles from an infant who blew saliva bubbles and lay contented with this perfect world on the rim of which were these fine, strange, ghastly, fun monsters who loved to hold his body in their arms. And they made sounds as he and they swallowed each other's sounds sometimes with great glee; and sometimes they offered his sounds to swallow along with sweet utter milk. Sound swallowing in his mind full of the fertilized cell of language—God knows where fertilized and by whom, whom, but an angel?—that was multiplying and growing, these were the ongoing memories after all, of multiplication and formation of limbs, spinal cord, liver, the baby felt his inestimable brilliance, an intelligence never before conceived. Agatha followed the baby, she thought, closely—watching, half dreaming, half seeing with the inner self.

Would she tell them this inner self…it is one thing—for we are indeed one in the beginning. There is no more than one—Eve. It is only later that we come to be split, ask for a soul. And the soul we receive at the culmination of toil, to retroactive sorrow and pain, and then we are two, three, four, five. Then two again through love. Then love, then one, Christ.

She had come out of misery suddenly and loved whomever her eyes rested upon. She thought it was Jason, but her eyes skipped over his dull, plate-like white face and settled on Dimitri. It was not choice. When had she ever known choice? The baby son who had lain like a burning coal in her belly and whom she had hated with all her heart, was a man she suddenly turned into a girl for. Her smile followed him, all wistful, joyous. She had a nagging, tearing unnameable feeling for this other person, his wife, whom she otherwise quite delicately respected—a sick American come forever to the island to live out her years in quiet by the sea.

While they lived in her house almost a year, singing to the baby, and amusing him with their antics, Agatha ruminated and thought her outlandish thoughts, sometimes voiced them low, her talking to, cooked, made beds, cooed over the baby and touched its skin soft and humid like the insides of flower petals. It was his baby and she decided she, at least, would die for him.

Die for him? Die for him? Live for him, rather, said Anna. You don't want to fill your insides with thoughts of death. Come kiss me, darling. You never minded this body ebbing away like a stinking fish, disintegrating that's the word. You can see that

Tia minds although she doesn't say anything. Slight motion of her lips, grimace—disgust.

No, said Agatha with a fresh, calm voice. I don't mind your body. You do smell a little, urine mostly. I suppose you can't always make it to the bathroom. But here is a kiss, Agatha bent down and kissed Anna's neck.

Ah, she said, how cool it is. Your lips I mean; as if you had just eaten melon. What delicious secret times we have had together while I've been ill. There are times you have come and stood against the window and there you have been something homey, sweet like lemon curd, taste a little mysterious and the moon outside flooding you with its light. Do you know that I delight in the sound of your voice?

Agatha laughed; it is as if you have the hots for me.

Perhaps it is the result of combining thanatos with eros. But I must say you have that sweet suppleness about your body with none of the mercilessness of youth. And you have kissed me even on the bare breast. Ah, there is still a little appetite for flesh even in a dying person. But it is not accompanied by that old anxiety. With my husbands, although I acted the role of indifferent, hilarious, availability to perfection, I was always tense, never knew if they would continue with our marriage. And I knew well that once or twice they had found better female company; but the thing toiled on. Marriage. But with you I breathe easy. There is something incredibly loyal about your character. You don't count slights or imagine wrongs. Cling a little like a child who has never been betrayed.

It may seem very foolish, a whim on my part, but I want to leave this house to you. Here you can set up shop with the family. And it makes me laugh to think that this village, which has so oppressed you, called you cursed, made you into something of an outcast, an object of scandal and gossip, should suddenly find you the richest on the island. Should suddenly have their notion of respectability thrown in their faces and watch you step from a marble floor out on to a tile porch and looking at you behold not only your face and the look of ease and comfort in it but a gold dome rising up behind. And your son has married into the rich Americans' home. So you see, you, outcast, are just now in a sphere slightly too good for the others. What do you think?

Agatha thought that the vengeance tasted sweet. She didn't tell Anna that she was engaged to Leo. There was no need and she sensed that in a funny way it would break her heart. She knew Anna was not exactly possessive but she wanted to think that Agatha was a discovery of her own and there were moments when Anna liked to imagine that it was she who had brought Agatha out of her stoop and stupor. That Agatha lived somewhere along that thread between them not that she had just invested half her mind and heart there. And she wanted it not for physical attraction but just for the passionate idea that had gotten into her—the passion to live utterly, truly —beyond all living that ordinary people know; in fact it is as if they had never lived. Agatha was this vehicle of life for Anna. But there were also moments when she drew away from her and complained over and over again in haunting little cries—I have not loved, I have not loved.

Agatha was half intrigued by this assertion that was more of a terrible lonely cry. It was, she thought, with a shudder, the soul facing eternity, perhaps the soul facing God. But there was something, all things considered, immeasurably sweet in the sound. So sweet that it seemed to defy the emptiness of the infinite journey since the music was in each step. She knew that Anna did not mean love as it is usually defined. She knew somehow that she had gone and conceived of something godly, the aspirations of one in mystical communion with. But she doubted that Anna could do more than cry out. That although she had hit the target mystically she could never realize her goal. She is at present a bag of bones. She cannot alter this dying in her. Where, how, when can she transform? But what would in some become depression contemplating these things, in Anna became a steady gaze, a determination to keep on living for it no matter that one could see her skull through her face now, no matter the crucible of pain she lived through when the morphine wasn't enough.

Paul was preening himself for the Easter dance. These were the days where one had to be prepared—that is, to pull off the right face, the right body. He had always managed in Church—the week of the Lord's Passion, to be somber, thoughtful with his wife on his arm, sometimes, in the front of the church with the whole congregation behind him, his hand waving his wife off impatiently as she invariably bent her face into his, he would kneel down and press his forehead to the floor and up and down. It was obnoxious her peering into his face like that; was he not a devout believer? What did she expect him to do, stand up and rejoice? Was it not necessary to confess oneself a sinner? Then, he would be the first. And images ran through his head—a gold chalice of blood, hot blood for some reason, held up before him. And he would think solemnly with a sense of petty satisfaction—and so, I am worthy.

Why the petty satisfaction—it was a question that bothered him later. Ah there are saints and there are saints. Some look up on God with wonder. And some…but he would later push all reflection aside. It was time for the dance. He had to be prepared. He could still do the back flip, the leap, although a little lower, the pirouette. He could do the cartwheel without hands. There was no question he would win the crown on Easter. And he would wear it with that same triumph, that victory—as if the island was an enemy territory that he, a foreign potentate, was conquering. And the crown would glint in everyone's eyes and above everyone's heads; because he was a tall and stately man cut out for a kind of rule—not only of dancing parties.

So he would pull his muscles until they stretched again long, impossibly long, and jump and run and get himself generally into shape for the dance. But it was as if written in his body, he had done it so often before. As he was practicing on the lawn behind his tower-study, he thought now and then of Agatha with a kind of smirk imagined that she would creep into a hole when he danced; she for whom nearly ten years had been barely enough to straighten her spine. And they say she was dancing. Witches don't dance. They hop and skip as if they are landing barefoot on hot coals.

But nonetheless, there was talk, and Paul had felt, yes, even he, uneasy in her presence. And what with the coming and going, the near possession of Agatha of the island through the sale of so much of it to the rich man by the intervention of her son, and then, the rich man's sudden departure, and Little Paul's fight with Dimitri that they had to hastily apologize for—he had felt that in some inexplicable way he was coming nearer to her. She like he apparently had ambition. She like he danced, apparently more and more spectacularly. And although he didn't quite believe it when the old men simply lusted and clouded over when they saw her, still it may be that she was up to something; and there was at heart a strange sense in him of ostracizing, since this had happened. He, of course, was not frowned on like Agatha, but he stood apart. He was, in a sense, watched. The village didn't treat him as one of themselves. And although he said to himself that this was because he was the natural leader, deep down it felt like being outcast. It felt as if there were suspicions. He always said to himself, because he told nobody of this, that this was the price for being superior in intellect, talent. And that one day the island would fall into his hand, his guiding hand, like a ripe plum off a tree. But so far it had not fallen and now there was trouble: Paul's son was getting more and more violent. There were whisperings. Apparently his son had a band of six to ten twenty some year olds who said things in low voices, which he could never hear, looked and laughed behind his back at him, an old fogey. This made him uneasy—for one can go from the promise of the island to old fogey as one can suck out a raw egg and leave behind a meaningless shell. The one proof that this had not happened was the Easter dance. He was crowned every year. He beat even Little Paul on the dance floor— twenty years younger than he who didn't have a single dance move in him.

As spring rolls in again—we are in the thick of March, rains and winds, but not always cold winds—we still have some of the old stirrings. Zoe continues abstracted—she begins a long sermon on the love of a woman, just like that, yes, looks at us, begins with those very words, and then cracks up and begins to weep. We don't think she has anything at all to say. These are just words that she got from somewhere and they suddenly appear in her brain, which is fixed on some other place besides earth, the spiritual home perhaps that we all one day will be a part of. But now and then, it is one might say, earth to Zoe! She pops up with these phrases that we have heard uttered by men and women and there is always some sequel that doesn't quite wrap up the mystery, but leaves it dangling in our faces with those half visions…Zoe didn't even bother to try to wrap up with words. She wept.

There are times we think that Zoe has hit upon something extraordinarily deep. Foti, who is a bit witless, pipes up with: what is the difference between the brain and the soul? If wickedness is just a physical thing like a big nose, how is it we are so held to account? We think that Foti has been reading some of the science magazines that Katrina spends her nights devouring. These magazines try to convince you that everything is mechanical and material that the universe is like a big machine and that it somehow produces itself. Then, I suppose said Cleo with dignity, that there is no distinguishing good and evil for everything arises from the same electrical activity in the brain.

But that is true, said Foti triumphantly. The only difference is whether or not a community survives. And the instinct to survive is…

Yes, yes, said Cleo—but so, they say, is the fascination to destroy.

And so it is like one color flame shot into the atmosphere and then another. Where is the good or evil? Out there it doesn't matter which is which.

Foti was so excited, thinking that she had finally reasoned something out that she wouldn't listen to anybody and became almost as bad as Zoe, enveloped in her own thoughts, oblivious to everyone and everything else.

When Cleo served us apricot brandy and little sugar cookies, and we took up our crocheting and embroidery, Foti could be heard to murmur —out there it doesn't matter. That is key. There is no oxygen and no good and evil.

Cleo kept on with a grim face. She said to Agatha once, you know about this. We thought it was unfair because Agatha didn't.

What? Asked Agatha looking steadily into her eyes.

Oh, this coming to life of Foti, coming to intellectual life, sneering emphasis on the word 'intellectual'.

Has she?

If you want to call it that. She doesn't know, of course, what she is doing or saying.

It is very similar to this lifting of your foot high above your head. Of course, it is not what we do. The dance was made a certain way by our forefathers; our bones even are laid out this way in the particular dance steps, one way for women, another way for men. There is a reason.

I thought skeletons were skeletons.

Ah, if you could see what I mean. The dance is in our bones, Agatha. And you come with your Gypsy blood and say but I…Even the Muslim bible doesn't tell you that. We are like frail little baby grass beneath your big feet. You would crush us and not hear our pitiful cries. Slide our lives, the whole fabric of our existence, the sons and daughters of those who saw the resurrected Jesus into the sea, and put something of your own in its place. Poor Foti, she sees the end of time and just doesn't know what to do other than babble.

It may be the end of time, Cleo, said Agatha, sternly. And the fact remains that we will all find ourselves in one configuration or another. This island as long as I remember has never opted for moral beauty and…

What do you know about moral beauty? Snapped Cleo.

Agatha was silent. It was useless to say that lifting her leg to the sun had anything to do with it. You know I did repent, she put in at last.

Ah, said Cleo ironically.

Yes, this is all repentance. It took sweat and tears and constancy to God.

And breaking into pieces all that nurtured you.

Nurtured? You would have burned me to death.

That is false like any one of your many falsehoods. The island has decayed, practically disintegrated. There are owing to your activities, for the immorality takes on a life and energy of its own and seeps into the environment like a poison—there are immoral men, violent men who rise up at the mere whisper of some contention, some fractious phrase.

You mean Paul.

Paul saved your life and when little Paul attacked Dimitri, Paul apologized.

But never mind the surface. It is the hate underneath.

That you have caused. All the way back to when you were almost a child and for some obscure reason, the pampering of that vagrant father and his wild ways, you went to Paul and…

And what?

Everything was set off balance. Yes, the dance was set off balance.

All because I lifted my foot to the sun, years later as I wanted to then.

You have a way with you, said Cleo fiercely to her.

Die or live, Foti came up to Agatha, smiling. It doesn't matter. It is like one color or another out there in the dark outer space.

Yes, maybe you can't even see it, said Agatha, nodding her head at her a little brusquely. Cleo looked the other way with a sniff that was half contemptuous, and half self-pity. Agatha felt the old depression suddenly slide into place on her back like a lead weight. But she didn't bow down to it. She fought off that temptation. She lifted her body erect from the small of her back; there were many voices in this depression that seemed to be like silence but in fact was a kind of dumbness or muteness instead. There were many voices…if one could let them free--. She glided out of Cleo's house more softly than a shadow.

It was time to listen to the voices. One was saying that she could rule the world. How rule? Well, there are ways and ways, and the voice laughed, a silvery laugh. For one thing, conquer. How that? Asked Agatha. At Easter, at the dance competition. Wear the ancient gold crown. It will have an effect. You know that will never happen. Even if I danced, even if I won against Paul and no one has beaten him for more than twenty years, they would not permit that on an unbaptized head, at Easter, the crown would be planted. Don't you want the crown? Think how it would silence them, the bitches and bastards. You now, the king of dancers. How could I be a king? Easy. The king is not about sex at all; it is about ability, strength, pliancy, lightness—the ability to make of your body a stepladder up to the stars. A cartwheel towards the sun.

I will do it, said Agatha dreamily. And then a chorus of other voices chimed in. You have been living life all wrong, like from the wrong end of a telescope. You want to live as if you are the one guilty. But your hips when you walk, those are hips of a queen, and your head, your chin. Why not become king as if the hips of dance are government not marriage? Put the world in its place. A little to the side, a little like a sleepy child falling over the arms that hold it. You know the proper direction. Your lifted foot, the toe pointing above the horizon like an arrow into the clouds, then, in a circle as you spin, your back arched, toe of the other foot firm on the ground. This, you see, is all that humanity desires, the pure ache of man or woman, randomly selected, as high as the sun. This deepening and at the core finding that uncreated light of dance when it becomes nature—this is man or woman, selected randomly. Thus if you can only do it without the slightest ruffle, tilt, accident, you will have in your hand the entire world; that is, not the world out there as Foti puts it, but the world as it is—humanity! One stumbles sometimes on it. You will have in your heart the crowning.

These were the many voices. Each sentence spoken by a different one with a timbre of voice distinct from the others. Not one was harsh. It sounded rather like a passage of music played on the piano when one hears the keys pressed, the note played and it sounds somehow like what a pure running stream would sound like were it articulated instead of mostly mute.

Agatha entranced by the beauty of the different voices in her head went along with them, was carried by the stream down, down past the village, out into sea and far away to a dawn country where there was nothing but dance, and the whispering of many dancing creatures, human and bird and beast—and although she didn't know the language, she knew that they were all saying: she will do it. She is one of us.

Agatha was walking home when the voices swelled in her mind and became a trance. She turned automatically down the front walk. She could see the profile of Dimitri's head in the window in the dim light. She came into the front door to the sound of singing, then arguing—something about the milk not being warm enough. She breathed on the threshold. Here was a world, which was gradually more and more alien to the dance of God. The magic of love was such that it did cast out the world to a certain degree. Despite Dimitri's philandering, he and Catherine were enclosed together in a shell of love into which nobody else could ever come. Agatha felt that with pain. Here in this house she had lost Dimitri, because the love had happened in her house, after the baby, when the homeless family had all camped out in her wedding bedroom with the photo of Alex staring mindlessly out at them. How odd it was. And Catherine had become utterly lush, sweet smelling, and it was clear that a mere glance of her eyes was in fact everything that Dimitri had ever wanted. So here, at last was marriage.

She had had a kind of straining with her husband. Cruelty, resentment, pity. And now Catherine who had been all long chest, attenuated, waif-pale, was suddenly more like a ripe apple, a perfect dancer with none of the labor, a cloud of the most delicious perfume. And Dimitri had grown handsomer if it were possible, secretive, laughing lightly, tenderly at nothing. He laughed a little, thought Agatha, as if he were hurt by her perfection.

She stepped into a house that contained another sphere—something not quite earthly, despite the constant smelling of baby's bottom, the warming of milk and minced baby foods. Dimitri was talking about a new version of the hotel into which he planned to sink his last savings. A house like the others, only divided up into little rooms. He would put his mother to work there, cooking and cleaning. Catherine would be at the front desk. Agatha laughed at him. I won't do any cooking and cleaning for a hotel, she said, but she smiled.

But mother, said Dimitri, his brow wrinkled in consternation, here I cut short my career, my life because of your incessant pleas for me to come home. I am home, married with a son—what more can you ask? And I simply ask for a logical return, an input. Do you expect me to just sit here like a carcass of beef until the flies gather? Aren't you glad that I have begun to think about standing up as a man of business once more? Here on the island, by your side. The least you could do is help me. It would then be a family affair.

He has a point, said Catherine, smiling like a rose. Remember it would be serving at most ten rooms, and some of them families, but not all.

I have my own life, now, said Agatha airily. I will be dancing, marrying.

Well, said Dimitri, it seems like life has finally worked out for all of us. Who will you be marrying?

A man, a friend. In fact, Agatha up until this point, had quite forgotten Leo. She remembered him more because here he conveniently fit into the argument against cooking and cleaning for Dimitri's bed and breakfast rather than because of some latent passion for him.

I will, Mother, support you and your marriage to Leo, Dimitri was saying to her, but Agatha wasn't listening. She was looking at him and thinking things that cannot be put into words and she breathed a soft, sad sigh.

Thought came and went quick and light like a feather blown by—life had passed her by. She was nothing; she was nobody, worse, she was futile. She had danced more than ten years with nothing to show for it. What constituted passing the time for her for the past thirty-five years had been waiting. Waiting that is all. Waiting for the moment when—she would cast off the oppression, the depression—when she would have life as others did—a perfect fulfillment, in one outcry. Yes, something that would be heard and remembered. She had been crippled early on. Like a serpent with its back end crushed, a dog or a cat, with its hind legs broken, she had dragged herself from that time, from that house that was now built up, white washed, the only white one in the village, with a tower on the east side, she had dragged herself up and down the road, through her chores as a housewife and mother.

Then one day, looking at her son, she had suddenly been healed. Uncrushed. And of course, feeling inestimably guilty, she had damned herself. And a spark had ignited a huge, beautiful fire. And the thought had come—take this fire and dance out of hell with it. And then had come the various chores she had done for Matrona, Martha, Leo. And the sheep-like eyes of Martha now were constant; she adored her and arrived every day on her doorstep at three to be fed, to touch the baby, to open her mouth wide and laugh and jump up and down and unzip and tear off clothes that Agatha quietly, with her finger on her lips at Martha, put back on her. And Martha with her finger on her lips in response accepted. So Martha was undressed and dressed. And to her it all made perfect sense. Whereas Leo looked at her with a half removed gaze as if she knew something he knew particularly intelligent, lazy, and gratifying. So in the end, she had gone from loneness with children whom she loathed, to healing, love, soundness, friendship—a little circle despite the antagonism like a miracle and a tabooed love that was the start of the healing and the perfection.

How could he be so beautiful? He was the start and the finish. He the one she had almost torn out of her body. She had thought about it constantly, when she was pregnant in the early stages and even in the later. Alex was supremely attentive, there was no denying that. But she had hated the child in her body. Who was it? A cousin of Anna's she thought, come over from the other island, who said—do you want me to get rid of it for you? I know of a place where they do such things. Agatha looked up. The woman was dark, all eyebrows on a white white forehead with black lank hair. How did you know? I can read any woman's eyes—the eyes are the window to the soul.

Agatha had arranged, paid the woman the money and then at the last minute, not gone. She had not shown up at the appointed place on the other island. Why? It was just an instinctive reaction against the surgery. As she remembered, Agatha simply didn't want to be invaded again. She did drink a powder— that was supposed to kill the fetus —that another woman gave her, another woman who also read her eyes. The powder was horribly bitter, but did nothing at all. And then she stopped. She sighed. She was used to misery. For eighteen years she continued used to it.

Jason would have kept her that way, she knew and she pitied him. But Dimitri had become handsome in a way that ate into her a bit, that flayed the inner skin. One day she thought, seeing Dimitri escape and escape, as beautifully as a long necked bird flying, the cut of Jason's knife, rather than misery why not joy? She shuddered remembering the razor against Dimitri's neck! And since the misery was far more habit than the joy, she called out hell to quench the fire of joy of Dimitri's expert evasion, physically expressed so light like the dance. She didn't really remember the rest of it. It was just a hoarse, dreadful cry that came out of her. And the boys stopped; Jason looked at her sweating, open mouthed with fear and shock. Dimitri now snatched the razor from his brother's hand and walked over to her and kissed her. She was frozen with her arms in front of her like a soldier marching. Dimitri moved her arms gently back and forth. I am leaving, Mother, he said. Tomorrow.

It took time to come out of the trauma of that hoarse dreadful cry that came right out of her heart. To come out of the question: What was she? What could she possibly be? And then, the vision—the hairy wild woman with purple ribbons. And then that free feeling, the climb up to Simon's house in the late evening. And the beginning. It was the beginning, Simon said, of sewing together the torn pieces that made up her heart until they were as smoothly one as if a dream.

How was it possible to do? She spoke like a child to him as if she hardly had command over her mouth uttering the words. Magic, said Simon. For a minute she thought he was old and silly. Magic, he repeated. You have to work until dancing is magic. And Agatha went home. When she was alone, she thought it was like a fairy tale where the princess had been assigned an impossible task. But there was no funny, little, diabolical man to help. It was all her sweat. And when she had at last come together, oh, they wanted to tear her apart again. Even Dimitri did not understand, sitting at breakfast, Catherine leaning towards the child in the high chair.

You will have to hire someone to do all that cooking and cleaning, she said shortly to Dimitri and Catherine. Well, that is no problem. But you said you are marrying just as a joke, hinted Dimitri, hopefully. Or a metaphor, he said to Catherine. Agatha was silent.

Irrationally, Agatha wanted Dimitri and Catherine both in the house and somewhere else. She thought vaguely that she would, should give it to them, Jason would have to live somewhere else, or perhaps he would stay, a reclusive, clammed up figure fending for himself every morning now, in the back room that had always been his bedroom. She would live with Leo. But towards Dimitri and his wife and child, how could she express it? She was embarrassed and ashamed. There were moments of proper tenderness and moments of violence. And when she retired at night, she thought she heard, just barely the sounds of love making between her son and daughter in law, and she much as she tried to repress herself found herself aroused and even over the peak, as it were.

She knew well that she was in love with her son. It was that kind of tabooed love that tore tears from her. There was nothing actually between them—but oh so many times she had felt it. She had thought it was all just jest and freedom, the sort of thing that would make Barbara turn away all sour faced from the window and scrape her kitchen chairs—this kissing of him, closed mouth but long and tender, this wrapping of one leg around him, this putting her face softly against his bosom. She thought the whole idea that she had proclaimed round about and that first even Zoe smiled about albeit wanly—that she was in love with her son—was just so much fluff, puff, laughter; it was a little dream as lacking in obscenity as a little white summer cloud. It was proprietorship, mother claiming son and the beauty on him like heaven claims dawn, like clear midnights. Mother not wanting to let go. And he had gone and she had survived on his letters. How odd, they seemed to be outpourings of his inmost self for her alone. As if in a dark shadow, he was saying, yes, I know this love and you know, although I will never say it, is ours alone.

Dimitri had never been surprised at her outrageous kisses and leg-twinings around his body. No, he had continued in a rather meek, perfect son demeanor—affectionate, patient, and protective. Then, she would think it is nothing at all. But it was the sight of that face, suddenly provocatively handsome, a jewel, or a brilliant sculpture out of the invisible, a light out of darkness, hanging in her vision, as it were, threatened by her other son, that had made her scream out the terrible curse. And then the face came back with a penitent air, though he was victim, saying away I'll go—even more the hero of a romance—their romance. But this no one was to know. No one was to see. Away I'll go—it was this that had made them lovers, passionate lovers, the greatest lovers that ever were—this unspoken, of course, in the margin of his eyes looking into hers and this vast tract of sea between them and the margin of his eyes.

But of course, all mothers and sons are lovers. Clandestinely, in their souls. And her heart had fled with him, brimming up from her loins, breaking free from her breast, scampering over the water. And he like a conductor of an orchestra had waved a hand at her invisibly, an interior invisible hand, and raised her each morning from her bed with sweet arousal like birds rustling, singing and popped her on her legs, with the will to lift one high…How was that? Odd, the things that the inner self, the other body did suddenly!

She would behave like a young girl around him—scampering around the kitchen; cooking for him was more of a love act than anything else. He was her young stranger—handsome man appearing, lost, needing of home comfort. He was nothing like the child she had frankly disliked who had been morose but relatively docile with her; who had thought, no doubt, that it was quite normal for mothers to hate their children. Now it was something different: it was as if a whole new creature had materialized with a wonderful polish on it. This polish conjured up other lands with different smelling air and a long voyage thither, which consisted mostly of finding that one door in the universe through which one had to pass were one to go beyond the limitations, the boundaries of all knowledge. And he had gone through, simply opened and walked, on water, on air…There were undoubtedly half human half beasts in that walking through space, fabulous conversations with stars, books that told of the signs that were written in human bodies, in gardens, seas, animals. Of course, coming back through the door, he had forgotten but he still looked like that knowledge. There was something in his eyes. She thought he was on this journey before he had actually, physically, sailed to Athens and then on to London. He had read a book, he had become a man with a woman in the forests—and there he was. But the going away, the slip of him, here today, gone tomorrow had also made him so much more a through-the-door creature. That one unsolvable door.

Now here he was forgetful of all that, with a woman, a wife, of course, what else would make him so forgetful? It was as if there was still a hum around his head from that land of the door, one could hear it faintly if one stood close to him, but otherwise, he was cut off, the door was all but shut in his face. And she felt in her heart of hearts, where one doesn't stay long for the fear of it, that were he her love, the door would open again.

It was half agony, half amusement to her. Imagine being caught up in an incestuous infatuation! She had thought long ago when she still hated him that she would get rid of her son—not the same way in which she tried to kill him when he was inside her, a fetus, but in another way—that she would send him away to a boarding school. She had talked it over with Alex. This one is intelligent; this one ought to receive a better education—a school thus and so. But he is a non talker, a mute; where could he go? Asked Alex. And so Dimitri at seven had hung around the house like a little thief, said Agatha miserably to herself. But there was presentiment there. But when things changed and that one door opened in the universe, when she had looked up and loved, because it had been that sudden, in fact, she had blushed scarlet as his eyes caught hers, then his going away was another matter. Her lower belly opened, her upper belly was tied into something inextricable. The sweat poured down the sides of her face.

She understood between that look and his decision violence would occur. It seemed natural; it was part of a logical sequence that she had not taken time to properly consider, somehow. And then hell on her head, hell, the curse. Then she had forgotten everything, except for Dimitri who still stood with an uncertain look and soft little smile, saying to her—Mother, mother—I am going. It was an attempt to patch things up with God for her, she intuited, not with Jason or Holy Island.

And things were and weren't. Here she was cursed. The whole village knew. She wore it bravely on her brow, she thought—that is, of course, you could read it there. In between the sheets, she would dream of her son, she would become aroused. Over time, it became more of an emotional thing. His beauty was suddenly to her like a fragile basket in which she was trying to carry her most treasured possessions. She held him in her heart. She was an adolescent girl. He, he was going to break…

Then she had bowed her head to the powers that made this happen. This strange confluence of the two of them their new harmony and their secret harmony. She simply decided that it was ok. She had a son; he was her beloved. She was not grossly fleshly. She didn't exactly dream of fornication or masturbate. Their love making, that is, her imaginary adoration of him, was like the embrace of sky and earth. Delight, adoration. It rose and fell softly in her belly like waves, it spread out in her belly like smooth seas.

There was no solving this riddle. The village knew of it vaguely. They believed anything could come of not being baptized. And they also believed, in their obstinate, folklorish way, that the bond between mother and son could be more powerful almost than God. One day Agatha said to herself in a number of ways: if it is thus and so, and the book opens on my page in God's hand, why not lift my leg high? A salute to the sun.

And the priest laughed and said to her long before Dimitri returned—in the tangled skein of what a human is, there are only a few things, a few recourses. One of them is to dance to the sun because of the sea.

Now Dimitri, the cut off boy, whom her soul clung to like a vine, was in and out of the house with Catherine and Tock or without them; Catherine was unperturbed about it though she had been cheated on twice, she was lost in the rhythm of feeding and changing Tock, the confines of the day, thought Agatha. Dimitri would leave or take his jacket. Agatha would smell the jacket, close her eyes and think a minute.

One afternoon, when Catherine and Tock were taking a siesta, Dimitri walked into the kitchen and picked up his jacket that was lying there and said to her—I've got it all worked out with the sisters of the monastery on the cliff; we are to purchase the Elder's shack for little money. We will be living there. Leaving here! We will no longer be underfoot.

Agatha swallowed. But, she said, vaguely, that house is so small. You could wait until I marry Leo and go to his home; then you will have this one.

Of course, said Dimitri stiffly; and then he became reflective. Something tells me I ought to get away though. From this house, yes from this house—he said, although Agatha had not said anything. This is a place where a strange feeling lurks. You have been a target of the villagers' hate, don't say you haven't! And there is something in general unwholesome. It isn't so much you. I don't know what it is. We never as a family quite mixed well. Face it, you don't act like other mothers. Not that I don't ardently admire you. I know you have your dancer's ways. It is just that I am lost here. I really would like an entirely fresh start. Here the walls remind me even...and think of poor Jason—to see me successful without lifting a finger. I thought also it might be good for Catherine and me to spend time together in a home we made ourselves.

Agatha froze and trembled. Of course, she said. Earth and sky reeling around her. I thought, oh I thought that...she ejaculated passionately.

But we would come often, and when you are at Leo's—Catherine will be there every day. Dimitri twirled his jacked behind one shoulder, winked at her and left.

The house was the house. The sun still came into the kitchen too strongly. There was a smell of coffee lingering—she had just made some. Her life too was in place. There was Leo, a comfortable, comforting kind of man, more or less like a cushion; there was Jason—he would be left with the house. She imagined it dark and Jason wandering into the kitchen with a newly caught fish dangling from his fist to cook, switching a dim light on. He would fill the halls with emptiness. And stonily, doggedly live.

Agatha wanted to cry out. Despite her cursed nature, the fact that her one beloved was not her husband to be but her son, she had filled the air with aliveness. She had managed to lift her leg high, and point her toe towards the rising sun and hold it there. She had leapt three feet off the ground, pirouetted on her bare toes with her back arched. She had done such things despite, despite—the murderous anger still lurking in Jason, the obscene impassivity in him, the terrible sins in her—one, two, three, and so on to infinity. And she had sprung up tall from her stoop; and the beauty had begun on her again. Now he was going to leave that house—he, being the only he. And she had crept around him so faithfully, quietly, unobtrusively! Her joy had almost been complete. It was she that knew him—his ways, his needs! Catherine did not. It was she that came up out of the shadows to provide and sink back into the shadows to watch his beauty. And it was she and he that walked with that slight similarity, that flesh of flesh in body and face.

Besides it was not all a dreadful thing. There were times she knew for the first time her son, her baby: Times she came up out of her womb it seemed, emerged through her waiting, blind flesh to Dimitri and saw something like her maker. These times had paradoxically in the middle of the worst of sins, brought back the holiness.

She breathed out a long breath and put her tips of her fingers to her lips. The thought that they were going was just a little painful. But when they actually left, the pain was unbearable. And to make it almost unbearably sweet, he had left her a pair of dancing slippers, God knows where he had found them—grey pink with rose red ribbons and pink pearls, real pearls on the tops of the toes. They were the color of love, innocent, tabooed love. And their color danced like a beautiful spice, like the white-hot brilliant eleven o' clock of an island August morning: bursting into the opening bubble of the sky.

The Easter dance was upon them. First there was Palm Sunday and the week of the Passion, the Pascha vigil. The little church had all the icons out. Max carried armfuls of wild grass crosses —that substituted for palms— that the old women had made, Cleo, Foti and some of the others, into the church narthex, really a side room next to the entrance and deposited them on a counter there next to the candles for sale.

The priest was preaching with increased ardor; he seemed to thrust out the words in his harsh voice so that they would take root in the little audience's minds. And these same folk, village folk, who lay down their cloaks before Jesus on the donkey would rise up against him and shout crucify him! Imagine a man groaning, with his head hanging, still loving like a child loves. You who want to rejoice so much with God—having kept the commandments—but defiled yourselves with self-righteous-ness...Do you think it is you that God loves?

Agatha listened in the back; she never dared to come closer to the altar, except when she went to bow and pray before the Crucifix. No God did not love her. Think of her sins! And the proud way she had of talking to! No, it was all a delusion that she had won. There was her path, down, down with her back bent, her leg dragging into the pitch- black outer darkness. Even prayer was hard for her now; her talking-to strained. Often she only repeated 'have mercy, have mercy' in a whisper. Perhaps she would receive a lighter sentence of hell.

Outside of the church, she felt lighter, almost gayer. She decided to go on danc-ing; it made her feel like she could stand on two feet. When she thought of Dimitri, the pain came back, sometimes she felt his absence like a presence that hurt her deep down in the middle of her body. But she continued her dancing. There was a power greater than her own that lifted her mornings and set her in position. Perhaps, she thought, this is what it means to have a soul. This power despite all the odds.

She went to visit Anna and found that she had miraculously, as it were, recovered a bit. She had ceased to lose weight and was doing rather well, sitting up on the side of the bed and going to the bathroom unaided. Agatha had gone to her, full of melancholy, creeping down the road that curved along the beach, down to the stately yellow house, and turning the key, for Anna had at last provided her with one, in the lock, opening up the door on the rooms full of massive furnishings, Venetian tables, sideboards, paintings; her own house was so flimsy it could hardly bear the weight of these things. And she had quietly mounted the staircase to the small bedroom where Anna was barely a lump on the white bed. Anna had said: Ho there, and laughed a little.

In a matter of twenty minutes, Agatha had forgotten her melancholy and was telling her about dance. I am not sure what it was in me that wanted dance, she said, sitting on the edge of the bed and taking off her jacket; the sun was strong. I started out of instinct. I could have been of course an entirely different person if....

You mean long ago—Paul.

Yes, I merely asked him to teach me...the tears rose in her eyes. Well, there is no point in crying about it. It was all a petty thing, really. I never hardened up. That's all.

You mean in a perfect world, Paul would have taught you, supported your instinct. Maybe then the island would have permitted women to dance beyond the line dance, the little steps. And you would have been...a thoroughly lost person.

What do you mean? Everything would have worked out.

Look, I don't have much right to speak, being mostly unbeliever. But I do know that often these people who are so 'saved' in your opinion and the opinion of the world, the ones for whom everything has 'worked out' are really the ones going to the devil. Don't you see? Whereas you, sinner-outcast, carrying the cross, refusing baptism on the theory that you will connect to the true Jesus, minus rituals, ghostly churches who 'confer' it on you, as if they hold God hostage—merely by the strength, there's the test, of your love for him—you are the one with the chance; the little daredevil spirituality.

So you think, said Agatha, that I should dance! She said it out of the blue but Anna laughed as if she was expecting it.

You should win, she said, the gold crown.

For what reason?

Superior dancing. You are better than Paul.

I? I'm a slut, a rebel, a renegade...

You are a dancer in the eyes of God. No more, no less. You are not bathed in Church water, but in your sweat.

What are dancers?

Oh, they are there. Remember the parable of the Prodigal Son. At the end there was singing and dancing in the house of the Father.

You know that Dimitri left.

No, Anna shook her head.

Yes, he went off with Catherine and Tock. They are living in the old Elder's shack on the mountain.

I never saw the Elder. Heard that he had died, she reflected a minute. You see, they live so as to die. Won't stand for the dissatisfactions of life. It is just death and then something infinitely better. But they allow for things. I've heard that even he joined the Easter dance in his younger days. Danced a honey of a dance though he never won anything. I think I saw him once. Faded, strained sort of smile. Old, pale face even when he was young. All hairy—long beard, hair. He moved very quickly through the village. Didn't stop to talk. I think he bought some medications from the supply boat. One person talked to him. I think it was Foti. She was an imbecile always about men, tried to snare this one too, although he clearly wasn't in the least interested. He said to her that he was on this island because it was as good as any other. And now—gone. Makes you think of the mystery of existence. One sentence on his lips, one movement in the midst of us, a dance that no one remembers, then up the cliff, then dead, having nothing to show for it but a love for medications.

But I believe, said Anna with a strange smile, that now he is in heaven, and he has got over all the prejudices against women, he is saying to you, Agatha, dance, dance, dance! The Holy Trinity is saying it to you. Dance, says the Father like a kettle drum, Dance, says the Son, singing a beautiful tenor, Dance peeps the Holy Spirit like a chime... Then they pause for it. It's as if you could add something to God.

Agatha laughed and stayed on to talk to Anna about this and that. How she would come to her with roast lamb at Easter. Anna protested, my son is coming. It is to be his one outing to this island, don't disappoint him by feeding me lamb before he arrives. He is bringing his two wives. The one he divorced to fuss, the other to provide chit chat.

Tia came in with some lemonade at around five. She had made herself quite a nest in the other room and was enjoying herself amidst the beautiful oak wardrobe and the tall French bed with canopy curtains. It was clear as Agatha went in to see her room on invitation that Tia was holing up happily, perhaps happily as never before. She confessed that she liked Anna—she had a personality that stood a mile tall, she said. No one could bring her down.

Then Agatha thought and said to her: You haven't heard her complain that she hasn't loved?

Yes, now and again. I have offered her myself, said the girl, pensively. But she says it is not that kind of love. I have wondered what kind there is.

Something closer to what we would call justice, I think, said Agatha—righteousness. But not what is usually considered...

She went back into the room with Tia following. Her lemonade was waiting on the little table. Anna was sipping hers.

I particularly relish this lemonade made of our lemons, said Anna. Tia does a wonderful job of concocting this old drink. She knows exactly how to strike a balance between sour and sweet.

How I want to creep into you, into your body, I think, said Agatha to Anna, suddenly. You have it made: a mind, an interpretation, even down to your toes.

Oh what a love letter said aloud, said Anna crinkling up her face into a smile. But what do you mean interpretation?

A way of living, said Agatha. A life of life, the sun's own secret knowledge. I never had anything like it. I just fumbled, rolled from time to time.

But you have your dancing.

It isn't much more than gymnastics, I've discovered.

Come to bed, with me, said Anna, stretching out one attenuated arm. Agatha crept into the bed with her. Here we have learned things, haven't we? And here you cannot honestly say that a woman who has done absolutely nothing with her life but savor the sweet and the sour, lovely sour, not bitter sour, has suddenly discovered the secret of living where you who have sweated and toiled on the greatest thing life has to offer—love—is somehow a great nothing.

But it is true. You have a way with you Anna that no one else can even come close to, even my son, with all his intellect. It makes me suddenly want to have cancer of the lung and to lie in bed stinking a little of urine. Others have reared up at me—you know, Paul, Zoe, Barbara and I have shrunk back all dutiful, but they have been-- how can I say it—like walls, imposing, fighting me off mentally-- sometimes you almost believe that they have something, contain something—but there has never been joy. You are like a window all full of light and beauty on the inside. One wants to keep it somehow, in love and jealousy—in hope, faith, tenderness—to guard it. To be it. Imagine being a window and people seeing--. It is the greatest joy, I think, to be like a window...

There is one joy greater, said Anna, reflectively, smiling. To be a door, the door.

Ah, Agatha shuddered a little; my son.

Then why when you come to me do you open up a great whale of light?

I? Agatha said in a hushed wondering voice.

You.

Why? What have I ever done or said?

I am not sure. I am not sure that it matters. Look, you must dance because win or lose it will mean something. It will turn heads. Turn a village; a world! Even the little butterfly's wings fluttering conjure up a storm on the other side of the world!

The dance was traditionally held on Easter eve up on the hill near the little church, precisely on the spot where the villagers had burned Father Isaac's writings. The little plot consisted of a square of weedy grass, mown down to stubble about fifty by fifty feet, a flat ledge in the hill. Usually, for the most part it was humdrum dancing. The village women got together and put on their best performance, which was just a mechanical repetition of steps they'd learned from their grandmothers. Musicians used to play for them—in Agatha's girlhood, her father was considered the best, although also, by some, demonically possessed. Now they had nothing but Simon with a recorder and a tape.

Last year, they had arranged so that two tape recorders would play the same tape at full blast and the viewers would sit around in white plastic chairs on the periphery of the dance floor. The judges, picked from among the men, always, for women in the island tradition knew nothing of fishing, dancing or decision making, being 'imprecise creatures,' according to Paul, had preferred seating up in front close to the action. From there they could see a leg wobble, or a knee bent when it was supposed to be straight.

That evening people assembled with more than the usual interest. News had flown around like a messenger pigeon from house to house the night before that Agatha was going to compete with the men.

Stavros was rather jolly about it which got Barbara's goat. Here it is all resolved most beautifully, he said and sat down in the only overstuffed armchair of maroon leather and crossed his leg so that the knee poked up, and opened the newspaper. The whole thing made Barbara burn with fury. That knee was entirely demonstration for one thing; it was as if to say one gets the better of contemptible people so easily, with such ease, to speak plainly. And she, of course, writhing with inexplicable anguish and anger over Agatha's dancing, was a contemptible person. It really is not rational, said Stavros that you should hold it against her that she has done a simple thing like dance and reach a certain expertise in it. I wouldn't hold it against you had you done it.

But the point is one didn't just do a thing like that. Agatha did it because, because...

She was outcast from all other joy, Stavros finished her sentence for her.

Not at all not really. We never held her parentage against her. No, it was that she should use this island to make a sort of statement. It isn't so much who she is, at all, at all. You know that I have been a good neighbor to her.

Hardly. Poking and prying but very little friendly talking to.

But you see, she has kept herself aloof. She has joined what you might call the 'militant feminists'—Barbara had once read the expression in an old magazine from the seventies that had percolated into the pile that was delivered to them from the other island's library. I mean it is the audacity—the desire to-- as it were --exhibit themselves... It is nothing more than that. It is feminist exhibitionism. And you know, Agatha is, well, you know—she touches people: Anna, Simon; and it is all for free.

Would you have it be for money? Stavros chuckled.

Even with Anna, though, don't you understand?

No; so she gives the poor lady a caress. You don't even visit her.

She has sex with everyone, blurted out Barbara, finally. I have seen her even with her own son. This dancing is no more than to say—see, I can do it! In the face, our face—of an island that believes in Christ.

Are you sure she is having sex (bravo, I must say, you wouldn't ordinarily express yourself so forthrightly) with everyone?

(I don't know why you say bravo! I had to express myself you are so thick headed...) As good as. And the dancing, you see, is to spread sexual wings...

Hmm. Well, you may have a point there. But oh, wife, you know it in your bones—one builds one's life on a foundation of sexual wings. The difference between you and her is you never were honest with yourself about it.

What went reeling through Barbara's head the night of the Easter vigil and all through the chanting and candle holding was that she really couldn't stand Stavros at all, that it was all humiliation but that it would be worse to leave him for then Agatha would have won….Much as it burnt her like a hot brand down in her belly, she would stay and be the demure, long skirted little stepping dancing wife; after all the real reward was not in this life.

But you, Stavros said, kissing her in bed in the dark, much to Barbara's indignation, will go up to God like a lion roaring. Everything for you is done out of anger and resentment and will explode after death because in life you denied yourself your own spirit.

Easter came and went. They sang the hymn Christ is risen; Barbara heard Agatha in the background and looked around at her full of annoyance, but she was so calm-eyed and quiet-faced that Barbara turned around again her anger muffled for the moment, the solemnity of the occasion. For the meal there was a village cook out, lamb and other foodstuffs that the village ladies prepared and the smoke from the lamb roasting wafted and down from the hillside where the spit was turning in front of the church and filled the little village.

Paul who received the nods of the villagers, especially of the ladies—Cleo came down to him from her perch in a white plastic chair above the spit and with the smoke of roast lamb cooking over a fire blowing all over her, in her hair and on her dress, rearranged his shirt collar flirtatiously, smiled into his face and said to him—you are a little lamb; it takes just crack with the Shepherd's staff to get you into the flock—Paul stuffed his face with grape leaf balls filled with rice and mint and ambled away to practice for the night, leaving instructions with Ella to set aside a plate of lamb meat.

And I said, said Cleo, satisfied, to Foti, and Zoe who was staring absent-mindedly at the fire, that Paul was the little lamb who needed just a crack from the Shepherd's staff…

Why how terrible, said Foti, alarmed.

Not at all, said Cleo, it makes allowances for the little excesses of the flesh. The little riots of carnality. Not all are so lucky. Peter I think is not even one of us. He has chosen sin, you see, no matter how many cracks…. Although, mind you, I blame Maria; now there is a wolf in sheep's clothing! Peter I would say is more or less devoured.

Peter? Cried Foti, really trembling. Our Peter? But how is it that one of us can be, can be…

Ah, said Cleo closing her eyes. It has to come to this pass. The end of the world is a terrible thing, Foti. We are divided—true from false.

And what happens?

Signs, portents. Some will visit death, Cleo said grandiosely. And some will be left to rot, having fed to the full and not hungered. Then there are some, she said, slowly gazing around the company, but not letting her eyes rest on anyone—who have self worshipped, who have made themselves big under the sun, bigger than they should be—the proud in the imagination of their hearts: these will be scattered.

And where will they go?

They will go to the far ends of the earth and never find rest because God will be after them. They will be marked...

Like Jonah?

No, no, said Cleo angry at Foti's simple-minded confusions. Jonah was a great prophet. No, I was thinking of Cain...

There needn't be a murder, precisely, for a person to have blood on his or her hands. One has, in a sense, being in the midst of holy people, and owing to one's refusal, willing disobedience, and thereby evil seduction of those same holy people—well, you see, it is Christ's blood that one has on one's hands. And in reality, it was, you see, Christ's blood that Cain had on his hands, mystically speaking, when he slew his brother.

Yes, said Foti, looking at Cleo with awe. She had always thought Zoe the intelligent one and now Zoe drifted off, undoubtedly to realms of thought they could not comprehend.

Yes, you see, the blame is not here or there exactly, but in one particular. And yet it looks so remote, so removed, so peaceful. There has been a slight off, a misalignment. Years ago, and Paul simply fell into the trap. Ah, it was a cunning trap.

Foti didn't know what Cleo referring to but she began in her simple way to see that Paul was better off cracked, as it were, with a little wooden shepherd's staff, than being scattered, that is, racing away with God after him.

People dispersed at around three, the usual hour of the siesta and the remnants of the feast were gathered. Agatha had not been at the feast and the villagers breathed a sigh of relief; she had been granted by Simon the right to dance but there were tensions in the air over this and the Easter liturgy had been rife with people darting angry, hard looks at the priest, whom they felt was behind it all with his leniency on Agatha, and muttering to one another darkly. But humanity being what it is, the villagers were also intensely curious. They wanted to see her dance. They had heard and seen glimpses. Some of the old village men harbored a secret pride in the girl who had been so mopey for so many years and then suddenly had picked herself up, flown up towards the sky, they said to themselves, like a tree branch that you pull down and then release.

At seven after a light refreshment of goat's cheese and a swallow of wine, the villagers again gathered. A fire was again lit and a little iron stool was placed near it. The ancient bejeweled, engraved, gold crown was to be brought out from the church and placed on the little iron stool. Everyone was in their places and the women in light tunics and skirts were dancing the line dance, Barbara and her cousin, Foti and other village women and one saw hips slightly moving and feet stepping, back stepping, skipping a beat, and arms thick with flesh raised, and lips covered with red red lipstick in round Os and little rose bud smiles. At one point, surreptitiously, with secret movements that nobody saw, Simon did place the crown on the little iron stool with its back rim over the edge so that by the end of the line dance when the women were bowing and restarting for an encore, there it was in the solitude of exceptionally gold, brilliant, jeweled beautiful things, a public solitude, but nevertheless solitude it was there for all to see.

It looked a little more than the worth of these dancers. It was engraved with birds holding jewels in their mouths; birds that seemed alive on branches of trees that seemed to sway. The gold was polished regularly and shone it seemed there by the fire with a light of its own. The crown had always blessed the person who wore it, it seemed; at least, Paul over the years had not diminished in his ability and it had appeared that he had only grown in his capacity to impress.

Already, he had papers for every aspect of governing the island. He was clearly waiting for Simon to die or to become such an imbecile that he would be forced down from his position of first among the islanders. Then there would be what they called a selection, democracy was an open invitation to atheism, the villagers believed. They had selections, rather than elections—and Paul was sure, the villagers he had talked to were sure, that it would fall to him to govern. Ah, then things would change. For one thing there would be none of this arrogance—women dancing like men! They would live according to the Bible, women in long skirts at home. They would have a men's station—a hall where the men would come and voice their opinions. And they would get a good priest who would lead them back—men first, women obedient. And he would win the crown so often, it would be considered his.

This evening he was prepared but tense. He knew that Simon had granted that slut, he had told his brother and others at the tavern, permission to dance her dance. It is not just her, he continued, referring to the word 'slut,' but her man too.

Leo? Asked Peter.

Leo? What Leo? That is just a façade. No, her son. Agatha has sex with her son.

Ah, po! The men said in disgust. Give her hell, they said, fiercely.

First, I must win this round. Then she must go. We must make it so bitter for her to stay.

But they have the only baby.

Import people. People who want to find their holiness again.

Just like that.

Advertise. Are you missing something in life? Along those lines. We'll have babies enough. Do you think I can't have babies if I want to? Import women, fertile women.

But the evening in which he would have to win the crown one more time loomed large for Paul. He was convinced that he would easily beat the others; Michael hadn't practiced and was busy with his motor scooter and diary, Nico had plumped a little and turned lazy under the hand of his new bride, Simon, who insisted on joining, was an old goon who wasn't up to much. No, it was, Agatha—the thought of competing with her secretly terrorized him. He knew she was readying herself for a showdown that would avenge her, and reinstate her regarding him after so many years. She wanted, he knew in his heart of hearts, to be back at that window, asking for him to teach her to dance, and when he invited her in with a lying smile, to turn away, to refuse, to have the strength to be undeceived and remain innocent and intelligent.

Her win would also somehow make him a hypocrite regarding the chieftainship of the village. It would be moreover his emasculation at least as master of them all, if not as man.

When the time came for the dance, Paul's dance, he stepped out not seeing Agatha anywhere. He thought to himself, maybe she won't come, she is a coward, afraid of competition; so he danced rather well in his usual style, leaping, flipping, crouching. It was all over in a few minutes but it did take the villager's breath away. It always did. As he finished and looked around to the applause, he saw Agatha looking at him with a steady, penetrating, iron eye. His heart flew into his mouth, and embarrassed at his terror, while in the middle of it, he began to feel as if he was suffocating and his face went red.

He left the dance floor with shaky knees and almost cursed the person, his son, Little Paul, who screamed out, the crown! The crown!

Agatha stepped firmly on to the floor. People were preparing themselves to hiss, but she turned her hips to the music with such vigor and power that they quieted down instantly. And then her foot went up in a flash and she held it there like a spear pointing at the moon, shod in that beautiful grey pink dance shoe with its little squat heel and rose-red straps and pearls sewn in on the toes! (Someone has come down from heaven or from Paris and completed our circle, wrote Michael—Agatha in those dance shoes with rose red straps and pink pearls given her by Dimitri) her arms went out to either side and she kicked her leg around her so that the knee was out, the leg bent and curved in back of her; she arched her back, then dropped her leg and kicked it so that she twirled in a pirouette. Then she was leaping little leaps down the dance floor, flying just above it, and then she soared—a leap four feet high, higher than she had ever leapt. And back and again she leapt, four feet again. Then she was crouching on her toes hopping, then raising her leg again in a perfect split. After that a million twirls it seemed, pirouette after pirouette. She cartwheeled and cartwheeled, faster and faster, one on her fingertips, until it seemed that she would never stop. The end was a slow body roll on her hips, her legs going out to either side of her until she landed in a split.

There was silence and then the old men started the clapping and whistling and calling bravo. The old women, Cleo included, and Foti, watching, clapped despite themselves. Zoe stood up like one of the old blood, before there had ever been prejudices and clapped her heart out. Who gave her those dancing shoes? Someone yelled, possibly little Paul. It suddenly seemed to Michael whether it was the old antagonism now exacerbated to delirium or gracious acceptance turned extraordinarily sweet in the extremity it was all one ecstasy.

The judges were divided three to two in Agatha's favor. Stavros, Timos, and Nisos voted for her, while Little Paul and Peter voted in favor of Paul.

Then came the hour of the coronation. The people sang the Easter hymn. Christ is risen, and there was joy in not a few faces while Agatha was crowned. But she cried out ah, and removed it immediately. The crowd was in consternation. It appeared that sitting on that iron stool near the fire the rim of the crown had gotten fiery hot.

A sign, muttered Cleo ominously. What's a sign?! Said Zoe. Some fool put the gold crown on an iron stool near the fire. There was muttering among the villagers. Put the thing in water, shouted Stavros. A bucket was brought from the church and the crown dunked in it.

And this is what comes of our Easter when you invite the likes of her, said Barbara.

You shouted bravo, said her husband.

Well, she had practiced; she did a good job dancing.

Paul stood up. Let the winner say a few words—he wanted to be remembered as the gracious one, suddenly.

Agatha was ushered on to the dance floor. But there were hisses and boos from those villagers who supported Paul and were angry that a woman should have had the effrontery to compete. Nevertheless Agatha was allowed a few words. The villagers heard: One should be allowed to be one's rightful self—holy truth...and the rest was drowned in boos.

Simon went to Agatha who was blushing and put his arm around her, put the now cooled, dripping wet crown on her head and walked with her to her house. Agatha by village tradition was permitted to keep the crown for a day, Easter Monday.

The next day was relatively quiet. Dimitri and Catherine came down—they had not been at the Easter Liturgy or the dance because Tock had been sick, Dimitri said the draughts in the Elder's house were at fault—and Robert joined them smiling at

Agatha's crown. She had on her best green dress instead of black, black can be laid aside now for a while, she said to Catherine.

And what do you feel? Asked Catherine

I am at last alive, said Agatha.

I too, said Catherine.

How you? Agatha asked, wrapping an arm around her waist.

Just seeing you. Knowing that it has been pain, upon pain. Remember I study love and my feelings by now have to do with others' joys and sorrows.

I am king, not queen, laughed Agatha, crowned by my virtue and merit, alone, my warrior conquest, not by inheritance, but you are greater than I.

Yes, so you are king, mother, laughed Dimitri, hearing this first part and coming up to her as they walked down the road towards the village square. Then he looked at her, took her hand and kissed her lips. How is that? He saw the angry red mark on her forehead of the burn.

The crown's rim was burning hot; it has been place by accident near the fire.

You know, I am nothing; not a real dancer, said Agatha, suddenly sad. Just a beater of Paul.

Don't you have something? Catherine asked. Maybe it is the script of the Lord on the brow of the elect.

Or, the mark of the beast.

At about two, the day after the Easter dance, when the family were gathered at home for the noon meal, there was a knock at the door and Agatha stood up as if alarmed at something. Catherine went to the door and ushered in Little Paul. Agatha stood rigidly and looked at him.

There has been a vote, he began in a slightly sneering voice. At eleven o' clock this morning the men gathered, even Nisos, Timos and Stavros. We decided that women should not dance and what you did was therefore illegal. Illicit, I mean, he looked at her uncertainly, no, illegal!—the word didn't sound accurate. Therefore, he continued, you must sacrifice this crown. It isn't yours. It goes to Paul. He stepped up to her with his hand outstretched to take it from her head.

Agatha stepped back. By rights it is mine, she said. Simon permitted me to dance in competition with the men.

He has retracted, said Little Paul. He sees the error of his ways. If you begin to allow women to dance the dances of the men, then all the island will be full of women dancing big dances and then correspondingly thinking big thoughts, saying big things like men and our homes will be disrupted.

Dimitri laughed. And be filled with big people, he said, with big minds instead of small ones.

Little Paul disregarded him. Come, hand it over. Otherwise it will be taken from you by force. We will bind your arms, hold you down....The crown is ours.

Agatha was quiet a minute. And Little Paul waited with a sickly look of triumph on his face.

You can have this gold crown, she said at last, taking it from her head.

Why mother? It is unfair.

I don't dance to put gold crowns on my head. In fact, you are welcome to this gold crown. I dance to win dance in my soul, which, indeed, I have. She took off the crown and held it out to him with a deep curtsey of servitude. Suddenly, Agatha had gold fire leaping in her eyes that made her face majestic; she stood erect and vibrant, calligraphically graceful like a lioness fighting, her head thrown back, one leg behind the other, foot cocked on the ball; she seemed slightly hesitant, expectant, amazed, yet serenely joyful instead of resentful or depressed; it was as if she was receiving a gift from God who is God, the lioness, as well as God, the lamb, and therefore dance, the larger category, in returning the crown and she felt it--as they took it from her with mock respect; it was as if rather than suffering this defeat she was being only now crowned with dance everlasting in her Body, holy vessel of dance, and seated on a throne that was inherently now irrevocably hers precisely for having proven and failed the victory of cheats and swindlers of the dance with regal humility and poise and discomposed them, really— such perverse gold crown worshippers, infantile intemperate fools of pride and lies; she was the dancer of the Spirit of love among the somersaulters for gold crowns, the kickers of legs for a usurped awe; she was the One whose gesture merely of putting her hand to her head in submission was the crowning, it was so beautiful and beautifully dancer-like and she looked holy wisdom midst absurdity, for the slow but sure rhythm of this yielding up of fools' gold was in fact the only dance of the celestial king.

Indeed, sneered little Paul, taking the gold crown from her.

Of course the next day, after Paul had worn it a few hours, the crown was back in its secret hiding place in our little ancient church. Agatha was forced to relinquish the prize money to Paul too and she needed it.

Everyone heard the story, though, of how the crown had been removed from Agatha and sent once again to Paul. Maria said to Peter with some discomfiture—so he's really in charge of things; I never knew. And yet I really did know. Peter was uncomfortable and didn't want to talk about it. He said to her, changing the subject, what we really want is an island—yes, you know, the real thing. In any case, another island a getaway and there we will go just you and I and this time I'll give you some real sweet living like heaven.

Maria sat on his knee and ate jam as he fed it to her on a little spoon—he was both gruff and gentle—and told him this was typical of before the war on Agatha—this calm, this strange, uncanny peace and really this sorrow. For it was not gladness that drew her to her lover, despite the fact that he was paying a little extra, but the kind of sorrow that takes the wind out of you. She knew the kind of sorrow that makes the surroundings look what they are—little, broken and faint. Figures in the distance bowing under a large load. And even those with their little hoards of money, their claims to respectability, a silk stockinged foot perhaps, but still the bowing under the load. And it was sorrowful this frittering away of time on trivial pursuits, or this clutching vainly to frivolous things; this seeking to become....this falling back into futility. And it had always been this way, and then the hatred of Agatha had all made them remark on it as if it was that woman's fault.

Maria had heard that Agatha had given away the crown almost gladly. Girl of light, she thought to herself; although Peter had qualms about saying the truth—there was no question, Agatha was upper caliber. Maria thought Agatha could stand up to any of them. And it was all an inner 'anointing,' she thought, from nowhere—through the loins of her son.

We saw Maria and Peter with a little disdain, that was our usual way with them. What can we do—this sort of immorality we know we have to answer for. Foti said something very like the sort of imbecile she is:—I think, she said, Maria is more human and Peter touched on it too.

I suppose she has hands and feet like the rest of us, said Cleo acerbically. But anyone who goes and plucks the egg out of the nest...

But she didn't pluck the egg, said Foti.

I meant it metaphorically. In marriage there is an egg—the marital contract, the marital life. Peter rarely goes home now.

Paul says nothing against his brother, said Foti.

What he says, said Cleo, is that Agatha has 'rubbed sex all over the island' just like a witch would do. Maria is a whore, she simply waits on men. But Agatha does something more and more insidious. She opens her sex and goes free with it, entirely free. Free as a bird in a tree.

Foti laughed and then looked uncomfortable.

What he is saying is that Agatha is corrupt. It has gone to the center of her soul. She no longer even wants baptism, no longer, that is, even considers it. It is no wonder that she and Leo hit it off, you see. The stories of Leo turning chaste are pure rubbish. The antics he and Agatha get up to in that house half way up the hill! And then she and Dimitri! Were a woman to have those sorts of feelings for her son, she should tie a millstone around her neck and drown herself in the sea.

But do you say it or Paul? Foti asked, uncertainly.

What I say hardly matters. It is what I want--. I am an old woman now. I hardly know what I say…. Talking is such an effort. And often it is quite useless; one can never express the truth inside. God has set his hand against it. Words flit from our mouths like moths, like flies… There are no light bearers anymore. To whom can we turn?

Fireflies, said Foti, smiling. Because you know there is no good or evil. In the end, only the winking, twinkling, blinking.

Cleo gave her a look. Agatha has corrupted all of us. Of course, when there is no God, there is all manner of things bumping and flitting against one in the darkness. But it is what I want…What you want…What love wants…Where does this love want come from?

And yet the perfect want whether in God or outside of God is one thing, the taboo—to die. Zoe had joined them. She had been listening behind Foti's elbow. As for her abstraction, where Cleo had thought to have lost her forever, at the time of Agatha's coronation, she had just sighed and broken with it. Her eyes had refocused on the circlet of gold, so exquisitely engraved, brought out for a day and a half every year. Suddenly, she was in the world again but with a difference: She was no longer the brisk, get things done Zoe. Certain of herself, fighting a little like a cat, bitter, stinging like a cat's scratch wound to be around. Now she was languorous, wispy. It was as if she had come away from, well, a kind of fairy tale, she said to us. But oddly, the fairy part was not that other, which was all she would say of the 'place' where she had been abstracted to in thought; no the fairy part was this island that had gone and become a thing of dreams.

Her being 'off' had to do with that 'before Zoe' whom we had known as our Zoe. Cleo said it was all rot. The material now Zoe was simply a little depressed. Not really altered. And yet it seemed the central pillar of our circle was in fact broken. Death was preferable, she said. Look around at this island—all death.

In fact, said Foti, it always has been. But that doesn't matter.

Zoe said—I have finally understood the secret. We all gathered around, metaphorically, for we were physically seated at Cleo's little iron balcony table. It was getting hotter and Foti was wearing her black silk dress without sleeves. We get annoyed, all of us, by the sight of her fleshy upper arms.

We are born to die. That is, we have no other purpose on this planet. None at all. Our struggle is just one: How to die. Agatha believes that by pointing her foot high, it brings a certain joy to the last moments. That one has in essence conquered the dilemma. Paul believes that by wearing the crown, Easter after Easter, he has done so. What do you believe? Piped up Foti.

What I believe is of no importance. It is what I know. I know it is all absurdity.

Dying and living, Foti screamed out joyfully, are exactly the same—in the out there, she ended, faltering.

I didn't say that. And we do have a maker. There is a soul. At least, I have one. The things we say and the things we do—they are recorded. Oh, not the pointing of the foot, or the wearing of the crown. What counts, is recorded. All that Agatha screamed out when Dimitri was being threatened by her other son. God notices these things. God is not like us who are inclined to pass it by. We do Him best credit when we design a mythological creature—like an eagle with the face of a man. And Agatha's thoughts at night, croaked Barbara—she had joined our group for once and was sitting until now in the far off chair, silently. They are all about her son.

The wheat will be separated from the chaff, said Cleo ominously.

To me, said Zoe, suddenly, Agatha is closest to having a soul.

Cleo made a face and was silent. Five minutes elapsed and it was seen that there were tears rolling down her face. We've been friends for years, she murmured. And now this.

Oh, bother, said Zoe, seeing her friend. What can I say? There is friendship and friendship. You, she spoke to Cleo but kept her eyes straight in front of her, have simply not been daring. You saw me as a kind of crust—the outer shell, and became all shell. Who said you had to take on my external personality?

For years, sniffed Cleo, inconsolable.

Zoe humphed, drew her legs under her, got up, and left. She was seen hobbling down the road in front of us towards her house.

We gathered around Cleo, immensely sympathetic. She's not herself, said Barbara with a slight bitter edge to her voice. The things she says—they in themselves are reprehensible. We do not judge as the Almighty judges: this determining of who has a soul! I can't say for certain, of course, that I or anybody does that I know—but we must have hope, as the apostle says. What do we know about Zoe's pronouncement except that she had been wandering in the brain? This seeming lucidity, might it not be another form of madness?

Father Raphael, another one, mad too, but at least a priest, ordained from on high—he told us that Agatha had lost her soul. And now Zoe, mad too, it would seem, at least for a time, mad, tells us that Agatha has almost a soul. What does that mean but a lot of nothing?

Why Agatha? Foti chimed in. It doesn't make sense.

Have you been on another planet, Cleo began viciously. She had recovered from her weeping. Haven't you seen how it is always Agatha who turns our people against themselves? How it is always Agatha who for over forty years has made us barren, sick, angry, violent?

But that doesn't make sense, objected Foti.

To you, to you. But to everybody else here on the island it does. It seems that in Agatha's household anything, mind you—let me say it again—anything can go on. Murder, blasphemy, incest, the refusal of God.

What do you mean?

Don't you remember how Jason poor lamb, provoked, naturally, but he did almost kill his brother? Don't you remember the terrible curse that Agatha invoked? And now don't you see the incestuous behavior with her son? The steady refusal to be baptized? What do you think it all means? Surely Zoe is out of her mind to say that Agatha almost has a soul—the only one among us. Humph, poor Zoe.

Foti protested: All that that you speak of was just accident! And nothing really happened. It was all terribly, wonderfully sad.

What on earth--? Wonderfully?

Well, you know; Agatha is just a human being and…

And so?

Well, it is a tragedy of course but it also seems to me to be profound. I mean on the part of Agatha. And out there it doesn't matter at all. Neither you nor her. But in here—oh, it stirs deep—Agatha, that is.

I see, said Cleo her face distorted slightly. I am to be cast out and this this stray is to be admitted. I, baptized and believing…

We gathered around. No, Foti had gone too far. But you can hardly listen to Foti, we said. What kind of nonsense is this—this 'out there' business? No, no one gives her half an ear.

But to think I have been steady friends…Cleo began to weep again.

Actually, we soothed her, you are to be the one in command now. Think of that. Zoe is wandering in mind, Foti has always been as foolish as a cow—no it is you now who lead us, the women of Holy Island. Don't let us down.

I shall hold fast to the traditions of Mother Dora, said Cleo, but she was practically sobbing.

She always smiled, said Barbara, the bitter edge still in her voice.

There had been a distinct, definite evolution in the marriage of Catherine and Dimitri. They had become instead of two wary animals, irresistibly attracted yet still unsure whether friend or foe, pacing around one another, one creature with two manifestations—mankind, as it were, male, female. They knew each other almost perfectly and the part that each didn't know about the other was the intimate secret, the mystery that kept them endlessly in love. For it is not the knowledge, direct and plain, the factual phenomenon about another that keeps them lovable, but, of course, the mystery, the profound strange, alienness: For Dimitri, Catherine was a hardly there kind of person that had grown flesh and was seated beside him. Her inner essence though was a different kind of thing entirely. He didn't know where she was native to in that sense—another world, indeed, he thought. And periodically, he pondered on God. Loved him, as a theory that that remote, estranged, yet close beauty was something of his, perhaps. This thought made him calm next to his wife. And he knew well the form of her and the part that he caressed day and night with the barely touching, warm, slipping palms.

Catherine knew and didn't know Dimitri. She was aware of his alienness to marriage in the conventional sense; she pardoned it; she had learned to almost be at ease with it. But she didn't quite know that he would stay. There was a turn about his inner self—and she reasoned that one day, he could turn away from her. As for his love, she was sure of that. But love would not necessarily hold him. There was something else. Her own mother urged her to regard this as selfishness. But Catherine would not. One has a right to be, she told Ellen. Ellen looked at her with a sick face in return.

There was no question that between the awe of Dimitri for his wife, and the response of utter receptivity of Catherine for Dimitri that the marriage had passed from being a superficial joy to a shaping, molding, differentiating thing—where they two were indeed one. If Catherine so much as moved her foot, Dimitri knew about it and it rose in his body like electricity and turned into that powerful sexual desire of a young man. They made love in the dead Elder's shack morning, noon and night on a mattress on the floor under a heavy orange woolen blanket that Agatha had provided that kept a body warm in the worst temperatures. The baby would lie in his crib, quite quietly, as if aware of this great imperative in the little circle of three between the two people who peered into his face.

The baby proved to be a kind of tonic for Catherine and Dimitri, emotionally. They were physically more tired, often exhausted, especially at first, but the fact remained that there was a certain reconciliation for the peccadillos against one another in this small, fragrant third flesh of theirs. For Dimitri it was a jolly thing that Catherine could bring forth his child. He saw her as brilliant, blindingly so. Every moment of lassitude when she had frustrated him—the weakness, and sickness, the times she had withdrawn into herself to breathe—and left him on the outside—just a poor feeble man after all, now seemed to have a great purpose. He even supposed in his wild moments that Tock had godly eyes, meaning seeing as God sees.

For Catherine, the baby meant that Dimitri was decidedly one with her. That there was no doubt—love, which had exhausted her in many ways, was not idle and vain. She now came to him a little more wantonly, exercising her whole realm of sexual fantasies on his body and driving him into half laughter, half-mad titillation.

Dimitri indeed felt that he was entirely unfinished with Catherine. Their crazy sex games in the little shack left him only desiring her more and more. Whereas Catherine felt that she had each time, a little more body resurrected from illness, loneliness and fear that had conspired to stamp her out.

But there was, Catherine and Dimitri knew, behind their sparkling eyes, in the back of their mesmerized brains, a final metamorphosis. A final, oh, perhaps in the sex match, when they will have each and together hit the target. Then waking from the great after sleep, they would see one another in their blindingly beautiful real forms.

Agatha slept fitfully—dreamed of marvelous things: it was as if first she was walking on water, on the sea just off their shores and she felt as if she had a mirror in her feet and could walk over infinite tracks of water reflecting one water but then in a trice, as if she blinked in her dream, she was in a boat heaving and swaying and she seemed to be rowing it, but over sand, over more sand and it was grinding heavily, it was crunching the sand; but she woke several times disturbed for all the miracles of dreams, having in the back of her mind a sense of the expansiveness of love they were doing up on the cliffs in the shack. She did not dare go to find them. When they had come down on Easter Monday and promenaded around town with her wearing the crown and the crowds strangely dispersed—strangely, because the weather was only a little cloudy, smoky and cold—they had looked both bright and shiny as Christmas ornaments, and she had made the connection to very fulfilling love making immediately.

Her breast was on fire, her brains boiled, but the calm thought had percolated out—they need to spend so much money to make a real house! Dimitri will use up all his savings and then? But she had kissed his lips with her slightly trembling ones, kissed the baby, kissed Catherine and sent them away saying nothing. And then that night back in her big marriage bed, which Catherine and Dimitri had recently vacated, and which, she thought, or maybe imagined, still smelled of lovemaking, she sweat, and agonized. It seemed to her like her body should be split open. Her heart should be pulled out live, beating and molted lead poured over it under heaven.

She became addicted to coffee. In the morning now, instead of her usual single cup with Jason, she made herself at least three or four cups. Jason for once opened his mouth and remarked that she looked haggard and wild. Are you up dancing at night? He asked.

No, my son. Agatha was silent. She had finally definitively taken to calling Jason 'my son' and Dimitri Dimitri. He was, she reasoned born from 'different loins', magical, bitter, after death loins for having tried to kill him in the womb. Jason was the usual baby, born from reconciled loins. Agatha was calm with Jason now. She sometimes ran her hand over his hair. But he was a great big hulking man now. He still talked rarely. But she knew that the villagers said he was often with Little Paul. For this she could not love him. It was a kind of justice in her—mother-justice—that made her run her hand across his head. She was picking him out, saying goodbye, perhaps. And the fact that he was talking—although she wondered a little: Did she detect a sneer in his voice when he spoke to her?

Whatever Jason really felt and thought was still kept under guard in his heart. His talking to his mother had to do with petty things, the weather, the kitchen to be cleaned, here and there a kind of solicitous inquiry but all the bare periphery of intimacy for one who was after all son in the house of his mother. And it had been worse when he was little. He was an unknowable it seemed, but Agatha feared that underneath it all lay violence and she had feared that before he had laid hands on Dimitri that frightful night. She had feared that Jason was a brute in reality; something she had never feared about Dimitri, silent though he had been for years. It was of course mother instinct but Dimitri was tender, Jason violent. And now Dimitri had her overflow of love, undisguised, sweet, beautiful love hiding in her. Jason, her justice. It was for Jason's sake that she had condemned herself twice to hell rather than let her sons be condemned, Dimitri made hell seem like an opera or a strange act in a theater. Jason kept a steady eye on her, seemed to know in that thick slow moving brain of his that she had this sweet passion for Dimitri the very second that it was born when he had removed the razor from his brother's neck. Ah, he was right to remove himself from the object of this passion. Right to be a brute; he had merely defended her perhaps holding the knife to Dimitri's throat.

She began by laughing about this love pain with Dimitri. This was the genesis, this laughter; for it really did not matter so much. It was not life or death. It was a temptation if you like but she could overcome. Not so much by not feeling arousal when she thought of her utterly lovely son with his dark, fathomless eyes, the glitter as it were all over him, the slender limbs, the strength—the man sweetness. No, but by just laughing about it. It was after all, another moment in the room that she didn't really want to be in, not quite like this. What she had really wanted was merely that beauty to get through the agony of the sin by toil—to reach grace with her body instead of her soul. And so laughter that was really tears or sweat. And soul that was really a Body of sweat and tears.

She went to the priest and he said to her: Why not? Utterly artlessly and innocently. Don't you think it was the same for Mary who wept at Jesus' feet. Somewhere against all recommendation, she thought to herself—He is beautiful; I will go to Him. She gave Him her sexual heart as you give the dance your heart. And let me tell you, she walked away with His crown. Yes, of course, it was envied her by Martha later—but there it was shining on her head—she, a sinner even a sinner against His body but out of passionate love—she wept enough for the whole Passion.

She wept. You danced. Where is the difference?

And are there not wicked tears? Self-pitying tears. Tears that someone tries, ah those desert monks, to conjure up so as to prove to God they are worthy of being pardoned. Water poured out?

No one said that dance was good or evil. Nor tears. It has to do with what is offered from your heart. How for you dance is love, and executed with truth, your self offered up perfectly and purely. Note how you lost the crown, the contest with Paul—the matter has been all over town, said the priest looking at her face. Even the villagers were impressed and angered. You gave it up with no evil in your heart at all. And I felt then the tears of Christ. Tears of love: crucifixion-resurrection, the pouring of the dance into the island, pain and light light motion.

No you, for reasons unrevealed, you danced, soft as tears, as if on tears without the drops breaking, before us, before God. And Easter night, you were judged. Worthy! Just as we call out for the priest.

They say I am the worst sinner.

And I? Am I not? Have I not mocked and laughed and judged? Are not these the real sins?

I wanted only to dance… murmured Agatha—to dance so much that it takes root and every move is dance, even the lame, the failing, the graphic and grotesque.

I to write, said the priest. Ah, you should have seen my storm and stomp and gnash my teeth when my files were burnt. You, child, were asleep. He turned to Max.

Max looked down without saying anything. He had the appearance of someone who could not keep still in his chair. The priest told Agatha right in front of him that he was acting like a wild animal in a cage, had been for months, pacing up and down the room. He looked at Agatha furtively, dark, hard looks now and then. Agatha tried not to notice.

They were in the little Eden, as the priest called it—the trap, as Max had taken to calling it—the little chamber of the priest with the solitary window and lace curtains. The priest had turned the wicker armchair so that its back was against the window. Agatha was seated on the little iron stool that had held the crown and had been given to the priest. In fact, different gifts from the villagers, some of which were obviously just items that people wished to throw out, were scattered around the little room. An iron flowerpot, a small bureau with the paint scraped off here and there, an old coat stand. The room was much more cluttered now than it had been just a couple of years ago. Max said it was too crowded, under his breath when Agatha mentioned it.

A funny Eden, said the priest full of odd things. I never thought that Eden was only beautiful. I thought there was a certain strangeness about it—imagine all the different species—they are not regular in their beauty. Imagine too the insects and the reptiles. Here we have bookshelves that are uneven, drawers with the paint coming off, a coat stand that falls down if you put a coat on it.

Mind you the strangest thing of all is what is beautiful: Max, who by smell alone can detect desire in flesh and blood and condemn it. Has not yet detected it in me, however hard he snuffs me. Then there is me, of course, a riotous sinner, now practicing the straight and narrow, happy though, happy as a clam about it.

What am I? murmured Agatha, as though she had not heard him— as a mother, I have failed, utterly failed.

That is more in God's hands than yours, said the priest softly. After all, it was he who made you a mother. I can understand when women say no, no, it cannot be and abort their children. Who said they can accomplish what God tells them to do? No, let them rant and rave all they like. They do not do God's proposals either. A simple thing—be kind to your neighbor! Look at the deplorable way they treated your own father! I wouldn't have blamed you for aborting Dimitri. But a part of you did not want to. Your body clung to him. There is the origin of your madness.

How did you know?

Prophecy. But it is really love, the great surrender. All prophecy is. Allowing for the simple truth: It is God's call. Surrender.

Agatha sat very still staring at the floor in front of her feet for a long time. The priest said nothing after the word surrender. And he went and turned on the tape recorder that had an old tape of Don Giovanni in it and began to sing along with the different characters as it played, singing both sides of the duets. When it came to 'la ci darem la mano', he did a little funny dance while singing, holding Max's hand, laughing a little, crying after. It is so sad and funny that a poor little twit of a woman should be seduced by the great Don, he finally murmured. It wasn't fair. It never is. Hallelujah. For if it was fair the true dances would never be danced, the true tears never wept.

Agatha sat still looking at the floor not listening. At the end of an hour or so, she rose and sighed. It is still not fixed. Not fixed at all, she said.

Max extricated himself from the old priest who had one arm thrown about his shoulders, and went up to her; she looked at him and wondered if he was like Jason, silent as a stone and equally immovable emotionally, thinking only of paradise, but she saw that he was silent in a different way. He was sweating, breathing audibly, his fingers were twitching, sometimes he put them together in a kind of gesture of supplication, which the priest seemed to ignore. Max opened his mouth as if he was about to say something and then breathed—nothing but breath came out. He looked at her, closed his eyes and then retreated towards the smiling, and sometimes singing priest.

Agatha laughed and went out. Thus, Agatha began. She began to laugh remembering all those moments of misery, the crying, the despair and the adolescent rages. Zoe passed a woman on the street, peered into her face, saw Agatha, and later told her crowd of women that Agatha has grown up. She was not in her infancy. She was pushing now—out, said Zoe. Is she going to go? Cleo asked, acerbically. Why? Zoe answered, and stared off her balcony past her friend who had come to forgive her by the sea.

Agatha decided, simultaneously with her laughing off her incestuous passion, that she would study the dance in a more rigorous form. She would be a dancer down to the tips of her fingers and toes. In her dance, she would be the gold crown, the crown of dance, dancing! …Not just the big moves. Not those moves, which elicit a cry of amazement from the audience; but the little moves, obscured, hardly seen, and even the daily moves. She would not only dance as a dancer but walk, sit, bend as a dancer; she would spell out dance in her body. For it was dance that had made her grow up. Her dance would be the softness of gold even in the high leaps, the brilliance of gold, even in the subtle footwork; for she had chosen a body of freedom and truth—the open door.

And like a long flower, the top of it swayed, tipped, leaned—which way would it go—she thought to herself—shall it be towards, away from…Agatha had begun. Would it be rot or an immortal soul? Would rot be at the center, at the core of her— or soul—something, what is part of—? She hesitated to say God. It had all been too desperate. She was the God-ostracized, the desperate one. Controlling herself, but sinking in a morass of misery for years and years. She had whittled her humanity with a relentless soul-knife down to a little little piece. That was soul—the thing with soul knife blunt, absurd but sucking on this passionate taboo and filling herself with sugar. And then just as she was about, plainly to say the truth, to plunge that soul knife into her heart, she eluded, evaded—she danced. Just as Jesus eluded, evaded the crowds with their loud words and angry bodies.

So that was how she began. By evasion. It was evasion what they saw: the back arched and straight, the legs stepping lightly as willows, the eyes like rain. Evasion— the village's big sinner, the outcast one, the sure as hell damned forever one, turning her waist like elegance itself and raising her leg in a sun salute! Even Agatha didn't know what it meant. Oddly, she felt as if she almost could see the pearl of great price, not so much as a pearl, but as light—the morning light that she danced to—almost white, brilliant white but soft and light. What if it was the dance that brought her closer, dance the pearl in the crown, the morning light in the circlet of gold, and she seemed to see herself, the pitiful and pathetic creature, destined to writhe in horrible, maddening torture for eternity, softly approaching new created out of this light, dancer, like she was gypsy before God. And she would steal back the vote in the competition. They would vote for her, clap for her, ravished out of their hard against her hearts as if they were amber heated and melted into a fragrant resin by her passion.

There was Paul. For years Agatha had looked at him with a muddied look. Even when Dimitri had come home, bringing promises of riches to the island folk, and for a minute crazed islanders had let go of their hearts and bid for more and more money as if they were children at the jam pot. Even then Agatha had retained towards Paul, although not to the others, defiantly not to the others, the same old muddied look. But since the Easter dance, when they had placed that crown on her head instead of on his, her eyes had cleared even towards him.

And how was it, she heard them say—how was it? That their Agatha, the pet damned one, the one that they surely were not—was suddenly aloof, clear, her voice steady as a healthy shouter's? Had they missed something? Agatha's thoughts ran on mimicking their minds.

In any case, there was now dance for life, and Tock who was in reality only beautiful. Other babies had their moments—not so cute, the chin undershot, the eyes too small, the fat accumulated in a gross way! Tock was beautiful. A little crinkled when he was an infant, red, mushy. But now, delicate, graceful, a little kicker and talker of an unknown language. A waker in the night, a dark eyed delightful puddle of sweet flesh. Agatha for some reason sometimes forgot his sex and called him 'her' and 'she'. He had only the softest breath of light gold hair settled on the otherwise bald, exquisite head. The parents were sometimes spirited away by their golden sex—everything seemed exquisitely at one between the two, with the little feelers of the one moving, sensing the light as dust leaves, and the wings of the other waving, lifting in the silken breeze; they had their thinking time, the spell of a cogitation, their sudden revelation and the joy that lit up in them like the summer noon! Then she, Agatha would take over the baby, the little package of humanity left behind. It was something to open and open, and she sang this song to little Tock—we are to open and open and find out who we are. It was a silly, unimaginative song. Who I am, sang the boy. I am a star.

But she secretly saw him, when she saw him as a him, becoming another Dimitri. Perhaps just a little shorter, and a 'cleaner' look to him. Sometimes, she saw little Tock forming and becoming a man like Max. What you might call angelic—at least, he had been. Something had downed him and dimmed him. The village felt it through and through. He wasn't quite his own original hymn of praise to Jesus now. Of course, they had always put him down behind his back. Where was his mind wandering, his flight of fantasy going? But the beauty had come right out of his transparent heart. Kooky though it was. It was beauty, no question; and now too dull for beauty.

Amen Max, she called him to herself and also poor Max. His garments were torn in places; no one was mending now. For some reason he and Father Isaac where going through the village in a hurried and abstracted air—clearly they had no time for mending. Max was still uttering the beautiful words, still seeing a shape in the air so perfect, so sublime, that left thirst, profound, irreconcilable thirst in this life and only the hope of drinking in the other. Agatha saw it on him, his body, his face, his hands and feet—this thirst. Amen Max, poor Max—she thought now and again—ah, he has no mother, little worth of a father. And then she thought how she was to marry this father shortly, sometime, they hadn't set a date, she thought again poor Max— perhaps I can bring Leo 'round.

It was the first effort of the new Agatha. And she went to Leo with her arms full of towels and scented soap. He greeted her and approved of all that she carried to him. I suppose a bath is the first thing, he said, in a betrothal. A sweet thing, this thought, he said, kissing her on the lips.

Yes, I want it done right, said Agatha with a simple, childlike look at him. Every-thing in place. Every stone for the builders. One thinks it will be a magnificent palace. Or just a room, said Leo, even more simply—with that one window, you know how it is: That one window out of which I can see—that you-world, the us-love. And it becomes the knowledge and the center of every action, every delight. Ah, what can I say? I can chortle, cook; look at you like a little expectant frog.

That's it: that is all love is, said Agatha, happy despite herself. She put the towels inside on the dining table. Leo was standing on the other side of the table by the window. His hair was a mess, frizzy, with a bit of bread sticking in it. His face was slightly leaner than Agatha remembered it a month ago when he had pronounced that they were engaged. But it was still the same half baby, half philosopher face— aloof, comic, hiding an enormous mind, Agatha suddenly thought.

I have come, she said, briskly, to ask you to reconcile towards Max.

With clean puffy towels and scented soaps?

Yes, wash away the old rancor. What earthly good does it do you?

You mistake, said Leo. Gravely mistake. There is no rancor. I have sacrificed, absolutely denied myself—cut myself off from my own heart. What do you think of that? He asked looking at her with his head thrown back, from under half closed lids. Call me a buffoon, a clown—a mockery of myself, if you like. Max was my sole treasure—the living in me. It was death to let him go.

You are mocking.

No, you see, it is true that I beat him often unjustly. But I loved him. Ah, my ethereal Max. What happened was that he found his life; I could not stand in the way. His life, my death. Just as with his mother, only more, if you will metaphorical. After losing my life, and being cast into the realm of death, I found nothing at all but cruelty and savagery, until, for some reason—you. Now what are you made of? Mother of pearl? I think of you like a mother. Mother of pearl and pearl is beautiful. So life—you know, where beauty is.

I think purple—that under your eyelids, in your eyes when you look at me with those deep gazes.

They continued talking in this way, a kind of exotic banter. Agatha threaded in by Leo's smoke thread of imagination and sweetness. They found themselves, both rapt in their fantasies and soft words, entwined—Agatha sitting on Leo's lap, leaning back against his chest, and Leo with his arms wound around her. They had been chit chatting in this dreamy way for three hours.

When they came to Agatha suddenly seemed struck by something; she hopped off his knees and stood up and faced him. I came with gifts of bath soap, she said to him, and a decision. What was it? Oh that you were to make up with Max. But there was something else. Oh, I remember now. If something happens to the priest, or to me, or to both—to take Max in.

Leo sat up suddenly, alert and tense. What exactly is going to happen?

You know I danced at the Easter dance with Dimitri's dance shoes and…

I see, he said softly. The island fell apart. There is a civil war going on over dance shoes with red ribbons and pearls sewn in the toes. Those in favor of exotic-erotic women leaping and pointing their pearled toes at the sun…and the many more who hate the sight of these female ecstatics whose hieratic spirit is completed by their truly beloved sons.

More or less. There is a brutal atmosphere. One doesn't actually see much difference. Just something off and the priest and Max whipping through the village chanting a little, and Max lifting his head like a heron and letting out of his mouth a stream of praise for our Lord Jesus Christ.

But the people gather with shifting feet and eyes. Dark in their eyes. The kind of dark where there is no relief.

Do you want to stay with me? Leo asked in a high pitched anxious voice.

No, I am a heretic that has survived being burned at the stake, that is, I have survived the sentence of burning and the burn of our fiery crown. I don't fear. But since it is the end of things….Although it is all in place and of course I love you, the puzzle piece isn't always the one we imagine.

You mean—what? Not our marriage?

Oh, these are just strange fears. This island these days is the place to have them. I have begged, although no one knows, but I have begged Catherine and Dimitri to go somewhere else. In the middle of lunch, bringing it up like a proposal for a Sunday picnic. It hasn't worked; they are cozy enough in the old Elder's shack.

You fear for the baby.

A strange kind of fear. It doesn't seem real at all. You see, the land is quiet. Simon comes around a grin all over his face to talk and when the baby comes with his parents, Simon is all over him. The baby must see strange smiles floating in the air. You have the impression that he smiles so much at the child that he leaves the smiles behind like the Cheshire Cat. I would say that everything is alright—except for the times, even with Barbara now, I can't quite understand but there seems to be something stirring underfoot.

The impression I get from her, from some of the people passing; old timers, with houses down by the beach—Vera, and Lucy and their husbands. The kind that doesn't come out much usually except to do the grocery shopping. It seems they are now coming out of the woodwork.

I really wanted to tell you that there is a different atmosphere. And the flavor is dark and bitter. People, like Barbara, are all isolated now. Stavros goes by without a word and frowning. Everybody is seeing to his own soul, in a sense. But they are congregating with anger in little groups and they do not seem to see the baby. Of course, when Dimitri and Catherine go out with Tock, the island town is deserted somehow. Then the strange people whom we never knew much of—like Vera and Lucy. We were content to know they were bowing before their icons, picking hand engraved crosses wrapped in tissue paper out of boxes. We were content to think them holy or hanging on to holiness as best they could.

We imagined, Dimitri and I, he and I come together in our imagination, that these people would just rejoice—the baby, after all, what the island wants. But now it is not even that. There is something hard and cruel in their souls. They are like alien birds congregating in the air, hovering vulture-like...

Leo looked into Agatha's eyes; she was suddenly startled at finding him, peering down into her and looked down. Hovering, vulture like—but there is no death here, said Leo with forced jollity. No—I wanted the simple things, responded Agatha, a little incoherently—just a mother walking down the beach with her baby and people thinking it is so sweet, you know how they do? What does it have to do with death? But it makes me scared. Not that anyone has said anything. You know how they are. Mute about the things that matter. But it comes out in their eyes—phantom eyes suddenly in the crowd. Of course I know them as I said—Vera and Lucy; but it suddenly strikes me that I haven't taken pains to know them and consequently I don't know them. I don't know what is in them—you know, life or death? I only see death seeking in their eyes. Then it becomes all complex, you know, what was supposed to be the first easy solution for the island in years—a baby, a longed for baby.

...it is simply horrible. I begin to see the tiny skeleton at the bottom of the sea, and the fish that nibbled away the pink sweet flesh swimming obliviously by. Then, you know I dream of going.

They have entirely forgotten the longed for baby, said Leo.

When he was born it seemed that quite a few people rejoiced even our Zoe and Cleo. But then Zoe, how can I say it—changed, lately it seems she has changed in my favor but it is a strange pitying change as if she is convinced that something is irremediable in the whole equation. She exhibits a kind of latent rebellion. Her Church says I am anathema and so the baby, and so she comes out with a tear in her eye. Just to show them! Just to be the last one in the ark before the flood sweeps me off, so that she can weep. I really think it is a kind of flirtation.

To stare truth in the eye? Leo cocked his head. Interesting.

She says, I have heard, when she wakes from her long sleeps, and her open-eyed sleeping as well, that I have a soul.

This you don't want to lose.

No, never.

Sometimes we are given second chances, murmured Leo. Give over believing imaginatively. Just act. Marry me, Agatha. The island will no doubt settle down. In any case, no one ever comes up to this house on the hill. The village has forgotten me. I shamed so many wives and husbands, they don't want to look me in the eye. I once thought I'd be killed for being as it were the hub and core of adultery on the island. But the act of murder turned into a mirror when they approached. They were nothing more than the worst sorts of sinners—not wishing justice, just revenge, or not even that; they wished for a way to cover themselves for their petty, inept husbanding of their wives. For their failure as men. So one and all they let me go. They wished for a hush to descend over me, not an uproar. Thus they bury me here—yes, alive, on a hill, at my prayers, and my new found chastity. No one comes near.

But I! shouted Agatha, she meant joyfully but it came out painfully.

Leo took her hand and held it softly, kissing it.

Should we…? Agatha began, tentatively; should we tonight? After all, we are getting married. It seems to be the fruit of the marriage tree and that is growing despite ourselves and despite all attempts on the part of others to get us to the court…

The marriage tree, mused Leo. You still won't be baptized so that we could do it here? Ah my dear, I would love to lie in your arms naked, light from sex as a puff of smoke, sweet as a rose—but no, wait, I say, wait.

Should I be baptized? Asked Agatha, thinking of love making.

Don't you think that that will do it, said Leo. Settle the island once and for all. And then we might be married with reconciled looks on the village faces.

Technically speaking, said Agatha, choosing her words carefully, they would come 'round.

Remember Agatha, it is not a refusal to deny you my body tonight. It is rather a more mystical event—that is, you see, it begins now as our two bodies come into proximity and several candle flames light up mysteriously in each one of our pores. It becomes, I become, you become, we become a leaping flame on the wedding night.

A good flame, a pure enough almost holy flame.

As I see it, God sees everything in terms of fire. The quality of fire—hellish, heavenly—dying down or leaping up. People have fire in them, you know. I have secretly heard, at windows listening at night, when I was a rampant Casanova, wives weeping because of the burning in their corroded loins—this was after I had ditched them. There really is, you see, hell fire. But when my last lady of the blonde hair, slanting eyes, the pregnant one left on the little unsteady boat and went abroad to have or have not our baby, to grow or uproot my seed, then the old rampant nerve snapped in my body. I became a limp, listless, helpless man. I determined to start a new career—chaste, low voiced, nerveless, perfect for the holy society that the island desires. As I said, they could have killed me; they preferred to leave me solitary, a recluse, just like some holy hermits although in my case not as popular among the believers.

They leave you alone because they don't know if you are really reformed or not. And out of respect for they remember Magda. They think perhaps you have grown from a devil to a widow. But when they see me coming and staying day and night, in our hollows, in our nooks, eating, drinking, and whatever they believe we do together, they don't know if you are so sincere.

Of course, of course, said Leo. They have a right to their doubts, cantankerous as they are as people on the whole. Their doubts are sickly, withered, dry, choking things in the live imagination—not something you'd want to run across as a lover. But I completely permit, no, not permit, who am I to permit, but open the way, pave the way for their doubts.

Things are changing for the worse, said Agatha, and yet you are so engagingly light hearted, merry, gay. And, she put her hand on Leo's pink lips as he appeared about to speak, I do not believe for a moment that our marriage would bring things back to normal. Oh, we could live normally enough as people do live in desert wastes. Clinging together, with the rest of the family. There is Robert and Ellen too—although I hear that they are on the path to division. I hear that Ellen has written to a lover from way back and he has invited her for a 'rest' from marriage—can you imagine? She is going. There is no question, but she wanted to haunt the shack where her daughter is living now for a few nights and days.

No we are entering a shadowy phase in our history. People gather secretly and scatter suddenly in our faces. Agatha brought her hand before Leo's face as a fist and opened it in front of his eyes to demonstrate what she was saying.

Oh, said Leo turning his head away, it is quiet enough. The human animal is odd. We really have no form. Our mind turns one way, then another. What does it say in Ecclesiastes: All is vanity.

No, said Agatha, moving towards the door and speaking in a low voice so that Leo could barely hear. All is not vanity. There are human mistakes in the Bible, lies, short sightedness. There is the progression from zero to one. I learned that dancing. In the beginning, I had no ability. I could not even balance on one leg. How is it then that in ten years I won the dance away from Paul who was an expert gymnast? And if it had been the fancy crown I wanted, it would have been vanity. But that gold crown they took away. And every dawn I am up as I have been for ten years—dancing to the sun rising. Sometimes I toil for a fistful of dust in my face but sometimes…

Sometimes? Leo was listening.

New creation, the old talking-to meaning much more than I ever thought possible. Not even a stretch of the imagination; no, something entirely new. Re-rooting—plant I thought dead re-planting in living water. Agatha opened the door and looked around at him, pensively.

He looked back with his foggy look and putting his head on one side like a big seagull watched as she went out.

Spiritual point and counterpoint, she thought, as she left. It is quite impossible to leave him. We must marry and live somewhere which is nowhere, on a point, just a point in the universe, which has no mass or volume. Almost, for all one can see it, a theoretical point in the vast seas filled with points, so full that to mankind the points are infinite. And we make one, living and doing—what? Dancing and cooking but like the old ascetics of this former island, the land on which once God shed His glory—like they prayed—radiant, singing, welling up with prayer. We are lesser but good and that is love.

It was with that good taste in her mouth that was not a taste but a thought but also a taste— transmuted to a taste, Agatha went home to Jason.

The man looked like a person outfitted—everything washed for him and mended, the holes perfectly patched up. Michael thought that he had never lifted a finger, was some kind of helpless misfit at home—and this because his mother, Stefania, had taught him all sorts of home industry like cooking and sewing. He was eighteen the time when men are close to angels, beautiful, virile, agile, mentally alert and capable. He had a motor scooter, which Catherine had fixed once—it was before her marriage; a matter of toying a bit with the engine, she had said. And he had learned to twiddle and toy and had started it going a number of times since then. Around about the island he had flown on it, feeling like an angel, heedless of what was before or behind. Once he had almost collided with a donkey. Another time he had slid down into the dirt driving on the hill where there was no road. But Michael chafed at the bit so to speak because it was all so toy like—that is, driving this little motor scooter on an island that was so small it really only had one road. A road that went from one side between forest and beach where no one lived but dead men in their graves, around to the town and down the length of it, and then up the mountain, or the fragment of it that ended in the cliff over the two rocks that stuck up like daggers out of the water. Michael wanted to fly off that cliff sometimes, that confining cliff into a real reality, as he called it in his writing.

But here was a man, first, who looked hopelessly helpless. Stuffed probably with chicken and goat meat, filled with wine! He was fiddling with his nets. Michael noticed that the one thing he seemed able to do was to mend nets. He looked into his face. White, round, smooth, impassive like a stone. And then he remembered: this was the other son of Agatha, the one he must have seen, because one sees everyone on the island, but he had overlooked. This was the son that they said fit in, had the approval, Michael laughed to himself, of the powers that be. He watched him: Moving very slowly by his boat, getting up, sitting down. No power of thought, or writing. Perhaps never thought of it. Perhaps a word was traced on him: what was this word?

Michael was curious. Imagine a literally dead person. A relic of sorts of the stone age only part of this new one. A man of the beginning time, but only cast up on the shore of the end time dead but living, that is, breathing. Perhaps, he thought, he was an innocent. Watching the sun rise and set on his fishing boat—fishing was one thing Michael did to honor his father, he felt that he really had no part in it—but one could see those who did it for labor, unquestioning labor, like the sun coming up and going down, great labor of the cosmos.

Michael was standing a little behind this curious, new man, as he called him—a bit like machine. For the thought had struck him like a revelation that this was exactly as we should be. It was a Biblical reality; not that of quarrels and argument, strange thoughts, words coming from God knows where, the sense of a nothing place with nothing people wandering about, attacking him, them, riling them up for a nothing war where real blood would be shed and people, would go, dead and alive to nothing land. No this one, perhaps the one and only, sat, real, unalterable, and solid—killing or dissolving all the rest by his machine-reality, percolating out of their natural-nothingness, where one could not be both dead and alive, in other words—and he was, Michael thought or discovered, Biblical, a sign.

He looked up, this man, looked really around, screwed his head at an awkward angle and perceived another man. A glint came into his eyes. Odd, that glint. Perhaps it was just the life, that is, the machine filament in him. Running through like electricity.

Months and months had gone by and Michael had not gone to the priest. The last time he had seen him, before the great penitential climb, the priest had been a sad figure, shadowy; the villagers burning of his files had, Michael thought, washed him out. And Michael himself had been 'on his side' when with him, but had switched sides as soon as he was away from him. But there had been the fact of the diary. It was odd, a lot of things had changed from normal, everyday occurrences on Holy Island to odd, and they weren't much different—but it was odd on the island now. Michael had continued the diary and he could only say now again and again—there is something; there is nothing. I had in mind to write only of the most important things—the meaning of Holy Island. And now all that I say is just twitter. Yet I am sure I was on to something.

He toiled up the hill to ask the words for this strange man, the other son of Agatha. Michael had felt that here he was—Biblically, somehow. He wondered if the priest would concur. A material presence when the rest, quibbling, twittering had gone down into the darkness and become nothingness. But it was odd to see the glint in his eyes when Little Paul had come. What exactly was that?

Michael had come to an impasse. He had written and written because he believed he had grasped the whole meaning of Holy Island and his own existence. And then after a time, months and months of toiling partly by candlelight because the night lights on the island were dimmed by the electric company to save money, Michael discovered that he had written nothing worth anything at all. That suddenly, walking out and imagining that he had met a foreigner, he had seen—what was his name? Jason!—by his fishing boat at an odd hour—one in the afternoon—and he had known a different kind of reality that was only words and meaning but not their island meaning although a fixture of the island.

He was half way up the hill when he stopped, suddenly realizing. Of course, he had assumed that the priest would know exactly…that he didn't need more explanation, more words. Now, he realized that the priest would not necessarily understand a thing. And then, he thought a minute—did he understand it? How was it possible anyway for him, except if this were a hallucination and he was going mad—to see a man, Jason, the one that had been hidden all this time, sitting there like the word of the Bible? Holy, and wholly material but a machine?

Of course, the priest said to this when Michael reiterated it at the doorway of the chamber. Max was washing dishes and had his back turned; he didn't turn around when Michael walked in but Michael noticed he was alert and tense like a young tree and the ends of him, fingers, hair, ears, seemed to quiver slightly.

There was a sweet smell in the air like figs and a fresh smell like leaves. Michael wondered abstractly where it came from. But the priest didn't respond as he had hoped. There was no answer no specific wording that he could hang on to the way one does in writing. It was not all said, all argued. There were instead silences, soft senses—visions, almost, or was it touch? And what stopped it from being obscene?

Michael wanted to say that he was standing naked in the priest's chamber and Max and the priest were busy about one thing or another, something completely trivial at the time of this immensely important event—his nakedness. He felt on the one hand as if he was a god, on the other, as if he was the worst devil. Then they went on talking and Michael blurted out but of course it is all untrue—meaning his crimes against the priest of long ago. The priest softly reiterated, of course. And Michael was aware of his nakedness again as if the sensation were a bell that rang again as the priest quietly intoned his words. The priest smiled and Michael felt a warm sensation on his thigh; he was suddenly afraid that he had peed a little on himself for shame. He was not quite sure what exactly made him ashamed. Why should he be ashamed when he had tried to write the truth?

Even about his vacillating—now for the priest, now against him—he had after all confessed. Confessed with searingly cruel comments about himself in his diary...

You can sit down, said the priest. Take Max's chair, he said airily—right across from me. What did you come about?

There is an odd fellow, began Michael, hardly noticing his words, his mind was so confused. I think he is both good and evil.

You mean, said the priest, he quietly fishes, reads the Bible, but something sinister catches you out.

Because you can't quietly fish and read the Bible in this place even though it appears made for it.

You mean you are not sure if it can be—this Eden.

Things happen interiorly. I have been writing my diary for at least four years now. I know that people exist on two levels. The one—the active and contemplative. The other—the place of evil. It is still a great journey—to be human, that is, to contemplate coming away from evil. And there are, I must say, roads to be built, cities to be made—even if you just fish and read the Bible click click click, this word, that, as if it was a machine and you an answering machine.

You caught a glimpse of something, said the priest, and you can't say what. But you saw it very clearly. Father Isaac was leaning forward, half smiling, excited.

I can't say that it is because he fishes and reads the Bible. I want to say that he simply wants to be saved, the way we all do here pulled away from something we don't half understand—built but in a way that works. But then I think he wants to use the Bible and fishing and...here Michael became almost hysterical. He felt his nakedness was protruding somehow from his clothes. He pulled himself together and stated: He sat there until Little Paul came. Then he said to Little Paul—do you know Moses commanded the Levites to kill their brothers? They had worshipped a god calf, an object of beauty, for beauty's sake, he said. No harm, would you say? But not the will of God. My brother worships Man-god-girl love for beauty's sake. You know it is time to reclaim the island. We worship the man who is God. There is no mixing. Do you want mixing? Perversions. A girl-man giving birth to the golden calf of Ba'al. That is the way they are.

What do you think of this? Fr. Isaac asked, when he had finished.

He wants to drown the island out with his idea of righteousness. Look, it sounds crazy; but anything else would sound even crazier.

And you wanted to alert me, inform me? Father Isaac asked. To do something about it, I suppose. No, I won't do anything about it.

It wasn't my original intent coming here. I thought I'd pass by and patch up the old wrong doings. But as I was coming I just noticed Jason, you know, Agatha's other son and then Little Paul. Jason seemed to be delegating a task.

Ah, said the priest. He looked at Max who was clattering the dishes as he dried them, thoughtfully.

Do you think there is such a thing as evil despite—the attempt to be kind, the feeding, the clothing and doctoring? Not evil of course in the sense of violent crime, but something insidious and inner that can tilt the balance, can result in death, a sort of falling from innocence of the island, a sign of final corruption.

Yes, you are right. Perhaps I had not noticed. I was busy with my joy. It is a shocking oversight. I always knew about Jason. He wants heaven as a sort of final place—a place for the select people. The people God has built according to God-Jason. Another island. A golden palace. A golden road. But yet the truth is that he withdraws, imagines himself superior religiously. I can't say that he is evil, though he displays a confident lack of humility. I imagine that it is hard for him to weep. He thinks tears are soft, a resource for women, children, gays or the superannuated and silly.

Or gays? Said Michael, stupefied. Since when have gays—I mean they have come as tourists a few times but...

Sh, said priest, warily. Perhaps the walls will hear. Yes, homosexuals, the poor green children—the shadowy ones, the ones not yet sturdy. The ones that somehow people recognize as sinners and the horror of sin in them they see too. Ah, poor persons—less than ourselves, built not so high and mighty; I say they sin—yes, they sin less than we do.

Max had gone over to the one bed and was straightening it; then he leant down and fixed the covers on his own mattress. He looked at the priest with an impassive gaze, then to the door as if he had something in mind. Then softly and quickly with utter grace he sunk to the ground and lay himself out on the mattress and stared up at the ceiling.

Michael realized that Max was used to the oddities of the priest, and responded with his own. As he was thinking this, Father Isaac looked at him with a glint in his eye, almost exactly as Jason had when he had seen him staring but just slightly sweeter: l'estro in me he said—the whim in me, he said, indicating Max.

Michael, we are all evil; so our Savior says. There is no putting one above another; for instance, me above Jason. But you feel something queasy. I suggest to you it is nothing more than torment of a kind. And perhaps the thread runs through the island. When God withdraws and leaves us torn, the needle in our hand to sew it up again. Sew, sew say the angels; you heard God. Without the weave whole again he will not accept you at the gate of heaven. Jason sews conscientiously. What does he do? His faith is based on the knowledge of sin—there the tear goes, and there. Rout it out let the thread cover it so that it doesn't ever appear again. Rout it out. Perhaps Jason was thinking when you saw him: ah, I have found the way, sewing blamelessly, but relatively absurdly.

The priest was creeping noiselessly around the room, pacing a little, back and forth; his hand was at his lips; periodically, he stroked his beard. Michael thought he had a sort of tired white look. It is as if, thought Michael, sainthood has been too much for him.

Yes, said the priest in response to his thought again: God wakes me up at all hours, you know. Rout it out, he says; rout it out! But I, unlike Jason, have not found the way to be in pure knowledge of evil.

Michael left the priest pacing and lost in thought. He went home, took his diary and went up the hill and sat and wrote until there was no more light. He wrote that he had finally understood a few things. What he was there for, what he was born to do. It all seemed very grand and yet, weary and sad. The fact remains, he did not quite understand what he was writing. It wasn't quite like before when he wrote poetically, mystically. It was not like when he wrote that all of flesh was a question to him. He now felt—what was it? Boredom, wistfulness…The island seemed like a land of thorns, though it was June and all flowers. Or else there was on the land an inexplicable wound—he didn't exactly see how there could be—and it had healed up a bit in ugly scabs that kept peeling off and bleeding. What was it? The slave's back after many lashings.

He looked down at the main street that ran by the beach and saw a figure, stooped, and frail, a network of bones—who was it? Simon? Zoe? It was the figure of the lost person, blown a little in this effortless wind, tripping one two along the street, turning back—having as it were, no direction. He thought and wrote that we are lost creatures, naturally—to be torn apart; it is not so bad as all that, an inner voice seemed to say to him. Just a kind of wasteland figure of humanity. They don't mean, no they don't mean at all to be destroyed, to be barren. And what is it? A kind of lunacy, a near death madness. Michael wrote that we were all in that fix and that it wasn't the thinking, in the end, that got us out—unless thinking came from the core motion of love.

Agatha? Who was she? She had been very tired looking of late. Was she too passing into that barrenness? Of course, she was. The village had all along suspected that she had brought it like a disease to the island. But he had seen her dance from afar on Easter; and he had thought to himself—a flame of life, of love! It is not wrong to pour out your soul even if the thing is not right in the usual sense, criminal to the Church. He had heard too how she had shamelessly doted on her son, wrapped her leg around his middle and kissed him all hot on the lips! Here she was, he reasoned in his diary, showing herself—but it was not insolence or ostentation. It was, he suspected the priest would agree—shouting to God! Beauty! Beauty! And it was building, he suspected, a roof over Dimitri's head, and now over little Tock. So should God choose in his wrath at the village to rain down fire, she would have covered her little ones; she would have danced out the flames.

Sinners, they were, yes. Noah too was a sinner. But Agatha was confessing: her pointed toe was towards God bosom, her private parts were open to the crowd... The shout—surely God had heard it.

At the same time the little, wretched, miserable men headed by Paul who had lost the crown of the Easter dance to Agatha and had had to repurchase it ignobly by some quibble in the rule—that women were not allowed to compete—they were creeping around like shadows that had acquired a kind of cruel gray flesh. One could see it on them—the flesh, that is, and that their intent could only be violent and evil.

Would the island disappear to nothingness directed by these insignificant cruel quibbling men? Humanity dissolved into a shadow and then quite obliterated one fine day of the Lord, as it were. At least, Agatha was not that.

Anyway, the shadow was becoming larger and larger. One didn't quite understand how it happened. Michael himself had almost lost his head and become part of it. There were rumors—voices—words: Agatha needs to be chastened. This is an assault on our dignity, our very faith. Dimitri has brought the world into our midst with its vile sins. And to think that first he would try to seduce us with money—to change our homeland forever...first jet boats, then air conditioning, then free sex, perversions...We were right to say no. To deceive as God deceives righteously, through the spirit of deceit when evil comes our way.

Are we so enervated? We must rise up once again like the men of the Lord that we are. Ah we see Agatha dancing—whore of Babylon, that she is, drinking the blood of the prophets, cursed all the more for her rearing up in the sun. Her son Dimitri, with that false humility, walking so quietly with that American who fixes old machines, his wife and not his wife! Which wife would undertake to accept a husband who does the unspeakable, breaks chastity with a demon's hand?

They have come from another world—the world of jet boats and free sex! Send them back, send them back—our island is still following God. We simply cannot accept. Look at Zoe, she has lost herself. Cleo is alone. Simon has no more wisdom. Something must be done.

...

Michael was not with the band of men that suddenly rose up and swooped like black crows around the island. Anna heard of them and one night she rose up suddenly, miraculously appeared on the roof of her house thin and freezing in the winter weather in a little bluish purple nightgown. She saw them gathering around Simon's house, a little distance away. They were holding flashlights, and their murmurings were rising in volume to a roar like the sea: Death, death to Dimitri, Agatha, death, death.

Anna took a breath into her skeletal body wracked with pain and shouted so that the pain burst her body—Damn! Damn you! It seemed to warm her because she continued shouting Damn you, and the men could hear her as they climbed the mountain. The shout had this effect: That the men on the fringes of the crowd looked back and saw a tiny figure on the roof of Anna's house all haloed with white hair, and what looked like a storm cloud colored nightgown billowing around her; her fist was raised and she shouted again: Damn you all. Damn you.

The crowd set their faces away from her and pressed grimly on, down the street. They swept through the village, dim lights were on, white faces pressed to the windows, but the doors were tightly shut. There were no weapons except for a knife here and there; no it seemed that the men were out to destroy only with their hate. They circled Agatha's house when they came to it. Torches were flashed in the windows. Jason stood calmly in the kitchen drinking cold tea despite the freezing temperatures. Agatha rushed outside in an agony of fear.

Where is it you are going? She shouted, what are you doing? Ha, said one of the men, although it was as if they were all one body, one face turned away and looked at her. Then it shoved itself under her eyes and said in a hiss—Max has declared to us that Dimitri raped him. If I were you, I would get him, yourself and the wife and child off the island. Go to the other island and live with the gypsies, or with any filthy people who are ruled by sexual perversion.

Agatha fell into line behind the moving mass of men. She was afraid, but the soul in her was slow somehow. It was too impossible to think of the islanders doing anything. This was the usual antagonism. She had encountered it before. The sullen warriors would not make a real, flesh and blood move. They would be called off; the island was after all a peaceful enclave dedicated to Christ. She almost raised her head and laughed a little at them. These were boys of thirty or forty—she knew them all, after all—family men, fisher boys—frustrated maybe, misunderstanding Dimitri, of course, set in their ways, yes, but they had and would settle; bristle up sometimes when Dimitri walked by, and well, yes, they hated her for being unbaptized, not a regular one of the faith, but they would simply go on their way with a cold look. One or two of them had always given her the time of day.

Strangely, she feared, despite all this. There was a colder atmosphere about the crowd than she had ever known before except for when the men had almost burned her house down. But that was so brief and so unreal a moment. And the perpetrators—where were they? Who were they? The faces she had seen that night, she had never seen again. They had vanished. But these faces, she knew them. And she saw that they were changing and yet they were what they had always been somehow. There was Tasos with his curling lip—she had thought it a tic, and now it was clear that it was hatred—hatred! There was Stefanos, strange man with three children in their twenties who had gone off island and entered business, medicine, and the theater. One would have thought him sane, normal. But the strangeness about him— now Agatha saw—the cold dead eye, it was hate.

The crowd began to climb the narrow cliff stairs one by one. Agatha was in the rear. Now she felt desperate with fear, cold in the January air. Wait, she called out in a thin, high voice. Come back, she called but her chest was constricted and only a whisper came out. She went up after the crowd.

Dimitri and Catherine were passing the evening quietly in the dead Elder's shack. They had reconstructed the little house so that it was sturdier, had plumbing and an extra room. They were living with the baby in a single bedroom and sitting room that they had both decorated with rugs, curtains, tables, chairs—sparsely but sweetly. Father Isaac had visited once and blessed them without comment. He had said to Dimitri, now you are on a rope, you can't get lost. Tonight, Dimitri to Catherine appeared both sad and happy. His eyes looked peculiarly peaceful as if he had found, thought Catherine, inner ground. But his face looked like a sad face. Periodically, he smiled up at her, her back was longer and when she sat straight she was taller— for they were seated in little wooden chairs. Outside the window they could see big snowflakes falling and melting as soon as they hit the ground. They seemed, to Catherine, to be marooned in the middle of a disintegrating cloud—that soon all the confusion would be cleared up.

The fact is that evening Catherine looked to Dimitri like a queen. For once, he had been so absorbed in her face that all thought of himself had disappeared. He came back to himself a moment, sat quietly, and said to her, Dear, what I thought was ful-filling myself as a man was just hardening the outlines of a sickly sweet narcissism. I really want there to be nothing between love and you. I heartlessly have taken you along a hard, stony path. The forgiveness part—it is entirely up to you. Catherine, remember one thing—I have always loved you more than anyone. I know what you are thinking: It is not only that. All that is part of putting myself at the core center. I knew no other way, you understand.

I think this is more about you than about me. I knew what I was getting into when I married you.

Have you ever regretted? Dimitri said with a smile, though his face was still sad.

Never. I have loved you all the way through.

A strange murmuring sound came to them through the windows.

What is it? Asked Catherine, a little nervously.

The crowd, said Dimitri after listening a minute. I knew they'd come.

What do they want? Asked Catherine, anxiously.

Nothing of any importance, said Dimitri, smiling. I will go out to meet them—you make a tea or something, and tend to Tock. One thing: You don't believe that I raped Max do you?

You didn't intend violence; that I know.

Ah, said Dimitri, bitterly—one is less than a man... no matter...

Dimitri put on his black jacket and went out.

He found himself in the midst of a swirl of men who stopped murmuring when they saw him. The moon was high and he could see quite well. He caught sight of Agatha a little below on the cliff, for the Elder's shack was just up from the monastery, which loomed over the Isolets, large white villa. Robert had joined her and was calling anxiously for Catherine, and telling the men in their dialect in a harsh voice to stop the nonsense, to come to their senses, to redirect their energies, to remember the peace of their Creator. Dimitri turned and looked at the men. They seemed to smile at him, and he felt reassured.

You have come to tell us to leave, he said. For what reason?

Max has said to us—that you raped him, and one of the men spit on the ground at his feet.

I am not a rapist, said Dimitri; Max lied.

Max is innocent, said another man, a thin sallow man whose long fingers played on his lips.

Yes, said Dimitri, coldly. Max is innocent. Nevertheless, he lied. But it has been two years in any case. You thought nothing of it before. Why do you bring it up now?

Our island needs to be purged. We are losing our old life. We are rapidly losing the light of God. Why don't you leave the island with your mother and wife and boy? We would not stop you. Just tell us that you are intending to leave, to go—who knows? Into the world where they do these things...You have come from that world after all. You are not part of this world. Why do you insist? Force yourself on us? We are not so great! As you can see, we are simple folk, the kind you think of as nothing, dust beneath your feet. We haven't got that intellect, that gift for business that you have.

I wanted to revive my old home, said Dimitri, your old home. What is wrong? I wanted to lift the little island from its ashes. Not to disturb the holiness. But to bring it to the contemporary...

You lie, spat the thin man and another man joined him, a fat man who looked so like him that he could have been his twin except for his fatness so Dimitri was almost inclined to laugh at the comedy. The fat man said—we embrace holiness here, remote from the world that embraces profanity. Dimitri thought for a minute; this bore arguing it out. I am not quite sure, he said.

In any case, Paul struggled through the other men and bore down on the little group, we hold you accountable for bringing something worldly and loathsome to God to our island. For being a different type of man. We define manhood in one way, godliness. You have waylaid, destroyed our definition. With the snowflakes in his hair, he looked holy, thought Dimitri.

How? Dimitri was surprised.

It is not worth even entering into discussion with you, said Paul in disgust. We want you off the island.

Dimitri had unconsciously moved himself to the little clearing behind his house. He could see the sea stretched out below him out of the corner of his eye glittering in the moonlight. He felt, oddly, rather lazy.

The men were smiling and they did not after all look so enraged. It seemed rather that they were embarrassed by homosexuality—it was something they didn't want to know about, something shameful that one doesn't discuss generally. They suddenly began to sing a silly little song: Where does the cock go? To the hen, to the hen. And the others kept singing this all the while one or two of them were talking. Dimitri smiling, joined in to show the others his bonhomie and to make it clear that he didn't despise them.

So you love us? Shouted another man, dark faced with a huge mustache.

Of course, I love you, said Dimitri; where do these men come from at these times? I never see them usually— and smiling foolishly he began singing again. Where does the cock go? To the hen, to the hen.

There was a shout more like a blood curdling scream from the corner of the crowd and out burst Little Paul, whom Dimitri had not seen and had not even imagined present. The crowd began singing louder and the men clapped their hands; Dimitri thought to quiet him down by retreating at his charge. Where does the cock go? Dimitri stepped backward, and backward. And then lost his footing at the edge of the cliff. He thought somehow calmly-- this must not be, must not be—he heard: Only to the hen, the singing fainter; he fell--then darkness.

Agatha let out a terrible scream. It was so bad that some blood vessel broke inside her and blood came from her mouth. She fell on the ground and writhed in the dust, eating the dust and bloodying it. Robert knelt beside her. The men fell back. They silently crept away back down the cliff. It was the judgment of God, Paul shouted aloud, not our murder. We didn't touch him. See Little Paul stopped without laying hands on him.

Somehow Agatha came to rising in a little throng of Robert, Ellen, Catherine, the baby in her arms and Kali. They were talking in low voices. Catherine looked like death boiled over. Agatha studied her face and found not a trace of her former flush, the rosy red beauty that just a few days ago—and then she thought of her son again, and let out a terrible tearing cry. It was endless weeping, days, nights, days of it. She exhausted herself lying in Catherine's old single bed in the blue-walled room where the girl used to go to breathe; it seems of late during the heyday of the marriage, she hadn't required so much time out time; she breathed now in company.

In any case, she was the one who tended to Agatha dry eyed while Agatha wept incessantly. Agatha moaned too; she felt physical agony, as if someone had opened her up with a knife and ripped out her womb, she said. Something was gone from within. A living human, a man of utter beauty. Dimitri, she said, was the meat in her. Now it had been torn off the bone, suddenly disemboweled of her.

In fact, she ate almost nothing and dropped thirty pounds in a few days. Catherine began to nurse her and sit by her day and night, sleeping on the floor beside her, sometimes leaving the baby in the crib, sometimes with Robert. Ellen wafted in once or twice and then one evening when the light was dim, caught her daughter in the hall going to her mother in law, and said to her—I'm out. I've made arrangements. It would be hypocritical for me to stay and mourn with you in this deep, single-minded way. I have not lost anyone. I am trying to lose…but she bit her tongue. Even you. It is grisly of me, perhaps, but there you have it. I am interested only in writing and in a peaceful haven where the slop of human emotion doesn't come too near. Catherine nodded. You must go, Ellen. It is only right.

She proceeded then to Agatha, sat down on the bed beside her and held her in her arms.

That evening she didn't see Ellen; she heard voices, perhaps an argument, she was too tired to listen—in her parent's bedroom. The next morning, she heard from Robert that Ellen was gone. He sat in the kitchen with the cup of coffee that Catherine had made him, staring at the floor. I don't understand the sense, that is my problem. I would even believe in God if I understood the sense—of existence, of things that happen…

The house inside rotated. Catherine and Tock now slept in the double bed in what had been her parent's room. Robert slept in Stephen's room, as they called it, though Stephen had never yet shown up. Agatha still wailed, moaned and slept out of exhaustion in Catherine's bed. On about the twentieth day, Catherine went to Agatha who had become so thin her face had caved in around the cheekbones and said to her: You must get up. You have shed the tears of a host of mourners, me included. It is time that you face the world again. You had thirty-three years of love of Dimitri. You are going to have to count on those thirty three years that somehow changed, reconfigured you. And you are going to have to count that the impression in your flesh is such that it will still be there. In other words, he made a dent in your substance—that is what is left.

Ah, you know he didn't marry properly, said Agatha, rudely. But he married for love. He should have had a woman that he could have looked at with amusement and affection and she him. But he was distracted by you. Yes, so it became tragedy. You are so tragic, Catherine.

Catherine wisely ignored all this. Yes, Agatha went on getting ruder and ruder—I knew it all along. I know there would have been reconciliation…And what is this? Living on the cliffs? Putting oneself above the others. That is what it is. He would have never asked… I think he even wanted to die…It was all a death wish. Sometimes those are very compelling.

Catherine looked at her. Agatha didn't look herself. Her eyes were so dark and large! They looked like the depths of water look—without light, without sound. There was a bottom down in her, the end of the chasm—what was it? Death, the body of Dimitri—the death of everyone?

Catherine helped Agatha to dress. She noticed that she had a large rib cage and that big breaths went through her body. The ribs looked cruel. Now, said Catherine, sitting beside her and taking her hand, whatever the truth is, you must eat. I will bring you some fish and rice with lemon, pepper and tomato.

Agatha sat down on the side of the bed, and bowed her head. It seemed for the moment that she had wept herself dry of tears. Her son's death had given her pain, but a strange relief also. It was relieving to not be in that world that had cost her so much. It was relieving to be granted by all the powers in the universe that she knew, time to weep and to detach. As she ate, obediently, the fish with pepper, lemon and tomato slapped Body against her side, driving hunger out; as she swallowed, she felt she was a child to Catherine, who was stronger than the strongest tree, she thought, she felt herself lightly, wearily, slightly warily coming back from the other end—coming up from the dark depths, full, and whole. Light filled her and for a time, she sat utterly peaceful, that is, devoid, staring at Catherine, abstractly, a piece of fish still unswallowed in the back of her throat.

Actually, I am not surprised that it would end this way, said Catherine. Oh, don't get me wrong; I am not one of those who believe in curses. No, rather in cures, you see. I mean that Dimitri should have left us to be together—you what I would call rather than mother, his 'other' and me his wife. Licit and illicit, the illicit one weeping much more, of course. I can't say that I didn't love him that much. But my own mother instructed me to be not much of a weeper, if you understand. Tears, she said, were not how one understands things, or comes to any enlightened conclusion. I guess there are better natures than my own. But just to say—that two lovers—one physical— of Dimitri should come together in the end and help one another, stumble through life together…because in the end, it won't even be about Dimitri, although he stands beautiful as a Christmas tree between us—no love will be about me and you. How something hit us and we helped one another to stand up. You doing the weeping…I doing the enduring…

At first, Agatha in her heart of hearts was incensed that Catherine didn't see it her way—the utter loss, the tragedy, the need for tears, to wail in the vale of sorrow.

How could she be so stony-faced when she had had his entire love? But bit by bit she began to see Dimitri reappear unaccountably in Catherine—in her very expressions, her movements. She even said to herself perhaps she has internalized my son with such love genius that whether he is physically present or not, he is with her, in her. Perhaps it is a matter of getting the hang of him so entirely that she has dispensed with the need for his bodily self, or it is so thoroughly imprinted on her body, that he, separately, is unnecessary.

But one day Catherine sat down with Agatha in two little chairs outside of the front door overlooking the sea from on high as it were and said: I miss him as much as you do. When I was little my mother always said to me: Don't cry. Don't. I grew up that way—I told you this—you see, there was a greater virtue in not weeping always. Robert is different. He wept many a tear in sympathy not knowing Dimitri.

There is something I must at last tell you, now that you are eating and drinking. I went down to the town and asked. Dimitri for now is gone. The body didn't wash in. It is as if he took a backward misstep into the invisible.

It almost seems tedious to me to mourn. He is part of the invisible. That is all.

Agatha murmured—I cried spasmodically; the thought that he missed his footing and fell so far. That he might have been dashed against the rocks—but apparently fell clean into the sea in between. It made me enormously frightened. I literally cried thinking he might have hurt himself. That his body might have suffered. I didn't think so much that he was dead as that he might be. I have never been so weak. I beg you to understand. I cried too because the love wasn't finished. He had been in my way of thinking artificially removed. He wasn't home—it wasn't what I imagined; I thought I would know and feel in my heart of hearts peaceful and sweet. But I only felt questions when he married you. I felt that he broke from me there—traveled away; I felt then that there was a deal of water between us. I held my breath hoping for his return, I must admit—put it that way. This of course makes the water breach wider and wider...Something I can't accept. I look out on the back of the water to the horizon, see the clouds and there is nothing but that emptiness of water—his body mysteriously plunged in, mine drawn out. I keep thinking I should have been the one to go over the cliff. My death would have filled up the breach. But somehow there is a familiarity, a love in the water space.

But you, though you are pale, rest behind with your attractiveness intact.

There is something else I have to tell you, began Catherine, a little hesitantly. I went down to the village and it appears Father Isaac has called for a criminal investigation. It appears the villagers went around once too often saying things like it was the will of God against men like that for his taste. You are murderers, he told them from the altar. They shouted back at him, there is no blood on our hands. No blood has stained our soil.

Simon went up for Holy Communion before the others. He had not been at the cliff. Father Isaac gently ministered to the poor old man, who is now half insane, but the priest refused a number of the men who had boasted that they had not shed blood. You should have seen them, kneeling and gaping like fish before the chalice and Father Isaac, stern, lofty, blazing white light withholding the spoon—just the tiniest frown but something like a lightning bolt. They back off. And then they began murmuring that they would have another priest, they would.

I received Holy Communion, myself. I noticed the men who had been excommunicated watching me. I asked Father Isaac later—it is perhaps righteous of you, but this kind of righteousness is so fragile.

Child's play, he said. Yet when we stand weak as children with our holiness…

I questioned him further: It is not so much the murder that Little Paul committed—who by the way didn't show in church, not so much for shame of his action but because he hates me; it is, from my perspective the way they do not take responsibility—the inability to take blame for—not murder—but hate—being anti-love.

Dimitri, I said, a little anxious, did not rape Max.

Of course not, said the priest—it was mutual consent, his lips seemed to caress the words. I do not know who coaxed Max to say it was rape. Work of the devil. Perhaps he was threatened. He has not spoken to me, not a word. When he heard what had happened, he went to bed and wouldn't get up. Slept maybe four or five days. Got up with what he called a headache. And there were signs of his squinting, crouching and cringing again—not very pronounced. I say almost nothing to him, but when I speak of Dimitri, I do so softly, holding his hand. He eats almost nothing at meals--only a little bread and complains that it tastes too salty. I think the boy is holding many tears in his stomach. And tastes now are all salty to him.

Catherine stopped because Agatha had begun to cry again but she arrested the sobs. It is odd, she said, you spoke of Holy Communion, which I have never tasted and of the men being rejected and of Max tasting salt in his bread—well, it is just that, perhaps of no consequence—I taste that sweet warm blood when I weep. Sweet warm blood. Before I could only taste water.

Christ's mercy comes in different forms, said Catherine. I thought for me it had to do with loving little green leaves, worms. I had a great gift for insects, loving them, you know, before I married. The question is will you, as it were, eat this mercy of Christ Jesus?

More pertinently than little green leaves—how will I help you? Agatha grasped Catherine's arm.

Tock, she said, slowly, looking down. It was all fun and fancy while Dimitri was there to father; now I am at a loss. I look at my baby boy with a troubled eye now. I always thought Dimitri would…she stopped. Strange, I almost cried just then. It is strange how we are made of we know not what. A material that surfaces amidst the shadows now and then, out of the dead water. I would like to have it be different.

Agatha sobbed a little quietly. Then she said, it is all as if a nightmare did come true. But I will take care of that material—of Tock; don't worry. If you have the confidence to entrust to me...

Yes, said Catherine, suddenly, softly—I do. You are the most human of all of us.

I? Agatha in her amazement looked a little wildly around her.

I would say so. Even your despair—it is not cold hearted. Nor your sins, she said again very softly. Rather a full-blooded person with many sins, than a sterile person with few. Wasn't that what the Jesus said to the Pharisee about Mary who wept at His feet? What is love? Full bloodedness, shame of passionate desire! I learned that one with Dimitri. You are the kind that would fall in the dust before our Lord and tear your hair and weep. That is most human. You are the kind that would rear up in the end with the cross on your back and dance to give courage to the Christ of the Passion. You again, most human. You would weep seeing Him, a mother's son, on the cross until you had tasted blood in your own mouth, until, resurrected, you had sweet warm wine. Again, Agatha, the human one. Woe to us who have lost humanness.

Humanness! That is as if you were to say to a person in the chasm—pointing upward to the edge where a little dandelion is smiling all yellow in the sun—there you are—that is the real you. But that little dandelion doesn't feel the pain, never will never has and when you say to it—here is pain, it will reply—ah, how wonderful and curious, terrible and great—but I don't know it.

No, no—the pain makes you human, humanness in the dream of crossing over to dandelion reality.

Rather it makes me into a beast, said Agatha, and she hung her head. The knot in my heart used to be fearlessness. I used to be solid, spinning, beautiful. Now a nothing person. I used to be like a star. You mistake pain; you would glorify it.

I realize it is the twilight of your old self. I realize that.

Anna must have died, said Agatha, suddenly. Check and see. I've not been myself, as you know, now suddenly, like all disoriented and dizzy—I come back—here is the day, there the table and chairs. I am in a different house. Didn't mean to be. Where is my house? And, ah, Dimitri is gone—but where is Jason? Help me to put the pieces back together. She leaned towards Catherine from her chair.

It has been a little odd, she whispered. God or the devil, I have pushed on—dancing, you know. No wonder they called me a witch, some thought me from the other side of the coin a saint. Now, I came to a dead halt. It is the thought of looking down, you see, into that sea that swallowed him. The sea he didn't emerge from. Everything paused—that is all the dances in me, millions on millions—they all paused like a mighty swarm of bees. They hang golden in the air: yet I begin to see, now, that too is the dance, the bee silence and stillness. I have been dancing lying here with the tears trickling down under the moon. Sometimes I have only raised one arm and with my hand wiped my face. Still it was dance. Incredible, isn't it? This gold in the air in my uplifted nose by day, weeping, one-armed in the night. Deformed, bestial with my passionate sorrow, I dance, you see, dance and it is crazy, blundering, awkward, rough and sugar fine like old folks are. I wonder is it the curse again? I thought I had it solved.

The curse, said Catherine. What do you think? We all have it. But you have felt it flesh and blood. Let's start from there. I haven't heard from the village about Anna.

Go and find out. And I have forgotten Leo too. Ha, death and love—I have forgotten. And you talk of my humanness.

Catherine checked. She went down to the village; pausing a little as she stepped down the staircase, putting her hand to her heart. It was again the way it had been when she had gone to bed to breathe for ages, it seemed. The little cloud nine with Dimitri was over and the old ordinary pain was there. The weight of the village stare, as she called it, because of a kind of dim collective guilt towards the widow of the man whose death they were responsible for, she bore rather well, with dignity and peacefulness. Above all, she was unafraid. There was the man whose refrigerator she had fixed. There the woman whose outlet she had rewired. Here was a woman whose storage hole high above the kitchen sink, she had climbed into to retrieve two decrepit, cobwebby fans that she had coaxed to life one hot summer. Now they stared at her and then half closed their eyes. Simon, she met in the streets, coming to her slowly, haltingly. He approached her, stood in front of her, and the tears came; he kissed her hand and then went down on his hands and knees, laboriously and kissed one foot and then the other.

You have not died, then, like we have, he said, standing up slowly. There were times even now he had attacks of sanity.

I had no time to, said Catherine, warmly taking his hand. Agatha collapsed; there was Tock to consider.

Agatha, Tock, said Simon—I rarely feel pleasure these days but thinking of them… Not so much that things have changed, but we have all grown suddenly old, older, can you believe it? Than we were. We are each and every one of us, almost, antiques. We should be exhibited, sold at auctions.

Ha! But not your baby. He has a real, live father. Simon began to wander in his thoughts. Catherine grasped his arm affectionately. You are a great friend to Agatha, she said. Agatha, he said, perplexed. Yes, Agatha—the bride of Dimitri, the one the war was over.

Tell me Simon, said Catherine in a low, gentle voice: How is Anna?

Oh, Anna, that is an easy question to answer: She died with me last night. We died smiling like highborn ladies. And the winged roses of love greeted us and bore us away.

Catherine walked with Simon back to his house along the beach. It turned out that Tia was there, and confirmed to Catherine that Anna had in fact died twenty-four hours ago. She said Anna had died peacefully and murmured to her that it was alright, life had tried to 'get her off' but she had come back—she had done it. She had loved! She had loved on the rooftop the night the thugs were going for Dimitri. She said that Agatha would understand.

Tia was hired now by Stavros to help Simon. She had been checking in on him anyway out of the kindness of her heart. There were so many old and so few to help them. Simon was wonderfully colorful—a poet when he was off, a good, kind old man when he was on. And there were so many brilliant paintings, all of strange shapes shining, she thought she was in a hall of wonders where there were pictures and pictures of God.

Catherine handed her Simon who stood holding her arm and looking at Catherine as if he didn't know her, patient and a little perplexed. Quite the lady, aren't you? He shouted at her suddenly. Put me to shame, will you?

Tia smiled at her apologizing. He sometimes thinks he is a woman, she said. And then she took him into the house.

Catherine walked past Anna's mansion and looked around. It looked somehow as if the old lady was still there, as if her aura, her air was still filling the rooms, the porch. Catherine sat down on the steps. She hadn't known Anna well but what she remembered of her—tall, severe, beautiful—was distinct in her mind. She remembered coming in to Agatha's house for coffee five years ago when she had just come to Holy Island and seeing—it was Anna, not Agatha, so much—she had thought how remarkable—these people look a little like icons. The sense of the island had been so peaceful then. Oddly, she suddenly felt she was now going to cry about Dimitri, thinking suddenly of the old woman damning everyone who would kill him as rapist, and knowing she would have long ago have had Paul killed, because it wasn't the killing of a man that bothered Anna at all, but the killing of a truly beautiful man. Catherine couldn't help herself. The tears ran down, she sobbed as if her heart would break. And through it all, she was not even thinking much of Dimitri, her husband, but of Anna—the severity and the beauty; it was as if Anna was gazing at her darkly knowing and sweet and sad invisibly but there.

After about half an hour, Catherine took out a tissue from her pocket and blew her nose, wiped her face with her hands, sighed and stood up. It was getting late and she wanted to be back home by sundown. She sighed again and walked pensively on down the road, stopping and looking out to sea now and then. It seemed to her then that she had taken hold of life for those four years with Dimitri—she had raced with him with the kind of muscles in her thighs that make for light running not falling—

Tock had appeared more than three years ago and he too, he had lived half thrown up into the air above them, caught as he came down and thrown high again.

Now it was something different entirely. A winded sensation, the heaviness of Tock. Tock an almost alien creation, she deflated, thin, flabby. The boy had 'gone with her' only a month before when Dimitri was with them. Tock had been part of her, her cheer, her rosiness, her bosom, her light. Now he was a strange staring little boy, rather big-headed. He didn't ask about his father. He sang the chicken soup song over and over again until Catherine, who would have delighted in it before, wanted to scream.

Catherine got back about six when it was still light. She found Agatha trying to make something passable for dinner. A hard-boiled egg salad with olives and chives on a bed of tomatoes. Tock was playing with two spoons at her feet. Robert was sitting at the table looking somehow stiff all over, with an apologetic expression on his face.

When Catherine came in, instead of greeting her, he said—don't you think we must make decisions?

Yes, said Catherine sitting down for a minute.

What are you sitting down for? Piped up Robert a little crankily. Are you ill?

Of course, not, said Catherine. Why—I just sat down a minute after climbing those cliffs. You know I have a heart condition—why should that be strange?

You never sit down when you come in, muttered Robert a little angrily. You know you always go straight to work, housework of all sorts. I have no right to demand it, but you know that is the way you are.

Where is Tock? Catherine asked ignoring him.

Playing. He gets along very well with Agatha. He doesn't cry at all with her— laughs rather. He likes especially to spin round and round with his arms held out like a little top. Agatha shows him how to do it—teaches him spinning. When he gets dizzy and falls down she teaches him how to rise up again gracefully and go back to it. He learns very readily.

Catherine nodded and leaned her elbow on the table.

Well? Don't you have anything to say? Robert continued petulantly.

I went down to Anna's house, Catherine explained, patiently; you know, she is dead; Simon is in and out of madness. We have no more friends except the priest.

Ah, this island is mysterious. No one quite seems to ever be friends with anyone. Just open friends. Everyone is slightly reserved and then there are those bastards the Paulines.

Catherine wanted to say: I cried Daddy. But for years and years she had grown up without referring to Robert that way and although her father when she was a child had always comforted her in a heavy, almost inarticulate way as if the language of love and tenderness was known to exist but not known well enough to carry on a conversation—he had not expected her to need comforting since coming of age, and especially since her marriage. Catherine therefore hovered near saying those three confiding words that would have put a little of her pain in his hands to be held and soothed, but then she sighed and veered away to silence.

Agatha—of what use was Agatha? She was so close to tears every second that Catherine knew she would unloose another waterfall. She could out cry anyone at this time and she was needed to help look after Tock. Odd how when there should have been such sympathy between them, there should exist a kind of sterility, a kind of impossibility of comfort and support in their relationship. There came to her a soft thought, a gentle perception: She wants me dead! Odd, that it did not fill her with horror at all. It was a light filled thing in fact, like an angel. Perhaps it was an angel.

Late that night after dinner had been eaten and Tock had been put to bed in the slender double bed of Robert and Ellen where Catherine slept with him, Catherine wandered out into the back patio and looked off the cliff to the sea in the moonlight. She wants me dead—how is it I know this? But it seemed entirely peaceful. It isn't resentment; she doesn't hold a grudge. It is she feels the right way—the immolation of the wife after husband and master are drowned. She feels I should not live on to grow inevitably into another person. And even more than that—she wants the coast clear to remember Dimitri in a single-minded way without his wife. It is passion too: she would throw herself after him into the sea were she not ashamed to have the village talk. But I? Oh, it is natural and would get rid of the obstacles, the alien inter- ferences! She could be alone with her memories then. She holds out the sea to me as a beautiful, shining path. She asks: Don't you too want death?

I am not built to want it, no. But I don't fear it. One proceeds down down a road to the vanishing point. Now, it is true in this house all is grey and dark except Tock. Even the white plastered walls are grey and dark somehow. The marked emptiness, which I used to think was filled with my father and mother's creative genius—the one spiritual, the other artistic—I used to think there was a great meaning to the void in the house—now it is gloomy.

Catherine turned away and walked into the house to her bed where her little son was asleep. She lay down and put her arm around him softly. Lying there next to him, touching his softest hair, she delighted for a minute in him and then oddly, suddenly, just like at Anna's house, the tears came again and she cried violently until she was exhausted and slept.

We have changed a bit. We are willing to admit that things are not the same. Of course, things have not been the same for the past half a century—not the same as they were for ages and ages—two thousand years or so. Nobody is sick, thank God, but everyone is slightly weak and grey-fleshed. Simon is a little off. But to counter that, Zoe is on again. She is walking down the road every day with drive and determination. She goes to the grocery store, buys a bottle of wine, eggs and bread, some vegetables, olives and cheese. She seems to say with her little old, stiff body: Life is the important thing now.

We rarely go to her house for a chat. She says we have grown old and useless, flabby, idle in mind; she says she wants someone who has something to say not just words thrown out like trash, becoming trash, having no life behind them.

She however doesn't refuse to come to Cleo's house and so we gather there. Cleo mumbles: It is all absurd anyhow. Perhaps Foti is right. We are just a swarm of dust specks out there—there is nothing meaningful about us at all. Perhaps our minds too, movements of brain chemistry that we cannot control. (Cleo's son had sent her an article on the mind and brain connection from the world out there.) It is all absurd—she said, referring to and not referring to Dimitri's 'fall' as we put it. The mind having failed or misfired in Little Paul and Dimitri. And to think one different movement of the brain chemistry and they would have loved one another. But of course it isn't about that. No, it is about all of us. We haven't a clue. Yet, I know there is something to be known. That much is clear: We haven't had a tradition for thousands of years for nothing. And it tells me that if I love or hate there is suddenly a difference, even a profound difference. Bah, this is a puzzle on many levels.

But at last I know why I didn't take that million and go to Paris. Yes, I know. Because here I see that there is something to be known. Here on this island I know that there is something to be known. In Paris, the swarm of dust specks becomes the only level of the puzzle. It blots out the out there, perhaps the out there is nothing but a swarm of dust specks. Why, I would addle my brain.

We feel rather glum, listening to Cleo. There are times we feel that nothing terrible has really happened. Of course, we pity Agatha, we mourn Dimitri a little. We fear the priest though he has gone back to giving Holy Communion to us. Here is the sand, we say to ourselves; there is the brilliant, blazing whitish sun. It is September, hot and the cicadas buzz. The quality of the light is just beginning to change. How odd, it seems that we slept all summer. There was that terrible January—when was it? January 20th, that he died—the heat and the men milling around—our men, the old familiar faces, strained, looking to see what they couldn't see—but somehow it was part of a great sleep. Summer is like that.

Now we are awake. It is over. There is a light feeling as well as a heavy feeling among the villagers. There is the dark side of life—the fact that killing Dimitri, of course, we refer to him and do not refer to him here, brought us a kind of new livingness. Also, he totally disappeared. It has been a month and he has not washed up on our island. There is no news of him on the other island either. Some of us think he was just removed by God. When we think like this the light feeling and the heavy feeling come back.

We can say we have a sort of seasickness. We do not know where this seasickness if from—people with headaches and nausea. We are not settled back into our old selves. Our bodies are not unwell, as we have said, but they are not quite the same. Barbara says that her skin has grown thick. Nisos' wife says that she has incessant hunger pains that no amount of food will quell. Paul stares at us out of eyes that have not known sleep for weeks. Jason who now lives by himself in Agatha's house forgotten—Agatha is up at the Isolet's villa with Tock—has grown extremely fat. His face has grown smaller and rounder in the fatty folds around it. But he walks around with a little smile, a little red smile. He is also growing a rather ugly sparse beard.

When we woke up from our long summer 'sleep', that dull, slow, hot, nightmarish summer, we found ourselves faced with Anna's death. She had never recovered from her stand on the balcony, the terrible high-pitched scream-shout damning the men that were going after Dimitri. Tia said that she took her to bed and she dwindled there gasping for the pain for four weeks. When she died, she said, she was fully conscious and her eyes were bright like a child's but she looked like some kind of insect, she was so tiny with emaciation. When we put her in her coffin, she looked like a baby. She had lost all her hair and her face was little and thin like an infant's. The coffin was light —hardly more with the body than without. It was a coffin of pine and looked clean and simple. Stavros had it made by some of the same men that were up there yelling and singing that ludicrous song on the cliff. We all gathered around for her funeral. A kind of love seemed present, even in all those men she had damned so heartily. She was the oldest among us and she had held on to life for so long after she got sick. She also seemed to all of us like the main link to the old island as it once was when that light that was not the sun's light, filled everything. The thirty and forty year olds would ask Zoe and Cleo or any one of us older folks—did she, Anna, actually see that light?

Well, we don't know but given Anna, the way she was so humorous and sweet, severe and kind, we say yes. Of course, she was half way on the way to being atheist, but there were times she turned back. And isn't that the case with all of us? We want to voyage out not in—away, how can we not? There is this little land, cramped, dry, not what it used to be and the vast sea with other lands…. That is what killed Dimitri. Anna had gone away with a string tied to her and the rock under the cliff of this island. Dimitri—he had let go entirely. One saw it in the way he was. And Anna had come back. Dimitri, well yes, physically—but not really. He had kept the alienness the world had rooted in him. No Anna was our own in the end. So we thought when the priest conducted the Liturgy. But after? There were murmurings and arguments.

Why were we giving Anna a land burial—the kind we reserved for saints, and nuns, and priests and a very few proven holy? Someone has paid, her son, yes, well, there he was at the funeral kissing the priest's hand—but this was an affront. And gradually, though some of us remembered Anna's baby head and the clean, simple pine coffin, we also thought back on the days she condemned our faith. And here she would rest in earth like one of the holy. Little Paul said it was a kind of mockery. But no one knew who was doing the mocking. It just happened that way. Jason murmured to Little Paul that this above anything else would change Holy Island. Little Paul nodded. And from that day we saw them together. Both of them 'extremists' for our holy little land.

So the island seems to toil on in the usual way. But we know there is a difference. We feel it in the air, and in the men's bodies. Everyone is really uncomfortable. We don't quite fit anymore. Everything that seemed natural, our work, fishing in the little boats at dawn, milking the goats, picking lemons, mending clothes, sewing, carpentering, painting, cooking now seems a little forced as if we are doing it to no avail. There is a certain restlessness round about and meetings at Paul's house to all hours. We don't attend but we hear that they are unhappy with the priest who after all did nothing to chastise Dimitri after the affair with Max. Even if it hadn't been a real rape, which of course it was, Max declared it so, it would have been something so evil and perverse to countenance on this very Holy Island. Father Isaac acted as if he was entirely unconcerned and denounced even the idea of his own deacon having been raped as totally false. Max was utterly desirous of that love affair, he had the effrontery to say. He calls it a love affair.

Here was this priest who from the first had been scientific rather than spiritual, casually lounging about; his deacon of course hiding in the church, but he strolling out with an almost blissful look on his face—he says he loves the sun on the island—going to buy eggs or milk, or cheese…it's as if nothing in the world can touch him.

So Paul and Little Paul gather a group of men who are going to shake him up. Father Isaac looks, Zoe said, as if he would spit in the face of death. It makes us all mad. And I have no faith any longer in his so-called miracles. The fruit grew more abundantly for a natural reason; the goats produced a lavish supply of milk because it was in their breed. Father Isaac had nothing to do with it. In fact, I am sure that penitence was just a performance for our benefit and God will have nothing to do with it. For it is clear that a saint would never behave as he is behaving.

A saint would be lowly and meek.

A saint would be strong, upright, stern—in command of Holy Island.

A saint would never just sit in his chambers, content with his tea, smiling a little as if he knew something great.

A saint would never speak of love affairs…

The voices came from all sides. Our little crowd was growing excited.

Well, said Zoe, I don't know what a saint would look like. Maybe no more extraordinary than me, she laughed a little vague, vaporish laugh. But to countenance what I have seen him countenance! Our first duty as you all know is not to sin. But he seems to take sin in stride. Why not reprimand Fr. Isaac instead of well—almost encourage him.

Everyone was silent for a minute. I for one, piped up one of the old women in the back, I, for one, would, would pack him off.

Zoe pondered for a minute. Perhaps that is what we should tell Paul. That we, the congregation, are exercising our God given right to dismiss him, that is all.

It is all peaceful that way, said Cleo, and according to plan.

What plan? Asked Foti who had joined the group a few minutes ago. She was wide eyed with terror, had been since Dimitri died.

The plan for our redemption. We have to encounter Jesus. We have to catch the bull by the horns, so to speak. We are guilty of sins but we never, never would have had—a—well, what can I say—a mess, an iniquitous mess on our island.

You mean a homosexual, Foti paused…

Yes, you know what I mean. We would have been—had not this accident occurred to us—upright at least as far as the psalm says. No good thing is denied those who walk uprightly in the Lord.

Do we think of it as an accident? Zoe asked sharply. Or do we rather not repent for knowing from a long time ago that no good thing would come to us from Agatha and her brood. I might myself have thought of expulsion or scourging, but…I have always had the heart of a mother.

But I think, said Foti, that you are very sharp for a mother. I think of fangs, not caresses.

After all these years, retorted Zoe, but you are a weakling, so unfit, never understanding reality.

No, there should have been chastisements—that is what made the Holy Spirit leave us. We should have whipped them—a few pains in the flesh, a little blood— they would have learned what it meant to be in holy prayer for the Holy Spirit to return to us. But we were as lax as the tourists that come to admire our sea and eat our red snapper. All flesh and no bone we were. And flesh simply rots away.

We were soft, moaned Cleo. It was afternoon and the winds had picked up. We were sitting on the balcony at Cleo's house drinking cold lemonade. We felt somehow that we had been left behind. But we knew that it was the result of God walking by on the water with huge steps, and when he came Dimitri fell—perhaps it was like that. Or perhaps we are still there, he is still there, somewhere, stuck on some giant's kneecap. But in any case, God had gone by and left us in a perverse world or grotesque phantoms, vast things; he had left us even more squalid and insignificant. We were ready to bite our hands with frustration. What does it all mean?

There are our ever there Cleo and Zoe dressed in yellow and white, respectively, looking like they might fade or blow away or melt. But still being what they are our persons, our stand by women, the faces and figures of familiarity and sweetness. We might sound odd saying that: Of course they are not sweet the way people think of sweet. But they are to us—a single drop of honey in the air, landing now and then on our tongues—like the smell and savor of jasmine. They are our females, even though we'd be scoffed at to say it—the beauties of the island. Cleo, now taller than Zoe although it used to be the other way around, matron-like, imposing! Zoe now like a little shriveled apple with her large, clear eyes—clear recently, as she precipitated out of her 'abstraction'! Foti is the lowly one, no one thinks much of her. She hovers around them with her wide, comfortable hips, making those silly comments, trembling like a little lamb with fear. We call them the three Fates, sometimes for fun—who spins? It must be Foti, she is the kind that brainlessly works day by day; who measures the thread? It must be Cleo, for she is resentful of the least excess in life. Who cuts? It would be Zoe, sharp, bitter, one would say cruel, but one hesitates. It is just the way of things. Perhaps our fault.

Where will we be if we have no bone in us? Zoe continues two hours after she left off, as if there had been no interruption. Only the bones rise clothed with flesh.

But we have bones in our bodies, exclaimed Foti in her foolish-high voice.

I can still remember the vigor of Mother Dora—all bone derived. The holy part is locked in the bones, said Zoe, decidedly; this I have learned. That scientific priest up on the hill who thinks he can talk! Humph. No, that is not what we do. The learned folk are not the ones God picks.

Who do you think should be our leader? Our guide? Cleo asked in a very low tone. Aren't we tired of these fallen priests, these delusions of holiness? Do you think Paul would be fit?

Paul? Zoe snorted. But then again, Paul attracts. He attracts the island men and among them—I wonder. Even Jason…He looks all wrong; he looks even unseemly; but he has a way of tenaciously hanging on—the Word of God, you know. He will not talk much for fear of idle words. Just think of that. A man who obeys to such an extent the word of God! A man who lives in solitude, despite what is going on around him. They say that holy monks live in perpetual isolation with only God no matter what occurs in their vicinity. Zoe looked off into the distance. I wonder, she said again.

Well, we sorely need a true spiritual guide, said Cleo, suddenly interrupting the quiet. We'd better be quick and business like about it; we are getting on.

The end will come like a lightning bolt, said Zoe in response. We must be ready to die.

I am afraid, whispered Foti in a high voice. We thought she sounded kind of silly but secretly, we felt something of the same fear. Where would we be in the afterlife?

Certainly not drinking lemonade, sitting out on the balcony, watching the little black figures move down the streets! (Not that they are all dressed in black, but something about them is dark, perhaps we see them dark, now after what happened.) But what happened really? We don't know. Dimitri was once with us, a man full of iniquity, and then boom, silently, of course, and he was gone. We were left staring at the space, the glittering water. The sun is still so hot and brilliant, the houses bright, the rose vine still blooming—but the creatures, how can we say it—look dark, somehow. All except Jason and Little Paul. They have taken to wandering around the streets in the evening together. We hear that Jason is a regular guest at the Pauls' house for dinner and lunch even, and ambles home only to sleep. He looks lighter than the other men –has a pair of dark grey trousers; Little Paul wears blue jeans. Jason looks a little self-satisfied—a little like all knowledge stems from him. He is untouchable, has never known a woman. Something about him and little Paul that is clean and sour, burns a little— like antiseptic on the tongue, so to speak. Jason has an airy demeanor, despite his fat cheeks. A look as if to say—I could teach you the way of the Lord. But his eyes are cold and hard. Never mourned his brother. Little Paul always seems to be cross at the world, arguing, talking it out with Jason, although he may as well talk to himself for all that Jason answers.

We have seen them suddenly in our midst—we never used to. Jason was always down by the fishing boats; little Paul closeted up in his house. But now at, twenty-five, they have come out, so to speak; we might see them turning the corner and coming down the street right in front of us. They show themselves, we say on purpose. There is some kind of method to their madness.

A vague rumor has it that they wish to oust the priest—that is, send him away now by force. The whole purpose of their going among us is to rid us of Father Isaac as soon as possible. Something about their presence quails all spirit of dissent among us. We go to Simon's house still out of respect for our convention, that the leader is leader as long as he lives, and we sit in wicker chairs and Tia serves us tea. We hear at last the proposal: Paul says this man must go. He says 'this man' not this priest. Little Paul stands up and says we will remove him by force if he refuses! There are a few cheers; then a few more.

Agatha has come. She looks like half herself, winded, pale. She wanders in as if she had been wounded in the lower belly, stooped a little, staring with those hurt eyes that she acquired after the accident. What is she doing here? One person compassionately rises from his seat. Catherine is just behind. She too looks quite ill. Someone murmurs that she doesn't have long in this world. Another asks in a low tone: Who does?

Hands are raised in agreement to remove the priest, Father Isaac. The motion is past. Agatha still has her hand in the air. We look at her. She clearly does not know what she is doing. Everyone is preparing to leave and Agatha is still sitting with her hand raised.

Catherine speaks to her in a low voice (Dimitri's wife did not raise her hand but she is not a resident of Saints village) and she tries to shake her half caressing her at the same time, kissing her shoulder, the edge of her cheek under the ear. Agatha gets up, walks straighter now, wanders out at the very end of the throng of people.

One or two of us turns back, murmuring to us later when we have gathered together again: Agatha now is Agatha with the lights turned out.

We, the women, want more than what is given us. Zoe walks about nervously, wringing her hands every once in a while and saying—I would not have been like this, really I would not if things had been different. What can we do when we are set to crocheting for hours with a glass of lemonade or brandy, bits of chocolate, cookies, fruit? We end up like ghosts.

We don't know exactly what she is talking about, but deep down she strikes a chord in us. We feel we have been cheated, neglected, grown up but remained little and shadowy creatures inside, never quite a self. We would never have harmed a soul, Zoe says. And we agree. The island isn't the same as it used to be—even last year. We forgot the luxury God gave us—the smelling of the jasmine without a care. Barbara's still purplish black hair. Now it is all gone. We still smell the jasmine but we can't enjoy it at all. Nor do we see for a moment Barbara's gift. No, everything is dreary.

Father Isaac is as mysterious as the moon. He has pain, they say, great pain. It is cancer, has always been cancer; he walks slowly. Yet he is packing his belongings all alone. He has refused Max's assistance. It now seems to us a terrible thing that he is being forced to leave, indeed that he is going. Yes, he was scientific and all that, but he had a forceful way about him—he taught us forcefully—like when he refused us Holy Communion until we had come to him and confessed after the affair with Dimitri. At least here was a peg firmly in the ground. We believed this, and so easily let it go—as if, ah well, a firm peg in the ground but so many indignities. What indignities? This was the scientific priest with his files and his infusions against sin. If we had had our way.

Agatha said she watched Father Isaac get in to the boat with his belongings. He had an attachment to his old stuff and he even brought his wicker chair. She said he stayed on the beach for a long time; for part of that time she talked to him.

Why didn't you save Dimitri? Agatha asked him, a little hollowly. You could have so easily. You broke me, betrayed me...! One word from you, one threat to excommunicate....Dimitri, my dear, he said to her, was on the path. And he died innocently loving his tormentors. You others want a good whipping, he said, but he smiled. It is nothing. For me the island is ever beautiful, and the people, rare little children. One wants to just jar them a little, so they leave their grip on the old bones of the Church. And you have inherited Anna's house, that huge mansion with many bright rooms.

Yes, a lawyer wrote me. But, precisely because of Anna, I can't live in it.

Agatha said she saw the boat leave and Father sitting there on the sand; she guessed another boat would come but she watched from further up on the beach and the boats left and the priest was left alone.

Agatha said later, weeping that he had simply gotten up and walked across the water. We asked how was it possible? When had he done this? And Agatha in a rare meeting with Zoe and Cleo said in the evening, the sun had gone down, the first star was out. And they said: How do you know you ever saw such a thing?

The rumor went around Saints Village that Agatha was definitively broken, yet gasping with joy. Yet again the curse had shown itself in bits and pieces. The faces like little round stones gleaming on the shore were grim; she was a lost soul irremediably; she had gained her just deserts. But Zoe and Cleo were tenderer than most. They showed up at her house with chicken and rice and onions steaming hot in a casserole; Jason opened the door, however, and stood in his huge baggy jeans with rope suspenders holding them up because the zipper had broken owing to his bulging belly and took the casserole from them. Agatha wasn't there. She wasn't up on the cliff inside the Isolets' villa, either, with Robert and Catherine and the baby. She had strayed apparently to Leo's; so the two women rather tired-faced accepted the inevitable. She and he would pair up and live quietly together as a nut in its shell.

They thought we have had enough of stigmatizing her. The fire against her in our hearts has simply worn out over time. There was a coal for a while, and then it went cold. We think now—why not let her alone? What difference can it make that Agatha's unholy feet walk the same walk as Mother Dora's where every footstep was filled with the uncreated Light? We have a sudden burst of latent affection for our Agatha. She has been with us so long—more than fifty long years and it seems like an eternity. She was old throughout her young years, stooped and lame with sparse hair and a hollow face; she transfigured, that is what we must call it—lifting her leg towards the sun, and something in her suddenly shining out, gleaming, smiling, lofty—but these are all the wrong words. She became for a minute like a cool forest—impenetrable, powerful in the legs the way trees are powerful. The old men wanted to get their hands on her, but that is their way of affection—Nisos fell in love, kissed the ground she walked on, went mad. It was all an impossible thing—as if a stone had suddenly floated on water. We realized that this was our miracle—not the eggs and milk of Father Isaac, but our Agatha's sudden beauteous transformation. And now she has lapsed back. It makes us rub our eyes and wonder.

Yes now there is nothing. A cracked and eaten nut. We are witnessing death—in her case, not as someone dying slowly, as Anna did, with a little glow to her, pale-faced staring, the stink too of the sick flesh. No, in Agatha's case death as someone literally not there—the not thereness of death. Such a morbidity argues rot in her. Past rot.

Yes, there is a living being of sorts. Her hips move along as she walks. There is a living tear between right eye and left hip. Out of her body darkness looks. Her teeth are more visible, perhaps she is snarling a little for the pain. Pain can make someone an animal, Cleo says. It depends, said Zoe—some have the ability to make of pain a fine spiritual instructor. That is all bosh, said Cleo, and for the first time in sixty years they had a real argument.

Agatha was no longer a real person in Saints Village. I mean she lived, there were whispers surrounding her presence; she wasn't buried like dead people. But she was another creature—a sub-creature, it seemed to us. Jason took over the house and home. Barbara said he 'pushed her around' as if she was distasteful to him and did not offer her the respect he should as her son.

The spiritual side of him all came out. He had loathed Dimitri, for spiritual reasons; he disliked his mother because he believed that she had a secret filthiness to her in her gypsy blood that she had passed on to him. Baptism had rid him of this secret filth, for he had been baptized when she and Dimitri would not; but she still carried it around and could potentially contaminate him. Since his spiritual side consisted in hating his mother, an unbaptized person, he felt justified. Hadn't the Lord commanded us to hate mother and father? His mind was clear. His body had gotten so large as to be on another order of human. Jason walked with Little Paul through the few streets of Saints Village bulwarked round by an enormous body and the justification of those whose prejudices and intolerances have been fulfilled. Few people talked to him. Nobody loved him. Everybody followed him.

Holy Island was in utter decline. But some of the elder men still enjoyed their wits and their apricot brandy. They made briefer and briefer conversation. About Simon who had taken to peeing and pooping anywhere in the street, they laughed a little, painfully—become a little child in God, they said, and blessed him. About Katrina, they said—ah a perpetual widow, deserving the compassion of Christ. Little Paul they didn't talk about except to shrug—killed the cat! It was a story that he had taken the family cat and drowned it just for cruelty's sake. Weak, they said; but stopped there. It was difficult thing on the island to speak of the Pauls. Paul was St. Paul now. He had 'won' this subtle battle with Agatha, the anathema, and had transcended blame: Dimitri had to die; it was God's will. Man should rule, they said to one another, about his transgression of years ago. And Agatha was Agatha. Of course, even as we fall into line with the Pauls and Jason, we know we all feel like a million when women are head. When Agatha was sweet and lovely as cream—didn't you just feel like honey in your gut? Now, shrug again. We have come back to the real truth of Christ. Agatha put us all under a spell. Unbaptized, undoubtedly a witch, half Christian—half is heresy, said St. Paul. Why won't she after all these years go to the font of living water? Now—St. Paul. He was an elder at fifty-three, tacitly accepted as an elder, that is. He had thrown out the priest. He was going to take command.

St. Paul went to Agatha's house to talk to her about putting the house in the hands of Jason to sell. In any case, it would happen after her death. She could marry and move in with Leo. Agatha sat and cracked seeds with her front teeth and stared off to sea as he talked. She had moments when she would not utter a sound. She would stare off somewhere, actually it looked like she was trying hard to see.

St. Paul stayed for about an hour; before him was a cup of coffee Agatha had prepared for him. St. Paul said to Little Paul in private but it got around as everything does on this island that he had been in the den of death: Agatha is not coming out. She is making her habitation among ashes and bones. It is indeed a sign of wickedness. Isn't wickedness death? But 'I would rather be a doorkeeper in the house of my Lord than dwell in the tents of wickedness.' I have converted and I seek conversion of this island. Agatha is stiff necked and stubborn. The death of Dimitri of course we had nothing to do with. That accidental backward step—God willed it. Neither I, nor Little Paul. The Holy Spirit struck him down like Sapphyra. He did not give his all to God, but let the rich man go.

Agatha, however, did not see night and did not see day. When Catherine came with Tock walking slowly down the stairs of the cliff to the village, the villagers quieting respectfully, for here was a quiet girl that had always loved the island, an American transplanted, having blossomed in the arms of a man and lost him, a widow with a look like business and soft sorrow, all frank her eyes caught their eyes without timidity—when Catherine came, Agatha would come to life a little. Once she even put on a red blouse above her black skirt. The two women looked so delicate, so breakable. Foti went to visit Agatha and Catherine was there so there were sparks like stars in her night eyes. She said it was like Christmas.

Impossible, said Zoe. She is for all purposes dead. No, no, said Foti in an absentminded way. It was Christmas and Easter being there; they have together woman and woman life that we don't have.

Nobody listened to Foti. Who was she but what St. Paul called the woman that should keep silent? Zoe scoffed at St. Paul: I, for one, am too old even to be called a woman anymore. Foti turned her plump, heart-shaped face in her direction and looked at her with her grey cloudy eyes, then turned away and quietly began to cry.

Catherine was sick—some trouble about her heart. The doctor came and ordered her to bed. He said to Robert: In some cases, in a love marriage when wife or husband dies, the one or the other left behind does not live long. Soul calls to soul and whoever it is, even one with a strong constitution, cannot resist but turns away and follows. I see it in her—that turning away. She didn't cry much, you say? All the more reason. Her grief is not about tears, but about earths slipping away off of her heart, falling from her eyes, about the coming of heaven and it reestablishing ownership in her like a perfect and beautiful rose red apple.

A perfect apple?

Before it was earth—the perfect apple had a spot.

She still smiles.

Why not? asked the doctor, though we only look at the perfect apple through a veil of pain. Why not? He went back to the other island without advising the transferal of Catherine to the other island hospital. Let her make up her own mind about it, he said. Catherine looked at Robert's face, which was several times whiter than it used to be, saw the pain in it, and said to him—if you want me to go....But I feel that the move might kill me. I feel as delicate as the throat of a little bird. I think, Robert, that in fact, I was born to be your hearty little girl all appetite, strong-willed, but that something, a supernatural knife stabbed me into my spirit. I suffered a wound—not sure exactly how or why—couldn't keep a grip anymore. Marriage with Dimitri was the kind of hilarity that happens sometimes when you are faint, half-mad with faintness. I was dizzy, delirious. Then she reflected—it left behind a little package of flesh and blood. Poor little creature. I worry about him. Be a good grandfather to him, Dad.

Robert stroked her hair, his fingers enjoying its softness. You called me Dad, he said. We did things a little too unconventionally. I made you all odd, unchildlike. And now...

Yes, and now... said Catherine. But I think one chooses parents all over again—the one who stayed loyal...why not start over, a clear understanding...

Catherine actually did not decline right away. Agatha took one look at her and said that she would not die. She just seemed to have little air and little ability to talk. She was like someone after a long race, although she didn't pant. She lay in bed, often muttered to Agatha a few fragment sentences that amounted to her being frustrated that she was so out of commission. She ate little but was mindful of her eating—everything had to be nutritious. She said, again in fragments, that it felt like there was a huge weight on her chest.

Some of the villagers dropped by—Zoe, Cleo, Timos. Zoe said to her you are one of the few that really grew roots in this stony soil like those persistent flowers—even a rose or two, a jasmine, but it must be a special rose, or jasmine.

It was all Dimitri, said Catherine, looking at them soberly. There was rich soil for all that he was wanton in the estimation of Saints.

Yes, said Zoe—well, you knew him. We did not and I believe we wronged him with our suspicions. We have a suspicious nature—you must have seen it. But it would be a terrible thing to hold something against us—we are so little, frail and, and impossible.

Nothing, said Catherine, nothing. And Zoe said that she looked as if she had a secret in mind that made it all, well, fine.

Yes, Zoe said to Cleo and I am not surprised. Cleo also went to 'examine' Catherine about this and to pay her respects and get forgiven.

I for one, she said after greeting the sick girl, was very happy about what Anna did. As you know, probably, with her last strength she went up to the roof—it was strength you understand of bone and will, nothing else—and she shouted them down, bursting her weak lungs—Damn it, no damn you, she shouted at the crowd on that terrible night. I tell you that it was a martyrdom.

Catherine smiled. It must have been. I can see him coming back all incarnate love out of the death he died for her damnation martyrdom for love.

It's like he isn't dead, said Cleo. I know. We weren't part of it.

Part of it or not, said Catherine with a touch of asperity, I am not holding grudges. I hand out a free pardon. As you say, I don't feel death when I think of him. Just wit, love, tenderness. I get a little frustrated, she said, that's all, she said; her voice broke a little, it was a soft, sweet voice—but she didn't cry.

It is all oddness, said Foti, who was the last to come. She clambered up the cliff panting and red-faced, stumbled into the villa and looked around ready to say something polite and ingratiating to Robert but could think of nothing and so curtseyed and was silent as he led her to Catherine.

We are the odd ones, she said to her, not you, not even Dimitri. I see that we are all twisted and distorted, as if God came down to a pile of bones and put them together all wrong. But it doesn't matter. If you see it from the outside, the darkness, you know, the out there side, it doesn't matter in the least. Laughter is the same as crying, living as dying. And here Foti grinned for she had rhymed for the first time in her life. But don't think I don't know how painful it must be. It is just a comfort to know that true existence, I mean, reality, is not this division.

They say that I am a little, you know, crazy, stupid—something they would say about me. I haven't been so smart as they are. But it is a wonderful thing that I found the truth in the end. I mean I found out that if you were out there you would find that your pain is the same as your joy was. I believe it would all come down to a feeling that we have never felt, or perhaps an emptiness, no feeling, but not in the least uncomfortable. You don't mind talking of this, do you? I mean of grief and dying... One conventionally whispers and keeps a straight face; and I don't mind doing that. But you know, my heart is singing the same song I always sang. A song of life—a beautiful song. That is one thing I am sure of: It is beautiful—this dying, grieving. The thing that does not exist is ugliness.

Catherine kept Foti for some time, coaxing her to stay with tea and snack cakes from America. When she finally released her, she was tired but happy. The fat, old woman stumbled out into the evening, scrambling to get down the cliff stairs while it was still partially light. Catherine said to Robert, I have just been listening to an imbecile who gave me gems of wisdom. More and more I don't think it comes from the mind at all. I am beginning to wonder what in the world the mind is good at, really. But who am I to know? I am not a scientist nor a saint. I don't think it can be analyzed in any case. I am, for all I know, just a wonderer. Yes that is all I have. I never was good at anything; my study of love broke down when I married and had Tock. My machine fixing was all very well but it was just tinkering that went well here and there, perhaps an attempt to see inside people's houses—a flash of affection, the inside of love. In the end, and on my tomb, they must just inscribe the truth—I was a wonderer. I wondered at things and didn't judge them.

I'll think along the lines of Foti and give my gems of wisdom: the brain is just a tinker toy. Yes that is all. And all truth is seeing past. I've wondered about this. The machinery of body, brain, nature invites one to see past. How does it work? What is the intent? Let's see the ingenuousness—of a Foti, for example. And I have wondered about that.

Agatha finally came. She saw Robert—a peculiar expression, as if his face was broken in several places, a smile all teeth and pain. She is dying, Agatha said. She chooses to remain on the island. She says she is involved in a meditation that must take place here. To die, she says, may only be the climax, the finishing point—the proper finishing point if all goes well; Robert explained things to her.

I never got anywhere with anything, Catherine complained a little when Agatha came. I thought this and I thought that. I stopped down by people's hearth sides in the village, tinkered with their old refrigerators, sometimes got them to work better. I peeked in, you know, to their little kitchens, watched them cook the red snapper in oil and lemon, fry up the fresh sardines and potatoes. I was searching for something. With Dimitri, I thought I had it; it was as if my fingers closed around it—I could feel something—I was perfect, I had hit the nail--the way-- on the head. The way of what? I wondered later. Of love? Or was it simply a kind of passivity, what Foti calls—the same whether I died for it or didn't die and went on most contented making red snapper, fried sardines? I was on a journey, on an arc of a bridge over shining water, a bridge suspended in mid-air with no beginning and no ending.

You know that Dimitri and I quarreled for the first time just before he died. It frustrates me. It was about the way I said something. I never had the chance to say—you are love, to me, you are holy. But you know, I think the words would have been off, completely off. Saying them to you is better, is perfect. You know now that I venerated him. He was an icon, one that I partially wrote, but you did too. He was an icon of God. At least, that is what I saw in the end. It was not that he always knew what to do, how to handle....

It must have been especially hard for you, said Agatha, swallowing down tears. I made a mess of myself; I let the burden simply fall on to you. It wasn't fair. As for my son, I know there was an attraction in him, a magnetism, electricity. It tore me, his own mother. But I thank you for saying he was holy. I can only say I don't think there was a hating bone in him.

But now the pain sticks like a spear inside. I have been evil—ah, there it is.

God only wants your turn about, you know. I have been studying 'metanoia', the virtue of tears, seeing the holy before seeing God. The pre purity. Something tells me, you have been in fact more virtuous in your passionate mourning because of your tabooed holy love.

But how can I rid myself of the sense that it was in fact my heart, my desire, my love?

What?

That son.

Nothing but a matter of time, I believe, said Catherine and turned away from her exhausted.

Agatha went down off the cliff at four in the afternoon, thinking of Leo. She would go to him, she would be with him, she would drink a beer with him, kiss him, fall into bed with him, such like. All this beauty and intensity, it would simply be swept away in his embrace. There would be nothing left but a little kitchen garden in her soul—a basil or two, a flower, the sun coming down into the dust. The earth would swallow up her evil and depravity—monster that she was. The village would give way, as it were, they would not bother her. She would be safe, unjudged—a simple woman with a husband and she knew she could tend him. They could talk the talk of newly wedded folk and little by little with coaxing here and there, as it always is, they could walk the walk.

She arrived at his house, walking slowly and thinking, at five; it was beginning to get shadowy now that it was October. The breezes had picked up; the air had that translucent grey look that makes one relax a little, breathe, and that restores the inner person. She knocked on his door and no one answered. She knocked on the kitchen window. It had been a month and a half and there had been no contact between them. She wondered if he had gone back to his old slobbish ways, if his living room was a mess, if he was sleeping on the floor with an open can of peas, a bottle of wine lying on its side with the contents spilling on to the rug.

She went around the back to the garden and found him sitting there on a white plastic chair, wrapped up in a blanket, with a half drunk cup of coffee in his hand.

Oh, he said seeing her. I suppose you knocked.

Yes, how are you? I am sorry that… but Agatha stopped; she was weary suddenly and couldn't go on.

Yes, I know, he said. Who knows how it got like this? We once had everything. Did we have everything? I feel like death came and took—the flesh and blood of it. Of course, he wasn't my son, but…I feel as if there just wasn't a death, an actual death until now. Silly, isn't it? I mean my own wife died, the perfect one, the one that is both saint and witch on this ridiculous island, the one I was not so much lover to as fearing little slave. And yet, you, to whom I am lover, though I have not swept you into my naked, hairy hide and made love to you—you, a stranger, a most marvelous creation—Woman, the last, the best—how could I love you if you were not the last and best of all, better than myself, better than all men....

Well? Said Agatha, since Leo did not finish.

Oh yes, I only mean that your son, you, somehow plunked life and death in my little garden. And it all seems very obvious: We were to get married, and your son died but in such a way that death strode right into the midst of us and took up residence. None of us are guiltless except you.

Oh, said Agatha, the pain coming back again; but you wouldn't know.

But here, little sweet, this is where I act as your mate, you know. I tell you now and forever, engrave it in stone and in blood: None of us are guiltless except you.

How is it possible? Agatha gasped, and her face went white.

We didn't push him technically over the cliff, did we? But every little monstrous hair hide wanted him punishe'd-dead instead of blesse'd-dead. Every little gyre of mind in these little holy, unholy villagers wanted him in hell. Everyone was judging him because he was the lover.

And I wanted him like a lover, madly perfumedly—Agatha responded softly.

Poor babe, said Leo. You are like a little lamb who made a bit of a mistake, followed the one instead of the other. Got your little thread like nerves full of sense and sensation, crossed. I wish I was as attractive, Agatha. Your son was beauty itself.

Thank God, you are alive, he said, suddenly, and throwing off the blanket put his arms around her middle.

You have nothing on but your pajamas, she said. And where on earth did you find them? How odd they are all green and purple.

Design of fig leaves, he laughed. Doesn't it strike you that here were men and women somehow in a kind of paradise, oh yes, with the goats giving milk and the trees fruit, especially the golden apricot trees, and then, what happened? One hardly knows. Did one eat of the forbidden fruit? Was it Dimitri? Was it, my little treasure, the divine Max? Was it you? I say no. I say it was them, all those who went after him to kill him. You sinned in mind, but they double sinned. They with the outside of the cup so clean and the inside writhing with worms.

In any case, as I mentioned to you, somehow Paradise was lost with the cup full of rot. Let us build it again. They won't disturb us. Let us simply close out this little island, close off everybody. My son Max can live with us again—he is mourning and lying on the cold sand every night. I don't think he has eaten. In our little house, we will have wine and dancing. You are all that is necessary. You with your life—isn't it true that you won the crown and wear it still just here—a mark of fire? He indicated with his thumb her mind in her forehead. Ah, you will win the crown of life. And we will plant roses, jasmine, lilies. We will have a lemon tree and a cherry tree, a plum tree, camellias. The garden will grow thick.

But this soil sometimes is stony, said Agatha.

Their soil is stony. Ours is not.

Come dance a little with me. Leo put down his coffee cup and held out his arms.

But Agatha backed away. You don't understand something. That old way is blocked off. I can't follow it. Don't you see that as you said, death has entered here? I will marry you, of course, I promised that, but everything has changed. I can't find the person I used to be. There's a lead-weight scar inside my belly where there used to be a pregnancy. How can there ever again be gaiety in my heart? We will live like the blind and deaf, holding on I think to half dirty plates and cups, drinking coffee for consolation while our hearts are screaming—at least, my heart.

If you could only see things my way, said Leo. He had folded his arms and was looking at her smiling. She seemed to him very young and agitated, like a girl who is afraid of everything, not knowing anything about the world.

To Agatha, he seemed different, his voice more sonorous, and he more wrapped up in his own thoughts. Perhaps that was the result of her having neglected him for so long and his having to get along—the way men never seem capable of doing. She still saw him as her bridegroom—anything was fine—his turns and twists as he went down the road with her. But he had been right, so right, to say there was death now. Death and life. There had only been life before even though so many had died. Oh, of course, there had been the dead. Her father, her mother, Anna but they had just slipped away. Dimitri had hung heavily on the skirt of her belly. His going had left death behind.

And so there was nothing that Leo could do. Smile and look loftily, dress himself in fig leaves for a jest, rebuild Eden, plant jasmine, and apricot trees despite God, as it were, death had come like an axe and hewn down before it was even physically planted, hewn it down in Paradise—when it was still in God's eye. Anything they did now would be odd, out of place—any love making, that is, whether sex or talk, or cooking. Dancing, Agatha saw as sheer madness.

She went into his house and looked around the living room for signs of the slob. But the house, strangely was neat; everything was in order. There was not even a beer can left on the table, or a paper bag full of raisins on the couch. Leo came in behind her—a bridegroom can learn to make a place tidy, he said into her ear and then kissing it. But the very neatness depressed Agatha. When Leo was in soiled clothes and his room full of scraps of half eaten things, when he lived like a pig, she had found him, as he had said about her, living. It was not that she enjoyed cleaning up after him, but there was something ghostly about this clean house and about his having waited in it for a month and a half. It was not a bright, cheerful clean house. Rather it was clean the way a morgue is clean. It was gloomy-clean, lonesome-clean. She now saw that none of the furniture was pretty. On the contrary, it was ghastly dark and grey. It looked in fact, on this close examination without the mess, like a house for the old and frozen dead.

But strange! How sure she was that it had not been thus when it was a huge impossible mess. And Leo's mess had been a way of talking to, as well as a way of living, just as her dancing had been for her.

She turned around to Leo following in after her and said to him: What to do?

The sunlight came in behind Leo's bulky form, lighting up his grey hair. Agatha noticed that he was the same pudgy, cute man with the soft white face and sleepy-intelligent eyes that he had always been.

Can you still marry me, given your feelings?

Of course, of course. I suppose death is just part of the picture now. We have to live with it; that is the second narrative. It is, you know, a kind of child to us—came out a bit strange. As far as Eden is concerned, well, it won't be quite Eden with death in it and all, but…

Yes, yes, we will just live around it! said Leo.

And we will invite Max.

Naturally.

I forgot to tell you, said Agatha, looking down. Catherine is dying. It is not death but---I mean, well, you know what I was going to say.

Perfectly. She will soon cease to breathe.

It is hard to think of her as gone.

And the baby?

I will take him, that is, we will, if you don't mind. He, of course, won't see death, if you know what I mean. At least, it won't get the better of his feelings.

Of course, we will take him. Tock, I believe his name is?

Yes, Tock for the clock's tick tock.

I would have you move in now, but I am remaining chaste for…well, said Leo, smiling sheepishly—I just thought, given my past, you'd want to trust me in some tangible, real way.

Oh yes, said Agatha, not like herself; no I would like to wait. I must go back to Catherine. I am not living with her now. I stay with Jason. I don't advise you come there.

For what reason?

It is the wrong atmosphere. Jason is, Jason does not want me gadding about, happy, as it were.

But you are not happy.

In a strange way, I am relieved. You see it is different now that we are living with death.

I'll stay the same, on my heart and hope to die.

Yes, said Agatha and raised herself on her toes and kissed him on the lips. I am going back to Catherine.

All the way up the cliff stairs Agatha thought that the meeting with Leo had not been satisfactory. She loved him, she thought, of course, she loved him. He was entirely cozy, comfortable, reliable and solid. The past was—well, what of it? His peccadillos were all swept away now; and she had some of her own. There was a sense that if you can forgive me mine, I can forgive yours in her heart. She knew Leo felt differently. He felt that she was actually innocent, simply a waylaid little lamb.

A waylaid little lamb—for a minute she shuddered. Who is the wolf? Who had been the wolf in her life. On the top of the cliff, she saw a huddled figure of a man. Oddly, she felt that she must be a foreigner, but that she knew him. He turned around and looked at her in the face and she saw a shriveled, old man who had a look of appeal in his eyes. She pieced the eyes together with the face and the chin and said aloud—Paul.

Agatha, he said. I came to offer my condolences. I am sorry for what happened. It was just circumstances, you know. No one meant any harm.

The villagers, said Agatha slowly, should not have been egged on. Things should have been handled differently. The priest....! That kind of thing is just an explosion of raw nerve, imagination, prejudice into anger that knowns no reason just madness.

Paul leant over and spat to the side like an old dolt of a villager. It was also God's justice.

Agatha looked at him. Their eyes met—blue and brown and locked together. Paul's gaze stubborn and defiant, Agatha's steady.

Agatha walked up to him; she could hear the waves crashing against the rocks. He was your son, too, she said, in a low voice that cut in.

Paul's mouth quivered. Impossible! You had Dimitri nine months after you married. We, our affair was over almost a month before.

Dimitri was late. I had a ten months' pregnancy.

You do not know this.

I do.

Paul tore off and ran to the edge of the cliff, with Agatha running behind afraid he would throw himself off. But he stopped at the edge and roared, a terrible fierce, tearing roar. He dropped on his knees and roared again and then put his face into his hands.

Agatha came over and put her hand on his shoulder. It is finished, she said, and bowed her head. Paul grasped her hand and looked up into her face. Agatha stooped down and put her cheek against his forehead.

There was never any trying to get away in my heart, he said. I just had to, just had to…

I can forgive, I have forgiven you. Yes, I have forgiven. God help me, I too had become a bit inhuman.

What do you want? Asked Paul—my house? It is yours. Ah, my son! My son! And he wept like a child.

I don't want anything, said Agatha. What can I ask for? She caressed his face. Perhaps this island is not the right place for me.

Paul stood up—nor for me. There is something about this island, a kind of cloud hangs over it. We were supposed to be one way—true hearted. I thought somehow that Dimitri had taken it away….

No, said Agatha. It is not him or the island. Just that over time, people became so set in their ways, developed stiff, cantankerous personalities, prejudices against what was irregular and strange. It is what happens when people let little evils accumulate—and then my son and life and death on me became like a great mysterious burden. My life is over. But you, and she slid the palm of her hand gently over his eyes, closing them for an instant, you can go on –differently; taking the helm as it were. But one thing I do ask of you—remember, just for new friendship's sake—don't let Max be hurt. It is something I think we can both agree on.

Was it rape? Paul whispered, hot tears still on his face.

Agatha bowed her head—no. I am sure not.

What do you think happened?

Passion, Agatha stared him in the eyes again. Just passion!

Paul's eyes clouded a bit. He was that way?

He was passionate with anyone beautiful.

Perhaps it is just-- Paul looked down, then he said-- finding something in oneself. Something beautiful, despite that it is, well, not sinless.

And who am I, you, everybody—Agatha gestured over the village. Beautiful, not sinless. Who is black but beautiful? The sinner, the whore, the homosexual…Wake up, for heaven's sake. Who did Christ come for? Beware judgment. Don't throw stones.

No, no! Dimitri! He was beautiful! My poor son. Paul turned and started down the cliff stairs. He stopped, breathed, and then exhaled, shook the tears away and continued.

After a few days, word got around that Agatha was to marry; the new priest—who had been selected under the guidance of Little Paul and Jason-- had impressed on her the necessity of baptism, not just as a technical part of Orthodox marriage, but as a spiritual experience, opening the way to what he called 'independent acknowledgement' of Church teachings on salvation. It was a sacrament in which sins were remitted and all the old was made new—a sacrament also in which the Church was triumphant...

This could have been a point of contention for Agatha, but the priest couched it in such words—for the Church was not the old men saints, the controllers, the watchers, the curtailers of freedom; the Church was the warrior bride of Christ, composed of all those who had in fact risen up though the cross was bearing them down in the strength and grace of God, for all those who did, in one way or another, wear the crown of victory. And Agatha had to affirm that this was in a factual sense true. One just stands up at the call, even paralyzed, because paralysis doesn't stop the rising.

On earth, he continued, the Church was that crown worn in the heart of the believers—those who had triumphed over falsehood, and had glorified Christ with truth. All this, Catherine said, was true, of course, but there was something nebulous about it nonetheless. I love you as you are, she said, weakly to Agatha.

Still, said Agatha, kissing her, this has to do with whether or not I am going to accept the religion as it is dictated to me by the Orthodox Church. There is a level where I do, of course, a strange, personal, mystical thing. I think I am still governed by my own perceptions of truth, however. And you know, the priest yielded to that: Oh yes, he said, ultimately you must use all your forces for your own sake and for others. Even if you do not enter the Church it will haunt; here there have been a sorrowful group of friends, penitent and sweet to you; and all the little monk-nun saints in heaven even in hell for you to burn a while in penitence, emitting a wonderfully sweet and sorrowful odor.

But on this note, Agatha decided she would move into the Isolets' villa. Catherine was dying. There was no doubt about it. The heart that had barely held on, but that she had thought, during her marriage, healed up—she had been full of energy, brimming, brilliant, she had known every way to handle Dimitri's will—now suddenly with his death, could not continue. It was what it always had been, a broken machine, one that she could not fix.

She looked on detached to the symptoms. Weakness, wasting, shortness of breath, irregular beat. When she got up from bed she was immediately out of breath. She saw her bowed, bony form as if from on high—a creature, while she herself was akin to its Creator; she felt deep pity for this body but thought it really a good thing that it was dying.

Agatha was aghast at this strange cheer in Catherine, or perhaps not cheer but indifference. But it also gave her a new kind of hope, as if she was peering through a door and seeing that in fact this was not the only reality—that there was a whole infinite and endless sweet world built on little insignificant things on this earth, like joy and patience. The material of the obscure soul in this little beaten down place—grace, love, endurance—suddenly appeared to her in another light—as robes of gold, mantles of silver. She suddenly thought that they should stand up on those podiums she had imagined listening to radio announcements of races and say about the victors of the marathons--what we are awarding here is not the strength of a body, the superior quality of a meat, focus of an intelligence, the better brain, the fact that this one not that one was half a foot in front of the others, what we are awarding is long suffering, endurance, humility…But no, pride kept entering into it. In her mind, pride kept entering into the speech, it was somewhere along in the discourse—pride of the country, pride of the people, pride of the athletes, the runners, the historical doers and achievers…and so the original sense was lost.

But Catherine had outshone the others—this she thought after secret hatred and envy; they had reconciled, it was Catherine who did it, she had fixed the old broken wires, misfiring things, uselessness between them. She had used one word—she had called him holy! And all the pain that was churning in her heart as a mother and an imaginary lover to her son, all of it, had, as it were, smoothed out; the wires had reconnected, the light was on, the blades were spinning. She was able to think again in peace about Dimitri, her son, her stranger- child that had driven her half wild. Yes, she could just barely see it—but Catherine knew all about this. He was holy—yes because he didn't do anything but fall and then rise up again with the rhythm of a wave and he had died rising up loving like a man, like the real man, one beautiful woman, beautiful because perfectly loving. There had been the last slight indignation, Catherine said, and then Stavros said—Dimitri loved, that is all. In the end, he loved with a passionate love his wife and child. Ah, he made a few mistakes but you see he loved. A few of us knew—Catherine, Anna—a few of us. He loved. I challenge anyone who pretends to know God to love—that is all, simply to love.

At first this was not enough for Agatha, but she went around town savoring the phrase—Dimitri was holy; and for reasons unknown she accepted it. Oh, of course, she was his mother—but she knew Jason, also her son, was entirely different. Perhaps it was that Dimitri was born of a rape and that she had been carrying him first in her belly as death and hate and then in her mind and heart, as her only love, on the road to forgiving the rapist, a terrible ordeal, an agony at times as much as the rape itself had been.

It was Catherine who said to her—you know, you think you live in darkness, and that you have just managed to stand upright despite invisible and visible foes. But I tell you, that is what a saint does. Only that. No, they don't see bright lights, visions, or engage in nuptial ecstasies. They manage to stand upright for God in the midst of the battle in the dark. The foundation was this: your son is holy. At the end, he said, he had made a mistake having affairs with others. Alright, a mistake, but he made you forgive.

How is this possible? But you knew it, Agatha, didn't you? Not for his mistakes, not for sins, but because all along he was carrying more love in him, fire hot, martyrdom love in him than he ever carried evil, though he carried evil. Loved his enemies with the same sweetness that he fell in love with Max. God said to us: She sinned much, but she loved much. The will of God is love for God is love. Mary must have been like Dimitri—loving intensely, making this and that mistake whether fornication or other, kissing the feet of the men she succumbed to, finally kissing the Lord Jesus Christ's feet along with the men she committed whoredom with but with tears, many tears for Him as opposed to the others. These things startle the devils, you know who know only the sin, not the love of the act. Maria in the café is like Dimitri, and he would have been happy about this. He, sweetly singing the killers' song, a little child—given up to them, happy, innocent in their midst. I think, actually, that he knew they wanted him dead, I think his heart bowed to them, to their feet; and I think, pardon me for being obscure, that is why he sang their song. And for those few minutes, he was one with them, loving them who hated him. This you see is the straight gate, singing, exalting their piteously crude child song.

Amazing, Catherine lay back, panting. It was the most she had said in a couple of weeks. For another week she said fragments of sentences, as she had when she had first gotten sick. Come Sunday and Agatha found her still alive, still smiling, although it was a little smile. Sunday marked the week. Agatha thought she would go on forever. Not as a human being but rather has an ancient piece of clockwork that you find still running. Someone has wound it up, and wonder of wonders, it begins the tick tock.

Speaking of tick tock, Tock played at the floor in front of Catherine's bed. Agatha peered into his face and saw that he looked a little like her son, but he also had a long face that Dimitri didn't have, studious looking—not Catherine's either; she didn't know where it came from. He had begun to talk a little, fragments—so that when his mother spoke to him in fragments, he talked back with a word.

Once he ordered Catherine—Mamma, get up. Get up, Mamma. I love you, she said to him; her voice was sad but also slightly indifferent. It was as if she didn't have the energy to focus on her child. She became languid and listless, eating only broth now and a little orange. More and more she was at war inside herself with her failing organ. She couldn't get comfortable. She died on Tuesday, her body flung on the side of the pillow against the wall as if she had just been in battle with her insides. Her eyes were staring but empty, like two beautiful mirrors and her mouth was open as if she was struggling for breath.

Agatha was tired. She took Tock out of the room with her and informed Robert that his daughter had died. She looked around at the big barren, white villa. The sun was shining in but there were shadows from the blind drawn down half way. The light seemed both tearful, kind, and also obdurate. Catherine had not been a big personality like Anna, and yet she and Anna had died almost the same—how can one say it? With little. They had seen, experienced—Anna her hot moment, Catherine her pure marriage, as Agatha called it—and then nothing. Yet it wasn't true, she thought watching Tock who wasn't aware that his Mamma was dead, that the world was the same without them. No something had been taken away on the outside, unlike when Dimitri had died, and ripped something out of her on the inside, as if she had just given birth, a terrible birth. She could see in her imagination, in her mind's eye, the big world losing a little—what? A sort of color, as if the blueschist color on the cliff—that beautiful, startling blue but not the real blue—no more like the blue of Simon's paintings, a blue with a kind light in it, like the light in God's kind eyes to the sinner. She was thinking that way now.

Slowly, the world was losing her color. (Simon still painted but strange black and red paintings like anger with a little white.) Agatha knew that she had a color— it was not exactly the blueschist color in Simon's old paintings but something like. She liked the fact that it belonged to a bygone time. Anyway, the world had hung on to it for a while and now it was fading from it and the colors of the world now were spiritless cruel and cold.

It was agreed, though never in words, that Agatha would take Tock. Robert was not saying much in any case. Agatha made all the funeral arrangements for Catherine's body to be buried, at the wish of Robert, in the forest. It was an expensive proposition, but Robert dug into his mysterious wealth somewhere in a bank in Switzerland and came up with the money. Catherine was buried in a plot all alone with a little stone cross marking her grave that Simon, half mad though he was, carved perfectly. His hands obeying the order though his mind wandered. It was a beautiful cross with a circle in its center; the sun of the island, he said. On it, Robert had inscribed—faithful daughter and wife.

Agatha wanted to ask shouldn't it be 'faithful wife and daughter'? But she hadn't dared. Robert, although he looked almost exactly the same abandoned by his wife and bereaved at the death of his daughter, was in fact rearing up like a lion inside. His was a pitch against death that expressed itself in physical ways: He took to climbing the cliffs, a little at a time. At first, he couldn't get up much above sea level. But slowly he went up higher and higher until finally he had climbed the whole way to the peak from the sea. No one asked why an old man would have in mind to perform these death defying physical feats. The villagers knew, watched him with reverence, doffed their caps when he came down to the village café. They began to think of him with a kind of hope; before they hadn't thought of him at all. The idea of the sheer grit in him and the bodily act of climbing the cliff made the villagers of Saints see the island holding together, welded by this man of muscle back into a working creation. They began to look at him as the real root of their world for now and the future.

. . .

Paul had retired. There was no announcement, but it was understood that Paul somehow had mixed with Agatha and had gone all-feeble. We village men saw it our way. There had been something between them, more than a kiss, and it had never quite been extinguished. Agatha had called it rape, but so do all women who feel jilted—no, she had gotten the better of him at last. He would never dance again, we decided; but sit in a chair and be spoon fed coffee. Perhaps he would still live a good long life, but always in that chair, unable to stand up and take command as he once had. And who would be feeding him coffee but Ella…We thought she was a poor, beaten down wife. Now she would have her say.

But Little Paul was angry and he and Jason were conspiring to bring the island under their command. The priest was on their side—but he was a well-meaning type, maybe slightly foolish; he sided with everybody. He said very little; but one thing, he repeated over and over again: Holy Island has gone to the dogs. This made Little Paul furious because he thought that Holy Island or holy anything should not be in the same sentence with dogs. Jason who was contemptuous of him asked him in a sneering tone—who do you think Robert is? And he said, I would say a dog, yes. A dog. And Agatha? Persisted Jason, who now since his conversion, called her Agatha instead of Mother. A dogess, said St. Paul, sucking his lower lip into his mouth and looking at them vacuously. But then he asked Ella when the young men had gone, a dogess? And his face went all broken and a few tears trickled down out of his eyes. You don't know what you are saying, she said primly and wiped his face with the towel that she always held draped over her arm. You are like a baby.

The village came together to celebrate two funerals in one—funerals that made them feel like they were the same old island village that they had ever been. Katrina's parents both died on the same day and though for all practical purposes they had been dead already, and the villagers had abandoned them, when they finally stopped breathing they spoke of them as they had been twenty years before, kindly, full of life. And one or two stood up and said—these knew something of the Gospel and followed in the old style, so should really be hailed. When they became ill, we wandered. But just think how Katrina slaved for them day and night. And a mighty cheer was sent up for Katrina, who, however, turned her face away in disgust.

The women looked at her with sympathy; old Zoe put her arm around her waist, but their eyes were sparkling with what had been said, in any case. It was the old village again; it sounded like the old village and it smelled like the old village. A few of the men danced a little dance, leftover from the days when we danced with genuine innocence. Agatha wearing her blue shirt with her black skirt watched Katrina, thoughtfully. She came up to her, sidling through the throng, and asked her—what is it going to be now? You have been living one way for so long.

How do I know? She shrugged. Ah, said Agatha, and we watched her kiss Katrina lightly and sidle away again.

Some of us got up the courage to ask her as she went by, little and bent but vigorous. Another competition, eh, Agatha? And one of us kicked out his leg. Agatha looked up, stood erect for a minute—it was all there again, the queenliness, the peace and beauty—and then slouched and moved on. Death ate her heart, said one of us, I think Nisos. Without heart you can't dance.

Now the island looked like this: A strange place, brimming with sun, hot and dry for the summer with a few figures in skirts, dotted here and there, in trousers milling around. Maria had grown graver and stockier, the affair with Peter now was mostly cuddling—they both said the old passion that had once been so sweet and sticky like fig juice and hot as pepper had subsided; in fact, they just clung together dolefully, Maria heavier on his lap with her arm around Peter's shoulder and he arguing to her for the thousandth time that well, after all, she was a woman who had been his special friend and it wasn't adultery, no, not adultery which was a cruel, cold-hearted, devilish thing and which they say Paul fell into once because of Agatha. The outcome was a son, a son so strange and wild no one quite knew what to do with him…who had stepped out, one fine morning, said Maria, completing the sentence, one fine morning over the cliff and into invisibility, the other life.

The island looked like this: Barbara in her kitchen, her glorious hair thinning rapidly so that she would put it into a red turban to hide the bald patches, cooking up squid for Stavros, his favorite meal. The fried squid on paper towels and chilled white wine in an earthenware jug made them feel as if things were going well. It hit the spot, according to Stavros and one felt less stranded, one felt as if one was building and rebuilding home. Indeed, for them this was so; there were fierce arguments, Stavros coming and going slamming doors, Barbara red-faced over the stove. But the fact remains they remained loyal to one another. Oddly, they could shout until they were heard all over the meager village, until Michael poked his head out from his bedroom window and shouted: Hey there, Ho—don't you know I am trying to study? But it was in quality a cozy thing in the end. Stavros and Barbara expressed themselves loudly. It is merely the groaning under the martyrdom of marriage, said the priest. Perfectly permitted. And when the family seemed devastated, and the sons showed up at the fishing boats early in the morning with worried faces, though certainly plump and finely fed, then Stavros would invariably arrive two days later at the café and say—we have swept everything out of the old marriage and are rebuilding something new.

Little Paul and Jason were gathering families in the church house and no one could stop them. They were announcing that it would be better for us to die out as staunch followers of the Gospel than to accept any more builders and developers. There had been suspicion from the first about Jason, son of Agatha, a cursed woman. Let us not fall into another cruel temptation. But Cleo said, he won't be so resigned to poverty. All through his speeches, she said—ah, hypocrite! The others looked at her surprised. There seemed no evidence as yet of his hypocrisy. Katrina who was standing near one time said to Cleo—yes, probably, he is destined to be a hypocrite; but then, you know, it is perfectly natural. One might try to follow the Gospel, but then this, that arises, the pain and suffering of poverty. Still, one must preach it, mustn't one?

What about you? Cleo asked, a little aggravated. What are you doing?

Retiring, selling the house, the priest is interested. He has good money. It is located in a spot that gets both sun and shade, winds off the sea. He wants to live well. And I am retiring too from Christianity. I simply can't do it. I believe that this whole thing is a machine, you see, and it just happens to be here—the universe that is, with us in it.

Is this Dimitri's doing? You doted on him.

No, Dimitri said he was an atheist but was really a believer. I am the other way around. He tried to convert me.

You fell apart at the seams, said Cleo bitterly. The whole cause is his death. I know the other woman feels it more, it burns, corrodes.

You have never felt anything, snapped Katrina. You have sailed through life accomplishing everything that you were supposed to accomplish—husband, old age in comfort, the possibility of living in Paris....

Ha. You hardly know the grief. Who am I but a pale reflection of Zoe, wandering around town, seen out of the corner of an eye, forgotten instantly. A nothing on earth, a nonentity in heaven. You young ones think we old people have no indignation, no passion. Why, I have walked in your shoes more than once in my soul. Yes, tempted, tortured....faith almost blasted. What is left worth living for?

I am an atheist, responded Katrina, a little coldly. I live for life now.

All those wasted years, Cleo half mocked, half sorrowed. But I wouldn't throw away my soul. And I realize it would have been easier if you had been Catherine. Lord knows, though, she too...

Little Paul and Jason convinced the village families-- of which there were sixty now, twenty having either died or moved away—to establish a mini Constitution as if they were a nation, or a nation in miniature. Few people ever came this way from the government. Taxes were something that paid or not paid, no one of the government agency seemed to notice. There were no controls or checks. A solitary policeman had arrived after the death of Dimitri and asked questions and then gone away. The electrical company gave them reduced fees for less service, not asking if they were content with this arrangement. The gas company which sent out canisters by boat, never offered to install gas lines. The thought was that they were a broken down little organism, grinding slowly to a halt. The government, they knew, from some notice or other, would welcome them all dying off. They would put up Holy Island for sale so that a multimillionaire could build on it, make it his own getaway island and the strange, contorted, quirky little history would be first written down, with everything expressed in impoverished language, as if the writer was giving it half a mind and writing too hastily, then stuffed into some library where no one would find it or read it for ages. But Little Paul and Jason were convinced that they could rekindle the old flame. They imagined Holy Island in renewed glory with people arriving to live simply, modestly, perfectly in the way of the Lord. After all, they said there has been no blood shed, no stealing, the adultery has been punished. We have done well not to covet; we have honored our mothers and fathers, look at Katrina, and others, and as far as worshipping idols, Agatha worshipped the sun so it was good for her that—that is all a mistake on the part of—one who shall be nameless. Katrina sighed audibly.

Here and now we must gather together and pick up the remains of what we had. The Constitution named the priest as the titular head, and the fellowship of the Saints, Little Paul and Jason as the two executors. Simon waggling his head in a corner, smiling and spitting, was, of course, put out of business. For those sorts of casual governing bodies, said Little Paul to the assembly, resulted in our weakening. The Constitution went on to establish a little electorate of old men and women. The electors were all to be fathers and mothers and over sixty baptized, and communing regularly.

Since all this appeared to the islanders to be just the right kind of stuffy, twisted bureaucracy for old folk who were dwindling down—already there had been three, four, five funerals in only half a year—this 'Constitution' passed without a murmur. Zoe only said, sarcastically, that all is perfectly well when people can be hoodwinked for their own good. Jason, a weighty fellow but young, who moved his mass around uncomfortably, and Little Paul, vigorous, acrimonious seemed to be exactly the right duo for the government of the island. Why? Well, we don't know; aren't quite sure. For one thing they seem passionate, fired up—aware of things and we like to drift, to dilly dally in the sun. But one thing is for sure: These two encapsulated the very spirit of the island and they had determined to forge out of this spirit, the new holiness. We knew in our heart of hearts, that the existing spirit was yes—massive, uncomfortable and bitter. It was the counterpart to Mother Dora and her light, slender footsteps. And here it was prominent, evident, obvious to us—ha, ha—a caricature, but a solemn one. We were facing ourselves in a mirror. For it was we who were fat on our abundant goat's milk, and uncomfortably fleshed, we who were bitter, thrashing….In Little Paul and Jason we were in one person, for it was one spirit, finding our ways back to the straight and narrow. It was we, who, once holy, were facing the terrible and ugly truth of our waywardness.

Voting for Little Paul and Jason was mortification; we all felt that. But we had ceased to hold out any hope that our finding the way back again would be joyful. No, we expected, needed, as a kind of strenuous spiritual exercise to the weak, fat, indolent body—as one needs to sweat to feel that one is working at one's greatest capacity, as one needs to strain—the grim, painfully rigid, oppressive atmosphere that Little Paul and Jason promised us in ways more penetrating and profound than words. We were facing a climb from down below the cliff. We had to prepare. It was not an easy, light, carefree endeavor.

The new priest was a good priest. He said nothing beyond the few words, which he uttered for a sermon and these were directly relating to the Gospel reading. We felt that Jason and Little Paul were satisfied, therefore we were satisfied.

Only Agatha had not voted. She was busy shuttling from villa to Leo's in a dark green skirt; she still wore her grief as if carrying the cross in her backbone; she bent over like a young pine covered with snow. Not that we hadn't seen such a sight often. We watched her going to and fro. We wondered what she was doing alone with one man, Robert, and then another, Leo. The women's circle was encouraging her to get baptized. We should rephrase that: the woman's circle had been given permission to encourage her to get baptized. There was a tacit understanding, all of us creatures were now under one command. Of course, of course, it was loose—we could simply cease to support Little Paul and Jason. We could as one body, turn away. But we were a bit stuck. We had no idea of our own. The island had to be reformed; we wanted once more to be holy. It was no use saying anything would make it so. We had become loose, languid, all flesh, sweet, no spirit. This new arrangement was like hot pepper to the dulling palate. We had that much left us—a little taste. So we listened: so little Paul and Jason had their fingers shortly in everything we did, even in the old women's circle, even in ours.

The point was things were being straightened out. We were not meandering any more. The spiritual path was being shown to us—clearly: a straight line from A to B. Agatha was given permission to be baptized. We all felt that it was time. We all felt that once immersed into the holy waters, the past would fall away. She would be back in joint instead of out of joint. The island would feel it; we would feel as if leavening had been given us, a missing coin of the treasury had been found. Complete—risen bread, our full sum would be there.

We knew that Agatha felt as though she was dead to her son, Jason, and that he felt dead to her. And it was not the kind of dead that living comes out of. It was the kind of dead that gets buried by the dead, whereas Dimitri, to Agatha, was never anything but living.

Robert told her: You must carry on. It is what we do. Fix the old broken place as best you can.

Leo told her: You are both dead and alive. I am no source of divine wisdom, but it seems that it is you who are in possession of the first step.

I suppose that I will be baptized, will be married, said Agatha in a dreamy tone. Leo knew from a lover's instinct that his lady felt marginalized on the island, where she had been born and suffered so, despite the new 'understanding' between her and Paul, that filtered down in some form to Little Paul, that she felt in fact insubstantial, ethereal, as if her footstep had no weight. Perhaps, said Leo, if you went back to dancing…Don't you think that dancing and weddings go hand in hand?

Dancing, murmured Agatha—I fear it. I fear the taking on of this body and blood…

Now listen, spoke Leo, a little crossly. We are to be married soon. You have to wake up a little, be a good girl along with me, a good boy—and of course, that means accepting the body and blood…yours, mine, God's! You don't expect that you are really to be made of air and sort of waft about in my house from corner to corner do you?

He was looking at her in the eyes but Agatha, frowning and peering, did not see him. She had in his opinion an old, strained, cross face—something between mad and thinking high thoughts. She came back to him in her eyes looking weary.

It is still your two sons, Leo whispered.

I have always worked like a machine. It is what life sometimes gives. On with it, so be it. I'll be baptized tomorrow.

Ah, it is just a little trick, said Leo. We can be as free as you like within the walls of this my house. We just give them the official rite, ceremony, whatever you might call it, and then we are home free. Here you will have a foothold. You won't be oppressed. You will be safe in my arms. And above all you know that once you are a married woman, no one will bother you. But his voice had a note of falseness about it.

We women are a little miffed about all these formalities. Oh, Jason and Little Paul are organized enough. They have brought in a new priest who does things properly. We are not some fancy-free half-dream place that we were under Father Isaac. Yes, Jason and Little Paul they were responsible for getting in this new priest. They organized the letter to the Bishop in Athens explaining everything. Father Isaac, in any case, was too sick to carry on his duties and needed the kind of attention he could only get on the other island. Oh, they made it sound proper, dignified and above all compassionate. But they are also all official, all stuffed shirts. And it is interesting how dreary our island is, even the sun that used to be the pride of the island, because there is a quality of sun, and the way it finds its way into all the corners here, blanches things white, bakes things dry as bones—even the sun does not cheer us as it always used to. Agatha is in her house under the thumb of Jason now, although he doesn't spend much time there. She is ordered to 'refresh' the place for he wants to bring in some new men to talk about the important part of governing the island. They are entering a new phase, he says. A phase in which we become Christian again through the efforts of concerned lay people. We create responsible government—we get electricity, gas—we regulate tourism; we establish a working community of Christians. And we open ourselves to those who choose to emigrate here, and live far away from the world according to our Church.

Agatha is to purchase new cloth and sew new curtains, buy a new rug. Everything is faded. Agatha doesn't want to tell him, her own son, that she rather liked the faded cloths. It was the character of the island—the sun 'got in' everywhere. She feels another break in the invisible backbone that bows her still further---that she has to obey her child. And yet another break that the baptism will give her a little acceptance into the community that she once imagined, with Dimitri's help to semi-possess. It was not a baptism, she thought of faith at all; it was a baptism of necessity, one, if she wanted to marry Leo in Church, and a baptism of conformity, two, if she wanted to live with these folks, her own people, among them, her own son. It was to be a baptism, she thought, and there may be many, where God is entirely absent. The curtains, the rugs were symbols of the new life after baptism. The dictatorship of her son, in other words, worse in many ways than the rape she had suffered at the hands of Paul, for she would have to submit to it, rather than dancing, as the new life of Christ. She was expected, she thought, watching Jason burping after a huge meal of fried fish and potatoes, to attribute this oppression to the will of the God in which Jesus delighted. Needless to say Jason no longer helped in the kitchen. For among other things, Agatha is to refresh the house and her own behavior. She is entering on a new phase—that of following the living God.

As a result, Agatha's flesh is different. She can't stand to be touched. She once threw an egg at Jason; she just exploded as he swayed his huge body closer. The egg cracked and broke on his holy head. Jason uttered a sound like 'phew' and held out his hand for a towel, Agatha gave him one, and he wiped the raw egg off his face as best he could. Agatha imagined that he would 'punish' her either physically or mentally. But he did nothing at all. Just turned and with a staring gaze, marched out the door. He was back for dinner, on purpose, thought Agatha, usually he stayed at Little Paul's; he fed on a mountain of rice and tomato and squid stew that Agatha heaped up on his plate on purpose. She thought I will just feed and feed him until he bursts an artery. But there were times she felt sad—she had not loved him as she had loved Dimitri, perhaps she had not loved him at all. Children grow knowing these things even when they are never said, even when the opposite is assured them.

Thinking to herself these sad thoughts, and rumination, Agatha decided to let herself 'fall into a new humility', as she put it to the priest. She prefaced her words to Jason: May I offer you a word? A thought? And bowed her head and sat in silence if Jason sonorously intoned—it is not amenable to me now.

But the whole world except for us, the women of long acquaintance, old fossils that we are—thought that Agatha had accepted new life in Christ. They thought at last that she was broken in. They thought that she had become what they called 'Woman', a broken, tearful, half human, half shadow.

There was another creature haunting us besides this new woman Agatha; that was a newborn Max, as it were. Having been set free from the old fantastical priest and his dreams of the other world, Max no longer preached—that is, told us tales of blue mountains, topped by white clouds, and castles of gold light as lace. Max hid. He went up the cliffs and into the monastery where the sisters gave him food; he stayed in the old cell where Father Isaac had confessed a long confession lasting a month, and hugged his sides on the rubber-sheathed mattress, and rocked his body back and forth. He grew a long beard, golden in the sun, his hair was light brown, and he ate very little, becoming skinny and pointed looking like a nail. When he stood erect, which was not often, he looked like a strange composite of figures—body, face— that would if it were not recognizable as Max, be like a hieroglyph—a human being, perhaps, but something else entirely also. No one, we think, could understand Max now at all. For we too secretly knew, in the deep parts of ourselves, that Dimitri had never raped Max at all. We secretly knew in the place where maybe the sun comes, maybe not—through tissues and brain cells—that Max and Dimitri had loved but Dimitri could love again and Max could not. Yes loved, in the way a human being loves—tenderly, with fire, pain, and sweetness. Many of the old men turned away in shame. But we, the women—said, ah, well, it is just body and blood.

Max, of course, did not talk about it. He made himself an outcast. Everyone said nothing to him or about him. There was a consensus, even among the two—Jason and Little Paul—that he might come and go. But come and go he did not do. He stayed up with the sisters who treated him with gentleness and demanded of him nothing.

There is a rumor now that Agatha has been to see him. How is it that these rumors descend on us, like sudden storms? He admitted to her what we expected-- that Dimitri never raped him—he was forced to make that confession by Jason. Why? They wanted an excuse, you see, to 'get' him. And if Max would not confess—he too would be....Jason had never told him what; it was something in his manner, his tone that told him. It would be much easier to confess, said Jason; you know, we are talking about the whole island rising up, we are talking about the kind of anger that can tear a man physically limb from limb, we are talking about the kind of punishment where eyes, tongue are torn out....

Max was weak and he lied. He had never been strong. When Dimitri died, he had considered suicide. He had been so utterly ashamed of himself.

Agatha said to him in this day on Holy Island there is nothing but humiliation, cruelty, something worse than rape, something worse than the ripping out of eyes, ears, tongue. There are two who tear the soul. The rumor has it that Agatha had called him her son, and cried over him.

But no one ever saw her go up the cliff to the monastery to see Max or come down from seeing him. In any case, if we saw her go up the cliff, she went sometimes to see Robert we must have thought it was that. Nothing changed in her demeanor. Nothing was said. But Agatha came to and fro among us with a dreamy look sometimes in her eyes. She had always had that dreamy look. And she murmured to herself. She had always murmured to herself.

She went to Leo, we imagined it the case was closed, so to speak. She would be baptized, shortly, we would come bearing that special soft apricot candy rolled in confectioner's sugar that we had always made for occasions like these—baptisms and weddings. We imagined, and waited. There is nothing to be done, anyway, said Zoe, and sighed. Why not simply reflect on the good health we have, hold up our hands in gratitude. Foti sensed that there was something strange about Zoe's tone.

It was about two days later that we found out what Agatha had said to Leo. She had left him, had very quietly gone home. There she had cooked several dishes. Made herself some coffee. Nothing, not a peep from her. And then lo and behold one morning, she was gone.

Oh, it was nothing mysterious; Leo told Jason, with something of his former self-reasserted—she feels that she did wrong to the last priest. She has gone to the other island to confess to him. She will be back soon.

She could have and should have confessed to the new priest, said Jason. We have allowed her baptism at last, she shouldn't push the envelope too far.

Baptism, said Leo, with a little sparkle in his eyes like amusement, is for no one but the catechumen and the priest to decide.

This island is no longer in the hands of the priests exclusively. We have seen what priests do. We are judges, judges. We can dismiss priests, tear down churches. Erect one of our own. We are the ones with the precious history. We are the bloodlines of those who actually beheld the risen Christ. We are the ones.

Well, said Leo, Agatha now is on the way to beholding someone she loves and trusts. She is going to beg his forgiveness. Odd, how I see Jesus going with her.

Well? Jason retorted impatiently. Is she or is she not going to be baptized?

I thought you said just now you would tear down churches....

Oh well, we have a priest now we can work with. And baptism is a must, you know. The goal is still of course sainthood.

As far as I know, said Leo carelessly, avoiding the cold eyes staring at him, the marriage is on. I am awaiting my bride; I am going to teach her for as long as we last together to kick her feet up to the sun, yet again, although the sun knows and I do not the correspondence between them. Her secret lover, this intense, summer white sun! As far as I know, Leo allowed his mind to roll around to what Jason was waiting for—she is going to be married in Church and therefore baptized.

Well, said Jason, after a moment's thought—we don't know about the dancing, it is on this island reserved for men except for the line dances—we'll have to see about that, you know, but she is perfectly welcome to be baptized and married. We might wrap up everything that way. And then for the new beginning.

What new beginning? Leo asked, innocently. Everybody is old here and no one is a baby except for Tock—There is nothing little, new or fresh…

You see but you don't see, said Jason majestically. This is something entirely spiritual. A shut down of all things carnal, liberal…but a new advent of the Lord.

…

We women didn't have much to do in terms of this recreation of Holy Island so Jason and Little Paul in conjunction with the priest asked us to decorate the church for Agatha's wedding. There will be, of course, said Jason to Zoe, a real need, which he emphasized, for the women to concern themselves with food and flowers. We are going to have lots of festivities to keep people happy. The men will dance again as they used to. The electrical company will give us more light, the gas company put in lines. We feel that God is directing us here.

And the money, snapped Zoe?

There are certain ideas that women can't enter into, said Jason, he was leaning forward a little as he spoke and then he rocked back so that his huge bulk protruded in front of him.

We women found out that Katrina was leaving—she was going to live in Athens with a cousin who was getting on and needed some assistance. Little Paul was buying the house for a pittance and the plan, we found out secretly listening in to the men when they sat round and gabbed at the café, was to build—would you believe it—a little hotel. Oh yes, before they had killed Dimitri, they had learned a thing or two from him. Tourism was really the only hope for us, except for the monastery which depended entirely on God, but which, as we had seen with Anna, was deteriorating spiritually—at least, it wasn't the same friendly place that it had always been, the place we knew would get us into heaven.

For Little Paul it was as if heaven decided a few things as well. Just a month before Katrina made no sign of moving; in fact, it was known throughout the village that she had gone down to the boats with Agatha, bending over to pick up her luggage, to help her with Tock. Katrina, said Michael, who had seen her, looked youthful, tender. He had felt a pang that she had been used so lousily—he faulted Dimitri there. Couldn't he have left well enough alone—chosen another for his youthful indiscretions—a tougher bird.

There she was in a grey skirt, and it seemed to him that she was slimmer—a truly poetic figure on the beach in the evening under the stars, the wind stirring her clothes. He had even seen her face, a placid face—the kind that is like some of those

English garden landscapes, not even those—perhaps the watercolors that girls try to paint. Nothing at all violent or passionate; Michael has assumed Katrina was violent and passionate and had never thought again about it until seeing her on the beach with her arm around Agatha. In any case, she was selling and moving. She had found buyers, first the priest, then Nico and Elizabeth who had been living in Nico's too small house should children come along. But the priest didn't want it in the end, and Nico and Elizabeth decided to leave. Michael felt rather sorry now that he had seen the new Katrina. She was even rather pretty, calm—the kind of woman one would like to have around like a picture. For woman were necessary, he decided. Yes, necessary. This opinion, he felt, in his heart of hearts, put him at odd with Little Paul and Jason and some of the rough men for whom women existed as a kind of unfortunate fact; and since they were here, one had to make the best of it. Pitying them, of course, and trying, although it really was impossible, to teach them.

Katrina had seen Agatha and Tock off in the boat. The three figures on the shore Michael categorized in his mind as the last three figures—the antediluvian figures on the lone shore of the world. Little Tock had played in the sand as the women talked. Agatha had bent over and put her head on Katrina's bosom, for a brief moment. Michael suddenly determined to write in his diary: Love once, briefly—a moment between women on the shore. You have gone your whole life at odds with this person—everywhere you turned she seemed to get in the way; (this was Katrina!) Now you have laid your head innocently against her bosom, yes innocently—all the pain and contention floating above your mind and body, and the bosom is holding your whole entire organism in your head as if it is the palm of a mighty hand.

But no, no woman's bosom would ever convey such an idea. The space on a woman's breasts is limited, one rests one's head briefly, barely. The wind is blowing, the sea is beckoning—there is the mighty hand—over the endless waters. Nothing can resist that call onward. But it seemed as if Agatha wrenched her head away, uprooted something deep inside Katrina; one could see the earth, the heart as if torn out of her bosom.

All these thoughts Michael wrote in his diary, which was really bits and pieces, full of fragments of thoughts, and incomplete sentences. He wondered about Katrina who like a chameleon for so many years had fit anonymously into the environment, but who, underneath had a different soul. No one had 'seen' her, he thought. Dimitri had probably been attracted to all that underneath, what Michael didn't want really to call soul but rather power; Dimitri had welcomed it into his entrails where it had caused a little conflagration but Dimitri too in his way was a powerful man. He was swayed, blown over by what one could only call passion; and then he righted himself like a tree after a storm. The fire still burned him, Michael suspected, when he confronted the many men leering and grimacing at him, and it took greater strength of mind and soul to overcome this fire and to say softly—I love you, because the news of that utterance had roused the village for a while—yes, I love you to those ugly men, he had said, and then he had sung the lousy, foolish song of theirs.

I am a seer, I am, thought Michael; a seer means a knower. I see Dimitri correctly. He was never tempted by lust, lasciviousness; rather it was beauty and love—incomplete, you might say. He loved in one way here, in another there. The passionate part was for Max, the idling, amusing, intellectual interest was Katrina. His heart and body were for his wife, to whom he was ever 'steady'—that is kept with unfailing affection and dearness. I see the whole thing, suddenly. Perfectly human, properly man. Of course, everybody would object to it. And we have crumpled into a little ball over it. Dimitri must die over it. Agatha must leave over it. And the village is dying, turning to ashes, dust—with the crumpled little ball of two women and a boy on the shore: all because one man lived, lived the life of love. And then we have a religious war over it. Not a war of killing bodies so much as killing spirits. Agatha is permitted baptism and marriage (she doesn't merit them) by whom? Her own outgrown son—grown out not up--to the proportions of an incestuous bishop, says mad Simon. He is no bishop. What is he but an enormous cage keeper who puts her into a cage, closes the door, permits her her incestuous baptism, food, drink, as if those things answer for wind and sky, for the God of slight creatures in corners who danced once? Now the bird has flown.

Leo received a letter from Agatha about a month later—a month of worrying and wondering. The letter said nothing about coming home. It was full of joy and sorrow, though, full of life, he said—the thought was painful to him for she was not at his side—she had found Father Isaac. He was living in a one room flat near an encampment of gypsies without water or electricity. The three story white house stood up in the dust-covered fields all solitary and alone. Who had built it? No one knew. Father Isaac had signed the lease on a burst of willpower, he had been doubled over by pain. He had accompanied the landlord to the door and then collapsed on the bare floor. Some of the older gypsy children helped him the next day to bring a mattress in from an apartment upstairs; the old woman living there had pity on him. It could be my destiny as much as his. I am handling my own flesh when I tend to him, she said. I brought very little.

Father Isaac is dying from liver cancer, said Agatha. He knew before he left. He told Jason and Little Paul to let him die in peace—but you see what happened. In any case, I intend to stay and care for him. We have no pain pills, she said, but someone from the gypsy camp brings us marihuana. It does him a world of good. I give what I have.

Mostly he smokes and drinks the hard liquor and lousy red wine of this island. He won't eat much so I make fried bread to try to get fat inside him. There is nothing to do but wait. Death plays a hard, hard number on flesh. I have not brought up my role in sending him away; there is no mention of the island-wide vote. He sits, puffs at the joint, blows and fills the entire room with smoke, and then grins at me, white faced out of the smoke like an attenuated ghost, drinks a sip of bad wine.

We talk very little and only strange commentary—about the goodness of sunlight, the kindness of it, or about the deliciousness of water when I can buy it in bottles. In my mind, he is praising God in the deliciousness of water. I often kiss his hand. In my mind, he knows about Dimitri. Not that there is anything to know—this is where we have a soul: it is something about the soul. I tasted life in Dimitri. Call it eternal for that savor! It is true he was terrible. But what I tasted in him was meekness like a lover tastes meekness in her beloved; he died meek; he was meek, and his sins just washed out! Once Fr. Isaac kissed me, not I him, on the forehead, and then on the lips. It was a chaste kiss, tasting like smoke in return for soul like fire. It seemed to me that he was in fact blessing me, as an agonized body struggling to be born unearthly out of earthly, blesses an earthly body. The non-existent smoke on my lips after tasted so bitter yet so beautiful.

I once asked him about baptism. He nodded, just nodded and began to weep at the thought. Pulled my head down towards him and, not finding water, weeping, baptized me in his tears murmuring the Name of Father, Son and Holy Spirit-- rubbing the tears across my brow-- with a kind of gasp as if calling them like a child who is trying to keep up. I can't say whether or not I have been baptized. I think so. But it has been baptism of a sort, communion too, birthing-dying—God, out of his seamy body, the wine of our nuptials changed to weeping, as it were, to lie on the floor and watch him die, eating his dying bread-body—with my heart which has no sight or smells of food to feed on; it is gay and it is bitter like the crap of an old person. It is a baptism that I accept.

For there is such light-heartedness, such absence of rancor and resentment. He regrets nothing, fears, but doesn't hate the disease, even blesses it. And God willing, he smiles, and his eyes glitter. There is something like excitement, even fire in them. And even later, when the thought has passed, his eyes continue to burn and then he weeps. He weeps for God willing passing. As I, for a minute when I thought the dance over....I wept as if the end had come. For Dimitri died, you know, I thought he would never--and now, I have been baptized in a dying man's tears, a man, who sent Dimitri to his death, whom I've forgiven who forgives me everything, stirs the ashes, as it were, raises up life in me of pain but of sweetness through tears raining on me at night when he kisses me for we hold each other at night. I've been baptized; he told me pre-baptized in precisely my taboo passion. I kiss him on the forehead, and on the smidgeon of hair that he has. I hold him in my bosom like wine. There is very little of him left and he stinks and shrinks but I hold him all the more with delicacy like you would hold a bird; there is a bad taste with him but such a beautiful burn of him in my heart, held up to his mouth like the best wedding wine--a bright stern scorch! I forgive him again and again and again and I watch him again and again forgiving like the dying child forgives God—so passionately absolutely that the word itself is effaced by its meaning; like an old person forgives life: To forgive and forgive like a mirror reflecting a mirror of forgiveness how it reflects infinitely—for the child is God, God the child; the old person is life, life the old person; and the middle aged woman, love, murmurs Fr. Isaac, the one who steps in heaven when she walks, stepping on earth. Outside the door of the apartment building, I smile at the gypsy children, and lift my leg and pirouette; yes, dirty, shrunken, humpbacked, tired, destitute in the loss of Dimitri, I dance; I can dance again—like one of those shiny new coins, a very little girl says, that you suddenly find long lost in the dust: how you dance-shine and they are in awe! But I am shy of her and them and run away, hearing them laughing with joy of their still unbelief on the verge of knowledge and mischief of freedom and running after, a humpback who can dance. And Fr. Isaac laughs too. His laughter is exactly like his weeping, a light sobbing, wracked with pain. And we live if you can call it living on a single mattress and tomatoes and bread. And yet I dance not shiny new dances, but shrunken, humpbacked, tired, sad, lame, childless dances within the mandala of the smoke of the bitterly perfumed joints. And the little girl claps her hands ecstatically at my heaven stepping on earth, as the Fr. Isaac calls it! I almost feel the gypsy children write my story of passion and exhaustion, my story of dead ends and loss with their bare feet in the dust, lovelier than the sparkles of crystals, as dancers write stories, and like the best writers of stories, leave them unforgivably incomplete. I've left almost all my money. And given most of the rest to the gypsies. Even for, contrary to all my instincts as a mother, bad ice cream. The taste of Heaven, to them!

Leo read the letter again and again. It was a beautiful letter, he thought, although all scratchy with Agatha's bad handwriting. At the end there had been only an affectionate and friendly salutation. She had said nothing about returning or marrying him. He was inclined to write to her, a big, long letter full of fun. He wanted to tell her, open up his brain and let the words flow out to her—of course, they would be together, of course. But just as he was about to get started, he suddenly decided to put the whole endeavor on hold.

He would let her return to him naturally—when the mood, the very blood, began to flow his way again. There was definitely love between them—not the adolescent variety, but good love. Meanwhile, he would get to know his vagrant son Max better, hidden up in the hills for shame and fear. He had heard Little Paul was calling him— 'that deposed sodomite of a deacon'. The words were horrible to him and made his son appear to him like a ghastly piece of half-diseased meat.

The island has changed drastically, he told himself. Years ago, no one would have used such language. The words would not even have been part of our vocabulary. Leo felt he had lost his innocence unwittingly owing to Max—not because of anything his son had actually done but because of this kind of phrase. Leo had read widely—in fact, he had read during his childhood—any books that came on the boat—because he was fat and ungainly and it was difficult for him to keep up with the boys. And he remembered now various points of Italian history that he had read—how he would say that such phrases as Little Paul used to describe his son were more appropriate in the papal court of Rodrigo Borgia, thick and murky with intrigue, than on their little clear island.

He was almost surprised when Max did come home to him all of one piece and looking a little like an Ariel figure, slim-legged, fresh faced, with a beautiful torso on which, as the boy showered, and he peeked in, he counted delicate, delightful ribs.

Max kissed his father's hand, bowing his head down quickly and quietly. Leo reached out his fat fingers and caressed his face. There were no recriminations on either side. Leo cooked up some chicken in tomato and onion, baked with a little hot pepper and plenty of olive oil; Max feasted as if he had finally gotten food after a long period without. When he looked up his beard was yellowish with oil and tomato stains.

Leo said at that point: Look, it is all the same to me whether you stay or not. What I mean is, I don't mind in the least for however long. I am waiting for a woman with a little child. When she comes I will be married to her. But you are still welcome to stay.

I know you are waiting for Agatha to come back, said Max, staring straight ahead.

Yes, said Leo, looking at him with gentle eyes.

Say whatever you want to say.

Did you ever tell her, she suffered a lot, you know—that Dimitri did not rape you?

Max was silent for a moment. Dimitri loved me, he said in a low, broken voice. What is the point though? What is the point?

Ah, said Leo: Two men can never love one another. Kill one another—yes, that is alright, in the eyes of the world.

Did I kill him? Asked Max in a low tone. And then, he suddenly shouted: Did I kill him? He ran out on to the little terrace and shouted down the hillside that ran down from the house: Did I kill him? Did I kill him?

Leo followed him out and said to him in his ear, taking his elbow: If you did, you had to. Better you, who loved him than those people on their own…

Max put his hand in front of his face and crouched down. Leo bent down and took his arm, pulling him up. Look, he said, tenderly; Max still had his hand in front of his face. He wants you to live. Not because you didn't do anything wrong. It is just one of those foolish, little gifts of love.

Yes, said Max solemnly; I actually realize that. I mean that he would want me to live. He was not jealous or vengeful, not in the least. Ecstatic, more than anything else, as I knew him. He didn't, couldn't hold a grudge, couldn't resent. It was a quiet kind of ecstasy; no one would imagine Dimitri like that. But that is what it was. He was filled up to the brim with it. Sometimes I imagine that he is still. I never thought however of myself as the one to survive.

What is it for you? Leo asked, after he had led him inside to sit on the sofa in the living room.

Straining, longing. I am the cooped up goose in the farmyard. He was the wild goose who passed overhead and called down to me.

Is it sexual, physical, mental, or spiritual?

How should I know? Dimitri treated me as one package. He said I had wings to fly with. But I find that they don't work somehow.

Did you love Dimitri?

How could I not love Dimitri? Isn't he the beloved round here really? Oh, they say they hate him but that is merely because they all resent really loving, and they are frightened at the idea of tenderness and beauty between men as if it is a kind of impotence. The jealous one was Little Paul. This Jason knew. He came to me with a knife. Deliver him to us, he said. I know what I did. But I don't know why. How much easier it would have been just to die.

I believe, said Leo, slowly, ruminating, that we will talk this out for many years. But you, you must trust that above everything else that Dimitri wants—notice I speak as if he is alive—he wants you, Max, to live. As for me, I would understand your throwing yourself off a cliff, but if my word is worth anything, I swear that, after all these years, and seeing you from a distance, and then coming to my house like the sun in miniature, no matter what it is on your conscience, still, you understand, to me like a little sun in my house—to me your death would be endless, unfathomable night. Such night, you understand that I could not find my hand in front of my face; the soul in me would be blind and lost.

I didn't think you cared for me, said Max, quietly.

Then you don't know anything about a father's wiles to deceive himself and his child.

After this the two men sat on the sofa until evening, smoking. Leo went into the kitchen and took out some white wine from the refrigerator. They drank that night and didn't eat both towards midnight feeling light and dizzy. Neither one even imagined food. The darkening room filled with smoke and the moonlight came in so that they could see the veils of smoke in the air. Leo wanted to talk about many things: About Magda, for one thing, the intoxication of her, body and mind—how he had heard, from here and there, the wind carries talk on the island—how Max had sometimes preferred her to God, how in the throes of his deaconship, how even at the altar reciting the prayers, his inner mind had strayed to her—the woman whose blood bond to him was deeper than life.

For this Max had felt—an affinity, a kinship of all things, the priest, laughing, had said it—to the Lord Jesus Himself who had a mother and the whole thing was similar. Only for Jesus His mother supplied a blood bond with God and for Max—he didn't know, but it seemed to him to begin and end with him and his mother, which was somehow more than life.

But Leo didn't talk. Thoughts like this came and went but he didn't permit himself the liberty of opening his mouth.

Max on his account was imagining first Dimitri, and then his mother and father—Leo out of place, his mother golden in the darkness, half seen, like a secret that has been heard of. She just stood suspended as it were from the night full of stories, intimate, elegant, beautiful…she was like a golden glove lying on the table—one wondered where it had come from. And it seemed as if there was a whole dramatic act before and to follow. This is what made the scene in his imagination so exhilarating—his mother was definitely thespian, adept at wearing masks, at telling the truth through a false impression.

And his father said, although Max hadn't opened his mouth about all this—yes, she was all strength and bravery to the manly eye; but within she was meek, feminine, motherly: One had merely to crack her like a nut. Love did that like one sharp, inexorable blow.

There is argument about whether or not she went to heaven. I see her slipping through the narrow gate—she had, after all, embraced death, taking along no baggage, no rancor or resentment, no bitterness or pride. She was like a child when she died, talkative, smiling, a little, eyes large as saucers, but peaceful, knowing something. She had no charisma at the time—which some people, like Paul, used to blame her for. She had spellbound the people, he used to say, quite different from a saint! But no there was nothing; she was simple, when she died like a wheel detached from a cart, lying against a wall. Pretty…nothing fancy; besides, everybody knows a wheel. But there was for a long time a contention between resentment of her and utter adoration. Some went to their prayers loving her, she was beautiful, remember! Others, struggling, remembering this thing and that. But she did exert some kind of appeal—it was as if one wanted to pray to her as a saint, as a microcosm of God that would move that would help. Because who can move the earth back into alignment with God? It seemed she was, for a long time, what the islanders thought of as a bridge.

Now the island has changed. It is for you and me to remember her. We believe that wheel left behind—supposed to turn earth into heaven?—is reattached in heaven. And the amazing thing is that it isn't divided either from us. Not divided. Only it is seen differently. It is seen as in yes—that is exactly…Barbara, Nisos, Timos, Paul! And you see there Magda holds out her Creator-hands, welcoming –across the bridge.

There are probably a few who still pray to her. What a woman we all knew become a saint! Nothing remarkable—everything remarkable about her; a wheel is remarkable after all, so is a human being! But we know that it wasn't for the strength and the bravery. We know it is more for the eyes like saucers so meek and peaceful.

Max leaned over on the couch and bent his head and kissed his father's hands. Then he reverentially kissed his knees and putting out his hand to the floor leaned on it as he bent down further and kissed Leo's puffy white ankles.

You don't think, said Leo gruffly, looking at him as he settled back on the couch— that I am worthy of all that veneration?

I see that I had in some dark hallowed hall with candles flickering, two holy people fragrant as the night, laughing holy laughter as my parents.

What do you intend to do?

Perhaps my mother has taken a spiritual step with me on her back. Odd, how we come to it.

Leo didn't understand Max, but sitting there the huge affection that he had had for him as a baby flooded back, and yet, mixed in, something different now, a certain terrible timidity. He was still little, never tall, or muscular— vulnerable, fragile—but there was no question that he knew more.

Together, unable to express themselves better than that, they sat on the sofa and drank cool white wine until dawn. Then they went to their beds and slept until noon, at which point Leo remembers nothing but being served fragrant coffee which spilt over the side of the little cup and which he drank up from the saucer.

Zoe said to Cleo that the island had become little clusters of people like wild grasses, a little windblown with a distant look in their eyes at times. And these clusters of people talked in low voices about luncheons, fishing, and how the sun rotted everything dead but sometimes made dried fruits, which could be put into very sweet desserts after all. Simon said that the sun knows something! Zoe thinks that he is getting at something in his madness. She said to Cleo—this is what we have been seeking: the question is—is it Agatha? Have we really done her wrong? I think the sun knows that it is blind and doesn't know. When she comes back to marry Leo we must altogether make it up to her even though the whole thing is absurd. Is there something about what Little Paul and Jason say? That we have strayed so far we wouldn't know true holiness and we must now simply crush ourselves, you know. I suppose the women go first as is usually the case in the work of humility. We must break ourselves down until the bones of contention and pride are broken. And then the bones which the Lord has broken may rejoice. Poor Maria had to go. And there is talk of limiting the amount of apricot brandy, which we are able to buy. It seems as chief they will requisition the whole lot and sell it off as they see fit.

Bandits, said Cleo—hypocrites!

Ah, no, they drink hardly anything. But they will put by some money, obviously. Little Paul and Jason call it 'reorganization'. They are going to build a hotel. A cement addition will be made to Katrina's place and a few more rooms. All in all there will be fifteen rooms, ten double and five single for tourists. And our exercise will be meekness and asceticism. The fish will be sold to the other island for profit and we will have fish in our markets every Tuesday and Friday. Otherwise we will eat the barley and cheese of our island farms, the eggs of our chickens.

Cleo said—but that house has been sold to Little Paul for his wife and children.

Ah, they will never live in it.

What I want to know, said Zoe, reflecting for a space, is whether or not this new government is based on truth—whether or not what Jason and Little Paul are offering is Christ. At times I think it is. How can it not be? We have hospitality and only eggs to eat ourselves—a chicken or two for guests. Is this not what we want—the track back to holiness? Mother Dora preached: hospitality forever and for all, irregardless. Of course, there are rules—you know the way it is. People who disrupt are to be politely sent away. These rules are iron rules. Our freedom is bought with a price, and bound with a chain.

For one thing, there are to be no other gods, no other love affairs than those prescribed by our traditions. Thank God, Nico finally married Elizabeth or those two would have heaped up fornication on fornication. No, our traditions of Christ for a lifetime of eighty-eight years, I have accepted. But as I sit back, having observed the rules, and even now, with a hoary head, bowed under the budding dictatorship of Little Paul and Jason, mere chickens when we were in the prime of life, as I sit back to savor, for now even they would say—yes, go ahead, it is your right, I taste nothing sweet in our traditions. Isn't the savor of holiness fragrant and beautiful—sweet as the jasmine blossom? What is lacking, what is missing?

Then my thoughts guiltily and secretively turn to Agatha. She who accomplished something extraordinary—on the night of that dance, competing against Paul and the Pauls—ah she brought not only him but all of us to our knees, weeping and beseeching, laughing and jumping up high as we could! She made us live—she was flesh as it should be. Dancing seemed to be the only way to us. How was anything else possible, we asked, after she had finished and was receiving the crown? And ah, it burned her. So it should have—searing the flame in her with flame, fire coming to fire. It was the most beautiful thing I have ever seen, although she cried out in pain. They say she has stopped dancing now—feeds the priest, tends him, wipes the spittle from his mouth, sits by him while he smokes his joints and gets high, inhaling herself, greedily the toxic fumes, letting them go to her head, and circle around in her brain like a halo and make her high.

In any case, we are awaiting her return. Surely, one like she will come back and marry. She can't go without the very meat of a man—one like she. Even I used to dream of passion, the kind of passion with a man that surely she will have with Leo. Cleo and I will begin to craft the decorations for the little church. Deep in the recesses of it, in the shadows there is a painting. They say it is of Christ dancing on the water—that is walking, but in such a way—taking not just any step, but a dance step….And there will be a marriage, an occasion. I suppose it suits, I suppose so. Agatha should marry as she loves—and then that will be….she didn't marry as she loved before. Alex was just, hum, well, it has all come out now. Alex covered for… but those were just youthful indiscretions. And so, we shall go dancing home. I look forward to Agatha's return as I never did her presence all these years.

Jason and Little Paul went away on a little boat to the other island to present a 'plan' of payment and implementation to the electrical company so that Holy Island could have full power back at night. We, the men and women of the island, the old-timers, soon to be ancestors in the graves—we thought that Jason would see to it that Agatha came home with him. He was now her only son and the one that 'had things in mind' the way no one else did except Little Paul. Although they had confiscated her property, there was Tock to consider: He couldn't live for very long in the unhealthy atmosphere of the sick priest—not, of course, because of his physical ailment, but because he was a reversed saint, as it were. Tock had to come home, if Agatha was still in her right mind she would bring him so that he could go to school with the new priest who was young, pink in the face from health, settled and calm. Oh, how pink they can be on a desolate island. He said in his sermons the usual thing. Foti said—I could give his sermons. Of course, that was not the point. We milled around him, the one left in charge, when Jason and Little Paul were gone. We sat on our balconies, the women did, and the men sat down by the boats or up in the seats of the closed tavern and we drank our hidden stores of apricot brandy. Peter came to preside. He said Paul was closed up in his house an invalid; he had a disease of weeping—that is what he said. Ella had become sharp, pale and full of newfound righteousness. Peter said that there had been a general loss of passion—the old kind—the kind that burned in one, larger than life. We realized that he had really loved Maria and that perhaps there was something to it. And what are we without holiness, anyway? Or what are we without passion? Always God and man, the Spirit and the flesh—if now, neither, what then? We had our Spirit transfusing our flesh, our flesh in the light of Spirit.

No one changed position even, at these words. We sipped and murmured. We all somehow had gotten together and were sitting around Peter at the old closed tavern which still had all the chairs and tables laid out neatly as if to host a crowd. We drank and murmured. But we all of us knew that there was a kind of dread in our hearts. What were we becoming? And then we all simultaneously had the same thought; one of us, maybe Timos, shouted suddenly Magda—ha, Magda—she would have known the answer…but we weren't thinking Magda. We were all thinking Agatha. We knew it and felt ashamed. I suppose, said Peter—voicing something, which preyed on our consciences—we don't have to hate one who loves another of the same sex. Maybe loving one of the same sex can be enlightening, can be—well, sweet. We knew in that well he was leaving out the word 'holy.'

All love is holy, said Nisos; but, retorted Cleo, Dimitri is dead. Maybe and maybe not said Nisos. That is assuming that life is just this machine of a body and brain. But everything is spiritual. Life is in the Spirit not in the machine.

Life is in the soul, murmured Zoe.

In any case, what if there is a separate reality from the mechanical thing—the same that we've always believed in—what if it is true and we have simply stopped believing in it. And in that separate reality, it is Dimitri who is alive. And it is we who are dead. This is where our conscience enters in and tells us the truth.

This is all nonsense, said Cleo brusquely. A matter of words to make children afraid. Maybe it would be good to think about Agatha coming home in a few weeks or days, even. She is such a comfortable person now. Reconciled, I think is, in fact, the word. Cleo was happy that she could still choose good words at her age—her mind at least was not all confused and clouded. Barbara suddenly said in a loud voice—Agatha still has a will in her that I have never seen the likes of. Will like iron, I'd say. Barbara said in a stentorian tone. If she were to come back she would crack the very walls with her presence.

Agatha, said Nisos, grandly, is alive— she loves—look at her humpback and twisted leg.

She found love with Dimitri, Zoe said, and Cleo smirked. You are out of line, said Zoe to her in an aside, but there is no out of line in this crowd, of course. There is no pushing you over a cliff. Cleo narrowed her eyes and spat at her—you would come with me.

Zoe glared at her, but proceeded, calmly. Yes, with Dimitri—she took a sip of apricot brandy and savored the sweet-tartness and the burn of the alcohol in her throat. Yes, while we sit here and because of rules can't have passion or holiness.

Catherine would say, piped up Michael who was ever ambivalent—friend, not friend, his own person, a loner and a thinker—Catherine would say that love is a wild mysterious thing—to be respected, not tamed, you know—like a white tiger.

Maria would say, said Peter with a hoarse voice, that our Lord Jesus respected the love, wild and mysterious in the flow of tears of Mary at his feet while the Pharisee rejected it because it came out of sinfulness.

Tiger's tears.

Everybody sat silently for a few minutes, absorbing not only what was said but the poetic twist of Michael, the writer. Barbara spoke up finally: Well, I have to cook. We have fish today. I am stuffing the sea bass with bread and onions and sage. At least, we have fish; it is good, I say to be thankful.

A number of things ran through Barbara's head as she walked home that afternoon. Things were still the same. There had been no earthquake, she jested to herself grimly. And if there were—what of that? She had lived by the grace of God, thankfully; thankfulness was in her heart and also eroding that, although she fought it off, was the sense that she was in the midst of the most petty and ridiculous life one could possibly conceive of. But then life was petty and ridiculous for the most part. People now and then made grand gestures. They discovered things or wrote music that made you a little excited—but that was all after an extraordinary amount of pettiness and ridiculousness. It was a moment when the sun got to you, she thought—even in those cold countries, the sun could 'get to you.'

She had once told Father Isaac about this theory of the sun—getting to people. And he had said—yes, yes, God put into the sun some secret knowledge. And then Barbara continued with her musing, people thought that the light was more than the light actually is. She was gentle on herself—was that atheism, she softly asked. Of course, but light is more than light actually is. At least, on this island one saw it. One lived in a crucible of light; there was so much light sometimes that one didn't see at all—that is, one saw only light. And then rising out of the heart—this person, that person—for her it had been Stavros, Agatha—her husband and her neighbor; her children she had loved of course but barely noticed also. What was God then? Light? Of course, for the sun had told her that—there is light that lets one see only light.

She had been trying to see for centuries it seemed—maybe fifty years—but that can have a different time measurement when it is lived; they all thought ill of her—Barbara with the vicious temper, the pettiness, the snooper—it was all true, she would be the first to admit. But yet it wasn't her—it was an alien soul that entered her—perhaps the soul of her sister, a woman who had died young—seventeen, bone thin, arrogant, happy to be arrogant, who spat once into the chalice instead of receiving Holy Communion. Why shouldn't we throw stones? She asked.

No one spoke of her. The scandal had been hushed up. The priest had quickly drunk up the wine, prayed and gotten more wine for the communicants. Bitter, angry girl she was like a thorn. But to the end grinning with triumph. And this soul entered like the devil. It questioned, tormented made love impossible. Why shouldn't you snoop on Agatha, it asked her, she makes such a show of meekness, and then, she ah now made you die for her triumph, lazy, good-for-nothing, Barbara. This soul, as she called her sister, this soul, one of the muted knowledges of the island, this soul was not even atheist. This soul was antagonist. Her parents had put their two venerable heads together and asked themselves if she, this sister, wanted beating, breaking of bones. But they were afraid she would go on to the death.

Barbara loved her. She made Barbara laugh. You should have seen the faces in church—the looks of shock; the stiffness towards the family after. The elaborate rituals they undertook to bar her from communion. Bah, she had said, when the priest had told her—mishandling the communion, taking it with less than awe means that you burn in hell especially. Why? And she had curled her lip with disgust, she a mere slip of a thing, so thin and stinking a little, yellow for thinness while the priest was so full fleshed, staring down at her over his ugly, greasy, few hairs beard.

Barbara had gone home and considered running away from home. For there was no question, this soul was condemned. But when she had died it had all seemed different. There were no mourners. Her mother wept just a little. Barbara had no words. Her father turned away from the grey sea as they lowered the body in from the boats. A favorite bracelet of this sister was given her and she held it in her hand for a day and a night. Perhaps there was something wrong—just wrong, she told her mother.

Her mother and father acted like this sister was nonexistent even while she was sick. She had no pain—oh, that her bowels might be disgorged on the sheets, her breath come short, the sweat cover her, that sort of thing. But no real pain like a man befriending and she wanting more. In the end, she was flat and skeletal like the figures in the icons. Only she was unholy and no one was much convinced by the priest's sermon of merciful God. Barbara held the bracelet for one night, then the next. In any case, every so often a deep lassitude overcame her and then the cruelty, vanity and spite of this sister, the arrogance, insolence—and all this made Barbara hard. Yet it wasn't her. No, it wasn't. It wasn't real. But as she thought this, a jangle of bones and bracelets in her ear and a familiar mocking voice came—neither is communion. Foolish collection of hags and monsters gaggling around to sip—what? And it was true. As for Agatha, Barbara bitterly squinted at her, half envious.

But the real creature, the reality, dead center, was sweet in Barbara. This her husband knew. And this the other soul said was because, ultimately, she was so stupid.

She loved God. She thought God had made it such that every leaf and every blade of grass spoke some higher language of delicate and magnificent courtship to God. That God had given them words and this was the greatest gift. One could see these words for the silence of night wasn't silence. The muteness of the living thing wasn't muteness.

Only Barbara's husband knew that Barbara had poetry in her. But Barbara mourned and twisted in her soft bed thinking of that sister and saying nothing.

It was Barbara who had the insights. Agatha has cut ties, she knew. They would have to go on without her. And they would be forever trying to cut off—the 'soul'. Bone thin, rebellious, arrogant, anti-Christ—when is the punishment going to stop? Crucifixion on the one end, and rains of fire on the other. Good, bad—this was the soul. Mostly we are promised hell, a distant perhaps of heaven…for the few!

Barbara simply loved in her other self. And she saw that this love tucked down inside made her beautiful still. It is beauty no matter, said Stavros looking at her wilted purple black hair.

Barbara thought she would just live ignoring Little Paul and Jason. They were, she told her husband, very righteous. She was sure they didn't sin.

Violent, and tyrannical. We'll be a seemingly holy haven—one will be quiet and respectful here, leave a tip at the church…We will be given 'our ways' at last. And there will be no women dancing, no magical women. Just long skirted, little, automatic, toe tapping women. And you, who know things, will have no voice.

What should I do? He asked her leaning on her chest one night. I have no heart to kill them. No heart, anymore; no heart.

Were you ever in love with Agatha, Barbara asked curiously.

I thought she was sagacious, passionate, richly dignified. If I had loved her, I would have been a free man.

A free man?

Not so holy, he said kissing her on the ear.

There are no words, no words for the Almighty, intoned the priest. He was having, after having asked permission, little get-togethers at the church concerning the nature of God.

And yet, thought Barbara we enter into an intimate relationship with Him.

She and Stavros along with Paul and Ella were some of the few parishioners who had come. Others had pleaded busy. People were staying close—that is, among themselves, not wanting anymore, since Agatha's departure and before that since Dimitri's death, to go out and socialize even with the priest who was not making waves. In fact, everyone appreciated him—he was nondescript, absolutely plain, with no imagination. He was rotund, pink-faced and gazed like a little rabbit looking into headlights upwards, spellbound during the Divine Liturgy. He was not unintelligent, however, and had learned his lessons well at Seminary. He was introducing the parishioners in a very mild, sugar-coated way to lessons from apophatic theology.

So there is no way to say that we love God? asked Barbara.

God is unlovable, said the priest—no, in fact, you see, He is infinitely lovable. But we must learn the spirit of the Commandments. Otherwise, what are we loving? Our own mistakes, really.

The lesson went on in this way and Barbara and Stavros and Paul and Ella felt at the end of it very edified. But somehow milling around after and talking outside, Barbara felt that they all had become smaller. Something vast and furious had, as it were, sloughed them off here on this little island, or rather, right here in front of the church, remnants of something, a great golden age of knowledge about God. knowledge that the priest had told them, laughing, only came as a result of loving God. So that they had been thoroughly confused and back at the beginning.

But things were beginning again in life on the island, in little. At Easter there had even been dancing—Little Paul had danced, won the crown! Secretly several islanders had shifted their feet as they pronounced his victory. Little Paul couldn't split his legs or leap; he hadn't really practiced, and just jumped a little, stomped, turned red in the face, roared, somersaulted—in short he had impressed nobody. But everyone felt, as Zoe said, too old to do anything—to rise up against...

St. Paul was talking to Stavros in slow measured tones. His voice, Ella said, was shaky; several times in the church listening to the lecture, he passed his hand in front of his eyes and shook tears off his face. He was a changed man and very feeble. But Barbara said to Stavros, he has found his heart. Better find it broken, have it break you down for good and ever than...Stavros bowed his head.

People were kind to St. Paul. Ella received packages—chicken, salt, potatoes, warm sweaters. It was whispered around town that the man in St. Paul was gone. He was womanly, soft; no longer a big eater, never more a shouter, he sat in a chair by the window with a glass of milk or held Ella's hand out walking the way a blind person holds hands. Nothing had happened to his brain, Ella insisted; but it was hard to see it that way. Ella said, everyone carries a house inside—his had come tumbling down. Little Paul, she said, 'took good care of him,' but Ella was caught between two violent men—first Paul now little Paul; she was so used to the violence that she may have herself been somewhat shocked to find it gone. Little Paul, the whisper went around, really bullied his father now. And his father submitted like a sheep led to slaughter; one could almost hear him bleat. He was utterly penitent.

St. Paul had said to Stavros: and the Lord God said to Mary Magdalene when He was resurrected: I go to my God and your God. Then his voice had broken and he stopped. It is just, he whispered, that I wish he wouldn't keep reminding me of the humiliation of going to Agatha's to ask forgiveness of Dimitri. He seems especially to hold that against me.

Stavros said later to Barbara, I would have thought St. Paul would be all plump and pathetic, but he is thin like the old style among men here. Thin, and simply helpless.

Little Paul spent the summer on the other island, supposedly negotiating with the electrical company in order to say that Holy Island still existed and its inhabitants still married and some produced children. He rounded up folks that had come from Holy Island and were living on the other island, fishing and operating small businesses, some were even working in the electrical company and showed them their children, saying that it was a malicious rumor that the families on Holy Island had been cursed by God and were infertile. Yes, families had left, it is true, but might they not return? Should not there be a bridge, the bridge of good will, he called it, considering they were Holy Islanders really and had found refuge on this other island while the folks of the other island might at any time take up residence on Holy Island. Now they were, he said proudly, living up to their name. They had settled back into that one primary pursuit—that of holiness. And they claimed almost nothing—fish, lemons, goats, chickens, apricots—just enough to keep the strings of the instrument humming and by instrument Little Paul poetically represented village life.

Well, he went and argued and petitioned, we heard about it later, we men of Holy Island, and he came back at the end of August while the heat was still brimming over from day into night and the usual cool at dawn, and he came bringing with him a yellow haired doll whom he intended to marry. We think her name was Celeste—one of her parents was a stray French island lover! She was not a beauty: Snub nosed, round blue eyes, thin hair hanging limply, but she was entirely docile and in love with Little Paul. She followed him around wherever he went, not walking and talking side by side as lovers do, but keeping one step behind until she was called like a dog on a leash.

Little Paul sometimes walked with Jason too and then Celeste looked on to the backs of two men—one little and one large, as she followed behind. The wedding date was set, Little Paul knew and did it deliberately—for on the night of the wedding day, at the very dinner in the new inn, which had yet to be opened to the public, but was being used to show case Little Paul's success, suddenly the whole island was illumined by electric light.

People had forgotten how bright light bulbs can be. They gasped, smiled in disbelief and then cheered, throwing rice, confetti and a few honey cakes that Zoe and Foti had made at the happy couple. But really it was Little Paul that took the most of the confetti, rice and cakes; he smiled to in the way that one does when one is conscious of being in the spotlight.

The brightness of the lights now in the homes convinced people that Little Paul was entirely worth his salt. Worthy, they called out, as he passed, as if they were in church presenting himself for an ordination. Timos in particular was impressed—he said that Little Paul had kept the savor of his salt the way the Lord said we should. He smacked his lips after as if tasting Little Paul's salt and finding it very good.

Celeste seemed a little dazed, the first few days after the wedding night. It was reported all around town that she was a virgin. Little Paul clothed her—that is he decided on her garments—even the wedding dress—and when she was a married woman he dressed her all in grey and black in wide long skirts that made her trip. This he did to keep her pure, he said, and not tempted to lure other men with her newfound sexuality. But he couldn't help smirking a little over her slight, girlish body. There was a bit of a stir when someone found out that she was fourteen. But Little Paul denied this. He claimed loudly and drunkenly at one point—we think that he often got into the stores of apricot brandy that he intended to regulate and sell in small amounts to maintain our sobriety—any way, loudly and drunkenly he said one evening eating dinner at Peters with a group of others: that his wife was sixteen, the right age for bearing children. The older a woman gets, he said, the sourer her eggs become.

He committed the indiscretion of saying that he had paid off Celeste's grandmother, her guardian, after her mother and father were killed in a tragic accident. This caused a little rustle among the women. But then again for years no one had brought such a great blessing to the island as light, bona fide electric light the kind that you can rely on, and so the fact that Little Paul had bought a wife, as the saying went, was overlooked entirely. And then his wife after a few tries was already pregnant, disproving our theory that only Agatha's one son was potent (because so passionate!) and produced children. And Little Paul was triumphant for now he truly rivaled Dimitri.

You can see how we all forgot for a while about Agatha and the old priest of ours who went up the cliff on his knees in the days when the lights at night were dim—we now talk of the past like that. But Simon went around, dear, little Si, Little Paul called him with a wink and a screwing of his hand by the side of his head—and Simon said—we have a devil in our midst, meaning Little Paul; in fact, two devils, he would say immediately after—meaning Jason too. Three, meaning Little little Paul, as the baby was called already.

We learned that they had bigger ideas too than we had thought for the inn that used to be Katrina's house. They were going to enlarge it and make it for fifty beds instead of thirty with a swimming pool where the garden used to be. The proceeds would go into Little Paul and Jason's pockets. There would be Internet and wide screen television, twin jet boats for them—and for us, a penitence that lasted, and then our women would have to go around dressed in befitting garments—long, long sleeved dresses, with their heads down. They would be embroidering, cooking, lace making. It was, they explained to us, our tradition, a kind of marginal embroidery. For it is women who cause God to remove His Holy Spirit! When women get out of line—and here there was a slight reference to Agatha—dancing or asserting themselves, looking you in the eyes like sailors do, dead center, coring, and not in the margins—ah then....

But we wanted Agatha to come back rather more desperately than we were willing to admit publicly. Some of us missed the old days of dim lights and real dead center passion—Peter of course meant Maria—and we still gathered around him sitting in the chairs of the closed tavern, Nisos meant Agatha, for all that he had been publicly shamed and insulted for loving her, he still remembered her, he said, like an exquisite boat sailing offshore, a boat that made him wish he was a pirate to capture and escape with. We were initially content with Jason and Little Paul—because whatever sins they were guilty of, we were back repenting, walking on our path to holiness, to recapturing the uncreated light from God.

Nisos hung around Leo who looked at everyone with a little ironic, though entirely playful smile. Leo was treated a little like a woman by Little Paul and Jason a moral castrato for being the father of a man—can you call them men?—who had that inclination. Although they were not molested because, after all, Max had claimed that the whole thing was not his initiative but rather forced upon him.

There was one day a rumor—Celeste ghastly pale and swallowing hard, running to throw up in Zoe's bathroom (of course, she was pregnant, but still--)that Little Paul had gone to Max one day when Leo was out and Max was lying on the sofa in his underwear with a knife and had done the unspeakable yet again. It was Max who said it, whispered it to Peter—Max unkempt, eyes staring, half mad…

Little Paul affirmed that Max was mad! Why, he had never been 'like that.' He had a wife, he was faithful to her and in short the whole thing was impossible. Whatever it was, Leo did not come out of his house for many days. Tia who brought them eggs and rice said that he was sitting with Max in his arms and Max was shaking and crying, not eating, walking around the house with a butcher's knife ready to kill himself or another, she wasn't sure who.

Nothing was done to Little Paul, however; Celeste said that he was 'our savior' small s, faintly, repetitively like a machine making beeps. Feed her and she would beep: He is our savior look at the lights in the night! He had brought electricity and was bringing tourists to the island. Above all, he was getting us to repent. Little Paul and Jason took the first seats in church still with Celeste right behind them. The island appeared to have an energized two leaders, and a priest that knew the old ways well. There were suspicions that people went to bed with. But when anyone brought up Max to little Paul he would say mad, mad, mad. It was all part of the old disharmony with Scripture, he would say. Besides, who can prove anything against me? I spend my nights at home with my wife and father, my days managing and getting ready for the great opening of the inn. We are going to live, we will be a place on the map; our folks will survive as they wish to as the elect of Christ. Let anyone who wants come to see: The women are dressed with long skirts, our church is attended every Sunday by all, our business of fishing is lucrative enough but we fast, and fasting—bread and vegetables-- is built into our Constitution. Let them come and see—there is nothing to hide. We have our holiness. We don't listen to voices of mad people.

And with this note of absolute confidence in his voice, people began to quietly speak less and less of that strange rumor about Max. And, also, wasn't it possible that the whole thing with Dimitri was also false? That Max, in short, was diseased in mind and making things up? Then why was Dimitri killed? But Dimitri was not killed. The men went to tell him to stick to his wife—the man was just by the looks of him a libertine. The men went to him outside where he lived on the cliff to tell him that our ways must be adhered to—else why come to Holy Island, the one place where the elect have lived generation after generation….It was God's will that Dimitri slipped and fell. Why we gave him a choice: Why didn't he just fall to his knees and promise repentance? Fall to his knees before Little Paul. He was proud and arrogant. And what would that have meant but child rearing with his wife, a quiet life…

Little Paul and Jason were absolute authorities. No one got in their way. Only Simon voiced discontent. Max has stuck that knife into all of us morally. If he is mad, why did Dimitri have to die? If he is not why again did Dimitri have to die? And, they say that I am mad.

But his voice was to us a little like the sound of the sea at night. You hear it constantly on one level, on another, you never hear it.

The fact is no one wants to hear or know of Dimitri anymore. His face in our memory is synonymous with a shadow on the island; it is in our minds—for the island continues to be bright, bright, bright like a jewel of fire. It has an independent soul to our souls; how can I say it? It goes on living, and deep words come out of its interior, words like perfect poetry where we become vulgar, superficial, fantastic. For some odd reason, it seems as if we are in fact too heavy for this little place that is delicate like love, burning with a fire we are ignorant of. That is what Zoe says. In any case, we have ruined it. Dimitri is part of this ruination. His face is like a jewel of shadow. It was always handsome; but we remember, how can we ever forget? How he tilted his head back just before he fell—there was an odd smile on it, but perhaps it was a grimace. Some console themselves thinking he welcomed death.

Perhaps we don't want to know of Dimitri any more but we have to confess that the thought of him never leaves us. Some people think to themselves that the force of his memory is such that he will become an island folk hero. Little things will be remembered—the way he gallantly forgave Little Paul, but as if it was natural, natural the affection with which he treated everybody even when they turned against him. Could he be the saved soul, the holy one of our island….it was natural!—we shudder at the thought and yet it is a little funny.

Agatha wrote to Leo; the news filtered out even though that house was closed like a prison and very little was seen or heard of Leo, nothing of Max. She, whom we all secretly called 'she'—it used to be Magda, but now Magda was being put gently to rest—she was part of the island that was young and hopeful and had, we hate to say it, at least in that guise, died;--she was happy. That is, something had transpired: the priest, Father Isaac was very ill, he was breathing his last no doubt on a mattress on the floor where now and then a dirty draught came through at the bottom of the door; the room was filled with marihuana smoke; there was a glass of red wine, some uneaten rice. Wasting from being unable to eat had picked his bones. He looked like a skeleton –just as naked. In fact, said Agatha, his nakedness was so little, so anguished, so pathetic—it looked, she had the effrontery to say—like Jesus' on the cross. For all this, she and he were happy. The anathemas of the island together in the worst of straits somehow were happy. If you want to know of a miracle…began Nisos, and Timos humphed. We don't know anything real of the matter. She wrote to Leo we are in a little ring of fire—sickness, heat, famine, grief. And I simply won't go anywhere else. Don't mistake: This is not only my sentimental side, the pitying side that keeps me here. The pain of the one thing cancels the pain of the other. Pain is a constant. I eat bitter. But oh, the sun cracks open the day like an egg of white gold all around me. I love like never before. I have learned to reinterpret things. My brain is literally re-wired. Pain means joy. And this suffering, life.

Father Isaac talks a lot about Jesus. He says again and again that Jesus was tender—like a child. His brave words he shouted out like a child might shout that he has fought the terrible white tiger in the bathroom. They were beautiful words, sharp as daggers, entirely fanciful and free, but true, real. He was a child enjoying this other reality—the son in his father's house. His child heart is ablaze and when he sees another person made of fire….And the child's reality is above and below the world, of good beyond good.

Agatha therefore bears, as part of her happiness, the crown of thorns—anticipation, anguish of mind, and on her bosom the heavy weight of Dimitri's body that in her mind she rescues from the sea at dawn every day and drags before Jesus dancing on the water. She writes, however that that pain is part of her newfound dance. Oh yes, she too is dancing her way to life, she says as if she too is dying; it is a lowly dance—not so high-minded as before; once she asked of the sun to tell her things; now, she says, she is blind to the sun; does it heat them? Is that the sun out there where the white fire and white tiger reigns?

The dance is that which a mother does when she has lost her child, when she is the lost child-pain. Of course, at first the wind is knocked out of you. Then the pain sits heavily on you. The pain knifes through your very skeleton into the soft part of the vertebrae to paralyze. Down it goes through you into your bowels and twists your leg. I once thought, she said, that life came from my bowels, from Dimitri, now from the pearl dance of a grief-paralysis. I thought that my legs would never come back to the dance. I don't know how they work.

Now I don't know where life, that is, reality comes from, she said in her letter, contradicting herself. I go grinning, for the pain, out amongst the gypsy children who hand me around in their soft hands. Off we go skipping down the road, the road of dust and thirst. I learn to step lightly, as if all disincarnate, that is all. I teach them to step down lightly as they skip in case there is a thorn. This stepping lightly is above and below the world. This stepping lightly, coming to step lightly, is the dance. All dance is the prelude to walking on water. I learn from the little children.

The gypsy children are smudged, eat cookies when they can get them, barefooted, one five, they count, one three, one seven, hurrah--wear yellow or blue smocks, grey sweat pants made in China, laugh, chatter, squat and pee; and when they suffer hunger or pain or fever from the heat throw back their heads in their mothers' arms and scream all taut until they are screamed out and go sweetly limp-damp; I stuff cannabis leaves into their mouths; it's all I have except vegetables and bread; we all are hungry; we are all dancers; we can still lift our legs to skip beautifully, ethereally; how many can? and everything is dance—the bending the weeping—not the mimic of the prance but the step of heaven of the walker on water….to step not only lightly, impalpably lightly but with the spirit of the foot, of the Spirit of creation. Lightly as if the feet were wounded incarnated and we raised by superhuman effort drenched in sweat to walk incorporeally on them—as if balancing the body on a feather, on a whisper: so and so is dying; let's last another minute in veneration.

So I dance with poor gypsy children. That is my occupation now. That and feeding the dying priest his milk, cleaning up the soiling on the sheets. Washing it out of the yellowish cottons. We are light, you know; we live lightly and we step lightly. This is Christ-life, this love, this lightness. We are learning to be dancers. There is only one dance—if you ever come to it: the living dance as opposed to death it is living life that Jesus calls eternal life. (I learn dance from the children.) The children say that with my lame leg, I dance like a dragon with a most beautiful dragging tail. I whirl out of me, skipping, whirling, until I return from the dance as if bodiless, landing like a feather. How can a humpback dance like a wing of a dinosaur bird lifting, like a dragon broken, yet weightless as ash? And return dancing-less still dancing…even when not? A feather with a foot attached to it. Dancing, even when not, like ash which blows— the silence and the stillness carved out by the sun-fire, dancing, dancing—in every posture, every gesture. That is the Holy Spirit, says Father Isaac, when weight has become noetic, of the spiritual intellect, the intellect of ever-mourning, so infinitely light, but, now and then, heavy, not earthly— gravity, grace—. But the thought of reconciliation: it is all muscle, sweat that drenches me—body poured out like water. Then I am heavy, full of agony, but dance as if on water. For the pain floats.

Little Paul, yes Little Paul and Jason have in cold language invited me back-- to marry you, to 'settle down', that is not to leap in the air, to have someone near me who is a man, that is, not to go dancing solo, leg tilted crazily up, head back in an arch, in the dawn. Of course, I am to respect the new/old rules and not to point my foot at the sun or and God forbid I should straighten my back after Dimitri. They would be glad to bend me until I broke like a tree with too much snow on its branches, cripple my legs, crush my mind. Yet I love them. I think—ah you want crushedness all around to show off yourselves—how sad, but my weeping is a form of the dance of dance, as death, in any case, when I know how to walk on water, which is the goal of dance, to step so lightly, to live in the buzzing lightness of the sole of the foot... And the little dumb, lame, mad, rough, poor creatures outside are the angel dancers, says Jesus, the true one. These are the beauties, the dragon's tail-lame dancers, the shriveled, withered, one hand-claw griffin of the unspeakable air dancers whom you see human suddenly, human for tears and sweat and laughter. Talking of mad, I hear Martha cries for me in her wanderings and that you take her in. The song is incessant like the cicada's.

Do I have a will any longer? Can I say I will one day or will not marry you? I don't know. One thing is sure all those considerations are now in the margin—the place of the empty tomb, the eternal dance of eternal life. Dance is the architecture of heaven.

Do I love you? Ah that is a reality—I know this reality. I begin to see and to know. The priest and I are both bubbling babies in this. He sleeps on his mattress, I on the floor beside him. We exist to pray the Jesus prayer: It is much like a song—a sad, disharmonious song; at least, it was at first; now it gathers up and dissolves; and pours forth like wine—silent, sweet, wordless, for it is wordless-- with a burn giving life—an ache, no more. An ache of both tremendous sorrow and also of nuptial love, one rising up under heaven; one raining down from heaven—the rape, Dimitri's after death, my heart ejected out with dancing, living with fall out—feeling my light light failing falling soul-- sometimes, for I love my son passionately, it happens after death: on the serene dance floor sea that Dimitri vanished into. I know the sweetness and beauty of it and I sweat the sweetness and beauty of it: Lord Jesus Christ, Son of God, have mercy on me, a sinner.

We couldn't glean anything more out of Leo who seemed to be telling us this as some sort of vindication. We knew that Agatha had been baptized, in what we called 'dirty tears,' that she was tending the priest—in short we knew that she was doing the 'righteous things' that made us Christian. The rest we didn't dare consider. It was, Nisos said, Agatha's madness. She has gone mad in the sun over there. The gypsy camp is so exposed—it stinks, everything is rotting; The children get fevers from the heat. There, they are inland; it takes an hour by bus to get to the sea. Here we simply walk down on the beach and plunge into the water, or amble around in the cool forest. There are winds blowing constantly.... He didn't say more; there was a troubled look on his face.

Of course, Zoe, Cleo and Foti said—and there are other women who have joined the group now to embroider and knit together on the balcony—she is perfectly welcome. It is an uncomfortable fit, piped in one of the newer women—she must blame—

Do we blame? Asked Zoe peremptorily. No, of course not. We have laid down the spears, said Cleo colorfully. It is all bygones. We are in reality one flesh, even though hers is a bit mixed. Zoe and Cleo were tolerating one another again.

But there were never any spears, said Foti, it was just the injustice...

She was quiet for Cleo was glaring at her.

In any case, said Zoe, I feel that for the likes of her we are rather small—she said this without resentment. We have been, you see, left behind and are fast fading into the distance. If she returns, it will be because all this nonsense about Jesus, who is the Lord, you know, not some kind of nirvana toy, will have crashed all around her. She will have come to her senses—that of an ordinary woman with one child left, and some reconciling to do still. That is the reality.

But perhaps she has found something... Murmured Foti.

Zoe took off her glasses and stared at her.

We have all found something beyond. But we sit here still, sipping our brandy or our tea, now that our brandy is being rationed—I hear that Little Paul is doing a business selling it to the mainland for exorbitant prices—but ah, in any case—she shrugged; I have seen these prospective money makers come and go; we thought immediately Dimitri but kept silent. You see, the beyond, is here—right here, not there.

But Jesus had to leave, persisted Foti.

Did he leave? Zoe asked; ha, yes and no. Not really, he stayed close even to where he was born. He left pharisaical Judaism.

We are Pharisees, said Foti.

I wouldn't go that far. We are just little people living from day to day; timid people, really, not wishing to make waves. Comfortable, you might say with our ways, but you know this comfort makes us suffer too. How many of us haven't wanted to flee to the other island and do exactly what we please?

We have upheld the traditions. Who would not? Descended as we are from a group at Jerusalem itself who beheld the risen Christ—imagine the glory all around him—a body no longer mortal but of God?!

You see in the Resurrection, life changes entirely. All the pain, all the bitterness— well, it is joy, in actuality, you see. We must hold that joy right here, said Zoe, putting her hand on her abdomen, like a twirling bird in our hands.

Ah, there is a sweetness there, said Cleo.

That is the brandy, said Zoe. They would be friends again but not quite. They would come together for the time being to sew and knit and sip a drop or two of whatever brandy was left, or drink tea, and then they would go home and say things—sharp words—thinks the world of herself, Cleo would say, always has about Zoe—stupid, stupid old girl, Zoe would reiterate under her breath.

Foti who was considered to witless to even count in terms of her opinions, said that it was all petty and meaningless. The waters, she said, were stagnant but it didn't matter. Nothing mattered because out there it didn't matter. She had said this so many times that it had begun to convince even other witless old fools like Nisos, but it sounded strange to her to say it now. She saw Zoe as outlasting the disturbance that was on all of their minds—that of Dimitri and Agatha. Outlasting Zoe, she thought to herself and she would live somehow to see the Apocalypse—one in heaven or possibly ten in heaven would remember what she had to say—as a stubborn old woman, which was Foti's private thought about her—and then possible she would go to heaven, laughing, you know. But she doubted it. In any case, she would be remembered.

Yes, Foti saw it: Zoe remembered. Not only remembered but refusing to fade as the grass. She had read somewhere that all flesh faded as the grass. Not Zoe. She would print herself in some extraordinary way on fire and water just like heroes do; in fact, more than heroes do—more like saints do—pieces and parts of God, the priest told her. Only Zoe was Zoe and not so very godly. Was it all that stubbornness that made her feel this way? As if Zoe would print herself, her very character and being, on fire and water. No she was not quite a saint.

Agatha was not the saint. How they would ridicule her, if they knew she was entertaining such a thought when the blinds where down and a little moonlight drifted into the hot room, cooled just a little by the night breezes and she on her pillow –how they would say—you have no brains in a number of ways, one two three she knew all the ways. Yet perhaps Agatha was a saint.

A saint is not what you do or whether or not you don't sin. A saint is someone who finds love in agony…Seek and ye shall find.

What had Agatha sought? It could not be love. We know what love is. All she really knew for sure was what she had said to Leo on leaving that he had shared among the old men at the tavern: to ease her bosom she was going to the other island. Her bosom…!

About what? They had all asked astonished.

Voting to throw out the priest. He had been kind, so kind about Dimitri. Said that he never condemned him. Given me life. Given me back my son.

Why then did she vote to throw him out?

Anger, general anger. That nothing had been done to save his life. She had for a minute expected the priest dying of cancer to rush up the mountainside and into the fray around Dimitri, take his hand and lead him home. Wasn't that the way holy men worked?

She had wanted a miracle to restore him. What use were miracles making abundant goats' milk and fruit on the trees when you couldn't restore a man to life? One mother's son?

But after she had risen up against the priest as if someone had to pay for what they had done, she remembered him—I mean as he really was. The same way we sometimes remember Dimitri. Was he a moody rebel or was he our most affectionate one? This had made the men uncomfortable of course but they just kept staring at Leo and saying: And so?

Leo drew a long breath—she went to the priest in her sorrow and repentance. Why take a scapegoat and heap on him the anger due to ourselves and our own impotence? Our false teaching? No, she stayed with him.

For what? What can she possibly do for the priest? He is old and ill and used up, Timos said harshly. He makes no more miracles.

For love, said Leo.

And you just sit there, said Peter.

What do you think I am? Leo challenged them. I am not a beast but a man. If she was not like this I think I would have never found…

Bah, said Timos. You romanticize. I know people on this island sometimes say it—God this, God that…It is not difficult at all. It was never meant to be. Life is a little thing. And where we go hereafter? Rest, peace, that is all. Perhaps we will see our relatives and friends. It is true there are tales of some people specially picked out for God—monks, saints, so on. But we just live as best we can. It has nothing to do with me anyhow.

Foti thought about all this on her pillow. Love, the idea had once been a tall, shadowy fisherman with something of a mood on him, a thinker, a deep man. And she was to be in his arms every night—that was when she was a young girl. Love now, that was something that still had that face—moody, deep and the airiness of the young girl too, a combination, love was. A combination of two, and a combination lock with a particular number to open it up.

This would make the out there unimportant. Yes, the locus would shift from the utterly infinite out there to the little and finite in here. Yes, Zoe was right it was here, only here, but it largely depended on where you define, 'here.' For Agatha, it was right off her, Foti's, center. And, sighing, Foti felt she was probably right. She had probably found the combination number with that priest, although everyone knows she had loved her son so much, we thought she'd die with him.

…

Agatha wrote to Leo again; she was in an epistolary passion: We breathe, we pray, we talk—oh about fantastical things; we make up God knows what—the purple Lazarus naked life, as Father Isaac calls it. It is the life in which one is fully alive and gone beyond death…the life, he says of the penitent. He says it is not Dimitri who is taboo in me; I meant nothing but love. He says it is Paul. Have you, can you live?

I begin to think life is a fool's love, as far as the world is concerned—love that gets in the way of everything useful, sober and real. Ah, that is penitence when you sit before the little stool plain and unornamented with Jesus Christ on top of it and there you worship Him, the King of Kings, who died a fool. And Fr. Isaac leaning forward on his knees with a frown on his unkempt and battered face, saying dance eternal life.No, rather Dance, Eternal—to you. A fool's love—not Dimitri, or you; but Paul. Ah, not in that sense…I did not save Dimitri, because at the thought of his death, I had the most majestical laziness. He was alive; what is there to save?

I have lived lived, died lived, he said to me: All the miracles are gone now; I am wounded and bitter and dying, dying but you have a marvelous way of making a man feel forgiven even for an asshole presumptuous penitence charade. It's as if my heart finally goes through that door—is it you, at last? For I have always loved you passionately, passionately! Do you hear? Yes, Dimitri passed through easily. It was just that you were door for him too, and for Alex and Paul.

Loving him is like loving through him. He makes life sweeter like some lamp-shades do the light—by his ugliness, his pain. I don't know, can't say exactly what. God? Really? In such a place as this where we have been liars and cheaters? And I, originally, only gave up everything provisionally, to ask forgiveness, satisfy my con-science with a few good deeds, and then sail away with you, dear. But of course, humanly, seeing him crawl across the floor to get the bottle of milk delivered at the door-- and paid for by the friendly gypsies—I could not go. And it became clear to everyone, and they wrote up the tale too, although it was all fabrication, that I was his long lost love. And I couldn't go for that reason either. It set everything in place and gave me something to think about—ah that I had abandoned him once in youth, and that he had betrayed, that now I would abandon him no more because I would not abandon; that for the sake of not being able with Paul, and of having failed with Alex, of being in the future with you, I will love this old shrouded-with-pain man. He says, by way of a Valentine, his penitence was not at all going up the cliff on his knees—that was all a macabre show of self torture; the penitence is now when from the midst of pain, let's say, sometimes it is as if there is no pain at all—but so let's say to embellish the story, love just is—with me humpback and wizened with sorrow and passion. Our love in amidst the taste of the cannabis and our preposterous chastity is belief in Jesus Christ, the only truehearted man, son of the most high, defying grav-ity, which I once thought consisted of leaping high above Paul's head.

You must think we are both 'high'. Sometimes-- laughing crying, that is, our cry-ing is laughter, our crying crying-- not always. We are slaves of earth and we breathe, pray, —sometimes live feeding on a bowl of rice—he smiles at that, and it means everything to me—to watch his purple lips turn soft and sweet, softer sweeter than a rotten pear with a reticence however, an enormous reticence. But life turns to grey. I somehow did not save all the people!

The elderly ladies found Agatha's dancing shoes floating on the waves a little way out from the beach. Walking on water, said Foti—see one is in front of the other like the pace of a dancer. It ripped through the town like tearing an old cherished letter that Agatha had committed suicide. Agatha! For a while we were aghast. She had nothing left, of course. But that is exactly why she would live, said Zoe. But then Leo received a letter, kind of finishing where she had left off with no explanation.

By the way, he ran out of money long ago. I have been paying for the milk and bread and vegetables, for the marihuana out of my own pocket. Can you send a do-nation? I only ask you for pity's sake.

I threw my pearly pink shoes into the water; they were too hard and crude, garish, and of the time when I was fighting rather than dancing. I dance, I skip, bounce- flut-ter on my feet-- I walk barefoot one foot weightlessly now forever tender bare like the poor gypsy children. Why bother with shoes? It is as he said once to me, cough-ing for the marihuana smoke: Life, living. We are the incarnation of thought without gravity—of feet—and the building up from feet in the sudden cold sun-washed seawater. You can tell when they are grown up: their feet get all calloused, soles, hard like leather. Mine still feel. I have soft feet like a miracle. Walk-on-water feet they call me for my dancing—so dizzyingly, tenderly, we step like babies unsure on our feet: As if the ground is a baby's face and our soles the tips of a mother's fingers barely balancing on the cheek. We aim to feel light enough, serene enough, to step on to the top of water and not to sink, to leave the barest of prints on the surface. I've learned dancing out, crooked, unreal like a basilisk lizard or water strider: to step all shivering hideous on top of a pure sea-pool of sweat in the white sun. This is the dance where all weight is eviscerated out of you, strung up behind you. Not just the weight of your body, but the weight of pain, of what we call life but which is really heaviness—the 'chastisement' of Holy Island. I spend hours learning to step—and it takes hard muscle!—so that I am scooped up and lighter than it. My body isn't any-thing but worse bitterness, crookedness, and so inhumanly agonizing when the pain of love is drowned upward (yes up in the air drowned) in a worse agony--up in the air-heart-diaphragm drowned where the tears and sweat erupt: I didn't save him. The weight of Dimitri is there, but that steps up in heaven and I like an awful grotesque dance lighter than light; I am the ugly wood that floats on a pool of sweat.

I feel, dearest friend, finished Agatha, that I have caught the tail end of a strange kind of salvation precisely for my recalcitrance as it passes us by, the world like a hell of a dragon storm of tears and fury and I have wept horribly furiously until—I am small, soft, high and still—I am scooped out of me with my heart, my dance, my dance is inexpressibly soft and light, totally humanely pre-gravity as insects and children are, as my son is in my heart, though heavy in my belly. My pain, by the way—was it for what Paul did? Or was it for my father, long before—.

And I, said Leo, reading aloud the letter and coming to this finishing point—have only begun to live in this earthly world. I cut up such exquisite tomatoes and douse them with olive oil for my and my son's delectation to put on golden weight. He said it with a groan...

Simon and Nisos were by his side in the deserted tavern.

I brought you here, he said, to answer this question: What does this mean? Surely Agatha only means that she is doing a good deed for a holiday—suffering perhaps, but seeing justice and mercy done. And then she is going to come home, of course. What else could she do?

Why are you asking us? Nisos said gloomily. Us, us, us, said Simon. You know that she is a fish that has learned to fly.

A fish can't breathe in the air, retorted Nisos. And a fish needs pan-frying.

No, said Simon. She is not breathing; she is dancing. A hunchback formerly straight as Diana, now crooked, dragging one leg, but rising up on the beach! Copper to copper and tin to bronze—they see the bronze! What are we but steel to be pummeled and never to alter!

Then again, I tremble—what can she come back to: a man who lives as a loner, with a hated son, a son who has been attacked, and no one will listen, no one will open that can of worms. They wish to continue in their margin of comfort, their two nights a week of fish, their staticky TVs, their women in their long skirts and believe against all counter argument that they are at last on the right track again. Although, we rose up against Dimitri, for some reason, he was a free spirit, the son of Agatha, who was so despised, so out there, until she came dangerously close to having us in hand financially—and then, lo, her son trips and falls into the abyss, and it is God's doing, of course, an abyss to disappear into that is not set out by man, and she is well, destroyed, muted, pardoned, at last, we don't have enmity only those things which don't go quite...She leaves and lives the life of a—well, sick, crazy, tin crazy person. Naturally, she would do that. Smoking marihuana with the cast off priest. And imagining things...

She writes continued Leo, half to himself with smoky lips, to come with Max—to come, do you understand? Live the free life on a mattress on the floor, teaching dancing in the sun to gypsy children who listen off hand, for they don't need lessons, in a flash they skip like gold. We will get married, somewhere, anywhere. But Max is too frightened; he cannot come out of the corner where he is trying to be unreal. She said, ah, that is easy, just get him once across the chasm...But you know, Max! I reply. He hides, he dies. He loves Christ, his love oh so beautiful—but now can it be realized? Was it realized once?

And she will come back to this island where the women cannot lift their skirts for the sake of some Jesus that we tremble before. And for the sake of this same Jesus we eat fish only once a week and no meat. Yet for Him, Agatha steps so lightly she is like a puff of snow.

Living, you see, means trying to protect one's only child after years and years of scoffing at him in the bosom of this same priest, babbling about the life to come. Now he is back, thrown on me. I tell you that Max, my child, is not such a bad body. He is a humble boy; he likes his wine. He cries now and then. But I have done nothing to harm him. And I will do nothing. I actually love him. I listen to his tears. I see through them. Dark, distorted place, once holy.

They have come, said Nisos, meaning vaguely Little Paul and Jason and all the reformers and money makers and power grabbers which ganged up in invisible masses behind Little Paul and Jason and gave wonder of wonders electricity, bright, ecstatic light where there was once only dimness; they have come and there is nothing we can do. We must go along with them, shining with our bulbs.

Max is only the necessary victim by product of our advancement. Ah, I tell you, said Leo, I have begun to live. You others, perhaps, are comfortable and sure—the way, you know, people have of being comfortable and sure. Diminished, they are, yes assuredly. The joy was well, once, long ago—perhaps during the Easter dances when Agatha picked up her leg high and held it there and then swung it around slowly to the rear of her and held it up arching her back: it was fantastic, you must admit, achingly glorious, burnished gold! But those things are memories. They have been somehow deleted from our existence along with too much apricot brandy and the supplies of fish for daily consumption; Little Paul and Jason freeze the fish now and send it to Greece. And then before that we had—ah—magic: A girl who could tell the future and fight like a man. And before her, she died heroically, when heroism existed—we had holiness, yes that is right, sheer holiness—in the form of a girl so full of light that traces of it were left behind in her footsteps.

But of all that—who cares? We have our electricity—it was tedious and straining to live with dim lighting and we defer to two men who slink about sly and possibly violent, corrupt and evil who permit us, however, rations of fish and apricot brandy and a long length for women's skirts and we imagine, yes—that because we are now comfortable and sure—we are on the track back to our lost holiness. Secretly, though, we have become like individuals who will give up everything for pleasure— whose super island of islands in the world, refuge of refuges, haven of havens, is an island of pleasure in the brain cells, the thought that for our rations and our women's skirts we are right, heaven bound—and a misdemeanor here or there is nothing now. We all sin. Before it was death but now.… Its brandy like sugar in our brain, that's all.

I never saw anything, said Nisos, but a little island cracked by the sun; dried, faded, bristling with heat. I knew that it was my place—that is all that I can say. It is the same island you know. I see the same sun—white and fragrant. You know, how heat is sometimes fragrant. I remember Anna who said that things were changing on the island, flowers didn't grow so much. In my way of looking at things, men are always evil, but the earth changes rarely. Now the earth is changing, as Anna said. I don't know where to go. Maybe it is a sign though. That there is no place to run. Best to just bend one's head down and go about one's business.

A few fish learn to fly, said cracked up old Simon, shaking his head. It is the sign of God.

Do you think she'll come home? Leo asked Max. They were standing together in the little church. Max was in a little crouch, swaying from side to side; his eyes were half closed. He had been this way since the rape. What he called the rape. More like, said Leo, the apocalypse of violence and hate—one man against another. He spent most of his time in the house lying in bed.

There had been a time when Max walked straight as goldenrod. It was between the two crushed times—the beatings of his father, whom he had run away from, and this, the rape. In the midst he had stood tall, and yes, he was beautiful. He and Dimitri were like gold and fire. The whole island saw it. Why was there no rejoicing? Leo asked. Zoe and Cleo said: Well, you know, our island is so narrow-minded. Beauty is really relegated to children and girls. And women as soon as they marry are old and frowzy even if they are sixteen. Men are only strong arms, dictating voices. It is what we imagine that they are supposed to be.

Max and Dimitri were men. Men. They were our flowers blooming again. They were so beautiful when they loved as to be holy. They were so beautiful no wonder they loved. And they had the graciousness in them that goes along with beauty when it shines from the inside.

Well, it is odd then that you did nothing about...about...

What could I do? I never thought they would kill Dimitri, and do such unspeakable violence to my own son.

You will get nowhere with such talk and you know it well. Better not to speak, and we will say we have not heard. It is for your own sake, for that of your son. Keep to your hill with him. No one will bother someone inside their own house.

Nonsense, they almost burned Agatha in her own house.

That was so long ago. And as I remember Paul called the men off. Well, now we have Little Paul, his own son.

It was little Paul who raped....Leo couldn't go on. I found him, he finally blurted out, lying in a crumpled heap. Since then he hasn't been able to straighten his back.

As before when you beat him.

Things are so different now, said Leo, pleading.

Ah well, we can't be so sure of that, snapped Zoe.

But you know! Yes, you know—isn't it obvious now?

Our lives will be calmer now. We have a good business going with the hotel—think of that. Perhaps, just perhaps, if you get along with our leaders, you can take some role in it. They are talking of hiring people as managers, cleaners.

To me this island is completely destroyed. We have become cruel beyond compare.

No, there is no cruelty. We are living a lesser life than in the world. We follow our leaders and our priests hoping for our heavenly reward. As far as Max is concerned—he was let off lightly, don't you think? What if it was he who seduced, God forbid, or assaulted, Little Paul? Now, you don't really know what happened. Chances are nothing happened at all.

But a rape—and to come home to find him crumpled, shaking, weeping...

Ah hum hum. Yes, there are dreadful things about this earthly life. But someone like Max can only expect...When he well, announces the way he is....And he did get justice, if you remember, in one instance...Can you expect such justice in two instances? Besides, isn't it a little much? Rape almost never happens to a man.

But you know Max lied about Dimitri assaulting him and you know why. Jason threatened to expose his tendency.

Ah well then, you know the truth. He has a tendency. Nothing ever happened. It is all fantasies and lies. It is after all so easy for him to lie.

Leo looked at the group of elderly ladies silently. His mind was throbbing with pain. But a little sliver of it like a silver fairy part of his brain said to him: What are they really? Just some kind of old sugar ornaments from a wedding cake; the kind of thing nobody ever eats and that are used again and again. I must say they look like poison sitting in their sweet little grey outfits with their carefully curled hair.

Someone says Leo and Agatha exchange missives now, the letters go back and forth tenderly and swiftly like the calls of mating birds.

We are an insignificant people, a diminishing people. We have learned through the grapevine that our old priest is dead. Agatha is in the apartment clearing out things. She is with the gypsy children, teaching them dance steps. Tock is wild, longhaired and naked and happy. But of course, this sort of situation can't last forever—one of our daughters, a servant to gypsies! We, the old women, wonder about her, a vagabond and a half gypsy, half baptized—do tears count as baptismal water? Apparently, she wanted to trace her roots and this gypsy clan says that her father was a wanderer, and it wasn't known where he came from. We are not surprised that Agatha is with gypsies, but we have, with the permission of the priest extended her a warm hand of welcome back to our island, Holy Island. She could come back and marry Leo and cook and clean and take care of Max who is a poor child. There are some like that. Our leaders have talked with the priest and permitted him to permit it. She would have to comply with the rules, of course. There are no women individual dancers anymore although women are allowed to dance in the line dances. Celeste says that she enjoys her 'humbling' by Little Paul, although the rumor is that she was seen with a knife against her jugular. Little Paul tossed it from her hand and spat in her face, effectively killing that wickedness. That is love, that spit on her, such love, said crazy St. Paul. Celeste dances in our Easter dances with the long skirted mini stepping women, but in little jolty movements. Ella said she looks like there is something poisonous in her that makes her body jerk and twitch, but so sensitively. What if, Ella asks, Ella afraid of no man now, she has imbibed something of Agatha, baptized in her baptism—the baptism of real dance, the Holy Spirit? And we are holding her back? Our houses are like snow, without dance. Once the Holy Spirit was poured out like water on us. Then we danced.

Our decorations made for Agatha were quickly appropriated and used by Little Paul and Celeste at their wedding. We made new ones and set them up. The lilies, the white roses and the wreaths of jasmine give off a lovely perfume. We have decorated even the little altar on the side in back with the fresco of Jesus walking on water. It is a queer little painting and has Jesus with his foot up, smiling as if in ecstasy, although it is an odd face, someone might call it torture. Painful somehow to do a miracle! Agatha saw it differently used to say he was dancing, the pain was travail of which was born Body, or, the dance. Ah, but he is a man, Agatha, Cleo said. He is God, she said in a loud voice that filled the church with a rich, harsh sound. And thus male, female--one holy, painful, ecstatic One, Body at last--fragment that has lost its wholeness except in the dance of light Light that is God, mad, crooked, wild dance on water.

We know, ah yes, we know that, despite what Leo has to say, she will be back. While she is dancing her dance of deformed beauty which is beauty straight and pure—a grotesque snowflake, which is the ultimate flake of snow-human, they call her at the gypsy camp, as her lame sorrow-leg is dragged so well in her 'Purple Dragon Pirouette,' and her twisted arm is bent so perfectly as she lifts it into the Silver Crystal Bras Bas' light, light as light and even lighter, they say— she learned off of our little children, and the white snow tiger—and they laugh and cry for joy! A miracle, say the children, the lightness of tears and child's laughter—though, we ask ourselves, how can deformity in dance be—let alone a miracle? Fr. Isaac wrote Leo—something not of us but intrinsic to us— her body, twisted and deformed, but light as a cloud, is her journey back, dancing on water. And she will only go back, she says, when she can. And in the dance the pain of learning heaven-stepping is visible, for dancing on the sea, though for now, she dances on the sand leaving barely a footprint. And so beautifully that fish leap out of the water when she steps and razor blades appear in their mouths with drops of blood on them. But she says, when they ask, will you dance on water—it is my ambition, she says, but, I confess, and it makes me sweat and gasp in my lame-grotesque-beautiful-dragon body— it is bigger than me. So the beautiful fish and razor blades come in our dreams along with the little gypsy children stepping so lightly, some of them dragging one leg imitating her. And she becomes a kind of fairy-human-saint, capable of beauty and that other life after death, spirit when spirit has been crushed— that is, art. There are ranks of saints, says Fr. Isaac, some with fish leaping in their footsteps, some dancing on water. But they all become light as little children from sorrowing for love.

We have permission to keep the floral decorations until she returns and they marry—perhaps she will be in the kitchen with her distorted knee and contorted shoulder enfleshed real woman as if quilted on the hobgoblin dancer, of course we don't believe Fr. Isaac. She is evil like all women and needs a man. It has been a number of weeks but we insist that Leo not give up hope. Strangely we don't see Leo's fat body, but Jason's advancing to hers flailing helplessly before him like a stinkbug turned on its back. Meanwhile we have our Divine Liturgy after Divine Liturgy and we notice in the yellow darkness of the church, lit now not only by candles that the purple white orchids are withering and fading a bit and need changing, even their leaves are turned, the ribbons are dusty.

The End.

Made in the USA
Columbia, SC
09 January 2018